THE TOTAL INCOMES SYSTEM OF ACCOUNTS

ROBERT EISNER

The University of Chicago Press • Chicago and London

Robert Eisner, past president of the American Economic Association, is currently the William R. Kenan Professor of Economics at Northwestern University and is the author of *How Real Is the Federal Deficit?*

The University of Chicago Press, Chicago 60637
The University of Chicago Press, Ltd., London
© 1989 by The University of Chicago
All rights reserved. Published 1989
Printed in the United States of America

98 97 96 95 94 93 92 91 90 89   5 4 3 2 1

Library of Congress Cataloging-in-Publication Data
Eisner, Robert.
    The total incomes system of accounts / Robert Eisner.
        p.   cm.
    Bibliography: p.
    Includes index.
    ISBN 0-226-19638-0
    1. National income—United States—Accounting.   I. Title.
HC110.I5E47   1989   89-4681
339.373—dc19   CIP

⊗ The paper used in this publication meets the requirements of
the American National Standard for Information Sciences—Permanence of
Paper for Printed Library Materials, ANSI Z39.48-1984.

Contents

HC
110
I5
E47
1989

Introduction: Motivation for Change

The national income and product accounts for the United States (NIPAs), and kindred accounts in other nations, have been among the major contributions to economic knowledge over the past half century. Wedded to the great innovations in macroeconomic theory dating to the 1930s, their value has perhaps been underestimated. We know the pitfalls of measurement without theory, though we may forget the strength and life that theory must draw from measurement. Several generations of economists and practitioners have now been able to tie the theoretical constructs of income, output, investment, consumption, and saving to the actual numbers of these remarkable accounts with all their fine detail and soundly meshed interrelations.[1]

Yet, the accounts are not set in concrete. From the early days of their formulation by Sir William Petty and Gregory King in seventeenth-century England[2] there have been lively debates as to just what they should include,

I am especially indebted to Moses Abramovitz for his detailed, insightful, and most useful comments on an earlier draft of the substantial portions of this volume that were published in my "Extended Accounts for National Income and Product," *Journal of Economic Literature* 26 (December 1988): 1611-84. Very helpful comments were received as well from Carol S. Carson, F. Thomas Juster, John W. Kendrick, Richard Ruggles, and James Tobin. I am further indebted for collaboration and assistance over many years on this work to Steven Bender, Carol S. Carson, Marsha Courchane, Gerald F. Donahoe, John A. Gorman, George Jaszi, John Keating, Hilarie Lieb, Wilson Lim, John C. Musgrave, Rene Moreno, David Nebhut, Paul J. Pieper, Gerald Silverstein, Emily Simon, Helen Stone Tice, Arthur B. Treadway, Stuart Weiner, and others too numerous to mention. Molly Fabian, as ever, has been of enormous help in multiple tasks of typing, word processing and proofing, as well as keeping up the good cheer of several generations of indefatigable research assistants. My efforts have enjoyed the financial support of a number of grants from the National Science Foundation which, of course, like all of the individuals acknowledged, is in no way accountable for this output.

how items ought to be measured and how they are to be put together.[3] They have been modified over the years. Many of the far-reaching changes and extensions which a varied band of economic and statistical explorers has worked to implement were originally suggested four decades ago by Simon Kuznets,[4] to many the father of modern national income accounting, but there have been notable contributions by others.[5]

Remarkable as are the NIPAs as a measure of the economic health of the nation, much concern has been expressed in the body politic, among social scientists in general, and by economists as to their adequacy if not accuracy. Do changes in national income and product over time or differences among nations really measure appropriately changes and differences in "well-being" or, perhaps more to the point, "economic well-being"? Do our measures show correctly the distribution of income and output within the population, their cyclical fluctuations, and their allocation to current consumption and accumulation of capital for the future? Are we on the one hand measuring all of income and output and on the other properly avoiding significant double counting? Do our measures really fit the theoretical constructs they are presumed to serve?

Among major motivations for the construction of extended accounts for national income and product are the development of better measures of economic activity contributing to social welfare, more inclusive and relevant measures of capital formation and other factors in economic growth, and better and/or additional data to fit concepts of consumption, investment, and production relevant to economic theory and structural econometric relations. Pursuit of these goals raises certain basic issues of national income and product accounting, which may be categorized as:

1. Definition of the production boundary or what activities will be considered to result in economic output
2. Definition of primary incomes, which will in turn relate to measures of the distribution and redistribution of income
3. Definition of final and intermediate output
4. Definition of investment and consumption as the two ultimate uses of final output
5. Application of the appropriate valuation to production

We address first the definition of economic production or output. As indicated in 1954 by what is now the Bureau of Economic Analysis (BEA), "the basic criterion used for distinguishing an activity as economic production is whether it is reflected in the sales and purchase transactions of the market economy."[6] A clear, tradition-based exception to that rule of including market transactions, as there acknowledged, is the exclusion of illegal transactions, so prominently exemplified today in drug traffic, prostitution, and gambling, which come to hundreds of billions of dollars.

Market and Nonmarket Output

Of much bigger magnitude than excluded market transactions, though, is the value of nonmarket output. This includes, in particular, a vast amount of household activity. The work of paid domestic servants is counted in the official accounts; that of housewives or other unpaid workers in the home is not. The preparation of meals in restaurants and the washing of clothes in laundries or laundromats are included; home-cooked meals and the services of user-owned washers and dryers are not. And the transportation services of taxis, buses, and rented cars are included while those of the family car are not.

Gross national product in the BEA NIPAs of the United States is essentially production for the market, and valued at market prices. National income then is the remuneration of the factors of production of that gross national product. Where we do not count production we do not have a component of national income, with the curious exception of output related to government subsidies or losses in government enterprises.

The difficulty with exclusion of nonmarket output is not merely that it results in lesser totals of GNP and national income. It is also that it tends to vitiate international and intertemporal comparisons.[7] Thus, again as Kuznets pointed out a long time ago ([1947] 1951a, for example), the availability of goods and services in less developed economies, in which a large proportion of production is in the home or on the subsistence farm, will not be as much less than in highly developed economies as would appear from viewing only market economic activity.

The growth of total output in the United States is similarly exaggerated if we ignore the shift of production from the old spinning wheel in the parlor to the textile factory and from the wood stove and fresh farm produce to frozen foods and restaurants. Most recently, the vast increases in conventional GNP associated with the major movement of women into the labor force may signify a much lesser gain in total output, as nonmarket child care gives way to the paid baby sitter and nursery school, care of the aged to nursing homes, care of the sick to hospitals, and home cooking to McDonalds. There is also some offsetting movement out of market activity, as tax considerations, changes in relative prices, and other factors have encouraged do-it-yourself house maintenance and repairs. A major shift to nonmarket output has taken place in the field of transportation, as the bulk of Americans get around in their own owner-driven cars. And while current lack of adequate quarterly or even annual series on use of time precludes accurate measurement, there is probably substantial movement between market and nonmarket activity in connection with cyclical fluctuations in employment.

Inclusion of nonmarket output may also bring significant changes to measures of income distribution, by size, by sex, by age, and by rural-urban status. It is reasonable to conjecture that the proportions of income related to nonmarket output in the home are larger among the poor and among women, the aged, and those on farms or in rural areas. Full imputation of the value of education would appear likely to bring further, dramatic changes in our views of the distribution of saving and investment as well as of income.

Final and Intermediate Product

Critical to the measurement of output in income and product accounts is the issue of duplication or "double-counting." We clearly do not want to count the rubber and tires and steel and paint going into an automobile as well as the total value of the automobile itself. The matter is resolved in official accounts essentially by restricting the measure of output to "final product." This in turn is defined as the total of purchases of goods and services not resold. For households and government, not generally in the business of reselling what they buy, that essentially means the inclusion of "personal consumption expenditures" and "government purchases of goods and services." (There are no fundamental problems in netting out government or household sales of used cars or the like, which generally become the purchases, not resold, of another economic entity or household.) For the business sector (including government enterprises), final purchases are generally taken to be purchases on capital account, that is, goods lasting more than one year. The only purchases on current account that are "final" for the period of measurement are increases in inventories; all other goods and services purchased are resold.

The identification of household and government purchases with final product, and goods and services bought by business as intermediate product, unless they are deemed "capital" or accumulated in inventories, raises some critical questions and indeed a number of anomalies relating to the sometimes shifting identities of purchasers. Thus police services purchased by government are final product and included in GNP while the services of guards or watchmen purchased by a business are not; they are presumably resold as part of the business production in which they are instrumental. The repair of state-owned highways is final product, while repair of private railroad tracks is intermediate. If the highways were private tollways and the railroads were nationalized, the classifications would be reversed. A great part of government activity is in fact clearly devoted to direct service to business as well as maintenance of the system and infrastructure essential to private production.

The amusement or entertainment services of movies watched in theatres, on cable television sold by subscription, or on public (government) television are generally included in GNP. Similar services provided by regular commercial television in the United States are not included since they are paid for by purchases on current account by one business firm, in the form of advertising expenses, from another.

But what about travel expenses in connection with work, including the commuting costs of getting from home to job? If these are paid directly by a business firm they will be intermediate product, included in the value of the "final" output of the firm. If firms pay their employees higher wages and let them pay their own travel costs, these expenditures will be counted as personal consumption and their value will enter independently into gross national product in addition to the value of whatever output the firm is producing.

Gross Private Domestic Investment and Total Capital Formation

The broad importance attached by many to investment contrasts sharply with the narrowness of its definition in the BEA NIPAs. Gross investment in the BEA accounts includes only "gross private domestic investment," which is the sum of plant, equipment and inventories acquired by private business and nonprofit institutions, and "net foreign investment," which is merely the addition to net claims of Americans on foreigners resulting from the excess of exports of goods and services over the sum of imports and of payments to foreigners in the form of government interest and of net transfers by persons and government. If Hertz, Avis, or any other private company buys an automobile, that constitutes investment. If a police car or any other automobile is purchased by any branch of government, that shows up merely in "government purchases of goods and services." And automobiles purchased by households are part of personal consumption expenditures. Yet, in terms of economic theory and analysis, the automobile in each case, like any other durable good, is investment in that it will provide future services.

There are, however, further matters of concern in the definition of investment. Our official accounts in the United States not only exclude all acquisitions of tangible or physical capital by government, including government enterprises, and by households, they also exclude the acquisition of intangible capital in all sectors. Thus, research and development efforts by business are treated as intermediate products, subsumed in some other final output. Research and development expenditures by nonprofit institutions turn up as consumption as a consequence of the peculiar consolidation of household and nonprofit accounts (exclusive of nonprofit capital expenditures, which are, as noted above, included in gross private domestic investment), and government expenditures for research are buried in that catchall, government purchases of goods and services. Yet, current research and development expenditures may well prove more of an economic investment in future output than much of what is currently treated as "gross investment." And what are we to make of the vast amounts of expenditures, market as well as nonmarket, for education, training, and health, let alone for the raising of our children, which create the human capital on which our future depends?[8]

These exclusions of so much of capital formation from official measures of investment may also vitiate international and intertemporal comparisons. Can we confidently say that the United States is lagging far behind other nations in investment without counting R&D, education, government capital, and expenditures for household durables in ways that are comprehensive as well as comparable across countries? Is a nation really investing less if it builds highways and produces automobiles than if it invests in trains and busses? And is American investment declining if capital formation shifts from business spending for plant and equipment to education and research? The answers to these questions are not found in the conventional accounts.

Issues of Valuation

Assignment of values to production and associated incomes on the basis of the market prices of sales and purchases raises a number of problems. There are of course the familiar ones with regard to capital consumption allowances and the evaluation of changes in inventories. But in general, difficulties arise from the inadequacy of market sales and purchases as measures of production. Thus, what is the value of production when it is paid for only in part by market sales and in part by government subsidies? What is the value of production of government enterprises when the government in effect subsidizes them by making up their losses? And how should we evaluate government services, which generally are not sold? What about the value of housing services of owner-occupied dwellings or, if we are to extend the accounts, the great amount of productive activity within the household?

Further, how are we to handle various vexing changes in relative prices? Since the net investment component of national product constitutes an addition to the value of capital, how are we to treat changes in the real value of capital stemming from changing relative prices of capital and output? If saving is to correspond to accumulation of wealth, should we ignore accruals of wealth from capital gains? And what values are we to place on real product and income when terms of international trade change so that we give domestic output in exchange for more or less in the way of imports from other countries?

All of these issues and others that follow logically from the NIPA framework have been taken up by one or another of those who have endeavored to construct new, extended, or alternative accounts of national income and product. They are illustrated and discussed further in the course of a survey[9] of six such sets of accounts for the economy of the United States—by Nordhaus and Tobin (1972, 1973), Zolotas (1981), Jorgenson and Fraumeni (1987),

Kendrick (1976, 1979, 1987a, 1987b), Ruggles and Ruggles (1973, 1982a, 1982b), and Eisner (1985).[10]

Our focus, it should be stressed, is on measures of all economic activity related to welfare, but not of welfare itself. And we seek measures which capture as fully and distinctly as possible both the flow of current consumption and the accumulation of capital contributing to future welfare.

2

Guiding Principles for Extended Accounts

What set of principles should guide us in meeting all of these issues arising out of the conventional accounts? Just what should we be measuring and how? I would argue first—and all those working with extended accounts would, I believe, agree—that the conventional accounts should be retained, to be viewed alone or as a central component of revised and expanded measures. They offer and should continue to offer historical series of enormous value for economic analysis. The market transactions that form their core are of course essential to any meaningful measure of a largely market economy. And further, we need not focus on one "bottom line." Different components, or different measures, will be appropriate for different purposes.

Measure Final Product

Expanded accounts should retain one central focus of the conventional accounts: the measure of final product. A frequent complaint about the conventional accounts is that they do not measure "welfare" or "well-being." It must be quickly conceded that there are many aspects of human well-being that conventional economic accounts do not measure. But I do not believe that it is an appropriate task of national income and product accounts to measure all aspects of welfare. We can leave some things to psychologists and sociologists. Our accounts may better seek to measure not welfare itself but the nation's output of final goods and services, which are presumed to contribute to welfare. We focus on the final product, those goods and services that are the penultimate ingredients of human well-being, and try to avoid double counting by separating out the intermediate product, which constitutes a cost, possibly a varying cost, of producing the final output with which we are concerned.

In this effort, a guide to definition of final product may be found in a statement by Kuznets, ". . . the final goals are provision of goods to ultimate consumers, the living members of society, and net additions to capital stock relevant to ultimate consumption current and future." (Moss 1979, 579). This offers a plausible basis for considering police and defense services as intermediate rather than final, and commercial media entertainment information as final rather than intermediate. It does leave uncertain the answers to many questions. Is driving to the supermarket intermediate in the acquisition of food? Is eating itself intermediate to the creation or maintenance of human capital?

There would seem to be a strong case for viewing a considerable portion of government output as intermediate. We may again cite Kuznets, who had early questioned, with regard to government provision of "guns, planes, ships, roads, public buildings, judicial, legislative, and administrative services . . . How much of all this is the mere cost of maintaining the social fabric, a *precondition* for net product rather than the net product itself?" (1953, 197–98). He answered, "Only those parts of government activities of direct welfare to individuals as individuals (education, health services, and the like), can be considered as yielding net product" (p. 199).

The NIPA definitions of final product are neat but make our measures of income and output hostage to particular institutional arrangements. They also suggest serious limitations as to the validity of official measures in both international and intertemporal comparisons. Thus, as indicated earlier, police services are counted as final product if provided by government or purchased by households but as intermediate product if purchased by business. If a large company were to arrange with a municipality to provide for its own watchmen or security force in return for a reduction of the property taxes it pays the municipality, the real gross national product would decline. The police services formerly purchased by the local government would now be subsumed in the value of the company's output, with the company paying for them directly rather than in taxes.

The point may well be made that police services, however useful or necessary, are in fact intermediate in nature no matter who pays for them. The final output is always the goods and services being produced and the police necessary to protect the activity and profits of production are simply a cost of that final output. Treating police services on this basis would enable us to avoid the anomaly of showing increases in real GNP as both crime and the police efforts to hold it in check rise apace.

It may be argued that many police services directly benefit households, facilitating consumption and leisure activities by directing traffic to the ball game or protecting us in our sleep and recreation at home. Should they then not, in part, be viewed as themselves consumption and final product? Except to the extent, which I would judge trivial or immeasurable, that we view police services as a product enjoyed or consumed for its own sake—for example, we like to look at attractive police uniforms—my answer would be negative. It must be understood that as intermediate product it is not then excluded from consumption or GNP. If police services increase, nominal GNP rises as the cost of producing final product rises. But when we deflate nominal GNP to arrive at a measure of real output, the cost and price increases are washed out.

It may be conceded, though, that more police may improve the quality of the consumption activities they serve. We may enjoy the ball game better if we do not miss the first two innings because of a traffic jam outside of the ball park. But here we are running into the perennial problem of measuring quality improvement and adjusting our price deflators accordingly. And, of course, to the extent more police are provided because there is more traffic or more potential for crime, we have no quality improvement in the final output we are measuring.[11]

The argument against viewing police (and fire) services as final product may obviously be extended to what is in the United States the very large category of national defense expenditures. However necessary (or not), the services of national defense are intermediate in character, except again for the joy given to those who love a military parade. They are better viewed as provided generally to protect the capital and labor utilized in the production of the consumption and investment goods that constitute final output. Such treatment of the output of military services as intermediate would also, at least for those who do not literally glory in arms, make the resultant GNP a more meaningful measure of economic welfare. It would be hard to argue that a nation whose military expenditures are very large, and contribute to a high conventional GNP per capita, is better off than another nation whose conventional GNP per capita is the same but enjoys a larger total of consumption and investment per person.[12]

It is of course also true that a country with a good climate that does not have to devote a large amount of resources to heating and warm clothing may be better off than another country with harsh weather. No subtraction of these ''defensive'' expenditures against nature is warranted, however, by our criterion of including, as we indicated above, ''those goods and services that are the penultimate ingredients of human well-being.'' Warm clothes are then to be included and cold cannon are not. Both may (or may not) make us better off, but the one is final product in contributing to our welfare and the other is not.

Once we recognize clothing as final product, as all accounts generally do (except perhaps for uniforms or other work clothes provided by employers), we count it in cold climates and warm alike. The nation facing worse Arctic blasts may then have a greater GNP while enjoying it less. That should cause us no problem if we recognize, once more, that we seek to measure the final product contributing to welfare and not welfare itself.[13]

The boundary between final and intermediate product may also well be shifted in the case of expenses related to work, which are currently counted as consumption because they are incurred by employees and not directly reimbursed by their employers.[14] A major item in this category is travel or commutation expenses from home to job. One might add additional expenses of lunch or other workday meals over and above the cost of meals at home and, to the extent they do not also serve as a source of consumer satisfaction, the clothes that must be purchased for the factory or office. Employers in some instances do provide workers transportation to and from their jobs, as well as other work-related goods and services. Extended accounts might move most expenses related to work from final product (generally consumption) to intermediate, regardless of who incurs them, and make corresponding reductions in national income.

The final/intermediate product boundary may need to be moved in the other direction, however, to include in consumption some output now viewed as intermediate. Business furnishes many consumption services not purchased on their own account by those who enjoy them. Some may be symbolized by that tax-reform target, the three-martini business lunch. But there is much more: business conventions appreciated as much for their entertainment value as for managerial enlightenment, the perquisites of executive suites and company-supported club memberships, boxes at sports stadiums, athletic facilities and subsidized lunch rooms, and a host of employee insurance and health and welfare benefits which are at best picked up only in part as consumption in the conventional NIPAs.

Another anomaly of the final/intermediate product categorization is the media services supported by advertising. In the United States, the vast amount of entertainment and information provided by commercial television supported by business advertising is not now counted in real GNP. The movie paid for in a movie theater or on government-financed public television or direct-pay television is counted. It enters into real GNP as consumption services if paid for by households and as government purchases of goods and services if paid for by government in its provision of public television. In other nations where most television is government-supported and paid for directly by government funds, GNP is to that extent larger. As nations "privatize," as in Britain and France, and turn payment over to business advertisers, real GNP by official measures in the United States would decline. And, of course, this issue emerges as well in the case of all media services supported by advertising, including newspapers, magazines, and radio. A measure that distinguishes consistently between the consumption services provided by the media and the truly intermediate marketing costs of advertising would appear to be in order.

Include Market and Nonmarket Output

The BEA NIPAs include a number of "imputations" of output not produced for the market.[15] The largest of these relate to the value of housing services provided by residential units occupied by their owners. In addition to the imputations for owner-occupied housing, there is one for "the rental value of buildings and equipment owned and used by nonprofit institutions serving individuals," another for "services furnished without payment by financial intermediaries except life insurance carriers and private noninsured pension funds," and still others for "farm products consumed on farms," for "food furnished employees, including military and domestic service," and (recently) for "employer contributions for social insurance for Federal Government employees." But except for the housing imputations, which came to $305 billion or 7.2 percent of GNP in 1986, and the financial intermediaries imputation of $71 billion, which amounted to 1.7 percent, these are quite minor. There are huge amounts of nonmarket production not included at all in the official accounts.

We may begin in households, where the generally uncounted economic activity is epitomized in the old sexist Econ-1 joke about the man who depresses GNP by marrying his housekeeper. As the joke suggests, almost all nonmarket household work has some market counterpart, so that the measures of output and income in our NIPAs become dependent upon whether the work is done for the market or not. As may readily be imagined, and as various estimators make clear, the value of nonmarket household product, if it were purchased in the market, would be huge. It includes major activities such as meal preparation, home cleaning and maintenance, child care, care of the sick, transportation services in the family car, the services of household goods, and a great deal more.[16]

The great bulk of services of government are not produced for the market. They are distributed to the population without direct charge, but the NIPAs do in effect impute a partial value to them. Government output is counted on the basis of market inputs of labor services. Our immense (if insufficient) product of public education is measured only by the wages and salaries paid to janitors, clerks, administrators, and teachers. The value of government output is understated by the extent to which it ignores inputs of capital and land. There is no imputation for interest or return on capital, capital consumption allowances, or rent. And there is no imputation for the value of labor time not paid for. In earlier years this involved a substantial understatement of the economic or opportunity cost of conscripted military services and currently involves some understatement in compulsory jury service. Of much greater magnitude is the opportunity cost of students' time in both public and private educational institutions.

In the American economy there is now a substantial nonprofit sector. Its current account in the NIPAs is subsumed with that of households while its capital expenditures are included with business investment. Nonprofit current expenditures, while included in personal consumption, do not include imputations for taxes or capital income. Services of nonprofit schools, hospitals, and churches, financed in considerable part by public and private subsidies and donations and further supported by the labor of volunteers, where not free are generally provided below social opportunity cost. Their value may hence be considerably understated in conventional accounts and there have been efforts to correct this in extended measures.

While preserving a clearly identified core of market transactions, extended accounts should include all economic activity productive of final output, whether market or nonmarket. This is clearly indicated for output that is currently partly market and partly nonmarket, as the BEA recognizes in the case of housing services. But the general importance of including nonmarket output is accentuated by its varying significance in different periods of time and different economies. International and intertemporal comparisons that ignore nonmarket activity risk domination by particular and changing institutional arrangements and are for many purposes seriously misleading.

In looking for a measure of comprehensive product, there is a question of how far to go. Margaret Reid (1934, 11, as cited by Murphy 1980, 6), proposed that we take nonmarket economic activities to include

> those unpaid activities which are carried on, by and for the members, which activities might be replaced by market goods, or paid services, if circumstances such as income, market conditions, and personal inclinations permit the service being delegated to someone outside the household group.

Hawrylyshyn (1977, 89) invokes a "third-person criterion" to state:

> Economic services are then defined conceptually as those producing indirect utility, and identified in practice by reference to the criterion: is it conceivable to have a third person (e.g., market) do it?

Consistent with these concepts, extended accounts generally include housework and child care but exclude what Kuznets (1941, 6–7), as cited in Murphy (1980, 7) refers to (and would also exclude as overly extensive) as "acts that might be called 'personal,' such as washing, shaving, and playing for amusement on the piano. . . . "

Critical to decisions regarding the production boundary is the fungibility of resources as between market and nonmarket output. Where labor and capital can serve in similar production with or without market transactions, exclusion of nonmarket output will result in incomplete and possibly misleading measures of product. This point acquires particular force where production has in fact been undertaken with and without market transactions at different periods of time in any one economy or, when we are concerned with international comparisons, where production has been undertaken in greater degree with market transactions in one country than in another. It acquires all the more force where the proportions of production with and without market transactions are changing, as would appear to be conspicuously the case in the economy of the United States and more generally as economies move through the path of economic development.

Impute Incomes from Extended Output

As we extend production boundaries it is necessary, in complete sets of accounts (such as Kendrick's adjusted GNP and the Ruggleses' IEA, discussed in Appendix E, and those presented in this volume), to make corresponding extensions on the income side. As we impute additional production we impute additional income or nonincome charges to keep our books balanced but more fundamentally to indicate the identities of the factors of production and their remuneration or of ultimate claimants of the additional output. We thus affect our measures of income and its distribution.

The measures of income distribution are affected in many dimensions. If nonmarket output is more labor intensive, for example, extended accounts will show a different distribution in terms of factor shares. If women, the poor, and the aged engage disproportionately in nonmarket work, distribution by sex, size of income, and age will be different. If nonmarket output is relatively stable in the face of cyclical fluctuation of market production, or even related inversely to it, distribution of aggregate income over time and our measures of instability will be affected. And extended measures may also alter our perception of the proportions of income that are rewards to capital and to labor and the proportions received by primary producers as against those received in the form of transfers.[17]

Develop Comprehensive Measures of Investment

Interest in investment stems in major part from its relation to productivity and growth. Net investment is indeed the growth or time derivative of capital, where capital is an argument of the production function.

From this perspective a much broader view of investment than the gross private domestic investment or gross investment of the BEA's national income and product accounts would seem in order. But how far should it reach and, where market transactions are not available, how should investment be evaluated?

As we have noted, gross private domestic investment in the U.S. NIPAs includes only plant and equipment purchased by business and nonprofit institutions and the change in business inventories. Extended accounts would include in investment acquisitions of durable goods of all kinds by households and government as well as additions to inventories in all sectors of the economy. In addition, they might include, by way of tangible capital, additions to the value of land as it is developed as well as expenditures that look to the discovery or development of natural resources. They might count changes in inventories of oil and coal below the ground as well as above it. Further, extended accounts would include intangible investment in research and development by both business and government. They would include intangible investment in health, education and training,[18] and information.[19]

There are further extensions which have been implemented. John Kendrick includes investment in mobility and in tangible human capital in the form of rearing costs. Dale Jorgenson and Barbara Fraumeni count as capital formation the present value of all of the additions to future labor income resulting from birth and immigration as well as education. Both Richard and Nancy Ruggles and Jorgenson and Fraumeni take into account revaluations as a source of changes in wealth, and Eisner includes net revaluations, that is, real capital gains in physical assets, in measures of both capital formation and product.

The extension to government and household acquisition of structures, equipment, durable goods, and inventories apparently commands considerable support. Market transactions and data are readily available and, except for inventories, relevant series are to be found in the NIPAs themselves or in other tables produced by the BEA.

Land and natural resources begin to raise some difficulty. While in classical theory they may be viewed as exogenous to production, in fact they are not. Productive effort may develop land and natural resources and hence increase their input to production. Economic activity that increases the value of land and natural resources may hence be seen as investment. But then economic activity that exhausts the land or natural resources may be seen as capital consumption. On the usual assumption that producers equate at the margin the cost of their investment to the present value of its expected returns, one could evaluate investment in land or natural resources either on the basis of costs or changes in value. The observed changes in capital value—to the extent they are observed—would be ex post, though, and may not equal the costs of investment. More generally, because of externalities, changes in value of capital need not in the aggregate equal the costs of investment, which producers relate to the increases in value of their own capital.

Include Investment in Intangible and Human Capital

A comprehensive measure of investment would include, however, not only acquisition or development of the tangible capital of structures, equipment, inventories, and land. It should also extend to the vastly greater and in many senses more important intangible and human capital created by education, training, the acquisition of knowledge, and raising the level of health in the population. Intangible investment, that is, investment with no immediate tangible output, like tangible investment, is characterized as product which contributes to future output. Inclusion of intangible investment would seem essential for measures of total capital accumulation that would indicate the proportions of output going to current consumption as against provision for the future. Such measures would better inform society and policymakers on the perennial and critical choices between today and tomorrow and this generation and the next.

There are, however, major problems, both conceptual and empirical, in estimating investment in human capital. With regard to education, for example, are we to measure the value of investment by the market costs of schooling, with or without imputation for value of services of government capital? Are we to include as well the very substantial opportunity cost of the time of those students who, if not in school, would be involved in market output? General considerations of economic theory would suggest so. But can all that time be considered devoted to investment? Is a considerable part of educational experience, at least in colleges and universities and perhaps in secondary schools as well, to be viewed as current consumption? At least to some of the students, some of the time, school is fun.

The issue is similarly difficult in the case of expenditures for health. How much of them should be viewed as current maintenance rather than investment? How much really contributes to *future* productivity, that is, to output in a future accounting period?

Should one go further and count human beings themselves as capital? Should all of the costs of child rearing then be viewed as investment? Should one count birth itself—and immigration—as formation and accumulation of capital? What then are the costs of this investment? Or should we report such investment as the present value of the future earnings of the new-born, or the newly arrived immigrants? But if humans are to be viewed as capital, as they might be in a slave economy, should not their "earnings" be taken net of maintenance and other costs of production, that is, net essentially of consumption? Or is this extension of investment to the production of human beings themselves one that would better, as I believe, be omitted from income and product accounts?

Take into Account Revaluations or Capital Gains and Losses

Conventional accounts measure output in terms of the current use of resources in production. Gross investment is then the value of resources currently devoted to the portion of production that constitutes goods to be used in future production—in the BEA accounts, business and nonprofit institution structures and equipment, including those in newly constructed owner-occupied housing, and accumulation of business inventories—and in the net accumulation of foreign claims. Net investment is the value of additions to "capital" minus an estimate of capital consumption, the depreciation in the value of existing capital.

This, it may be noted, is different from the net addition to the value of capital. Values of assets change, in both absolute and relative terms, quite aside from current capital expenditures and depreciation. The changes may stem from alterations in income flows, absolute and relative prices of inputs and outputs both within the country and vis-à-vis other nations, technology, discount rates, and risk. These last may change the value of current wealth even with no change in the mathematical expectations of future income, with significant effects if agents have different horizons for consumption and income.

One kind of capital may gain in value at the expense of another—tangible as against intangible and human, for example. Changes in international terms of trade may affect the aggregate value of a nation's capital. If world prices of sugar fall, the value of Cuban capital declines. If the demand for airline travel throughout the world grows rapidly, the value of American know-how and plants involved in plane production rises. And such changes in the value of capital may prove just as significant as and in many senses equivalent to contributions to changes in the aggregate value of capital brought on by the current production of capital.

If we accept the Haig-Hicks-Simon concept of income as that which can be consumed while keeping real wealth intact, saving is the difference between this measure of income and actual consumption. Both income and saving will then include real capital gains. To preserve the saving-investment identity, investment would also have to include these capital gains. Failure to include them causes a disparity between income statements and balance sheets that reflect market values. It further distorts measures of the distribution of income within nations and the distribution of income and wealth among nations. Changing relative prices of oil, for example, have had enormous effects on current and expected *future* incomes of various developed and less developed countries.

It is *real* capital gains or what may be called "net revaluations," that is, changes in capital values net of those changes necessary to keep real value intact, that would be included in saving, capital accumulation, and income. The revaluations ideally should reflect market prices. In work with financial assets and liabilities and land, Eisner and Pieper (1984 and elsewhere) and Eisner (1986) did present estimates of market prices of stocks. It is generally practicable, however, in the treatment of tangible reproducible assets, to rely on "replacement costs" based on prices of flows of current output. Capital stocks so calculated are indeed now provided by the BEA, in both current and constant dollars. With corresponding series on gross capital expenditures and capital consumption allowances, the calculation of real and nominal capital gains, or gross and net revaluations, is then fairly straightforward. Appropriate price deflators may also be applied to nominal asset values of successive years to convert nominal capital gains to real.[20]

Net revaluations so calculated do show some sharp year-to-year variation. In terms of the concept of permanent income, net revaluations appear to have a considerably larger transitory component than do other types of current income. This suggests the usefulness of separating net revaluations from other income for many kinds of analysis. It suggests, similarly, the advisability of showing separately the rest of investment or capital accumulation as well as GNP and other aggregates exclusive of revaluations in those accounts that include them.

Inclusion of net revaluations in measures of income, product, and investment does entail a significant conceptual departure from conventional accounts, which focus on the direct output of current productive activity. It may well be argued further that different elements of revaluations have different implications for economic behavior. Changes in terms of trade or exchange rates may alter the wealth position of the nation as a whole. Changes in rates of discount may alter the wealth distribution among generations and among sectors and agents in accordance with the differences in expected streams of income and the consumption streams generated by intertemporal utility functions. Technological innovation may change both expected future incomes and the value of existing physical capital, not necessarily in the same directions. Changes in tastes may alter the value of existing capital, with price adjustments minimizing changes in expected income and output.

All of these considerations emphasize the need for caution in any integration of revaluations with income and output and saving and investment. But if then for many purposes it may be best to utilize measures that exclude revaluations, it may prove, for many purposes, particularly where the focus is on the accumulation of capital, seriously distorting to ignore them.[21]

Other Adjustments

Various other modifications to conventional accounts have been undertaken. There have been adjustments for the "disamenities" of urban life. In one case, to take into account the changing relative price or costs of the imports that we "buy" with our exports, a "terms of trade" correction has been provided for real GNP.[22] There have been adjustments for pollution and changes in natural resources. And there have been attempts to impute values of leisure time, a major, if problematic, effort.

Surely from the standpoint of welfare, if two economies have the same total output of final goods and services the one that produces this output with less sacrifice of leisure will be viewed as better off. But should leisure be viewed as an output itself or something that is used up as an input to the final product with which we are concerned? Whatever the preference in this regard, there are perhaps overwhelming problems in including leisure in a measure of output. In particular, estimates of its value as the product of its quantity in hours and its marginal rate of substitution—some vector or mean of wage rates—are enormous. Estimates of changes in its value over time prove acutely sensitive to the choice of deflators for wages, which carries with it assumptions as to the growth in "productivity" of leisure. As a consequence, extended measures of income and product that include a component of leisure are dominated by this component. Estimates of the value of leisure might therefore better be kept separate from other extensions of income and product accounts, offered as addenda below the bottom line, if included at all.

Methods of Estimation

In considerable part, revised accounts have involved rearrangement of items already to be found in the conventional NIPAs. Thus, personal consumption expenditures for durables and semidurables may be reclassified as investment. Estimates of the services of these goods would then be put back into consumption. Government output of services may be broken down into consumption, capital accumulation, and intermediate product. Along with this, however, come imputations for the services of government capital. Activities of nonprofit institutions may be taken from the household sector and, with imputations for services not sold in the market, classified separately or combined with an expanded business or "enterprise" sector.

Imputations of income and product from household and government capital generally entail assumptions of depreciation rates to measure capital consumption on bases of historical, constant, and current or replacement cost, and application to net capital of estimated real rates of return. The latter may involve assumed real rates of interest or their calculation from nominal interest and inflation rates. More complicated methods involving estimates of total return from a variety of assets have also been tried.

Issues arise as to the interest rates or opportunity costs applicable to different kinds of capital and to capital in different sectors. Are government interest rates appropriate for government capital? These indeed differ as between federal and state and local governments because the latter issue securities at generally lower, nontaxable rates of interest. What is appropriate for household capital? Is it borrowing costs on installment buying or rates of return on alternative investments such as savings accounts, pension funds, and stocks and bonds? What adjustments are to be made for taxes and price changes?

Reallocation of government output to consumption, capital formation, and intermediate product has been undertaken on the basis of a classification of government activities by function. This entails decisions as to a mapping of government functions to these three major categories of output.

Calculation of investment in human and intangible capital has generally been on a cost basis, as in conventional measures of investment in physical capital by business. There have also been attempts, however, to estimate investment in human capital in terms of its presumed effect on the present value of expected income.

Imputations of value of production by nonmarket labor have been attempted on the basis of opportunity costs and the costs of comparable market labor. Those costs or rates of remuneration per hour have then been applied to time use estimates to get the value of the output of nonmarket labor. Estimates may differ, depending on whether they are based on opportunity costs of existing nonmarket labor or on the wages of market labor devoted to similar market output. Should housework be evaluated at what a household member might earn in the market or at what would be paid in the market for someone to do the housework? Is my time reading with my grandson to be balanced at my marginal return as an economist, or at the rates of pay of a kindergarten teacher or a baby-sitter? The output of nonmarket household labor may also be estimated on the basis of the prices of comparable market output: hotel, restaurant, laundry, and private school services, for starters.

Net revaluations or real capital gains have been estimated by subtracting from changes in the market value of existing assets the increases in market value that would be necessary, on the basis of some measures of the general rate of inflation, to keep real values intact. In general, of course, wealth increases as a consequence of both current capital expenditures for investment and revaluations. Estimation of revaluations for land hence requires allocation of changes in value among pure revaluation and investment in land development.

3

The Structure of TISA:
The National Accounts

The "Total Incomes System of Accounts" (TISA) attempts to implement all or almost all of the extensions which have been discussed with the major exception of leisure. TISA offers estimates of total income and product and associated capital stocks in current and constant dollars for all of the years from 1946 to 1981. It is designed to include the income corresponding to all consumption and capital accumulation, market and nonmarket, in all sectors of the economy.

First, TISA expands the production frontier to include such major items of nonmarket product as the services of government, household capital, unpaid household labor, and the opportunity costs of students' time.

Second, TISA sets up new measures of final product. The services of national defense, roads, and police are classified as intermediate. A portion of commercial media services of television, radio, newspapers and magazines—intermediate in the BEA accounts—is counted in TISA as final product. Expenses related to work are subtracted from income and product while the values of employee training and human capital formation are added. Business product is reduced by the amount of intermediate product deemed to be received from government.

Third, TISA generally values output as the value of all of the factor services and resources from which it flows, regardless of the form of payment or nonpayment. It includes government subsidies and the deficits of government enterprises in the market value of output along with the services of volunteer labor and the difference between the opportunity costs of military conscripts and jurors and what they are paid.

Fourth, TISA breaks down the national income and product account into five separate sector accounts of income and product: for business, nonprofit institutions, government enterprises, government, and households. This entails separating the current accounts of nonprofit institutions from the BEA household or personal sector and separating government enterprises from BEA's implicit business sector. Investment in and income from owner-occupied housing is included in the household sector, along with major imputations for the opportunity costs of students 14 years of age and over, included in investment in human capital, the value of nonmarket household labor, allocated among consumption and investment in human capital, and the services of consumer durables.

Fifth, TISA vastly increases the measure of capital accumulation. It includes, in addition to the BEA's gross private domestic investment, which comprises business and nonprofit institution expenditures for structures and equipment and business accumulation of inventories, acquisition of structures and equipment and additions to inventories by government and government enterprises, and acquisition of durable goods and additions to inventories by households. TISA offers, as a supplement to conventional capital accumulation, net revaluations of tangible assets, that is, increases in the market values or replacement costs of tangible assets over and above changes in the general level of prices. TISA also includes in capital accumulation very large amounts of investment in intangible capital in the form of research and development, education and training, and health.[23]

TISA thus offers a complete set of integrated national income and product accounts with debits and credits for the economy and each of the sectors. These are presented in this volume for all of the years 1946 to 1981, along with associated measures of capital stocks, with the text discussion indicating relative magnitudes by focussing on 1981 estimates. Full details for all years are also available on IBM-compatible 5.25 inch diskettes, with software to facilitate their use in statistical analysis.[24]

National Income and Product

TISA national income and product shows gross national product (GNP) as the sum of credits, and charges against GNP as the sum of debits. As in the BEA accounts, GNP in TISA is a measure of the value of goods and services produced by labor and property supplied by residents of the United States.

Debits

TISA income and nonincome charges on the debit side of the accounts, shown in table S.1A (and in full detail for all years, in table 1), include first a vastly expanded measure of labor income. TISA supplements BEA's $1,769 billion

Table S.1A   TISA National Income and Product Account, Debits

		Billions of Dollars		Average Annual Percent Change	
		1966	1981	1966–81	1946–81
1.	Labor income	841.3	3,208.7	9.335	7.341
2.	Compensation of employees	439.3	1,769.2	9.732	8.042
3.	Additional imputations	416.1	1,502.0	8.934	6.729
4.	Employee training	25.4	73.7	7.360	5.996
5.	Expense account consumption	6.3	24.6	9.506	7.607
6.	Labor income of self-employed	55.6	138.8	6.289	3.987
7.	Opportunity costs of students	60.9	284.2	10.815	9.559
8.	Unpaid household work	267.9	980.7	9.036	6.888
9.	Less: Expenses related to work	14.1	62.5	10.436	9.184
10.	Rental income owner-occupied nonfarm dwellings	0.9	9.3	16.847	12.714
11.	Capital income	82.2	369.8	10.545	9.796
12.	Interest paid	43.5	332.1	14.512	11.917
13.	Net imputed interest (excluding business)	37.3	11.8	−7.386	1.322
14.	Net interest, rest of world	1.4	26.0	21.504	15.864
15.	Net operating surplus	108.9	247.7	5.631	6.945
16.	Corporate profits	85.1	192.3	5.585	7.254
17.	Proprietors' capital income	4.9	−18.6	n.a.	n.a.
18.	Gross business investment in research and development	7.2	33.9	10.881	11.499
19.	Government enterprise surpluses	3.8	12.1	8.027	6.772
20.	Net rental income of persons	7.8	28.0	8.894	5.946
21.	Net revaluations	12.0	−153.7	n.a.	n.a.
22.	Net surplus (15 + 21)	120.8	94.0	−1.658	n.a.
23.	National income (1 + 10 + 11 + 22)	1,045.2	3,681.8	8.787	8.226
24.	Less: Intangible capital consumption	78.5	402.3	11.510	9.064
25.	Net national income (23 − 24)	966.7	3,279.5	8.485	8.138
26.	Business transfer payments	8.2	33.5	9.837	9.483
27.	Media support	4.0	15.8	9.591	9.634
28.	Health and safety	1.2	4.7	9.529	8.265
29.	Other	3.0	12.9	10.213	9.876
30.	Uncompensated factor services	17.1	18.7	0.598	4.945
31.	Net indirect business taxes	10.4	98.0	16.130	n.a.
32.	Indirect business taxes	56.4	219.3	9.476	7.765
33.	Less: Intermediate product transferred from government business	46.0	121.3	6.678	3.563
34.	Statistical discrepancy	1.4	−4.9	n.a.	n.a.
35.	Net national product (25 + 26 + 30 + 31 + 34)	1,003.8	3,424.7	8.525	8.487
36.	Capital consumption allowances	243.0	1,135.5	10.825	7.405
37.	Tangible	164.6	733.1	10.471	6.777
38.	Intangible	78.5	402.3	11.510	9.064
39.	Charges against gross national product (35 + 36)	1.246.8	4,560.1	9.030	8.179

Source: Eisner (1985), table 1, p. 36.
n.a. = not available.

23

for compensation of employees in 1981 with $1,502 of additional imputations, to bring total labor income, after deduction of $63 billion for expenses (for travel) related to work to $3,209 billion. These imputations include employee training, expense account items of consumption, and labor income of the self-employed, which last entails a corresponding subtraction from proprietors' income. The largest imputations of labor income are opportunity costs of students ($284 billion) and unpaid household work ($981 billion), the latter alone over one-half as much as the BEA total compensation of employees.

Several forms of income from property are measured separately. Imputed rental income of owner-occupied nonfarm dwellings, as in the BEA accounts, is included in national income. For the TISA measure, however, the BEA rental income is reduced by net imputed interest, which, in TISA, is part of capital income. Hence TISA rental income in 1981 amounted to only $9 billion.

Capital income ($370 billion) encompasses monetary and imputed interest. In addition to business interest paid, it comprises imputed interest on nonbusiness land, dwellings, structure and equipment, consumer durables and semidurables, and inventories.

Also among the debits is then a net operating surplus composed of corporate profits, a negative figure for proprietors' capital income (after the subtraction of imputed labor income of the self-employed from the BEA figure of proprietors' income), the amount corresponding to gross business investment in research and development ($34 billion, which is expensed and hence reduces current income in conventional accounts), government enterprise surpluses, and net rental income of persons.

Rounding out the components of national income are net revaluations of tangible capital, which are included in an effort to get closer to a consistent theoretical Hicks-Haig-Simon measure of income as what can be consumed while keeping real net worth intact. The net revaluations are the changes in the nominal value of existing land, owner-occupied dwellings, other structures and equipment, consumer durables and semidurables, and inventories minus the changes in nominal value which would be necessary to match changes in the general level of prices.

Tangible capital prices over 1946–81 have generally increased more rapidly than the implicit price deflator for GNP, which is the measure of the general price level used in TISA. Net revaluations were thus generally positive and frequently very substantially so. They also did fluctuate sharply. They were a negative $154 billion in 1981, but they came to a positive total over the 1946–81 period as a whole.

TISA national income is then the sum of labor income, rental income, capital income, net operating surplus, and net revaluations. From this total of $3,682 billion in 1981 it is then appropriate to subtract additional capital consumption allowances for the additional investment of TISA, thus bringing us to a TISA net national income of $3,279 billion, which is 38 percent greater than the comparable BEA national income of $2,373 billion (table S.1C).

Next on the debit side of the TISA national income and product accounts is business transfer payments, which include in addition to the BEA transfer payments, those for commercial media services to consumers[25] and for worker health and safety benefits that are paid for by business. The debits further include uncompensated factor services of volunteers,[26] jurors[27] and (in time of conscription) military draftees.[28]

Because TISA considers government product in part intermediate and subtracts from BEA's GNP and gross business product the value of intermediate product estimated to be transferred to business, it must correspondingly reduce the charges against GNP. It is convenient to view indirect business taxes (nonprofit and government enterprise taxes are treated separately) as a way of paying for government services to production, for which the income and nonincome charges have already been included. Accordingly, TISA subtracts the value of intermediate product transferred from government to business, $121 billion in 1981, from indirect business taxes. Finally, TISA adds nothing (except trivial rounding errors) to the BEA statistical discrepancy.

TISA net national product of $3,425 billion is then only 30.5 percent more than the BEA NNP of $2,625 billion. Capital consumption allowances remain to be added. They are broken (in table 1) into components relating to the original cost of capital and those relating to revaluations (BEA's capital consumption adjustment of consistent accounting at original cost to current replacement cost). In 1981 they summed to $733 billion on tangible capital and $402 billion on intangible capital, bringing total charges against TISA GNP to $4,560 billion, 54.4 percent more than BEA GNP of $2,954 billion. The GNP figures are perhaps less comparable than the NNP's, however, because of TISA's added capital consumption allowances relating to non-business and intangible capital.

Credits

The credit side of the TISA national income and product accounts, shown in table S.1B, is an allocation of total product to consumption, gross domestic capital accumulation, and net exports. The last item in current dollars is identical with that in the BEA accounts. In constant dollars, TISA makes a terms-of-trade adjustment, shown in table S.1D, similar to that in BEA's calculation of GNP on a "command basis." The TISA measures of consumption and gross domestic capital accumulation are substantially different, in both current and constant dollars, from personal consumption expenditures and gross private domestic investment in the BEA accounts.

Table S.1B   TISA National Income and Product Accounts, Credits

		Billions of Dollars		Average Annual Percent Change	
		1966	1981	1966–81	1946–81
1.	Consumption	742.0	2,856.0	9.402	7.182
2.	Household expenditures for services and nondurables	267.4	1,044.2	9.507	7.298
3.	Expense account consumption	6.3	24.6	9.506	7.607
4.	BEA imputations other than housing	7.4	44.5	12.705	6.542
5.	Subsidies allocated to consumption	2.4	7.3	7.698	5.765
6.	Transfers	72.6	280.1	9.419	6.582
7.	Nonmarket services produced in households	358.9	1,455.4	9.253	7.252
8.	Gross domestic capital accumulation	498.3	1,677.9	8.431	12.066
9.	Original cost	483.4	1,823.0	9.253	8.483
10.	Tangible	282.6	972.8	8.590	8.147
11.	Structures and equipment, household durables, and semidurables	271.9	953.8	8.727	7.910
12.	Business	77.6	344.5	10.447	8.567
13.	Nonprofit institutions	5.0	10.3	4.936	9.359
14.	Government enterprises	5.6	22.3	9.650	10.704
15.	Government	38.3	102.7	6.797	8.113
16.	Households	129.3	444.3	8.577	7.019
17.	Fixed gross private domestic product reconciliation	8.3	19.1	5.713	n.a.
18.	Government capital accumulation reconciliation	7.8	10.6	2.066	n.a.
19.	Change in inventories	10.8	19.0	3.838	n.a.
20.	Intangible	200.7	850.2	10.103	8.919
21.	Research and development	21.8	68.5	7.932	11.324
22.	Education and training	153.9	640.1	9.968	8.606
23.	Health	25.1	141.6	12.226	9.702
24.	Subsidies and government enterprise transfers allocated to investment	3.0	8.5	7.190	6.601
25.	Net revaluations	12.0	−153.7	n.a.	n.a.
26.	Net exports	6.5	26.3	9.766	3.515
27.	Export	44.6	368.8	15.123	9.557
28.	Imports	38.1	342.5	15.766	11.633
29.	Gross national product	1,246.8	4,560.1	9.030	8.179

Source: Eisner (1985), table 1, p. 37.
n.a. = not available.

Table S.1C   TISA National Income and Product Accounts, Addenda

	Billions of Dollars		Average Annual Percent Change	
	1966	1981	1966–81	1946–81
1. GNP minus NR	1,234.9	4,713.8	9.341	7.572
2. NNP minus NR	991.8	3,578.4	8.931	7.627
3. NNI minus NR	954.8	3,433.2	8.906	7.344
4. GDCA minus NR	486.4	1,831.6	9.242	8.470
5. NDCA minus NR	243.3	696.1	7.259	11.991
6. NDCA	255.3	542.4	5.152	n.a.
7. NDCA at original cost	240.3	687.5	7.259	12.180
8. NDCA, tangible, at original cost	118.0	239.7	4.838	n.a.
9. NDCA, intangible, at original cost	122.3	447.9	9.039	8.795
10. GDCA − NR/GNP − NR, percent	39.4	38.9	− 0.085	0.835
11. NDCA − NR/NNP − NR, percent	24.5	19.5	− 1.510	4.054
12. NDCA, tangible, at original cost/ NNP − NR, percent	11.9	6.7	− 3.757	n.a.
13. NDCA, intangible, at original cost/ NNP − NR, percent	12.3	12.5	0.108	1.085
14. BEA GNP	756.0	2,954.1	6.536	7.849
15. BEA NNP	695.3	2,624.6	9.260	7.697
16. BEA NI	628.1	2,373.0	9.266	7.671
17. BEA GPDI	125.7	474.9	9.266	8.145
18. BEA NPDI	65.0	145.4	5.514	6.391
19. BEA PCE	465.1	1,857.2	9.670	7.583
20. BEA GPDI/BEA GNP, percent	16.6	16.1	− 0.204	0.274
21. BEA NPDI/BEA NNP, percent	9.4	5.5	− 3.510	− 1.213
22. GNP	1,246.8	4,560.1	9.030	8.179
23. CCA	243.0	1,135.5	10.825	7.405
24. CCA, tangible	164.6	733.1	10.471	6.777
25. CCA, intangible	78.5	402.3	11.510	9.064
26. NNP	1,003.8	3,424.7	8.525	8.487
27. Business transfer payments + uncompensated factor services + net indirect taxes + statistical discrepancy	37.1	145.2	9.523	n.a.
28. NNI	966.7	3,279.5	8.485	8.138

Source: Eisner (1985), table 1, p. 38.
Notes:
BEA   Bureau of Economic Analysis
CCA   Capital consumption allowances
GDCA   Gross domestic capital accumulation
GNP   Gross national product
GPDI   Gross private domestic investment
NDCA   Net domestic capital accumulation
NI   National income
NNI   Net national income
NNP   Net national product
NPDI   Net private domestic investment
NR   Net revaluations
PCE   Personal consumption expenditures
n.a. = not available

Table S.1D   TISA National Income and Product Accounts, 1972 Dollars, Credits

		Billions of 1972 Dollars		Average Annual Percent Change	
		1966	1981	1966–81	1946–81
1.	Consumption	993.6	1,430.0	2.457	2.200
2.	Household expenditures for services and nondurables	340.3	500.1	2.600	2.734
3.	Expense account consumption	7.8	13.3	3.622	3.587
4.	BEA imputations other than housing	10.6	23.0	5.300	2.191
5.	Subsidies allocated to consumption	3.3	4.1	1.458	1.387
6.	Transfers	102.8	125.7	1.350	0.749
7.	Nonmarket services produced in households	528.8	763.9	2.482	2.181
8.	Gross domestic capital accumulation	654.5	866.8	1.891	7.127
9.	Original cost	634.9	936.1	2.621	3.750
10.	Tangible	360.1	521.5	2.500	3.935
11.	Structures and equipment, household durables and semidurables	347.2	512.8	2.634	3.833
12.	Business	101.0	166.3	3.380	3.438
13.	Nonprofit institutions	7.2	5.2	−2.146	4.447
14.	Government enterprises	8.1	9.9	1.347	4.873
15.	Government	53.5	48.7	−0.625	2.321
16.	Households	157.8	264.5	3.503	3.800
17.	Fixed gross private domestic product reconciliation	10.2	12.7	1.472	n.a.
18.	Government capital accumulation reconciliation	9.5	5.5	−3.578	n.a.
19.	Change in inventories	12.8	8.7	−2.541	n.a.
20.	Intangible	274.8	414.6	2.780	3.534
21.	Research and development	30.4	34.0	0.749	5.932
22.	Education and training	208.2	318.0	2.864	3.380
23.	Health	36.1	62.5	3.727	3.451
24.	Subsidies and government enterprise transfers allocated to investment	3.9	4.6	1.107	2.271
25.	Net revaluations	15.7	−73.9	n.a.	n.a.
26.	Net exports	8.5	13.5	3.132	−0.806
27.	Net BEA exports	6.5	43.0	13.424	3.430
28.	Terms of trade effect	2.0	−29.6	n.a.	n.a.
29.	Net exports in current dollars, deflated	8.5	13.5	3.132	−0.806
30.	Less: net exports in constant dollars without terms of trade effect	6.5	43.0	13.424	3.430
31.	Gross national product	1,656.6	2,310.4	2.242	3.215

Source: Eisner (1985), table 7, p. 43.
n.a. = not available.

28

Table S.1E   TISA National Income and Product Accounts, 1972 Dollars, Addenda

	Billions of 1972 Dollars		Average Annual Percent Change	
	1966	1981	1966–81	1946–81
1. GNP minus NR	1,640.9	2,384.2	2.522	2.677
2. NNP minus NR	1,323.6	1,836.6	2.208	2.736
3. NNI minus NR	1,273.9	1,752.7	2.150	2.459
4. GDCA minus NR	638.8	940.7	2.614	3.741
5. NDCA minus NR	321.5	393.1	1.349	7.772
6. NDCA	337.2	319.2	−0.365	n.a.
7. NDCA at original cost	317.5	388.5	1.355	7.971
8. NDCA, tangible, at original cost	146.6	174.6	1.172	n.a.
9. NDCA, intangible, at original cost	171.0	213.8	1.500	3.230
10. GDCA − NR/GNP − NR, percent	38.9	39.5	0.102	1.036
11. NDCA-NR/NNP-NR, percent	24.3	21.4	−0.844	4.902
12. NDCA, tangible, at original cost/ NNP-NR, percent	11.1	9.5	−1.032	n.a.
13. NDCA, intangible, at original cost/ NNP-NR, percent	12.9	11.6	−0.706	0.481
14. BEA GNP	984.8	1,513.8	2.908	3.347
15. BEA NNP	906.2	1,357.9	2.733	3.244
16. BEA NI	816.0	1,212.6	2.676	3.204
17. BEA GPDI	163.0	227.6	2.251	3.388
18. BEA NPDI	84.3	71.6	−1.083	1.910
19. BEA PCE	585.7	956.8	3.326	3.359
20. BEA GPDI/BEA GNP, percent	16.6	15.0	−0.673	0.040
21. BEA NPDI/BEA NNP, percent	9.3	5.3	−3.679	−1.292
22. GNP	1,656.6	2,310.4	2.248	3.215
23. CCA	317.3	547.7	3.706	2.490
24. CCA, tangible	213.5	346.9	3.289	1.911
25. CCA, intangible	103.9	200.8	4.490	3.897
26. NNP	1,339.3	1,762.7	1.848	3.483
27. Business transfer payments + uncompensated factor services + net indirect taxes + statistical discrepancy	49.7	83.8	3.544	n.a.
28. NNI	1,289.6	1,678.9	1.774	3.151

Source: Eisner (1985), table 7, p. 44.

Notes:

BEA   Bureau of Economic Analysis
CCA   Capital consumption allowances
GDCA   Gross domestic capital accumulation
GNP   Gross national product
GPDI   Gross private domestic investment
NDCA   Net domestic capital accumulation
NI   National income
NNI   Net national income
NNP   Net national product
NPDI   Net private domestic investment
NR   Net revaluations
PCE   Personal consumption expenditures
n.a. = not available.

29

For consumption, the BEA measure is basically changed, as shown in table S.2, to arrive at one that includes, rather than expenditures for consumer durables and semidurables, both of which are treated as investments in TISA, the value of their services. These capital services are measured as the sum of capital consumption and a net imputed return. TISA thus subtracts from BEA personal consumption expenditures purchases of consumer durables and semidurables. TISA also subtracts current expenditures of nonprofit institutions, expenditures for medical care considered investment, changes in household or consumer inventories, and travel expenses related to work.

TISA adds to consumption the value of expense account items, including but not limited to the ill-famed business lunch. Also, because the TISA measure of output is generally at factor cost rather than market prices, TISA

Table S.2   Reconciliation of BEA and TISA Measures of Consumption, 1981 (Billions of Dollars)

1.	BEA personal consumption expenditures	1,857.2
2.	Less: Durables	236.1
3.	Semidurables	125.6
4.	Current expenditures of nonprofit institutions	123.5
5.	Medical care investment not included in durables	60.0
6.	Change in household inventories	0.1
7.	Net space rent, owner-occupied nonfarm housing	178.6
8.	BEA nonhousing imputations	44.5
9.	Equals: TISA gross household expenditures	1,088.1
10.	Less: Expenses related to work	43.9
11.	Equals: Household expenditures for services and nondurables	1,044.2
12.	Plus: Expense account items of consumption	24.6
13.	BEA nonhousing imputations	44.5
14.	Subsidies to market consumption	7.3
15.	Transfers	280.1
16.	From business	14.8
17.	From nonprofit institutions	81.0
18.	From government enterprises	6.0
19.	From government	178.2
20.	Nonmarket services produced in households	1,455.4
21.	Net space rent, owner-occupied nonfarm housing, including subsidies	178.9
22.	Other capital services	332.3
23.	Labor services	944.3
24.	Equals: TISA consumption	2,856.0

BEA sources (U.S. Department of Commerce, *Survey of Current Business,* July 1983):
Line 1: National income and product accounts (NIPA) table 2.2, line 1.
Line 2: NIPA table 2.2, line 2.
Line 3: NIPA table 2.4, lines 12, 13, and 33.
Line 4: Unpublished detail underlying NIPA table 2.4.
Line 5: NIPA table 2.4, 0.5 (line 44 − line 46 − line 53 − line 54 − 0.76 line 50).
Line 7: NIPA table 8.8, line 74.
Line 8: NIPA table 8.8, line 7.

consumption includes the portion of subsidies related to consumption. And TISA includes in consumption substantial amounts, coming to $280 billion in 1981, for what are then taken to be transfers of consumption services from other sectors. These include the value of media support and provisions for health and safety from business; health, education, and religious services, in excess of what consumers pay for, from nonprofit institutions; similar unpurchased services provided by government enterprises; and a large item, $178 billion in 1981, for a variety of services of government, such as those of roads and parks, for which households would presumably have had to pay directly, rather than by taxes, had they been furnished by private industry.

Consumption includes as well the bulk of nonmarket services produced in households from tangible capital and unpaid household work. Thus, TISA includes $332 billion in 1981 for the capital services of consumer durables and semidurables and of inventories. As noted these are substituted for the BEA items for corresponding expenditures for durables and semidurables. The value of the services actually proves smaller in 1981 because the net imputed return was less than the excess of current expenditures over capital consumption; a great deal of BEA's personal consumption expenditures were thus net investment in durables.

The TISA value of nonmarket labor services in households was no less than $1,265 billion (the sum of lines 7 and 8, the opportunity cost of students and unpaid household work, in table S.1A) in 1981, but of this total $321 billion was allocated to investment, generally in the form of health and education of household members. This left $944 billion as the value of preparation of meals, cleaning clothes, care of children, and other unpaid housework counted as provision of consumption services.

The sum of TISA's additions was much more than the subtractions. TISA consumption hence came to $2,856 billion in 1981, 53.8 percent greater than BEA personal consumption expenditures.

TISA's gross domestic capital accumulation, as shown in table S.3, is vastly increased over BEA gross private domestic investment by the inclusion of household and government investment in tangible assets as well as the intangible investment of research and development, education and training, and health. The total is broken down into tangible and intangible investment at original cost, subsidies and government enterprise transfers allocated to investment, and net revaluations.

BEA gross private domestic investment, $475 billion in 1981, includes only investment in structures and equipment by private business and nonprofit institutions, additions to inventories by private business and (what TISA counts as household) investment in owner-occupied nonfarm dwellings. TISA sets forth explicitly the nonprofit institution investment in structures and equipment, $10 billion in 1981, and includes also $22 billion of such investment by government enterprises, $103 billion by government (including

Table S.3   Reconciliation of BEA and TISA Measures of Investment, 1981 (Billions of Dollars)

1.	BEA gross private domestic investment	474.9
2.	Less: Structures and equipment owned by nonprofit institutions	10.3
3.	Owner-occupied nonfarm dwellings	82.5
4.	Change in business inventories	18.5
5.	Fixed gross private domestic investment reconciliation	19.1
6.	Equals: TISA business investment in structures and equipment (original cost)	344.5
7.	Plus: Nonprofit institutions	10.3
8.	Structures	8.6
9.	Equipment	1.7
10.	Government enterprises	22.3
11.	Structures	20.1
12.	Equipment	2.2
13.	Government	102.7
14.	Structures	32.6
15.	Equipment	43.4
16.	Product accumulated	26.7
17.	Households	443.3
18.	Owner-occupied dwellings	82.5
19.	Durables	236.1
20.	Semidurables	125.6
21.	Reconciliations	29.7
22.	Fixed gross private domestic investment	19.1
23.	Government capital accumulation	10.6
24.	Equals: TISA gross domestic investment in structures and equipment and in household durables and semidurables (original cost)	953.8
25.	Plus: Changes in inventories	19.0
26.	Business	18.5
27.	Government	0.4
28.	Households	0.1
29.	Equals: TISA gross domestic tangible investment (original cost)	972.8
30.	Plus: Intangible investment	850.2
31.	Research and development	68.5
32.	Education and training	640.1
33.	Health	141.6
34.	Subsidies and government enterprise transfers to households	8.5
35.	Net revaluations	− 153.7
36.	Equals: TISA gross domestic capital accumulation	1,677.9

BEA sources (U.S. Department of Commerce, *Survey of Current Business*, July 1983):

Lines 1 and 4 (and 26): National income and product accounts (NIPA) table 1.1, lines 6 and 15.

Lines 2, 3, 7–15, and 18: BEA updates and revisions of *Fixed Reproducible Tangible Wealth in the United States, 1925–79.*

Line 19: NIPA table 1.1, line 3.

Line 20: NIPA table 2.4, lines 12, 13, and 33.

Line 21: These reconciliations are necessary because some of the investment series by sector are from BEA tangible wealth presentations that differ from the NIPA investment series in their valuation of export sales of used equipment and business capital account transactions with government.

$27 billion of product accumulated in natural resources) and the additional investment by households of $236 billion in durables and $126 billion in semidurables.

Reconciliation items are needed to bring sector sums in line with corresponding BEA totals because the prices at which intersector transactions are carried in the two data sources differ. These items, plus investment in inventories, including that by government and households, are part of the $973 billion in total gross domestic tangible capital accumulation at original cost in 1981. Intangible investment is almost as large, $850 billion. This total consists of: $69 billion in research and development investment by business, nonprofit institutions, and government; $640 billion of investment in the "stock" of education of the American people; and $142 billion of investment in their health. The value of subsidies and government enterprise transfers allocated to investment comes to another $9 billion.

TISA's gross domestic tangible investment at original cost was thus more than twice BEA's gross private domestic investment. Total gross domestic capital accumulation without net revaluations ($1,832 billion) was almost four times BEA's gross private domestic investment. And while BEA gross private domestic investment was only 16.1 percent of BEA GNP, TISA gross domestic capital accumulation was 36.8 percent of TISA GNP, as seen in chart 1. Net domestic capital accumulation at original cost, $687 billion, was 4.7 times BEA's net private domestic investment of $145 billion (table S.1C).

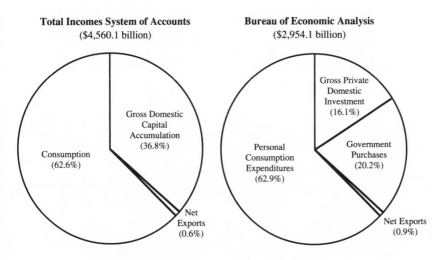

Total Incomes System of Accounts
($4,560.1 billion)

Consumption (62.6%)

Gross Domestic Capital Accumulation (36.8%)

Net Exports (0.6%)

Bureau of Economic Analysis
($2,954.1 billion)

Gross Private Domestic Investment (16.1%)

Personal Consumption Expenditures (62.9%)

Government Purchases (20.2%)

Net Exports (0.9%)

Chart 1   Gross National Product by Type of Product, 1981. Taken from Robert Eisner, "The Total Incomes System of Accounts," *Survey of Current Business* 65, no. 1 (1985): 26.

To arrive at total capital accumulation, that is, the increase in the real value of capital, TISA adds net revaluations on tangible capital—in 1981, as already noted, a negative figure of $154 billion. The negative net revaluations were due to capital losses (after adjustment for general inflation) of $142 billion on land, $35 billion on consumer durables and semidurables, and $28 billion on inventories, as shown in the detail in table 1. There were, however, capital gains of $18 billion on structures and equipment owned by business and $51 billion on government structure and equipment. Homeowners lost $14 billion after adjustment for inflation, and nonprofit institutions lost $4 billion.

Net exports are added to the totals for consumption and gross capital accumulation to arrive at a TISA GNP of $4,560 in 1981 (table S.1B). Without net revaluations, TISA GNP of $4,714 billion (table S.1C) was 59.6 percent larger than BEA GNP. Because much of TISA product is additional capital accumulation that requires additional capital consumption allowances, the excess, again without net revaluations, of TISA NNP of $3,578 billion over BEA's NNP is considerably less, 36.3 percent.

4

The Sector Accounts

Total TISA GNP is the sum of the product of each of the domestic sectors plus the BEA's net product attributed to the rest of the world. Because the TISA measures reflect a substantial amount of nonmarket output of nonbusiness sectors, it is useful to set forth the full sector accounts. They make clear the greatly expanded role, in total product, of households and, to a lesser extent, government, and the contrasts to be drawn with the corresponding BEA sectors. While some 85 percent of total BEA GNP was accounted for by business in 1981, the corresponding figure for TISA was only 47 percent, as shown in chart 2. Households and nonprofit institutions accounted for only 3.3 percent of BEA GNP but 40 percent (37.5 percent from households alone) of TISA GNP. Government produced 11.1 percent of TISA output but only 10.1 percent of BEA GNP.

Unlike the basic income and outlay accounts of the BEA NIPAs, the TISA sector accounts relate income and *product*. In each account, TISA credits total to gross sector product—the sector's contribution to GNP or value added. TISA debits are the charges against gross sector products. In the business sector, the foundation is the BEA's gross business product and the charges against it. Various additions and subtractions on the credit side bring us to TISA gross business product, and corresponding adjustments are made to the debits. In all of the other sectors, total product is calculated on the debit side, utilizing accounts of market transactions from the BEA and a number of imputations for labor and capital income and nonincome costs or charges. Gross product of each sector other than business and, in part, government enterprises, is allocated, along with intermediate product from other

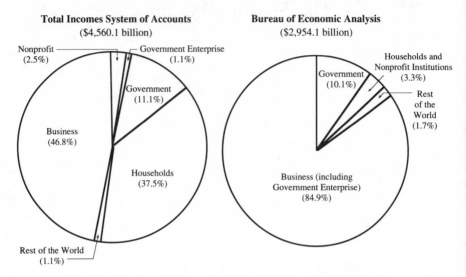

Chart 2   Gross National Product by Sector, 1981. Taken from Robert Eisner, "The Total Incomes System of Accounts," *Survey of Current Business* 65, no. 1 (1985): 29.

sectors, to consumption and capital accumulation and, in the case of government, to intermediate product.

Business

The TISA business sector comprises the BEA business sector less owner-occupied nonfarm dwellings, government enterprises, and buildings owned by nonprofit institutions. The TISA business sector account (table 2) entails subtractions, corresponding to these exclusions, from BEA's gross domestic product of business, along with a number of additions.

As in the national account, additions to BEA-type product are made to reflect the altered scope of final product. Subsidies received by business are included in the value of final product so that product, not merely income, is at factor cost. Expense account items of consumption and the value of employee training are included in labor income and in final product. Business R&D is also counted as final product, to go into the total of investment rather than to be expended as in BEA practice. The portion of expenditures for advertising that results in provision of entertainment to viewers, listeners, and readers is allocated to final product rather than wiped out as intermediate purchases of one firm from another. Business provisions for health and safety of employees is also counted, as noted earlier, as a business transfer payment entering into final product.

Among the items subtracted, several are moved to nonbusiness sectors: space rent of owner-occupied nonfarm dwellings, to the household sector; the product of government enterprises, to the government enterprise sector; and the rental value of buildings and equipment owned and used by nonprofit organizations serving individuals, to the nonprofit sector. Expenses related to work are subtracted, as they would be in the BEA accounts if employers incurred them, as in employer provision of transportation to the job. Finally $121 billion of intermediate product from government, covering services such as those of police, defense, and roads, is also subtracted.

With negative net revaluations of $107 billion in 1981, the BEA gross domestic product of business of $2,509 billion is thus reduced to a TISA gross business product of $2,134 billion. Without net revaluations, TISA gross business product of $2,241 billion is 10.7 percent less than BEA's gross domestic product of business.

Nonprofit Institutions

Total product of the nonprofit sector (table 3), as in the case of all the nonbusiness sectors, is estimated on the debit side of the account. It is the sum of the incomes of the labor and capital the sector uses, net revaluations, and capital consumption allowances. Labor income of $86 billion in 1981 consists overwhelmingly of compensation of employees, with a small addition for employee training and a $4 billion subtraction for expenses related to work. The value of output produced by labor also includes, however, $18 billion that is imputed, on the basis of estimates of time spent in volunteer activities and the average wage of nonsupervisory service industry workers, to volunteer services.

Capital income of $6 billion is imputed gross interest on land, structures and equipment, and residential property. It is calculated by applying to the average of each year's beginning and ending stocks a weighted average of the after-tax rate of return to household and business capital. This rate is obtained by dividing an estimate of total return—the sum of after-tax corporate profits, proprietors' capital income, interest paid by business and on owner-occupied housing, rental income, and imputed interest on household capital, less personal taxes on business capital—by the total stock of business and household tangible capital. Negative net revaluations of $5 billion and capital consumption allowances of $8 billion are then added, to bring total gross nonprofit product to $113 billion.

On the credit side of the account, the total of this product, plus expenses related to work, intermediate product purchased, and intermediate product transferred from government is allocated among consumption and capital accumulation. Consumption includes $63 billion accounted for by expenditures in the BEA's personal consumption expenditures and an additional imputation, amounting to $18 billion, of a portion of the services of capital, as measured by net imputed interest, and of volunteers. The capital accumulation total of $66 billion includes $1.5 billion in R&D, $34 billion in education and training, $36 billion in health (which is, by assumption, one-half of the value of health product), and again $5 billion of negative net revaluations.

Government Enterprises

Product of government enterprises (table 4), like that of nonprofit institutions, estimated on the debit side of the account, is the sum of labor income, $37 billion in 1981, measured net of expenses related to work, capital income and surpluses of $12 billion, and trivial net revaluations. The ''surpluses'' are the sum of $6 billion of BEA surpluses and the almost equal sum of absolute values of negative BEA surpluses for those classes of government enterprises that were running losses. The latter, again, are included in order to measure product in terms of factor cost rather than, necessarily, the market value of sales.

There are no capital consumption allowances, and imputed capital income is very small, because all of the product of tangible government enterprise capital, other than inventories, is attributed to government itself. One consideration underlying this procedure is that governments often incur direct expenditures for the provision of fixed capital to government enterprises, so that the enterprises do not, in fact, then cover capital costs in their sales. The most important consideration, however, was the need to allocate the imputed product of this capital by functions in which it was employed, and information for this allocation was generally available only for capital of government and government enterprises combined.

As with the business sector, the credit side of the government enterprise account starts with sales, minus of course the purchase of intermediate goods. Because there is no independent information on this latter magnitude, it becomes the balancing item between total credits and total debits. Credits must also include, then, the value of product not paid for by the $43 billion of sales net of purchases.

Thus the credit side shows $11 billion of transfers, stemming from imputed capital income and negative surpluses that government enterprises do not cover in their receipts, intermediate product from government less indirect taxes, and employee training expenditures. The allocation of these transfers between consumption and capital accumulation, admittedly ad hoc, is based on proportions in the rest of the economy.

Government

The TISA government sector account (table 5 and S.4) differs fundamentally from that of BEA. TISA product originating in government includes not only the value of compensation of employees or, more generally, labor income, which came to $318 billion in 1981. It also includes the value of capital services, the sum of $69 billion of imputed capital income, calculated (as for nonprofit institutions) on the basis of a weighted average of the after-tax rates of return to business and household capital, and $91 billion of capital consumption allowances, as well as $25 billion of net revaluations.[29] In addition,

Table S.4   TISA Government Income and Product

Debits	Billions of Dollars		Average Annual Percent Change
	1966	1981	1946–81
1. Labor income	85.5	318.2	7.485
2. Capital income	30.8	69.4	6.413
3. Net revaluations	5.0	24.7	n.a.
4. Income originating (1 + 2 + 3)	121.3	412.3	11.902
5. Uncompensated factor services	10.2	0.7	−1.958
6. Charges against net government product (4 + 5)	131.5	412.9	11.424
7. Capital consumption allowances	22.1	91.3	3.018
8. Charges against gross government product (6 + 7)	153.6	504.3	7.387

Credits	Current Dollars (in Billions)		1972 Dollars (in Billions)		Average Annual Percent Change (1972 Dollars)
	1966	1981	1966	1981	1946–81
9. Consumption (to households)	27.8	129.5	37.4	60.3	2.970
10. Capital accumulation	77.9	314.9	113.8	151.6	2.820
11. Intermediate product	86.0	233.6	120.1	110.5	−1.464
12. Gross credits exclusive of change in inventories and net revaluations	191.6	678.0	271.3	322.4	0.572
13. Change in inventories	−3.6	0.4	−4.3	0.2	n.a.
14. Less: intermediate purchases from other sectors	36.7	187.5	47.4	80.0	6.804
15. Less: Expenses related to work	2.7	11.4	3.3	5.0	4.055
16. Gross government product exclusive of net revaluations	148.6	479.5	216.3	237.5	−0.030
17. Net revaluations	5.0	24.7	6.6	11.9	n.a.
18. Gross government product	153.6	504.3	222.8	249.4	0.964

Source: Eisner (1985), table 5, p. 41, and table 11, p. 46.
n.a. = not available.

TISA includes the value of uncompensated factor services (the difference between opportunity cost and actual compensation)—the tiny item of $0.6 billion for jury duty in 1981, but a larger amount in earlier years when military conscription was in effect.

The total of these debit items is gross government product, $504 billion in 1981. This product plus the value of intermediate purchases from other sectors and expenses related to work, but minus change in inventories and net revaluations, must then be allocated among consumption, capital accumulation, and intermediate product to other sectors. The allocation involves a complicated procedure related to the functions or activities into which government output can be categorized. The functional classification also determines the sectors to which government output—which is not, of course, generally sold—is transferred.

First, BEA government expenditures by type of function are reclassified into ten broad categories: defense (including police and fire protection); space; education and training; health; housing and community services; transportation and mobility; local parks and recreation; natural resources; welfare; and general administration. Second, the published and unpublished data on expenditures and capital[30] are adjusted by somewhat complicated (resourceful!) procedures to derive TISA measures of product by function. Third, the allocation to consumption, investment, intermediate product, and among sectors is undertaken for each of the ten categories or functions.[31]

In this allocation, defense, transportation, and general administration are generally counted as intermediate to other government production or to the output of other sectors. One-half of the cost of manned space flights, which may be taken as their entertainment value, is viewed as consumption, along with major portions of the product associated with local parks and recreation and of the transportation product going to households. Education and training is considered an output of capital which is transferred to households. Health services, following Kendrick, are counted as one-half going to capital accumulation in households and one-half maintenance or current consumption. Investment in natural resources is considered capital accumulated by government. Housing and community services and welfare are designated as consumption. R&D expenditures, associated with the defense and space functions, are viewed as creating an output partly retained in government as a stock of R&D knowledge and partly transferred to business.

The intermediate product of government is thus taken to include half of government sanitation services, a share of transportation services estimated to be going to enterprises, the portion (33.2 percent) of the household share estimated to be devoted to travel to work, all of the final product of general administration, all of space product except that allocated to consumption (its entertainment value) or to investment in research and development, and all of national defense not allocated to research and development. The defense services are allocated to sectors in proportion to the capital stocks in the sectors—on the convenient assumption that defense serves to protect the nation's productive plant. General administration services are allocated to sectors in proportion to their output.

The intermediate product transferred to business is viewed as a purchase paid for by indirect taxes. It is hence excluded from GNP. To include it would be, by this logic, to double-count the output of government and its input into whatever business is producing. That business output goes into consumption or investment (capital accumulation) as it is purchased. The intermediate product that goes to the other sectors (mainly to households) is imputed to these sectors' product in the form of consumption or investment and is thus not subtracted from GNP.

On the basis of these allocations, government was deemed to contribute to households $130 billion of consumption services, equal to 4.4 percent of BEA GNP, in 1981. Government production of capital came to $315 billion, 10.7 percent of BEA GNP, of which $25 billion was in the form of R&D expenditures viewed as a transfer to business and $255 billion went to households. The latter included $225 billion in education and training, mainly the cost of public schools, and $30 billion in health services. Government retained $35 billion of the capital it produced—$8 billion in R&D capital and $27 billion in natural resources investment. Government intermediate services to other sectors came to $121 billion to business and $103 billion to households.

Households

Gross household product (table 6 and S.5), also estimated from the debit side, is the sum of labor income, $1,271 billion in 1981, $143 billion of capital income, and $361 billion of tangible capital consumption, plus negative net revaluations of $66 billion. Gross household product in 1981 was thus put at $1,709 billion—only moderately smaller than gross business product of $2,134 billion.

Actual compensation of employees in households is, of course, very minor—only the $7 billion, in 1981, denoted by the BEA as household product. The big items in labor income in households are the imputations for the opportunity costs of students, $284 billion, and for unpaid household work, $981 billion. In view of the size of these items an extended discussion of their derivation may be in order.

Opportunity costs of students relate to those 14 years of age and over. The estimates were originally prepared by Kendrick (1976) for the years 1946 to 1969 and 1973. They are based on wages estimated to be available at the relevant ages and school enrollments. Kendrick's series were extended largely on the basis of later enrollment figures and changes in average annual compensation of the total labor force, which were taken to be proportional to changes in compensation available to students.

The value of unpaid household work is taken conservatively to be the product of annual hours in relevant household activities and the average hourly compensation of household domestic workers.[32]

The capital income attributed to households consists of two items. The largest is $101 billion for owner-occupied nonfarm dwellings. Of this, $91 billion is gross imputed interest, leaving only some $9 billion for net rental income. The remaining $43 billion is imputed interest on the stock of consumer goods held by households.[33]

Capital consumption allowances on intangible capital amounted to $351 billion. These are subtracted to get a measure of net income originating, after including net revaluations, of $997 billion. The intangible capital consumption allowances, along with tangible capital consumption allowances, are added back to get total gross household product.

Before this product is allocated between consumption and capital accumulation, $103 billion of intermediate product transferred from government and the $1 billion for expenses related to work must be added. After accounting for $19 billion of services related to travel to work, $1,511 billion of final

Table S.5   TISA Household Income and Product

Debits	Billions of Dollars		Average Annual Percent Change
	1966	1981	1946–81
1. Labor income	332.4	1,271.4	7.269
2. Compensation of employees	4.0	7.0	3.489
3. Imputations	328.9	1,265.0	7.312
4. Employee training	0.1	0.1	0.744
5. Opportunity costs of students	60.9	284.2	9.559
6. Unpaid household work	267.9	980.7	6.888
7. Less: Expenses related to work	0.5	1.0	6.809
8. Capital income	36.8	143.1	9.990
9. Owner-occupied housing	22.9	100.5	10.857
10. Consumer goods	13.9	42.6	8.589
11. Net revaluations	1.4	−66.0	n.a.
12. Income originating (1 + 8 + 11)	370.7	1,348.1	7.974
13. Less: intangible (human) capital consumption	68.3	351.1	8.750
14. Net income originating and charges against net household product (12 − 13)	302.3	997.0	7.743
15. Capital consumption allowance	158.7	711.7	8.009
16. Tangible (nonhuman)	90.3	360.6	7.429
17. Intangible (human)	68.3	351.1	8.750
18. Charges against gross household product (14 + 15)	461.0	1,708.7	7.851
			(*continued*)

Table S.5   (*Continued*)

Credits	Current Dollars (in Billions)		1972 Dollars (in Billions)		Average Annual Percent Change (1972 Dollars)
	1966	1981	1966	1981	1946–81
19. Consumption	410.0	1,511.1	566.1	786.1	1.814
20. Market (labor services in households)	4.0	7.0	5.9	3.1	−1.742
21. Nonmarket	385.9	1,455.4	529.8	763.9	2.181
22. Intermediate product of government to consumption	20.1	48.7	31.4	19.0	−2.944
23. Capital accumulation	82.7	282.5	107.3	146.6	n.a.
24. Intangible at original cost	81.3	348.6	105.5	178.3	3.886
25. Education	78.0	335.5	100.8	171.9	4.030
26. Health	3.2	13.0	4.6	6.4	1.628
27. Employee training	0.1	0.1	0.1	0.1	−3.643
28. Net revaluations	1.4	−66.0	1.8	−31.7	n.a.
29. Services to expenses related to work	5.8	18.6	6.9	8.2	3.690
30. Less: Intermediate product transferred from government	37.0	102.5	51.9	48.7	−0.709
31. Less: Expenses related to work	0.5	1.0	0.6	0.5	1.636
32. Gross household product	461.0	1,708.7	627.9	891.7	2.693

Source: Eisner (1985), table 6, p. 42, and table 12, p. 46.
n.a. = not available.

household product is consumed and $283 billion of product is invested. Of the nonmarket output, $179 billion is the net space rent of owner-occupied nonfarm dwellings and $332 billion is the value of other capital services, essentially from the stock of consumer durables and semidurables. Of imputed labor services, $944 billion are counted as consumption, with the remaining $321 billion going to capital accumulation.

Most of that capital accumulation is the $284 billion for education equal to the opportunity cost of students, considered intangible capital accumulated in the household. In addition, $27 billion is for the value of time devoted to teaching children in the home and $18 billion is for intermediate product of government to education. One-half of the value of time devoted to health, $13 billion, is also counted as investment. Net revaluations in 1981 amounted to capital decumulation of $66 billion.

5

Constant-Dollar Accounts and Capital
Stock Series

The constant-dollar accounts, tables 7 to 12, are generally analogous to the credit sides of the current-dollar accounts. The addenda to table 7 show constant-dollar NNP and net national income and the nonincome charges against product that must be subtracted from gross national product to derive them.

Constant-dollar series for the BEA components of the TISA accounts are taken directly, where possible, from (usually unpublished) BEA tables in millions of dollars. For other items, implicit deflators provided by BEA, or constructed from BEA series or from combinations of BEA series and non-BEA TISA components, are used to deflate current dollar measures.

With regard to capital accumulation, constant-dollar sectoral investment figures were taken from BEA capital stock tapes.[34] Investment in household inventories is the difference between successive end-of-year stocks calculated on the assumption that nondurable household goods have a two-week life. Net revaluations in constant dollars are calculated with the implicit price deflator for fixed investment.

As in the BEA accounts, components of income are not generally offered in constant dollars. Since, however, in all of the sectors except business, total product is estimated on the debit side, in a number of important instances current-dollar debit figures must be deflated in order to get the constant-dollar credit items that depend upon them. Thus, the deflator for personal consumption expenditures is applied to the opportunity costs of students, which has the effect of imputing increases in ''productivity'' of student time in proportion with increases in the real wage. A domestic wage deflator is applied

44

to unpaid household work, and this makes changes in the constant dollar value of that output depend only upon changes in the inputs of time.

TISA departs from conventional practice for net exports, and applies essentially the alternative "command" measure presented by BEA.[35] Instead of defining net exports as constant-dollar exports minus constant-dollar imports, TISA defines them as current dollar net exports divided by the GNP implicit price deflator. With this measure of net exports, constant-dollar GNP better reflects the goods and services actually available to the residents of the United States. TISA net exports in constant dollars thus equal the conventional BEA net exports plus a "terms of trade effect," reflecting the fact that more or less U.S. goods must be produced to get a given real quantity of foreign goods. In 1981, the terms of trade effect amounted to minus $30 billion 1972 dollars, converting a $43 billion BEA net export surplus to one of only $13 billion in TISA.

The capital stock series, in current and constant dollars, shown in tables 13 and 14 with corresponding implicit price deflators in table 15, with 1981 estimates and 1945–81 growth rates in table S.6, are in principle consistent with the income and product accounts. Constant-dollar capital stocks at the end of each year in each sector might then be expected to equal capital stocks at the end of the previous year plus gross capital accumulation, including net transfer of capital into the sector, minus capital consumption allowances. In fact, discrepancies generally arise (except where investment figures are directly related to changes in stocks, as in the case of business and government and government enterprise inventories), essentially because 1972 dollars for component flows of investment during the year are not the same as 1972 dollars pegged to end-of-year, aggregated stocks.

Current-dollar capital stocks equal previous stocks plus gross capital accumulation plus net transfers, minus current cost capital consumption allowances, plus gross revaluations. Net revaluations of tangible capital in the income and product accounts may then be calculated from the gross revaluations by netting out the portion accountable to changes in the general level of prices.

Tangible capital stocks other than land were generally taken from BEA series. Consistent with the inclusion of all investment in the income and product accounts, the capital stock series include residential and nonresidential structures and equipment in all sectors—government, government enterprises, and households, as well as business and nonprofit institutions. For households, capital stocks include durables, semidurables, and inventories, along with houses. We add separate estimates of land in all sectors, usually taken from series provided by the Flow of Funds section of the Board of Governors of the Federal Reserve System.

Intangible capital relates either to R&D which, wherever originally produced, is assumed to be of ultimate use to business and hence credited to

Table S.6   Capital Stocks, 1981, and Average Annual Percent Change in Capital and Implicit Price Deflators, 1945–81

| | Capital Stocks | | | | | | |
| | Billions of | | Percent of Total | | Average Annual Percent Change | | |
	Current Dollars	1972 Dollars	Current Dollars	1972 Dollars	Current Dollars	1972 Dollars	Deflators
1. Total capital	23,746.4	11,487.8	100.0	100.0	8.656	3.857	4.621
2. Business	6,085.9	2,893.1	25.6	25.1	8.423	3.616	4.639
3. Tangible	5,528.9	2,496.6	23.3	21.7	8.240	3.262	4.821
4. Land	1,465.1	731.1	6.2	6.4	7.319	2.684	4.514
5. Structures and equipment	2,668.4	1,188.0	11.2	10.3	9.870	4.433	5.206
6. Residential	557.7	228.9	2.3	2.0	6.229	1.163	5.007
7. Inventories	837.8	348.6	3.5	3.0	8.082	3.412	4.516
8. Intangible (research and development)	557.0	396.5	2.3	3.5	11.412	8.782	2.148
9. Nonprofit	248.2	111.7	1.0	1.0	8.833	3.487	5.166
10. Land	41.7	20.8	0.2	0.2	7.867	3.208	4.514
11. Structure and equipment	180.8	80.5	0.8	0.7	10.459	4.548	5.653
12. Residential	25.7	10.4	0.1	0.1	5.290	0.220	5.059

13.	Government	2,309.9	1,030.1	9.7	9.0	6.420	1.522	4.824
14.	Land	552.6	275.7	2.3	2.4	9.374	4.651	4.514
15.	Structures and equipment	1,502.8	621.7	6.3	5.4	6.400	0.900	5.450
16.	Residential	20.0	7.1	0.1	0.1	6.488	0.883	5.556
17.	Inventories	145.0	56.7	0.6	0.5	2.545	−1.156	3.745
18.	Intangible (research and development)	89.5	68.9	0.4	0.6	10.962	9.322	1.467
19.	Government enterprise	476.3	194.3	2.0	1.7	9.605	3.784	5.609
20.	Structures and equipment	421.8	172.1	1.8	0.6	9.673	3.721	5.738
21.	Residential	45.2	18.2	0.2	0.2	10.952	5.597	5.071
22.	Inventories	9.3	4.0	0.0	0.0	5.673	1.602	4.006
23.	Household	14,625.0	7,258.4	61.6	63.2	9.330	4.566	4.556
24.	Tangible	3,949.7	1,914.6	16.6	16.7	9.425	5.094	4.121
25.	Land	615.1	306.9	2.6	2.7	11.640	6.818	4.514
26.	Residential	2,078.8	842.4	8.8	7.3	9.976	4.687	5.052
27.	Durables	1,052.7	625.4	4.4	5.4	8.919	5.977	2.776
28.	Semidurables	179.6	129.3	0.8	1.1	5.737	2.812	2.845
29.	Inventories	23.4	10.5	0.1	0.1	6.910	2.362	4.443
30.	Intangible (human capital)	10,676.3	5,343.9	45.0	46.5	9.296	4.398	4.691

Source: Eisner (1985), tables 13 and 14, p. 47, and table 15, p. 48.

the business account, or to health or education and training. Stocks related to these latter, wherever produced, are deemed to be human capital owned by households.

The methodology for intangible capital stock series is largely similar to that employed by Kendrick (1976). Where possible, his series are used for the years he covered, and they are extrapolated and interpolated, with the aid of associated series, for other years. His investment in mobility and basic child-rearing is excluded, however, while TISA adds the value of time spent in education and in medical care in the home, which Kendrick does not include.

TISA employs the gross simplifying assumption that most human capital is general—that is, not tied to any particular job or occupation—and that general human capital has a service life of 50 years. For employee training, military education, and safety and health spending by business, though, 40 percent of the investment is assumed to be specific, that is, useful to employees only as long as they remain in the activity for which the capital was provided. Service lives for specific capital are assumed to be equal to the average length of employment in the sector in which it is produced.

As indicated earlier, only one-half of the output of health services is considered investment. The inference that much of the noninvestment half is for "maintenance" of the elderly may support the reasonableness of the assumption of the 50-year average life for general health capital.

R&D investment series are generally taken from the National Science Foundation. Applied R&D is assumed to have a service life of 20 years, and basic R&D capital is assumed to last forever.

6

Substantive Highlights and Conclusions

In 1981, TISA NNP was 30 percent more than the BEA NNP, and 36 percent more if the negative net revaluations of that year are excluded. Constant dollar TISA GNP was 53 percent more than BEA GNP in 1981, 57 percent more if the negative net revaluations are excluded.

The differences between TISA and BEA measures of national product relate preponderantly to TISA's inclusion of nonmarket output. Over one-half are accounted for by the TISA imputation for the product of unpaid household labor. The remainder is made up mostly of opportunity costs of students and capital services—defined as depreciation plus a return to capital—in households, government, and nonprofit institutions. The latter was 14.9 percent of TISA GNP in 1981. TISA imputations of labor income of $1,502 billion in 1981 were 32.9 percent of TISA GNP, thus bringing total labor income, even after deduction of expenses related to work, to 81 percent more than the $1,769 billion of compensation of employees taken from BEA.

TISA picks up a great deal of what may be viewed as capital formation that is not encompassed in the BEA definitions of gross and net private domestic investment. BEA's gross private domestic investment—tangible investment by business and nonprofit institutions along with housing—accounted for only 25.9 percent of TISA gross capital accumulation excluding net revaluations in 1981. The constant dollar figure was 24.2 percent. TISA net domestic capital accumulation in current dollars was 19.5 percent of net national product, both excluding net revaluations. BEA net private domestic investment, by contrast, was only 5.5 percent of BEA NNP. And BEA net private domestic investment was only 20.9 percent of TISA net domestic capital accumulation excluding net revaluations and 60.7 percent of TISA net tangible capital accumulation at original cost.

Similar proportions show up in the measures of capital stocks. Business nonresidential structures and equipment, to which much attention is usually given as a source of productivity, amounted to 11.2 percent of total TISA capital in all sectors, including intangible capital and land and reproducible tangible capital—$23.7 trillion at the end of 1981, as shown in table S.6. Structures and equipment in government came to 6.3 percent and in government enterprises to another 1.8 percent, and household durables and residential capital amounted to 13.2 percent. The stock of intangible capital in the form of research and development, $646 billion, was 2.7 percent of the total while human capital from investment in education and training and health came to 45.0 percent. Intangible capital thus came to almost half— 47.7 percent—of the total stock of capital and land in 1981, while tangible capital amounted to only 41.1 percent and land 11.3 percent.

Over the long run, there has apparently been some substitution of the market output generally measured in the BEA's GNP for the nonmarket output also included in TISA. Thus, while the average annual rate of growth of BEA real GNP was 3.35 percent from 1946 to 1981, that growth rate for TISA GNP excluding net revaluations was only 2.68 percent (table S.1E). Corresponding growth rates for BEA and TISA NNP were 3.24 percent and 2.74 percent. Including net revaluations, the average growth rate of TISA GNP was 3.21 percent, but that reflected considerably the negative net revaluations for 1946. These comparisons should be taken with some reserve, however, because they are sensitive to our choice of deflators and the consequent implicit assumptions about trends in productivity of time spent as students and in unpaid household labor.

Substantially negative net revaluations in 1981 contributed to lower real rates of growth in the 1976–81 period for TISA measures of total product and, particularly, capital accumulation. Excluding net revaluations, however, we still note a marked decline in the real rate of growth of TISA gross domestic capital accumulation, to only 3.04 percent for 1966 to 1971, 2.37 percent for 1971 to 1976, and 2.43 percent for 1976 to 1981, from rates of growth of 4.36 percent and 4.83 percent in the 1946–56 and 1956–66 decades.

Despite much concern expressed in some quarters, BEA gross private domestic investment actually had a substantially larger real rate of growth from 1976 to 1981, 4.28 percent, as compared to 3.39 percent over the entire 1946–81 period. (BEA net investment grew less rapidly but that, again, may reflect some distortion in the capital consumption adjustment.) The rate of growth of tangible government capital accumulation at original cost was only 2.32 percent (4.87 percent for government enterprises) as compared to 3.44 percent for business, 4.45 percent for nonprofit institutions, and 3.80 percent for households.

Of particular note are the relative growth rates of tangible and intangible investment. Over the entire 1946–81 period, constant dollar tangible capital accumulation at original cost grew at an average annual rate of 3.94 percent while intangible capital accumulation grew at a rate of 3.53 percent. Contrasts over subperiods, however, are sharper. Tangible capital accumulation showed declining growth rates in the first three decades—6.06 percent and 4.00 percent in the first two decades and 1.55 percent from 1966 to 1971—before rising to 2.40 percent in 1971–76 and 3.56 percent in 1976–81. The intangible investment pattern, though, was a rise from growth of 2.24 percent in 1946–56 to 6.01 percent in 1956–66, followed by declines to 4.92 percent in 1966–71, to 2.39 percent in 1971–76 and to 1.07 percent in 1976–81. This last stemmed from a falloff to 0.49 percent in the rate of growth of capital accumulation in education and training.

TISA suggests some substantial correction to the views of those who have asserted that Americans have been enjoying more and more consumption at the expense of investment. When nonmarket product going to consumption—chiefly from the household sector but also from government, nonprofit institutions, and business—is taken into account, a different picture emerges. In contrast to the rates of growth of 3.94 percent and 3.53 percent over the 1946–81 period noted above for constant dollar tangible and intangible capital accumulation, respectively (at original cost, that is, excluding subsidies and the sometimes major item of net revaluations), and 3.36 percent for BEA personal consumption expenditures, TISA total consumption grew at an average annual rate of only 2.20 percent. (Gross domestic capital accumulation grew at a much larger rate still, 7.13 percent, chiefly because in the initial year, 1946, it included very large negative revaluations.) In the first two decades, the growth rates of TISA consumption were, consecutively, 1.38 percent and 2.64 percent, and then 2.24 percent in 1966–71 and 2.39 percent in 1971–76. In 1976–81 that growth rose to 2.74 percent, but this was still well below the corresponding 3.56 percent rate for tangible capital accumulation at original cost. Again, however, the negative impact on growth rates of holding constant the productivity of time spent in household labor must be noted.

TISA gross business product in current dollars in 1981 was still less than one-half— 46.8 percent—of TISA gross national product. The share of the nonprofit sector was 2.5 per cent, that of government and government enterprises combined was 12.1 percent, and that of households 37.5 percent. Rates of growth of the business sector, however, were considerably larger over the entire 1946–81 period than those of government and households. In constant dollars, the growth rates were 5.07 percent for business,[36] 0.96 percent for government, and 2.69 percent for households. The low government-sector figure reflected, in part, the relatively large government product in 1946, before World War II demobilization had been completed.

All real growth rates must be interpreted with caution, however. As with the BEA figures, the value of TISA growth rates depends critically on the relevance and accuracy of underlying price deflators. Many price deflators are essentially input-based, and may well omit or understate significant effects of changes in productivity. It may be observed in particular that while TISA implicit deflators for consumption and intangible capital accumulation moved in quite parallel fashion, that for tangible capital formation rose more slowly. Over the entire period from 1946 to 1981, as may be calculated from table 21, deflators for consumption and intangible capital accumulation rose at average annual rates of 4.87 percent and 5.20 percent, respectively, but that for tangible capital formation rose at only a 4.05 percent average annual rate. If the increase in the relative price of intangible capital is overstated, the rates of growth in real intangible and total capital formation relative to BEA investment figures are also correspondingly understated.

Whatever the caveats in this very summary presentation, a number of salient findings demand attention. Nonmarket output provides an enormous, if declining proportion of total U.S. product. Correspondingly, business product, while growing at a more rapid rate than nonbusiness product, is still less than one-half of the total.

Similarly, the great bulk of capital accumulation takes place outside of the business sector, and more of it takes the form of intangible than tangible capital. Analysts and policymakers cannot properly ignore the major contributions of the household and government sectors to capital accumulation and to total product. And consideration of the nation's perennial, fundamental set of choices between current consumption and investment for the future may well take into account the suggestion that total consumption has in fact been growing less rapidly than total capital accumulation.

While capital accumulation, broadly defined, looms large, the measure of labor output is significantly expanded. The greater role of labor is seen in imputations of labor income to the work of independent proprietors, in the activities of volunteers and of others who do not receive full remuneration for their services, and, most important, in the major imputations for the value of housework and the opportunity costs of students.

All this suggests reconsideration of conventional measures of the shares of income and output accountable to "labor" as opposed to "capital." And it calls into question oft-repeated assertions that, by some historical or international standards, saving and investment in the United States are "too low," that we are consuming too much now at the expense of the future. Reasonable support for those assertions would require appropriate analysis of differences in comprehensive measures of capital formation and their trends across nations and over time.

There are other sets of extended national accounts, which are described and compared with each other and with TISA in appendix E. This presentation should serve as an important reminder that it can be done. A comprehensive, consistent enlargement of the traditional national income and product accounts can be put together to offer a moving picture of total output and income, market and nonmarket, of all sectors of the economy. It may be hoped that they will enhance our ability to measure the state of the nation's welfare and its progress and to estimate basic macroeconomic relations of the economy. A set of first efforts at the latter is presented in appendix D.

The apparent rigor of integrated sets of accounts should not obscure the multiplicity of options and choices in their construction. Difficulties abound, in concepts and in data, as should become abundantly clear on examination of the voluminous "Sources and Methods" at the end of this volume.

More relevant measures for some purposes may prove less useful for others. Some of the revisions introduced, such as reclassification of government and household expenditures for tangible reproducible capital as investment and the corresponding capital consumption as output, are straightforward. Indeed, BEA estimates for much of this are readily available. But other major revisions and imputations, such as for income from government and household capital and from nonmarket labor, are relatively speculative. A critical question to many will be how much to sacrifice in the way of precision in the interest of relevance. The market transaction core of conventional accounts can be very exact, where data are available, although even here accuracy becomes uncertain when we move to the real, constant dollar measures crucial to much economic analysis. Without market transactions, as indeed in the bulk of capital consumption allowances in conventional accounts, but certainly in the imputations for nonmarket income and product which loom so large in extended accounts, confidence in the precision of estimates is certainly lost. Comprehensiveness essential for explaining and predicting economic behavior, however, may be gained.

The views and reactions of theoreticians, producers, and users of national income and product accounts have been varied. Simon Kuznets, as I pointed out earlier, argued repeatedly during his distinguished career for many of the revisions and extensions here discussed—inclusion of nonmarket output, subtraction of government and other intermediate products as "regrettable necessities," and comprehensive measures of intangible as well as tangible investment in all sectors of the economy. Edward Denison (e.g., 1971, 1973) and George Jaszi (e.g., 1973), with decades of expertise as pioneers in national accounts, have cautioned against the introduction of imputations of uncertain methodology and accuracy and the submerging or distortion of relatively precise if more limited accounts that have served us well. Arthur Okun (1971a, 1971b) insisted on the primacy of market transactions and argued eloquently that the NIPAs were not and could not be measures of social welfare and that the BEA (then the OBE) should not get into the business of trying to make them so. He also cautioned against the danger of critical losses of input to analysis of cyclical fluctuations and the development of effective stabilization policy. Robert Solow (1973) welcomed extended accounts with the reminder that the new may complement and supplement without replacing the old.

I may conclude on a note that I hope will not appear unduly self-serving. The efforts in preparing these sets of extended accounts have generally been prodigious. While there has been generous government support in a number of instances, particularly from the National Science Foundation, they have approached the limits of what is feasible with essentially private research. The Bureau of Economic Analysis did over several years include a Measures of Economic Well-Being Branch in the Environmental and Nonmarket Economics Division. Some very useful work in accounting for nonmarket economic activity was then accomplished. But budgetary stringencies led to the elimination of the branch and the scattering of its personnel.

There is more to economic activity than what is measured in conventional accounts, in the United States and elsewhere. What is covered is important and should in no way be lost or hidden from view. But perhaps private research has shown enough in the way of possibilities for presenting a systematic set of accounts of a greater totality, along with informative rearrangements of existing data. It is time for the major resources of government to be put to the task. The payoff can be great, for the economy as a whole as well as for national income accounting.

Appendix A
Valuation of Household Work

Variety of Approaches

Valuation of nonmarket household labor presents a number of options. Hawrylyshyn (1976) notes three basic methods. He lists first one, following the formulation of Gary Becker (1965), by which time is allocated to household work so that at the margin its value equals the opportunity cost market wage. This method is hence dubbed "wage equals opportunity cost of time" (WOCT). Employed (see Appendix E) by Nordhaus and Tobin, by Zolotas, and by Jorgenson and Fraumeni, it generally entails multiplying the time spent in housework by appropriately weighted average wages of those, perhaps classified by sex or age, who are involved. As Hawrylyshyn points out, the wage rate to be used in the imputation should be net of taxes. Jorgenson and Fraumeni went through the difficult effort of estimating and applying average marginal tax rates. Nordhaus and Tobin and Zolotas did not, and their estimates of the value of household labor on that account would be biased upward.

A second method, employed by Kendrick and in TISA, is that of the "market alternative = housekeeper cost" (MAHC), as labelled by Hawrylyshyn. This involves multiplying the time spent in nonmarket household labor by the wage rate for domestic workers. Since the result is what the product of nonmarket labor would cost if market labor could be substituted, it is the before-tax wage that is required.

A third method is described by Hawrylyshyn as "market alternative = individual function costs" (MAIFC). This involves multiplying the

This appendix and appendix B, which follows, were essentially produced by John W. Keating, building on an earlier version prepared by Stuart E. Weiner.

time spent in each household activity by the wage that would have to be paid for that activity in the market. There could thus be different rates imputed for cooking, cleaning, child care, and the like. These wage rates also would be without subtraction for taxes.

Hawrylyshyn indicates the danger of upward bias in implementation of the individual function approach but reports that estimates using it, where the value of nonmarket labor is normalized as a ratio of GNP, are at the low end of the range. In a later survey including estimates in France and a number of other nations as well as the United States, Chadeau (1985) reports that the individual function approach yields higher estimates. Chadeau finds estimates based on the prices of market *output* still higher, however, and the opportunity cost measure at the top of the range.

Murphy (1982a, 1982b) categorizes methods of estimation as the market cost approach, with variants of "housekeeper cost" and "specialist cost," and the opportunity cost approach, utilizing gross compensation, after-tax compensation, and net compensation, the last netting out costs of child care and commuting to work. Murphy's estimates showed the housekeeper variant to yield estimates 45 percent less than the gross compensation variant and 25 percent less than the net compensation variant. The specialist variant was about equal to the after-tax variant, midway between the gross and net compensation approaches. The housekeeper method of valuation utilized by Kendrick and in TISA was thus at the low end of the range.

Chadeau refers to results as "remarkably consistent" (p. 251), a judgment that Hawrylyshyn, after a number of adjustments of coverage to insure comparability, would apparently share. Hawrylyshyn attributes particularly high estimates from the opportunity cost method to its failure in a number of instances to apply an after-tax wage rate and concludes, "Generally empirical estimates have indicated that HW . . . the value of economic services produced by household members . . . is equal to about one-third of [conventional] GNP" (1976, 129). This is confirmed in later work surveyed in Appendix E and Eisner (1988), and particularly in TISA. In 1981, the TISA imputation of $980.7 billion for unpaid household work was 33.2 percent of BEA GNP.

TISA calculates the value of unpaid or nonmarket labor output in the household as a product of the average hourly compensation of paid household employees (domestic workers) and the number of hours devoted to unpaid household work. The compensation rates are derived from published and unpublished data of the Bureau of Economic Analysis. Mean time per adult per day spent in unpaid household work was estimated from the results of time-use surveys made available by the Inter-University Consortium of Political and Social Research (ICPSR) at the University of Michigan. Appropriate population data were applied to individual time-use means to calculate the aggregate of hours devoted to unpaid household work in the economy as a whole each year.

Individual Time Use

Our basic source of data as to time devoted to household activities was the Michigan surveys[37] of 1965, 1975, and 1981. It was necessary to adjust for a number of differences in sample and categories of time use in the three years in order to obtain comparable data. The general procedure was to calculate annual rates of change, from 1965 to 1975 and from 1975 to 1981, in the time devoted to several groups of household activities by four sex and employment-status categories of individuals. These rates of change were applied to mean time estimates from the unrestricted 1975 survey sample in order to interpolate and extrapolate estimates of mean time use for the years 1946 to 1981.

In all three surveys, individuals were asked to report time spent in various activities over a 24-hour period. In the 1965 survey, eligible respondents were between 19 and 65 years of age. The sample was drawn from households with at least one employed adult in a nonfarming occupation in cities with populations of 30,000 to 280,000. The 1975 sample contained respondents aged 18 years or older and had no restrictions as to city size or occupation. The 1981 survey involved a follow-up on a 620 family subset from the 1975 survey.

To make the 1965 and 1975 data comparable, the University of Michigan provided a "comparison tape," with the data of the 1965 survey and that of a subset of respondents in the 1975 survey who met the restrictions imposed in drawing the 1965 sample. The 1965 sample had 1,241 respondents. Of the original 1,159 respondents in the 1975 survey, 812 were included in the comparison tapes.

The Michigan surveys endeavored to offer a complete report on the allocation of time by household adults. They thus include accounts of time spent in a vast number of specific activities within the household. For our purposes it was necessary first to arrive at a working definition of activity deemed to contribute to nonmarket output. Essentially we follow the definition proposed by Margaret Reid (1934, p. 11, as quoted by Murphy [1980, p. 6]): "Those unpaid activities which are carried on, by and for the members, which activities might be replaced by market goods, or paid services, if circumstances such as income, market conditions, and personal inclinations permit the services being delegated to someone outside the household group." We have hence defined household labor output as derived from the following activities reported in the Michigan surveys:[38]

Housework
    Meal preparation, serving, and cleanup
    Indoor and outdoor cleaning
    Laundry and clothing care
    Repairs and maintenance, indoors and outdoors

Gardening, care of house plants, pet care, and livestock care by nonfarmers

Other housework, including household paperwork, home improvement, preserving food, home production or maintenance of clothes

Obtaining goods and services

All forms of shopping, including for groceries, clothing, durables, and housing

Repair services for auto, clothing, appliances, and other household goods

Government and financial services, e.g., banking, visits to post office; other professional services such as obtaining legal advice, therapy, or counselling

Travel related to obtaining goods and services

Care of family and others

Child care, including helping and teaching children, disciplining children, playing indoors and outdoors with children, medical care provided to children, unpaid baby-sitting for friends and relatives

Care of others than children, including medical care to self and other adults in household, nonmedical care to friends and relatives

Travel related to care of family and helping others

Subcategories under child care, both specified in the 1975 and 1981 surveys only, were health care, consisting of medical care for children, self, and other adults, and child education, which included helping, teaching, disciplining, coaching, conversing with, and reading to children.

The four sex and employment-status groups were defined as employed males, employed females, nonemployed males, and nonemployed females. Respondents who classified themselves as employed were so designated. Respondents who classified themselves as unemployed, laid-off, retired, or disabled were designated as nonemployed. Respondents who classified themselves as students or housewives were designated as employed or nonemployed depending upon whether or not they reported time spent in "normal work."

Our procedure involved calculating mean times per day devoted to various sets of activities for each of the sex and employment-status groups. Time allocation depends, however, on the day of the week, with clear differences among time allocations on weekdays, Saturdays, and Sundays. To avoid bias and noncomparability resulting from differences in days for which time use was reported, we calculated separate means of daily time use for weekdays, for Saturdays, and for Sundays. Means for all days of the week were then calculated as the weighted average of the means for weekdays, weighted five, for Saturdays, and for Sundays. The results of these calculations from the 1965–75 comparison tape for each of the sex and employment-status groups are shown in tables A.1, A.2, A.3 and A.4. As indicated above, the full, unrestricted sample of the 1975 survey was used to calculate our benchmark time-use estimates.

Table A.1   Time Use: Employed Males, 1965–75

	Comparison Tape (Average Minutes per Day)		1965–1975 Exponential Rate of Growth per Annum
	1965	1975	
Housework	(521)	(331)	
Meal preparation and cleanup	10.465	12.754	
Indoor cleaning	3.125	2.683	
Laundry	1.650	1.871	
Outdoor cleaning	3.681	7.722	
Repairs and maintenance	9.271	11.753	
Gardening and pet care	2.163	4.732	
Other	6.360	3.655	
Total	36.715	45.170	2.09%
	[39.5%]	[45.6%]	
Obtaining goods and services	38.350	32.299	−1.70%
	[41.2%]	[32.6%]	
Care of family			
Child care	14.752	12.717	
Care of others	3.214	8.930	
Total	17.966	21.647	1.88%
	[19.3%]	[21.8%]	
Total unpaid household work	93.031	99.116	0.64%
	[100.0%]	[100.0%]	

Note: Sample sizes in parentheses. Percent of total in square brackets.

Calculation of rates of change per annum in time use from 1975 to 1981 involved use of the full set of data from the 1975 survey and the 1981 followup of a subset of the 1975 families. From these surveys we were able to use data reported by respondents for both themselves and their spouses. The resultant increase in the size of the data set for 1981 was particularly welcome.

Both the 1975 and 1981 surveys were done in four "waves" staggered roughly over the four quarters of each year. Taking data from all four waves may be expected to reduce seasonal variations as well as the effects of cyclical variations within each year. Unfortunately, we were unable to utilize data of the second wave of the 1975 survey because information as to employment status was inexplicably omitted.

The 1975 survey lumped together time spent in personal travel and time spent in travel to help others. We do not consider time devoted to personal travel as contributing to household output but we do wish to include time spent in "helping travel." The 1981 survey fortunately reports separately the time devoted to these two types of travel. To calculate the time spent in

Table A.2   Time Use: Employed Females, 1965–75

	Comparison Tape (Average Minutes per Day)		1965–1975 Exponential Rate of Growth per Annum
	1965	1975	
Housework	(352)	(225)	
Meal preparation and cleanup	73.140	61.431	
Indoor cleaning	40.587	33.531	
Laundry	26.862	16.572	
Outdoor cleaning	0.917	3.449	
Repairs and maintenance	1.902	4.704	
Gardening and pet care	2.896	3.744	
Other	12.954	4.023	
Total	159.258	127.454	−2.20%
	[66.5%]	[62.1%]	
Obtaining goods and services	47.706	39.237	−1.94%
	[19.9%]	[19.1%]	
Care of family			
Child care	25.391	31.122	
Care of others	7.042	7.530	
Total	32.433	38.652	1.77%
	[13.5%]	[18.8%]	
Total unpaid household work	239.397	205.343	−1.52%
	[100.0%]	[100.0%]	

Note: Sample sizes in parentheses. Percent of total in square brackets.

helping travel in 1975, we applied to each sex and employment-status group the 1981 ratio of helping travel time to total time devoted to personal and helping travel. These ratios are shown in table A.5.

The weekly averages for total time spent in unpaid household work are shown in table A.6, along with subsets for time spent on child education and health care in the household. For total unpaid household work time, the 4.04 percent rate of increase for employed males from 1975 to 1981 is substantially greater than the 0.64 percent rate from 1965 to 1975. The rate of change for male-nonemployed shows a small increase, however, from 2.65 percent in 1965–75 to 2.84 percent in 1975–81. The per annum change for employed females went from −1.52 percent to +0.69 percent, a somewhat surprising reversal. And the negative change in unpaid household work for nonemployed females also shows a significant moderation, from −1.89 percent per year in 1965–75 to −0.19 percent in 1975–81.

Household time reported devoted to child education declined sharply from 1975 to 1981. The drop appears too large to be accounted for by the decline in children per family in the U.S. population. A prime explanation

Table A.3   Time Use: Nonemployed Males, 1965–75

	Comparison Tape (Average Minutes per Day)		1965–1975 Exponential Rate of Growth per Annum
	1965	1975	
Housework	(20)	(39)	
Meal preparation and cleanup	38.824	12.359	
Indoor cleaning	9.679	12.351	
Laundry	0.0	2.143	
Outdoor cleaning	7.667	9.107	
Repairs and maintenance	5.107	35.806	
Gardening and pet care	2.000	10.135	
Other	2.786	12.506	
Total	66.063	94.407	3.63%
	[53.7%]	[59.1%]	
Obtaining goods and services	46.393	41.412	−1.13%
	[37.7%]	[25.9%]	
Care of family			
Child care	6.643	18.204	
Care of others	3.929	5.747	
Total	10.572	23.951	8.52%
	[8.6%]	[15.0%]	
Total unpaid household work	123.028	159.770	2.65%
	[100.0%]	[100.0%]	

Note: Sample sizes in parentheses. Percent of total in square brackets.

may be found in sampling bias in the selection of families for the 1981 survey. As mentioned previously, all families in the 1981 study were also in the 1975 study. Thus, both the average age of respondents and the distribution of ages were pushed six years higher. Given the age distribution of our 1975 sample, the number of respondents in the typical child-rearing and child-bearing age group had to decline by 1981. Further, since the 1981 sample is composed of 1975 families who were easily relocated by the ICPSR, many had probably started raising children by 1975. Consequently, both the average age and the distribution of children were shifted six years higher. At the high end of this distribution will be children who move out or go to college. Thus the average number of children in families declined and the average age increased from 1975 to 1981. Both the increase in average age and the decrease in average children per family could be expected to contribute to a reduction in time spent in child care in general and in child education in particular.

The problem of sample aging, while most obvious for child education, manifested itself in all aspects of our empirical work on time use. In an effort to adjust for the aging in our sample, we adopted a weighted difference

Table A.4   Time Use: Nonemployed Females, 1965–75

	Comparison Tape (Average Minutes per Day)		1965–1975 Exponential Rate of Growth per Annum
	1965	1975	
Housework	(347)	(214)	
Meal preparation and cleanup	139.122	108.185	
Indoor cleaning	72.614	73.607	
Laundry	61.212	37.922	
Outdoor cleaning	4.165	3.604	
Repairs and maintenance	4.516	6.866	
Gardening and pet care	5.165	5.699	
Other	18.902	6.372	
Total	305.696	242.255	−2.30%
	[66.7%]	[64.0%]	
Obtaining goods and services	60.457	55.994	−0.76%
	[13.2%]	[14.8%]	
Care of family			
Child care	82.575	64.026	
Care of others	9.435	16.348	
Total	92.010	80.374	−1.34%
	[20.1%]	[21.2%]	
Total unpaid household work	458.163	378.623	−1.89%
	[100.0%]	[100.0%]	

Note: Sample sizes in parentheses. Percent of total in square brackets.

Table A.5   Ratio of Time Use for Selected 1981 Subactivities

	Male		Female	
	Employed	Nonemployed	Employed	Nonemployed
Travel Related to Helping Others as a percent of Total Personal and Helping Travel	21.85%	47.19%	31.42%	48.11%

Note: The 1975 study lumped Personal and Helping Travel together. Personal Travel included vacation and other travel which is not household work. The 1981 survey had these as separate categories. Hence, we used the 1981 average value of Travel for Helping Others as a percent of Total Personal and Helping Travel to estimate Travel for Helping Others for 1975. The percentages are multiplied by the average Total Personal and Helping Travel for 1975 to obtain the 1975 estimates of average Travel for Helping Others for each gender and employment status group. (This method was not needed for the 1965–75 estimation since the time-use categories were identical in these two studies.)

Table A.6   Time Use Estimates 1975–1981 (Minutes per Week)

Time-Use Activity	Group	1975 Unrestricted Sample	1981 Sample	1975–81 Exponential Rate of Growth per Annum
Unpaid household work	ME	748.20	948.70	4.04%
	MN	1276.20	1509.50	2.84%
	FE	1660.34	1730.70	0.69%
	FN	2598.57	2568.60	−0.19%
Child education in the	ME	25.92	15.93	−7.79%
household	MN	14.58	4.48	−17.85%
	FE	82.43	37.83	−12.17%
	FN	116.19	48.57	−13.53%
Health care in the	ME	6.55	4.08	−7.59%
household	MN	7.22	10.57	6.56%
	FE	12.95	9.95	−4.30%
	FN	30.20	26.94	−1.89%

Group abbreviations:
M = Male
F = Female
E = Employed
N = Nonemployed

approach. We illustrate the method for a particular time-use, sex-employment category.

Define X_{ti} and N_{ti} as mean time use and number of valid cases, respectively. The t and i reference the sample year and six-year age bracket, respectively, where $t = 1975$ or 1981 and $i =$ age brackets 17 to 22, 23 to 28, 29 to 34, . . ., 77 to 82 and over 82. The age-adjusted weighted mean change in time use from 1975 to 1981 may then be written as:

$$\Delta XW = \frac{\sum_i (N_{75,i} + N_{81,i}) (X_{81,i} - X_{75,i})}{\sum_i (N_{75,i} + N_{81,i})}.$$

The weighted differences in means are added to the 1975 sample means for each sex and employment-status category to calculate 1981 time use. Table A.7 shows the weighted differences and the 1981 estimates.

Comparing the weighted difference rates of change for child education in table A.7 to the sample rates of change in table A.6, we see that for three of the sex and employment-status groups the weighted-differences rates of change are substantially less negative. The male-nonemployed rate of change for 1975–81 remains essentially unchanged from the nonweighted estimate.

Table A.7   Weighted Difference Calculations, 1975–1981 (Minutes per Week)

Time-Use Activity	Group	1975 Unrestricted Sample	Weighted Differences	1981 Estimate	1975–81 Exponential Rate of Growth per Annum
Unpaid household work	ME	748.20	57.49	805.69	1.24%
	MN	1276.20	93.86	1370.06	1.19%
	FE	1660.34	0.13	1660.47	0.001%
	FN	2598.57	−36.99	2561.58	−0.24%
Child education in the	ME	25.92	−4.91	21.01	−3.44%
household	MN	14.58	−9.82	4.76	−17.02%
	FE	82.43	−28.46	53.97	−6.81%
	FN	116.19	−36.85	79.34	−6.16%
Health care in the	ME	6.55	−0.28	6.27	−0.72%
household	MN	7.22	3.69	10.91	7.12%
	FE	12.95	−2.88	10.07	−4.01%
	FN	30.20	4.38	34.58	2.28%

Group abbreviations:
M = Male
F = Female
E = Employed
N = Nonemployed

The 1981 survey included only six *un*employed males. With most nonemployed males retired, the median age of this group was almost 66 years in 1975 and just over 70 in 1981. In neither year did nonemployed males devote much time to child education.

Weighted difference estimates for time spent in unpaid household work yield more credible rates of change for 1975–81. For the male-employed category the per annum increase in time use was 1.24 percent. This is nearly double the rate for 1965–75, but the unweighted estimate for 1981 indicated a rate of increase for 1975–81 over six times greater than the rate in 1965–75. The weighted difference increase of 1.19 percent per annum for male-nonemployed is slightly less than half the rate of 1965–75. For female-employed, the large rate of decline disappears; in fact the 1975–81 trend is slightly positive. For female-nonemployed, the negative rate of change becomes less negative in 1975–81. The upward movement in annual rates of change from 1965–75 to 1975–81 for females in both employment status categories is just over 1.5 percent.

An average time-per-week series for 1946 to 1981 was constructed for unpaid household work by each group. We used the weighted difference rates of change to interpolate estimated values for the 1975 to 1981 period. The

1965–75 rates of change were used to extrapolate back to 1965 from the 1975 unrestricted sample estimates. We assumed, however, that average time use for unpaid household work was constant at its 1965 value for each group during all years prior to 1965, as extrapolating the 1965–75 rates of change back to 1946 produced results that appeared unreasonable. Extrapolating back the large rate of increase for household work time by nonemployed males would result in a very small 1946 value. The large decrease for the female-nonemployed category conversely implied a huge value in 1946. The assumption of no change in average time use prior to 1965 seemed for our purposes a more appropriate, conservative approach.

On the basis of these interpolations and extrapolations from the 1965, 1975, and 1981 data, we thus produce estimates of average individual weekly time use for each of the years from 1946 to 1981. The four series for unpaid household work are in table A.8. Similar series for child education and health care are presented in tables A.9 and A.10, respectively. Lacking 1965 data, however, we assumed time use in these categories were at their 1975 values in all prior years.

Table A.8   Average Household Work, by Gender and Employment Status (Minutes per Week)

Year	Employed Males	Nonemployed Males	Employed Females	Nonemployed Females
1946–65	702.266	982.715	1935.690	3144.470
1966	706.730	1008.734	1906.215	3085.078
1967	711.221	1035.442	1877.189	3026.808
1968	715.742	1062.857	1848.605	2969.638
1969	720.291	1090.998	1820.457	2913.548
1970	724.869	1119.884	1792.736	2858.518
1971	729.476	1149.535	1765.438	2804.527
1972	734.113	1179.971	1738.556	2751.556
1973	738.779	1211.213	1712.083	2699.585
1974	743.475	1243.282	1686.013	2648.596
1975	748.200	1276.200	1660.340	2598.570
1976	757.489	1291.384	1660.361	2592.368
1977	766.894	1306.749	1660.382	2586.182
1978	776.415	1322.296	1660.402	2580.010
1979	786.055	1338.029	1660.423	2573.852
1980	795.814	1353.949	1660.444	2567.710
1981	805.694	1370.058	1660.465	2561.582

Table A.9   **Average Child Education in the Home, by Gender and Employment Status (Minutes per Week)**

Year	Employed Males	Nonemployed Males	Employed Females	Nonemployed Females
1946 to 1975	25.920	14.580	82.430	116.190
1976	25.029	12.098	76.813	109.033
1977	24.169	10.039	71.578	102.318
1978	23.338	8.330	66.701	96.016
1979	22.536	6.912	62.155	90.102
1980	21.762	5.735	57.920	84.552
1981	21.014	4.759	53.973	79.344

Table A.10   **Average Health Care in Household, by Gender and Employment Status (Minutes per Week)**

Year	Employed Males	Nonemployed Males	Employed Females	Nonemployed Females
1946 to 1975	6.550	7.220	12.950	30.200
1976	6.503	7.734	12.419	30.889
1977	6.456	8.285	11.909	31.593
1978	6.409	8.875	11.420	32.314
1979	6.363	9.507	10.951	33.051
1980	6.317	10.183	10.502	33.805
1981	6.272	10.909	10.071	34.576

Aggregate Time Use and Value of Output

It was then necessary to convert average weekly time use per individual to annual time use in the economy. This was accomplished by multiplying the individual weekly mean by the census population in each category and in turn multiplying those products by the number of weeks in the year.

The population data for the four sex-employment groups are shown in table A.11. Economy-wide estimates of hours spent on unpaid household work and the subcategories of child education and health care are shown in table A.12. The total hours are then valued at the average hourly domestic wage (also in table A.12) to obtain the value of total unpaid household work and of time spent in the household in education and health care. The domestic wage rate was calculated for 1956 to 1981 as

$$DW_t = \bar{X}_t \times \frac{C_t}{X_t},$$

Table A.11   Population Statistics, U.S. Adults 16 and Older, by Gender and Employment Status (In Millions and as a Percent of Total Population)

| | Males | | | | Females | | | |
| | Employed | | Nonemployed | | Employed | | Nonemployed | |
Year	Number	% of Total	Number	% of Total	Number	% of Total	Number	% of Total
1946	42.145	40.9	8.402	8.2	16.064	15.6	36.386	35.3
1947	42.145	40.9	8.402	8.2	16.064	15.6	36.386	35.3
1948	42.875	40.4	8.269	7.8	16.636	15.7	38.454	36.2
1949	42.075	40.0	9.397	8.9	16.742	15.9	36.948	35.1
1950	42.728	40.2	9.145	8.6	17.359	16.4	36.930	34.8
1951	43.892	41.1	7.946	7.4	18.212	17.1	36.713	34.4
1952	44.030	40.9	8.017	7.4	18.606	17.3	36.959	34.3
1953	44.625	40.8	8.319	7.6	18.785	17.2	37.556	34.4
1954	43.727	39.6	9.775	8.8	18.523	16.8	38.435	34.8
1955	44.654	40.0	9.488	8.5	19.582	17.5	38.024	34.0
1956	45.315	40.1	9.344	8.3	20.447	18.1	37.808	33.5
1957	45.278	39.6	9.959	8.7	20.741	18.2	38.236	33.5
1958	44.243	38.3	11.612	10.0	20.640	17.9	39.078	33.8
1959	45.227	38.6	11.327	9.7	21.191	18.1	39.373	33.6
1960	45.737	38.4	11.760	9.9	21.902	18.4	39.709	33.3
1961	45.528	37.7	12.630	10.5	22.119	18.3	40.396	33.5
1962	46.208	37.8	12.654	10.4	22.554	18.5	40.796	33.4
1963	46.636	37.5	13.264	10.7	23.132	18.6	41.389	33.3
1964	47.465	37.5	13.374	10.6	23.858	18.9	41.806	33.0
1965	48.260	37.6	13.441	10.5	24.775	19.3	41.983	32.7
1966	49.012	37.6	13.343	10.2	26.006	20.0	41.820	32.1
1967	49.665	37.6	13.427	10.2	26.925	20.4	42.076	31.9
1968	50.333	37.5	13.734	10.2	27.841	20.7	42.373	31.6
1969	51.022	37.4	14.080	10.3	29.118	21.3	42.353	31.0
1970	51.041	36.7	15.301	11.0	29.704	21.4	43.067	31.0
1971	51.178	36.1	16.491	11.6	29.914	21.1	44.169	31.2
1972	52.402	36.1	16.828	11.6	31.113	21.4	44.796	30.9
1973	53.688	36.3	16.781	11.4	32.495	22.0	44.745	30.3
1974	54.177	36.0	17.572	11.7	33.480	22.3	45.091	30.0
1975	52.830	34.5	20.173	13.2	33.631	22.0	46.313	30.3
1976	54.720	34.7	20.621	13.1	35.701	22.6	46.775	29.6
1977	56.291	35.0	20.464	12.7	37.381	23.3	46.551	29.0
1978	58.010	35.5	20.098	12.3	39.669	24.3	45.764	28.0
1979	59.096	35.5	20.413	12.3	41.325	24.8	45.626	27.4
1980	58.665	34.6	22.212	13.1	42.241	24.9	46.231	27.3
1981	58.909	34.3	23.114	13.5	43.133	25.1	46.618	27.1

(*continued on next page*)

Table A.11   *(Continued)*

Derivation of Population Data Used in Table A.11

Employed males are the sum of:

a. Employed male civilians, aged 16+ (1947–1974: Table 1, *Handbook of Labor Statistics, 1975;* 1975–1977: Table A-2, *Employment and Earnings,* June 1979 and March 1983).

b. Male military personnel stationed in the United States (*Employment and Earnings,* March 1983).

Employed females are the sum of:

a. Employed female civilians, aged 16+ (1947–1974: Table 1, *Handbook of Labor Statistics, 1975;* 1975–1977: Table A-2, *Employment and Earnings,* June 1979 and March 1983).

b. Female military personnel stationed in the United States (*Employment and Earnings,* March 1983).

Nonemployed males are the sum of:

a. Unemployed male civilians, aged 16+ (1947–1974: Table 1, *Handbook of Labor Statistics, 1975;* 1975–1977: Table A-2, *Employment and Earnings,* June 1979 and March 1983).

b. Male civilians, aged 16+, not in the labor force, including nonworking students and retirees (1947–1974: Table 1, *Handbook of Labor Statistics, 1975;* 1975–1977: Table A-2, *Employment and Earnings,* June 1979 and March 1983).

Nonemployed females are the sum of:

a. Unemployed female civilians, aged 16+ (1947–1974: Table 1, *Handbook of Labor Statistics, 1975;* 1975–1977: Table A-2, *Employment and Earnings,* June 1979 and March 1983).

b. Female civilians, aged 16+, not in the labor force, including nonworking students and housewives, and retirees (1947–1974: Table 1, *Handbook of Labor Statistics, 1975;* 1975–1977: Table A-2, *Employment and Earnings,* June 1979 and March 1983).

Because employment data are lacking for the year 1946, we assumed that the population statistics were identical to the 1947 numbers. Also, data on military personnel were avaible back to 1950. Numbers for earlier years are assumed to be equal to the 1950 figures.

and for 1955 to 1946, working recursively backwards, as

$$DW_{t-1} = DW_t \times [\frac{C_{t-1}/H_{t-1}}{C_t/H_t}],$$

where

DW = domestic wage, including all compensation, in private households,

$\overline{X}$ = mean cash earnings of employees in private households,

C = total employee compensation, private households (NIPA table 6.5B, line 75 in U.S. Department of Commerce (1976), *National Income and Product Accounts of the United States, 1929–74,* and *Survey of Current Business,* July 1983.)

X = total earnings of employees in private households and

H = hours worked by full and part-time employees in private households (NIPA table 6.10, line 72 in *National Income and Product Accounts of the United States, 1929–74,* and *Survey of Current Business,* July 1983).

X and $\overline{X}$ are unpublished data from Robert Parker at the BEA and were available from 1956 to 1981.

Table A.13 presents the current dollar figures for the total value of unpaid household work, child education, and health care in the home. The

Table A.12   Total time Spent in Household Work, Child Education, and Health Care in the Home, and Household Domestic Wage

Year	Total Household Work[a]	Child Education in the Home[a]	Health Care in the home[a]	Household Domestic Wage[b]
1946	159.352	5.881	1.428	0.598
1947	159.352	5.881	1.428	0.662
1948	166.753	6.162	1.496	0.666
1949	162.835	5.997	1.457	0.675
1950	164.007	6.051	1.465	0.687
1951	164.536	6.101	1.468	0.736
1952	166.471	6.175	1.484	0.796
1953	168.569	6.249	1.503	0.848
1954	171.226	6.317	1.527	0.890
1955	172.205	6.368	1.532	0.921
1956	173.826	6.439	1.543	0.944
1957	175.517	6.493	1.557	0.980
1958	178.428	6.568	1.583	1.004
1959	180.518	6.656	1.600	1.044
1960	183.816	6.776	1.627	1.107
1961	186.171	6.849	1.648	1.132
1962	188.432	6.936	1.667	1.154
1963	191.807	7.055	1.695	1.178
1964	195.302	7.189	1.725	1.221
1965	197.336	7.271	1.740	1.287
1966	197.004	7.359	1.753	1.360
1967	197.383	7.466	1.774	1.435
1968	198.619	7.602	1.803	1.572
1969	198.593	7.690	1.818	1.670
1970	200.310	7.820	1.851	1.800
1971	202.467	7.965	1.891	1.893
1972	205.376	8.168	1.935	1.974
1973	205.457	8.268	1.951	2.106
1974	206.835	8.394	1.979	2.315
1975	209.840	8.531	2.021	2.487
1976	216.651	8.245	2.095	2.826
1977	219.319	7.825	2.128	3.047
1978	222.089	7.440	2.157	3.261
1979	225.794	7.085	2.199	3.540
1980	231.459	6.762	2.269	3.844
1981	234.789	6.409	2.319	4.177

[a] Billions of hours.

[b] Current dollars.

Table A.13   Current Dollar Value of Household Work, Child Education, and Health Care in the Home (Billions of Dollars)

Year	Total Household Work	Child Education in the Home	Health Care in the Home
1946	95.292	3.517	0.854
1947	105.491	3.893	0.946
1948	111.058	4.104	0.997
1949	109.914	4.048	0.983
1950	112.673	4.157	1.007
1951	121.098	4.490	1.081
1952	132.511	4.915	1.182
1953	142.947	5.299	1.275
1954	152.391	5.622	1.359
1955	158.601	5.865	1.411
1956	164.091	6.079	1.457
1957	172.007	6.363	1.526
1958	179.142	6.594	1.589
1959	188.461	6.949	1.671
1960	203.485	7.501	1.801
1961	210.746	7.753	1.865
1962	217.450	8.004	1.924
1963	225.948	8.311	1.997
1964	238.463	8.777	2.106
1965	253.972	9.358	2.239
1966	267.925	10.008	2.384
1967	283.245	10.714	2.546
1968	312.229	11.950	2.834
1969	331.651	12.843	3.036
1970	360.557	14.076	3.332
1971	383.269	15.077	3.579
1972	405.412	16.124	3.820
1973	432.693	17.412	4.109
1974	478.824	19.433	4.581
1975	521.871	21.217	5.027
1976	612.254	23.300	5.919
1977	668.266	23.844	6.484
1978	724.231	24.262	7.034
1979	799.312	25.080	7.785
1980	889.728	25.993	8.720
1981	980.711	26.771	9.684

constant dollar series shown in table A.14 are based on the 1972 domestic wage. Table A.15 includes the per capita average hours per day spent in unpaid household work, and shows current dollar ratios of unpaid household labor output to BEA and TISA GNP. Table A.16 assesses the relative importance, in changes of aggregate household time, of individual changes in time use and of changes in the distribution of population among sex and employment-status groups.

Findings

The time-use data (tables A.1–A.4) reveal a definite pattern: from 1965 to 1975, women performed a decreasing amount and men an increasing amount of household work. Between 1965 and 1975, the annual rate of change for time spent in total household work were − 1.52 percent for employed women, − 1.89 percent for nonemployed women, + 0.64 percent for employed men, and + 2.65 percent for nonemployed men.

These trends hold as well for the more narrowly defined "housework," which includes only the traditional in-home activities (meal preparation, cleaning, etc.). Between 1965 and 1975, the average annual rate of change was − 2.20 percent for employed women, − 2.30 percent for nonemployed women, + 2.09 percent for employed men, and + 3.63 percent for nonemployed men. Clearly, men are doing some of the housework previously performed by women.

In 1975, nonemployed women spent 933 more minutes per week in household labor than employed women, while nonemployed men spent 528 more minutes per week than employed men. These spreads are roughly the same in 1981. However, differences due to employment status were considerably less in 1965 for males, 280 minutes per week, and considerably more for females, 1,209 minutes per week. We note also that employed and nonemployed women generally spent more than twice as much time in household labor than their male counterparts.[39] (The exception was the 1981 female-nonemployed to male-nonemployed ratio which was slightly less than two.)

In 1975, for employed and nonemployed women and nonemployed men the "housework" portion of household labor time ranged from 59 percent to 64 percent while that for "obtaining goods and services" ranged from 15 percent to 21 percent. Employed men, on the other hand, devoted only 46 percent of their lesser household labor time to housework, but 33 percent to obtaining goods and services.

All groups spent more time in repairs and maintenance in 1975 than in 1965. This presumably reflects the increased service required of a larger stock of consumer durables.[40]

It is interesting to compare the changes for unpaid household work (excluding child education and health care) from 1965 to 1975 with those

Table A.14   Constant Dollar Value of Household Work, Child Education, and Health Care in the Home (Billions of 1972 Dollars)

Year	Total Household Work	Child Education in the Home	Health Care in the Home
1946	314.561	11.608	2.820
1947	314.561	11.608	2.820
1948	329.171	12.164	2.954
1949	321.437	11.838	2.875
1950	323.751	11.944	2.892
1951	324.794	12.044	2.898
1952	328.614	12.190	2.930
1953	332.756	12.335	2.968
1954	338.000	12.469	3.015
1955	339.932	12.571	3.024
1956	343.132	12.711	3.046
1957	346.471	12.817	3.074
1958	352.217	12.966	3.124
1959	356.343	13.139	3.159
1960	362.853	13.377	3.212
1961	367.502	13.520	3.252
1962	371.964	13.692	3.291
1963	378.626	13.926	3.347
1964	385.525	14.191	3.404
1965	389.542	14.354	3.434
1966	388.886	14.526	3.460
1967	389.634	14.738	3.502
1968	392.074	15.006	3.559
1969	392.023	15.180	3.589
1970	395.411	15.437	3.654
1971	399.669	15.722	3.732
1972	405.412	16.124	3.820
1973	405.573	16.321	3.851
1974	408.293	16.571	3.906
1975	414.224	16.841	3.990
1976	427.668	16.276	4.135
1977	432.936	15.447	4.201
1978	438.403	14.687	4.258
1979	445.718	13.986	4.341
1980	456.900	13.348	4.478
1981	463.472	12.651	4.577

Table A.15   **Per Capita Unpaid Household Work and Unpaid Household Work as a Percent of BEA GNP and TISA GNP**

Year	Per Capita Time Spent in Unpaid Household Work (Hours-per-Day)	Current $ Unpaid Household Work as a Percent of BEA GNP	Current $ Unpaid Household Work as a Percent of TISA GNP
1946	4.24	45.4	32.7
1947	4.24	45.3	24.8
1948	4.29	42.8	24.4
1949	4.24	42.6	24.9
1950	4.23	39.3	23.8
1951	4.22	36.6	21.6
1952	4.23	38.1	23.6
1953	4.23	39.0	23.6
1954	4.25	41.5	24.7
1955	4.22	39.6	23.2
1956	4.21	38.9	22.6
1957	4.21	38.7	23.1
1958	4.23	39.8	23.4
1959	4.22	38.6	23.3
1960	4.22	40.2	24.1
1961	4.23	40.2	23.9
1962	4.22	38.5	23.2
1963	4.22	37.9	23.0
1964	4.22	37.4	22.2
1965	4.21	36.8	22.2
1966	4.15	35.4	21.5
1967	4.09	35.4	21.5
1968	4.04	35.7	21.6
1969	3.98	35.1	21.5
1970	3.94	36.3	21.8
1971	3.91	35.6	21.6
1972	3.87	34.2	19.8
1973	3.81	32.6	18.5
1974	3.77	33.4	19.3
1975	3.76	33.7	21.2
1976	3.75	35.6	20.0
1977	3.74	34.8	19.9
1978	3.72	33.5	19.2
1979	3.72	33.1	19.5
1980	3.73	33.8	21.0
1981	3.74	33.2	21.5

Table A.16   Unpaid Household Work Time per Capita: Estimates Reflecting Changing Population Distribution among Sex-Employment Categories, Changing Time Use within Categories, and Both Changes (Mean Hours per Day per Person)

Year	(1) Changes in Population Distribution only	(2) Changes in Time Use within Categories Only	(3) Both Changes
1965	4.209	4.209	4.209
1966	4.195	4.159	4.146
1967	4.191	4.111	4.094
1968	4.184	4.065	4.041
1969	4.170	4.019	3.984
1970	4.173	3.975	3.945
1971	4.181	3.932	3.913
1972	4.174	3.890	3.866
1973	4.155	3.849	3.811
1974	4.148	3.810	3.770
1975	4.167	3.772	3.759
1976	4.147	3.779	3.751
1977	4.125	3.786	3.739
1978	4.094	3.794	3.721
1979	4.077	3.802	3.716
1980	4.080	3.810	3.734
1981	4.077	3.818	3.745
Differences:			
1975 − 1965	− .042	− .437	− .450
1981 − 1975	− .089	.046	− .014
1981 − 1965	− .131	− .391	− .464

Note: Column (1) is calculated holding time use within sex-employment categories at 1965 averages. Column (2) is calculated holding the population distribution at 1965 proportions. Column (3) is the estimate of per capita unpaid household work time, based on reported variation of time use within categories as well as changes in the distribution among categories.

from 1975 to 1981. For nonemployed females the per annum decline of 1.52 percent leveled off to essentially zero. The change was from − 1.89 percent in 1965–75 to − 0.24 percent. This indicates that the major reduction in female household work time between 1965 and 1975 was not repeated from 1975 to 1981. Employed males, however, experienced an acceleration in the annual rate of increase in household work time from 0.64 percent to 1.24 percent. In the small male-nonemployed group, the increase fell from 2.65

percent per annum to 1.9 percent. Thus as the decline in household work of women virtually ended, the increase in household work time of men continued.

For the period from 1946 to 1965, our estimates of per capita unpaid household work are fairly flat as we assume, for lack of data, no change in individual time use within each sex-employment group. Hence changes in the composition of the labor force are the sole source of changes in average time devoted to unpaid household work. In 1946, employed males were 40.9 percent of the population and nonemployed males were 8.2 percent. These figures become 37.6 percent and 10.5 percent, respectively, in 1965. The percentages of employed women and nonemployed women were, respectively, 15.6 percent and 35.3 percent in 1946 and 19.3 percent and 32.7 percent in 1965. Population shifts account for only small changes in per capita unpaid household work, however, from 4.24 hours in 1946 to 4.21 hours in 1965. The increasing proportion of nonemployed males relative to employed males raised the per capita amount of unpaid household work, since nonemployed males perform more household work. Conversely, the increasing proportion of employed females to nonemployed females lowered the overall per capita figures because employed females perform less unpaid household work. These effects tended to cancel each other out as can be seen from an examination of per capita household work from 1946 to 1965.

From 1965 to 1975, we show a decline in per capita unpaid household work time from 4.21 hours to 3.76 hours. The reduction in household work time of women over these years substantially overbalanced the increases for men.

We may look to population shifts as another factor in the decline in the per capita household work time figures from 1965 to 1975. Even in the absence of the changes in time use within sex and employment-status categories, per capita averages could have declined because of the shift of women into the labor force. In fact, the population shifts were of lesser importance in the decline in per capita household work time, as shown in table A.16. Of the decrease of 0.450 hours per week from 1965 to 1975, 0.437 hours are attributable to changes in average time use within sex and employment-status groups and only 0.013 hours to shifts between groups.

From 1975 to 1981, we observe a leveling off in per capita unpaid household work from the downward trend of the prior 10 years. In fact, from 1979 onward we observe a small increase in per capita time in household work. This reversal in trend stems from increases in male time in household work which were sufficient to compensate for a small further decline in female time within the nonemployed group and the continuing shift into the labor force.

Despite the decline and then leveling off in per capita time, total time spent in unpaid household labor has increased, and with it, the current and constant dollar values of that labor. From $95.3 billion in 1946, as shown in table A.13, the current dollar value has risen to $980.7 billion in 1981. As a percentage of BEA GNP, however, unpaid household work has declined. From a high of 45.4 percent in 1946, this ratio has fallen to 33.2 percent in 1981. We observe a similar trend for the ratio of the current dollar value of unpaid household work to TISA GNP. This ratio goes from 24.8 percent in 1947 to 21.5 percent in 1981. (These percentages may be calculated from table 1. We consider the TISA GNP value for 1946 to be an outlier since it appears abnormally low in comparison to TISA GNP from 1947.) Both of these ratios reach their minimums in 1973.

Our estimates of the value of household labor by these techniques would be greater with an opportunity cost approach, where time spent in household work is valued at the wages of those employed outside of the household. Similarly, our estimates would be greater if we took into account the household labor time of children. Walker and Gauger (1973, 10), in a study completed in Syracuse, N.Y., in 1967–68, found that children ages 12 to 17 perform, on average, approximately one hour per day of household work.[41]

Appendix B
Expenses Related to Work

Method

Major expenses related to work include in principle costs of travel from residence to job site and added costs of clothing and meals. With data as to the latter not readily available, we have in practice included only travel costs. And with separate data not generally available on work-related and non-work-related travel expenses, we have allocated total travel costs on the basis of time devoted to various kinds of travel. Thus annual travel expenses related to work are calculated as

$$(1) \quad ERW_t = \text{Total Travel Costs}_t \left[\frac{\text{Travel Time Related to Work}}{\text{Total Time Spent Traveling}} \right]_t .$$

Denoting BEA NIPA table sources by "N," with table and line numbers following (so that, for example, N2.4-69 refers to NIPA table 2.4, line 69), total travel costs are the sum of

1. Personal vehicle maintenance expenses, which include
   (a.) repair, greasing, washing, parking, storage, and rental (N2.4-69 for current dollars)
   (b.) gasoline and oil (N2.4-70 for current dollars and N2.5-31 for 1972 dollars)
2. Bridge, tunnel, ferry, and road tolls (N2.4-71 for current dollars)

This appendix was largely prepared by John W. Keating, building upon an earlier version of some portions by Stuart E. Weiner.

3. Insurance premiums less claims paid (N2.4-72 for current dollars)
Note: The constant (1972) dollar sum of (1a), (2), and (3) is N2.5-57, user operated transportation.
4. Purchased local transportation for transit systems, taxis, and commuter railroads (N2.4-73 for current dollars and N2.5-58 for 1972 dollars)
5. Purchased intercity transportation: railroads, buses, airlines, and others (N2.4-77 for current dollars and N2.5-61 for 1972 dollars)
6. Consumption services of the net stocks of autos and other motor vehicles
These services are computed as the sum of imputed interest and depreciation. Interest is calculated as

$$INT(t) = \left[\frac{STOCK\ (t)\ +\ STOCK(t-1)}{2} \right] i_t,$$

where

$STOCK(t)$ = year-end net current and 1972 dollar stock of autos and other vehicles in year t, and
i_t = household real interest rate.

Stocks and depreciation of autos and other motor vehicles, in current and 1972 dollars, were obtained from Jerry Silverstein of the Bureau of Economic Analysis. Derivation of the household real interest rate is explained in line 22, section 6 of Sources and Methods.

Time series for the ratios of work-related travel time to total travel time were generated from the surveys of time use, in 1965, 1975 and 1981, furnished by the Inter-University Consortium for Political and Social Research at the University of Michigan.

Respondents and spouses were allocated to sex- and employment-status groups as described in appendix A on the valuation of household work. For the purpose of estimating changes in travel time from 1965 to 1975, the male and female nonemployed were lumped together in a single "nonemployed" category. As in preparing the household labor time estimates, we utilized the comparison tape which included 1975 families which met the restrictions imposed on the 1965 sample. Responses for employed males, employed females and the nonemployed were again weighted so as to secure an equal weight for the means for each day of the week. The time-use estimates and 1965–75 percentage rates of change are reported in table B.1. The full, unrestricted 1975 time-use study was used to obtain the 1975 point estimates. Rates of change calculated from the comparison tape were then applied to derive travel times for the years 1965 to 1974.

The 1975 and 1981 estimation of total travel time and travel time related to work utilized both respondent and spouse data. There were four waves of

Table B.1   Time Spent on Total Travel and Travel Related to Work, 1965–75

	Comparison Tape (Average Minutes per Day)		1965–75 Percentage Rates of Change per Annum
	1965	1975	
Male employed			
Travel time related to work	41.41	38.18	−0.809
Total travel time	89.70	95.99	0.680
Female employed			
Travel time related to work	28.84	24.90	−1.459
Total travel time	73.94	76.38	0.325
Nonemployed			
Travel time related to work	0	0	—
Total travel time	60.25	70.32	1.558

interviews each in the 1975 and 1981 surveys. The employment status variable was inexplicably omitted, however, in the second wave of the 1975 survey, so that we were able to use the data of only seven waves. Respondents and spouses were divided among the categories of employed male, employed female, nonemployed male and nonemployed female for each survey; our procedure thus differed from that with the data of the 1965–75 comparison tape, where we lumped nonemployed males and females together. Averages for total travel time and work travel time were again calculated for weekdays, Saturdays and Sundays. In the 1975 and 1981 surveys, data were available regarding travel time spent in job research, which we counted as work related. Hence, travel time related to work was not zero for the nonemployed categories. Weekly time spent on total travel and travel related to work categories was calculated by appropriately weighting the weekday, Saturday, and Sunday averages. Weekly averages for 1975 and 1981 are presented in table B.2.

Because the 1981 survey was restricted to households which had been included in the 1975 survey, we observed a sample bias due to aging. To correct for this bias, we adopted a weighted difference method for identical six-year age categories. (A detailed description of the methodology and its rationale can be found in appendix A.) The results and the 1975–81 per annum percentage rates of change are reported in table B.3.

An average time-per-week-per-adult series for each group was constructed for total travel time and travel time related to work. For total travel time, 1975–81 weighted difference rates of change were used to interpolate estimated values for the intervening years. The 1965–75 rates of change were used to extrapolate back to 1965 from the 1975 unrestricted sample estimates. Since the nonemployed males and females are lumped together in our analysis of the comparison tape for 1965 and 1975, their rates of change for total

Table B.2   Time-Use Estimates 1975–1981 (Minutes per Week)

Time-Use Activity	Group	1975 Unrestricted Sample	1981 Sample	1975–81 Percentage Rates of Change per Annum
Total travel time	ME	596.97	650.80	1.45
	MN	477.59	449.63	−1.00
	FE	540.79	558.18	0.53
	FN	437.33	448.15	0.41
Travel time	ME	238.95	233.48	−0.39
related to work	MN	20.12	11.70	−8.64
	FE	166.80	165.27	−0.15
	FN	6.75	3.28	−11.33

Group abbreviations:
M = Male
F = Female
E = Employed
N = Nonemployed

Table B.3   Weighted Difference Calculations, 1975–1981 (Minutes per Week)

Time-Use Activity	Group	1975 Unrestricted Sample	Weighted Differences	1981 Estimate	1975–81 Percentage Rates of Change per Annum
Total travel time	ME	596.97	20.33	617.29	0.56
	MN	477.59	−12.84	464.75	−0.45
	FE	540.79	12.78	553.57	0.39
	FN	437.33	−16.40	420.93	−0.63
Travel time	ME	238.95	0.42	239.37	0.03
related to work	MN	20.12	−4.16	15.96	−3.79
	FE	166.80	4.48	171.28	0.44
	FN	6.75	−0.45	6.30	−1.14

Group abbreviations:
M = Male
F = Female
E = Employed
N = Nonemployed

travel time are identical over these years. For each group during the years prior to 1965, we assume that total travel time is equal to the 1965 value.

With little change in work-related travel time from 1975 to 1981, we assumed, for each sex-employment group, that it was constant at the 1975 unrestricted sample value for all years up to 1975. We could not readily utilize 1965 estimates for travel time related to work since they did not allow for the time spent in job search and were hence not fully comparable to the 1975

Table B.4   Average Travel Time, Total, and Related to Work, by Gender and
Employment Status (Minutes per Week)

| Year | Total | | | |
	Employed Males	Nonemployed Males	Employed Females	Nonemployed Females
1946–65	557.863	409.185	523.515	374.692
1966	561.656	415.560	525.217	380.529
1967	565.474	422.034	526.925	386.457
1968	569.318	428.608	528.639	392.477
1969	573.189	435.285	530.358	398.592
1970	577.085	442.067	532.082	404.801
1971	581.009	448.953	533.813	411.107
1972	584.958	455.947	535.548	417.512
1973	588.935	463.050	537.290	424.016
1974	592.939	470.264	539.037	430.622
1975	596.970	477.590	540.790	437.330
1976	600.310	475.426	542.899	434.554
1977	603.668	473.271	545.017	431.795
1978	607.045	471.126	547.142	429.054
1979	610.441	468.991	549.276	426.330
1980	613.856	466.866	551.418	423.623
1981	617.290	464.750	553.569	420.934
	Related to Work			
1946–75	238.950	20.120	166.800	6.750
1976	239.020	19.358	167.538	6.673
1977	239.089	18.624	168.280	6.596
1978	239.159	17.919	169.024	6.521
1979	239.229	17.240	169.772	6.446
1980	239.299	16.586	170.523	6.372
1981	239.369	15.958	171.278	6.299

and 1981 figures. From 1975 to 1981, we used the weighted difference rates of change to interpolate estimates for each group's work travel time. The total travel time and travel time related to work series are reported for each group in table B.4.

For a given year, we have, for each population group, i, mean weekly travel time related to work (TW_i) and mean total weekly time spent traveling (TT_i). To find the economy-wide estimate of the ratio of work-related total time to total travel ($RATIO$) for a given year, we applied U.S. population data to these figures. Thus,

$$(2) \quad RATIO = \frac{ME \cdot \text{TW}_{me} + FE \cdot TW_{fe} + MN \cdot TW_{mn} + FN \cdot TW_{fn}}{ME \cdot TT_{me} + FE \cdot TT_{fe} + MN \cdot TT_{mn} + FN \cdot TT_{fn}}$$

where

ME = number of employed males in the U.S.
MN = number of nonemployed males in the U.S.
FE = number of employed females in the U.S.
FN = number of nonemployed females in the U.S.

The population data are shown in table A.11 of appendix A.

Estimates for economy-wide current and constant dollar expenses related to work are calculated in accordance with equation (1), by multiplying $RATIO$ by total travel expenses, in current and constant dollars, respectively. The two expenses related to work series can be located in table B.5, along with the expenses related to work implicit price deflator.

We distribute the total current and constant dollar expenses related to work, on the basis of employment, among four of the five sectors of the economy: household (HH), government (G), government enterprise (GE), and nonprofit (NP), using equation (3).

$$(3) \qquad ERW_i = ERW \times \frac{EMP_i}{EMP},$$

where

ERW = total expenses related to work,
ERW_i = expenses related to work for sector i,
EMP = total number of employees in domestic industries,
EMP_i = number of employees in sector i,

and the sources of our data are

for EMP, N6.7-2,
for EMP_{HH}, N6.7-5,
for EMP_G, N6.7-78 + N6.7-83,
for EMP_{GE}, N6.71 + N6.7-86,

where, again, "N" indicates a national income and product accounts (NIPA) table.

NIPA data on the number of employees in the business and nonprofit sectors are aggregates in the BEA's "Business" category. Hence, we were

Table B.5 **Ratio of Work Related to Total Travel Time, Current and Constant Dollar Expenses Related to Work, and the Expenses-Related-to-Work Deflator**

Year	Ratio of Work Related to Total Travel Time	Current Dollar Expenses Related to Work	Constant Dollar Expenses Related to Work (1972 Dollars)	Expenses-Related-to-Work Deflator
1946	.269	2.89	7.26	39.80
1947	.269	3.30	7.43	44.50
1948	.267	3.76	7.55	49.83
1949	.266	4.15	7.72	53.76
1950	.268	4.53	8.06	56.21
1951	.273	5.17	8.68	59.61
1952	.273	5.86	9.19	63.79
1953	.272	6.59	9.77	67.40
1954	.267	7.13	10.25	69.58
1955	.270	7.80	11.20	69.64
1956	.272	8.75	12.27	71.36
1957	.270	9.39	12.52	74.98
1958	.264	9.61	12.40	77.51
1959	.266	10.41	13.00	80.12
1960	.266	10.86	13.42	80.90
1961	.264	11.03	13.50	81.74
1962	.264	11.48	14.05	81.73
1963	.263	11.91	14.58	81.72
1964	.264	12.50	15.28	81.80
1965	.265	13.29	16.05	82.80
1966	.265	14.12	16.92	83.47
1967	.263	15.18	17.77	85.41
1968	.262	16.26	18.64	87.23
1969	.260	18.01	19.99	90.09
1970	.256	19.55	20.75	94.19
1971	.250	21.13	21.38	98.82
1972	.249	22.40	22.40	100.02
1973	.249	24.35	23.63	103.03
1974	.246	27.56	23.54	117.05
1975	.238	29.39	23.49	125.12
1976	.240	33.02	24.66	133.94
1977	.243	37.86	26.30	143.98
1978	.247	42.37	27.79	152.45
1979	.248	49.93	28.59	174.63
1980	.245	58.60	28.30	207.15
1981	.244	62.52	27.64	226.20

forced to estimate their division into our separate nonprofit and business sectors.

The number of employees in the nonprofit sector was estimated as

$$EMP_{NP} = \left[\frac{.5(N6.7B\text{-}68) + .9(N6.7B\text{-}70) + N6.7B\text{-}71}{.5(N6.5B\text{-}68) + .9(N6.5B\text{-}70) + N6.5B\text{-}71} \right]$$

$$\times \left[N1.12\text{-}40 - N6.5B\text{-}75 \right],$$

where the indicated sources in NIPA tables relate to the following time series:

N6.7B-68 = full and part-time employees, health services
N6.7B-70 = full and part-time employees, educational services
N6.7B-71 = full and part-time employees, social services and membership organizations
N6.5B-68 = compensation of employees, health services
N6.5B-70 = compensation of employees, educational services
N6.5B-71 = compensation of employees, social services and membership organizations
N1.12-40 = national income for households and institutions
N6.5B-75 = compensation of employees in private households

We assumed that 50 percent of the employees in health services and 90 percent of the employees in educational services are in the nonprofit sector.

We applied equation (3) to total employment and sector employment data to allocate expenses related to work to the four sectors other than business. The business sector expenses related to work then equal total expenses related to work less expenses related to work in the other sectors.

Findings

Total travel time per employed person generally increased from 1965 to 1975 (table B.1) and from 1975 to 1981 (tables B.2 and B.3). Travel time related to work did appear to decline over the 1965–75 period before leveling off or rising slightly from 1975 to 1981 but, as noted above, the 1965 and 1975 data were not fully comparable. Thus, travel time related to work was assumed constant, for each sex-employment group, from 1946 to 1975 (table B.4).

In table B.3 we observe that for each group the growth rates for total travel time move in the same direction as the rates for travel time related to work. For both, the employed groups experience positive growth rates while the nonemployed groups experience negative growth rates in 1975–81.

In table B.5, we have the economy-wide time series of the ratio of time spent on travel related to work to total travel time. Our estimates yield a fairly constant ratio from 1946 to 1965. It fluctuates only between .263 and .273 during this 20-year period. It falls from 1965 to 1975, however, from .265 to .238. From 1976 to 1981, we again estimate little change in the economy-wide ratio, with a low of .240 in 1976 and a high of .248 in 1979. These patterns correspond generally with patterns observed in unpaid household labor. It would appear that changes in time use dominate changes in population. Before 1965, where we assume no time-use shifts within employment status groups, we observe small fluctuations in the ratio. Between 1965 and 1975, where we have allowed for changes in time use within groups we observe a decline in the estimated ratio. There is no clear trend between 1975 and 1981, a period in which time-use shifts exist for total travel time and travel related to work.

Appendix C

Capital Formation and Capital Consumption in Land, Natural Resources, and the Environment

Proper and consistent handling of natural resources and the environment is difficult. We should presumably take account of deterioration of our natural wealth or its associated flow of services. But then we should note as well investment to maintain or increase that wealth. And to the extent that the wealth is increased by discoveries or technological change we should recognize the accumulation, perhaps as capital gains or revaluations. Measurement of these revaluations, however, is challenging.

Conventional measures do clearly present a number of problems. Provision of oil or coal from inventories above ground does not essentially entail production but removal of stocks from below ground does. New discoveries do not enter into accounts at their market values, nor do we include in our accounts changes in market values of known reserves.

We do not measure in our national accounts the pollution of air and water, what Zolotas (Appendix E) calls the "damage cost." His estimates are fairly arbitrary, and relate to air pollution only. With regard to what he calls "control costs," we might at least move to some consistency. It seems foolish to treat antipollution expenditures as real consumption if incurred by households, as government purchases of goods and services if undertaken by government, and as not even a component of real product, in so far as they are on current and not capital account, if they are undertaken by business. Extended accounts would do well to treat all activities to maintain or improve our collective environment as investment or the provision of imputed consumption services. By excluding improvement of services of the environment from our measure of output, because they are not generally explicitly purchased, we not only detract from the usefulness of national income and product as a measure of welfare, we also give ourselves the rather troublesome problem of showing antipollution expenditures to be contributing to a decline in productivity or, at least, to a decline in its rate of growth.

As with capital consumption allowances generally, there is little that is reliable or in the way of market transactions to measure the value of exhaustion of soil or natural resources. If net investment is to be taken as the increment in value of capital, one way to approach the issue is to find measures of capital value or changes in value. These may be derived from sales of land and mineral rights (see Boskin et al., 1985 and 1987). One may also use projections of future flows of output to calculate present values of stock (see Soloday, 1980).

Landefield and Hines (1982) propose treatment of discovery of additional resources such as oil reserves as investment, and then charging capital consumption allowances for their depletion. They suggest three methods of valuation: present values on the basis of projected future flows, prices, and costs; land prices using data on bonus payments and royalties; and net price, applying the average price per unit to changes in reserves. Components of the changes in value of net stocks are then broken into discovery value, depletion, and price change.

Henry Peskin (1986) proposes that, in "expanding the conventional accounts to include environmental asset services . . . , investments that increase the environmental asset stock will be accounted for if they are not already accounted for in the conventional accounts." "Similarly," he adds, "there will be an entry measuring any depreciation in environmental assets" (Peskin, p. II-22). Peskin's measure of "value depreciation," defined as equal to changes in the present value of expected environmental service flows, would be, as he points out, the sum of conventional depreciation and capital gains or losses, or revaluations.[42]

Appendix D
Some New Estimates of Old Relations

Economists have offered countless estimates of the critical relations determining or explaining consumption, investment, and production. These have been based on time series and cross sections of households, firms, and industries, and of aggregates for the entire economy. They have most frequently, and certainly at the aggregate level, dealt in terms of the conventional, market measures of income and product. The TISA data offer an opportunity to go beyond this. In particular they permit consideration of the role of intangible capital and of nonmarket time in production functions. They lay the groundwork for introduction of capital and wealth arguments into a variety of consumption functions. And they permit a focus on much broader measures of investment.

Innovation in the TISA-based analysis is not in the forms of relations or methods of estimation but in the data. These, it will be seen, produce some considerable novelty in the results, which should generally be taken, however, as suggestive and hardly definitive. In many instances, careful and critical readers may see in them little more than the basic assumptions used in constructing the accounts. The imputations the computer puts in may be expected to be turned out in appropriate regression coefficients. But much of the story is provocative and should at the least command further effort to check its robustness and offer corrections where appropriate.

Production Functions

The basic lines of conventional production functions, going back to the seminal work of Cobb and Douglas, relate output to inputs of capital and labor.

In its simple log-linear form, output is positively related to capital and labor, with more capital increasing both output and the productivity of labor (and, as not widely recognized in popular or political debate, more labor increasing both output and the productivity of capital). The "capital" consists essentially of tangible structures and equipment, usually the structures and equipment accumulated by the chiefly business capital expenditures of gross private domestic investment. The "labor" is labor for the market. And the output, except perhaps for the few imputations in the official accounts, is the market output of conventional GNP.

In table D.1, we relate, in natural logarithms, conventional (BEA) real gross national product to the total of all tangible capital—of government, government enterprises, nonprofit institutions and households as well as business—and total labor market hours. In the ordinary least squares regressions (OLS), the coefficients of capital and labor are both positive, as expected, with the labor coefficient of 0.670 smaller, however, than the unusually large capital coefficient of 0.745. There is also the familiar indication of increasing returns, as revealed in the value of 1.415 for the sum of regression coefficients, this despite the fact that *KTAN* does comprise all kinds of tangible capital, including land, in all sectors.

The introduction of *KRD,* the total stock of R&D capital, brings a dramatic turn to the OLS story. Not only is this coefficient a highly significant 0.198, but its inclusion results in a higher value for the coefficient of labor market hours and a much lower—indeed no longer significantly positive—coefficient of 0.128 for tangible capital.

Finally, we include both *KRD* and *KHUM* in the regression. We then note highly significant positive coefficients for both of these components of intangible capital, and a significant negative coefficient of −.438 for tangible capital!

The Durbin-Watson statistics are extremely low in the OLS regressions. Cochran-Orcutt equations [AR(1)] were therefore also estimated. In regressions involving tangible capital and labor market hours only, the capital coefficient is a significantly negative −0.394, the labor coefficient about unity. The addition of human capital alone to the regressions again makes little difference to the other estimated parameters. R&D capital, when added to the relation, however, once more shows a significantly positive coefficient, of 0.221, with a tangible capital coefficient now about zero. And with R&D and human capital both in the regression, the coefficient of human capital is a substantially positive and significant 0.351. The tangible capital coefficient is again substantially negative, at −0.428, with a substantial standard error, though, of 0.233.

It is hard to accept that tangible capital should be *negatively* related to market output. The likelihood function in the AR regressions is indeed apparently fairly flat; with an autoregressive coefficient of 0.888, reached after

Table D.1 BEA GNP as Function of Tangible, R&D, and Human Capital, and Market Labor

$$\ln YBEA = b_0 + b_1 \ln KTAN_{-1} + b_2 \ln KRD_{-1} + b_3 \ln KHUM_{-1} + b_4 \ln LABMA$$

Regressor or Statistic	AR(1)				Ordinary Least Squares			
	Regression Coefficients and Standard Errors				Regression Coefficients and Standard Errors			
Constant	7.381 (2.227)	7.860 (5.577)	-0.611 (1.049)	0.717 (0.850)	-2.558 (0.415)	-3.014 (0.684)	-1.385 (0.313)	0.596 (0.494)
$KTAN_{-1}$	-0.394 (0.149)	-0.395 (0.152)	0.083 (0.171)	-0.428 (0.233)	0.745 (0.043)	0.846 (0.127)	0.128 (0.093)	-0.438 (0.144)
KRD_{-1}			0.221 (0.071)	0.263 (0.045)				0.273 (0.028)
$KHUM_{-1}$	-0.030 (0.314)			0.351 (0.130)		-0.101 (0.120)	0.198 (0.028)	0.331 (0.073)
$LABMA$	1.011 (0.085)	1.011 (0.087)	1.127 (0.123)	1.095 (0.104)	0.670 (0.145)	0.755 (0.178)	1.227 (0.122)	1.157 (0.096)
AR(1)	0.985	0.986	0.699	0.603	—	—	—	—
$\bar{R}^2$	.9990	.9990	.9986	.9990	.9939	.9938	.9976	.9985
D-W	1.93	1.92	1.56	1.61	0.54	0.57	0.81	0.75
n	34	34	34	34	34	34	34	34

Notes:

  $KTAN$ = Tangible capital.
  KRD = Research and development capital.
  $KHUM$ = Human capital.
  $LABMA$ = Market labor.
  AR(1) = Cochrane-Orcutt equation.

six iterations on a convergence interval of 0.01 (as opposed to the 0.985 shown in table D.1 after 19 iterations with convergence intervals of 0.001 and smaller), the tangible capital coefficient was 0.473 with a standard error of 0.210. (The labor coefficient was still about unity, at 0.977 with a standard error of 0.128.) But these results of time series regressions for real GNP from 1947 to 1981 should give some pause to purveyors of the conventional wisdom. Is the piling up of more and more bricks and mortar and other tangible capital the way to higher productivity or is more to be expected from investment in the intangible capital of human beings and knowledge?

Similar production functions for TISA output and the difference between TISA and BEA output are explored in table D.2. Since a major component of TISA output is nonmarket, it is appropriate to include nonmarket labor hour (*LABNM*) in TISA regressions. Doing so, we note first that with R&D and intangible capital excluded we have results roughly similar to those for BEA output. The coefficient of tangible capital is highly positive in the OLS regressions, but it is close to zero in the AR(1) relations while the sum of labor coefficients is 0.738.

When *KRD* and *KHUM* are added in the AR(1) regressions, however, the coefficient of tangible capital again turns significantly negative, to −0.447. We also note though that the coefficient of labor market hours rises to 0.746 while that of nonmarket labor hours declines to 0.054, very little above zero. This reflects perhaps the fact that the shift from nonmarket to market labor is generally a move from less to more productive activity. This is possibly accentuated in our imputation of the value of nonmarket household labor by our use of a wage deflator to calculate real output. This has the effect, as noted earlier, of assuming no productivity growth in nonmarket household labor. Our assumptions would thus tend to reduce the positive impact on TISA output of increases in nonmarket labor.

The differences between TISA GNP (excluding net revaluations) and BEA GNP consist largely, but of course far from entirely, of nonmarket output. Regressing the log of that difference on tangible capital and market and nonmarket labor gives results consistent with those earlier. The coefficient of market labor is virtually zero and that of nonmarket labor, now reflecting chiefly its role in nonmarket output, is a substantial 0.585. Introduction of the intangible capital variables, *KRD* and *KHUM*, does again reduce the coefficient of nonmarket labor hours but still leaves it at 0.331, just less than twice its standard error. The similarly positive, though smaller, coefficient of labor market hours in this regression is, however, somewhat perplexing. *LABMA* is apparently proxying for some omitted variable or correcting for nonlinearity (in the logs) relating to other variables in the regression.

Table D.2 TISA GNP and Difference between TISA GNP and BEA GNP as Functions of Tangible, R&D, and Human Capital, and Market and Nonmarket Labor

$$\ln Y = b_0 + b_1\ln KTAN_{-1} + b_2\ln KRD_{-1} + b_3\ln KHUM_{-1} + b_4\ln LABMA + b_5\ln LABNM$$

Regressor or Statistic	AR(1) — Regression Coefficients and Standard Errors — YTISA	AR(1) — YTISA	AR(1) — YTISA − YBEA	AR(1) — YTISA − YBEA	OLS — Regression Coefficients and Standard Errors — YTISA	OLS — YTISA	OLS — YTISA − YBEA	OLS — YTISA − YBEA
Constant	6.331 (4.454)	2.807 (0.576)	−0.497 (0.767)	3.458 (0.871)	1.157 (0.974)	2.557 (0.483)	3.469 (0.958)	0.309 (0.813)
$KTAN_{-1}$	−0.047 (0.166)	−0.447 (0.131)	0.455 (0.076)	−0.395 (0.203)	0.595 (0.095)	−0.414 (0.124)	−0.503 (0.247)	0.747 (0.079)
KRD_{-1}		0.247 (0.026)	0.234 (0.040)			0.232 (0.022)	0.206 (0.044)	
$KHUM_{-1}$		0.368 (0.065)	0.276 (0.116)			0.361 (0.057)	0.388 (0.113)	
LABMA	0.621 (0.091)	0.746 (0.075)	0.034 (0.122)	0.218 (0.100)	−0.040 (0.143)	0.749 (0.074)	0.203 (0.148)	0.411 (0.119)
LABNM	0.117 (0.201)	0.054 (0.125)	0.585 (0.222)	0.331 (0.173)	0.129 (0.308)	0.074 (0.122)	0.371 (0.242)	−0.202 (0.257)
AR(1)	0.991	0.420	0.807	0.582	—	—	—	—
$\hat{R}^2$	.9984	.9992	.9959	.9977	.9867	.9988	.9922	.9945
D-W	1.59	1.52	1.56	1.66	.43	1.01	.66	.56
n	34	34	34	34	34	34	3	34

Notes:

KTAN = Tangible capital.

KRD = Research and development capital.

KHUM = Human capital.

LABMA = Market labor.

LABNM = Nonmarket labor.

AR(1) = Cochrane-Orcutt equation.

Consumption Functions

In estimating consumption functions we have introduced variables for labor income after taxes, *YLAT*, and household and nonhousehold tangible capital, *KHTNCA* and *KNHTNC*, both taken as the average of previous and current end-of-year stocks. We have also adapted from my work with Paul Pieper on budget deficits a net federal debt variable defined as the debt of the federal government and associated agencies minus their financial assets other than gold and foreign exchange, *NDGFCA* (for net debt plus gold and foreign exchange in constant dollars, average of previous and current end-of-year figures). The after-tax labor income variable was constructed with the aid of a number of rather gross, simplifying assumptions, particularly with regard to the allocation of taxes.

In table D.3, we note the expected high coefficient of 0.923 for *YLAT* in the regression of BEA personal consumption expenditures, *CBEAPC*. We

Table D.3   **Consumption as Function of After-Tax Income, Net Federal Debt, and Household and Nonhousehold Tangible Capital**

$$C = b_0 + b_1 YLAT + b_2 NDGFCA + b_3 KHTNCA + b_4 KNHTNC$$

Regressor or Statistic	Dependent Variables Regression Coefficients and Standard Errors			
	CTISA	*CXSERN*	*CTSAOT*	*CBEAPC*
Constant	264.548	146.608	229.064	−62.907
	(68.766)	(98.543)	(50.158)	(39.475)
YLAT	0.119	0.270	−0.190	0.923
	(0.235)	(0.069)	(0.151)	(0.107)
NDGFCA	0.131	0.120	0.031	0.281
	(0.130)	(0.051)	(0.083)	(0.051)
KHTNCA	0.239	0.026	0.179	0.184
	(0.124)	(0.082)	(0.081)	(0.063)
KNHTNC	0.153	−0.001	0.129	−0.028
	(0.084)	(0.032)	(0.059)	(0.047)
AR(1)	0.791	0.999	0.723	0.297
$\hat{R}^2$	.9988	.9989	.9984	.9993
D-W	1.11	1.79	0.96	1.96
n	33	33	33	33

Notes:

YLAT = Labor after-tax income.
NDGFCA = Net federal debt (net debt plus gold and foreign exchange in constant dollars, average of previous and current end-of-year figures).
KHTNCA = Household tangible capital.
KNHTNC = Nonhousehold tangible capital.
CTISA = TISA consumption.
CXSERN = Consumer expenditures for services and nondurables.
CTSAOT = TISA consumption other than expenditures for services and nondurables.
CBEAPC = BEA personal consumption expenditures.
AR(1) = Cochrane-Orcutt equation.

also find significant positive coefficients for the net debt and household tangible capital variables. These results are consistent with basic theory indicating that consumption should be a function of labor income and wealth. The role of the federal debt as a measure of net financial wealth of the private sector, as suggested in Eisner and Pieper (1984) and Eisner (1986) is confirmed.

In that last connection, it may be recalled that real federal deficits were shown to have been positively related to subsequent growth in investment as well as consumption. The rather high coefficient for the net debt variable in the BEA consumption relation may reflect in part a wealth-portfolio adjustment as greater holdings of financial assets generate acquisition of real wealth in the form of consumer durables included in the BEA measure of personal consumption expenditures.

Comparison of the BEA consumption relation with that involving TISA consumption, *CTISA,* is revealing. The major arguments of the latter turn out to be household and nonhousehold tangible capital. This makes some sense in that considerable portions of TISA consumption are of a nonmarket variety, perhaps relating negatively if at all to market consumption. This would appear

Table D.4   **Consumption as Function of After-Tax Income, Net Federal Debt, and Tangible Capital**

$$C = b_0 + b_1 YLAT + b_2 NDGFCA + b_3 KTANA$$

Regressor or Statistic	Dependent Variables Regression Coefficients and Standard Errors			
	CTISA	*CXSERN*	*CTSAOT*	*CBEAPC*
Constant	220.564	141.590	195.539	−131.771
	(44.032)	(89.443)	(32.181)	(17.933)
YLAT	0.176	0.272	−0.120	0.867
	(0.171)	(0.060)	(0.113)	(0.088)
NDGFCA	0.230	0.119	0.094	0.328
	(0.118)	(0.047)	(0.081)	(0.044)
KTANA	0.178	0.008	0.140	0.060
	(0.022)	(0.020)	(0.016)	(0.012)
AR(1)	0.861	0.999	0.790	0.248
$\hat{R}^2$	0.9990	0.9989	0.9987	0.9992
D-W	1.31	1.81	1.11	1.83
n	33	33	33	33

Notes:

  YLAT = Labor after-tax income.

  NDGFCA = Net federal debt (net debt plus gold and foreign exchange in constant dollars, average of previous and current end-of-year figures).

  KTANA = Tangible capital (the sum of household and nonhousehold tangible capital).

  CTISA = TISA consumption.

  CXSERN = Consumer expenditures for services and nondurables.

  CTSAOT = TISA consumption other than expenditures for services and nondurables.

  CBEAPC = BEA personal consumption expenditures.

  AR(1) = Cochrane-Orcutt equation.

to be somewhat confirmed in the relation involving the essentially nonmarket component of TISA consumption designated *CTSAOT* (for TISA consumption other than most expenditures for the services and nondurables). Here we find a negative if not particularly statistically significant coefficient for after-tax income. The regression of consumer expenditures for services and nondurables, *CXSERN*, does show a significantly positive coefficient for after-tax labor income but virtually no relation with the tangible capital variables.

Table D.4, like D.3 presenting results of AR(1) regressions, shows results with a single tangible capital variable that is the sum of household and nonhousehold tangible capital. The estimated parameters here are consistent with those above.

Investment Functions

Perhaps still the most widely estimated investment functions are those in the "neoclassical" family, in which net investment is a distributed lag function of changes in output and the relative price of capital and gross investment is the sum of net investment and depreciation. In table D.5 we present estimates

Table D.5   Investment as Function of Changes in Output and Relative Price of Capital

$$d\ln K = b_0 + b_1 d\ln Q_{-1} + b_2 d\ln(P/c)_{-1} + b_3 d\ln K_{-1}$$

Regression or Statistic	Regression Coefficients and Standard Errors			
	Business Structures and Equipment	Residential Capital*	Other Tangible Capital	Intangible Capital*
Constant	0.003	0.014	0.0007	0.0005
$[b_0]$	(0.004)	(0.056)	(0.0405)	(0.0024)
$d\ln Q_{-1}$	0.114	−0.166	0.062	−0.0224
$[b_1]$	(0.045)	(0.155)	(0.139)	(0.0227)
$d\ln(P/c)_{-1}$	0.077	0.009	0.051	0.0100
$[b_2]$	(0.020)	(0.008)	(0.014)	(0.0046)
$d\ln K_{-1}$	0.868	0.401	0.741	0.9851
$[b_3]$	(0.123)	(0.293)	(0.149)	(0.1025)
$b_1/(1-b_3)$	0.862	0.349	0.240	−1.496
$b_2/(1-b_3)$	0.586	0.021	0.198	0.671
$\hat{R}^2$	0.778	0.153	0.750	0.814
D-W	2.009	1.329	2.301	1.845
n	25	16	25	24

Notes:

* "Filtered" or AR(1) regression

$d\ln K$ = change in logarithm of capital, as indicated in column heads.

$d\ln Q$ = change in logarithm of corresponding output.

$d\ln(P/c)$ = change in logarithm of ratio of price of output to rental price of capital.

$b_1/(1-b_3)$ = long-run elasticity of capital with respect to output.

$b_2/(1-b_3)$ = long-run elasticity of capital with respect to its relative price.

of such functions for the traditional private investment, that is, the change in the stock of business structures and equipment, for residential investment, for other tangible investment, and for intangible investment. For each kind of investment we introduce the corresponding output variable. The relative price of capital is taken as the ratio of the price of the corresponding output to the user cost (or "mental price") of business structures and equipment for traditional private investment, to the user cost of residential structures for residential investment, to the user cost of other tangible capital for other tangible investment and, for want of a more appropriate measure, again to the user cost of business structures and equipment, for intangible capital. Each of these variables is entered with a one-year lag, along with the lagged value of the dependent investment variable. All variables are taken in logarithmic form to reduce heteroscedasticity.

The results are instructive. First, traditional business investment over the period from 1957 to 1981 shows significant response to changes in both output and the relative price of capital. The implied long-run elasticity of capital with respect to its relative price is 0.586, suggesting a substantial but not overwhelming role for interest rates and other elements in the relative price of capital that may have varied in relation to their expected future values during the period of estimation. The implied long-run elasticity of capital with respect to output is a larger 0.862 which, however, consistent with many previous findings, still suggests at least moderately increasing returns. The positive constant terms suggest that some net investment would be taking place even without increases in output or decreases in the relative price of capital.

The residential net investment equation proves a rather different story. With observations only from 1966, none of the variables proves statistically significant. As far as output is concerned, this may relate to the fact that our residential output variable is in considerable part a measure of capital services. Changes in the demand for that output are not realized in measured output until investment in fact takes place. Therefore there is no positive relation between investment and lagged changes in output. And a greater-than-unity elasticity of expectations in the relative price of capital over this period may have dominated in the effects of that variable.

Other tangible investment, which would be largely household and government acquisition of structures and equipment other than residential housing, was quite significantly related to changes in its relative price of capital. The indicated long-run elasticity of other tangible capital to its relative price was only 0.198, however. The not significantly different from zero coefficient of the output variable suggested a slightly higher long-run elasticity of 0.240, but the very low standard deviation in the change of this output variable indicates that it had little role in explaining the variance of investment.

In the case of intangible investment, the relative price variable, which was the ratio of the implicit price deflator for TISA GNP minus net revaluations to the user cost of structures and equipment, was statistically significant but with a coefficient of lagged investment close to unity; the suggested long-run elasticity of 0.671 has an enormous standard error. The coefficient of the output variable, which is TISA GNP minus net revaluations, does not differ significantly from zero and in fact shows up with a negative sign.

The robustness of these findings is certainly open to serious question. They do suggest, however, the advisability of caution in inferences about the determinants of capital accumulation as a whole from studies of its minor component of traditional business investment. Increases in market output may do little in themselves to generate the intangible capital on which future output may critically depend. Neither of the usual variables shows a clear, substantial relation to residential investment. Changes in the relative price of output and capital do appear, however, to be highly significant in the explanation of other, government, and household tangible investment, although the long-run elasticity does not appear to be large.

Appendix E

A Survey of Revised and Extended Accounts

The MEW of Nordhaus and Tobin

A major set of estimates of extended product has been provided by Nordhaus and Tobin (N-T 1972, 1973). Dubbed "MEW," a "measure of economic welfare," it attracted wide attention, quickly entering into economics textbooks and collections of readings.[43]

In departing from BEA GNP, Nordhaus and Tobin add imputations for government and household capital services, nonmarket work, and leisure. They subtract output regarded as "regrettables and intermediate," that is, "instrumental expenditures" for "activities that are evidently not directly sources of utility themselves but are regrettably necessary inputs for activities that may yield utility" (1972, 7). These include costs of commuting to work and government expenditures for police, sanitation, road maintenance, and national defense. They deduct as well for the "disamenities" of urban life.[44]

Viewing consumption, current and future, as the ultimate final product, Nordhaus and Tobin net out not only the output of capital goods measured by BEA capital consumption allowances and those for the additional capital for which they impute services; they also subtract the amount of investment that would be necessary to satisfy growth requirements. The net investment that is left in sustainable MEW is not all that is over and above what is necessary to keep capital intact and consumption constant, but only that in excess of what would be necessary to maintain a constant capital-output ratio with consumption increasing at a rate consistent with population growth and technological progress.

While including imputations for the services of tangible capital in households (consumer durables) and government, MEW does not add the services of education and health capital. They are taken to be intermediate in character, with their fruits already shown in labor productivity and earnings.

N-T impute a value to nonmarket work at home as the sum of the products of opportunity-cost earnings rates and nonmarket hours of various population groups. To secure a value of real output it is then necessary to have a product deflator. N-T's preference here is the deflator for the service component of BEA personal consumption expenditures. To the extent that the deflator measures the cost of living, this implies that the productivity of nonmarket work has been rising with the real wage. Alternative results based on deflating by nominal wages, thus allowing no increase in productivity, are also offered, however.

Nordhaus and Tobin argue that "those social costs of economic activity that are not internalized as private costs should be subtracted in calculating our measures of economic welfare" (1972, 49). Citing lack of data, they do not adjust for the depletion of per capital stocks of environmental capital but do adjust, among "the disamenities of urban life," for "pollution, litter, congestion, noise, insecurity, buildings, and advertisements offensive to taste, etc." (49–50).

In excluding defense expenditures, N-T argue first that they are input to the final output of whatever they are intended to defend and second that they are essentially input to a product of "national security." If national security is no greater now than it was, say, in 1929 when defense expenditures were minuscule, the increase in defense expenditures has not added to real final output but the cost of providing a given amount of security has risen. This second argument, it must be noted, is different from the one I have advanced above. It is tied to a measure of welfare, rather than the output which may contribute to welfare.

Nordhaus and Tobin make one additional major imputation which dwarfs all the others in amount. This is an estimation of the value of leisure, viewed as a component of consumption. N-T calculate this value by multiplying their estimates of the number of hours of leisure in the population 14 years and over (duplicating a similar exclusion of those under 14 years of age involved in nonmarket work) by wage rates presumed to be opportunity costs for the same population categories set up for estimating the value of nonmarket work. Calculating the real value of leisure again presents a deflation problem. N-T solve this, in their preferred measure, by assuming that the price of what leisure "buys" has risen with nominal wages, so that there is no increase in the "productivity" of leisure. They also present an alternative measure in which they use a consumer price index as the deflator, so the product of leisure rises with the real wage.

Since MEW or "actual MEW" is equal to "total consumption," it excludes all investment: the gross private domestic investment of the NIPAs, government or public investment, household investment in durable goods, and investment in the human capital of education and health. N-T offer as their ultimate preferred measure, however, "sustainable MEW" (MEW-S), which is the amount that would be left for total consumption after a deduction from total *product* of the investment necessary to cover both capital consumption allowances and the "growth requirements" explained above. "MEW net investment" is gross investment minus capital consumption allowances and the growth requirements. Sustainable MEW then is actual MEW plus MEW net investment, and is thus a measure of net national product. Its net investment component, however, may well be negative, as actual investment may be less than that necessary to cover capital consumption allowances and the growth requirements. In this case, MEW-S (or sustainable MEW, corresponding to NNP) is less than actual MEW (corresponding to consumption).

The magnitude of the innovations in MEW may be seen in table E.1. N-T almost exactly double the BEA's 1965 gross national product (in 1958 prices) of $618 billion to reach a sustainable MEW of $1,241 billion. This involves, as proportions of BEA GNP, subtractions of 8.9 percent and 15.0 percent for BEA and additional capital consumption allowances, respectively,

Table E.1   Nordhaus and Tobin: Gross National Product and MEW, 1965, in 1958
Prices, and Average Annual Percent Change in MEW

	Billions of Dollars	Percent of BEA GNP	Average Annual Percent Change	
			1929–47	1947–65
1. Gross national product, BEA[a]	617.8	100.0	2.36	3.91
2. Capital consumption, BEA	− 54.7	8.9	0.49	6.27
3. Net national product, BEA	563.1	91.1	2.60	3.72
4. BEA final output reclassified as regrettables and intermediates				
a. Government	− 63.2	10.2	6.50	6.37
b. Private	− 30.9	5.0	0.32	5.96
5. Imputations for items not included by BEA				
a. Leisure	626.9	101.5	1.79	1.65
b. Nonmarket activity	295.4	47.8	3.51	3.48
c. Disamenities	− 34.6	5.6	2.38	3.36
d. Services of public and private capital	78.9	12.8	1.18	4.34
6. Additional capital consumption	− 92.7	15.0	5.52	3.40
7. Growth requirement	− 101.8	16.5	4.50[b]	
8. Sustainable MEW	1,241.1	200.9	2.57	2.07

Source: Nordhaus and Tobin (1972), table A.17, p. 55.

[a]As indicated by Nordhaus and Tobin. The BEA national income and product accounts have of course been repeatedly revised over the years. In all of the tables which follow, BEA figures shown are either those presented by the original authors or are drawn, where possible, from series that were available when the original revised or extended accounts were prepared.

[b]For 1929 to 1965; growth requirement was negative in 1947.

16.5 percent for the growth requirement, 15.2 percent for regrettables and intermediate product, and 5.6 percent for disamenities. There are then imputations of additions equal to 47.8 percent of BEA GNP for nonmarket work, 12.8 percent for services of public and private capital and 101.5 percent—more than all of the BEA GNP—for leisure.

The estimates for the values of leisure and nonmarket activities vary greatly with the assumed deflator. The N-T preferred wage deflator for leisure yields an increase from $339 billion to $627 billion in 1958 prices, or 1.72 percent per annum, from 1929 to 1965 (table E.2). Use of a consumption deflator, thus allowing the productivity of leisure time to grow with the real wage, results in an imputation for leisure growing from $163 billion in 1929 to $713 billion in 1965, or 4.19 percent per annum. The total amount of the increase thus changes from $287 billion to $550 billion, a difference of some 91 percent. Similarly, for nonmarket activities, the preferred consumption deflator yields a growth per annum of 3.50 percent, from a 1929 figure of $86 billion to $295 billion in 1965, a difference of $210 billion, 158 percent more than the $81 billion growth with the money wage deflator.

The variety of possible assumptions of deflators for leisure and nonmarket activity results in a variety of estimated rates of growth for MEW-S. The N-T preferred combination, money wages for leisure and a consumption price index for nonmarket activities, yields a growth rate of 2.32 percent per annum, compared with 3.12 percent for BEA net national product (NNP) from 1929 to 1965. A more conservative estimate of growth of MEW-S, 1.79 percent per year, is obtained by using the money wage deflator for both leisure and nonmarket product, while use of the consumption deflator for both yields a more rapid rate of growth of 3.64 percent. Exclusion of the imputation for leisure, we may add, would give a value of MEW-S of $614 billion in 1965 compared to a NIPA net national product of $563 billion and a rate of growth of 3.11 percent from 1929 almost exactly equal to the NNP growth of 3.12 percent (in 1972 dollars).

N-T subtract $48 billion of "regrettables," including national defense, from 1965 government purchases of $115 billion of goods and services, as shown in table E.3. They also subtract $16 billion of intermediate goods and services of general government, sanitation, and civilian safety. Thus, $51 billion, or 44.9 percent of government purchases of goods and services, is left in final output, chiefly as gross public investment.

The N-T estimates of gross investment, provided for 1958 (table E.4), show conventional business investment of $40 billion to be only 25.4 percent of total gross investment of $158 billion. Residential construction makes up 13.2 percent and net foreign investment 1.4 percent, but government investment at 23.5 percent and consumer durables investment at 24.0 percent are each approximately as large as business investment, and "other consumer investments" in educational capital and health comes to 12.4 percent.

Table E.2   Nordhaus and Tobin: Measures of Economic Welfare, Actual and Sustainable (Billions of 1958 Dollars, except as noted)

	1929	1965	Average Annual Percent Change
1. Personal consumption, BEA	139.6	397.7	2.95
2. Private instrumental expenditures	− 10.3	− 30.9	3.10
3. Durable goods purchases	− 16.7	− 60.9	3.66
4. Other household investment	− 6.5	− 30.1	4.35
5. Services of consumer capital imputation	24.9	62.3	2.58
6. Imputation for leisure			
B Wage deflator	339.5	626.9	1.72
A Wage deflator	339.5	626.9	1.72
C Consumption deflator	162.9	712.8	4.19
7. Imputation for nonmarket activities			
B Consumption deflator	85.7	295.4	3.50
A Wage deflator	178.6	259.8	1.05
C Consumption deflator	85.7	295.4	3.50
8. Disamenity correction	− 12.5	− 34.6	2.89
9. Government consumption	0.3	1.2	3.93
10. Services of government capital imputation	4.8	16.6	3.51
11. Total consumption = actual MEW			
B (6B,7B)	548.8	1,243.6	2.30
A (6A,7A)	641.7	1,208.0	1.77
C (6C,7C)	372.2	1,329.5	3.60
12. MEW net investment	− 5.3	− 2.5	—
13. Sustainable MEW (MEW-S)			
B (6B,7B)	543.5	1,241.1	2.32
A (6A,7A)	636.4	1,205.5	1.79
C (6C,7C)	366.9	1,327.0	3.64
14. MEW-S per capita, dollars			
B (6B,7B)	4,462	6,378	1.00
A (6A,7A)	5,225	6,195	0.47
C (6C,7C)	3,012	6,819	2.30
15. Per capita NNP, dollars	1,545	2,897	1.76
16. MEW-S minus leisure	204.0	614.2	3.11
17. Net national product, BEA	183.6	563.1	3.12

Source: Nordhaus and Tobin (1972), table 1, p. 10, and N-T table 2, p. 12.

The EAW of Zolotas

Xenophon Zolotas (1981) constructed a measure of "Economic Aspects of Welfare" (EAW) for the United States economy for the years 1950 to 1977. In a number of fundamentals, it is similar to the work of Nordhaus and Tobin.

Zolotas's measure, like N-T's MEW, is one of consumption, but he has no measure akin to MEW-S to allow comprehensively for the investment

Table E.3   Nordhaus and Tobin: Reclassification of Government Purchases of Goods and Services (Billions of 1958 Dollars)

	1965
1. Public consumption	1.2
2. Public investment, gross	50.3
3. Regrettables	47.6
4. Intermediate goods and services	15.6
5. Total government consumption and investment	51.5
6. Total government purchases	114.7

Source: N-T table A.1, p.27.

Note: Based on current-dollar figures for federal, state, and local purchase of goods and services, BEA NIPA table 3.10, deflated by government purchases deflator.

    Consumption: postal service and recreation.

    Investment: one-half atomic energy development, education, health and hospitals, commerce, transportation, and housing, conservation and development of resources and agriculture.

    Regrettables: national defense less one-half atomic energy development, space research and technology, international affairs and finance, and veterans benefits and services.

    Intermediate: everything else, including general government, sanitation, and civilian safety.

Table E.4   Nordhaus and Tobin: Items of Gross Investment, 1958

	Billions of Dollars	Percent of Total
Conventional items		
1. Business investment	40.1	25.4
2. Residential construction	20.8	13.2
New items		
3. Government investment	37.0	23.5
4. Consumer durables	37.9	24.0
5. Other consumer investments	19.6	12.4
6. Net foreign investment	2.2	1.4
Total	157.6	100.0

Source: Nordhaus and Tobin (1972), table A.2, p. 29.

necessary to sustain future consumption. He begins with private consumption expenditures, deducts private expenditure on advertising and on consumer durables, and adds an imputation for the value of services from consumer durables. Unlike N-T, Zolotas deducts estimated costs of resource depletion and private costs of environmental pollution. He also subtracts the private costs of commuting and excludes those private expenditures on health and on education that are viewed as of a maintenance nature or as not raising the level of welfare. He then adds public health and education outlays deemed to contribute to welfare, the imputed value of household services, and like Nordhaus and Tobin, a major imputation for the value of leisure time. For

1977, with a BEA GNP of $1,333 billion in 1972 prices and personal consumption expenditures of $858 billion, as shown in table E.5, Zolotas thus subtracts a total of $413 billion, 31.0 percent of GNP, and adds $920 billion, 69.0 percent of GNP, to the consumption figure to reach an EAW index of $1,364 billion, just 2.4 percent more than GNP (or 6.6 percent more if, in an alternative measure, resource depletion cost is not deducted).

Zolotas offers rationalizations for a number of rather arbitrary decisions affecting components of his EAW index. Thus, apparently not recognizing that they are generally intermediate and not directly included in BEA final

Table E.5   Zolotas: Magnitudes Forming the EAW Index

	Billions of 1972 Dollars			Percent of BEA GNP	Percent Change per Annum
	1950	1965	1977	1977	1950–1977
Gross national product at market prices	533.5	925.9	1,332.7	100.0	3.45
Private consumption	338.1	558.1	857.7	64.4	3.51
Deductible items	83.9	217.2	413.2	31.0	6.08
Private expenditures on consumer durables	43.4	73.4	137.8	10.3	4.37
Private expenditures on advertising	6.0	10.3	13.5	1.0	3.05
Cost of resource depletion	—	24.0	55.7	4.2	—
Cost of environmental pollution (private)	23.0	52.7	71.0	5.3	4.26
Private cost on commuting	8.8	40.7	95.4	7.2	9.23
Private expenditure on health	—	9.6	29.1	2.2	—
Private expenditure on education	2.7	6.5	10.7	0.8	5.23
Additional items	541.1	764.8	920.0	69.0	1.99
Services from public buildings included in EAW-index	7.5	14.5	23.0	1.7	4.24
Imputed value of services from consumer durables	13.2	33.9	62.1	4.7	5.90
Imputed value of household services	143.4	249.3	260.7	19.6	2.24
Imputed value of leisure time	368.4	451.2	547.2	41.1	1.48
Public health and education outlays contributing to welfare	8.6	15.9	27.0	20.3	4.33
EAW index	795.3	1,105.7	1,364.5	102.4	2.02

Source: Zolotas (1981), tables 20 and 21, pp. 104–107.

product, he subtracts 50 percent of advertising expenditures on the grounds that they are "suggestive . . . causing dissatisfaction with those [goods] already possessed . . . merely . . . a factor promoting price increases and a proliferation of largely similar marketed goods" (p. 49).

Zolotas deducts control costs of air pollution "borne directly by private consumption in the form of increased demand for, say, domestic smoke eliminators, special filters for car exhaust fumes, etc." (pp. 65–66). He adds substantial "damage costs" of air pollution.[45] Total deductions for environmental pollution are half of control costs for air pollution and water pollution, all of the control cost for solid wastes, and the air pollution damage cost. With regard to commuting costs, Zolotas breaks down civilian employment by means of getting to work into the categories of "pedestrians, commuting by public transport, and commuting by private car."[46]

Zolotas deducts 50 percent of the increment in private expenditures on health per capita since 1950 as "corrective" in nature, merely compensating for other increasingly adverse factors, and thus not adding to consumer welfare. Similarly, Zolotas subtracts all of private expenditure for primary and secondary education as a form of gross investment necessary to maintain a stock of productive human capital. He allows 50 percent of private expenditure on higher education to remain in the EAW on the ground that it enhances personal well-being.

Zolotas evaluates the services of public buildings by summing capital consumption allowances and a return on capital based on applying "the average long-term interest rate in the private sector" (p. 87). He then includes 50 percent of that value in EAW as contributing to welfare.

The imputed value of services from consumer durables, or 4.7 percent of BEA GNP in 1977, is based on a variety of depreciation rates and adjustments for rapid obsolescence. The much larger imputed value of household (labor) services was 19.6 percent of BEA GNP in 1977.[47]

Zolotas's estimates of the value of leisure in part parallel those of Tobin and Nordhaus. He accepts the N-T assumption that productivity of leisure time is constant, but applies half (without explanation) of the average nominal hourly wage rate in the urban sector of the economy in 1972 as the price per hour of leisure. His imputed value of leisure time came to 41.1 percent of BEA GNP by 1977, after a 1.48 percent per annum real rate of growth over the previous 27 years.

Finally, Zolotas adds as "public consumption" 50 percent of the *increment* of public expenditure on health since 1950, taken to contribute to the improvement of welfare, along with 50 percent of all public expenditure on college and university education. He then finds that the average annual growth rate of GNP from 1950 to 1977 was 3.45 percent, while the rate of increase in the EAW index was 2.02 percent.[48]

Accounts of Jorgenson and Associates

In a series of papers with Barbara Fraumeni (1980 and 1987), Laurits Christensen (1969 and 1973), and Alvaro Pachon (1983), among others, Dale Jorgenson has set out a system of accounts with vastly expanded measures of consumption and investment.

As reported in Jorgenson and Fraumeni (J-F 1987), "full gross private domestic product" adds to BEA private GNP the value of subsidies, imputations for household physical capital services, time in household production and leisure, and investment in human capital, coming to an enormous 1982 total of $15,364 billion (table E.6). By 1984 this figure was $17,658 billion,

Table E.6   Jorgenson and Fraumeni: Gross Private Domestic Product and National Receipts and Expenditures, 1982 (Billions of Dollars)

	Product	
1.	Private GNP, BEA	2,822.1
2.	+ Subsidies less surplus government enterprise	8.7
3.	+ Imputation for physical capital services	339.2
4.	+ Other adjustments	247.5
5.	= Gross private domestic product	2,922.5
6.	+ Time in household production and leisure	4,200.7
7.	+ Investment in human capital	8,240.1
8.	= Full gross private domestic product	15,363.6
	Receipts	
9.	Gross private national income	2,980.0
10.	+ Nonmarket labor income	12,440.8
11.	= Full private national income	15,420.8
12.	+ Government transfer payments other than social insurance funds	99.6
13.	= Full gross private national consumer receipts	15,520.4
	Expenditures	
14.	Personal consumption expenditures	2,050.7
15.	− Personal consumption expenditures, durable goods	252.7
16.	+ Services of nonhuman capital	339.2
17.	= Private national consumption expenditure	2,137.2
18.	+ Consumption of nonmarket goods and services	4,200.7
19.	= Full private national consumption expenditure	6,337.9
20.	+ Personal transfer payments to foreigners	1.3
21.	+ Personal nontax payments	43.5
22.	= Full private national consumer outlays	6,382.7
23.	+ Full gross private national saving	9,055.9
24.	= Full private national expenditures	15,438.6

Source: Jorgenson and Fraumeni (1987), tables 1 and 9.

of which $7,335 billion or 41.5 percent was allocated to consumption and $10,323 billion or 58.5 percent was investment. Of full private national income in 1984 the labor share came to 92 percent and the property share only to 8 percent.

Consumption is BEA's personal consumption expenditures ($2,051 billion in 1982) less expenditures for durable goods ($253 billion) but plus imputed services of nonhuman capital ($339 billion) and a very large amount ($4,201 billion) for "consumption of nonmarket goods and services" (table E.6). This last is taken as the value of time spent in household work and leisure.[49]

The major innovation is in the measurement of investment in human capital. Jorgenson and Fraumeni take this investment in any year to be the sum of the present values "of lifetime incomes for all individuals born in that year and all [of that year's new] immigrants plus the imputed labor compensation for formal schooling for all individuals enrolled in school." The value of a year of formal schooling, however, is not imputed as the time spent in schooling times its opportunity cost, that is, the after-tax market wage, as is done with time deemed to be devoted to consumption. Rather it is calculated as the difference between the present value of projected labor earnings of a person with the schooling and without it.[50]

This method of treating gross investment of each year as the sum of the present values of all future *gross* incomes of additions to the population, making no deduction for living costs or human "maintenance," and the increase in present values of projected incomes associated with formal education, results in huge estimates of investment, far in excess, as Jorgenson and Fraumeni point out, of those of Kendrick based on *costs* of rearing and education.[51]

In their gross private national capital formation account for 1982 (table E.7), J-F thus move from the BEA gross private domestic investment of $447 billion to a gross private national capital formation of $816 billion, essentially by adding household investment in durable goods and government budget deficits (this last apparently the accumulation of private wealth in the form of government obligations of securities or money). They then add $8,240 billion of gross private national human capital formation to arrive at "full gross private national capital formation" of $9,056 billion. Human capital formation hence comes to over 90 percent of the total. Large as is the figure for "full gross private national saving," which is equal to full gross private national capital formation, it in turn is dwarfed by revaluations of $15,008 billion. After a deduction of only $2,216 billion for depreciation, the human capital portion of which is attributed to "aging, deaths, and emigration," the increase in private national wealth in 1982 was put at $21,848 billion.[52]

Table E.7   Jorgenson and Fraumeni: Gross Private National Capital Formation, 1982
(Billions of Dollars)

		Saving	
1.		Personal saving	153.9
2.	+	Personal expenditures for durable goods	252.7
3.	+	Other private saving	409.2
4.	=	Gross private national saving	815.8
5.	+	Human capital saving	8,240.1
6.	=	Full gross private national saving	9,055.9
7.	−	Depreciation	2,216.5
8.	=	Net private national saving	6,839.4
9.	+	Revaluation	15,008.2
10.	=	Change in private national wealth	21,847.6
		Capital Formation	
11.		Gross private domestic investment	447.3
12.	+	Personal expenditure for durable goods	252.7
13.	+	Consolidated government deficit	104.7
14.	+	Net foreign investment	− 1.0
15.	=	Gross private national capital formation	815.8
16.	+	Gross private national human capital formation	8,240.1
17.	=	Full gross private national capital formation	9,055.9

Source: Jorgenson and Fraumeni (1987), table 13.

Kendrick's Adjusted GNP

John W. Kendrick prepared a thorough and careful set of expanded income and product accounts in the course of his work on *The Formation and Stocks of Total Capital* (1976). The essence of these is shown in tables E.8 through E.11. This was supplemented in Kendrick (1979) by imputations for unpaid household labor and that of volunteers, as well as consumption services provided to employees, as shown in table E.12. It was further supplemented by imputations for leisure (Kendrick 1987a, 1987b) that are presented in table E.13.

A quick overview of Kendrick's original work may be gathered from Kendrick's reconciliation of the BEA GNP with his own "GNP, adjusted," shown in table E.8. For 1969, for example, starting with BEA GNP of $929 billion, Kendrick adds to household income and product $92 billion (9.9 percent of BEA GNP) for imputed student compensation, $16 billion (1.7 percent) for imputed compensation of the frictionally unemployed, $100 billion (10.8 percent) for imputed rentals on household durables and inventories, and $6 billion for imputed rentals on institutional plant and equipment and land in excess of NIPA depreciation and interest paid. In the business sector, he adds $2 billion for tangible investment and $35 billion (3.8 percent of BEA GNP) for intangible investment conventionally charged to current account. Finally, for the government sector, Kendrick

Table E.8   **Kendrick: Reconciliation of Adjusted GNP and Commerce Department GNP, 1969 (Billions of Dollars)**

1.	GNP, Commerce concept	929.1
	Plus	
	Households and institutions:	
2.	Imputed student compensation (less unemployment adjustment)	92.3
3.	Imputed compensation of frictionally unemployed (less subsidies)	16.0
4.	Imputed rentals (excl. maintenance and insurance) on household durables and inventories	100.1
5.	Imputed rentals (excl. maintenance) on institutional plant and equipment and land, over OBE depreciation and interest paid	5.7
	Business:	
6.	Tangible investment conventionally charged to current account	2.3
7.	Intangible investment conventionally charged to current account	35.4
	General government:	
8.	Imputed rentals (excl. maintenance) on land, durables, and inventories	67.0
	Equals	
9.	GNP, adjusted	1,247.9
10.	Ratio: Adjusted to Commerce GNP	1.343

Source: Kendrick (1976), table A-1, p. 158.

adds $67 billion (7.2 percent of BEA GNP) for imputed rentals on land, durables, and inventories. For 1969, all these additions move us from the BEA GNP of $929 billion to GNP, adjusted, of $1,248 billion, a 34.3 percent increase. Kendrick makes no subtractions for intermediate product of government, expenses related to work, "regrettables," or "disamenities."

Essential to Kendrick's framework is an integrated set of sector current and capital accounts. Investment includes outlays of all kinds "by all sectors that yield a flow of services over more than one annual accounting period . . ." (1976, 4). Thus Kendrick provides estimates of investment in the tangible nonhuman capital of structures, equipment, inventories, and land of all sectors (although with the constraint that the total quantity of land does not change). He also considers rearing costs of children up to the age of 14, including the full value of their consumption, as an investment in tangible human capital.

By way of investment in intangible capital, Kendrick counts R&D expenditures (basic, applied, and development), education (involving costs of schools plus foregone earnings of students 14 years of age and over),[53] and informal education (from libraries, museums, and the printed word).[54] He also includes costs of employee training borne by employers and considers 50 percent of expenditures for health and safety as medical investment, assuming the other 50 percent to be of the nature of current maintenance. And

Table E.9   Kendrick: National Income and Product Account, 1966 (Billions of Dollars)

Debits

1.	Labor compensation	547.48
2.	Wage and salary disbursements	394.50
3.	Wage accruals less disbursements	0.00
4.	Employer contributions for social insurance	20.29
5.	Other labor income	20.71
6.	Imputed labor compensation of proprietors	38.86
7.	Additional labor compensation imputations	73.22
8.	Net rental income of persons and institutions	28.13
9.	From auxiliary business activities	8.72
10.	From owner-used capital	19.41
11.	Profits of business enterprises	116.52
12.	Net rental income of government	6.17
13.	Net interest	45.79
14.	Personal interest income	43.64
15.	Less: Unproductive interest paid by consumers	0.19
16.	Government interest income	4.15
17.	Less: Unproductive interest paid by government	1.81
	National Income	744.19
18.	Less: Human capital consumption	101.15
	Net National Income	643.04
19.	Capital consumption allowances	272.57
20.	Personal	169.44
21.	Nonhuman	68.29
22.	Human	101.15
23.	Business	71.26
24.	Government	31.87
	Gross National Income	915.61
25.	Current business transfer payments	2.99
26.	Indirect tax and non-tax charges	67.60
27.	Less: Subsidies less current surplus of government enterprises	2.62
28.	Statistical discrepancy	− 1.01
	Charges against Gross National Product	982.57

Credits

29.	Personal consumption	381.57
30.	Government consumption	98.48
31.	Gross tangible nonhuman investment	244.36
32.	Structures	78.27
33.	Private residential	25.04
34.	Other	53.23
35.	Durable goods	144.02
36.	Change in inventories	22.07
37.	Gross tangible human investment	54.62

(*continued on next page*)

Table E.9   (*Continued*)

38. Gross intangible investment	198.26
39. Education and training	136.60
40. Health	21.47
41. Mobility	17.41
42. Research and development	22.77
43. Net exports of goods and services	5.28
44. Exports	43.36
45. Less: Imports	38.08
Gross National Product	982.57

Source: Kendrick (1976), table 2-1, p. 26.

Kendrick views as investment in mobility the opportunity costs of frictional unemployment, taken to be 3 percent of the labor force, or the actual rate of unemployment in those few war years when it was less, along with explicit job search costs and outlays linked to work-oriented travel, migration, and moving of household items.

Kendrick's investment estimates are all cost-based, as with conventional business accounts, rather than in terms of the present value of expected returns. Investment series are calculated in current and constant dollars. Gross capital stocks are then calculated as well in current and constant dollars and net stocks (and net income) reached by application of double-declining balance depreciation (usually switched to straight-line depreciation where that becomes larger).

Kendrick's much expanded view of investment and capital entails substantial imputations of additional income from capital. He thus includes in net income from owner-used capital not only imputations for such income from residences and institutional plant and equipment but also income from consumer durables and inventories. And along with the expanded measure of gross investment comes expanded capital consumption allowances, including those for human capital consumption necessary to move from "national income" to a "net national income" comparable to BEA national income.

As seen in table E.9, Kendrick's national income and product accounts include items of rental income, net interest, and capital consumption allowances for persons and government. There is no imputation for income from human capital, earnings from which are rather recognized in labor compensation. Under labor compensation we find, however, "imputed labor compensation of proprietors," calculated by multiplying the number of proprietors by average annual earnings per full-time employee in each industry. We also find "additional labor compensation imputations" based on the opportunity costs of students and of frictional unemployment. These imputations bring us from BEA wage and salary disbursements of $394 billion to Kendrick's total labor compensation of $548 billion.

In addition to imputations of additional income and product, Kendrick offers vastly expanded measures of capital formation. First, his gross tangible nonhuman investment of $244 billion in 1966 (table E.10) is almost twice the BEA gross private domestic investment of $126 billion. In addition to BEA business investment in structures, equipment, and additional inventories, which takes in household investment in new residences and nonprofit institution investment, both of which he includes in the personal sector, Kendrick includes all government and all household acquisitions of structures, equipment, durable goods, and inventories. Further Kendrick estimates gross tangible human investment at $55 billion in 1966 and gross intangible investment at $198 billion. With over $5 billion from accumulation through net capital transfers from the rest of the world and $2 billion from net foreign investment, Kendrick reaches a total gross accumulation of $505 billion, some four times NIPA gross investment.

This expanded total of investment is essentially in households and government, with quite modest changes in business investment as the result of

Table E.10   Kendrick: Consolidated Capital Formation Account, 1966

	Billions of Dollars	Percent of Gross Accumulation
Debits		
1. Gross tangible nonhuman investment	244.36	48.4
2. Gross tangible human investment	54.62	10.8
3. Gross intangible investment	198.26	39.2
4. Accumulation through net capital transfers from rest of world	5.48	1.1
5. Net foreign investment	2.45	0.5
Gross Accumulation	505.16	100.0
Credits		
6. Gross domestic investment	497.24	98.4
7. By persons and institutions	260.38	51.5
8. By business	127.03	25.1
9. By government	109.83	21.7
10. Accumulation through capital transfers	5.48	1.1
11. By persons	75.22	14.9
12. By business	−4.88	−1.0
13. By government	−64.86	−12.8
14. Net financial investment	3.46	0.7
15. By persons and institutions	20.28	4.0
16. By business	−16.24	−3.2
17. By government	−0.57	−0.1
18. Statistical discrepancy	−1.01	−0.2
Source of Gross Accumulation	505.16	100.0

Source: Kendrick (1976), table 2-6, p. 45.

inclusion of business intangible investment in education and training, health, mobility, and research and development. Thus, Kendrick's total gross domestic investment of $497 billion in 1966 breaks down into $260 billion or 52.4 percent by persons and institutions, and $110 billion or 22.1 percent by government, with only $127 billion, or 25.5 percent, by business. Analogous figures for net national wealth show business tangible wealth in 1969 of $1,252 billion, only 18.1 percent of the estimate of $6,920 billion for total domestic wealth in the nation (table E.11).

In a later report, Kendrick (1979) adds estimates of the value of non-market household labor. These begin with measures of time spent on five major types of activity: food and beverage preparation, care of home, making and caring for clothing and home furnishings, care of family including transportation, and household management, record-keeping, and shopping.[55] Total annual hours in household work are then multiplied by the average hourly labor compensation of household employees as estimated by the Bureau of Economic Analysis. Kendrick adds to his imputations for unpaid labor services those for volunteer labor.[56]

Kendrick includes in his adjusted measure consumption outlays charged by business to current expense and hence excluded from BEA GNP. They consist of certain expenses, largely for business travel and entertainment, viewed as a supplement in kind to wages and salaries, increasing the measures

Table E.11   **Kendrick: Net National Wealth of the United States, by Sector and Type, 1969 (Billions of Dollars)**

	Nation	Persons	Business	Governments
Nonhuman	3,220.5	1,103.0	1,306.5	811.1
Tangible	3,035.6	1,091.5	1,252.1	692.0
Land	686.8	174.3	393.7	118.8
Structures	1,376.1	515.9	423.0	436.3
Equipment	617.4	284.0	230.7	102.7
(Military)	(146.8)			(146.8)
Inventories	355.3	117.3	203.8	34.2
Intangible	184.9	11.5	54.4	119.1
Human	3,699.9	2,695.9	169.5	834.5
Tangible	1,146.9	1,146.9	—	—
Intangible	2,553.0	1,549.0	169.5	834.5
Education	2,267.3	1,334.1	162.4	770.9
Health	241.7	175.0	5.0	61.7
Mobility	43.9	40.0	2.0	1.9
Total, domestic	6,920.4	3,798.9	1,476.0	1,645.6
Net foreign assets	69.2			
Total, national	6,989.6			

Source: Kendrick (1976), table 2-11, p. 51.

of both labor compensation and output. Kendrick also includes the public consumption of radio and TV programs, and newspapers and magazines subsidized by business advertising expenses, which are viewed as a business transfer payment and thus increasing GNP but not gross national income. In obtaining real value (in 1958 dollars) of unpaid household work and volunteer services, 1958 average hourly labor compensation figures were applied. Hence, implicitly, there is no allowance for increased labor productivity in imputations of the value of their product.

As shown in table E.12, the imputation of the value of unpaid housework would have added 23.9 percent and 24.4 percent, respectively, to BEA GNP in 1966 and 1973. The value of volunteer labor would have added 2.0 percent in both years and that of school work, with increasing proportions completing high school and going on to college, rose from 8.1 percent of BEA GNP in 1966 to 11.3 percent in 1973. The imputation of consumption expense by business in the way of travel and entertainment was 1.6 percent of BEA GNP in 1966 and 1.3 percent in 1973. The consumption imputed to radio-TV and other media services was 0.8 percent of BEA GNP in 1966 and 0.7 percent in 1973.

Table E.12   Kendrick: Imputations by Sector and Type in Relation to Gross National Product

	Billions of Dollars		Percentage of GNP	
	1966	1973	1966	1973
GNP, official	753.0	1,306.3	100.0	100.0
Additional imputed values				
Personal Sector, total	349.5	663.4	46.4	50.8
Unpaid household work	180.1	318.4	23.9	24.4
Volunteer labor	15.4	25.8	2.0	2.0
School work	60.9	148.1	8.1	11.3
Frictional unemployment	12.3	24.1	1.6	1.8
Imputed rentals				
Household capital	76.5	138.5	10.2	10.6
Institutional capital	4.3	8.5	0.6	0.7
Business sector, total	46.9	75.5	6.2	5.8
Investments expensed				
Tangible	1.8	2.3	0.2	0.3
Intangible	27.0	45.6	3.6	3.5
Consumption expensed				
Employee	11.9	17.4	1.6	1.3
Public	6.1	9.2	0.8	0.7
Government sector				
Imputed rentals	49.9	91.2	6.6	7.0
Total Imputed Values	446.3	830.1	59.3	63.5

Source: Kendrick (1979), table 2, p. 357.

Taking together all of Kendrick's imputations of additional product of both labor and capital, BEA GNP of $753 billion in 1966 is raised by $446 billion, or 59.3 percent, to an adjusted gross product of $1,199 billion. For 1973 the change is even greater. To a BEA GNP of $1,306 billion, imputations of $830 billion add 63.5 percent, to reach an adjusted gross product of $2,136 billion. And in real *income* terms the changes were still greater than that. (The failure to impute prices to components of nonmarket output makes real GNP measures noncomparable.) In 1966, the adjusted total of gross national income in 1958 dollars was 68.6 percent larger than official gross income and in 1973 the difference was 74.1 percent.

Looking at sector breakdowns, the imputations were of course overwhelmingly in the personal and government sectors. Kendrick's imputations added $663 billion to BEA's 1973 personal sector output of $40 billion, a 16.4-fold increase, $91 billion to the BEA government sector product of $149 billion, an increase of 61 percent, but only $75 billion, or 7 percent, to the BEA business output of $1,108 billion.

Kendrick did not impute a value to leisure in his original work, but he has recently reported such estimates (1987a, 1987b). Included in table E.13, they are relatively similar to those of Nordhaus and Tobin, dwarfing all other imputations. Kendrick's values for leisure came to 95.9 percent and 94.5 percent of BEA GNP in 1984 and 1985, respectively. (The Nordhaus-Tobin preferred estimate for constant dollars in 1965 was 101.5 percent of BEA GNP.)

Richard and Nancy Ruggles and the IEA

Longtime specialists in national income accounting, Richard and Nancy Ruggles published in 1982 a comprehensive set of "Integrated Economic Accounts for the United States, 1947–80" (Ruggles and Ruggles, 1982a, 1982b). Reflecting in part the work by the Ruggleses on the United Nations System of National Accounts and a number of other earlier contributions,[57] the IEA entails an integration of income and product and capital accounts, essentially using data from the BEA NIPAs and the Federal Reserve Flow of Funds accounts.[58]

The BEA NIPAs are summarized in a set of five accounts: (1) national income and product; (2) personal income and outlay; (3) government receipts and expenditures; (4) foreign transactions; and (5) gross saving and investment. There is no explicit, separate account for business. The Ruggleses' IEA also include five current accounts: gross national product, enterprise gross product, household current income and outlay, government current income and outlay, and rest-of-the-world current account. In addition, the IEA provide a set of capital accounts: capital accounts for the nation, national and sector capital accounts, and separate capital accounts for enterprises, households, government, and rest of the world. The capital accounts indicate capital

Table E.13 **Kendrick: U.S. Full Personal Income (FPI), Total and Per Person (Billions of Dollars, except as otherwise noted)**

	1984	1985
Sources of FPI		
Income from current production[a]		
Wages, salaries, and other labor income	2,021	2,163
Proprietors and property income	767	815
Rental value of personal durable goods	420	458
Imputed value of unpaid time		
Household work	1,060	1,099
Schoolwork	530	550
Leisure	3,675	3,848
Total FPI	8,473	8,933
Disposition of FPI		
Personal taxes and contributions for social insurance, less transfers to persons[a]	118	150
Disposable FPI	8,355	8,783
Personal consumption		
Nondurable goods[a]	870	905
Services		
Expenditures[a,b]	1,227	1,336
Produced in households[c]	1,480	1,557
Leisure	3,615	3,790
Personal saving/investment	1,163	1,195
New residences[a]	130	138
Durable goods[a]	331	359
Human investments	596	610
Net financial investments	106	88
Total FPI	8,473	8,933
Population 16 years and over (millions)[a]	178.1	179.9
FPI per person ($)	47,578	49,652
Consumer price index (1984 = 100.0)[d]	100.0	103.57
Real FPI per person ($1984)	47,578	47,941
Percent change, 1984–85		+0.8

Source: Kendrick (1987a), table 1, p. 38.

[a]Department of Commerce estimates; other components of FPI estimated by the author.

[b]Includes a few imputations, primarily the rental value of owner-occupied residences.

[c]Comprises the imputed values of unpaid household work and the services of personal durable goods.

[d]U.S. Department of Labor, Bureau of Labor Statistics Index, converted to a 1984 base.

transactions, revaluations and end-of-year value for the reproducible assets of residential and nonresidential structures, durable goods and inventories, for land, gold and foreign exchange, and for fixed claim assets, along with financial liabilities and net worth of enterprises, households (including the value of corporate equity), government, and the rest of the world.

The Ruggleses' IEA distinguish between market transactions, generally viewed as more precisely measurable, and nonmarket activity. Segregated in nonmarket activity are the BEA imputations of rent of owner-occupied housing and nonprofit buildings, margins on owner-built homes, and farm income in kind. The Ruggleses add the major imputations of consumption of household and government durables.

As do the other builders of extended accounts, the Ruggleses include in capital formation government and household outlays for structures, durable goods, and additions to inventories. Their imputations for the value of services of household durables then include both capital consumption and net income. The services of government durables, however, are assumed equal only to capital consumption.

Government and household expenditures for structures, equipment, durable goods, and additions to inventories are viewed as investment, with a corresponding increase in gross saving. Net saving is of course increased by considerably less, as additional capital consumption allowances are included for the additional capital. Thus for 1978, as shown in a reconciliation table in detail by Denison (1982), BEA NIPA gross saving of $355 billion becomes IEA gross saving of $653 billion. BEA net saving of $134 billion becomes IEA net saving of $231 billion. For gross national product, the IEAs show in 1978 $2,020 billion in market transactions compared with $2,156 billion for BEA GNP, but record a total GNP, market and nonmarket, of $2,418 billion (table E.14).

The Ruggleses show in their capital accounts that a major factor in changes in wealth or net worth, generally dwarfing in current dollars the effects of saving and investment, are revaluations, that is, changes in the market value of existing assets and liabilities. These of course reflect very considerably the effects of general inflation. However, the Ruggleses also calculate real revaluations, which are, like Eisner's "net revaluations" (1980a and note 20, above), the changes in the values of assets and liabilities net of those changes necessary to keep up with the general price level (as measured by the GNP implicit price deflator). These reveal substantial and variable effects of revaluation of wealth. Thus, households generally showed major gains over and above inflation in their wealth in houses, land, and corporate stock and other equities as well as in the declining real value of fixed claim liabilities, but suffered losses in revaluations of fixed claim assets and consumer durables and inventories. While noting them as a significant

Table E.14   Ruggles, IEA: Gross National Product Account, 1978 (Billions of Dollars)

1.	Current consumption expenditures	1,346.7
2.	Enterprises	139.2
3.	Employee benefits in kind	62.3
4.	Nonprofit benefits in kind	42.5
5.	Financial services in kind	34.4
6.	Households	829.4
7.	Nondurable goods	508.8
8.	Services	320.6
9.	Government	378.1
10.	Purchases	148.8
11.	Compensation of employees	229.2
12.	Gross capital formation	673.6
13.	Enterprises	289.1
14.	Structures	111.6
15.	Equipment	164.9
16.	Change in inventories	22.6
17.	Households	309.4
18.	Owner-occupied houses	94.7
19.	Durable goods	199.3
20.	Change in inventories	15.4
21.	Government	65.1
22.	Structures	27.8
23.	Equipment	31.0
24.	Change in inventories	6.2
25.	Sales to rest of the world, net	− 30.5
26.	Sales to rest of the world	176.1
27.	Less: Purchases from rest of the world	206.6
28.	Gross domestic product (market transactions)	1,989.8
29.	Factor income from rest of the world, net	29.9
30.	GNP (market transactions)	2,019.8
31.	Imputed nonmarket outlays	398.9
32.	Enterprises	7.1
33.	Nonprofit building rent	7.1
34.	Households	342.6
35.	Owner-occupied housing	126.9
36.	Margins on owner-built houses	1.7
37.	Durables consumed	213.4
38.	Farm income in kind	.6
39.	Government	49.2
40.	Capital consumption of structures and durables	49.2
41.	GNP (market and nonmarket)	2,418.7

(*continued on next page*)

Table E.14   (*Continued*)

42. Charges against enterprise gross product	1,760.6
43. Compensation of employees	1,070.5
44. Net interest	20.6
45. Proprietors' income	112.2
46. Rental income	17.5
47. Net dividends	34.3
48. Indirect taxes and nontaxes	151.9
49. Corporate profits taxes	83.0
50. Surplus of government enterprises	5.9
51. Net transfers	− 30.6
52. Enterprise gross saving	289.0
53. Statistical discrepancy (BEA)	6.4
54. Charges against government product	229.2
55. Compensation of employees	229.2
56. Charges against gross domestic product (market transactions)	1,989.8
57. Factor income from rest of the world, net	29.9
58. Factor income received	43.8
59. Less: Factor income paid	13.8
60. Charges against GNP (market transactions)	2,019.8
61. Charges against imputed nonmarket gross product	398.9
62. Enterprises	7.1
63. Nonprofit building rent	7.1
64. Households	342.6
65. Gross income on owner-occupied housing	126.9
66. Margins on owner-built houses	1.7
67. Gross income on durables	213.4
68. Farm income in kind	.6
69. Government	49.2
70. Capital consumption of structures and durables	49.2
71. Charges against GNP (market and nonmarket)	2,418.7

Source: Ruggles and Ruggles (1982a), sample table 1.1, p. 19.

matter the Ruggleses do not, however, adjust fixed claims of interest-bearing securities (or gold) to their changing market values.

A Summary and Comparison

A compilation of the major extensions and revisions undertaken in each of these accounts and in TISA is offered in table E.15. Beyond the individual items, the fact to be highlighted is that we can put together consistent sets of

Table E.15   Extensions and Revisions of National Income and Product Accounts

	N-T MEW[1]	Z EAW[2]	J-F FGPDP[3]	K AGP[4]	R IEA[5]	E TISA[6]
Impute nonmarket product						
Services of household capital	Y	Y	Y	Y	Y	Y
Value of nonmarket household labor	Y	Y	Y	Y[7]	N	Y
Services of government capital	Y	Y	Y	Y	Y	Y
Services of volunteers	N	N	N	Y[7]	N	Y
Value of other uncompensated factor services	N	N	N	N	N	Y
Value of leisure	Y	Y	Y	Y[8]	N	N
Redefine final as opposed to intermediate product						
Subtract government expenditures for police and defense from final output	Y	Y	N	N	N	Y
Subtract commuting and other expenses related to work	Y	Y	N	N	N	Y
Subtract other "regrettables" and disamenities	Y	N	N	N	N	N
Adjust for changes in the environment, resources	Y	Y	N	N	N	N
Adjust for changes in terms of trade	N	N	N	N	N	Y
Add commercial media expenses and other intermediate business product	N	N	N	N	N	Y
Expand measures of investment to include						
Acquisition of tangible, nonhuman capital by government	Y	—	Y	Y	Y	Y
Acquisition of tangible, nonhuman capital by households	Y	—	Y	Y	Y	Y
Acquisition or development of land		—		Y	N	Y
Expenditures for research and development	N	—	N	Y	Y	Y
Expenditures for education	Y	—	Y	Y	Y	Y
Opportunity costs of time of students	N	—	Y	Y	N	Y
Expenditures for health	Y	—		Y	Y	Y
Costs associated with labor mobility search	N	—	N	Y	N	N
Child-rearing costs	N	—	Y	Y	N	N
Births − deaths + immigration − emigration	N	—	Y	N	N	N
Revaluations of existing assets and liabilities	N	—	Y	N	Y	Y

120

Table E. 15 (*Continued*)

[1] Nordhaus and Tobin, Measure of Economic Welfare.
[2] Zolotas, Index of Economic Aspects of Welfare.
[3] Jorgenson and Fraumeni, Full Gross Private Domestic Product.
[4] Kendrick, Adjusted Gross Product.
[5] Ruggles and Ruggles, Integrated Economic Accounts.
[6] Eisner, Total Incomes System of Accounts.
[7] Included in Kendrick (1979).
[8] Indicated in "Full Personal Income" in Kendrick (1987a and 1987b).
Y = Yes; N = No.

accounts for a vastly extended array of economic activities. Kendrick and Eisner (and associates), following the general methodology of conventional accounts, developed full sets of debits and credits involving income and outlay or income and product for the nation and for government and households as well as business. Kendrick also specified a foreign sector and Eisner presented separate sector accounts for nonprofit institutions and for government enterprises. Both prepared their accounts over long periods (1929 to 1969 or 1973 and 1946 to 1981, respectively) so that consistent time series are available. And both presented these series in current and constant dollars.

Jorgenson (and associates) prepared extended accounts of gross private product, reporting some of the detail for 1982 and broad aggregates for the postwar years. The Ruggleses offered one set of broadly extended accounts for 1966 and a complete series of revised but only moderately extended accounts for 1947 to 1980. Nordhaus and Tobin and Zolotas also presented data for a number of years but essentially limited themselves to expanded and revised development of the product side of the national accounts.

The major extension common to all of the accounts except the Ruggleses' IEA was the imputation of product of nonmarket household labor. Kendrick and Eisner also specifically imputed the opportunity costs of students' time in school. All of the accounts included the services rather than the acquisition of household durables in consumption. And all of the accounts except the EAW offered broader measures of capital formation or investment, including government and household expenditures for structures, equipment, and durable goods. Kendrick, Jorgenson and Fraumeni, and Eisner included investment in intangible or human capital, as did the Ruggleses (1970) in their 1966 accounts. Nordhaus and Tobin, Zolotas, Jorgenson and Fraumeni, and, recently, Kendrick had major imputations for the value of leisure.

Nordhaus and Tobin, Zolotas, and Eisner subtracted large portions of government output, particularly for the military, as in the category of "regrettables," or more generally product intermediate to the final output of current consumption and investment for the future. They also subtracted certain private expenditures, such as those for commuting to work, deemed intermediate to final output. Eisner offered a detailed reallocation of government product as consumption, capital accumulation, or intermediate output. The Ruggleses, Kendrick, and Eisner shifted certain intermediate expenses, such as some of business media support, to final consumption. And the Ruggleses, Jorgenson and Fraumeni, and Eisner highlighted the role of revaluations of existing assets and liabilities.

Expanded consumption measures tend to be reasonably close, as shown in table E.16, when adjustments are made for whether or not they include leisure, nonmarket household labor, and imputations for consumption provided by government. Expansions in measures of capital formation were major, with the accounts generally pointing to a much larger role for investment as a whole (table E.17) but a smaller relative role for the tangible business investment component on which much attention is traditionally focussed. Indeed, expanded accounts suggest a relatively smaller role of business in economic activity and a greatly expanded role of households along with the intangible investment in health, education, and research largely associated with households, nonprofit institutions, and government. Gross investment estimates (again table E.16), where based on similar coverage, as in the cases of Kendrick and Eisner, are understandably virtually identical at about 65 percent of BEA GNP. Eisner's net investment is somewhat more than Kendrick's because he applies straight-line depreciation while Kendrick uses the larger double-rate declining balance method. But except for the Nordhaus and Tobin MEW, where growth requirements along with ordinary capital con-

Table E.16   Consumption and Tangible and Intangible Domestic Investment as Percent of BEA GNP

Account	Year	Consumption	Gross Investment		
			Total	Tangible	Intangible
Nordhaus-Tobin, MEW	1965[a]	99.8[b]	38.9	—	—
Zolotas, EAW	1965	73.3[b]	—	—	—
Jorgenson-Fraumeni	1966	65.7[c]	290.1	27.8[d]	262.3[e]
Kendrick (1976)	1966	63.8[f]	65.8	39.8[g]	26.3[h]
Ruggles and Ruggles (1970, 1973)	1966	78.0	40.0	30.4	10.4
Eisner, TISA	1966	98.1	64.3	37.6	26.7
BEA	1966	61.5	16.6	16.6	0

[a] 1958 prices.
[b] Excluding imputed values of leisure.
[c] Excluding value of time spent in nonmarket household production and leisure.
[d] Nonhuman investment.
[e] Human investment, tangible and intangible.
[f] 87.7 percent if value of nonmarket household labor, reported in Kendrick (1979) is included in consumption.
[g] Human and nonhuman; 32.3 percent excluding human tangible.
[h] 33.6 percent if human tangible is, as with Jorgenson-Fraumeni, included here.

Table E.17   Gross and Net Domestic Capital Formation as Percent of BEA Gross and Net Private Domestic Investment and of Own Gross and Net Aggregates

Measure	Year	Percent of BEA		Percent of Own Aggregate	
		Gross	Net	Gross	Net
Nordhaus-Tobin, MEW	1929	194.6	−2.9	14.5	−1.0
Jorgenson-Fraumeni	1949	2,164.4	4,651.7	62.3	58.5
	1966	1,705.4	2,958.9	62.1	58.0
	1982	1,919.6	10,671.5	59.0	52.0
Kendrick (1976)	1929	339.1	306.7	43.1	21.5
	1949	371.9	279.7	41.4	17.2
	1966	385.5	361.6	50.5	31.6
Ruggles and Ruggles, IEA	1969	193.1	181.5	27.8	14.5
	1980	166.5	139.5	24.5	7.7
Eisner, TISA	1949	394.6	310.8	32.0	12.4
	1966	387.0	374.2	39.4	24.5
	1969	421.0	444.5	40.5	25.0
	1981	382.6	478.7	38.9	19.5
BEA	1929	100.0	100.0	15.7	6.9
	1949	100.0	100.0	13.7	5.7
	1966	100.0	100.0	16.6	9.4
	1969	100.0	100.0	15.8	8.0
	1981	100.0	100.0	16.1	5.5

sumption are netted out, net investment is a considerably larger share of net output than in the BEA accounts.

Labor's share of income is expanded significantly, as may be noted in table E.18, particularly in the accounts of Jorgenson and Fraumeni, Kendrick, and Eisner. Eisner's values of household labor services exceed Kendrick's apparently because of greater estimates of household labor time. Kendrick and Eisner shares of property and labor income are about the same for 1966 at just over 25 percent and about 100 percent, respectively, of BEA GNP. Eisner's property incomes vary substantially from year to year, however, if net revaluations are included.

The extended accounts generally encompassed considerably larger aggregates, to the extent that they included nonmarket activity, although those of Nordhaus and Tobin and Zolotas were particularly reduced by the exclusion or netting out of investment and by subtractions for regrettables, disamenities, and other social costs. Magnitudes of aggregates in the different accounts vary, however, with differences in concept as well as method. Thus, as shown in table E.19, the "extended" aggregates for the early years listed range from 112 percent of BEA GNP (for Ruggles and Ruggles, in 1969) to 468 percent (for Jorgenson-Fraumeni in 1966). But the latter is based on vastly expanded, present value concepts and measures of investment in human capital and

Table E.18   Household and Government Capital Services, Household Labor Services
and Property, and Labor Incomes as Percent of BEA GNP

Account	Year	HHCS	GCS	HLS	Property Income	Labor Income
Nordhaus-Tobin, MEW	1965[a]	10.1	2.7	47.8	—	—
Zolotas, EWA	1965[b]	3.7	—	26.9	—	—
Jorgenson-Fraumeni	1966	—	—	—	33.9	429.3
Kendrick (1974)	1966	10.2	—	23.9	26.0	98.3
Ruggles and Ruggles	1966	12.6	3.0	—	24.3	63.0
Eisner, TISA	1966	11.9	7.0	35.4	25.6	102.2
BEA	1966	5.4[c]	0	0.5[d]	24.3	82.6

HHCS = household capital services.
GCS = government capital services.
HLS = household labor services.
[a] 1958 dollars.
[b] 1972 dollars.
[c] Space rent of owner-occupied nonfarm dwellings.
[d] Compensation of employees in households.

includes the value of leisure while the former excludes both. Nordhaus and Tobin show an MEW-S equal to 201 percent of BEA GNP (table E.1) but that includes a full, presumably opportunity-cost value of leisure while the Zolotas EAW at 122 percent of GNP imputes leisure at only half the market earnings rate and makes a number of additional subtractions. And Nordhaus and Tobin and Zolotas exclude most if not all gross investment. The estimates that come closest to each other are those of Kendrick at 159 percent of BEA GNP in 1966 and Eisner's TISA at 163 percent. But then Kendrick and Eisner are generally similar in coverage and method and Eisner in fact uses some of Kendrick's estimates for earlier years.

The accounts of Zolotas, Kendrick, and Eisner (and of Nordhaus and Tobin when leisure is included in MEW) point, in varying degrees, to somewhat lesser real growth of extended and revised product than in conventional or official accounts. But except for Zolotas there is little claim or indication that the differences are major. They are in any event sensitive to critical decisions about proper deflation procedures, so that these results would have to be judged in doubt. The trend in rates of growth into the mid-1970s seems generally down for extended as well as official accounts, although Kendrick's growth rates were rising.

Table E.19   Extended Accounts: Aggregates in Relation to BEA GNP and Rates of Growth

	Year	Ratio of BEA GNP	Years	Average Annual Percent Growth	
				Current $	Constant $
Nordhaus-Tobin, MEW-S[a]	1929	2.67	1929–47		2.57
	1965	2.01	1947–65		2.07
Zolotas, EAW[a]	1950	1.49	1950–65		2.37
	1965	1.22	1965–77		1.92
	1977	1.02			
Jorgenson-Fraumeni, Gross	1948	4.50	1948–66	6.34	
private domestic product	1966	4.68	1966–76	8.27	
	1981	4.74[b]	1966–81	9.62	
Kendrick (1979), GNP,	1929	1.54	1929–48	5.15	1.40[c]
adjusted	1948	1.59	1948–66	6.12	2.32[c]
	1966	1.59	1966–73	8.60	2.66[c]
	1973	1.64			
Ruggles and Ruggles,	1969	1.12	1969–80[m]	9.65	2.76
IEA, GNP	1980	1.15	1969–80[t]	9.78	3.14
Eisner, TISA, GNP minus	1946	1.75	1946–66	6.26	2.79
net revaluations	1966	1.63	1966–76	8.60	2.47
	1981	1.60	1966–81	9.34	2.52
BEA, GNP			1929–48	4.95	2.33
			1946–66	6.60	3.68
			1966–76	8.56	2.80
			1966–81	9.51	2.91

[a] Constant dollars.
[b] Ratio of BEA *private* GNP in 1982 was 5.44.
[c] "Gross National Income."
[m] Market transactions only.
[t] Total GNP.

TISA Tables

		DEBITS					
		1946	1947	1948	1949	1950	1951
1	LABOR INCOME	268.907	289.245	312.315	305.165	326.234	371.487
2	COMPENSATION OF EMPLOYEES	118.048	129.171	141.439	141.317	154.843	180.999
3	DOMESTIC	118.088	129.102	141.353	141.259	154.765	180.985
4	REST OF WORLD	-.040	.069	.086	.058	.078	.014
5	ADDITIONAL IMPUTATIONS	153.746	163.378	174.638	167.999	175.923	195.660
6	EMPLOYEE TRAINING	9.600	7.555	7.681	6.549	8.345	12.435
7	EXPENSE ACCOUNT ITEMS OF CONSUMPTION	1.887	2.181	2.407	2.371	2.558	2.874
8	LABOR INCOME OF SELF-EMPLOYED	35.327	33.771	37.832	33.595	35.927	41.013
9	OPPORTUNITY COSTS OF STUDENTS	11.640	14.380	15.660	15.570	16.420	18.240
10	UNPAID HOUSEHOLD WORK	95.292	105.491	111.058	109.914	112.673	121.098
11	LESS: EXPENSES RELATED TO WORK	2.887	3.304	3.762	4.151	4.532	5.172
12	RENTAL INCOME OWNER-OCC. NONFARM DWELLINGS	.141	.249	.188	.130	.354	.305
13	GROSS RENTAL INCOME	1.754	1.436	1.522	2.019	2.541	2.940
14	LESS: NET IMPUTED INTEREST ON OWNER-OCC. NONFARM DWELLINGS AND LAND	1.613	1.187	1.334	1.889	2.187	2.635
15	CAPITAL INCOME	14.045	13.921	16.159	17.293	17.180	18.229
16	INTEREST PAID	6.455	7.388	7.844	8.501	9.420	10.148
17	NET IMPUTED INTEREST (EXCL BUS)	7.440	6.349	8.074	8.537	7.489	7.728
18	GROSS IMPUTED INTEREST	13.290	12.801	15.158	16.241	16.018	16.872
19	LAND	.801	.803	1.005	1.124	1.139	1.219
20	OWNER-OCCUPIED DWELLINGS	2.225	2.042	2.378	3.022	3.468	4.152
21	STRUCTURES AND EQUIPMENT	6.004	6.241	7.746	7.601	6.729	6.414
22	CONSUMER DURABLES AND SEMIDURABLES	2.315	1.988	2.215	2.868	3.310	3.890
23	INVENTORIES	1.873	1.641	1.693	1.488	1.240	1.067
24	GOVT R & D	.073	.086	.122	.138	.133	.130
25	LESS: INTEREST PAID (EXCL BUS)	5.850	6.452	7.084	7.704	8.529	9.144
26	NET INTEREST, REST OF WORLD	.150	.184	.241	.255	.271	.353
27	NET OPERATING SURPLUS	23.619	30.374	38.877	36.183	43.657	48.339
28	CORPORATE PROFITS	16.581	22.279	29.422	27.145	33.948	38.665
29	DOMESTIC	15.890	21.293	28.161	26.020	32.679	36.921
30	REST OF WORLD	.691	.986	1.261	1.125	1.269	1.744
31	PROPRIETORS' CAPITAL INCOME	1.357	2.127	3.032	2.781	2.776	2.216
32	PROPRIETORS' INCOME	36.684	35.898	40.864	36.376	38.703	43.229
33	LESS: LABOR INCOME OF SELF-EMPLOYED	35.327	33.771	37.832	33.595	35.927	41.013
34	GROSS BUSINESS INVESTMENT IN R & D	.750	.950	1.030	.870	1.070	1.240
35	GOVERNMENT ENTERPRISE SURPLUSES	1.218	1.202	1.214	1.290	1.333	1.448
36	NET RENTAL INCOME OF PERSONS	3.713	3.816	4.179	4.097	4.530	4.770
37	NET REVALUATIONS	-75.268	21.937	17.187	6.558	3.817	29.770

126

		DEBITS					
		1946	1947	1948	1949	1950	1951
38	LAND	-21.784	-2.851	2.003	8.476	8.738	10.441
39	OWNER-OCCUPIED DWELLINGS	-6.111	6.228	4.013	-1.476	1.395	3.337
40	STRUCTURES AND EQUIPMENT OTHER THAN OWNER-OCCUPIED DWELLINGS	-22.753	16.935	13.320	3.215	-2.595	17.457
41	CONSUMER DURABLES AND SEMIDURABLES	-13.895	-2.568	1.142	2.412	-6.394	1.412
42	INVENTORIES	-10.725	4.193	-3.291	-6.069	2.673	-2.877
43	NET SURPLUS (27 + 37)	-51.649	52.311	56.064	42.741	47.474	78.109
44	NATIONAL INCOME (1+12+15+43)	231.444	355.726	384.727	365.329	391.242	468.130
45	LESS: INTANGIBLE CAPITAL CONSUMPTION	19.306	20.325	21.493	22.827	21.468	23.070
46	CAPITAL CONSUMPTION ON ALL R & D	.665	.797	.918	1.019	1.174	1.375
47	CAPITAL CONSUMPTION ON HUMAN CAPITAL	18.641	19.528	20.575	21.808	20.294	21.695
48	NET NATIONAL INCOME (44 - 45)	212.138	335.401	363.234	342.502	369.774	445.060
49	BUSINESS TRANSFER PAYMENTS	1.404	1.680	1.927	2.027	2.189	2.545
50	MEDIA SUPPORT	.633	.749	.842	.894	.997	1.137
51	HEALTH AND SAFETY	.293	.351	.385	.382	.414	.474
52	OTHER	.478	.580	.700	.751	.778	.934
53	UNCOMPENSATED FACTOR SERVICES	3.449	3.225	3.707	3.961	4.177	6.122
54	VOLUNTEERS	2.132	2.408	2.747	2.775	2.914	3.167
55	DRAFTEES	1.281	.784	.924	1.142	1.212	2.901
56	JURORS	.036	.033	.036	.044	.051	.054
57	NET INDIRECT BUSINESS TAXES	-19.618	-13.806	-11.639	-4.897	2.238	-.730
58	INDIRECT BUSINESS TAXES	16.004	17.220	18.770	19.783	21.742	23.379
59	LESS: INTERMEDIATE PRODUCT TRANSFERRED FROM GOVT TO BUSINESS	35.622	31.026	30.409	24.680	19.505	24.109
60	STATISTICAL DISCREPANCY	.506	1.539	-1.552	.563	1.307	3.154
61	BEA STATISTICAL DISCREPANCY	.502	1.536	-1.553	.562	1.306	3.153
62	TISA STATISTICAL DISCREPANCY	.004	.003	.001	.001	.001	.001
63	NET NATIONAL PRODUCT (48+49+53+57+60)	197.879	328.039	355.677	344.157	379.684	456.151
64	CAPITAL CONSUMPTION ALLOWANCES	93.173	97.181	99.171	97.289	94.606	103.795
65	TANGIBLE	73.867	76.856	77.678	74.462	73.138	80.725
66	ORIGINAL COST	58.460	56.726	56.710	56.918	58.557	62.604
67	REVALUATIONS	15.407	20.130	20.968	17.544	14.581	18.121
68	INTANGIBLE	19.306	20.325	21.493	22.827	21.468	23.070
69	ORIGINAL COST	15.764	15.589	15.006	14.846	15.380	16.420
70	ON RESEARCH AND DEVELOPMENT	.521	.594	.684	.781	.885	1.005
71	ON HUMAN CAPITAL	15.243	14.995	14.322	14.065	14.495	15.415
72	REVALUATIONS	3.542	4.736	6.487	7.981	6.088	6.650
73	ON RESEARCH AND DEVELOPMENT	.144	.203	.234	.238	.289	.370
74	ON HUMAN CAPITAL	3.398	4.533	6.253	7.743	5.799	6.280
75	GROSS NATIONAL PRODUCT (63+64)	291.052	425.220	454.848	441.446	474.290	559.946

The complete set of accounts in tables 1–15 is available in machine-readable form on 5.25 inch diskettes on request to the author or by asking Member Services, ICPSR, P.O. Box 1248, Ann Arbor, Michigan 48106, telephone 313-763-5010, for the TISA data in Class V.

127

TABLE 1. NATIONAL INCOME AND PRODUCT ACCOUNT, BILLIONS OF DOLLARS, 1946-81

		DEBITS					
		1952	1953	1954	1955	1956	1957
1	LABOR INCOME	399.556	424.146	429.780	457.302	483.076	507.724
2	COMPENSATION OF EMPLOYEES	195.697	209.569	208.396	224.905	243.511	256.480
3	DOMESTIC	195.695	209.576	208.453	224.975	243.593	256.558
4	REST OF WORLD	.002	-.007	-.057	-.070	-.082	-.078
5	ADDITIONAL IMPUTATIONS	209.722	221.164	228.514	240.194	248.319	260.629
6	EMPLOYEE TRAINING	13.565	13.672	12.933	14.402	12.575	12.509
7	EXPENSE ACCOUNT ITEMS OF CONSUMPTION	3.085	3.300	3.342	3.629	4.010	4.223
8	LABOR INCOME OF SELF-EMPLOYED	41.781	40.605	39.508	40.622	42.273	43.590
9	OPPORTUNITY COSTS OF STUDENTS	18.780	20.640	20.340	22.940	25.370	28.300
10	UNPAID HOUSEHOLD WORK	132.511	142.947	152.391	158.601	164.091	172.007
11	LESS: EXPENSES RELATED TO WORK	5.863	6.587	7.130	7.797	8.754	9.385
12	RENTAL INCOME OWNER-OCC. NONFARM DWELLINGS	.245	.307	.340	.510	.480	.318
13	GROSS RENTAL INCOME	3.797	4.849	5.759	6.038	6.121	6.407
14	LESS: NET IMPUTED INTEREST ON OWNER-OCC. NONFARM DWELLINGS AND LAND	3.553	4.542	5.419	5.528	5.641	6.089
15	CAPITAL INCOME	21.960	25.448	30.310	33.493	33.886	37.451
16	INTEREST PAID	10.913	12.174	13.337	14.568	16.385	18.481
17	NET IMPUTED INTEREST (EXCL BUS)	10.675	12.874	16.529	18.455	17.066	18.477
18	GROSS IMPUTED INTEREST	20.497	23.806	28.262	31.249	31.632	34.553
19	LAND	2.000	2.305	2.817	3.331	3.528	4.113
20	OWNER-OCCUPIED DWELLINGS	5.232	6.341	7.432	7.833	8.380	9.244
21	STRUCTURES AND EQUIPMENT	7.074	7.585	8.860	10.270	9.761	10.427
22	CONSUMER DURABLES AND SEMIDURABLES	4.890	5.899	6.728	6.784	7.129	7.878
23	INVENTORIES	1.154	1.512	2.219	2.778	2.582	2.601
24	GOVT R & D	.147	.164	.206	.254	.253	.290
25	LESS: INTEREST PAID (EXCL BUS)	9.822	10.932	11.733	12.794	14.566	16.076
26	NET INTEREST, REST OF WORLD	.372	.400	.444	.470	.435	.493
27	NET OPERATING SURPLUS	45.905	46.474	46.253	57.360	56.224	56.354
28	CORPORATE PROFITS	36.089	36.317	35.156	45.486	43.744	43.253
29	DOMESTIC	34.201	34.519	33.194	43.132	40.923	40.161
30	REST OF WORLD	1.888	1.798	1.962	2.354	2.821	3.092
31	PROPRIETORS' CAPITAL INCOME	1.575	1.160	1.727	2.258	1.666	1.696
32	PROPRIETORS' INCOME	43.356	41.765	41.235	42.880	43.939	45.286
33	LESS: LABOR INCOME OF SELF-EMPLOYED	41.781	40.605	39.508	40.622	42.273	43.590
34	GROSS BUSINESS INVESTMENT IN R & D	1.720	2.200	2.320	2.460	3.277	3.396
35	GOVERNMENT ENTERPRISE SURPLUSES	1.515	1.620	1.780	1.924	2.024	2.169
36	NET RENTAL INCOME OF PERSONS	5.006	5.177	5.270	5.232	5.513	5.840
37	NET REVALUATIONS	-4.952	3.325	-2.684	19.516	27.749	8.193
38	LAND	7.001	8.082	11.419	19.611	21.651	18.882
39	OWNER-OCCUPIED DWELLINGS	-.525	-.836	-.068	-.273	-4.522	-5.567
40	STRUCTURES AND EQUIPMENT OTHER THAN OWNER-OCCUPIED DWELLINGS	.223	-1.509	-8.086	10.039	13.999	-3.015
41	CONSUMER DURABLES AND SEMIDURABLES	-.914	-2.481	-6.896	-7.428	-2.574	-2.850
42	INVENTORIES	-10.737	.069	.947	-2.433	-.805	.743
43	NET SURPLUS (27 + 37)	40.953	49.799	43.569	76.876	83.973	64.547
44	NATIONAL INCOME (1+12+15+43)	462.713	499.701	503.999	568.181	601.415	610.040
45	LESS: INTANGIBLE CAPITAL CONSUMPTION	27.709	30.037	34.079	33.848	38.385	42.368
46	CAPITAL CONSUMPTION ON ALL R & D	1.568	1.836	2.097	2.431	2.852	3.330
47	CAPITAL CONSUMPTION ON HUMAN CAPITAL	26.141	28.201	31.982	31.417	35.533	39.038
48	NET NATIONAL INCOME (44 - 45)	435.004	469.664	469.920	534.333	563.030	567.672

128

TABLE 1. NATIONAL INCOME AND PRODUCT ACCOUNT, BILLIONS OF DOLLARS, 1946-81

		DEBITS					
		1952	1953	1954	1955	1956	1957
49	BUSINESS TRANSFER PAYMENTS	2.823	3.157	3.137	3.543	3.878	4.175
50	MEDIA SUPPORT	1.256	1.378	1.476	1.677	1.855	1.963
51	HEALTH AND SAFETY	.521	.578	.584	.621	.657	.697
52	OTHER	1.046	1.201	1.077	1.245	1.366	1.515
53	UNCOMPENSATED FACTOR SERVICES	7.486	8.095	8.479	9.395	10.299	11.556
54	VOLUNTEERS	3.386	3.616	3.752	3.936	4.158	4.409
55	DRAFTEES	4.036	4.402	4.634	5.356	6.025	7.034
56	JURORS	.064	.077	.093	.103	.116	.113
57	NET INDIRECT BUSINESS TAXES	-.608	.838	2.171	.622	3.117	2.234
58	INDIRECT BUSINESS TAXES	25.566	27.350	26.977	29.166	31.561	33.520
59	LESS: INTERMEDIATE PRODUCT TRANSFERRED FROM GOVT TO BUSINESS	26.174	26.512	24.806	28.544	28.444	31.286
60	STATISTICAL DISCREPANCY	1.728	2.274	2.022	1.317	-2.134	-1.236
61	BEA STATISTICAL DISCREPANCY	1.727	2.273	2.021	1.315	-2.136	-1.237
62	TISA STATISTICAL DISCREPANCY	.001	.001	.001	.002	.002	.001
63	NET NATIONAL PRODUCT (48+49+53+57+60)	446.433	484.028	485.729	549.209	578.190	584.401
64	CAPITAL CONSUMPTION ALLOWANCES	114.435	121.307	130.088	134.764	148.313	159.221
65	TANGIBLE	86.726	91.270	96.009	100.916	109.928	116.853
66	ORIGINAL COST	68.343	74.336	80.507	86.203	92.229	97.038
67	REVALUATIONS	18.383	16.934	15.502	14.713	17.699	19.815
68	INTANGIBLE	27.709	30.037	34.079	33.848	38.385	42.368
69	ORIGINAL COST	18.001	19.793	21.303	22.623	23.971	25.465
70	ON RESEARCH AND DEVELOPMENT	1.159	1.365	1.611	1.900	2.262	2.690
71	ON HUMAN CAPITAL	16.842	18.428	19.692	20.723	21.709	22.775
72	REVALUATIONS	9.708	10.244	12.776	11.225	14.414	16.903
73	ON RESEARCH AND DEVELOPMENT	.409	.471	.486	.531	.590	.640
74	ON HUMAN CAPITAL	9.299	9.773	12.290	10.694	13.824	16.263
75	GROSS NATIONAL PRODUCT (63 + 64)	560.868	605.335	615.817	683.973	726.503	743.622

		1958	1959	1960	1961	1962	1963
1	LABOR INCOME	519.874	553.348	584.750	603.343	637.953	668.537
2	COMPENSATION OF EMPLOYEES	258.245	279.579	294.932	303.568	325.098	342.882
3	DOMESTIC	258.317	279.659	295.074	303.698	325.178	342.930
4	REST OF WORLD	-.072	-.080	-.142	-.130	-.080	-.048
5	ADDITIONAL IMPUTATIONS	271.242	284.179	300.674	310.810	324.333	337.566
6	EMPLOYEE TRAINING	12.863	13.922	14.455	14.414	16.247	16.141
7	EXPENSE ACCOUNT ITEMS OF CONSUMPTION	4.310	4.441	4.636	4.701	4.946	4.909
8	LABOR INCOME OF SELF-EMPLOYED	46.167	45.305	44.878	46.209	46.490	46.908
9	OPPORTUNITY COSTS OF STUDENTS	28.760	32.050	33.220	34.740	39.200	43.660
10	UNPAID HOUSEHOLD WORK	179.142	188.461	203.485	210.746	217.450	225.948
11	LESS: EXPENSES RELATED TO WORK	9.613	10.410	10.856	11.035	11.478	11.911
12	RENTAL INCOME OWNER-OCC. NONFARM DWELLINGS	.322	.500	.247	.395	.519	.222
13	GROSS RENTAL INCOME	6.697	7.425	8.150	8.601	9.245	9.669
14	LESS: NET IMPUTED INTEREST ON OWNER-OCC. NONFARM DWELLINGS AND LAND	6.375	6.925	7.903	8.206	8.726	9.448
15	CAPITAL INCOME	40.312	44.851	47.808	51.059	57.370	63.244
16	INTEREST PAID	19.885	22.049	24.575	25.809	28.342	31.520
17	NET IMPUTED INTEREST (EXCL BUS)	19.846	22.115	22.523	24.378	27.998	30.620
18	GROSS IMPUTED INTEREST	36.423	40.889	43.471	45.819	51.397	56.269
19	LAND	4.607	5.559	6.073	6.583	7.773	8.769
20	OWNER-OCCUPIED DWELLINGS	9.944	10.802	12.067	12.809	13.853	14.884
21	STRUCTURES AND EQUIPMENT	10.553	12.248	12.296	13.015	15.395	17.088
22	CONSUMER DURABLES AND SEMIDURABLES	8.423	8.989	9.832	10.218	10.861	11.734
23	INVENTORIES	2.573	2.876	2.748	2.678	2.869	3.036
24	GOVT R & D	.324	.415	.455	.517	.647	.760
25	LESS: INTEREST PAID (EXCL BUS)	16.577	18.774	20.948	21.441	23.399	25.649
26	NET INTEREST, REST OF WORLD	.581	.687	.710	.872	1.030	1.104

129

		DEBITS					
		1958	1959	1960	1961	1962	1963
27	NET OPERATING SURPLUS	52.025	64.565	63.462	64.922	74.559	81.391
28	CORPORATE PROFITS	38.484	49.611	47.644	48.585	56.584	62.136
29	DOMESTIC	35.961	46.946	44.643	45.426	52.980	58.243
30	REST OF WORLD	2.523	2.665	3.001	3.159	3.604	3.893
31	PROPRIETORS' CAPITAL INCOME	1.543	2.308	2.325	2.381	3.401	3.621
32	PROPRIETORS' INCOME	47.710	47.613	47.203	48.590	49.891	50.529
33	LESS: LABOR INCOME OF SELF-EMPLOYED	46.167	45.305	44.878	46.209	46.490	46.908
34	GROSS BUSINESS INVESTMENT IN R & D	3.630	3.983	4.428	4.668	5.029	5.360
35	GOVERNMENT ENTERPRISE SURPLUSES	2.198	2.451	2.729	2.862	3.031	3.407
36	NET RENTAL INCOME OF PERSONS	6.170	6.212	6.336	6.426	6.514	6.867
37	NET REVALUATIONS	13.177	-.527	-1.829	3.755	-.032	-7.303
38	LAND	24.515	27.183	13.864	22.617	22.629	17.066
39	OWNER-OCCUPIED DWELLINGS	-4.501	-5.206	-2.105	-4.121	-4.736	-10.228
40	STRUCTURES AND EQUIPMENT OTHER THAN OWNER-OCCUPIED DWELLINGS	-8.328	-12.596	-9.293	-6.819	-7.037	-5.854
41	CONSUMER DURABLES AND SEMIDURABLES	-.830	-4.527	-3.604	-4.384	-6.720	-4.627
42	INVENTORIES	2.321	-5.381	-.691	-3.538	-4.168	-3.660
43	NET SURPLUS (27 + 37)	65.202	64.038	61.633	68.677	74.527	74.088
44	NATIONAL INCOME (1+12+15+43)	625.710	662.737	694.438	723.474	770.369	806.091
45	LESS: INTANGIBLE CAPITAL CONSUMPTION	45.111	47.767	50.793	53.118	56.877	60.749
46	CAPITAL CONSUMPTION ON ALL R & D	3.856	4.450	5.065	5.699	6.388	7.141
47	CAPITAL CONSUMPTION ON HUMAN CAPITAL	41.255	43.317	45.728	47.419	50.489	53.608
48	NET NATIONAL INCOME (44 - 45)	580.599	614.970	643.645	670.356	713.492	745.342
49	BUSINESS TRANSFER PAYMENTS	4.275	4.735	5.383	5.227	5.547	6.024
50	MEDIA SUPPORT	2.019	2.214	2.616	2.362	2.512	2.688
51	HEALTH AND SAFETY	.696	.750	.793	.830	.891	.931
52	OTHER	1.560	1.771	1.974	2.035	2.144	2.405
53	UNCOMPENSATED FACTOR SERVICES	11.605	12.832	13.200	14.223	15.486	15.682
54	VOLUNTEERS	4.603	4.833	5.072	5.266	5.491	5.744
55	DRAFTEES	6.877	7.871	7.997	8.824	9.850	9.778
56	JURORS	.125	.128	.131	.133	.145	.160
57	NET INDIRECT BUSINESS TAXES	2.701	3.676	6.781	7.303	8.529	10.822
58	INDIRECT BUSINESS TAXES	34.232	37.021	40.144	42.216	45.207	47.631
59	LESS: INTERMEDIATE PRODUCT TRANSFERRED FROM GOVT TO BUSINESS	31.532	33.345	33.363	34.913	36.679	36.809
60	STATISTICAL DISCREPANCY	.162	-1.309	-2.390	-.122	2.132	1.717
61	BEA STATISTICAL DISCREPANCY	.162	-1.309	-2.390	-.122	2.132	1.717
62	TISA STATISTICAL DISCREPANCY	.000	.000	.000	.000	.000	.000
63	NET NATIONAL PRODUCT (48+49+53+57+60)	599.342	634.904	666.620	696.987	745.185	779.587
64	CAPITAL CONSUMPTION ALLOWANCES	165.985	172.660	179.013	185.000	192.556	201.218
65	TANGIBLE	120.874	124.893	128.220	131.882	135.679	140.469
66	ORIGINAL COST	101.386	105.771	110.503	115.471	120.347	126.126
67	REVALUATIONS	19.488	19.122	17.717	16.411	15.332	14.343
68	INTANGIBLE	45.111	47.767	50.793	53.118	56.877	60.749
69	ORIGINAL COST	27.112	29.030	31.319	33.706	36.291	39.152
70	ON RESEARCH AND DEVELOPMENT	3.173	3.713	4.301	4.913	5.555	6.256
71	ON HUMAN CAPITAL	23.939	25.317	27.018	28.793	30.736	32.896
72	REVALUATIONS	17.999	18.737	19.474	19.412	20.586	21.597
73	ON RESEARCH AND DEVELOPMENT	.683	.737	.764	.786	.833	.885
74	ON HUMAN CAPITAL	17.316	18.000	18.710	18.626	19.753	20.712
75	GROSS NATIONAL PRODUCT (63 + 64)	765.327	807.564	845.633	881.987	937.741	980.805

TABLE 1. NATIONAL INCOME AND PRODUCT ACCOUNT, BILLIONS OF DOLLARS, 1946-81

		DEBITS					
		1964	1965	1966	1967	1968	1969
1	LABOR INCOME	714.472	769.306	841.279	904.997	996.236	1083.147
2	COMPENSATION OF EMPLOYEES	367.957	396.544	439.289	471.396	519.892	572.854
3	DOMESTIC	367.996	396.521	439.242	471.339	519.850	572.799
4	REST OF WORLD	-.039	.023	.047	.057	.042	.055
5	ADDITIONAL IMPUTATIONS	359.010	386.051	416.114	448.776	492.604	528.301
6	EMPLOYEE TRAINING	18.055	20.669	25.364	25.953	29.106	32.218
7	EXPENSE ACCOUNT ITEMS OF CONSUMPTION	5.428	5.792	6.305	6.664	7.225	7.927
8	LABOR INCOME OF SELF-EMPLOYED	48.584	51.978	55.630	57.154	60.194	64.235
9	OPPORTUNITY COSTS OF STUDENTS	48.480	53.640	60.890	75.760	83.850	92.270
10	UNPAID HOUSEHOLD WORK	238.463	253.972	267.925	283.245	312.229	331.651
11	LESS: EXPENSES RELATED TO WORK	12.495	13.289	14.124	15.175	16.260	18.008
12	RENTAL INCOME OWNER-OCC. NONFARM DWELLINGS	.647	.644	.858	.714	1.421	1.078
13	GROSS RENTAL INCOME	9.855	10.280	10.878	11.411	11.025	11.124
14	LESS: NET IMPUTED INTEREST ON OWNER-OCC. NONFARM DWELLINGS AND LAND	9.208	9.636	10.020	10.697	9.605	10.046
15	CAPITAL INCOME	68.206	76.134	82.202	87.431	87.715	92.632
16	INTEREST PAID	34.838	38.800	43.516	47.429	52.603	61.210
17	NET IMPUTED INTEREST (EXCL BUS)	32.121	35.946	37.297	38.514	33.645	30.745
18	GROSS IMPUTED INTEREST	60.333	66.515	70.145	73.060	72.066	73.696
19	LAND	9.685	10.969	11.693	12.135	11.884	11.780
20	OWNER-OCCUPIED DWELLINGS	15.344	16.323	17.241	18.286	18.190	19.632
21	STRUCTURES AND EQUIPMENT	19.070	21.883	23.145	23.624	23.106	22.404
22	CONSUMER DURABLES AND SEMIDURABLES	12.138	12.832	13.641	14.778	14.825	15.912
23	INVENTORIES	3.195	3.419	3.230	2.984	2.820	2.765
24	GOVT R & D	.900	1.089	1.196	1.254	1.242	1.202
25	LESS: INTEREST PAID (EXCL BUS)	28.212	30.569	32.848	34.546	38.421	42.951
26	NET INTEREST, REST OF WORLD	1.247	1.388	1.389	1.488	1.467	.677
27	NET OPERATING SURPLUS	89.623	102.822	108.871	106.775	114.577	110.922
28	CORPORATE PROFITS	69.172	79.959	85.103	82.382	89.132	85.056
29	DOMESTIC	64.927	75.505	80.893	77.996	83.907	78.913
30	REST OF WORLD	4.245	4.454	4.210	4.386	5.225	6.143
31	PROPRIETORS' CAPITAL INCOME	3.877	4.958	4.886	4.055	3.784	2.808
32	PROPRIETORS' INCOME	52.461	56.936	60.516	61.209	63.978	67.043
33	LESS: LABOR INCOME OF SELF-EMPLOYED	48.584	51.978	55.630	57.154	60.194	64.235
34	GROSS BUSINESS INVESTMENT IN R & D	5.792	6.445	7.216	8.020	8.869	9.857
35	GOVERNMENT ENTERPRISE SURPLUSES	3.574	3.775	3.821	4.031	4.269	4.734
36	NET RENTAL INCOME OF PERSONS	7.208	7.685	7.845	8.287	8.523	8.467
37	NET REVALUATIONS	19.510	7.138	11.968	.752	12.071	-9.267
38	LAND	24.180	25.408	16.415	13.628	3.346	-10.410
39	OWNER-OCCUPIED DWELLINGS	3.016	-5.167	4.122	-4.106	14.082	-.069
40	STRUCTURES AND EQUIPMENT OTHER THAN OWNER-OCCUPIED DWELLINGS	.437	-1.324	3.490	2.599	8.987	16.979
41	CONSUMER DURABLES AND SEMIDURABLES	-6.548	-14.055	-7.320	-5.455	-9.276	-13.177
42	INVENTORIES	-1.575	2.276	-4.739	-5.914	-5.068	-2.590
43	NET SURPLUS (27 + 37)	109.133	109.960	120.839	107.527	126.648	101.655
44	NATIONAL INCOME (1+12+15+43)	892.457	956.044	1045.177	1100.669	1212.019	1278.511
45	LESS: INTANGIBLE CAPITAL CONSUMPTION	65.174	71.377	78.455	86.589	95.811	106.283
46	CAPITAL CONSUMPTION ON ALL R & D	8.003	9.004	10.108	11.351	12.781	14.377
47	CAPITAL CONSUMPTION ON HUMAN CAPITAL	57.171	62.373	68.347	75.238	83.030	91.906
48	NET NATIONAL INCOME (44 - 45)	827.283	884.667	966.722	1014.080	1116.208	1172.228

131

TABLE 1. NATIONAL INCOME AND PRODUCT ACCOUNT, BILLIONS OF DOLLARS, 1946-81

		DEBITS					
		1964	1965	1966	1967	1968	1969
49	BUSINESS TRANSFER PAYMENTS	6.590	7.531	8.238	8.539	9.285	10.356
50	MEDIA SUPPORT	2.929	3.630	3.992	4.102	4.462	4.867
51	HEALTH AND SAFETY	1.006	1.089	1.206	1.300	1.445	1.601
52	OTHER	2.655	2.812	3.040	3.137	3.378	3.888
53	UNCOMPENSATED FACTOR SERVICES	16.607	16.763	17.086	20.247	21.461	23.567
54	VOLUNTEERS	6.011	6.409	6.839	7.305	7.845	8.533
55	DRAFTEES	10.426	10.179	10.061	12.771	13.408	14.752
56	JURORS	.170	.175	.186	.171	.208	.282
57	NET INDIRECT BUSINESS TAXES	12.358	12.083	10.367	9.379	12.372	20.659
58	INDIRECT BUSINESS TAXES	51.118	54.261	56.361	60.223	67.570	73.924
59	LESS: INTERMEDIATE PRODUCT TRANSFERRED FROM GOVT TO BUSINESS	38.760	42.178	45.994	50.844	55.199	53.265
60	STATISTICAL DISCREPANCY	.144	-1.212	1.381	-.257	-2.113	-3.886
61	BEA STATISTICAL DISCREPANCY	.144	-1.211	1.380	-.258	-2.113	-3.886
62	TISA STATISTICAL DISCREPANCY	.000	-.001	.001	.001	.000	.000
63	NET NATIONAL PRODUCT (48+49+53+57+60)	862.982	919.832	1003.794	1051.988	1157.212	1222.924
64	CAPITAL CONSUMPTION ALLOWANCES	211.804	225.476	243.047	265.092	290.303	320.472
65	TANGIBLE	146.630	154.099	164.592	178.503	194.492	214.189
66	ORIGINAL COST	132.821	140.846	150.254	161.107	172.286	186.060
67	REVALUATIONS	13.809	13.253	14.338	17.396	22.206	28.129
68	INTANGIBLE	65.174	71.377	78.455	86.589	95.811	106.283
69	ORIGINAL COST	42.379	46.115	50.620	55.817	61.419	67.422
70	ON RESEARCH AND DEVELOPMENT	7.018	7.836	8.712	9.637	10.599	11.594
71	ON HUMAN CAPITAL	35.361	38.279	41.908	46.180	50.820	55.828
72	REVALUATIONS	22.795	25.262	27.835	30.772	34.392	38.861
73	ON RESEARCH AND DEVELOPMENT	.985	1.168	1.396	1.714	2.182	2.783
74	ON HUMAN CAPITAL	21.810	24.094	26.439	29.058	32.210	36.078
75	GROSS NATIONAL PRODUCT (63 + 64)	1074.786	1145.309	1246.841	1317.080	1447.515	1543.396

		1970	1971	1972	1973	1974	1975
1	LABOR INCOME	1162.186	1240.732	1354.751	1503.317	1636.112	1741.206
2	COMPENSATION OF EMPLOYEES	611.953	652.186	717.985	801.275	877.490	931.375
3	DOMESTIC	611.899	652.139	717.959	801.255	877.475	931.389
4	REST OF WORLD	.054	.047	.026	.020	.015	-.014
5	ADDITIONAL IMPUTATIONS	569.781	609.671	659.167	726.389	786.181	839.216
6	EMPLOYEE TRAINING	31.538	32.126	37.305	42.589	43.492	39.868
7	EXPENSE ACCOUNT ITEMS OF CONSUMPTION	8.375	8.890	9.782	10.887	11.952	12.476
8	LABOR INCOME OF SELF-EMPLOYED	65.454	68.488	75.091	92.120	91.972	90.425
9	OPPORTUNITY COSTS OF STUDENTS	103.857	116.898	131.577	148.100	159.941	174.576
10	UNPAID HOUSEHOLD WORK	360.557	383.269	405.412	432.693	478.824	521.871
11	LESS: EXPENSES RELATED TO WORK	19.548	21.125	22.401	24.347	27.559	29.385
12	RENTAL INCOME OWNER-OCC. NONFARM DWELLINGS	.919	1.209	1.887	2.625	2.380	1.690
13	GROSS RENTAL INCOME	10.946	11.173	10.855	10.926	10.562	10.831
14	LESS: NET IMPUTED INTEREST ON OWNER-OCC. NONFARM DWELLINGS AND LAND	10.027	9.964	8.968	8.301	8.182	9.141
15	CAPITAL INCOME	99.206	110.109	116.358	126.389	138.237	162.666
16	INTEREST PAID	69.700	74.647	81.390	95.424	113.151	123.380
17	NET IMPUTED INTEREST (EXCL BUS)	28.754	33.462	32.739	28.663	21.611	34.922
18	GROSS IMPUTED INTEREST	75.079	83.132	87.637	92.243	92.271	111.504
19	LAND	11.592	12.524	13.253	14.436	14.446	17.771
20	OWNER-OCCUPIED DWELLINGS	20.733	22.492	24.051	26.136	29.024	32.125
21	STRUCTURES AND EQUIPMENT	22.115	26.049	27.836	28.749	24.862	34.226
22	CONSUMER DURABLES AND SEMIDURABLES	16.858	17.927	18.342	18.945	20.558	22.880
23	INVENTORIES	2.600	2.750	2.673	2.492	2.161	2.841
24	GOVT R & D	1.180	1.389	1.482	1.485	1.219	1.660
25	LESS: INTEREST PAID (EXCL BUS)	46.325	49.670	54.898	63.580	70.660	76.582
26	NET INTEREST, REST OF WORLD	.752	2.000	2.229	2.302	3.475	4.364

132

TABLE 1. NATIONAL INCOME AND PRODUCT ACCOUNT, BILLIONS OF DOLLARS, 1946-81

		DEBITS					
		1970	1971	1972	1973	1974	1975
27	NET OPERATING SURPLUS	96.146	109.125	125.938	140.953	126.050	145.267
28	CORPORATE PROFITS	71.383	83.228	96.604	108.315	94.890	110.493
29	DOMESTIC	64.880	76.112	87.958	94.627	78.601	97.529
30	REST OF WORLD	6.503	7.116	8.646	13.688	16.289	12.964
31	PROPRIETORS' CAPITAL INCOME	.775	.896	1.765	1.675	-3.244	-.405
32	PROPRIETORS' INCOME	66.229	69.384	76.856	93.795	88.728	90.020
33	LESS: LABOR INCOME OF SELF-EMPLOYED	65.454	68.488	75.091	92.120	91.972	90.425
34	GROSS BUSINESS INVESTMENT IN R & D	10.288	10.654	11.535	13.104	14.667	15.582
35	GOVERNMENT ENTERPRISE SURPLUSES	4.942	5.284	5.887	6.205	6.760	7.413
36	NET RENTAL INCOME OF PERSONS	8.758	9.063	10.147	11.654	12.977	12.184
37	NET REVALUATIONS	1.740	-12.002	104.022	188.910	156.387	-55.536
38	LAND	-5.597	-9.913	71.217	97.749	32.850	50.384
39	OWNER-OCCUPIED DWELLINGS	-3.677	7.696	20.265	31.415	-3.148	-4.540
40	STRUCTURES AND EQUIPMENT OTHER THAN OWNER-OCCUPIED DWELLINGS	26.376	14.227	21.456	55.312	113.521	-19.174
41	CONSUMER DURABLES AND SEMIDURABLES	-7.860	-20.512	-15.613	-28.252	-10.505	-9.930
42	INVENTORIES	-7.502	-3.500	6.697	32.686	23.669	-72.277
43	NET SURPLUS (27 + 37)	97.886	97.123	229.960	329.863	282.437	89.731
44	NATIONAL INCOME (1+12+15+43)	1360.197	1449.174	1702.957	1962.194	2059.165	1995.292
45	LESS: INTANGIBLE CAPITAL CONSUMPTION	117.869	129.649	142.214	156.189	178.443	201.455
46	CAPITAL CONSUMPTION ON ALL R & D	16.069	17.766	19.588	21.907	24.837	27.678
47	CAPITAL CONSUMPTION ON HUMAN CAPITAL	101.800	111.883	122.626	134.282	153.606	173.777
48	NET NATIONAL INCOME (44 - 45)	1242.328	1319.525	1560.743	1806.005	1880.722	1793.837
49	BUSINESS TRANSFER PAYMENTS	10.660	11.243	12.494	13.747	14.610	16.790
50	MEDIA SUPPORT	4.918	5.029	5.607	5.986	6.415	6.890
51	HEALTH AND SAFETY	1.662	1.770	2.026	2.246	2.392	2.464
52	OTHER	4.080	4.444	4.861	5.515	5.803	7.436
53	UNCOMPENSATED FACTOR SERVICES	25.684	24.947	21.874	22.537	20.414	18.384
54	VOLUNTEERS	9.347	10.251	11.222	12.164	13.332	14.566
55	DRAFTEES	15.992	14.313	10.249	9.856	6.596	3.302
56	JURORS	.345	.383	.403	.517	.486	.516
57	NET INDIRECT BUSINESS TAXES	21.424	28.090	32.935	39.515	47.510	45.342
58	INDIRECT BUSINESS TAXES	79.953	87.935	94.458	102.623	109.699	118.846
59	LESS: INTERMEDIATE PRODUCT TRANSFERRED FROM GOVT TO BUSINESS	58.529	59.845	61.523	63.108	62.189	73.504
60	STATISTICAL DISCREPANCY	-1.495	4.096	3.304	.763	3.732	5.471
61	BEA STATISTICAL DISCREPANCY	-1.495	4.098	3.312	.764	3.736	5.477
62	TISA STATISTICAL DISCREPANCY	.000	-.002	-.008	-.001	-.004	-.006
63	NET NATIONAL PRODUCT (48+49+53+57+60)	1298.602	1387.901	1631.349	1882.567	1966.988	1879.825
64	CAPITAL CONSUMPTION ALLOWANCES	351.689	383.337	415.440	453.552	517.258	587.593
65	TANGIBLE	233.820	253.688	273.226	297.363	338.815	386.138
66	ORIGINAL COST	199.689	213.169	228.142	247.338	267.566	288.649
67	REVALUATIONS	34.131	40.519	45.084	50.025	71.249	97.489
68	INTANGIBLE	117.869	129.649	142.214	156.189	178.443	201.455
69	ORIGINAL COST	73.763	80.453	87.834	96.426	106.071	116.004
70	ON RESEARCH AND DEVELOPMENT	12.610	13.643	14.715	15.832	17.007	18.254
71	ON HUMAN CAPITAL	61.153	66.810	73.119	80.594	89.064	97.750
72	REVALUATIONS	44.106	49.196	54.380	59.763	72.372	85.451
73	ON RESEARCH AND DEVELOPMENT	3.459	4.123	4.873	6.075	7.830	9.424
74	ON HUMAN CAPITAL	40.647	45.073	49.507	53.688	64.542	76.027
75	GROSS NATIONAL PRODUCT (63 + 64)	1650.290	1771.238	2046.789	2336.119	2484.246	2467.418

133

TABLE 1. NATIONAL INCOME AND PRODUCT ACCOUNT, BILLIONS OF DOLLARS, 1946-81

		DEBITS					
		1976	1977	1978	1979	1980	1981
1	LABOR INCOME	1960.149	2158.287	2399.368	2670.654	2911.519	3208.715
2	COMPENSATION OF EMPLOYEES	1036.339	1152.061	1301.081	1458.139	1599.633	1769.248
3	DOMESTIC	1036.354	1152.101	1301.155	1458.176	1599.705	1769.283
4	REST OF WORLD	-.015	-.040	-.074	-.037	-.072	-.035
5	ADDITIONAL IMPUTATIONS	956.831	1044.087	1140.656	1262.446	1370.484	1501.985
6	EMPLOYEE TRAINING	46.585	52.427	61.003	66.693	66.428	73.697
7	EXPENSE ACCOUNT ITEMS OF CONSUMPTION	13.879	15.566	17.768	20.262	22.358	24.560
8	LABOR INCOME OF SELF-EMPLOYED	95.473	104.901	119.306	139.305	132.053	138.787
9	OPPORTUNITY COSTS OF STUDENTS	188.640	202.927	218.348	236.874	259.918	284.230
10	UNPAID HOUSEHOLD WORK	612.254	668.266	724.231	799.312	889.727	980.711
11	LESS: EXPENSES RELATED TO WORK	33.021	37.861	42.369	49.931	58.598	62.518
12	RENTAL INCOME OWNER-OCC. NONFARM DWELLINGS	2.902	3.551	5.208	3.681	4.244	9.287
13	GROSS RENTAL INCOME	10.659	8.110	8.028	7.252	8.461	13.347
14	LESS: NET IMPUTED INTEREST ON OWNER-OCC. NONFARM DWELLINGS AND LAND	7.757	4.559	2.820	3.571	4.217	4.060
15	CAPITAL INCOME	166.069	186.535	210.884	248.222	294.691	369.824
16	INTEREST PAID	130.821	149.984	178.082	217.800	262.983	332.081
17	NET IMPUTED INTEREST (EXCL BUS)	29.026	28.196	22.853	18.419	16.211	11.782
18	GROSS IMPUTED INTEREST	116.765	129.180	143.220	159.372	179.446	209.726
19	LAND	19.085	21.760	24.600	27.476	31.186	36.400
20	OWNER-OCCUPIED DWELLINGS	34.492	37.605	43.070	51.876	61.278	70.086
21	STRUCTURES AND EQUIPMENT	34.597	39.721	43.101	43.103	44.282	54.320
22	CONSUMER DURABLES AND SEMIDURABLES	24.072	24.946	26.834	31.232	36.803	41.820
23	INVENTORIES	2.815	3.222	3.608	3.768	4.011	4.859
24	GOVT R & D	1.705	1.925	2.007	1.916	1.886	2.241
25	LESS: INTEREST PAID (EXCL BUS)	87.739	100.984	120.367	140.953	163.235	197.944
26	NET INTEREST, REST OF WORLD	6.222	8.355	9.949	12.003	15.497	25.961
27	NET OPERATING SURPLUS	174.820	210.659	241.933	244.508	225.184	247.668
28	CORPORATE PROFITS	138.097	167.259	192.382	194.794	175.429	192.334
29	DOMESTIC	123.824	152.110	172.654	164.188	145.544	168.674
30	REST OF WORLD	14.273	15.149	19.728	30.606	29.885	23.660
31	PROPRIETORS' CAPITAL INCOME	-1.401	-1.047	-.764	-7.210	-14.607	-18.621
32	PROPRIETORS' INCOME	94.072	103.854	118.542	132.095	117.446	120.166
33	LESS: LABOR INCOME OF SELF-EMPLOYED	95.473	104.901	119.306	139.305	132.053	138.787
34	GROSS BUSINESS INVESTMENT IN R & D	17.436	19.407	22.156	25.655	29.940	33.850
35	GOVERNMENT ENTERPRISE SURPLUSES	7.842	8.334	9.587	10.612	11.368	12.067
36	NET RENTAL INCOME OF PERSONS	12.846	16.706	18.572	20.657	23.054	28.038
37	NET REVALUATIONS	248.434	237.605	294.086	237.193	9.325	-153.661
38	LAND	137.454	90.756	158.674	110.742	69.166	-142.350
39	OWNER-OCCUPIED DWELLINGS	51.489	69.848	93.339	4.239	-41.052	-13.679
40	STRUCTURES AND EQUIPMENT OTHER THAN						
41	OWNER-OCCUPIED DWELLINGS	12.470	96.848	62.632	100.128	-1.673	64.917
42	CONSUMER DURABLES AND SEMIDURABLES	-11.287	-17.870	-29.292	-27.465	-27.811	-34.893
	INVENTORIES	58.308	-1.977	8.733	49.549	10.695	-27.656
43	NET SURPLUS (27 + 37)	423.254	448.264	536.019	481.701	234.509	94.007
44	NATIONAL INCOME (1+12+15+43)	2552.374	2796.637	3151.478	3404.258	3444.963	3681.832
45	LESS: INTANGIBLE CAPITAL CONSUMPTION	221.326	247.319	276.127	312.194	356.336	402.333
46	CAPITAL CONSUMPTION ON ALL R & D	30.222	33.178	36.808	41.086	45.973	51.204
47	CAPITAL CONSUMPTION ON HUMAN CAPITAL	191.104	214.141	239.319	271.108	310.363	351.129
48	NET NATIONAL INCOME (44 - 45)	2331.048	2549.318	2875.351	3092.064	3088.627	3279.499

TABLE 1. NATIONAL INCOME AND PRODUCT ACCOUNT, BILLIONS OF DOLLARS, 1946-81

		DEBITS					
		1976	1977	1978	1979	1980	1981
49	BUSINESS TRANSFER PAYMENTS	19.017	21.232	23.948	26.760	30.018	33.463
50	MEDIA SUPPORT	8.490	9.656	11.277	12.680	14.141	15.832
51	HEALTH AND SAFETY	2.607	2.968	3.419	3.811	4.200	4.720
52	OTHER	7.920	8.608	9.252	10.269	11.677	12.911
53	UNCOMPENSATED FACTOR SERVICES	15.602	15.915	16.146	16.546	17.563	18.676
54	VOLUNTEERS	15.043	15.370	15.633	16.049	17.015	18.017
55	DRAFTEES	.000	.000	.000	.000	.000	.000
56	JURORS	.559	.545	.513	.497	.548	.659
57	NET INDIRECT BUSINESS TAXES	54.380	59.977	68.166	70.289	78.400	97.949
58	INDIRECT BUSINESS TAXES	128.645	140.324	152.379	163.531	185.542	219.272
59	LESS: INTERMEDIATE PRODUCT TRANSFERRED FROM GOVT TO BUSINESS	74.265	80.347	84.213	93.242	107.142	121.323
60	STATISTICAL DISCREPANCY	5.097	1.352	-2.556	-1.487	2.288	-4.903
61	BEA STATISTICAL DISCREPANCY	5.102	1.350	-2.556	-1.487	2.291	-4.902
62	TISA STATISTICAL DISCREPANCY	-.005	.002	.000	.000	-.003	-.001
63	NET NATIONAL PRODUCT (48+49+53+57+60)	2425.144	2647.793	2981.055	3204.171	3216.896	3424.684
64	CAPITAL CONSUMPTION ALLOWANCES	642.076	710.168	795.684	900.565	1021.773	1135.464
65	TANGIBLE	420.750	462.849	519.557	588.371	665.437	733.131
66	ORIGINAL COST	311.938	339.915	373.527	412.557	453.413	494.181
67	REVALUATIONS	108.812	122.934	146.030	175.814	212.024	238.950
68	INTANGIBLE	221.326	247.319	276.127	312.194	356.336	402.333
69	ORIGINAL COST	126.419	138.328	152.557	168.913	186.525	205.820
70	ON RESEARCH AND DEVELOPMENT	19.580	21.021	22.633	24.467	26.569	28.972
71	ON HUMAN CAPITAL	106.839	117.307	129.924	144.446	159.956	176.848
72	REVALUATIONS	94.907	108.991	123.570	143.281	169.811	196.513
73	ON RESEARCH AND DEVELOPMENT	10.642	12.157	14.175	16.619	19.404	22.232
74	ON HUMAN CAPITAL	84.265	96.834	109.395	126.662	150.407	174.281
75	GROSS NATIONAL PRODUCT (63 + 64)	3067.220	3357.961	3776.739	4104.736	4238.669	4560.148

135

TABLE 1. NATIONAL INCOME AND PRODUCT ACCOUNT, BILLIONS OF DOLLARS, 1946-81

		DEBITS					
		PERCENT PER ANNUM RATES OF GROWTH CURRENT DOLLARS					
		1946-56	1956-66	1966-71	1971-76	1976-81	1946-81
1	LABOR INCOME	6.033	5.704	8.081	9.578	10.359	7.341
2	COMPENSATION OF EMPLOYEES	7.509	6.077	8.224	9.705	11.290	8.042
3	DOMESTIC	7.509	6.073	8.225	9.707	11.290	8.041
4	REST OF WORLD	N.A.	N.A.	.000	N.A.	N.A.	N.A.
5	ADDITIONAL IMPUTATIONS	4.911	5.298	7.939	9.433	9.437	6.729
6	EMPLOYEE TRAINING	2.736	7.268	4.840	7.715	9.608	5.996
7	EXPENSE ACCOUNT ITEMS OF CONSUMPTION	7.828	4.629	7.115	9.317	12.091	7.607
8	LABOR INCOME OF SELF-EMPLOYED	1.811	2.784	4.246	6.869	7.769	3.987
9	OPPORTUNITY COSTS OF STUDENTS	8.103	9.150	13.934	10.044	8.544	9.559
10	UNPAID HOUSEHOLD WORK	5.585	5.025	7.423	9.821	9.881	6.888
11	LESS: EXPENSES RELATED TO WORK	11.732	4.900	8.385	9.345	13.617	9.184
12	RENTAL INCOME OWNER-OCC. NONFARM DWELLINGS	13.039	5.989	7.105	19.133	26.192	12.714
13	GROSS RENTAL INCOME	13.313	5.919	.537	-.937	4.600	5.970
14	LESS: NET IMPUTED INTEREST ON OWNER-OCC. NONFARM DWELLINGS AND LAND	13.337	5.913	-.113	-4.884	-12.143	2.672
15	CAPITAL INCOME	9.207	9.266	6.020	8.566	17.366	9.796
16	INTEREST PAID	9.763	10.261	11.397	11.875	20.480	11.917
17	NET IMPUTED INTEREST (EXCL BUS)	8.656	8.132	-2.147	-2.804	-16.500	1.322
18	GROSS IMPUTED INTEREST	9.058	8.290	3.456	7.031	12.426	8.201
19	LAND	15.975	12.730	1.384	8.790	13.784	11.519
20	OWNER-OCCUPIED DWELLINGS	14.181	7.481	5.462	8.927	15.235	10.359
21	STRUCTURES AND EQUIPMENT	4.979	9.018	2.392	5.840	9.442	6.495
22	CONSUMER DURABLES AND SEMIDURABLES	11.905	6.704	5.618	6.072	11.680	8.620
23	INVENTORIES	3.264	2.264	-3.164	.471	11.532	2.762
24	GOVT R & D	13.253	16.804	3.035	4.175	5.628	10.282
25	LESS: INTEREST PAID (EXCL BUS)	9.552	8.472	8.622	12.052	17.671	10.585
26	NET INTEREST, REST OF WORLD	11.235	12.311	7.564	25.482	33.069	15.864
27	NET OPERATING SURPLUS	9.060	6.831	.047	9.884	7.215	6.945
28	CORPORATE PROFITS	10.187	6.882	-.445	10.658	6.850	7.254
29	DOMESTIC	9.922	7.052	-1.211	10.223	6.377	6.982
30	REST OF WORLD	15.105	4.085	11.068	14.936	10.637	10.623
31	PROPRIETORS' CAPITAL INCOME	2.073	11.360	-28.769	N.A.	N.A.	N.A.
32	PROPRIETORS' INCOME	1.821	3.253	2.773	6.277	5.018	3.448
33	LESS: LABOR INCOME OF SELF-EMPLOYED	1.811	2.784	4.246	6.869	7.769	3.987
34	GROSS BUSINESS INVESTMENT IN R & D	15.889	8.214	8.104	10.354	14.188	11.499
35	GOVERNMENT ENTERPRISE SURPLUSES	5.210	6.561	6.698	8.216	9.002	6.772
36	NET RENTAL INCOME OF PERSONS	4.032	3.591	2.929	7.226	16.895	5.946
37	NET REVALUATIONS	N.A.	-8.066	N.A.	N.A.	N.A.	N.A.
38	LAND	N.A.	-2.731	N.A.	N.A.	N.A.	N.A.
39	OWNER-OCCUPIED DWELLINGS	N.A.	N.A.	13.300	46.248	N.A.	N.A.
40	STRUCTURES AND EQUIPMENT OTHER THAN OWNER-OCCUPIED DWELLINGS	N.A.	-12.970	32.456	-2.602	39.091	N.A.
41	CONSUMER DURABLES AND SEMIDURABLES	N.A.	N.A.	N.A.	N.A.	N.A.	N.A.
42	INVENTORIES	N.A.	N.A.	N.A.	N.A.	N.A.	N.A.
43	NET SURPLUS (27 + 37)	N.A.	3.707	-4.275	34.232	-25.986	N.A.
44	NATIONAL INCOME (1+12+15+43)	10.020	5.682	6.754	11.986	7.603	8.226
45	LESS: INTANGIBLE CAPITAL CONSUMPTION	7.114	7.410	10.568	11.289	12.697	9.064
46	CAPITAL CONSUMPTION ON ALL R & D	15.673	13.488	11.940	11.211	11.121	13.214
47	CAPITAL CONSUMPTION ON HUMAN CAPITAL	6.664	6.760	10.359	11.302	12.938	8.750
48	NET NATIONAL INCOME (44 - 45)	10.253	5.555	6.420	12.054	7.066	8.138

TABLE 1. NATIONAL INCOME AND PRODUCT ACCOUNT, BILLIONS OF DOLLARS, 1946-81

		DEBITS					
		PERCENT PER ANNUM RATES OF GROWTH CURRENT DOLLARS					
		1946-56	1956-66	1966-71	1971-76	1976-81	1946-81
49	BUSINESS TRANSFER PAYMENTS	10.694	7.825	6.417	11.084	11.966	9.483
50	MEDIA SUPPORT	11.351	7.965	4.727	11.041	13.273	9.634
51	HEALTH AND SAFETY	8.410	6.262	7.975	8.052	12.606	8.265
52	OTHER	11.071	8.328	7.890	12.251	10.267	9.876
53	UNCOMPENSATED FACTOR SERVICES	11.562	5.192	7.864	-8.960	3.662	4.945
54	VOLUNTEERS	6.908	5.102	8.431	7.973	3.674	6.288
55	DRAFTEES	16.746	5.261	7.304	N.A.	N.A.	N.A.
56	JURORS	12.548	4.820	15.554	7.867	3.335	8.696
57	NET INDIRECT BUSINESS TAXES	N.A.	12.768	22.062	14.124	12.490	N.A.
58	INDIRECT BUSINESS TAXES	7.027	5.970	9.304	7.906	11.255	7.765
59	LESS: INTERMEDIATE PRODUCT TRANSFERRED FROM GOVT TO BUSINESS	-2.225	4.923	5.406	4.412	10.314	3.563
60	STATISTICAL DISCREPANCY	N.A.	N.A.	24.290	4.470	N.A.	N.A.
61	BEA STATISTICAL DISCREPANCY	N.A.	N.A.	24.319	4.480	N.A.	N.A.
62	TISA STATISTICAL DISCREPANCY	-7.902	-6.697	N.A.	N.A.	N.A.	N.A.
63	NET NATIONAL PRODUCT (48+49+53+57+60)	11.318	5.671	6.695	11.809	7.146	8.487
64	CAPITAL CONSUMPTION ALLOWANCES	4.758	5.063	9.541	10.867	12.077	7.405
65	TANGIBLE	4.056	4.119	9.038	10.648	11.746	6.777
66	ORIGINAL COST	4.665	5.002	7.246	7.912	9.639	6.289
67	REVALUATIONS	1.397	-2.084	23.093	21.844	17.038	8.148
68	INTANGIBLE	7.114	7.410	10.568	11.289	12.697	9.064
69	ORIGINAL COST	4.280	7.761	9.709	9.460	10.239	7.617
70	ON RESEARCH AND DEVELOPMENT	15.815	14.436	9.385	7.493	8.152	12.166
71	ON HUMAN CAPITAL	3.599	6.799	9.776	9.844	10.605	7.254
72	REVALUATIONS	15.068	6.802	12.064	14.044	15.669	12.159
73	ON RESEARCH AND DEVELOPMENT	15.146	8.994	24.184	20.882	15.875	15.487
74	ON HUMAN CAPITAL	15.064	6.699	11.259	13.330	15.643	11.907
75	GROSS NATIONAL PRODUCT (63 + 64)	9.579	5.550	7.274	11.608	8.255	8.179

137

TABLE 1. NATIONAL INCOME AND PRODUCT ACCOUNT, BILLIONS OF DOLLARS, 1946-81

		CREDITS					
		1946	1947	1948	1949	1950	1951
1	CONSUMPTION	252.086	272.947	289.650	289.165	298.621	327.185
2	HOUSEHOLD EXPENDITURES FOR SERVICES AND NONDURABLES	88.720	100.053	107.177	108.154	113.758	124.698
3	GROSS EXPENDITURES INCLUDED FROM BEA PERSONAL CONSUMPTION EXPENDITURES	90.686	102.231	109.607	110.732	116.445	127.700
4	LESS: PCE EXPENSES RELATED TO WORK	1.966	2.178	2.430	2.578	2.687	3.002
5	EXPENSE ACCOUNT ITEMS OF CONSUMPTION	1.887	2.181	2.407	2.371	2.558	2.874
6	BEA IMPUTATIONS OTHER THAN HOUSING	4.840	4.621	4.538	4.008	4.041	5.000
7	SUBSIDIES ALLOCATED TO CONSUMPTION	1.026	.267	.202	.154	.228	.187
8	SUBSIDIES INCLUDED IN BUSINESS INCOME	1.459	.383	.301	.228	.357	.300
9	LESS: AMT. ALLOCATED TO INVESTMENT	.433	.116	.099	.074	.129	.113
10	TRANSFERS	30.085	26.675	26.748	24.134	22.766	25.705
11	FROM BUSINESS	.557	.658	.736	.773	.868	1.007
12	MEDIA SUPPORT	.410	.482	.543	.582	.661	.770
13	TOTAL MEDIA SUPPORT	.633	.749	.842	.894	.997	1.137
14	LESS: MEDIA SUPPORT ALLOCATED TO INVESTMENT	.223	.267	.299	.312	.336	.367
15	HEALTH AND SAFETY	.147	.176	.193	.191	.207	.237
16	FROM NONPROFIT INSTITUTIONS	5.083	5.517	6.092	6.182	6.404	6.955
17	FROM GOVERNMENT ENTERPRISES	1.133	.829	.935	.887	1.020	.968
18	FROM GOVERNMENT	23.313	19.672	18.986	16.293	14.475	16.776
19	NONMARKET SERVICES PRODUCED IN HOUSEHOLDS	125.528	139.150	148.579	150.344	155.271	168.721
20	NET SPACE RENT OF OWNER-OCCUPIED NONFARM DWELLINGS	5.611	6.062	6.861	7.943	9.070	10.468
21	OTHER CAPITAL SERVICES	28.996	32.436	35.761	37.518	38.692	42.726
22	DURABLES	10.257	11.609	13.182	14.800	16.502	19.270
23	TOTAL DURABLES	11.607	13.237	15.086	17.020	19.049	22.215
24	LESS: DURABLES ALLOCATED TO INVESTMENT	.429	.502	.572	.648	.702	.775
25	LESS: SERVICES OF DURABLES TO EXP REL TO WORK	.921	1.126	1.332	1.573	1.845	2.170
26	SEMIDURABLES	18.671	20.770	22.519	22.647	22.115	23.373
27	INVENTORIES	.068	.057	.060	.072	.075	.083
28	LABOR SERVICES	107.013	119.949	126.789	125.533	129.159	139.419
29	LESS: LABOR SERVICES ALLOC. TO INVEST	16.092	19.297	20.832	20.650	21.650	23.892
30	GROSS DOMESTIC CAPITAL ACCUMULATION	31.128	140.366	158.261	145.769	173.486	228.341
31	ORIGINAL COST	105.484	117.953	140.520	138.710	168.960	197.871
32	TANGIBLE	62.743	71.984	91.546	90.881	117.294	138.477

		CREDITS					
		1946	1947	1948	1949	1950	1951
33	STRUCTURES AND EQUIPMENT AND HOUSE-HOLD DURABLES AND SEMIDURABLES	66.416	82.273	95.857	97.419	113.040	126.292
34	BUSINESS	19.399	27.049	28.625	25.298	28.228	31.332
35	NONRESIDENTIAL	18.085	24.971	25.773	22.418	24.648	28.401
36	STRUCTURES	6.379	7.049	7.846	7.067	7.423	8.951
37	EQUIPMENT	11.706	17.922	17.927	15.351	17.225	19.450
38	RESIDENTIAL OTHER THAN OWNER-OCCUPIED NONFARM DWELLINGS	1.314	2.078	2.852	2.880	3.580	2.931
39	NONPROFIT INSTITUTIONS	.451	.595	.918	1.163	1.407	1.538
40	STRUCTURES	.402	.534	.821	1.038	1.256	1.374
41	EQUIPMENT	.049	.061	.097	.125	.151	.164
42	GOVERNMENT ENTERPRISES	.636	1.662	1.585	1.706	1.792	2.446
43	STRUCTURES	.598	1.541	1.486	1.600	1.670	2.259
44	EQUIPMENT	.038	.121	.099	.106	.122	.187
45	GOVERNMENT	6.695	6.131	7.355	9.307	10.029	15.550
46	STRUCTURES	1.793	2.326	3.385	4.601	5.210	6.785
47	EQUIPMENT	2.385	1.635	2.107	3.138	3.498	7.414
48	PRODUCT ACCUMULATED	2.517	2.170	1.863	1.568	1.321	1.351
49	HOUSEHOLDS	41.357	50.096	56.970	57.181	68.424	67.744
50	OWNER-OCC. NONFARM DWELLINGS	5.718	9.000	11.852	10.686	15.648	14.309
51	DURABLES	15.756	20.431	22.855	25.047	30.754	29.814
52	SEMIDURABLES	19.883	20.665	22.263	21.448	22.022	23.621
53	FIXED GPDI RECONCILIATION	-1.296	-2.230	-.248	1.205	1.743	1.705
54	NIPA FIXED GPDI	24.272	34.414	41.147	38.352	47.026	48.884
55	LESS: CORRESP. SECTOR TOTALS	25.568	36.644	41.395	37.147	45.283	47.179
56	GOVERNMENT CAPITAL ACCUMULATION RECONCILIATION	-.826	-1.030	.652	1.559	1.417	5.977
57	NIPA GOVERNMENT INVESTMENT	3.988	4.593	7.729	11.004	11.917	22.622
58	LESS: GOVERNMENT AND GOVT ENTERPRISE TOTALS	4.814	5.623	7.077	9.445	10.500	16.645
59	CHANGE IN INVENTORIES	-3.673	-10.289	-4.311	-6.538	4.254	12.185
60	BUSINESS	6.379	-.462	4.708	-3.075	6.789	10.296
61	GOVERNMENT	-10.189	-9.779	-9.014	-3.506	-2.608	1.790
62	HOUSEHOLDS	.137	-.048	-.005	.043	.073	.099
63	INTANGIBLE	42.742	45.970	48.974	47.828	51.666	59.394
64	RESEARCH AND DEVELOPMENT	1.603	2.006	2.392	2.377	2.674	3.160
65	BUSINESS	.750	.950	1.030	.870	1.070	1.240
66	NONPROFIT INSTITUTIONS	.043	.046	.052	.057	.064	.070
67	GOVERNMENT	.810	1.010	1.310	1.450	1.540	1.850
68	EDUCATION AND TRAINING	35.599	37.692	39.620	38.421	41.702	48.420
69	HEALTH	5.540	6.271	6.963	7.030	7.290	7.814
70	SUBSIDIES AND GOVERNMENT ENTERPRISE TRANSFERS ALLOCATED TO INVESTMENT	.911	.475	.554	.501	.709	.700

TABLE 1. NATIONAL INCOME AND PRODUCT ACCOUNT, BILLIONS OF DOLLARS, 1946-81

		CREDITS					
		1946	1947	1948	1949	1950	1951
71	NET REVALUATIONS	-75.268	21.937	17.187	6.558	3.817	29.770
72	LAND	-21.784	-2.851	2.003	8.476	8.738	10.441
73	BUSINESS	-16.545	-3.764	.852	6.055	4.781	7.470
74	NONPROFIT	-.225	.100	.006	.172	.132	.304
75	GOVERNMENT AND GOVT ENTERPRISES	-3.155	-.413	.291	1.227	1.265	1.512
76	HOUSEHOLDS	-1.859	1.226	.854	1.022	2.560	1.155
77	STRUCTURES AND EQUIPMENT	-28.864	23.163	17.333	1.739	-1.200	20.794
78	BUSINESS	-11.217	10.162	8.757	3.225	-.272	8.193
79	NONPROFIT INSTITUTIONS	.124	.788	.126	.013	-.001	.502
80	GOVERNMENT	-11.660	5.985	4.437	-.023	-2.322	8.762
81	HOUSEHOLDS (OWNER-OCC. DWELLINGS)	-6.111	6.228	4.013	-1.476	1.395	3.337
82	HOUSEHOLD DURABLES AND SEMIDURABLES	-13.895	-2.568	1.142	2.412	-6.394	1.412
83	DURABLES	-9.689	-2.228	.171	1.154	-3.161	2.075
84	SEMIDURABLES	-4.206	-.340	.971	1.258	-3.233	-.663
85	INVENTORIES	-10.725	4.193	-3.291	-6.069	2.673	-2.877
86	BUSINESS (INCLUDING NONPROFIT)	.000	6.569	-1.865	-4.844	3.847	-.897
87	GOVERNMENT ENTERPRISES	.279	.160	.327	-.739	.329	.030
88	GOVERNMENT	-10.676	-2.656	-1.840	-.455	-1.337	-2.167
89	HOUSEHOLDS	-.328	.120	.087	-.031	-.166	.157
90	NET EXPORTS	7.838	11.907	6.936	6.512	2.183	4.420
91	EXPORTS	15.114	20.224	17.463	16.295	14.389	19.683
92	IMPORTS	7.276	8.317	10.527	9.783	12.206	15.263
93	GROSS NATIONAL PRODUCT	291.052	425.220	454.848	441.446	474.290	559.946
	ADDENDA:						
94	GNP MINUS NET REVALUATIONS (NR)	366.320	403.283	437.661	434.887	470.473	530.176
95	NNP MINUS NR	273.147	306.102	338.490	337.598	375.867	426.381
96	NNI MINUS NR	287.406	313.464	346.047	335.944	365.957	415.290
97	GDCA MINUS NR	106.396	118.429	141.074	139.211	169.669	198.571
98	NDCA MINUS NR	13.223	21.248	41.903	41.922	75.063	94.776
99	NDCA	-62.045	43.185	59.090	48.480	78.880	124.546
100	NDCA AT ORIGINAL COST	12.311	20.772	41.349	41.421	74.354	94.076
101	NDCA, TANGIBLE, AT ORIGINAL COST	-11.124	-4.872	13.868	16.419	44.156	57.752
102	NDCA, INTANGIBLE, AT ORIGINAL COST	23.436	25.645	27.481	25.001	30.198	36.324
103	GDCA - NR / GNP - NR, PERCENT	29.044	29.366	32.234	32.011	36.063	37.454
104	NDCA - NR / NNP - NR, PERCENT	4.841	6.941	12.379	12.418	19.971	22.228
105	NDCA, TAN, O.C. / NNP - NR, PERCENT	-4.073	-1.592	4.097	4.864	11.748	13.545
106	NDCA, INTAN, O.C. / NNP - NR, PERCENT	8.580	8.378	8.119	7.406	8.034	8.519
107	GROSS BUSINESS PRODUCT	118.670	189.029	208.390	204.447	239.882	278.349
108	GROSS NONPROFIT PRODUCT	5.220	7.084	7.354	7.779	8.167	9.570
109	GROSS GOVT ENTERPRISE PRODUCT	3.421	3.355	3.911	3.190	4.473	4.560
110	GROSS GOVERNMENT PRODUCT	41.630	58.845	55.785	49.330	43.158	63.823
111	GROSS HOUSEHOLD PRODUCT	121.306	165.666	177.820	175.261	176.991	201.533
112	GROSS DOMESTIC PRODUCT	290.246	423.978	453.259	440.006	472.671	557.835
113	GROSS PRODUCT, REST OF WORLD	.801	1.239	1.588	1.438	1.618	2.111

TABLE 1. NATIONAL INCOME AND PRODUCT ACCOUNT, BILLINGS OF DOLLARS, 1946-81

		CREDITS					
		1946	1947	1948	1949	1950	1951
114	BEA GNP	209.845	233.054	259.504	258.316	286.457	330.765
115	BEA NNP	195.823	215.713	239.290	236.529	262.961	303.600
116	BEA NI	178.570	194.945	219.871	213.625	237.569	274.131
117	BEA GPDI	30.651	33.952	45.855	35.277	53.815	59.180
118	BEA NPDI	16.629	16.611	25.641	13.490	30.319	32.015
119	BEA PCE	143.808	161.742	174.749	178.135	191.966	207.066
120	BEA GPDI / BEA GNP, PERCENT	14.606	14.568	17.670	13.657	18.786	17.892
121	BEA NPDI / BEA NNP, PERCENT	8.492	7.701	10.715	5.703	11.530	10.545
122	TISA GNP / BEA GNP, PERCENT	138.698	182.456	175.276	170.894	165.571	169.288
123	TISA NNP / BEA NNP, PERCENT	101.050	152.072	148.638	145.503	144.388	150.247
124	TISA NNI / BEA NI, PERCENT	118.798	172.049	165.203	160.329	155.649	162.353
125	TISA GNP - NR / BEA GNP, PERCENT	174.567	173.043	168.653	168.355	164.239	160.288
126	TISA NNP - NR / BEA NNP, PERCENT	139.487	141.902	141.456	142.730	142.936	140.442
127	TISA GDCA - NR / BEA GPDI, PERCENT	347.120	348.812	307.653	394.621	315.282	335.538
128	TISA NDCA - NR / BEA NPDI, PERCENT	79.516	127.914	163.422	310.760	247.577	296.037
129	TISA NDCA, TAN, OC / BEA NPDI,PERCENT	-66.896	-29.331	54.086	121.715	145.638	180.389
130	TISA CONSUMPTION / BEA PCE, PERCENT	175.294	168.755	165.752	162.329	155.559	158.010
131	GNP	291.052	425.220	454.848	441.446	474.290	559.946
132	CAPITAL CONSUMPTION ALLOWANCES (CCA)	93.173	97.181	99.171	97.289	94.606	103.795
133	CCA, TANGIBLE	73.867	76.856	77.678	74.462	73.138	80.725
134	CCA, INTANGIBLE	19.306	20.325	21.493	22.827	21.468	23.070
135	NNP	197.879	328.039	355.677	344.157	379.684	456.151
136	BUS TRANS PAY + UNCOMP FACTOR SERVICES + NET INDIR TAXES + STAT DISCREPANCY	-14.260	-7.362	-7.557	1.654	9.910	11.091
137	NNI	212.138	335.401	363.234	342.502	369.774	445.060
138	GNP LESS SUM OF SECTOR & RW	.004	.003	.001	.001	.001	.000

		1952	1953	1954	1955	1956	1957
1	CONSUMPTION	353.017	375.394	395.531	416.374	437.597	464.699
2	HOUSEHOLD EXPENDITURES FOR SERVICES AND NONDURABLES	131.631	137.791	142.399	149.532	158.089	167.469
3	GROSS EXPENDITURES INCLUDED FROM BEA PERSONAL CONSUMPTION EXPENDITURES	134.838	141.328	145.957	153.418	162.339	172.055
4	LESS: PCE EXPENSES RELATED TO WORK	3.207	3.537	3.558	3.886	4.250	4.586
5	EXPENSE ACCOUNT ITEMS OF CONSUMPTION	3.085	3.300	3.342	3.629	4.010	4.223
6	BEA IMPUTATIONS OTHER THAN HOUSING	5.231	5.147	4.730	4.713	4.775	4.805
7	SUBSIDIES ALLOCATED TO CONSUMPTION	.237	.244	.333	.313	.528	.833
8	SUBSIDIES INCLUDED IN BUSINESS INCOME	.377	.391	.519	.497	.837	1.306
9	LESS: AMT. ALLOCATED TO INVESTMENT	.140	.147	.186	.184	.309	.473
10	TRANSFERS	27.874	29.483	31.345	35.566	37.395	41.580
11	FROM BUSINESS	1.119	1.242	1.335	1.505	1.664	1.764
12	MEDIA SUPPORT	.858	.953	1.043	1.194	1.335	1.415
13	TOTAL MEDIA SUPPORT	1.256	1.378	1.476	1.677	1.855	1.963
14	LESS: MEDIA SUPPORT ALLOCATED TO INVESTMENT	.398	.425	.433	.483	.520	.548
15	HEALTH AND SAFETY	.261	.289	.292	.311	.329	.349
16	FROM NONPROFIT INSTITUTIONS	7.585	8.037	8.603	9.149	9.866	10.807
17	FROM GOVERNMENT ENTERPRISES	.861	.858	1.035	1.333	1.733	1.627
18	FROM GOVERNMENT	18.310	19.347	20.372	23.580	24.132	27.383

141

		CREDITS					
		1952	1953	1954	1955	1956	1957
19	NONMARKET SERVICES PRODUCED IN HOUSEHOLDS	184.959	199.428	213.382	222.621	232.800	245.789
20	NET SPACE RENT OF OWNER-OCCUPIED NONFARM DWELLINGS	12.192	14.035	15.874	17.355	18.963	20.701
21	OTHER CAPITAL SERVICES	46.353	49.020	52.098	53.941	57.282	60.970
22	DURABLES	21.549	23.816	26.367	27.830	30.472	33.053
23	TOTAL DURABLES	25.045	27.778	30.906	32.753	36.054	39.042
24	LESS: DURABLES ALLOCATED TO INVESTMENT	.840	.912	.968	1.013	1.079	1.190
25	LESS: SERVICES OF DURABLES TO EXP REL TO WORK	2.656	3.050	3.572	3.911	4.504	4.799
26	SEMIDURABLES	24.701	25.083	25.595	25.976	26.671	27.765
27	INVENTORIES	.103	.122	.136	.135	.139	.152
28	LABOR SERVICES	151.367	163.657	172.788	181.622	189.517	200.362
29	LESS: LABOR SERVICES ALLOC. TO INVEST	24.953	27.284	27.378	30.297	32.962	36.244
30	GROSS DOMESTIC CAPITAL ACCUMULATION	204.668	228.687	217.756	264.606	283.628	271.645
31	ORIGINAL COST	208.968	224.700	219.677	244.122	254.557	262.057
32	TANGIBLE	145.039	154.760	146.963	163.086	168.744	168.156
33	STRUCTURES AND EQUIPMENT AND HOUSE- HOLD DURABLES AND SEMIDURABLES	134.967	143.377	141.931	155.531	162.950	168.614
34	BUSINESS	31.163	34.027	33.094	37.397	42.019	44.754
35	NONRESIDENTIAL	28.350	31.085	30.064	34.043	38.737	41.399
36	STRUCTURES	9.333	10.463	10.368	11.836	14.234	14.531
37	EQUIPMENT	19.017	20.622	19.696	22.207	24.503	26.868
38	RESIDENTIAL OTHER THAN OWNER- OCCUPIED NONFARM DWELLINGS	2.813	2.942	3.030	3.354	3.282	3.355
39	NONPROFIT INSTITUTIONS	1.444	1.576	1.887	1.958	2.254	2.499
40	STRUCTURES	1.291	1.412	1.688	1.759	2.023	2.241
41	EQUIPMENT	.153	.164	.199	.199	.231	.258
42	GOVERNMENT ENTERPRISES	2.688	2.908	3.196	3.233	3.477	3.513
43	STRUCTURES	2.505	2.738	3.016	3.001	3.272	3.298
44	EQUIPMENT	.183	.170	.180	.232	.205	.215
45	GOVERNMENT	24.487	25.369	24.170	22.804	22.906	22.806
46	STRUCTURES	8.322	8.511	8.703	8.737	9.530	10.787
47	EQUIPMENT	14.610	14.928	12.841	11.266	10.624	8.923
48	PRODUCT ACCUMULATED	1.555	1.930	2.626	2.801	2.752	3.096
49	HOUSEHOLDS	67.599	71.721	72.466	83.838	82.702	83.063
50	OWNER-OCC. NONFARM DWELLINGS	14.158	14.779	16.236	19.642	18.127	16.858
51	DURABLES	29.148	32.499	31.840	38.621	37.888	39.334
52	SEMIDURABLES	24.293	24.443	24.390	25.575	26.687	26.871

TABLE 1. NATIONAL INCOME AND PRODUCT ACCOUNT, BILLIONS OF DOLLARS, 1946-81

		CREDITS					
		1952	1953	1954	1955	1956	1957
53	FIXED GPDI RECONCILIATION	2.211	2.520	3.041	3.427	3.927	3.742
54	NIPA FIXED GPDI	48.976	52.902	54.258	62.424	66.327	67.853
55	LESS: CORRESP. SECTOR TOTALS	46.765	50.382	51.217	58.997	62.400	64.111
56	GOVERNMENT CAPITAL ACCUMULATION RECONCILIATION	5.375	5.256	4.077	2.874	5.665	8.237
57	NIPA GOVERNMENT INVESTMENT	30.995	31.603	28.817	26.110	29.296	31.460
58	LESS: GOVERNMENT AND GOVT ENTERPRISE TOTALS	25.620	26.347	24.740	23.236	23.631	23.223
59	CHANGE IN INVENTORIES	10.072	11.383	5.032	7.555	5.794	-.458
60	BUSINESS	3.133	.447	-1.543	5.953	4.695	1.335
61	GOVERNMENT	6.831	10.827	6.537	1.436	.966	-1.889
62	HOUSEHOLDS	.108	.109	.038	.166	.133	.096
63	INTANGIBLE	63.929	69.940	72.714	81.036	85.813	93.902
64	RESEARCH AND DEVELOPMENT	4.148	4.823	5.424	6.180	8.388	9.781
65	BUSINESS	1.720	2.200	2.320	2.460	3.277	3.396
66	NONPROFIT INSTITUTIONS	.078	.087	.096	.103	.116	.139
67	GOVERNMENT	2.350	2.536	3.008	3.618	4.995	6.246
68	EDUCATION AND TRAINING	51.203	55.689	57.161	64.013	65.872	71.495
69	HEALTH	8.578	9.428	10.129	10.843	11.553	12.626
70	SUBSIDIES AND GOVERNMENT ENTERPRISE TRANSFERS ALLOCATED TO INVESTMENT	.652	.661	.763	.969	1.322	1.395
71	NET REVALUATIONS	-4.952	3.325	-2.684	19.516	27.749	8.193
72	LAND	7.001	8.082	11.419	19.611	21.651	18.882
73	BUSINESS	3.426	1.114	5.569	7.902	11.552	5.251
74	NONPROFIT	.296	.070	.949	.557	.923	4.365
75	GOVERNMENT AND GOVT ENTERPRISES	1.014	4.271	2.066	5.264	4.035	5.673
76	HOUSEHOLDS	2.265	2.627	2.835	5.888	5.141	3.593
77	STRUCTURES AND EQUIPMENT	-.302	-2.345	-8.154	9.766	9.477	-8.582
78	BUSINESS	.270	.614	-2.923	5.193	5.905	-1.565
79	NONPROFIT INSTITUTIONS	-.036	-.191	-.211	.398	.399	-.504
80	GOVERNMENT	-.011	-1.931	-4.952	4.448	7.695	-.946
81	HOUSEHOLDS (OWNER-OCC. DWELLINGS)	-.525	-.836	-.068	-.273	-4.522	-5.567
82	HOUSEHOLD DURABLES AND SEMIDURABLES	-.914	-2.481	-6.896	-7.428	-2.574	-2.850
83	DURABLES	-1.607	-1.902	-6.332	-6.468	-1.124	-2.360
84	SEMIDURABLES	.693	-.579	-.564	-.960	-1.450	-.490
85	INVENTORIES	-10.737	.069	.947	-2.433	-.805	.743
86	BUSINESS (INCLUDING NONPROFIT)	-7.751	-.882	-2.825	-3.097	.814	.962
87	GOVERNMENT ENTERPRISES	-.365	-.130	-.498	-1.199	.196	.807
88	GOVERNMENT	-2.620	1.117	4.308	1.984	-1.720	-1.074
89	HOUSEHOLDS	-.001	-.036	-.038	-.121	-.095	.048
90	NET EXPORTS	3.183	1.254	2.530	2.993	5.278	7.278
91	EXPORTS	19.127	17.971	18.703	21.007	25.035	28.087
92	IMPORTS	15.944	16.717	16.173	18.014	19.757	20.809
93	GROSS NATIONAL PRODUCT	560.868	605.335	615.817	683.973	726.503	743.622

143

TABLE 1. NATIONAL INCOME AND PRODUCT ACCOUNT, BILLIONS OF DOLLARS, 1946-81

		CREDITS					
		1952	1953	1954	1955	1956	1957
	ADDENDA:						
94	GNP MINUS NET REVALUATIONS (NR)	565.820	602.010	618.501	664.458	698.754	735.429
95	NNP MINUS NR	451.385	480.703	488.413	529.694	550.441	576.208
96	NNI MINUS NR	439.956	466.339	472.605	514.817	535.281	559.479
97	GDCA MINUS NR	209.619	225.361	220.440	245.091	255.879	263.452
98	NDCA MINUS NR	95.184	104.054	90.352	110.327	107.566	104.231
99	NDCA	90.233	107.379	87.668	129.842	135.315	112.424
100	NDCA AT ORIGINAL COST	94.533	103.393	89.589	109.358	106.244	102.836
101	NDCA, TANGIBLE, AT ORIGINAL COST	58.313	63.490	50.954	62.170	58.816	51.303
102	NDCA, INTANGIBLE, AT ORIGINAL COST	36.220	39.903	38.635	47.188	47.428	51.534
103	GDCA - NR / GNP - NR, PERCENT	37.047	37.435	35.641	36.886	36.619	35.823
104	NDCA - NR / NNP - NR, PERCENT	21.087	21.646	18.499	20.828	19.542	18.089
105	NDCA, TAN, O.C. / NNP - NR, PERCENT	12.919	13.208	10.433	11.737	10.685	8.903
106	NDCA, INTAN, O.C. / NNP - NR, PERCENT	8.024	8.301	7.910	8.909	8.616	8.944
107	GROSS BUSINESS PRODUCT	268.438	288.897	286.297	322.898	347.087	347.442
108	GROSS NONPROFIT PRODUCT	9.694	10.059	11.597	12.746	13.823	17.472
109	GROSS GOVT ENTERPRISE PRODUCT	4.673	5.120	5.048	4.808	6.488	7.444
110	GROSS GOVERNMENT PRODUCT	62.000	69.793	70.527	86.028	88.149	86.496
111	GROSS HOUSEHOLD PRODUCT	213.801	229.273	239.999	254.737	267.781	281.262
112	GROSS DOMESTIC PRODUCT	558.605	603.143	613.467	681.216	723.328	740.116
113	GROSS PRODUCT, REST OF WORLD	2.262	2.191	2.349	2.754	3.174	3.507
114	BEA GNP	347.967	366.792	366.847	400.042	421.699	443.959
115	BEA NNP	318.698	335.813	334.145	365.255	382.971	402.252
116	BEA NI	287.898	302.122	301.087	330.452	349.405	365.175
117	BEA GPDI	52.109	53.349	52.715	68.377	71.022	69.188
118	BEA NPDI	22.840	22.370	20.013	33.590	32.294	27.481
119	BEA PCE	217.093	229.665	235.842	253.666	266.008	280.409
120	BEA GPDI / BEA GNP, PERCENT	14.975	14.545	14.370	17.092	16.842	15.584
121	BEA NPDI / BEA NNP, PERCENT	7.167	6.661	5.989	9.196	8.432	6.832
122	TISA GNP / BEA GNP, PERCENT	161.184	165.035	167.868	170.975	172.280	167.498
123	TISA NNP / BEA NNP, PERCENT	140.080	144.136	145.365	150.363	150.975	145.282
124	TISA NNI / BEA NI, PERCENT	151.097	155.455	156.075	161.697	161.140	155.452
125	TISA GNP - NR / BEA GNP, PERCENT	162.607	164.128	168.599	166.097	165.700	165.652
126	TISA NNP - NR / BEA NNP, PERCENT	141.634	143.146	146.168	145.020	143.729	143.245
127	TISA GDCA - NR / BEA GPDI, PERCENT	402.271	422.428	418.173	358.441	360.281	380.777
128	TISA NDCA - NR / BEA NPDI, PERCENT	416.744	465.150	451.467	328.452	333.083	379.284
129	TISA NDCA, TAN, OC / BEA NPDI,PERCENT	255.310	283.817	254.607	185.086	182.125	186.684
130	TISA CONSUMPTION / BEA PCE, PERCENT	162.611	163.453	167.710	164.142	164.505	165.722
131	GNP	560.868	605.335	615.817	683.973	726.503	743.622
132	CAPITAL CONSUMPTION ALLOWANCES (CCA)	114.435	121.307	130.088	134.764	148.313	159.221
133	CCA, TANGIBLE	86.726	91.270	96.009	100.916	109.928	116.853
134	CCA, INTANGIBLE	27.709	30.037	34.079	33.848	38.385	42.368
135	NNP	446.433	484.028	485.729	549.209	578.190	584.401
136	BUS TRANS PAY + UNCOMP FACTOR SERVICES + NET INDIR TAXES + STAT DISCREPANCY	11.429	14.364	15.809	14.877	15.160	16.729
137	NNI	435.004	469.664	469.920	534.333	563.030	567.672
138	GNP LESS SUM OF SECTOR & RW	.001	.001	.001	.003	.001	-.001

		CREDITS					
		1958	1959	1960	1961	1962	1963
1	CONSUMPTION	485.059	512.429	542.081	566.040	588.774	614.010
2	HOUSEHOLD EXPENDITURES FOR SERVICES AND NONDURABLES	175.348	184.878	193.527	201.085	210.519	219.635
3	GROSS EXPENDITURES INCLUDED FROM BEA PERSONAL CONSUMPTION EXPENDITURES	180.079	190.111	199.208	206.925	216.756	226.154
4	LESS: PCE EXPENSES RELATED TO WORK	4.731	5.233	5.681	5.840	6.237	6.519
5	EXPENSE ACCOUNT ITEMS OF CONSUMPTION	4.310	4.441	4.636	4.701	4.946	4.909
6	BEA IMPUTATIONS OTHER THAN HOUSING	4.855	5.136	5.421	5.291	5.028	5.557
7	SUBSIDIES ALLOCATED TO CONSUMPTION	.901	.703	.798	1.388	1.516	1.454
8	SUBSIDIES INCLUDED IN BUSINESS INCOME	1.391	1.107	1.239	2.137	2.399	2.322
9	LESS: AMT. ALLOCATED TO INVESTMENT	.490	.404	.441	.749	.883	.868
10	TRANSFERS	42.440	46.292	47.566	51.997	53.979	56.355
11	FROM BUSINESS	1.815	1.989	2.344	2.140	2.297	2.454
12	MEDIA SUPPORT	1.467	1.614	1.947	1.725	1.851	1.988
13	TOTAL MEDIA SUPPORT	2.019	2.214	2.616	2.362	2.512	2.688
14	LESS: MEDIA SUPPORT ALLOCATED TO INVESTMENT	.552	.600	.669	.637	.661	.700
15	HEALTH AND SAFETY	.348	.375	.397	.415	.446	.466
16	FROM NONPROFIT INSTITUTIONS	11.276	12.285	12.788	13.569	14.357	15.294
17	FROM GOVERNMENT ENTERPRISES	1.915	1.536	1.960	2.291	2.245	2.123
18	FROM GOVERNMENT	27.433	30.482	30.475	33.997	35.081	36.484
19	NONMARKET SERVICES PRODUCED IN HOUSEHOLDS	257.206	270.979	290.133	301.579	312.787	326.100
20	NET SPACE RENT OF OWNER-OCCUPIED NONFARM DWELLINGS	22.570	24.530	26.640	28.588	30.936	32.943
21	OTHER CAPITAL SERVICES	63.677	66.608	69.310	71.863	74.329	77.517
22	DURABLES	35.050	37.374	39.043	40.538	41.915	43.909
23	TOTAL DURABLES	41.201	43.880	45.619	47.189	48.666	50.888
24	LESS: DURABLES ALLOCATED TO INVESTMENT	1.269	1.329	1.401	1.456	1.510	1.587
25	LESS: SERVICES OF DURABLES TO EXP REL TO WORK	4.882	5.177	5.175	5.195	5.241	5.392
26	SEMIDURABLES	28.463	29.058	30.072	31.121	32.195	33.372
27	INVENTORIES	.164	.176	.194	.204	.219	.236
28	LABOR SERVICES	207.964	220.579	236.771	245.551	256.722	269.673
29	LESS: LABOR SERVICES ALLOC. TO INVEST	37.005	40.738	42.588	44.423	49.200	54.033
30	GROSS DOMESTIC CAPITAL ACCUMULATION	277.015	293.720	298.088	309.324	342.602	359.227
31	ORIGINAL COST	262.306	292.961	298.391	303.582	340.445	364.395
32	TANGIBLE	163.608	183.609	182.122	180.060	205.625	218.039

145

TABLE 1. NATIONAL INCOME AND PRODUCT ACCOUNT, BILLIONS OF DOLLARS, 1946-81

		CREDITS					
		1958	1959	1960	1961	1962	1963
33	STRUCTURES AND EQUIPMENT AND HOUSE-HOLD DURABLES AND SEMIDURABLES	164.502	180.272	180.039	181.949	198.402	210.869
34	BUSINESS	39.238	43.958	46.253	45.932	50.128	53.710
35	NONRESIDENTIAL	35.626	39.422	41.641	40.750	44.000	46.403
36	STRUCTURES	12.896	13.377	14.296	14.408	14.847	15.015
37	EQUIPMENT	22.730	26.045	27.345	26.342	29.153	31.388
38	RESIDENTIAL OTHER THAN OWNER-OCCUPIED NONFARM DWELLINGS	3.612	4.536	4.612	5.182	6.128	7.307
39	NONPROFIT INSTITUTIONS	2.758	2.851	3.040	3.319	3.958	3.903
40	STRUCTURES	2.473	2.559	2.718	2.977	3.561	3.509
41	EQUIPMENT	.285	.292	.322	.342	.397	.394
42	GOVERNMENT ENTERPRISES	3.548	3.672	3.742	4.314	4.619	4.657
43	STRUCTURES	3.320	3.442	3.463	4.006	4.331	4.299
44	EQUIPMENT	.228	.230	.279	.308	.288	.358
45	GOVERNMENT	24.147	25.669	26.463	28.966	29.766	32.219
46	STRUCTURES	12.214	12.719	12.565	13.477	13.989	15.423
47	EQUIPMENT	8.708	9.408	10.344	11.313	11.666	12.227
48	PRODUCT ACCUMULATED	3.225	3.542	3.554	4.176	4.111	4.569
49	HOUSEHOLDS	81.089	91.942	91.083	89.594	97.258	104.644
50	OWNER-OCC. NONFARM DWELLINGS	17.127	20.767	18.582	17.819	18.800	20.545
51	DURABLES	36.846	42.438	43.110	41.574	46.702	51.431
52	SEMIDURABLES	27.116	28.737	29.391	30.201	31.756	32.668
53	FIXED GPDI RECONCILIATION	4.284	4.893	5.056	5.386	6.278	6.781
54	NIPA FIXED GPDI	63.407	72.469	72.931	72.456	79.164	84.939
55	LESS: CORRESP. SECTOR TOTALS	59.123	67.576	67.875	67.070	72.886	78.158
56	GOVERNMENT CAPITAL ACCUMULATION RECONCILIATION	9.438	7.287	4.402	4.438	6.395	4.955
57	NIPA GOVERNMENT INVESTMENT	33.908	33.086	31.053	33.542	36.669	37.262
58	LESS: GOVERNMENT AND GOVT ENTERPRISE TOTALS	24.470	25.799	26.651	29.104	30.274	32.307
59	CHANGE IN INVENTORIES	-.894	3.337	2.083	-1.889	7.223	7.170
60	BUSINESS	-1.491	5.659	2.951	2.322	6.257	5.965
61	GOVERNMENT	.554	-2.497	-.946	-4.293	.833	1.101
62	HOUSEHOLDS	.043	.175	.078	.082	.133	.104
63	INTANGIBLE	98.698	109.352	116.269	123.522	134.821	146.355
64	RESEARCH AND DEVELOPMENT	10.767	12.318	13.510	14.340	15.390	17.243
65	BUSINESS	3.630	3.983	4.428	4.668	5.029	5.360
66	NONPROFIT INSTITUTIONS	.160	.177	.191	.223	.265	.294
67	GOVERNMENT	6.977	8.158	8.891	9.449	10.096	11.589
68	EDUCATION AND TRAINING	74.438	82.308	86.934	92.208	101.184	109.487
69	HEALTH	13.493	14.726	15.826	16.974	18.247	19.626
70	SUBSIDIES AND GOVERNMENT ENTERPRISE TRANSFERS ALLOCATED TO INVESTMENT	1.532	1.286	1.526	1.986	2.189	2.135

TABLE 1. NATIONAL INCOME AND PRODUCT ACCOUNT, BILLIONS OF DOLLARS, 1946-81

		CREDITS					
		1958	1959	1960	1961	1962	1963
71	NET REVALUATIONS	13.177	-.527	-1.829	3.755	-.032	-7.303
72	LAND	24.515	27.183	13.864	22.617	22.629	17.066
73	BUSINESS	14.694	13.380	9.392	10.418	10.660	6.461
74	NONPROFIT	.108	.176	-2.707	1.020	1.298	.146
75	GOVERNMENT AND GOVT ENTERPRISES	4.533	4.938	5.251	6.731	5.479	6.554
76	HOUSEHOLDS	5.180	8.689	1.928	4.448	5.192	3.905
77	STRUCTURES AND EQUIPMENT	-12.829	-17.802	-11.398	-10.940	-11.773	-16.082
78	BUSINESS	-2.885	-5.613	-5.220	-5.445	-6.056	-5.538
79	NONPROFIT INSTITUTIONS	-.419	-.542	-.434	-.022	-.140	.210
80	GOVERNMENT	-5.024	-6.441	-3.639	-1.352	-.841	-.526
81	HOUSEHOLDS (OWNER-OCC. DWELLINGS)	-4.501	-5.206	-2.105	-4.121	-4.736	-10.228
82	HOUSEHOLD DURABLES AND SEMIDURABLES	-.830	-4.527	-3.604	-4.384	-6.720	-4.627
83	DURABLES	-.365	-3.717	-3.492	-4.053	-6.066	-4.109
84	SEMIDURABLES	-.465	-.810	-.112	-.331	-.654	-.518
85	INVENTORIES	2.321	-5.381	-.691	-3.538	-4.168	-3.660
86	BUSINESS (INCLUDING NONPROFIT)	1.548	-3.116	-.225	-2.456	-2.270	-2.377
87	GOVERNMENT ENTERPRISES	.997	-.726	.263	-.190	.051	-.277
88	GOVERNMENT	-.270	-1.460	-.759	-.869	-1.907	-1.006
89	HOUSEHOLDS	.046	-.079	.030	-.023	-.042	.000
90	NET EXPORTS	3.253	1.415	5.464	6.623	6.365	7.568
91	EXPORTS	24.231	24.814	28.861	29.936	31.804	34.214
92	IMPORTS	20.978	23.399	23.397	23.313	25.439	26.646
93	GROSS NATIONAL PRODUCT	765.327	807.564	845.633	881.987	937.741	980.805
	ADDENDA:						
94	GNP MINUS NET REVALUATIONS (NR)	752.149	808.091	847.461	878.231	937.773	988.108
95	NNP MINUS NR	586.164	635.431	668.449	693.231	745.217	786.890
96	NNI MINUS NR	567.422	615.497	645.474	666.601	713.524	752.645
97	GDCA MINUS NR	263.837	294.247	299.917	305.568	342.634	366.530
98	NDCA MINUS NR	97.852	121.587	120.904	120.568	150.078	165.312
99	NDCA	111.030	121.060	119.075	124.324	150.046	158.009
100	NDCA AT ORIGINAL COST	96.321	120.301	119.378	118.582	147.889	163.177
101	NDCA, TANGIBLE, AT ORIGINAL COST	42.734	58.716	53.902	48.178	69.946	77.570
102	NDCA, INTANGIBLE, AT ORIGINAL COST	53.587	61.585	65.476	70.404	77.943	85.606
103	GDCA - NR / GNP - NR, PERCENT	35.078	36.413	35.390	34.794	36.537	37.094
104	NDCA - NR / NNP - NR, PERCENT	16.694	19.135	18.087	17.392	20.139	21.008
105	NDCA, TAN, O.C. / NNP - NR, PERCENT	7.290	9.240	8.064	6.950	9.386	9.858
106	NDCA, INTAN, O.C. / NNP - NR, PERCENT	9.142	9.692	9.795	10.156	10.459	10.879
107	GROSS BUSINESS PRODUCT	356.727	378.950	390.650	400.250	432.244	451.570
108	GROSS NONPROFIT PRODUCT	14.352	15.647	14.333	19.419	21.294	22.052
109	GROSS GOVT ENTERPRISE PRODUCT	8.130	7.071	8.810	8.737	9.567	10.106
110	GROSS GOVERNMENT PRODUCT	85.193	88.560	96.079	105.159	112.233	121.241
111	GROSS HOUSEHOLD PRODUCT	297.893	314.065	332.193	344.522	357.850	370.887
112	GROSS DOMESTIC PRODUCT	762.295	804.292	842.064	878.086	933.187	975.856
113	GROSS PRODUCT, REST OF WORLD	3.032	3.272	3.569	3.901	4.554	4.949

147

TABLE 1. NATIONAL INCOME AND PRODUCT ACCOUNT, BILLIONS OF DOLLARS, 1946-81

		CREDITS					
		1958	1959	1960	1961	1962	1963
114	BEA GNP	449.670	487.902	506.512	524.554	565.039	596.714
115	BEA NNP	406.180	442.966	460.245	477.044	516.073	546.125
116	BEA NI	366.876	400.782	415.694	428.779	461.998	488.485
117	BEA GPDI	61.916	78.128	75.882	74.778	85.421	90.904
118	BEA NPDI	18.426	33.192	29.615	27.268	36.455	40.315
119	BEA PCE	289.461	310.773	324.907	334.997	355.219	374.581
120	BEA GPDI / BEA GNP, PERCENT	13.769	16.013	14.981	14.256	15.118	15.234
121	BEA NPDI / BEA NNP, PERCENT	4.536	7.493	6.435	5.716	7.064	7.382
122	TISA GNP / BEA GNP, PERCENT	170.197	165.518	166.952	168.140	165.960	164.368
123	TISA NNP / BEA NNP, PERCENT	147.556	143.330	144.840	146.105	144.395	142.749
124	TISA NNI / BEA NI, PERCENT	158.255	153.443	154.836	156.341	154.436	152.582
125	TISA GNP - NR / BEA GNP, PERCENT	167.267	165.626	167.313	167.424	165.966	165.592
126	TISA NNP - NR / BEA NNP, PERCENT	144.311	143.449	145.238	145.318	144.402	144.086
127	TISA GDCA - NR / BEA GPDI, PERCENT	426.122	376.621	395.241	408.634	401.112	403.206
128	TISA NDCA - NR / BEA NPDI, PERCENT	531.057	366.313	408.252	442.161	411.680	410.051
129	TISA NDCA, TAN, OC / BEA NPDI,PERCENT	231.922	176.899	182.009	176.684	191.869	192.411
130	TISA CONSUMPTION / BEA PCE, PERCENT	167.573	164.888	166.842	168.969	165.750	163.919
131	GNP	765.327	807.564	845.633	881.987	937.741	980.805
132	CAPITAL CONSUMPTION ALLOWANCES (CCA)	165.985	172.660	179.013	185.000	192.556	201.218
133	CCA, TANGIBLE	120.874	124.893	128.220	131.882	135.679	140.469
134	CCA, INTANGIBLE	45.111	47.767	50.793	53.118	56.877	60.749
135	NNP	599.342	634.904	666.620	696.987	745.185	779.587
136	BUS TRANS PAY + UNCOMP FACTOR SERVICES + NET INDIR TAXES + STAT DISCREPANCY	18.742	19.934	22.975	26.631	31.693	34.245
137	NNI	580.599	614.970	643.645	670.356	713.492	745.342
138	GNP LESS SUM OF SECTOR & RW	.000	.000	.000	.000	.000	.000

		1964	1965	1966	1967	1968	1969
1	CONSUMPTION	649.945	694.035	742.000	786.520	856.270	919.985
2	HOUSEHOLD EXPENDITURES FOR SERVICES AND NONDURABLES	232.391	249.308	267.366	281.836	304.240	332.642
3	GROSS EXPENDITURES INCLUDED FROM BEA PERSONAL CONSUMPTION EXPENDITURES	239.350	256.961	275.719	290.807	314.004	343.473
4	LESS: PCE EXPENSES RELATED TO WORK	6.959	7.653	8.353	8.971	9.764	10.831
5	EXPENSE ACCOUNT ITEMS OF CONSUMPTION	5.428	5.792	6.305	6.664	7.225	7.927
6	BEA IMPUTATIONS OTHER THAN HOUSING	5.641	6.032	7.428	8.814	9.756	7.154
7	SUBSIDIES ALLOCATED TO CONSUMPTION	1.747	1.898	2.436	2.339	2.576	2.758
8	SUBSIDIES INCLUDED IN BUSINESS INCOME	2.810	3.088	4.032	3.896	4.306	4.643
9	LESS: AMT. ALLOCATED TO INVESTMENT	1.063	1.190	1.596	1.557	1.730	1.885
10	TRANSFERS	61.084	66.177	72.600	75.871	83.497	88.034
11	FROM BUSINESS	2.677	3.298	3.648	3.782	4.150	4.549
12	MEDIA SUPPORT	2.174	2.753	3.045	3.132	3.427	3.748
13	TOTAL MEDIA SUPPORT	2.929	3.630	3.992	4.102	4.462	4.867
14	LESS: MEDIA SUPPORT ALLOCATED TO INVESTMENT	.755	.877	.947	.970	1.035	1.119
15	HEALTH AND SAFETY	.503	.545	.603	.650	.723	.801
16	FROM NONPROFIT INSTITUTIONS	16.480	17.657	18.937	19.660	22.337	24.533
17	FROM GOVERNMENT ENTERPRISES	2.256	2.246	2.155	1.865	1.690	2.078
18	FROM GOVERNMENT	39.671	42.977	47.860	50.564	55.320	56.874

148

TABLE 1. NATIONAL INCOME AND PRODUCT ACCOUNT, BILLIONS OF DOLLARS, 1946-81

		CREDITS					
		1964	1965	1966	1967	1968	1969
19	NONMARKET SERVICES PRODUCED IN HOUSEHOLDS	343.655	364.829	385.866	410.996	448.977	481.470
20	NET SPACE RENT OF OWNER-OCCUPIED NONFARM DWELLINGS	35.060	37.586	40.294	43.224	46.019	50.181
21	OTHER CAPITAL SERVICES	81.015	84.868	90.039	97.787	105.513	115.517
22	DURABLES	45.867	47.725	50.270	54.786	59.154	65.331
23	TOTAL DURABLES	53.081	55.151	57.975	63.125	67.975	75.074
24	LESS: DURABLES ALLOCATED TO INVESTMENT	1.679	1.790	1.935	2.135	2.325	2.566
25	LESS: SERVICES OF DURABLES TO EXP REL TO WORK	5.536	5.636	5.771	6.204	6.496	7.177
26	SEMIDURABLES	34.905	36.884	39.495	42.711	46.079	49.890
27	INVENTORIES	.242	.258	.275	.290	.281	.296
28	LABOR SERVICES	287.015	307.693	328.908	359.092	396.172	424.017
29	LESS: LABOR SERVICES ALLOC. TO INVEST	59.435	65.318	73.375	89.107	98.727	108.245
30	GROSS DOMESTIC CAPITAL ACCUMULATION	414.785	442.499	498.331	524.251	586.988	619.242
31	ORIGINAL COST	392.840	432.762	483.355	520.701	572.053	625.205
32	TANGIBLE	230.763	255.680	282.625	294.327	322.133	349.893
33	STRUCTURES AND EQUIPMENT AND HOUSE-HOLD DURABLES AND SEMIDURABLES	226.474	248.805	271.870	282.419	312.690	334.527
34	BUSINESS	59.570	69.580	77.638	78.268	86.133	97.863
35	NONRESIDENTIAL	52.324	62.672	71.472	72.363	78.685	88.518
36	STRUCTURES	16.320	19.895	21.925	22.490	23.981	27.600
37	EQUIPMENT	36.004	42.777	49.547	49.873	54.704	60.918
38	RESIDENTIAL OTHER THAN OWNER-OCCUPIED NONFARM DWELLINGS	7.246	6.908	6.166	5.905	7.448	9.345
39	NONPROFIT INSTITUTIONS	4.287	4.809	4.978	4.743	4.800	5.290
40	STRUCTURES	3.858	4.319	4.457	4.232	4.394	4.801
41	EQUIPMENT	.429	.490	.521	.511	.406	.489
42	GOVERNMENT ENTERPRISES	5.120	5.395	5.569	6.193	7.282	7.562
43	STRUCTURES	4.831	5.105	5.199	5.810	6.823	7.053
44	EQUIPMENT	.289	.290	.370	.383	.459	.509
45	GOVERNMENT	32.767	34.413	38.333	38.931	40.136	40.727
46	STRUCTURES	15.578	16.952	19.003	19.822	21.015	20.826
47	EQUIPMENT	11.875	11.767	13.103	12.656	13.197	13.359
48	PRODUCT ACCUMULATED	5.314	5.694	6.227	6.453	5.924	6.542
49	HOUSEHOLDS	113.344	122.263	129.258	133.786	152.809	162.828
50	OWNER-OCC. NONFARM DWELLINGS	21.478	22.038	20.655	21.291	25.642	27.023
51	DURABLES	56.435	63.007	67.985	70.067	80.460	85.724
52	SEMIDURABLES	35.431	37.218	40.618	42.428	46.707	50.081

149

TABLE 1. NATIONAL INCOME AND PRODUCT ACCOUNT, BILLIONS OF DOLLARS, 1946-81

		CREDITS					
		1964	1965	1966	1967	1968	1969
53	FIXED GPDI RECONCILIATION	6.401	7.235	8.299	8.192	8.844	9.283
54	NIPA FIXED GPDI	91.736	103.662	111.570	112.494	125.419	139.459
55	LESS: CORRESP. SECTOR TOTALS	85.335	96.427	103.271	104.302	116.575	130.176
56	GOVERNMENT CAPITAL ACCUMULATION RECONCILIATION	4.985	5.110	7.795	12.306	12.686	10.974
57	NIPA GOVERNMENT INVESTMENT	37.558	39.224	45.470	50.977	54.180	52.721
58	LESS: GOVERNMENT AND GOVT ENTERPRISE TOTALS	32.573	34.114	37.675	38.671	41.494	41.747
59	CHANGE IN INVENTORIES	4.289	6.875	10.755	11.908	9.443	15.366
60	BUSINESS	5.620	9.887	14.117	10.332	7.863	9.831
61	GOVERNMENT	-1.535	-3.275	-3.622	1.453	1.296	5.333
62	HOUSEHOLDS	.204	.263	.260	.123	.284	.202
63	INTANGIBLE	162.078	177.082	200.729	226.374	249.920	275.312
64	RESEARCH AND DEVELOPMENT	18.886	20.005	21.822	23.073	24.472	25.765
65	BUSINESS	5.792	6.445	7.216	8.020	8.869	9.857
66	NONPROFIT INSTITUTIONS	.311	.349	.394	.423	.448	.478
67	GOVERNMENT	12.783	13.211	14.212	14.630	15.155	15.430
68	EDUCATION AND TRAINING	121.501	133.857	153.851	176.253	195.382	215.508
69	HEALTH	21.691	23.220	25.056	27.047	30.067	34.039
70	SUBSIDIES AND GOVERNMENT ENTERPRISE TRANSFERS ALLOCATED TO INVESTMENT	2.435	2.599	3.009	2.798	2.864	3.304
71	NET REVALUATIONS	19.510	7.138	11.968	.752	12.071	-9.267
72	LAND	24.180	25.408	16.415	13.628	3.346	-10.410
73	BUSINESS	10.294	13.324	5.400	4.602	-9.234	-9.977
74	NONPROFIT	.681	1.005	.577	.578	-.991	.407
75	GOVERNMENT AND GOVT ENTERPRISES	6.508	4.497	5.847	4.088	1.933	-2.151
76	HOUSEHOLDS	6.697	6.582	4.591	4.361	11.638	1.311
77	STRUCTURES AND EQUIPMENT	3.453	-6.491	7.612	-1.507	23.069	16.910
78	BUSINESS	-.219	-3.159	2.894	-.306	4.088	6.091
79	NONPROFIT INSTITUTIONS	.091	.302	.498	.427	.362	2.751
80	GOVERNMENT	.565	1.533	.098	2.478	4.536	8.137
81	HOUSEHOLDS (OWNER-OCC. DWELLINGS)	3.016	-5.167	4.122	-4.106	14.082	-.069
82	HOUSEHOLD DURABLES AND SEMIDURABLES	-6.548	-14.055	-7.320	-5.455	-9.276	-13.177
83	DURABLES	-5.953	-12.991	-5.792	-4.573	-8.051	-11.653
84	SEMIDURABLES	-.595	-1.064	-1.528	-.882	-1.225	-1.524
85	INVENTORIES	-1.575	2.276	-4.739	-5.914	-5.068	-2.590
86	BUSINESS (INCLUDING NONPROFIT)	-2.411	.428	-3.520	-4.856	-3.508	-1.430
87	GOVERNMENT ENTERPRISES	-.311	.582	-.311	-.132	-.081	.112
88	GOVERNMENT	1.166	1.289	-.924	-.822	-1.405	-1.197
89	HOUSEHOLDS	-.019	-.023	.016	-.104	-.074	-.075
90	NET EXPORTS	10.056	8.774	6.510	6.309	4.257	4.170
91	EXPORTS	38.825	41.086	44.560	47.310	52.355	57.519
92	IMPORTS	28.769	32.312	38.050	41.001	48.098	53.349
93	GROSS NATIONAL PRODUCT	1074.786	1145.309	1246.841	1317.080	1447.515	1543.396

150

TABLE 1. NATIONAL INCOME AND PRODUCT ACCOUNT, BILLIONS OF DOLLARS, 1946-81

		CREDITS					
		1964	1965	1966	1967	1968	1969
	ADDENDA:						
94	GNP MINUS NET REVALUTIONS (NR)	1055.276	1138.170	1234.873	1316.327	1435.444	1552.664
95	NNP MINUS NR	843.472	912.694	991.826	1051.235	1145.141	1232.192
96	NNI MINUS NR	807.773	877.529	954.755	1013.328	1104.137	1181.496
97	GDCA MINUS NR	395.275	435.361	486.363	523.499	574.917	628.509
98	NDCA MINUS NR	183.471	209.885	243.316	258.407	284.614	308.037
99	NDCA	202.981	217.023	255.284	259.159	296.685	298.770
100	NDCA AT ORIGINAL COST	181.036	207.286	240.308	255.609	281.750	304.733
101	NDCA, TANGIBLE, AT ORIGINAL COST	84.132	101.581	118.033	115.824	127.641	135.704
102	NDCA, INTANGIBLE, AT ORIGINAL COST	96.904	105.705	122.274	139.785	154.109	169.029
103	GDCA - NR / GNP - NR, PERCENT	37.457	38.251	39.386	39.770	40.052	40.479
104	NDCA - NR / NNP - NR, PERCENT	21.752	22.996	24.532	24.581	24.854	24.999
105	NDCA, TAN, O.C. / NNP - NR, PERCENT	9.975	11.130	11.901	11.018	11.146	11.013
106	NDCA, INTAN, O.C. / NNP - NR, PERCENT	11.489	11.582	12.328	13.297	13.458	13.718
107	GROSS BUSINESS PRODUCT	493.028	539.151	584.705	602.386	648.614	709.491
108	GROSS NONPROFIT PRODUCT	24.251	27.128	29.628	32.331	33.727	41.635
109	GROSS GOVT ENTERPRISE PRODUCT	10.749	12.403	12.227	13.117	14.522	16.283
110	GROSS GOVERNMENT PRODUCT	133.775	142.506	153.645	168.547	180.710	192.835
111	GROSS HOUSEHOLD PRODUCT	407.532	418.262	460.994	494.771	563.208	576.278
112	GROSS DOMESTIC PRODUCT	1069.333	1139.450	1241.199	1311.152	1440.781	1536.521
113	GROSS PRODUCT, REST OF WORLD	5.453	5.865	5.646	5.931	6.734	6.875
114	BEA GNP	637.719	691.051	755.981	799.585	873.392	943.996
115	BEA NNP	584.834	635.010	695.316	733.735	801.319	864.005
116	BEA NI	524.941	572.444	628.072	662.236	722.548	779.338
117	BEA GPDI	97.356	113.549	125.687	122.826	133.282	149.290
118	BEA NPDI	44.471	57.508	65.022	56.976	61.209	69.299
119	BEA PCE	400.497	430.378	465.118	490.262	536.883	581.781
120	BEA GPDI / BEA GNP, PERCENT	15.266	16.431	16.626	15.361	15.260	15.815
121	BEA NPDI / BEA NNP, PERCENT	7.604	9.056	9.351	7.765	7.639	8.021
122	TISA GNP / BEA GNP, PERCENT	168.536	165.734	164.930	164.720	165.735	163.496
123	TISA NNP / BEA NNP, PERCENT	147.560	144.853	144.365	143.374	144.413	141.541
124	TISA NNI / BEA NI, PERCENT	157.595	154.542	153.919	153.130	154.482	150.413
125	TISA GNP - NR / BEA GNP, PERCENT	165.477	164.701	163.347	164.626	164.353	164.478
126	TISA NNP - NR / BEA NNP, PERCENT	144.224	143.729	142.644	143.272	142.907	142.614
127	TISA GDCA - NR / BEA GPDI, PERCENT	406.010	383.413	386.964	426.212	431.354	420.999
128	TISA NDCA - NR / BEA NPDI, PERCENT	412.563	364.967	374.206	453.536	464.987	444.504
129	TISA NDCA, TAN, OC / BEA NPDI, PERCENT	189.185	176.638	181.528	203.286	208.532	195.823
130	TISA CONSUMPTION / BEA PCE, PERCENT	162.285	161.262	159.529	160.428	159.489	158.132
131	GNP	1074.786	1145.309	1246.841	1317.080	1447.515	1543.396
132	CAPITAL CONSUMPTION ALLOWANCES (CCA)	211.804	225.476	243.047	265.092	290.303	320.472
133	CCA, TANGIBLE	146.630	154.099	164.592	178.503	194.492	214.189
134	CCA, INTANGIBLE	65.174	71.377	78.455	86.589	95.811	106.283
135	NNP	862.982	919.832	1003.794	1051.988	1157.212	1222.924
136	BUS TRANS PAY + UNCOMP FACTOR SERVICES + NET INDIR TAXES + STAT DISCREPANCY	35.699	35.165	37.072	37.908	41.004	50.696
137	NNI	827.283	884.667	966.722	1014.080	1116.208	1172.228
138	GNP LESS SUM OF SECTOR & RW	.000	-.006	-.004	-.003	.000	.000

151

TABLE 1. NATIONAL INCOME AND PRODUCT ACCOUNT, BILLIONS OF DOLLARS, 1946-81

		CREDITS					
		1970	1971	1972	1973	1974	1975
1	CONSUMPTION	998.934	1065.348	1143.726	1238.531	1372.292	1515.376
2	HOUSEHOLD EXPENDITURES FOR SERVICES AND NONDURABLES	355.521	378.448	410.026	449.579	501.404	550.817
3	GROSS EXPENDITURES INCLUDED FROM BEA PERSONAL CONSUMPTION EXPENDITURES	367.353	391.328	423.914	464.724	519.017	569.497
4	LESS: PCE EXPENSES RELATED TO WORK	11.832	12.880	13.888	15.145	17.613	18.680
5	EXPENSE ACCOUNT ITEMS OF CONSUMPTION	8.375	8.890	9.782	10.887	11.952	12.476
6	BEA IMPUTATIONS OTHER THAN HOUSING	13.105	13.332	14.559	17.183	21.313	25.947
7	SUBSIDIES ALLOCATED TO CONSUMPTION	2.979	2.867	3.773	3.048	2.092	2.975
8	SUBSIDIES INCLUDED IN BUSINESS INCOME	4.896	4.788	6.406	5.249	3.529	4.900
9	LESS: AMT. ALLOCATED TO INVESTMENT	1.917	1.921	2.633	2.201	1.437	1.925
10	TRANSFERS	97.173	104.572	114.066	122.751	132.477	152.003
11	FROM BUSINESS	4.619	4.741	5.346	5.769	6.190	6.615
12	MEDIA SUPPORT	3.788	3.856	4.333	4.646	4.994	5.383
13	TOTAL MEDIA SUPPORT	4.918	5.029	5.607	5.986	6.415	6.890
14	LESS: MEDIA SUPPORT ALLOCATED TO INVESTMENT	1.130	1.173	1.274	1.340	1.421	1.507
15	HEALTH AND SAFETY	.831	.885	1.013	1.123	1.196	1.232
16	FROM NONPROFIT INSTITUTIONS	27.166	30.031	33.041	35.426	39.227	43.999
17	FROM GOVERNMENT ENTERPRISES	2.818	2.865	2.622	3.283	3.371	4.283
18	FROM GOVERNMENT	62.570	66.935	73.057	78.273	83.689	97.105
19	NONMARKET SERVICES PRODUCED IN HOUSEHOLDS	521.782	557.239	591.520	635.083	703.053	771.159
20	NET SPACE RENT OF OWNER-OCCUPIED NONFARM DWELLINGS	53.918	58.897	64.825	71.444	78.747	86.251
21	OTHER CAPITAL SERVICES	124.715	133.729	141.227	152.467	169.496	189.281
22	DURABLES	71.287	77.525	82.142	88.927	99.430	112.960
23	TOTAL DURABLES	81.854	88.947	94.100	101.851	113.530	128.351
24	LESS: DURABLES ALLOCATED TO INVESTMENT	2.852	3.177	3.446	3.722	4.154	4.686
25	LESS: SERVICES OF DURABLES TO EXP REL TO WORK	7.716	8.245	8.513	9.202	9.946	10.705
26	SEMIDURABLES	53.116	55.874	58.751	63.195	69.691	75.902
27	INVENTORIES	.312	.330	.334	.345	.375	.418
28	LABOR SERVICES	464.498	500.248	537.081	580.897	638.854	696.517
29	LESS: LABOR SERVICES ALLOC. TO INVEST	121.349	135.635	151.613	169.725	184.044	200.890
30	GROSS DOMESTIC CAPITAL ACCUMULATION	644.699	701.786	902.324	1083.378	1098.566	925.260
31	ORIGINAL COST	639.229	709.948	793.839	889.896	938.428	976.099
32	TANGIBLE	336.515	376.566	421.833	477.645	492.800	490.650

152

TABLE 1. NATIONAL INCOME AND PRODUCT ACCOUNT, BILLIONS OF DOLLARS, 1946-81

		CREDITS					
		1970	1971	1972	1973	1974	1975
33	STRUCTURES AND EQUIPMENT AND HOUSE-HOLD DURABLES AND SEMIDURABLES	336.893	370.154	416.888	464.377	477.252	499.640
34	BUSINESS	99.106	103.196	119.435	143.202	154.115	151.963
35	NONRESIDENTIAL	90.523	92.554	105.400	127.817	142.313	142.280
36	STRUCTURES	29.081	30.033	33.233	40.036	45.820	44.999
37	EQUIPMENT	61.442	62.521	72.167	87.781	96.493	97.281
38	RESIDENTIAL OTHER THAN OWNER-OCCUPIED NONFARM DWELLINGS	8.583	10.642	14.035	15.385	11.802	9.683
39	NONPROFIT INSTITUTIONS	5.270	5.529	6.071	6.132	5.949	5.699
40	STRUCTURES	4.768	5.036	5.463	5.411	5.181	5.027
41	EQUIPMENT	.502	.493	.608	.721	.768	.672
42	GOVERNMENT ENTERPRISES	7.936	8.318	9.091	10.171	12.954	13.894
43	STRUCTURES	7.378	7.647	8.206	9.221	11.847	12.587
44	EQUIPMENT	.558	.671	.885	.950	1.107	1.307
45	GOVERNMENT	42.049	44.919	48.619	50.161	55.015	60.766
46	STRUCTURES	20.823	22.784	23.192	24.895	28.527	28.191
47	EQUIPMENT	14.123	14.500	16.668	16.509	17.012	20.957
48	PRODUCT ACCUMULATED	7.103	7.635	8.759	8.757	9.476	11.618
49	HOUSEHOLDS	163.188	190.045	217.679	238.653	234.294	248.779
50	OWNER-OCC. NONFARM DWELLINGS	26.555	37.408	46.045	48.246	41.965	40.747
51	DURABLES	85.214	97.249	111.108	123.342	121.517	132.197
52	SEMIDURABLES	51.419	55.388	60.526	67.065	70.812	75.835
53	FIXED GPDI RECONCILIATION	10.061	12.635	13.254	13.728	12.476	14.594
54	NIPA FIXED GPDI	140.992	158.768	184.805	211.308	214.505	213.003
55	LESS: CORRESP. SECTOR TOTALS	130.931	146.133	171.551	197.580	202.029	198.409
56	GOVERNMENT CAPITAL ACCUMULATION RECONCILIATION	9.283	5.512	2.739	2.330	2.449	3.945
57	NIPA GOVERNMENT INVESTMENT	52.165	51.114	51.690	53.905	60.942	66.987
58	LESS: GOVERNMENT AND GOVT ENTERPRISE TOTALS	42.882	45.602	48.951	51.575	58.493	63.042
59	CHANGE IN INVENTORIES	-.378	6.412	4.945	13.268	15.548	-8.990
60	BUSINESS	3.219	7.651	10.225	18.479	14.146	-6.914
61	GOVERNMENT	-3.852	-1.335	-5.592	-5.316	1.597	-2.234
62	HOUSEHOLDS	.255	.096	.312	.105	-.195	.158
63	INTANGIBLE	302.714	333.381	372.006	412.251	445.628	485.448
64	RESEARCH AND DEVELOPMENT	26.053	26.689	28.388	30.604	32.865	35.096
65	BUSINESS	10.288	10.654	11.535	13.104	14.667	15.582
66	NONPROFIT INSTITUTIONS	.524	.575	.608	.638	.687	.765
67	GOVERNMENT	15.241	15.460	16.245	16.862	17.511	18.749
68	EDUCATION AND TRAINING	238.328	263.871	295.680	328.513	353.375	383.608
69	HEALTH	38.333	42.822	47.938	53.134	59.388	66.745
70	SUBSIDIES AND GOVERNMENT ENTERPRISE TRANSFERS ALLOCATED TO INVESTMENT	3.731	3.841	4.463	4.572	3.751	4.698

153

		CREDITS					
		1970	1971	1972	1973	1974	1975
71	NET REVALUATIONS	1.740	-12.002	104.022	188.910	156.387	-55.537
72	LAND	-5.597	-9.913	71.217	97.749	32.850	50.384
73	BUSINESS	-6.715	-5.731	36.210	55.949	13.131	40.506
74	NONPROFIT	.021	-1.465	.934	.265	1.371	-3.093
75	GOVERNMENT AND GOVT ENTERPRISES	-1.156	-2.048	14.714	20.196	6.787	10.410
76	HOUSEHOLDS	2.253	-.669	19.359	21.339	11.561	2.561
77	STRUCTURES AND EQUIPMENT	22.699	21.923	41.721	86.727	110.373	-23.714
78	BUSINESS	8.098	3.290	7.032	18.327	82.552	-4.583
79	NONPROFIT INSTITUTIONS	1.419	.367	1.517	3.147	8.103	-7.616
80	GOVERNMENT	16.859	10.570	12.907	33.838	22.865	-6.974
81	HOUSEHOLDS (OWNER-OCC. DWELLINGS)	-3.677	7.696	20.265	31.415	-3.148	-4.540
82	HOUSEHOLD DURABLES AND SEMIDURABLES	-7.860	-20.512	-15.613	-28.252	-10.505	-9.930
83	DURABLES	-6.637	-18.803	-13.595	-23.067	-2.888	-7.013
84	SEMIDURABLES	-1.223	-1.709	-2.018	-5.185	-7.617	-2.917
85	INVENTORIES	-7.502	-3.500	6.697	32.686	23.669	-72.277
86	BUSINESS (INCLUDING NONPROFIT)	-5.973	-2.516	5.906	26.217	19.498	-71.258
87	GOVERNMENT ENTERPRISES	-.498	.213	.596	.883	-.158	-.069
88	GOVERNMENT	-1.025	-1.067	.238	5.363	3.813	-1.112
89	HOUSEHOLDS	-.006	-.130	-.043	.223	.516	.162
90	NET EXPORTS	6.657	4.103	.739	14.210	13.388	26.782
91	EXPORTS	65.670	68.813	77.467	109.593	146.195	154.930
92	IMPORTS	59.013	64.710	76.728	95.383	132.807	128.148
93	GROSS NATIONAL PRODUCT	1650.290	1771.238	2046.789	2336.119	2484.246	2467.418
	ADDENDA:						
94	GNP MINUS NET REVALUTIONS (NR)	1648.551	1783.240	1942.767	2147.209	2327.860	2522.954
95	NNP MINUS NR	1296.862	1399.903	1527.327	1693.657	1810.602	1935.361
96	NNI MINUS NR	1240.588	1331.527	1456.720	1617.095	1724.335	1849.373
97	GDCA MINUS NR	642.960	713.788	798.302	894.468	942.179	980.796
98	NDCA MINUS NR	291.271	330.451	382.862	440.916	424.921	393.203
99	NDCA	293.011	318.449	486.884	629.826	581.308	337.667
100	NDCA AT ORIGINAL COST	287.540	326.611	378.399	436.344	421.170	388.505
101	NDCA, TANGIBLE, AT ORIGINAL COST	102.695	122.878	148.607	180.282	153.985	104.512
102	NDCA, INTANGIBLE, AT ORIGINAL COST	184.845	203.732	229.792	256.062	267.185	283.993
103	GDCA - NR / GNP - NR, PERCENT	39.002	40.028	41.091	41.657	40.474	38.875
104	NDCA - NR / NNP - NR, PERCENT	22.460	23.605	25.067	26.033	23.469	20.317
105	NDCA, TAN, O.C. / NNP - NR, PERCENT	7.919	8.778	9.730	10.645	8.505	5.400
106	NDCA, INTAN, O.C. / NNP - NR, PERCENT	14.253	14.553	15.045	15.119	14.757	14.674
107	GROSS BUSINESS PRODUCT	733.170	794.988	937.507	1104.096	1196.318	1118.522
108	GROSS NONPROFIT PRODUCT	43.583	45.616	53.808	59.494	70.623	57.729
109	GROSS GOVT ENTERPRISE PRODUCT	17.583	19.617	21.922	24.187	25.853	28.716
110	GROSS GOVERNMENT PRODUCT	217.267	225.712	259.493	307.115	290.679	290.042
111	GROSS HOUSEHOLD PRODUCT	631.378	676.144	763.166	825.219	880.999	955.101
112	GROSS DOMESTIC PRODUCT	1642.981	1762.077	2035.896	2320.110	2464.472	2450.110
113	GROSS PRODUCT, REST OF WORLD	7.309	9.163	10.901	16.010	19.779	17.314

TABLE 1. NATIONAL INCOME AND PRODUCT ACCOUNT, BILLIONS OF DOLLARS, 1946-81

		CREDITS					
		1970	1971	1972	1973	1974	1975
114	BEA GNP	992.734	1077.619	1185.923	1326.396	1434.220	1549.212
115	BEA NNP	904.675	981.108	1079.506	1209.927	1298.230	1389.912
116	BEA NI	810.717	871.515	963.649	1086.172	1160.743	1239.362
117	BEA GPDI	144.211	166.419	195.030	229.787	228.651	206.089
118	BEA NPDI	56.152	69.908	88.613	113.318	92.661	46.789
119	BEA PCE	621.721	672.242	737.054	811.964	888.111	976.449
120	BEA GPDI / BEA GNP, PERCENT	14.527	15.443	16.445	17.324	15.943	13.303
121	BEA NPDI / BEA NNP, PERCENT	6.207	7.125	8.209	9.366	7.137	3.366
122	TISA GNP / BEA GNP, PERCENT	166.237	164.366	172.590	176.125	173.212	159.269
123	TISA NNP / BEA NNP, PERCENT	143.543	141.463	151.120	155.593	151.513	135.248
124	TISA NNI / BEA NI, PERCENT	153.238	151.406	161.962	166.272	162.027	144.739
125	TISA GNP - NR / BEA GNP, PERCENT	166.062	165.480	163.819	161.883	162.308	162.854
126	TISA NNP - NR / BEA NNP, PERCENT	143.351	142.686	141.484	139.980	139.467	139.243
127	TISA GDCA - NR / BEA GPDI, PERCENT	445.847	428.910	409.323	389.260	412.060	475.909
128	TISA NDCA - NR / BEA NPDI, PERCENT	518.719	472.695	432.061	389.096	458.576	840.375
129	TISA NDCA, TAN, OC / BEA NPDI,PERCENT	182.887	175.771	167.703	159.094	166.181	223.369
130	TISA CONSUMPTION / BEA PCE, PERCENT	160.672	158.477	155.175	152.535	154.518	155.193
131	GNP	1650.290	1771.238	2046.789	2336.119	2484.246	2467.418
132	CAPITAL CONSUMPTION ALLOWANCES (CCA)	351.689	383.337	415.440	453.552	517.258	587.593
133	CCA, TANGIBLE	233.820	253.688	273.226	297.363	338.815	386.138
134	CCA, INTANGIBLE	117.869	129.649	142.214	156.189	178.443	201.455
135	NNP	1298.602	1387.901	1631.349	1882.567	1966.988	1879.825
136	BUS TRANS PAY + UNCOMP FACTOR SERVICES + NET INDIR TAXES + STAT DISCREPANCY	56.274	68.376	70.606	76.562	86.266	85.988
137	NNI	1242.328	1319.525	1560.743	1806.005	1880.722	1793.837
138	GNP LESS SUM OF SECTOR & RW	.000	-.002	-.008	-.001	-.004	-.006

		1976	1977	1978	1979	1980	1981
1	CONSUMPTION	1693.045	1859.704	2054.917	2299.307	2580.708	2856.000
2	HOUSEHOLD EXPENDITURES FOR SERVICES AND NONDURABLES	605.280	666.862	739.540	835.539	939.355	1044.195
3	GROSS EXPENDITURES INCLUDED FROM BEA PERSONAL CONSUMPTION EXPENDITURES	626.464	691.543	767.030	868.818	979.858	1088.105
4	LESS: PCE EXPENSES RELATED TO WORK	21.184	24.681	27.490	33.279	40.503	43.910
5	EXPENSE ACCOUNT ITEMS OF CONSUMPTION	13.879	15.566	17.768	20.262	22.358	24.560
6	BEA IMPUTATIONS OTHER THAN HOUSING	26.649	29.792	37.147	43.622	45.897	44.465
7	SUBSIDIES ALLOCATED TO CONSUMPTION	3.397	4.516	5.554	5.630	6.496	7.297
8	SUBSIDIES INCLUDED IN BUSINESS INCOME	5.628	7.587	9.416	9.437	10.586	11.977
9	LESS: AMT. ALLOCATED TO INVESTMENT	2.231	3.071	3.862	3.807	4.090	4.680
10	TRANSFERS	161.083	177.951	198.881	220.850	251.340	280.070
11	FROM BUSINESS	7.971	9.058	10.617	11.879	13.232	14.822
12	MEDIA SUPPORT	6.667	7.574	8.907	9.973	11.132	12.462
13	TOTAL MEDIA SUPPORT	8.490	9.656	11.277	12.680	14.141	15.832
14	LESS: MEDIA SUPPORT ALLOCATED TO INVESTMENT	1.823	2.082	2.370	2.707	3.009	3.370
15	HEALTH AND SAFETY	1.304	1.484	1.710	1.906	2.100	2.360
16	FROM NONPROFIT INSTITUTIONS	47.942	52.714	58.151	63.711	71.682	81.031
17	FROM GOVERNMENT ENTERPRISES	2.951	3.432	3.575	4.036	5.581	6.017
18	FROM GOVERNMENT	102.220	112.747	126.539	141.225	160.845	178.200

155

TABLE 1. NATIONAL INCOME AND PRODUCT ACCOUNT, BILLIONS OF DOLLARS, 1946-81

		CREDITS					
		1976	1977	1978	1979	1980	1981
19	NONMARKET SERVICES PRODUCED IN HOUSEHOLDS	882.756	965.016	1056.027	1173.404	1315.262	1455.413
20	NET SPACE RENT OF OWNER-OCCUPIED NONFARM DWELLINGS	94.890	105.853	119.660	135.528	155.324	178.872
21	OTHER CAPITAL SERVICES	204.831	221.225	243.432	271.429	304.924	332.285
22	DURABLES	123.863	134.707	149.296	168.170	191.873	209.489
23	TOTAL DURABLES	140.836	153.458	170.418	191.835	217.920	237.001
24	LESS: DURABLES ALLOCATED TO INVESTMENT	5.136	5.571	6.243	7.013	7.952	8.904
25	LESS: SERVICES OF DURABLES TO EXP REL TO WORK	11.837	13.180	14.879	16.652	18.095	18.608
26	SEMIDURABLES	80.527	86.065	93.658	102.699	112.371	122.006
27	INVENTORIES	.441	.453	.478	.560	.680	.789
28	LABOR SERVICES	800.987	871.300	942.697	1036.304	1149.746	1265.046
29	LESS: LABOR SERVICES ALLOC. TO INVEST	217.952	233.362	249.762	269.857	294.732	320.790
30	GROSS DOMESTIC CAPITAL ACCUMULATION	1360.395	1502.243	1722.938	1792.217	1634.012	1677.886
31	ORIGINAL COST	1107.792	1259.234	1422.505	1548.487	1617.084	1823.009
32	TANGIBLE	576.156	678.716	787.121	851.533	854.134	972.821
33	STRUCTURES AND EQUIPMENT AND HOUSE-HOLD DURABLES AND SEMIDURABLES	563.165	651.875	756.236	837.647	862.213	953.811
34	BUSINESS	167.485	202.399	248.430	287.628	307.576	344.467
35	NONRESIDENTIAL	156.580	187.769	230.866	266.991	287.011	322.871
36	STRUCTURES	46.341	52.724	65.498	80.354	94.808	113.358
37	EQUIPMENT	110.239	135.045	165.368	186.637	192.203	209.513
38	RESIDENTIAL OTHER THAN OWNER-OCCUPIED NONFARM DWELLINGS	10.905	14.630	17.564	20.637	20.565	21.596
39	NONPROFIT INSTITUTIONS	6.195	6.439	7.333	8.252	9.173	10.331
40	STRUCTURES	5.369	5.437	6.004	6.784	7.719	8.632
41	EQUIPMENT	.826	1.002	1.329	1.468	1.454	1.699
42	GOVERNMENT ENTERPRISES	13.875	14.722	19.519	19.803	22.275	22.346
43	STRUCTURES	12.540	13.311	17.866	18.212	20.581	20.141
44	EQUIPMENT	1.335	1.411	1.653	1.591	1.694	2.205
45	GOVERNMENT	61.252	63.417	76.688	87.925	95.018	102.663
46	STRUCTURES	26.060	25.060	28.569	30.575	34.571	32.641
47	EQUIPMENT	23.247	24.389	30.987	38.488	41.351	43.359
48	PRODUCT ACCUMULATED	11.945	13.968	17.132	18.862	19.096	26.663
49	HOUSEHOLDS	293.740	341.046	383.759	406.810	410.557	444.311
50	OWNER-OCC. NONFARM DWELLINGS	54.822	72.766	83.022	86.038	81.820	82.543
51	DURABLES	156.831	178.215	200.214	213.441	214.731	236.142
52	SEMIDURABLES	82.087	90.065	100.523	107.331	114.006	125.626

156

TABLE 1. NATIONAL INCOME AND PRODUCT ACCOUNT, BILLIONS OF DOLLARS, 1946-81

				CREDITS			
		1976	1977	1978	1979	1980	1981
53	FIXED GPDI RECONCILIATION	17.542	19.445	21.352	26.851	13.093	19.123
54	NIPA FIXED GPDI	246.044	301.049	360.137	408.769	411.662	456.464
55	LESS: CORRESP. SECTOR TOTALS	228.502	281.604	338.785	381.918	398.569	437.341
56	GOVERNMENT CAPITAL ACCUMULATION RECONCILIATION	3.076	4.407	-.845	.378	4.521	10.570
57	NIPA GOVERNMENT INVESTMENT	66.258	68.578	78.230	89.244	102.718	108.916
58	LESS: GOVERNMENT AND GOVT ENTERPRISE TOTALS	63.182	64.171	79.075	88.866	98.197	98.346
59	CHANGE IN INVENTORIES	12.991	26.841	30.885	13.886	-8.079	19.010
60	BUSINESS	11.823	23.007	26.455	14.261	-9.789	18.452
61	GOVERNMENT	.549	3.398	4.138	-.768	1.594	.411
62	HOUSEHOLDS	.619	.436	.292	.393	.116	.147
63	INTANGIBLE	531.636	580.518	635.384	696.954	762.950	850.188
64	RESEARCH AND DEVELOPMENT	38.839	42.539	47.651	54.325	61.412	68.483
65	BUSINESS	17.436	19.407	22.156	25.655	29.940	33.850
66	NONPROFIT INSTITUTIONS	.880	.977	1.117	1.237	1.365	1.491
67	GOVERNMENT	20.524	22.155	24.378	27.433	30.108	33.142
68	EDUCATION AND TRAINING	418.442	453.623	493.883	536.529	580.309	640.129
69	HEALTH	74.355	84.356	93.850	106.100	121.229	141.576
70	SUBSIDIES AND GOVERNMENT ENTERPRISE TRANSFERS ALLOCATED TO INVESTMENT	4.169	5.404	6.347	6.537	7.604	8.539
71	NET REVALUATIONS	248.434	237.605	294.086	237.193	9.325	-153.661
72	LAND	137.454	90.756	158.674	110.742	69.166	-142.350
73	BUSINESS	78.322	48.643	76.182	72.308	17.144	-94.096
74	NONPROFIT	-.014	.523	1.139	.457	-1.274	-1.196
75	GOVERNMENT AND GOVT ENTERPRISES	28.399	18.750	32.784	22.880	14.290	-29.411
76	HOUSEHOLDS	30.747	22.840	48.569	15.097	39.006	-17.647
77	STRUCTURES AND EQUIPMENT	63.959	166.696	155.971	104.367	-42.725	51.238
78	BUSINESS	19.052	58.673	40.544	35.797	-15.583	17.747
79	NONPROFIT INSTITUTIONS	-2.288	4.861	3.948	5.276	-1.274	-4.245
80	GOVERNMENT	-4.295	33.314	18.139	59.056	14.906	51.414
81	HOUSEHOLDS (OWNER-OCC. DWELLINGS)	51.489	69.848	93.339	4.239	-41.052	-13.679
82	HOUSEHOLD DURABLES AND SEMIDURABLES	-11.287	-17.870	-29.292	-27.465	-27.811	-34.893
83	DURABLES	-8.387	-13.043	-20.262	-17.670	-15.157	-25.526
84	SEMIDURABLES	-2.900	-4.827	-9.030	-9.795	-12.654	-9.367
85	INVENTORIES	58.308	-1.977	8.733	49.549	10.695	-27.656
86	BUSINESS (INCLUDING NONPROFIT)	61.090	-2.325	7.038	37.306	9.708	-30.616
87	GOVERNMENT ENTERPRISES	-.264	.033	.837	-.201	-.069	.038
88	GOVERNMENT	-2.342	.487	.992	11.760	.648	2.738
89	HOUSEHOLDS	-.176	-.172	-.134	.684	.408	.184
90	NET EXPORTS	13.780	-3.986	-1.116	13.213	23.949	26.262
91	EXPORTS	170.876	182.744	218.718	281.358	338.771	368.753
92	IMPORTS	157.096	186.730	219.834	268.145	314.822	342.491
93	GROSS NATIONAL PRODUCT	3067.220	3357.961	3776.739	4104.736	4238.669	4560.148

TABLE 1. NATIONAL INCOME AND PRODUCT ACCOUNT, BILLIONS OF DOLLARS, 1946-81

		CREDITS					
		1976	1977	1978	1979	1980	1981
	ADDENDA:						
94	GNP MINUS NET REVALUATIONS (NR)	2818.786	3120.357	3482.653	3867.543	4229.344	4713.809
95	NNP MINUS NR	2176.710	2410.189	2686.970	2966.978	3207.571	3578.345
96	NNI MINUS NR	2082.615	2311.713	2581.266	2854.870	3079.302	3433.160
97	GDCA MINUS NR	1111.962	1264.639	1428.852	1555.024	1624.687	1831.548
98	NDCA MINUS NR	469.886	554.471	633.168	654.459	602.914	696.084
99	NDCA	718.319	792.075	927.254	891.652	612.239	542.422
100	NDCA AT ORIGINAL COST	465.716	549.066	626.821	647.922	595.310	687.545
101	NDCA, TANGIBLE, AT ORIGINAL COST	155.406	215.867	267.564	263.162	188.696	239.690
102	NDCA, INTANGIBLE, AT ORIGINAL COST	310.310	333.199	359.257	384.760	406.614	447.855
103	GDCA - NR / GNP - NR, PERCENT	39.448	40.529	41.028	40.207	38.415	38.855
104	NDCA - NR / NNP - NR, PERCENT	21.587	23.005	23.564	22.058	18.797	19.453
105	NDCA, TAN, O.C. / NNP - NR, PERCENT	7.140	8.956	9.958	8.870	5.883	6.698
106	NDCA, INTAN, O.C. / NNP - NR, PERCENT	14.256	13.825	13.370	12.968	12.677	12.516
107	GROSS BUSINESS PRODUCT	1452.381	1564.398	1785.949	1999.608	2005.293	2134.510
108	GROSS NONPROFIT PRODUCT	70.779	83.999	91.892	100.996	103.666	113.305
109	GROSS GOVT ENTERPRISE PRODUCT	30.788	33.175	37.738	40.371	44.837	49.788
110	GROSS GOVERNMENT PRODUCT	326.387	385.092	416.502	486.307	459.414	504.257
111	GROSS HOUSEHOLD PRODUCT	1166.412	1267.833	1415.054	1434.882	1580.150	1708.703
112	GROSS DOMESTIC PRODUCT	3046.745	3334.498	3747.136	4062.164	4193.359	4510.563
113	GROSS PRODUCT, REST OF WORLD	20.480	23.464	29.603	42.572	45.310	49.586
114	BEA GNP	1718.018	1918.324	2163.863	2417.759	2631.688	2954.069
115	BEA NNP	1543.000	1723.152	1941.387	2161.717	2338.528	2624.558
116	BEA NI	1379.233	1550.510	1760.277	1966.710	2116.644	2373.026
117	BEA GPDI	257.867	324.056	386.592	423.030	401.873	474.916
118	BEA NPDI	82.849	128.884	164.116	166.988	108.713	145.405
119	BEA PCE	1084.271	1204.440	1346.474	1507.165	1668.059	1857.180
120	BEA GPDI / BEA GNP, PERCENT	15.010	16.893	17.866	17.497	15.271	16.077
121	BEA NPDI / BEA NNP, PERCENT	5.369	7.480	8.454	7.725	4.649	5.540
122	TISA GNP / BEA GNP, PERCENT	178.532	175.047	174.537	169.774	161.063	154.368
123	TISA NNP / BEA NNP, PERCENT	157.171	153.660	153.553	148.223	137.561	130.486
124	TISA NNI / BEA NI, PERCENT	169.010	164.418	163.347	157.220	145.921	138.199
125	TISA GNP - NR / BEA GNP, PERCENT	164.072	162.661	160.946	159.964	160.708	159.570
126	TISA NNP - NR / BEA NNP, PERCENT	141.070	139.871	138.405	137.251	136.341	136.341
127	TISA GDCA - NR / BEA GPDI, PERCENT	431.215	390.253	369.602	367.592	404.279	385.657
128	TISA NDCA - NR / BEA NPDI, PERCENT	567.159	430.209	385.805	391.920	554.592	478.720
129	TISA NDCA, TAN, OC / BEA NPDI, PERCENT	187.578	167.490	163.034	157.593	173.573	164.843
130	TISA CONSUMPTION / BEA PCE, PERCENT	156.146	154.404	152.615	152.558	154.713	153.782
131	GNP	3067.220	3357.961	3776.739	4104.736	4238.669	4560.148
132	CAPITAL CONSUMPTION ALLOWANCES (CCA)	642.076	710.168	795.684	900.565	1021.773	1135.464
133	CCA, TANGIBLE	420.750	462.849	519.557	588.371	665.437	733.131
134	CCA, INTANGIBLE	221.326	247.319	276.127	312.194	356.336	402.333
135	NNP	2425.144	2647.793	2981.055	3204.171	3216.896	3424.684
136	BUS TRANS PAY + UNCOMP FACTOR SERVICES + NET INDIR TAXES + STAT DISCREPANCY	94.096	98.475	105.704	112.108	128.269	145.185
137	NNI	2331.048	2549.318	2875.351	3092.064	3088.627	3279.499
138	GNP LESS SUM OF SECTOR & RW	-.005	.000	.000	.000	.000	-.001

158

		CREDITS PERCENT PER ANNUM RATES OF GROWTH CURRENT DOLLARS					
		1946-56	1956-66	1966-71	1971-76	1976-81	1946-81
1	CONSUMPTION	5.670	5.422	7.502	9.707	11.024	7.182
2	HOUSEHOLD EXPENDITURES FOR SERVICES AND NONDURABLES	5.947	5.395	7.196	9.847	11.523	7.298
3	GROSS EXPENDITURES INCLUDED FROM BEA PERSONAL CONSUMPTION EXPENDITURES	5.996	5.440	7.254	9.868	11.675	7.357
4	LESS: PCE EXPENSES RELATED TO WORK	8.014	6.991	9.047	10.463	15.694	9.280
5	EXPENSE ACCOUNT ITEMS OF CONSUMPTION	7.828	4.629	7.115	9.317	12.091	7.607
6	BEA IMPUTATIONS OTHER THAN HOUSING	-.135	4.518	12.410	14.857	10.782	6.542
7	SUBSIDIES ALLOCATED TO CONSUMPTION	-6.424	16.515	3.316	3.450	16.524	5.765
8	SUBSIDIES INCLUDED IN BUSINESS INCOME	-5.405	17.025	3.497	3.286	16.305	6.200
9	LESS: AMT. ALLOCATED TO INVESTMENT	-3.323	17.854	3.770	3.038	15.969	7.037
10	TRANSFERS	2.199	6.859	7.571	9.025	11.697	6.582
11	FROM BUSINESS	11.572	8.169	5.381	10.949	13.210	9.831
12	MEDIA SUPPORT	12.530	8.595	4.836	11.573	13.326	10.247
13	TOTAL MEDIA SUPPORT	11.351	7.965	4.727	11.041	13.273	9.634
14	LESS: MEDIA SUPPORT ALLOCATED TO INVESTMENT	8.835	6.178	4.373	9.219	13.076	8.067
15	HEALTH AND SAFETY	8.410	6.262	7.975	8.052	12.606	8.265
16	FROM NONPROFIT INSTITUTIONS	6.857	6.737	9.660	9.807	11.068	8.233
17	FROM GOVERNMENT ENTERPRISES	4.337	2.203	5.866	.594	15.312	4.885
18	FROM GOVERNMENT	.346	7.087	6.939	8.837	11.757	5.983
19	NONMARKET SERVICES PRODUCED IN HOUSEHOLDS	6.371	5.183	7.627	9.638	10.517	7.252
20	NET SPACE RENT OF OWNER-OCCUPIED NONFARM DWELLINGS	12.950	7.828	7.887	10.008	13.518	10.397
21	OTHER CAPITAL SERVICES	7.045	4.626	8.233	8.902	10.160	7.217
22	DURABLES	11.503	5.133	9.051	9.825	11.082	9.002
23	TOTAL DURABLES	12.002	4.864	8.938	9.627	10.970	9.001
24	LESS: DURABLES ALLOCATED TO INVESTMENT	9.670	6.017	10.431	10.083	11.632	9.055
25	LESS: SERVICES OF DURABLES TO EXP REL TO WORK	17.202	2.510	7.396	7.500	9.469	8.968
26	SEMIDURABLES	3.630	4.004	7.185	7.584	8.665	5.510
27	INVENTORIES	7.452	7.100	3.677	5.987	12.325	7.272
28	LABOR SERVICES	5.882	5.668	8.748	9.872	9.571	7.312
29	LESS: LABOR SERVICES ALLOC. TO INVEST	7.434	8.331	13.075	9.951	8.037	8.926
30	GROSS DOMESTIC CAPITAL ACCUMULATION	24.727	5.798	7.087	14.154	4.284	12.066
31	ORIGINAL COST	9.209	6.622	7.992	9.307	10.476	8.483
32	TANGIBLE	10.399	5.293	5.907	8.878	11.045	8.147

		CREDITS PERCENT PER ANNUM RATES OF GROWTH CURRENT DOLLARS					
		1946-56	1956-66	1966-71	1971-76	1976-81	1946-81
33	STRUCTURES AND EQUIPMENT AND HOUSE-HOLD DURABLES AND SEMIDURABLES	9.390	5.252	6.366	8.755	11.113	7.910
34	BUSINESS	8.036	6.332	5.857	10.170	15.514	8.567
35	NONRESIDENTIAL	7.915	6.317	5.306	11.088	15.574	8.583
36	STRUCTURES	8.357	4.415	6.496	9.062	19.591	8.569
37	EQUIPMENT	7.667	7.295	4.762	12.011	13.704	8.591
38	RESIDENTIAL OTHER THAN OWNER-OCCUPIED NONFARM DWELLINGS	9.586	6.509	11.533	.489	14.644	8.327
39	NONPROFIT INSTITUTIONS	17.457	8.246	2.122	2.301	10.770	9.359
40	STRUCTURES	17.538	8.219	2.473	1.289	9.962	9.158
41	EQUIPMENT	16.773	8.473	-1.099	10.873	15.516	10.662
42	GOVERNMENT ENTERPRISES	18.515	4.823	8.355	10.775	10.000	10.704
43	STRUCTURES	18.525	4.740	8.023	10.398	9.940	10.571
44	EQUIPMENT	18.358	6.083	12.643	14.750	10.557	12.302
45	GOVERNMENT	13.089	5.284	3.222	6.399	10.881	8.113
46	STRUCTURES	18.182	7.145	3.696	2.723	4.606	8.644
47	EQUIPMENT	16.113	2.119	2.047	9.901	13.277	8.640
48	PRODUCT ACCUMULATED	.896	8.511	4.161	9.364	17.420	6.976
49	HOUSEHOLDS	7.176	4.567	8.014	9.099	8.629	7.019
50	OWNER-OCC. NONFARM DWELLINGS	12.230	1.314	12.613	7.944	8.529	7.926
51	DURABLES	9.171	6.021	7.422	10.030	8.530	8.042
52	SEMIDURABLES	2.987	4.290	6.399	8.186	8.883	5.408
53	FIXED GPDI RECONCILIATION	N.A.	7.770	8.770	6.783	1.741	N.A.
54	NIPA FIXED GPDI	10.575	5.338	7.311	9.157	13.156	8.745
55	LESS: CORRESP. SECTOR TOTALS	9.332	5.167	7.190	9.352	13.864	8.451
56	GOVERNMENT CAPITAL ACCUMULATION RECONCILIATION	N.A.	3.243	-6.696	-11.011	28.002	N.A.
57	NIPA GOVERNMENT INVESTMENT	22.069	4.494	2.368	5.327	10.451	9.910
58	LESS: GOVERNMENT AND GOVT ENTERPRISE TOTALS	17.246	4.775	3.893	6.739	9.253	9.002
59	CHANGE IN INVENTORIES	N.A.	6.381	-9.827	15.167	7.912	N.A.
60	BUSINESS	-3.019	11.638	-11.530	9.094	9.311	3.081
61	GOVERNMENT	N.A.	N.A.	N.A.	N.A.	-5.626	N.A.
62	HOUSEHOLDS	-.296	6.933	-18.067	45.172	-24.989	.201
63	INTANGIBLE	7.219	8.869	10.679	9.783	9.845	8.919
64	RESEARCH AND DEVELOPMENT	17.998	10.033	4.109	7.792	12.012.	11.324
65	BUSINESS	15.889	8.214	8.104	10.354	14.188	11.499
66	NONPROFIT INSTITUTIONS	10.487	12.969	7.885	8.856	11.130	10.669
67	GOVERNMENT	19.951	11.024	1.697	5.830	10.059	11.187
68	EDUCATION AND TRAINING	6.347	8.853	11.393	9.660	8.875	8.606
69	HEALTH	7.627	8.049	11.314	11.668	13.746	9.702
70	SUBSIDIES AND GOVERNMENT ENTERPRISE TRANSFERS ALLOCATED TO INVESTMENT	3.790	8.571	5.003	1.656	15.414	6.601

TABLE 1. NATIONAL INCOME AND PRODUCT ACCOUNT, BILLIONS OF DOLLARS, 1946-81

		CREDITS PERCENT PER ANNUM RATES OF GROWTH CURRENT DOLLARS					
		1946-56	1956-66	1966-71	1971-76	1976-81	1946-81
71	NET REVALUATIONS	N.A.	-8.066	N.A.	N.A.	N.A.	N.A.
72	LAND	N.A.	-2.731	N.A.	N.A.	N.A.	N.A.
73	BUSINESS	N.A.	-7.322	N.A.	N.A.	N.A.	N.A.
74	NONPROFIT	N.A.	-4.592	N.A.	N.A.	N.A.	N.A.
75	GOVERNMENT AND GOVT ENTERPRISES	N.A.	3.779	N.A.	N.A.	N.A.	N.A.
76	HOUSEHOLDS	N.A.	-1.125	N.A.	N.A.	N.A.	N.A.
77	STRUCTURES AND EQUIPMENT	N.A.	-2.168	23.563	23.879	-4.338	N.A.
78	BUSINESS	N.A.	-6.884	2.603	42.083	-1.409	N.A.
79	NONPROFIT INSTITUTIONS	12.361	2.239	-5.924	N.A.	N.A.	N.A.
80	GOVERNMENT	N.A.	-35.360	155.017	N.A.	N.A.	N.A.
81	HOUSEHOLDS (OWNER-OCC. DWELLINGS)	N.A.	N.A.	13.300	46.248	N.A.	N.A.
82	HOUSEHOLD DURABLES AND SEMIDURABLES	N.A.	N.A.	N.A.	N.A.	N.A.	N.A.
83	DURABLES	N.A.	N.A.	N.A.	N.A.	N.A.	N.A.
84	SEMIDURABLES	N.A.	N.A.	N.A.	N.A.	N.A.	N.A.
85	INVENTORIES	N.A.	N.A.	N.A.	N.A.	N.A.	N.A.
86	BUSINESS (INCLUDING NONPROFIT)	N.A.	N.A.	N.A.	N.A.	N.A.	N.A.
87	GOVERNMENT ENTERPRISES	-3.469	N.A.	N.A.	N.A.	N.A.	-5.537
88	GOVERNMENT	N.A.	N.A.	N.A.	N.A.	N.A.	N.A.
89	HOUSEHOLDS	N.A.	N.A.	N.A.	N.A.	N.A.	N.A.
90	NET EXPORTS	-3.877	2.120	-8.819	27.418	13.767	3.515
91	EXPORTS	5.176	5.935	9.080	19.951	16.630	9.557
92	IMPORTS	10.505	6.773	11.205	19.409	16.868	11.633
93	GROSS NATIONAL PRODUCT	9.579	5.550	7.274	11.608	8.255	8.179
	ADDENDA:						
94	GNP MINUS NET REVALUTIONS (NR)	6.671	5.859	7.626	9.590	10.831	7.572
95	NNP MINUS NR	7.258	6.065	7.135	9.230	10.453	7.627
96	NNI MINUS NR	6.416	5.957	6.879	9.358	10.514	7.344
97	GDCA MINUS NR	9.172	6.633	7.975	9.271	10.496	8.470
98	NDCA MINUS NR	23.321	8.505	6.313	7.294	8.177	11.991
99	NDCA	N.A.	6.554	4.521	17.667	-5.463	N.A.
100	NDCA AT ORIGINAL COST	24.051	8.504	6.329	7.354	8.103	12.180
101	NDCA, TANGIBLE, AT ORIGINAL COST	N.A.	7.214	.808	4.809	9.053	N.A.
102	NDCA, INTANGIBLE, AT ORIGINAL COST	7.304	9.933	10.750	8.780	7.614	8.795
103	GDCA - NR / GNP - NR, PERCENT	2.345	.731	.324	-.291	-.303	.835
104	NDCA - NR / NNP - NR, PERCENT	14.975	2.300	-.767	-1.772	-2.061	4.054
105	NDCA, TAN, O.C. / NNP - NR, PERCENT	N.A.	1.083	-5.906	-4.047	-1.268	N.A.
106	NDCA, INTAN, O.C. / NNP - NR, PERCENT	.043	3.647	3.374	-.412	-2.570	1.085
107	GROSS BUSINESS PRODUCT	11.329	5.354	6.337	12.809	8.005	8.607
108	GROSS NONPROFIT PRODUCT	10.228	7.922	9.015	9.183	9.868	9.191
109	GROSS GOVT ENTERPRISE PRODUCT	6.610	6.543	9.916	9.434	10.091	7.952
110	GROSS GOVERNMENT PRODUCT	7.791	5.714	7.996	7.655	9.090	7.387
111	GROSS HOUSEHOLD PRODUCT	8.241	5.582	7.962	11.523	7.935	7.851
112	GROSS DOMESTIC PRODUCT	9.561	5.548	7.260	11.574	8.163	8.154
113	GROSS PRODUCT, REST OF WORLD	14.762	5.929	10.169	17.451	19.345	12.510

161

TABLE 1. NATIONAL INCOME AND PRODUCT ACCOUNT, BILLIONS OF DOLLARS, 1946-81

		CREDITS PERCENT PER ANNUM RATES OF GROWTH CURRENT DOLLARS					
		1946-56	1956-66	1966-71	1971-76	1976-81	1946-8
114	BEA GNP	7.229	6.011	7.347	9.777	11.450	7.849
115	BEA NNP	6.938	6.146	7.129	9.479	11.209	7.697
116	BEA NI	6.943	6.040	6.771	9.616	11.464	7.671
117	BEA GPDI	8.766	5.874	5.775	9.154	12.991	8.145
118	BEA NPDI	6.863	7.249	1.460	3.455	11.907	6.391
119	BEA PCE	6.344	5.747	7.645	10.033	11.364	7.583
120	BEA GPDI / BEA GNP, PERCENT	1.434	-.129	-1.465	-.568	1.383	.274
121	BEA NPDI / BEA NNP, PERCENT	-.070	1.040	-5.292	-5.502	.628	-1.213
122	TISA GNP / BEA GNP, PERCENT	2.192	-.435	-.069	1.667	-2.867	.306
123	TISA NNP / BEA NNP, PERCENT	4.097	-.447	-.405	2.128	-3.653	.733
124	TISA NNI / BEA NI, PERCENT	3.095	-.457	-.329	2.224	-3.945	.433
125	TISA GNP - NR / BEA GNP, PERCENT	-.520	-.143	.260	-.171	-.555	-.256
126	TISA NNP - NR / BEA NNP, PERCENT	.300	-.076	.006	-.228	-.680	-.065
127	TISA GDCA - NR / BEA GPDI, PERCENT	.373	.717	2.080	.107	-2.208	.301
128	TISA NDCA - NR / BEA NPDI, PERCENT	15.401	1.171	4.784	3.711	-3.334	5.263
129	TISA NDCA, TAN, OC / BEA NPDI,PERCENT	N.A.	-.033	-.642	1.309	-2.551	N.A.
130	TISA CONSUMPTION / BEA PCE, PERCENT	-.633	-.307	-.132	-.296	-.305	-.373
131	GNP	9.579	5.550	7.274	11.608	8.255	8.179
132	CAPITAL CONSUMPTION ALLOWANCES (CCA)	4.758	5.063	9.541	10.867	12.077	7.405
133	CCA, TANGIBLE	4.056	4.119	9.038	10.648	11.746	6.777
134	CCA, INTANGIBLE	7.114	7.410	10.568	11.289	12.697	9.064
135	NNP	11.318	5.671	6.695	11.809	7.146	8.487
136	BUS TRANS PAY + UNCOMP FACTOR SERVICES + NET INDIR TAXES + STAT DISCREPANCY	N.A.	9.354	13.024	6.594	9.061	N.A.
137	NNI	10.253	5.555	6.420	12.054	7.066	8.138
138	GNP LESS SUM OF SECTOR & RW	-13.771	N.A.	N.A.	N.A.	N.A.	N.A.

162

TABLE 2. BUSINESS INCOME AND PRODUCT, BILLIONS OF DOLLARS, 1946-81

		DEBITS					
		1946	1947	1948	1949	1950	1951
1	LABOR INCOME	129.984	142.943	157.714	149.374	164.055	189.550
2	COMPENSATION OF EMPLOYEES	90.911	105.285	116.008	113.332	124.755	143.691
3	ADDITIONAL IMPUTATIONS	41.236	40.244	44.628	39.189	42.728	49.709
4	EMPLOYEE TRAINING	4.022	4.292	4.389	3.223	4.243	5.822
5	EXPENSE ACCOUNT ITEMS OF CONSUMPTION	1.887	2.181	2.407	2.371	2.558	2.874
6	LABOR INCOME OF SELF-EMPLOYED	35.327	33.771	37.832	33.595	35.927	41.013
7	LESS: EXPENSES RELATED TO WORK	2.163	2.586	2.922	3.147	3.428	3.850
8	CAPITAL INCOME AND SURPLUS	21.957	28.699	36.683	34.047	41.367	45.495
9	INTEREST PAID	.605	.936	.760	.797	.891	1.004
10	CORPORATE PROFITS	15.890	21.293	28.161	26.020	32.679	36.921
11	PROPRIETORS' CAPITAL INCOME	1.357	2.127	3.032	2.781	2.776	2.216
12	PROPRIETORS' INCOME	36.684	35.898	40.864	36.376	38.703	43.229
13	LESS: LABOR INCOME OF SELF-EMPLOY.	35.327	33.771	37.832	33.595	35.927	41.013
14	OPPORTUNITY COST OF SELF-EMPLOY.	43.138	44.298	44.991	45.705	45.601	47.322
15	LESS: UNDERREMUNERATION OF LABOR	7.811	10.527	7.159	12.110	9.674	6.309
16	NET RENTAL INCOME OF PERSONS	3.713	3.816	4.179	4.097	4.530	4.770
17	TOTAL RENTAL INCOME	5.467	5.252	5.701	6.116	7.071	7.710
18	LESS: OWNER-OCCUPIED NONFARM RENTAL INCOME	1.754	1.436	1.522	2.019	2.541	2.940
19	NET BUSINESS INVESTMENT IN RESEARCH AND DEVELOPMENT	.392	.527	.551	.352	.491	.584
20	GROSS INVESTMENT	.750	.950	1.030	.870	1.070	1.240
21	LESS: CAPITAL CONSUMPTION ALLOWANCE	.358	.423	.479	.518	.579	.656
22	NET REVALUATIONS	-27.762	12.966	7.745	4.436	8.356	14.766
23	LAND	-16.545	-3.764	.852	6.055	4.781	7.470
24	NON-RESIDENTIAL STRUCTURES AND EQUIPMENT	-5.334	5.004	5.994	4.435	-1.157	6.394
25	INVENTORIES	.000	6.569	-1.865	-4.844	3.847	-.897
26	RESIDENTIAL STRUCTURES	-5.884	5.157	2.763	-1.210	.884	1.799
27	NET SURPLUS (8 + 22)	-5.805	41.665	44.428	38.483	49.723	60.261
28	INCOME ORIGINATING (1 + 27)	124.179	184.609	202.142	187.857	213.777	249.811
29	LESS: CAPITAL CONSUMPTION ON R & D TRANSFERRED TO BUSINESS	.237	.286	.334	.385	.462	.561
30	NET INCOME ORIGINATING (28 - 29)	123.942	184.323	201.808	187.472	213.315	249.250
31	BUSINESS TRANSFERS	1.404	1.680	1.927	2.027	2.189	2.545
32	MEDIA SUPPORT	.633	.749	.842	.894	.997	1.137
33	HEALTH AND SAFETY	.293	.351	.385	.382	.414	.474
34	OTHER	.478	.580	.700	.751	.778	.934
35	NET INDIRECT BUSINESS TAXES	-19.618	-13.806	-11.639	-4.897	2.238	-.730
36	INDIRECT BUSINESS TAXES	16.004	17.220	18.770	19.783	21.742	23.379
37	LESS: INTERMEDIATE PRODUCT TRANSFERRED FROM GOVT TO BUSINESS	35.622	31.026	30.409	24.680	19.505	24.109
38	STATISTICAL DISCREPANCY	.502	1.536	-1.553	.562	1.306	3.154
39	BEA STATISTICAL DISCREPANCY	.502	1.536	-1.553	.562	1.306	3.153
40	TISA STATISTICAL DISCREPANCY	.000	.000	.000	.000	.000	.001
41	CHARGES AGAINST NET BUSINESS PRODUCT (30+31+35+38)	106.230	173.733	190.543	185.164	219.048	254.219

163

TABLE 2. BUSINESS INCOME AND PRODUCT, BILLIONS OF DOLLARS, 1946-81

		DEBITS					
		1946	1947	1948	1949	1950	1951
42	CAPITAL CONSUMPTION ALLOWANCES	12.440	15.295	17.846	19.283	20.834	24.130
43	TANGIBLE	11.845	14.586	17.033	18.380	19.793	22.913
44	ORIGINAL COST	8.261	9.251	10.668	12.082	13.519	15.141
45	REVALUATIONS	3.584	5.336	6.365	6.298	6.274	7.771
46	INTANGIBLE	.595	.709	.813	.903	1.041	1.217
47	ORIGINAL COST	.466	.531	.610	.694	.784	.889
48	ON BUSINESS RESEARCH AND DEVELOPMENT INVESTMENT	.266	.299	.339	.376	.415	.461
49	ON RESEARCH AND DEVELOPMENT INVESTMENT TRANSFERRED FROM GOVERNMENT AND NONPROFIT INSTITUTIONS	.200	.232	.271	.318	.369	.428
50	REVALUATIONS	.129	.178	.203	.209	.257	.328
51	ON BUSINESS RESEARCH AND DEVELOPMENT INVESTMENT	.092	.124	.140	.142	.164	.195
52	ON RESEARCH AND DEVELOPMENT INVESTMENT TRANSFERRED FROM GOVERNMENT AND NONPROFIT INSTITUTIONS	.037	.054	.063	.067	.093	.133
53	CHARGES AGAINST GROSS BUSINESS PRODUCT (41 + 42)	118.670	189.029	208.390	204.447	239.882	278.349

		1952	1953	1954	1955	1956	1957
1	LABOR INCOME	200.304	211.396	207.497	223.361	238.131	248.906
2	COMPENSATION OF EMPLOYEES	153.830	166.321	164.306	177.853	193.141	202.638
3	ADDITIONAL IMPUTATIONS	50.799	49.953	48.424	51.223	51.397	53.093
4	EMPLOYEE TRAINING	5.933	6.048	5.574	6.972	5.114	5.280
5	EXPENSE ACCOUNT ITEMS OF CONSUMPTION	3.085	3.300	3.342	3.629	4.010	4.223
6	LABOR INCOME OF SELF-EMPLOYED	41.781	40.605	39.508	40.622	42.273	43.590
7	LESS: EXPENSES RELATED TO WORK	4.325	4.878	5.233	5.715	6.407	6.825
8	CAPITAL INCOME AND SURPLUS	42.855	43.421	43.132	53.743	51.929	52.061
9	INTEREST PAID	1.091	1.242	1.604	1.774	1.819	2.405
10	CORPORATE PROFITS	34.201	34.519	33.194	43.132	40.923	40.161
11	PROPRIETORS' CAPITAL INCOME	1.575	1.160	1.727	2.258	1.666	1.696
12	PROPRIETORS' INCOME	43.356	41.765	41.235	42.880	43.939	45.286
13	LESS: LABOR INCOME OF SELF-EMPLOY.	41.781	40.605	39.508	40.622	42.273	43.590
14	OPPORTUNITY COST OF SELF-EMPLOY.	49.096	51.301	52.364	55.387	58.035	59.796
15	LESS: UNDERREMUNERATION OF LABOR	7.315	10.696	12.856	14.765	15.762	16.206
16	NET RENTAL INCOME OF PERSONS	5.006	5.177	5.270	5.232	5.513	5.840
17	TOTAL RENTAL INCOME	8.803	10.026	11.029	11.270	11.634	12.247
18	LESS: OWNER-OCCUPIED NONFARM RENTAL INCOME	3.797	4.849	5.759	6.038	6.121	6.407
19	NET BUSINESS INVESTMENT IN RESEARCH AND DEVELOPMENT	.982	1.323	1.337	1.347	2.008	1.959
20	GROSS INVESTMENT	1.720	2.200	2.320	2.460	3.277	3.396
21	LESS: CAPITAL CONSUMPTION ALLOWANCE	.738	.877	.983	1.113	1.269	1.437

164

TABLE 2. BUSINESS INCOME AND PRODUCT, BILLIONS OF DOLLARS, 1946-81

		DEBITS					
		1952	1953	1954	1955	1956	1957
22	NET REVALUATIONS	-4.055	.846	-.179	9.998	18.271	4.647
23	LAND	3.426	1.114	5.569	7.902	11.552	5.251
24	NON-RESIDENTIAL STRUCTURES AND EQUIPMENT	.712	1.198	-2.631	5.489	8.202	.938
25	INVENTORIES	-7.751	-.882	-2.825	-3.097	.814	.962
26	RESIDENTIAL STRUCTURES	-.442	-.585	-.292	-.297	-2.297	-2.503
27	NET SURPLUS (8 + 22)	38.800	44.267	42.953	63.741	70.200	56.708
28	INCOME ORIGINATING (1 + 27)	239.104	255.663	250.451	287.102	308.331	305.614
29	LESS: CAPITAL CONSUMPTION ON R & D TRANSFERRED TO BUSINESS	.652	.753	.875	1.037	1.248	1.496
30	NET INCOME ORIGINATING (28 - 29)	238.452	254.910	249.576	286.065	307.083	304.118
31	BUSINESS TRANSFERS	2.823	3.157	3.137	3.543	3.878	4.175
32	MEDIA SUPPORT	1.256	1.378	1.476	1.677	1.855	1.963
33	HEALTH AND SAFETY	.521	.578	.584	.621	.657	.697
34	OTHER	1.046	1.201	1.077	1.245	1.366	1.515
35	NET INDIRECT BUSINESS TAXES	-.608	.838	2.171	.622	3.117	2.234
36	INDIRECT BUSINESS TAXES	25.566	27.350	26.977	29.166	31.561	33.520
37	LESS: INTERMEDIATE PRODUCT TRANSFERRED FROM GOVT TO BUSINESS	26.174	26.512	24.806	28.544	28.444	31.286
38	STATISTICAL DISCREPANCY	1.727	2.273	2.021	1.314	-2.135	-1.235
39	BEA STATISTICAL DISCREPANCY	1.727	2.273	2.021	1.315	-2.136	-1.237
40	TISA STATISTICAL DISCREPANCY	.000	.000	.000	-.001	.001	.002
41	CHARGES AGAINST NET BUSINESS PRODUCT (30+31+35+38)	242.394	261.178	256.904	291.543	311.944	309.292
42	CAPITAL CONSUMPTION ALLOWANCES	26.043	27.719	29.393	31.355	35.143	38.150
43	TANGIBLE	24.653	26.089	27.535	29.205	32.626	35.217
44	ORIGINAL COST	16.787	18.431	20.140	21.771	23.587	25.403
45	REVALUATIONS	7.866	7.658	7.394	7.434	9.039	9.814
46	INTANGIBLE	1.390	1.630	1.858	2.150	2.517	2.933
47	ORIGINAL COST	1.022	1.203	1.419	1.669	1.986	2.362
48	ON BUSINESS RESEARCH AND DEVELOPMENT INVESTMENT	.522	.609	.711	.827	.964	1.115
49	ON RESEARCH AND DEVELOPMENT INVESTMENT TRANSFERRED FROM GOVERNMENT AND NONPROFIT INSTITUTIONS	.500	.594	.708	.842	1.022	1.247
50	REVALUATIONS	.368	.427	.439	.481	.531	.571
51	ON BUSINESS RESEARCH AND DEVELOPMENT INVESTMENT	.216	.268	.272	.286	.305	.322
52	ON RESEARCH AND DEVELOPMENT INVESTMENT TRANSFERRED FROM GOVERNMENT AND NONPROFIT INSTITUTIONS	.152	.159	.167	.195	.226	.249
53	CHARGES AGAINST GROSS BUSINESS PRODUCT (41 + 42)	268.437	288.897	286.297	322.898	347.087	347.442

		1958	1959	1960	1961	1962	1963
1	LABOR INCOME	249.104	266.763	276.814	282.397	300.094	312.448
2	COMPENSATION OF EMPLOYEES	200.012	218.226	228.534	232.936	249.096	261.629
3	ADDITIONAL IMPUTATIONS	55.969	56.006	56.020	57.241	59.075	59.191
4	EMPLOYEE TRAINING	5.492	6.260	6.506	6.331	7.639	7.374
5	EXPENSE ACCOUNT ITEMS OF CONSUMPTION	4.310	4.441	4.636	4.701	4.946	4.909
6	LABOR INCOME OF SELF-EMPLOYED	46.167	45.305	44.878	46.209	46.490	46.908
7	LESS: EXPENSES RELATED TO WORK	6.877	7.469	7.740	7.780	8.077	8.372

165

TABLE 2. BUSINESS INCOME AND PRODUCT, BILLIONS OF DOLLARS, 1946-81

		DEBITS					
		1958	1959	1960	1961	1962	1963
8	CAPITAL INCOME AND SURPLUS	49.002	60.923	59.362	61.069	70.449	77.298
9	INTEREST PAID	3.308	3.275	3.627	4.368	4.943	5.871
10	CORPORATE PROFITS	35.961	46.946	44.643	45.426	52.980	58.243
11	PROPRIETORS' CAPITAL INCOME	1.543	2.308	2.325	2.381	3.401	3.621
12	PROPRIETORS' INCOME	47.710	47.613	47.203	48.590	49.891	50.529
13	LESS: LABOR INCOME OF SELF-EMPLOY.	46.167	45.305	44.878	46.209	46.490	46.908
14	OPPORTUNITY COST OF SELF-EMPLOY.	60.315	63.323	65.035	65.846	66.976	66.502
15	LESS: UNDERREMUNERATION OF LABOR	14.148	18.018	20.157	19.637	20.486	19.594
16	NET RENTAL INCOME OF PERSONS	6.170	6.212	6.336	6.426	6.514	6.867
17	TOTAL RENTAL INCOME	12.867	13.637	14.486	15.027	15.759	16.536
18	LESS: OWNER-OCCUPIED NONFARM RENTAL INCOME	6.697	7.425	8.150	8.601	9.245	9.669
19	NET BUSINESS INVESTMENT IN RESEARCH AND DEVELOPMENT	2.020	2.182	2.431	2.468	2.611	2.696
20	GROSS INVESTMENT	3.630	3.983	4.428	4.668	5.029	5.360
21	LESS: CAPITAL CONSUMPTION ALLOWANCE	1.610	1.801	1.997	2.200	2.418	2.664
22	NET REVALUATIONS	13.358	4.652	3.948	2.517	2.334	-1.454
23	LAND	14.694	13.380	9.392	10.418	10.660	6.461
24	NON-RESIDENTIAL STRUCTURES AND EQUIPMENT	-.738	-3.354	-4.016	-3.716	-3.961	-1.569
25	INVENTORIES	1.548	-3.116	-.225	-2.456	-2.270	-2.377
26	RESIDENTIAL STRUCTURES	-2.146	-2.258	-1.203	-1.729	-2.095	-3.969
27	NET SURPLUS (8 + 22)	62.360	65.575	63.310	63.586	72.783	75.844
28	INCOME ORIGINATING (1 + 27)	311.464	332.337	340.124	345.982	372.877	388.292
29	LESS: CAPITAL CONSUMPTION ON R & D TRANSFERRED TO BUSINESS	1.783	2.109	2.447	2.796	3.173	3.577
30	NET INCOME ORIGINATING (28 - 29)	309.681	330.228	337.677	343.186	369.704	384.715
31	BUSINESS TRANSFERS	4.275	4.735	5.383	5.227	5.547	6.024
32	MEDIA SUPPORT	2.019	2.214	2.616	2.362	2.512	2.688
33	HEALTH AND SAFETY	.696	.750	.793	.830	.891	.931
34	OTHER	1.560	1.771	1.974	2.035	2.144	2.405
35	NET INDIRECT BUSINESS TAXES	2.701	3.676	6.781	7.303	8.528	10.822
36	INDIRECT BUSINESS TAXES	34.232	37.021	40.144	42.216	45.207	47.631
37	LESS: INTERMEDIATE PRODUCT TRANSFERRED FROM GOVT TO BUSINESS	31.532	33.345	33.363	34.913	36.679	36.809
38	STATISTICAL DISCREPANCY	.162	-1.309	-2.390	-.122	2.132	1.717
39	BEA STATISTICAL DISCREPANCY	.162	-1.309	-2.390	-.122	2.132	1.717
40	TISA STATISTICAL DISCREPANCY	.000	.000	.000	.000	.000	.000
41	CHARGES AGAINST NET BUSINESS PRODUCT (30+31+35+38)	316.818	337.330	347.451	355.594	385.911	403.278

166

TABLE 2. BUSINESS INCOME AND PRODUCT, BILLIONS OF DOLLARS, 1946-81

		DEBITS				
		1958	1959	1960	1961	1962	1963
42	CAPITAL CONSUMPTION ALLOWANCES	39.908	41.620	43.199	44.655	46.332	48.293
43	TANGIBLE	36.515	37.710	38.755	39.659	40.741	42.052
44	ORIGINAL COST	27.035	28.580	30.253	31.891	33.528	35.379
45	REVALUATIONS	9.480	9.130	8.502	7.768	7.214	6.673
46	INTANGIBLE	3.393	3.910	4.444	4.996	5.591	6.241
47	ORIGINAL COST	2.785	3.257	3.770	4.304	4.860	5.464
48	ON BUSINESS RESEARCH AND DEVELOPMENT INVESTMENT	1.276	1.454	1.647	1.848	2.059	2.288
49	ON RESEARCH AND DEVELOPMENT INVESTMENT TRANSFERRED FROM GOVERNMENT AND NONPROFIT INSTITUTIONS	1.509	1.803	2.123	2.456	2.801	3.176
50	REVALUATIONS	.608	.653	.674	.692	.731	.777
51	ON BUSINESS RESEARCH AND DEVELOPMENT INVESTMENT	.334	.347	.350	.352	.359	.376
52	ON RESEARCH AND DEVELOPMENT INVESTMENT TRANSFERRED FROM GOVERNMENT AND NONPROFIT INSTITUTIONS	.274	.306	.324	.340	.372	.401
53	CHARGES AGAINST GROSS BUSINESS PRODUCT (41 + 42)	356.727	378.950	390.649	400.249	432.244	451.570

		1964	1965	1966	1967	1968	1969
1	LABOR INCOME	333.946	360.860	398.081	419.300	458.488	503.069
2	COMPENSATION OF EMPLOYEES	280.100	301.935	333.059	353.663	388.400	427.633
3	ADDITIONAL IMPUTATIONS	62.602	68.263	74.886	76.147	81.331	87.954
4	EMPLOYEE TRAINING	8.590	10.493	12.951	12.329	13.913	15.792
5	EXPENSE ACCOUNT ITEMS OF CONSUMPTION	5.428	5.792	6.305	6.664	7.224	7.927
6	LABOR INCOME OF SELF-EMPLOYED	48.584	51.978	55.630	57.154	60.194	64.235
7	LESS: EXPENSES RELATED TO WORK	8.756	9.338	9.864	10.510	11.243	12.518
8	CAPITAL INCOME AND SURPLUS	85.475	99.517	107.807	107.091	114.569	112.974
9	INTEREST PAID	6.626	8.231	10.668	12.883	14.182	18.259
10	CORPORATE PROFITS	64.927	75.505	80.893	77.996	83.907	78.913
11	PROPRIETORS' CAPITAL INCOME	3.877	4.958	4.886	4.055	3.784	2.808
12	PROPRIETORS' INCOME	52.461	56.936	60.516	61.209	63.978	67.043
13	LESS: LABOR INCOME OF SELF-EMPLOY.	48.584	51.978	55.630	57.154	60.194	64.235
14	OPPORTUNITY COST OF SELF-EMPLOY.	69.535	71.588	72.343	68.317	72.518	77.238
15	LESS: UNDERREMUNERATION OF LABOR	20.951	19.610	16.713	11.163	12.324	13.003
16	NET RENTAL INCOME OF PERSONS	7.208	7.685	7.845	8.287	8.523	8.467
17	TOTAL RENTAL INCOME	17.063	17.965	18.723	19.698	19.548	19.591
18	LESS: OWNER-OCCUPIED NONFARM RENTAL INCOME	9.855	10.280	10.878	11.411	11.025	11.124
19	NET BUSINESS INVESTMENT IN RESEARCH AND DEVELOPMENT	2.837	3.138	3.515	3.870	4.173	4.527
20	GROSS INVESTMENT	5.792	6.445	7.216	8.020	8.869	9.857
21	LESS: CAPITAL CONSUMPTION ALLOWANCE	2.955	3.307	3.701	4.150	4.696	5.330

167

TABLE 2. BUSINESS INCOME AND PRODUCT, BILLIONS OF DOLLARS, 1946-81

				DEBITS		
		1964	1965	1966	1967	1968	1969
22	NET REVALUATIONS	7.664	10.593	4.774	-.560	-8.653	-5.317
23	LAND	10.294	13.324	5.400	4.601	-9.234	-9.977
24	NON-RESIDENTIAL STRUCTURES AND EQUIPMENT	-.789	-.815	2.017	1.476	-.295	6.377
25	INVENTORIES	-2.411	.428	-3.520	-4.856	-3.508	-1.430
26	RESIDENTIAL STRUCTURES	.570	-2.344	.876	-1.781	4.383	-.286
27	NET SURPLUS (8 + 22)	93.139	110.110	112.581	106.531	105.916	107.657
28	INCOME ORIGINATING (1 + 27)	427.085	470.969	510.662	525.831	564.404	610.726
29	LESS: CAPITAL CONSUMPTION ON R & D TRANSFERRED TO BUSINESS	4.030	4.541	5.086	5.706	6.389	7.126
30	NET INCOME ORIGINATING (28 - 29)	423.055	466.428	505.576	520.125	558.015	603.600
31	BUSINESS TRANSFERS	6.590	7.531	8.238	8.539	9.285	10.356
32	MEDIA SUPPORT	2.929	3.630	3.992	4.102	4.462	4.867
33	HEALTH AND SAFETY	1.006	1.089	1.206	1.300	1.445	1.601
34	OTHER	2.655	2.812	3.040	3.137	3.378	3.888
35	NET INDIRECT BUSINESS TAXES	12.358	12.083	10.367	9.379	12.372	20.659
36	INDIRECT BUSINESS TAXES	51.118	54.261	56.361	60.223	67.570	73.924
37	LESS: INTERMEDIATE PRODUCT TRANSFERRED FROM GOVT TO BUSINESS	38.760	42.178	45.994	50.844	55.199	53.265
38	STATISTICAL DISCREPANCY	.144	-1.206	1.385	-.254	-2.113	-3.886
39	BEA STATISTICAL DISCREPANCY	.144	-1.211	1.380	-.258	-2.113	-3.886
40	TISA STATISTICAL DISCREPANCY	.000	.005	.005	.004	.000	.000
41	CHARGES AGAINST NET BUSINESS PRODUCT (30+31+35+38)	442.147	484.836	525.566	537.788	577.559	630.730
42	CAPITAL CONSUMPTION ALLOWANCES	50.880	54.315	59.140	64.598	71.055	78.761
43	TANGIBLE	43.895	46.467	50.353	54.742	59.970	66.305
44	ORIGINAL COST	37.468	40.049	43.188	46.605	50.119	54.272
45	REVALUATIONS	6.428	6.418	7.165	8.137	9.850	12.033
46	INTANGIBLE	6.985	7.848	8.787	9.856	11.085	12.456
47	ORIGINAL COST	6.114	6.807	7.551	8.336	9.160	10.012
48	ON BUSINESS RESEARCH AND DEVELOPMENT INVESTMENT	2.544	2.828	3.142	3.484	3.863	4.284
49	ON RESEARCH AND DEVELOPMENT INVESTMENT TRANSFERRED FROM GOVERNMENT AND NONPROFIT INSTITUTIONS	3.570	3.979	4.409	4.852	5.297	5.728
50	REVALUATIONS	.871	1.041	1.236	1.520	1.925	2.444
51	ON BUSINESS RESEARCH AND DEVELOPMENT INVESTMENT	.411	.479	.559	.666	.833	1.046
52	ON RESEARCH AND DEVELOPMENT INVESTMENT TRANSFERRED FROM GOVERNMENT AND NONPROFIT INSTITUTIONS	.460	.562	.677	.854	1.092	1.398
53	CHARGES AGAINST GROSS BUSINESS PRODUCT (41 + 42)	493.028	539.151	584.705	602.386	648.613	709.491

		1970	1971	1972	1973	1974	1975
1	LABOR INCOME	525.836	554.586	613.931	700.932	757.806	782.028
2	COMPENSATION OF EMPLOYEES	450.769	476.728	526.266	592.621	650.331	679.790
3	ADDITIONAL IMPUTATIONS	88.628	92.481	103.308	125.525	126.979	122.682
4	EMPLOYEE TRAINING	14.799	15.103	18.435	22.518	23.055	19.781
5	EXPENSE ACCOUNT ITEMS OF CONSUMPTION	8.375	8.890	9.782	10.887	11.952	12.476
6	LABOR INCOME OF SELF-EMPLOYED	65.454	68.488	75.091	92.120	91.972	90.425
7	LESS: EXPENSES RELATED TO WORK	13.561	14.623	15.643	17.214	19.504	20.444

TABLE 2. BUSINESS INCOME AND PRODUCT, BILLIONS OF DOLLARS, 1946-81

| | | DEBITS | | | | | |
		1970	1971	1972	1973	1974	1975
8	CAPITAL INCOME AND SURPLUS	102.053	114.976	130.389	144.380	135.702	160.651
9	INTEREST PAID	23.375	24.977	26.492	31.844	42.491	46.798
10	CORPORATE PROFITS	64.880	76.112	87.958	94.627	78.601	97.529
11	PROPRIETORS' CAPITAL INCOME	.775	.896	1.765	1.675	-3.244	-.405
12	PROPRIETORS' INCOME	66.229	69.384	76.856	93.795	88.728	90.020
13	LESS: LABOR INCOME OF SELF-EMPLOY.	65.454	68.488	75.091	92.120	91.972	90.425
14	OPPORTUNITY COST OF SELF-EMPLOY.	80.518	86.583	92.018	99.560	109.003	117.273
15	LESS: UNDERREMUNERATION OF LABOR	15.064	18.095	16.927	7.440	17.031	26.848
16	NET RENTAL INCOME OF PERSONS	8.758	9.063	10.147	11.654	12.977	12.184
17	TOTAL RENTAL INCOME	19.704	20.236	21.002	22.580	23.539	23.015
18	LESS: OWNER-OCCUPIED NONFARM RENTAL INCOME	10.946	11.173	10.855	10.926	10.562	10.831
19	NET BUSINESS INVESTMENT IN RESEARCH AND DEVELOPMENT	4.265	3.928	4.027	4.580	4.877	4.545
20	GROSS INVESTMENT	10.288	10.654	11.535	13.104	14.667	15.582
21	LESS: CAPITAL CONSUMPTION ALLOWANCE	6.023	6.726	7.508	8.524	9.790	11.037
22	NET REVALUATIONS	-4.591	-4.957	49.148	100.493	115.182	-35.335
23	LAND	-6.715	-5.731	36.210	55.949	13.131	40.506
24	NON-RESIDENTIAL STRUCTURES AND EQUIPMENT	9.474	1.099	1.127	9.560	85.252	-3.268
25	INVENTORIES	-5.973	-2.516	5.906	26.217	19.498	-71.258
26	RESIDENTIAL STRUCTURES	-1.377	2.192	5.905	8.768	-2.700	-1.315
27	NET SURPLUS (8 + 22)	97.462	110.019	179.537	244.873	250.884	125.316
28	INCOME ORIGINATING (1 + 27)	623.298	664.605	793.468	945.805	1008.690	907.344
29	LESS: CAPITAL CONSUMPTION ON R & D TRANSFERRED TO BUSINESS	7.873	8.596	9.367	10.350	11.584	12.695
30	NET INCOME ORIGINATING (28 - 29)	615.425	656.009	784.101	935.455	997.106	894.649
31	BUSINESS TRANSFERS	10.660	11.243	12.494	13.747	14.610	16.790
32	MEDIA SUPPORT	4.918	5.029	5.607	5.986	6.415	6.890
33	HEALTH AND SAFETY	1.662	1.770	2.026	2.246	2.392	2.464
34	OTHER	4.080	4.444	4.861	5.515	5.803	7.436
35	NET INDIRECT BUSINESS TAXES	21.424	28.090	32.935	39.515	47.510	45.342
36	INDIRECT BUSINESS TAXES	79.953	87.935	94.458	102.623	109.699	118.846
37	LESS: INTERMEDIATE PRODUCT TRANSFERRED FROM GOVT TO BUSINESS	58.529	59.845	61.523	63.108	62.189	73.504
38	STATISTICAL DISCREPANCY	-1.495	4.098	3.312	.764	3.736	5.477
39	BEA STATISTICAL DISCREPANCY	-1.495	4.098	3.312	.764	3.736	5.477
40	TISA STATISTICAL DISCREPANCY	.000	.000	.000	.000	.000	.000
41	CHARGES AGAINST NET BUSINESS PRODUCT (30+31+35+38)	646.014	699.440	832.842	989.481	1062.962	962.258

169

TABLE 2.   BUSINESS INCOME AND PRODUCT, BILLIONS OF DOLLARS, 1946-81

		DEBITS					
		1970	1971	1972	1973	1974	1975
42	CAPITAL CONSUMPTION ALLOWANCES	87.156	95.548	104.665	114.615	133.356	156.264
43	TANGIBLE	73.260	80.226	87.790	95.741	111.982	132.532
44	ORIGINAL COST	58.623	62.812	67.618	73.539	80.448	87.610
45	REVALUATIONS	14.637	17.414	20.172	22.201	31.534	44.923
46	INTANGIBLE	13.896	15.322	16.875	18.874	21.374	23.732
47	ORIGINAL COST	10.871	11.735	12.630	13.567	14.559	15.613
48	ON BUSINESS RESEARCH AND DEVELOPMENT INVESTMENT	4.733	5.198	5.694	6.234	6.827	7.470
49	ON RESEARCH AND DEVELOPMENT INVESTMENT TRANSFERRED FROM GOVERNMENT AND NONPROFIT INSTITUTIONS	6.138	6.537	6.936	7.333	7.732	8.143
50	REVALUATIONS	3.025	3.587	4.245	5.307	6.815	8.119
51	ON BUSINESS RESEARCH AND DEVELOPMENT INVESTMENT	1.290	1.528	1.814	2.290	2.963	3.567
52	ON RESEARCH AND DEVELOPMENT INVESTMENT TRANSFERRED FROM GOVERNMENT AND NONPROFIT INSTITUTIONS	1.735	2.059	2.431	3.017	3.852	4.552
53	CHARGES AGAINST GROSS BUSINESS PRODUCT (41 + 42)	733.170	794.988	937.507	1104.096	1196.318	1118.522

		1976	1977	1978	1979	1980	1981
1	LABOR INCOME	873.949	979.334	1119.208	1268.507	1358.242	1495.845
2	COMPENSATION OF EMPLOYEES	762.999	856.635	977.167	1105.517	1208.071	1336.317
3	ADDITIONAL IMPUTATIONS	134.138	149.515	172.307	198.914	192.094	204.311
4	EMPLOYEE TRAINING	24.786	29.048	35.233	39.348	37.683	40.964
5	EXPENSE ACCOUNT ITEMS OF CONSUMPTION	13.879	15.566	17.768	20.261	22.358	24.560
6	LABOR INCOME OF SELF-EMPLOYED	95.473	104.901	119.306	139.305	132.053	138.787
7	LESS: EXPENSES RELATED TO WORK	23.188	26.816	30.266	35.924	41.923	44.783
8	CAPITAL INCOME AND SURPLUS	183.585	222.545	254.902	262.525	263.530	323.184
9	INTEREST PAID	43.082	49.000	57.715	76.847	99.748	134.137
10	CORPORATE PROFITS	123.824	152.110	172.654	164.188	145.544	168.674
11	PROPRIETORS' CAPITAL INCOME	-1.401	-1.047	-.764	-7.210	-14.607	-18.621
12	PROPRIETORS' INCOME	94.072	103.854	118.542	132.095	117.446	120.166
13	LESS: LABOR INCOME OF SELF-EMPLOY.	95.473	104.901	119.306	139.305	132.053	138.787
14	OPPORTUNITY COST OF SELF-EMPLOY.	126.111	140.890	159.125	178.850	193.572	208.267
15	LESS: UNDERREMUNERATION OF LABOR	30.638	35.989	39.819	39.545	61.519	69.480
16	NET RENTAL INCOME OF PERSONS	12.846	16.706	18.572	20.657	23.054	28.038
17	TOTAL RENTAL INCOME	23.505	24.816	26.600	27.909	31.515	41.385
18	LESS: OWNER-OCCUPIED NONFARM RENTAL INCOME	10.659	8.110	8.028	7.252	8.461	13.347
19	NET BUSINESS INVESTMENT IN RESEARCH AND DEVELOPMENT	5.234	5.776	6.725	8.043	9.791	10.956
20	GROSS INVESTMENT	17.436	19.407	22.156	25.655	29.940	33.850
21	LESS: CAPITAL CONSUMPTION ALLOWANCE	12.202	13.631	15.431	17.612	20.149	22.894

170

TABLE 2. BUSINESS INCOME AND PRODUCT, BILLIONS OF DOLLARS, 1946-81

		DEBITS					
		1976	1977	1978	1979	1980	1981
22	NET REVALUATIONS	158.464	104.991	123.764	145.411	11.269	-106.965
23	LAND	78.322	48.643	76.182	72.308	17.144	-94.096
24	NON-RESIDENTIAL STRUCTURES AND EQUIPMENT	4.007	38.620	14.571	34.567	-5.308	20.953
25	INVENTORIES	61.090	-2.325	7.038	37.306	9.708	-30.616
26	RESIDENTIAL STRUCTURES	15.045	20.052	25.974	1.230	-10.275	-3.206
27	NET SURPLUS (8 + 22)	342.049	327.536	378.666	407.936	274.799	216.219
28	INCOME ORIGINATING (1 + 27)	1215.998	1306.870	1497.874	1676.443	1633.041	1712.064
29	LESS: CAPITAL CONSUMPTION ON R & D TRANSFERRED TO BUSINESS	13.714	14.845	16.190	17.703	19.393	21.160
30	NET INCOME ORIGINATING (28 - 29)	1202.284	1292.025	1481.684	1658.740	1613.648	1690.904
31	BUSINESS TRANSFERS	19.017	21.232	23.948	26.760	30.018	33.463
32	MEDIA SUPPORT	8.490	9.656	11.277	12.680	14.141	15.832
33	HEALTH AND SAFETY	2.607	2.968	3.419	3.811	4.200	4.720
34	OTHER	7.920	8.608	9.252	10.269	11.677	12.911
35	NET INDIRECT BUSINESS TAXES	54.380	59.977	68.166	70.289	78.400	97.949
36	INDIRECT BUSINESS TAXES	128.645	140.324	152.379	163.531	185.542	219.272
37	LESS: INTERMEDIATE PRODUCT TRANSFERRED FROM GOVT TO BUSINESS	74.265	80.347	84.213	93.242	107.142	121.323
38	STATISTICAL DISCREPANCY	5.102	1.352	-2.556	-1.487	2.288	-4.902
39	BEA STATISTICAL DISCREPANCY	5.102	1.350	-2.556	-1.487	2.291	-4.902
40	TISA STATISTICAL DISCREPANCY	.000	.002	.000	.000	-.003	.000
41	CHARGES AGAINST NET BUSINESS PRODUCT (30+31+35+38)	1280.783	1374.586	1571.242	1754.302	1724.354	1817.414
42	CAPITAL CONSUMPTION ALLOWANCES	171.598	189.812	214.707	245.306	280.940	317.096
43	TANGIBLE	145.682	161.336	183.086	209.991	241.398	273.042
44	ORIGINAL COST	95.184	104.615	116.776	131.505	147.218	164.507
45	REVALUATIONS	50.498	56.721	66.310	78.485	94.179	108.536
46	INTANGIBLE	25.916	28.476	31.621	35.315	39.542	44.054
47	ORIGINAL COST	16.738	17.980	19.385	20.995	22.857	25.008
48	ON BUSINESS RESEARCH AND DEVELOPMENT INVESTMENT	8.171	8.961	9.874	10.942	12.188	13.615
49	ON RESEARCH AND DEVELOPMENT INVESTMENT TRANSFERRED FROM GOVERNMENT AND NONPROFIT INSTITUTIONS	8.567	9.019	9.511	10.053	10.669	11.393
50	REVALUATIONS	9.178	10.496	12.236	14.320	16.685	19.046
51	ON BUSINESS RESEARCH AND DEVELOPMENT INVESTMENT	4.031	4.670	5.557	6.670	7.961	9.279
52	ON RESEARCH AND DEVELOPMENT INVESTMENT TRANSFERRED FROM GOVERNMENT AND NONPROFIT INSTITUTIONS	5.147	5.826	6.679	7.650	8.724	9.767
53	CHARGES AGAINST GROSS BUSINESS PRODUCT (41 + 42)	1452.381	1564.398	1785.949	1999.608	2005.293	2134.510

171

TABLE 2. BUSINESS INCOME AND PRODUCT, BILLIONS OF DOLLARS, 1946-81

		DEBITS					
		PERCENT PER ANNUM RATES OF GROWTH CURRENT DOLLARS					
		1946-56	1956-66	1966-71	1971-76	1976-81	1946-81
1	LABOR INCOME	6.241	5.273	6.856	9.523	11.347	7.229
2	COMPENSATION OF EMPLOYEES	7.827	5.600	7.436	9.863	11.861	7.982
3	ADDITIONAL IMPUTATIONS	2.227	3.836	4.311	7.721	8.780	4.678
4	EMPLOYEE TRAINING	2.431	9.737	3.122	10.415	10.570	6.856
5	EXPENSE ACCOUNT ITEMS OF CONSUMPTION	7.828	4.629	7.115	9.317	12.091	7.607
6	LABOR INCOME OF SELF-EMPLOYED	1.811	2.784	4.246	6.869	7.769	3.987
7	LESS: EXPENSES RELATED TO WORK	11.470	4.409	8.192	9.659	14.070	9.044
8	CAPITAL INCOME AND SURPLUS	8.989	7.578	1.296	9.811	11.975	7.986
9	INTEREST PAID	11.637	19.351	18.547	11.520	25.502	16.687
10	CORPORATE PROFITS	9.922	7.052	-1.211	10.223	6.377	6.982
11	PROPRIETORS' CAPITAL INCOME	2.073	11.360	-28.769	N.A.	N.A.	N.A.
12	PROPRIETORS' INCOME	1.821	3.253	2.773	6.277	5.018	3.448
13	LESS: LABOR INCOME OF SELF-EMPLOY.	1.811	2.784	4.246	6.869	7.769	3.987
14	OPPORTUNITY COST OF SELF-EMPLOY.	3.011	2.228	3.659	7.811	10.554	4.601
15	LESS: UNDERREMUNERATION OF LABOR	7.273	.588	1.602	11.107	17.793	6.443
16	NET RENTAL INCOME OF PERSONS	4.032	3.591	2.929	7.226	16.895	5.946
17	TOTAL RENTAL INCOME	7.844	4.873	1.566	3.040	11.979	5.954
18	LESS: OWNER-OCCUPIED NONFARM RENTAL INCOME	13.313	5.919	.537	-.937	4.600	5.970
19	NET BUSINESS INVESTMENT IN RESEARCH AND DEVELOPMENT	17.746	5.759	2.247	5.909	15.921	9.983
20	GROSS INVESTMENT	15.889	8.214	8.104	10.354	14.188	11.499
21	LESS: CAPITAL CONSUMPTION ALLOWANCE	13.490	11.298	12.691	12.651	13.412	12.615
22	NET REVALUATIONS	N.A.	-12.560	N.A.	N.A.	N.A.	N.A.
23	LAND	N.A.	-7.322	N.A.	N.A.	N.A.	N.A.
24	NON-RESIDENTIAL STRUCTURES AND EQUIPMENT	N.A.	-13.087	-11.444	29.538	39.212	N.A.
25	INVENTORIES	N.A.	N.A.	N.A.	N.A.	N.A.	N.A.
26	RESIDENTIAL STRUCTURES	N.A.	N.A.	20.124	47.003	N.A.	N.A.
27	NET SURPLUS (8 + 22)	N.A.	4.837	-.459	25.465	-8.765	N.A.
28	INCOME ORIGINATING (1 + 27)	9.521	5.175	5.411	12.843	7.082	7.785
29	LESS: CAPITAL CONSUMPTION ON R & D TRANSFERRED TO BUSINESS	18.072	15.084	11.067	9.793	9.061	13.694
30	NET INCOME ORIGINATING (28 - 29)	9.497	5.112	5.348	12.881	7.059	7.752
31	BUSINESS TRANSFERS	10.694	7.825	6.417	11.084	11.966	9.483
32	MEDIA SUPPORT	11.351	7.965	4.727	11.041	13.273	9.634
33	HEALTH AND SAFETY	8.410	6.262	7.975	8.052	12.606	8.265
34	OTHER	11.071	8.328	7.890	12.251	10.267	9.876
35	NET INDIRECT BUSINESS TAXES	N.A.	12.768	22.062	14.124	12.490	N.A.
36	INDIRECT BUSINESS TAXES	7.027	5.970	9.304	7.906	11.255	7.765
37	LESS: INTERMEDIATE PRODUCT TRANSFERRED FROM GOVT TO BUSINESS	-2.225	4.923	5.406	4.412	10.314	3.563
38	STATISTICAL DISCREPANCY	N.A.	N.A.	24.229	4.480	N.A.	N.A.
39	BEA STATISTICAL DISCREPANCY	N.A.	N.A.	24.319	4.480	N.A.	N.A.
40	TISA STATISTICAL DISCREPANCY	683.472	17.462	N.A.	N.A.	57.620	7.879
41	CHARGES AGAINST NET BUSINESS PRODUCT (30+31+35+38)	11.374	5.355	5.883	12.861	7.250	8.451

172

TABLE 2. BUSINESS INCOME AND PRODUCT, BILLIONS OF DOLLARS, 1946-81

		DEBITS					
		PERCENT PER ANNUM RATES OF GROWTH CURRENT DOLLARS					
		1946-56	1956-66	1966-71	1971-76	1976-81	1946-81
42	CAPITAL CONSUMPTION ALLOWANCES	10.943	5.343	10.070	12.424	13.067	9.694
43	TANGIBLE	10.663	4.435	9.763	12.673	13.387	9.379
44	ORIGINAL COST	11.062	6.235	7.779	8.669	11.564	8.923
45	REVALUATIONS	9.691	-2.297	19.438	23.730	16.536	10.235
46	INTANGIBLE	15.515	13.317	11.762	11.084	11.195	13.087
47	ORIGINAL COST	15.600	14.288	9.218	7.360	8.362	12.052
48	ON BUSINESS RESEARCH AND DEVELOPMENT INVESTMENT	13.742	12.542	10.593	9.468	10.751	11.901
49	ON RESEARCH AND DEVELOPMENT INVESTMENT TRANSFERRED FROM GOVERNMENT AND NONPROFIT INSTITUTIONS	17.718	15.741	8.195	5.558	5.867	12.243
50	REVALUATIONS	15.199	8.816	23.749	20.671	15.721	15.339
51	ON BUSINESS RESEARCH AND DEVELOPMENT INVESTMENT	12.733	6.246	22.276	21.411	18.146	14.090
52	ON RESEARCH AND DEVELOPMENT INVESTMENT TRANSFERRED FROM GOVERNMENT AND NONPROFIT INSTITUTIONS	19.837	11.596	24.915	20.110	13.669	17.270
53	CHARGES AGAINST GROSS BUSINESS PRODUCT (41 + 42)	11.329	5.354	6.337	12.809	8.005	8.607

		CREDITS					
		1946	1947	1948	1949	1950	1951
54	BEA GROSS DOMESTIC PRODUCT, BUSINESS	183.759	209.960	234.886	231.514	257.523	294.359
55	LESS: NET SPACE RENT OF OWNER-OCC. NONFARM DWELLINGS	5.611	6.062	6.861	7.943	9.070	10.468
56	LESS: BEA GOVT ENTERPRISE PRODUCT	2.517	2.570	2.780	3.058	2.955	3.419
57	LESS: RENTAL VALUE OF BLDGS. OWNED AND USED BY NONPROFIT INSTITUTIONS	.458	.561	.624	.643	.678	.777
58	BEA-TYPE GROSS DOMESTIC PRODUCT OF TISA BUSINESS SECTOR	175.173	200.767	224.621	219.870	244.820	279.695
59	SUBSIDIES INCLUDED IN BUSINESS INCOME	1.459	.383	.301	.228	.357	.300
60	EXPENSE ACCOUNT ITEMS OF CONSUMPTION	1.887	2.181	2.407	2.371	2.558	2.874
61	LESS: EXPENSES RELATED TO WORK	2.163	2.586	2.922	3.147	3.428	3.850
62	BUSINESS INVESTMENT IN RESEARCH AND DEVELOPMENT	.750	.950	1.030	.870	1.070	1.240
63	TRAINING PRODUCED IN BUSINESS SECTOR	4.022	4.292	4.389	3.223	4.243	5.822
64	MEDIA SUPPORT PLUS HEALTH AND SAFETY	.926	1.100	1.227	1.276	1.411	1.611
65	NET REVALUATIONS	-27.762	12.966	7.745	4.436	8.356	14.766
66	LESS: INT PRODUCT FROM GOVT	35.622	31.026	30.409	24.680	19.505	24.109
67	GROSS BUSINESS PRODUCT	118.670	189.029	208.390	204.447	239.882	278.349

TABLE 2. BUSINESS INCOME AND PRODUCT, BILLIONS OF DOLLARS, 1946-81

		CREDITS					
		1952	1953	1954	1955	1956	1957
54	BEA GROSS DOMESTIC PRODUCT, BUSINESS	307.328	324.890	323.947	354.025	372.126	390.815
55	LESS: NET SPACE RENT OF OWNER-OCC. NONFARM DWELLINGS	12.192	14.035	15.874	17.355	18.963	20.701
56	LESS: BEA GOVT ENTERPRISE PRODUCT	4.208	4.443	4.481	4.416	4.195	4.939
57	LESS: RENTAL VALUE OF BLDGS. OWNED AND USED BY NONPROFIT INSTITUTIONS	.829	.866	.893	.950	1.052	1.134
58	BEA-TYPE GROSS DOMESTIC PRODUCT OF TISA BUSINESS SECTOR	290.099	305.546	302.700	331.304	347.916	364.041
59	SUBSIDIES INCLUDED IN BUSINESS INCOME	.377	.391	.519	.497	.837	1.306
60	EXPENSE ACCOUNT ITEMS OF CONSUMPTION	3.085	3.300	3.342	3.629	4.010	4.223
61	LESS: EXPENSES RELATED TO WORK	4.325	4.878	5.233	5.715	6.407	6.825
62	BUSINESS INVESTMENT IN RESEARCH AND DEVELOPMENT	1.720	2.200	2.320	2.460	3.277	3.396
63	TRAINING PRODUCED IN BUSINESS SECTOR	5.933	6.048	5.574	6.972	5.114	5.280
64	MEDIA SUPPORT PLUS HEALTH AND SAFETY	1.777	1.956	2.060	2.298	2.512	2.660
65	NET REVALUATIONS	-4.055	.846	-.179	9.998	18.271	4.647
66	LESS: INT PRODUCT FROM GOVT	26.174	26.512	24.806	28.544	28.444	31.286
67	GROSS BUSINESS PRODUCT	268.437	288.897	286.297	322.898	347.087	347.442

		1958	1959	1960	1961	1962	1963
54	BEA GROSS DOMESTIC PRODUCT, BUSINESS	393.074	428.290	441.964	455.719	490.646	517.190
55	LESS: NET SPACE RENT OF OWNER-OCC. NONFARM DWELLINGS	22.570	24.530	26.640	28.588	30.936	32.943
56	LESS: BEA GOVT ENTERPRISE PRODUCT	5.094	6.174	6.436	6.357	6.985	8.036
57	LESS: RENTAL VALUE OF BLDGS. OWNED AND USED BY NONPROFIT INSTITUTIONS	1.171	1.228	1.302	1.377	1.476	1.590
58	BEA-TYPE GROSS DOMESTIC PRODUCT OF TISA BUSINESS SECTOR	364.239	396.358	407.587	419.397	451.249	474.622
59	SUBSIDIES INCLUDED IN BUSINESS INCOME	1.391	1.107	1.239	2.137	2.399	2.322
60	EXPENSE ACCOUNT ITEMS OF CONSUMPTION	4.310	4.441	4.636	4.701	4.946	4.909
61	LESS: EXPENSES RELATED TO WORK	6.877	7.469	7.740	7.780	8.077	8.372
62	BUSINESS INVESTMENT IN RESEARCH AND DEVELOPMENT	3.630	3.983	4.428	4.668	5.029	5.360
63	TRAINING PRODUCED IN BUSINESS SECTOR	5.492	6.260	6.506	6.331	7.639	7.374
64	MEDIA SUPPORT PLUS HEALTH AND SAFETY	2.715	2.964	3.409	3.192	3.403	3.619
65	NET REVALUATIONS	13.358	4.652	3.948	2.517	2.334	-1.454
66	LESS: INT PRODUCT FROM GOVT	31.532	33.345	33.363	34.913	36.679	36.809
67	GROSS BUSINESS PRODUCT	356.727	378.950	390.649	400.249	432.244	451.570

TABLE 2. BUSINESS INCOME AND PRODUCT, BILLIONS OF DOLLARS, 1946-81

		CREDITS					
		1964	1965	1966	1967	1968	1969
54	BEA GROSS DOMESTIC PRODUCT, BUSINESS	551.621	598.388	652.646	685.089	745.419	803.226
55	LESS: NET SPACE RENT OF OWNER-OCC. NONFARM DWELLINGS	35.060	37.586	40.294	43.224	46.019	50.174
56	LESS: BEA GOVT ENTERPRISE PRODUCT	8.494	9.345	10.103	11.452	13.222	14.102
57	LESS: RENTAL VALUE OF BLDGS. OWNED AND USED BY NONPROFIT INSTITUTIONS	1.743	1.919	2.161	2.423	2.689	3.047
58	BEA-TYPE GROSS DOMESTIC PRODUCT OF TISA BUSINESS SECTOR	506.324	549.538	600.088	627.990	683.489	735.903
59	SUBSIDIES INCLUDED IN BUSINESS INCOME	2.810	3.088	4.032	3.896	4.306	4.643
60	EXPENSE ACCOUNT ITEMS OF CONSUMPTION	5.428	5.792	6.305	6.664	7.224	7.927
61	LESS: EXPENSES RELATED TO WORK	8.756	9.338	9.864	10.510	11.243	12.518
62	BUSINESS INVESTMENT IN RESEARCH AND DEVELOPMENT	5.792	6.445	7.216	8.020	8.869	9.857
63	TRAINING PRODUCED IN BUSINESS SECTOR	8.590	10.493	12.951	12.329	13.913	15.792
64	MEDIA SUPPORT PLUS HEALTH AND SAFETY	3.935	4.719	5.198	5.402	5.907	6.468
65	NET REVALUATIONS	7.664	10.593	4.774	-.560	-8.653	-5.317
66	LESS: INT PRODUCT FROM GOVT	38.760	42.178	45.994	50.844	55.199	53.265
67	GROSS BUSINESS PRODUCT	493.028	539.151	584.705	602.386	648.613	709.491
		1970	1971	1972	1973	1974	1975
54	BEA GROSS DOMESTIC PRODUCT, BUSINESS	837.334	907.086	998.613	1118.656	1206.436	1301.670
55	LESS: NET SPACE RENT OF OWNER-OCC. NONFARM DWELLINGS	53.863	58.722	64.265	71.064	78.522	86.074
56	LESS: BEA GOVT ENTERPRISE PRODUCT	15.144	16.441	18.545	19.156	21.841	24.093
57	LESS: RENTAL VALUE OF BLDGS. OWNED AND USED BY NONPROFIT INSTITUTIONS	3.415	3.744	4.069	4.502	5.254	5.791
58	BEA-TYPE GROSS DOMESTIC PRODUCT OF TISA BUSINESS SECTOR	764.913	828.179	911.734	1023.935	1100.819	1185.712
59	SUBSIDIES INCLUDED IN BUSINESS INCOME	4.896	4.788	6.406	5.249	3.529	4.900
60	EXPENSE ACCOUNT ITEMS OF CONSUMPTION	8.375	8.890	9.782	10.887	11.952	12.476
61	LESS: EXPENSES RELATED TO WORK	13.561	14.623	15.643	17.214	19.504	20.444
62	BUSINESS INVESTMENT IN RESEARCH AND DEVELOPMENT	10.288	10.654	11.535	13.104	14.667	15.582
63	TRAINING PRODUCED IN BUSINESS SECTOR	14.799	15.103	18.435	22.518	23.055	19.781
64	MEDIA SUPPORT PLUS HEALTH AND SAFETY	6.580	6.799	7.633	8.232	8.807	9.354
65	NET REVALUATIONS	-4.591	-4.957	49.148	100.493	115.182	-35.335
66	LESS: INT PRODUCT FROM GOVT	58.529	59.845	61.523	63.108	62.189	73.504
67	GROSS BUSINESS PRODUCT	733.170	794.988	937.507	1104.096	1196.318	1118.522

TABLE 2. BUSINESS INCOME AND PRODUCT, BILLIONS OF DOLLARS, 1946-81

		CREDITS				
		1976	1977	1978	1979	1980	1981
54	BEA GROSS DOMESTIC PRODUCT, BUSINESS	1447.281	1623.976	1837.188	2052.144	2228.128	2508.986
55	LESS: NET SPACE RENT OF OWNER-OCC. NONFARM DWELLINGS	94.727	105.718	119.549	135.423	155.187	178.649
56	LESS: BEA GOVT ENTERPRISE PRODUCT	27.985	29.331	32.795	35.917	38.792	43.426
57	LESS: RENTAL VALUE OF BLDGS. OWNED AND USED BY NONPROFIT INSTITUTIONS	6.025	6.589	7.449	8.633	9.968	11.233
58	BEA-TYPE GROSS DOMESTIC PRODUCT OF TISA BUSINESS SECTOR	1318.544	1482.338	1677.395	1872.171	2024.182	2275.678
59	SUBSIDIES INCLUDED IN BUSINESS INCOME	5.628	7.587	9.416	9.437	10.586	11.977
60	EXPENSE ACCOUNT ITEMS OF CONSUMPTION	13.879	15.566	17.768	20.261	22.358	24.560
61	LESS: EXPENSES RELATED TO WORK	23.188	26.816	30.266	35.924	41.923	44.783
62	BUSINESS INVESTMENT IN RESEARCH AND DEVELOPMENT	17.436	19.407	22.156	25.655	29.940	33.850
63	TRAINING PRODUCED IN BUSINESS SECTOR	24.786	29.048	35.233	39.348	37.683	40.964
64	MEDIA SUPPORT PLUS HEALTH AND SAFETY	11.097	12.624	14.696	16.491	18.341	20.552
65	NET REVALUATIONS	158.464	104.991	123.764	145.411	11.269	-106.965
66	LESS: INT PRODUCT FROM GOVT	74.265	80.347	84.213	93.242	107.142	121.323
67	GROSS BUSINESS PRODUCT	1452.381	1564.398	1785.949	1999.608	2005.293	2134.510

		PERCENT PER ANNUM RATES OF GROWTH CURRENT DOLLARS					
		1946-56	1956-66	1966-71	1971-76	1976-81	1946-81
54	BEA GROSS DOMESTIC PRODUCT, BUSINESS	7.311	5.779	6.806	9.795	11.632	7.755
55	LESS: NET SPACE RENT OF OWNER-OCC. NONFARM DWELLINGS	12.950	7.828	7.823	10.036	13.529	10.393
56	LESS: BEA GOVT ENTERPRISE PRODUCT	5.241	9.187	10.229	11.224	9.185	8.477
57	LESS: RENTAL VALUE OF BLDGS. OWNED AND USED BY NONPROFIT INSTITUTIONS	8.671	7.465	11.619	9.981	13.268	9.573
58	BEA-TYPE GROSS DOMESTIC PRODUCT OF TISA BUSINESS SECTOR	7.103	5.602	6.655	9.747	11.533	7.602
59	SUBSIDIES INCLUDED IN BUSINESS INCOME	-5.405	17.025	3.497	3.286	16.305	6.200
60	EXPENSE ACCOUNT ITEMS OF CONSUMPTION	7.828	4.629	7.115	9.317	12.091	7.607
61	LESS: EXPENSES RELATED TO WORK	11.470	4.409	8.192	9.659	14.070	9.044
62	BUSINESS INVESTMENT IN RESEARCH AND DEVELOPMENT	15.889	8.214	8.104	10.354	14.188	11.499
63	TRAINING PRODUCED IN BUSINESS SECTOR	2.431	9.737	3.122	10.415	10.570	6.856
64	MEDIA SUPPORT PLUS HEALTH AND SAFETY	10.495	7.543	5.517	10.294	13.117	9.261
65	NET REVALUATIONS	N.A.	-12.560	N.A.	N.A.	N.A.	N.A.
66	LESS: INT PRODUCT FROM GOVT	-2.225	4.923	5.406	4.412	10.314	3.563
67	GROSS BUSINESS PRODUCT	11.329	5.354	6.337	12.809	8.005	8.607

TABLE 3. NONPROFIT INCOME AND PRODUCT, BILLIONS OF DOLLARS, 1946-81

		DEBITS					
		1946	1947	1948	1949	1950	1951
1	LABOR INCOME	2.380	2.788	3.214	3.501	3.811	4.199
2	COMPENSATION OF EMPLOYEES	2.368	2.789	3.235	3.566	3.864	4.237
3	EMPLOYEE TRAINING	.090	.093	.097	.074	.099	.130
4	LESS: EXPENSES RELATED TO WORK	.078	.094	.118	.139	.152	.168
5	CAPITAL INCOME	.410	.502	.702	.746	.708	.698
6	INTEREST PAID	.059	.063	.065	.071	.075	.077
7	NET IMPUTED INTEREST	.351	.439	.637	.675	.633	.621
8	GROSS IMPUTED INTEREST	.410	.502	.702	.746	.708	.698
9	LAND	.093	.109	.146	.154	.146	.142
10	STUCTURES AND EQUIPMENT	.182	.234	.337	.367	.358	.365
11	RESIDENTIAL	.136	.159	.219	.225	.204	.191
12	LESS: INTEREST PAID	.059	.063	.065	.071	.075	.077
13	NET REVALUATIONS	-.101	.889	.131	.185	.131	.806
14	LAND	-.225	.100	.006	.172	.132	.304
15	STRUCTURES AND EQUIPMENT	.446	.424	-.090	.027	-.108	.333
16	RESIDENTIAL STRUCTURES	-.322	.364	.216	-.014	.107	.169
17	INCOME ORIGINATING (1+5+13)	2.689	4.178	4.048	4.432	4.650	5.703
18	IMPUTED VALUE OF VOLUNTEER SERVICES	2.132	2.408	2.747	2.775	2.914	3.167
19	CHARGES AGAINST NET NONPROFIT PRODUCT (17 + 18)	4.821	6.586	6.795	7.207	7.564	8.870
20	CAPITAL CONSUMPTION ALLOWANCES	.399	.498	.559	.572	.603	.700
21	ORIGINAL COST	.225	.235	.253	.278	.312	.350
22	REVALUATIONS	.174	.262	.306	.294	.291	.351
23	CHARGES AGAINST GROSS NONPROFIT PRODUCT (19 + 20)	5.220	7.084	7.354	7.779	8.167	9.570
		1952	1953	1954	1955	1956	1957
1	LABOR INCOME	4.540	4.986	5.365	5.881	6.310	6.931
2	COMPENSATION OF EMPLOYEES	4.601	5.078	5.502	6.015	6.536	7.191
3	EMPLOYEE TRAINING	.133	.133	.123	.160	.113	.118
4	LESS: EXPENSES RELATED TO WORK	.194	.225	.260	.294	.339	.378
5	CAPITAL INCOME	.762	.796	.938	1.116	1.077	1.235
6	INTEREST PAID	.082	.084	.088	.092	.095	.099
7	NET IMPUTED INTEREST	.680	.712	.850	1.024	.982	1.136
8	GROSS IMPUTED INTEREST	.762	.796	.938	1.116	1.077	1.235
9	LAND	.157	.165	.205	.258	.257	.356
10	STUCTURES AND EQUIPMENT	.408	.433	.510	.610	.597	.653
11	RESIDENTIAL	.197	.199	.223	.248	.222	.226
12	LESS: INTEREST PAID	.082	.084	.088	.092	.095	.099

TABLE 3. NONPROFIT INCOME AND PRODUCT, BILLIONS OF DOLLARS, 1946-81

		DEBITS					
		1952	1953	1954	1955	1956	1957
13	NET REVALUATIONS	.260	-.122	.737	.955	1.322	3.861
14	LAND	.296	.070	.949	.557	.923	4.365
15	STRUCTURES AND EQUIPMENT	-.066	-.235	-.303	.309	.386	-.517
16	RESIDENTIAL STRUCTURES	.030	.044	.092	.089	.013	.013
17	INCOME ORIGINATING (1+5+13)	5.561	5.661	7.040	7.952	8.708	12.028
18	IMPUTED VALUE OF VOLUNTEER SERVICES	3.386	3.616	3.752	3.936	4.158	4.409
19	CHARGES AGAINST NET NONPROFIT PRODUCT (17 + 18)	8.947	9.277	10.792	11.888	12.866	16.437
20	CAPITAL CONSUMPTION ALLOWANCES	.747	.782	.804	.858	.957	1.035
21	ORIGINAL COST	.387	.424	.468	.514	.564	.620
22	REVALUATIONS	.360	.358	.337	.344	.393	.415
23	CHARGES AGAINST GROSS NONPROFIT PRODUCT (19 + 20)	9.694	10.059	11.597	12.746	13.823	17.472

		1958	1959	1960	1961	1962	1963
1	LABOR INCOME	7.658	8.491	9.683	10.309	11.363	12.320
2	COMPENSATION OF EMPLOYEES	7.938	8.792	10.036	10.672	11.725	12.723
3	EMPLOYEE TRAINING	.140	.167	.174	.185	.222	.216
4	LESS: EXPENSES RELATED TO WORK	.420	.468	.527	.548	.584	.619
5	CAPITAL INCOME	1.334	1.571	1.542	1.608	1.962	2.218
6	INTEREST PAID	.102	.110	.125	.140	.155	.175
7	NET IMPUTED INTEREST	1.232	1.461	1.417	1.468	1.807	2.043
8	GROSS IMPUTED INTEREST	1.334	1.571	1.542	1.608	1.962	2.218
9	LAND	.431	.500	.447	.427	.536	.604
10	STUCTURES AND EQUIPMENT	.679	.813	.839	.913	1.112	1.270
11	RESIDENTIAL	.224	.258	.257	.268	.314	.343
12	LESS: INTEREST PAID	.102	.110	.125	.140	.155	.175
13	NET REVALUATIONS	-.311	-.366	-3.141	.999	1.158	.356
14	LAND	.108	.176	-2.707	1.020	1.298	.146
15	STRUCTURES AND EQUIPMENT	-.513	-.636	-.543	-.153	-.461	.110
16	RESIDENTIAL STRUCTURES	.094	.094	.109	.131	.321	.100
17	INCOME ORIGINATING (1+5+13)	8.680	9.696	8.084	12.916	14.483	14.893
18	IMPUTED VALUE OF VOLUNTEER SERVICES	4.603	4.833	5.072	5.266	5.491	5.744
19	CHARGES AGAINST NET NONPROFIT PRODUCT (17 + 18)	13.283	14.529	13.156	18.182	19.974	20.637
20	CAPITAL CONSUMPTION ALLOWANCES	1.069	1.118	1.176	1.237	1.321	1.415
21	ORIGINAL COST	.683	.749	.819	.894	.978	1.071
22	REVALUATIONS	.386	.369	.357	.343	.342	.343
23	CHARGES AGAINST GROSS NONPROFIT PRODUCT (19 + 20)	14.352	15.647	14.332	19.419	21.294	22.052

TABLE 3. NONPROFIT INCOME AND PRODUCT. BILLIONS OF DOLLARS, 1946-81

		DEBITS					
		1964	1965	1966	1967	1968	1969
1	LABOR INCOME	13.445	14.834	16.743	18.780	21.197	24.472
2	COMPENSATION OF EMPLOYEES	13.853	15.243	17.126	19.244	21.691	25.001
3	EMPLOYEE TRAINING	.255	.311	.395	.400	.460	.539
4	LESS: EXPENSES RELATED TO WORK	.663	.720	.778	.864	.954	1.068
5	CAPITAL INCOME	2.503	2.933	3.166	3.265	3.165	3.065
6	INTEREST PAID	.223	.275	.356	.447	.540	.640
7	NET IMPUTED INTEREST	2.280	2.658	2.810	2.818	2.625	2.425
8	GROSS IMPUTED INTEREST	2.503	2.933	3.166	3.265	3.165	3.065
9	LAND	.666	.775	.824	.832	.770	.702
10	STUCTURES AND EQUIPMENT	1.455	1.717	1.874	1.958	1.937	1.930
11	RESIDENTIAL	.382	.441	.468	.474	.458	.433
12	LESS: INTEREST PAID	.223	.275	.356	.447	.540	.640
13	NET REVALUATIONS	.772	1.308	1.074	1.005	-.629	3.158
14	LAND	.681	1.005	.577	.578	-.991	.407
15	STRUCTURES AND EQUIPMENT	-.423	-.072	-.091	.131	-.179	2.647
16	RESIDENTIAL STRUCTURES	.514	.374	.589	.296	.541	.104
17	INCOME ORIGINATING (1+5+13)	16.720	19.075	20.984	23.050	23.733	30.695
18	IMPUTED VALUE OF VOLUNTEER SERVICES	6.011	6.409	6.839	7.305	7.845	8.533
19	CHARGES AGAINST NET NONPROFIT PRODUCT (17 + 18)	22.731	25.484	27.823	30.355	31.578	39.228
20	CAPITAL CONSUMPTION ALLOWANCES	1.520	1.644	1.805	1.976	2.149	2.407
21	ORIGINAL COST	1.164	1.270	1.387	1.499	1.600	1.700
22	REVALUATIONS	.355	.374	.418	.477	.550	.707
23	CHARGES AGAINST GROSS NONPROFIT PRODUCT (19 + 20)	24.251	27.128	29.628	32.331	33.727	41.635
		1970	1971	1972	1973	1974	1975
1	LABOR INCOME	27.106	30.056	33.288	36.627	40.362	44.827
2	COMPENSATION OF EMPLOYEES	27.763	30.811	34.000	37.306	41.256	46.047
3	EMPLOYEE TRAINING	.516	.547	.677	.805	.806	.707
4	LESS: EXPENSES RELATED TO WORK	1.173	1.302	1.389	1.484	1.700	1.927
5	CAPITAL INCOME	3.025	3.488	3.687	3.789	3.301	4.434
6	INTEREST PAID	.750	.825	.910	1.000	1.100	1.180
7	NET IMPUTED INTEREST	2.275	2.663	2.777	2.789	2.201	3.254
8	GROSS IMPUTED INTEREST	3.025	3.488	3.687	3.789	3.301	4.434
9	LAND	.666	.725	.736	.741	.626	.815
10	STUCTURES AND EQUIPMENT	1.955	2.312	2.486	2.585	2.297	3.126
11	RESIDENTIAL	.404	.451	.465	.464	.377	.493
12	LESS: INTEREST PAID	.750	.825	.910	1.000	1.100	1.180

179

TABLE 3.   NONPROFIT INCOME AND PRODUCT, BILLIONS OF DOLLARS, 1946-81

		DEBITS					
		1970	1971	1972	1973	1974	1975
13	NET REVALUATIONS	1.440	-1.098	2.451	3.412	9.474	-10.709
14	LAND	.021	-1.465	.934	.265	1.371	-3.093
15	STRUCTURES AND EQUIPMENT	1.515	.387	1.443	2.897	8.542	-7.370
16	RESIDENTIAL STRUCTURES	-.096	-.020	.074	.250	-.439	-.246
17	INCOME ORIGINATING (1+5+13)	31.572	32.446	39.426	43.828	53.137	38.552
18	IMPUTED VALUE OF VOLUNTEER SERVICES	9.347	10.251	11.222	12.164	13.332	14.566
19	CHARGES AGAINST NET NONPROFIT PRODUCT (17 + 18)	40.919	42.697	50.648	55.992	66.469	53.118
20	CAPITAL CONSUMPTION ALLOWANCES	2.664	2.919	3.159	3.501	4.154	4.611
21	ORIGINAL COST	1.805	1.910	2.023	2.146	2.274	2.398
22	REVALUATIONS	.859	1.009	1.136	1.356	1.880	2.212
23	CHARGES AGAINST GROSS NONPROFIT PRODUCT (19 + 20)	43.583	45.616	53.808	59.494	70.623	57.729
		1976	1977	1978	1979	1980	1981
1	LABOR INCOME	48.994	53.177	59.985	67.168	75.993	86.245
2	COMPENSATION OF EMPLOYEES	50.275	54.617	61.546	69.138	78.703	89.189
3	EMPLOYEE TRAINING	.877	.986	1.163	1.259	1.212	1.332
4	LESS: EXPENSES RELATED TO WORK	2.158	2.426	2.724	3.229	3.922	4.276
5	CAPITAL INCOME	4.298	4.910	5.357	5.314	5.322	6.282
6	INTEREST PAID	1.280	1.368	1.493	1.731	2.071	2.639
7	NET IMPUTED INTEREST	3.018	3.542	3.864	3.583	3.251	3.643
8	GROSS IMPUTED INTEREST	4.298	4.910	5.357	5.314	5.322	6.282
9	LAND	.775	.876	.943	.927	.911	1.059
10	STUCTURES AND EQUIPMENT	3.027	3.464	3.795	3.791	3.841	4.567
11	RESIDENTIAL	.496	.570	.619	.596	.570	.656
12	LESS: INTEREST PAID	1.280	1.368	1.493	1.731	2.071	2.639
13	NET REVALUATIONS	-2.301	5.384	5.088	5.732	-2.270	-5.441
14	LAND	-.014	.523	1.139	.457	-1.274	-1.196
15	STRUCTURES AND EQUIPMENT	-2.744	4.384	3.251	5.996	.240	-3.501
16	RESIDENTIAL STRUCTURES	.456	.477	.697	-.720	-1.236	-.744
17	INCOME ORIGINATING (1+5+13)	50.991	63.471	70.429	78.214	79.045	87.086
18	IMPUTED VALUE OF VOLUNTEER SERVICES	15.043	15.370	15.633	16.049	17.015	18.017
19	CHARGES AGAINST NET NONPROFIT PRODUCT (17 + 18)	66.034	78.841	86.062	94.263	96.060	105.103
20	CAPITAL CONSUMPTION ALLOWANCES	4.745	5.158	5.830	6.733	7.606	8.202
21	ORIGINAL COST	2.527	2.672	2.844	3.048	3.288	3.583
22	REVALUATIONS	2.218	2.486	2.986	3.686	4.318	4.618
23	CHARGES AGAINST GROSS NONPROFIT PRODUCT (19 + 20)	70.778	83.999	91.892	100.996	103.666	113.305

180

TABLE 3. NONPROFIT INCOME AND PRODUCT, BILLIONS OF DOLLARS, 1946-81

| | | DEBITS | | | | | |
| | | PERCENT PER ANNUM RATES OF GROWTH | | | | | |
		1946-56	1956-66	1966-71	1971-76	1976-81	1946-81
1	LABOR INCOME	10.242	10.250	12.414	10.266	11.974	10.802
2	COMPENSATION OF EMPLOYEES	10.686	10.112	12.463	10.288	12.148	10.924
3	EMPLOYEE TRAINING	2.302	13.332	6.728	9.901	8.718	8.003
4	LESS: EXPENSES RELATED TO WORK	15.827	8.662	10.848	10.634	14.656	12.120
5	CAPITAL INCOME	10.140	11.388	1.954	4.266	7.885	8.111
6	INTEREST PAID	4.879	14.123	18.304	9.182	15.570	11.470
7	NET IMPUTED INTEREST	10.836	11.089	-1.071	2.536	3.835	6.914
8	GROSS IMPUTED INTEREST	10.140	11.388	1.954	4.266	7.885	8.111
9	LAND	10.725	12.348	-2.519	1.336	6.445	7.202
10	STUCTURES AND EQUIPMENT	12.651	12.111	4.287	5.542	8.572	9.653
11	RESIDENTIAL	5.067	7.735	-.747	1.917	5.749	4.607
12	LESS: INTEREST PAID	4.879	14.123	18.304	9.182	15.570	11.470
13	NET REVALUATIONS	N.A.	-2.048	N.A.	N.A.	N.A.	N.A.
14	LAND	N.A.	-4.591	N.A.	N.A.	N.A.	N.A.
15	STRUCTURES AND EQUIPMENT	-1.445	N.A.	N.A.	N.A.	N.A.	N.A.
16	RESIDENTIAL STRUCTURES	N.A.	46.426	N.A.	N.A.	N.A.	N.A.
17	INCOME ORIGINATING (1+5+13)	12.468	9.193	9.108	9.463	11.299	10.446
18	IMPUTED VALUE OF VOLUNTEER SERVICES	6.908	5.102	8.431	7.973	3.674	6.288
19	CHARGES AGAINST NET NONPROFIT PRODUCT (17 + 18)	10.314	8.018	8.943	9.112	9.741	9.205
20	CAPITAL CONSUMPTION ALLOWANCES	9.143	6.552	10.091	10.202	11.567	9.022
21	ORIGINAL COST	9.614	9.421	6.617	5.754	7.236	8.229
22	REVALUATIONS	8.505	.621	19.246	17.061	15.799	9.822
23	CHARGES AGAINST GROSS NONPROFIT PRODUCT (19 + 20)	10.228	7.922	9.015	9.183	9.868	9.191

181

TABLE 3. NONPROFIT INCOME AND PRODUCT, BILLIONS OF DOLLARS, 1946-81

				CREDITS			
		1946	1947	1948	1949	1950	1951
24	CONSUMPTION	5.083	5.517	6.092	6.182	6.404	6.955
25	CONSUMPTION IN BEA PCE	2.890	3.139	3.426	3.494	3.741	4.045
26	ADDITIONAL IMPUTED CONSUMPTION	2.193	2.378	2.665	2.687	2.662	2.910
27	CAPITAL ACCUMULATION	2.756	4.186	3.834	4.026	4.146	5.226
28	RESEARCH AND DEVELOPMENT	.043	.046	.052	.057	.064	.070
29	EDUCATION AND TRAINING	2.008	2.311	2.577	2.651	2.734	3.016
30	INVESTMENT IN BEA PCE	1.182	1.408	1.565	1.650	1.731	1.897
31	ADDITIONAL IMPUTED INVESTMENT	.735	.810	.914	.927	.904	.989
32	EMPLOYEE TRAINING	.090	.093	.097	.074	.099	.130
33	HEALTH	.806	.940	1.075	1.132	1.217	1.334
34	INVESTMENT IN BEA PCE	.480	.580	.661	.715	.812	.895
35	ADDITIONAL IMPUTED INVESTMENT	.326	.361	.414	.418	.405	.440
36	NET REVALUATIONS	-.101	.889	.131	.185	.131	.806
37	LESS: INTERMEDIATE PRODUCT TRANSFERRED FROM GOVERNMENT	.772	.702	.609	.582	.424	.550
38	LESS: INTERMEDIATE PRODUCT PURCHASED	1.769	1.823	1.845	1.707	1.806	1.893
39	LESS: EXPENSES RELATED TO WORK	.078	.094	.118	.139	.152	.168
40	GROSS NONPROFIT PRODUCT	5.220	7.084	7.354	7.779	8.167	9.570
		1952	1953	1954	1955	1956	1957
24	CONSUMPTION	7.585	8.037	8.603	9.149	9.866	10.807
25	CONSUMPTION IN BEA PCE	4.453	4.740	5.066	5.327	5.902	6.315
26	ADDITIONAL IMPUTED CONSUMPTION	3.132	3.296	3.537	3.822	3.964	4.492
27	CAPITAL ACCUMULATION	5.055	4.983	6.212	6.922	7.700	10.978
28	RESEARCH AND DEVELOPMENT	.078	.087	.096	.102	.116	.139
29	EDUCATION AND TRAINING	3.253	3.436	3.663	3.995	4.263	4.739
30	INVESTMENT IN BEA PCE	2.053	2.180	2.318	2.498	2.770	3.032
31	ADDITIONAL IMPUTED INVESTMENT	1.067	1.123	1.222	1.337	1.380	1.588
32	EMPLOYEE TRAINING	.133	.133	.123	.160	.113	.118
33	HEALTH	1.464	1.581	1.716	1.870	2.000	2.239
34	INVESTMENT IN BEA PCE	.989	1.085	1.176	1.279	1.401	1.543
35	ADDITIONAL IMPUTED INVESTMENT	.475	.496	.540	.591	.599	.696
36	NET REVALUATIONS	.260	-.122	.737	.955	1.322	3.861
37	LESS: INTERMEDIATE PRODUCT TRANSFERRED FROM GOVERNMENT	.609	.587	.697	.791	.803	1.231
38	LESS: INTERMEDIATE PRODUCT PURCHASED	2.143	2.149	2.261	2.241	2.601	2.704
39	LESS: EXPENSES RELATED TO WORK	.194	.225	.260	.294	.339	.378
40	GROSS NONPROFIT PRODUCT	9.694	10.059	11.597	12.746	13.823	17.472

TABLE 3. NONPROFIT INCOME AND PRODUCT, BILLINGS OF DOLLARS, 1946-81

		CREDITS					
		1958	1959	1960	1961	1962	1963
24	CONSUMPTION	11.276	12.285	12.788	13.569	14.357	15.294
25	CONSUMPTION IN BEA PCE	6.807	7.456	7.920	8.229	8.587	9.213
26	ADDITIONAL IMPUTED CONSUMPTION	4.469	4.829	4.868	5.340	5.770	6.081
27	CAPITAL ACCUMULATION	7.239	7.915	5.586	10.524	11.476	11.490
28	RESEARCH AND DEVELOPMENT	.160	.177	.191	.223	.265	.294
29	EDUCATION AND TRAINING	4.983	5.446	5.678	6.189	6.657	7.048
30	INVESTMENT IN BEA PCE	3.281	3.587	3.825	4.138	4.403	4.699
31	ADDITIONAL IMPUTED INVESTMENT	1.562	1.692	1.678	1.866	2.031	2.133
32	EMPLOYEE TRAINING	.140	.167	.174	.185	.222	.216
33	HEALTH	2.407	2.658	2.859	3.113	3.397	3.793
34	INVESTMENT IN BEA PCE	1.725	1.913	2.123	2.283	2.476	2.808
35	ADDITIONAL IMPUTED INVESTMENT	.683	.745	.736	.831	.921	.985
36	NET REVALUATIONS	-.311	-.366	-3.141	.999	1.158	.356
37	LESS: INTERMEDIATE PRODUCT TRANSFERRED FROM GOVERNMENT	.879	.973	.793	1.303	1.425	1.412
38	LESS: INTERMEDIATE PRODUCT PURCHASED	2.864	3.113	2.722	2.823	2.530	2.701
39	LESS: EXPENSES RELATED TO WORK	.420	.468	.527	.548	.584	.619
40	GROSS NONPROFIT PRODUCT	14.352	15.647	14.332	19.419	21.294	22.052
		1964	1965	1966	1967	1968	1969
24	CONSUMPTION	16.480	17.657	18.937	19.660	22.337	24.533
25	CONSUMPTION IN BEA PCE	10.011	10.538	11.378	11.586	13.976	15.638
26	ADDITIONAL IMPUTED CONSUMPTION	6.469	7.118	7.560	8.074	8.361	8.895
27	CAPITAL ACCUMULATION	12.921	13.664	15.808	16.130	16.940	23.038
28	RESEARCH AND DEVELOPMENT	.311	.349	.394	.423	.448	.478
29	EDUCATION AND TRAINING	7.647	7.432	9.299	10.084	10.985	12.104
30	INVESTMENT IN BEA PCE	5.123	4.671	6.223	6.762	7.538	8.396
31	ADDITIONAL IMPUTED INVESTMENT	2.269	2.449	2.681	2.922	2.987	3.168
32	EMPLOYEE TRAINING	.255	.311	.395	.400	.460	.539
33	HEALTH	4.192	4.576	5.041	4.619	6.136	7.299
34	INVESTMENT IN BEA PCE	3.121	3.368	3.743	3.263	4.693	5.727
35	ADDITIONAL IMPUTED INVESTMENT	1.071	1.208	1.298	1.356	1.443	1.572
36	NET REVALUATIONS	.772	1.308	1.074	1.005	-.629	3.158
37	LESS: INTERMEDIATE PRODUCT TRANSFERRED FROM GOVERNMENT	1.517	1.708	1.890	2.229	2.321	2.677
38	LESS: INTERMEDIATE PRODUCT PURCHASED	2.970	1.764	2.450	.366	2.275	2.191
39	LESS: EXPENSES RELATED TO WORK	.663	.720	.778	.864	.954	1.068
40	GROSS NONPROFIT PRODUCT	24.251	27.128	29.628	32.331	33.727	41.635

183

TABLE 3.   NONPROFIT INCOME AND PRODUCT, BILLIONS OF DOLLARS, 1946-81

		CREDITS					
		1970	1971	1972	1973	1974	1975
24	CONSUMPTION	27.166	30.031	33.041	35.426	39.227	43.999
25	CONSUMPTION IN BEA PCE	17.637	19.686	21.884	23.695	26.835	30.234
26	ADDITIONAL IMPUTED CONSUMPTION	9.529	10.345	11.158	11.731	12.391	13.766
27	CAPITAL ACCUMULATION	23.442	23.373	29.393	32.839	42.377	26.239
28	RESEARCH AND DEVELOPMENT	.524	.575	.608	.638	.687	.765
29	EDUCATION AND TRAINING	13.080	14.221	15.647	17.032	18.743	20.463
30	INVESTMENT IN BEA PCE	9.208	10.061	11.099	12.195	13.719	15.099
31	ADDITIONAL IMPUTED INVESTMENT	3.357	3.614	3.870	4.032	4.218	4.657
32	EMPLOYEE TRAINING	.516	.547	.677	.805	.806	.707
33	HEALTH	8.398	9.674	10.687	11.757	13.473	15.720
34	INVESTMENT IN BEA PCE	6.697	7.797	8.659	9.642	11.274	13.200
35	ADDITIONAL IMPUTED INVESTMENT	1.701	1.877	2.028	2.115	2.199	2.521
36	NET REVALUATIONS	1.440	-1.098	2.451	3.412	9.474	-10.709
37	LESS: INTERMEDIATE PRODUCT TRANSFERRED FROM GOVERNMENT	2.965	2.922	3.057	2.924	3.276	3.123
38	LESS: INTERMEDIATE PRODUCT PURCHASED	2.888	3.564	4.181	4.363	6.005	7.459
39	LESS: EXPENSES RELATED TO WORK	1.173	1.302	1.389	1.484	1.700	1.927
40	GROSS NONPROFIT PRODUCT	43.583	45.616	53.808	59.494	70.623	57.729

		1976	1977	1978	1979	1980	1981
24	CONSUMPTION	47.942	52.714	58.151	63.711	71.682	81.031
25	CONSUMPTION IN BEA PCE	33.988	37.833	42.909	48.160	55.260	63.227
26	ADDITIONAL IMPUTED CONSUMPTION	13.954	14.881	15.242	15.550	16.422	17.804
27	CAPITAL ACCUMULATION	38.137	49.917	54.554	60.769	59.641	65.768
28	RESEARCH AND DEVELOPMENT	.879	.977	1.117	1.237	1.364	1.491
29	EDUCATION AND TRAINING	21.656	23.092	25.441	27.884	30.700	34.035
30	INVESTMENT IN BEA PCE	16.114	17.125	19.190	21.445	24.033	26.798
31	ADDITIONAL IMPUTED INVESTMENT	4.665	4.982	5.088	5.180	5.455	5.905
32	EMPLOYEE TRAINING	.877	.986	1.163	1.259	1.212	1.332
33	HEALTH	17.903	20.464	22.908	25.916	29.847	35.683
34	INVESTMENT IN BEA PCE	15.347	17.576	19.907	22.833	26.563	31.952
35	ADDITIONAL IMPUTED INVESTMENT	2.557	2.889	3.001	3.083	3.284	3.731
36	NET REVALUATIONS	-2.301	5.384	5.088	5.732	-2.270	-5.441
37	LESS: INTERMEDIATE PRODUCT TRANSFERRED FROM GOVERNMENT	3.114	3.902	3.960	4.350	5.186	6.171
38	LESS: INTERMEDIATE PRODUCT PURCHASED	10.028	12.304	14.129	15.904	18.549	23.046
39	LESS: EXPENSES RELATED TO WORK	2.158	2.426	2.724	3.229	3.922	4.276
40	GROSS NONPROFIT PRODUCT	70.778	83.999	91.892	100.996	103.666	113.305

TABLE 3. NONPROFIT INCOME AND PRODUCT, BILLIONS OF DOLLARS, 1946-81

		CREDITS					
		PERCENT PER ANNUM RATES OF GROWTH					
		1946-56	1956-66	1966-71	1971-76	1976-81	1946-81
24	CONSUMPTION	6.857	6.737	9.660	9.807	11.068	8.233
25	CONSUMPTION IN BEA PCE	7.401	6.784	11.589	11.541	13.218	9.216
26	ADDITIONAL IMPUTED CONSUMPTION	6.099	6.668	6.474	6.168	4.993	6.166
27	CAPITAL ACCUMULATION	10.822	7.458	8.135	10.288	11.515	9.488
28	RESEARCH AND DEVELOPMENT	10.490	12.973	7.884	8.856	11.131	10.671
29	EDUCATION AND TRAINING	7.821	8.111	8.869	8.774	9.463	8.423
30	INVESTMENT IN BEA PCE	8.890	8.430	10.085	9.880	10.708	9.327
31	ADDITIONAL IMPUTED INVESTMENT	6.494	6.868	6.153	5.237	4.829	6.132
32	EMPLOYEE TRAINING	2.302	13.332	6.728	9.901	8.718	8.003
33	HEALTH	9.512	9.688	13.923	13.101	14.790	11.438
34	INVESTMENT IN BEA PCE	11.302	10.330	15.809	14.503	15.797	12.744
35	ADDITIONAL IMPUTED INVESTMENT	6.276	8.039	7.649	6.378	7.849	7.212
36	NET REVALUATIONS	N.A.	-2.048	N.A.	N.A.	N.A.	N.A.
37	LESS: INTERMEDIATE PRODUCT TRANSFERRED FROM GOVERNMENT	.405	8.932	9.103	1.285	14.658	6.121
38	LESS: INTERMEDIATE PRODUCT PURCHASED	3.930	-.597	7.784	22.988	18.107	7.610
39	LESS: EXPENSES RELATED TO WORK	15.827	8.662	10.848	10.634	14.656	12.120
40	GROSS NONPROFIT PRODUCT	10.228	7.922	9.015	9.183	9.868	9.191

TABLE 4. GOVERNMENT ENTERPRISE INCOME AND PRODUCT, BILLIONS OF DOLLARS, 1946-81

		DEBITS					
		1946	1947	1948	1949	1950	1951
1	LABOR INCOME	1.890	1.965	2.318	2.540	2.693	2.995
2	COMPENSATION OF EMPLOYEES	1.896	1.965	2.316	2.564	2.695	2.999
3	EMPLOYEE TRAINING	.039	.048	.061	.045	.071	.076
4	LESS: EXPENSES RELATED TO WORK	.045	.048	.059	.069	.073	.080
5	CAPITAL INCOME	.034	.028	.051	.099	.118	.087
6	SURPLUSES	1.218	1.202	1.214	1.290	1.333	1.448
7	BEA SURPLUS	.608	.592	.449	.482	.243	.402
8	SUM OF ABSOLUTE VALUES OF NEGATIVE SURPLUSES	.610	.610	.765	.808	1.090	1.046
9	NET REVALUATIONS	.279	.160	.327	-.739	.329	.030
10	NET SURPLUS (6 + 9)	1.497	1.362	1.541	.551	1.662	1.478
11	CHARGES AGAINST GOVERNMENT ENTERPRISE PRODUCT	3.421	3.355	3.910	3.190	4.473	4.560

		1952	1953	1954	1955	1956	1957
1	LABOR INCOME	3.458	3.511	3.549	3.814	4.003	4.193
2	COMPENSATION OF EMPLOYEES	3.489	3.545	3.597	3.862	4.054	4.282
3	EMPLOYEE TRAINING	.066	.072	.070	.078	.087	.061
4	LESS: EXPENSES RELATED TO WORK	.097	.106	.118	.126	.138	.150
5	CAPITAL INCOME	.065	.119	.216	.269	.265	.275
6	SURPLUSES	1.515	1.620	1.780	1.924	2.024	2.169
7	BEA SURPLUS	.701	.878	.843	.515	.103	.614
8	SUM OF ABSOLUTE VALUES OF NEGATIVE SURPLUSES	.814	.742	.937	1.409	1.921	1.555
9	NET REVALUATIONS	-.365	-.130	-.498	-1.199	.196	.807
10	NET SURPLUS (6 + 9)	1.150	1.490	1.282	.725	2.220	2.976
11	CHARGES AGAINST GOVERNMENT ENTERPRISE PRODUCT	4.673	5.120	5.047	4.808	6.488	7.444

		1958	1959	1960	1961	1962	1963
1	LABOR INCOME	4.646	5.008	5.492	5.751	6.164	6.640
2	COMPENSATION OF EMPLOYEES	4.741	5.093	5.561	5.828	6.243	6.726
3	EMPLOYEE TRAINING	.065	.092	.120	.120	.125	.128
4	LESS: EXPENSES RELATED TO WORK	.160	.177	.189	.197	.204	.214
5	CAPITAL INCOME	.289	.338	.326	.314	.321	.336
6	SURPLUSES	2.198	2.451	2.729	2.862	3.031	3.407
7	BEA SURPLUS	.308	1.037	.817	.454	.641	1.202
8	SUM OF ABSOLUTE VALUES OF NEGATIVE SURPLUSES	1.890	1.414	1.912	2.408	2.390	2.205
9	NET REVALUATIONS	.997	-.726	.263	-.190	.051	-.277
10	NET SURPLUS (6 + 9)	3.195	1.725	2.992	2.672	3.082	3.130
11	CHARGES AGAINST GOVERNMENT ENTERPRISE PRODUCT	8.130	7.071	8.810	8.737	9.567	10.106

TABLE 4. GOVERNMENT ENTERPRISE INCOME AND PRODUCT, BILLIONS OF DOLLARS, 1946-81

		DEBITS					
		1964	1965	1966	1967	1968	1969
1	LABOR INCOME	7.164	7.714	8.459	9.067	10.188	11.262
2	COMPENSATION OF EMPLOYEES	7.251	7.782	8.490	9.108	10.211	11.271
3	EMPLOYEE TRAINING	.136	.168	.219	.229	.267	.309
4	LESS: EXPENSES RELATED TO WORK	.223	.236	.250	.270	.290	.318
5	CAPITAL INCOME	.321	.332	.258	.151	.146	.175
6	SURPLUSES	3.574	3.775	3.821	4.031	4.269	4.734
7	BEA SURPLUS	1.152	1.478	1.536	2.277	2.952	2.764
8	SUM OF ABSOLUTE VALUES OF NEGATIVE SURPLUSES	2.422	2.297	2.285	1.754	1.317	1.970
9	NET REVALUATIONS	-.311	.582	-.311	-.132	-.081	.112
10	NET SURPLUS (6 + 9)	3.263	4.357	3.510	3.899	4.188	4.846
11	CHARGES AGAINST GOVERNMENT ENTERPRISE PRODUCT	10.748	12.403	12.227	13.117	14.522	16.283
		1970	1971	1972	1973	1974	1975
1	LABOR INCOME	12.995	13.983	15.305	17.011	19.213	21.328
2	COMPENSATION OF EMPLOYEES	13.039	14.039	15.276	16.903	19.135	21.365
3	EMPLOYEE TRAINING	.313	.334	.424	.529	.565	.504
4	LESS: EXPENSES RELATED TO WORK	.357	.390	.395	.421	.487	.541
5	CAPITAL INCOME	.144	.137	.134	.088	.038	.044
6	SURPLUSES	4.942	5.284	5.887	6.205	6.760	7.413
7	BEA SURPLUS	2.041	2.332	3.191	2.180	2.637	2.657
8	SUM OF ABSOLUTE VALUES OF NEGATIVE SURPLUSES	2.901	2.952	2.696	4.025	4.123	4.756
9	NET REVALUATIONS	-.498	.213	.596	.883	-.158	-.069
10	NET SURPLUS (6 + 9)	4.444	5.497	6.483	7.088	6.602	7.344
11	CHARGES AGAINST GOVERNMENT ENTERPRISE PRODUCT	17.583	19.617	21.922	24.187	25.853	28.716
		1976	1977	1978	1979	1980	1981
1	LABOR INCOME	23.150	24.668	27.084	29.751	33.344	37.444
2	COMPENSATION OF EMPLOYEES	23.093	24.582	26.916	29.616	33.384	37.468
3	EMPLOYEE TRAINING	.639	.728	.871	.958	.942	1.013
4	LESS: EXPENSES RELATED TO WORK	.582	.642	.703	.823	.982	1.037
5	CAPITAL INCOME	.059	.140	.230	.209	.193	.239
6	SURPLUSES	7.842	8.334	9.587	10.612	11.368	12.067
7	BEA SURPLUS	4.818	4.666	5.779	6.189	5.252	5.763
8	SUM OF ABSOLUTE VALUES OF NEGATIVE SURPLUSES	3.024	3.668	3.808	4.423	6.116	6.304
9	NET REVALUATIONS	-.264	.033	.837	-.201	-.069	.038
10	NET SURPLUS (6 + 9)	7.578	8.367	10.424	10.411	11.299	12.105
11	CHARGES AGAINST GOVERNMENT ENTERPRISE PRODUCT	30.787	33.175	37.738	40.371	44.836	49.788

TABLE 4. GOVERNMENT ENTERPRISE INCOME AND PRODUCT, BILLIONS OF DOLLARS, 1946-81

		DEBITS					
		PERCENT PER ANNUM RATES OF GROWTH CURRENT DOLLARS					
		1946-56	1956-66	1966-71	1971-76	1976-81	1946-81
1	LABOR INCOME	7.793	7.769	10.575	10.609	10.095	8.907
2	COMPENSATION OF EMPLOYEES	7.896	7.672	10.582	10.466	10.163	8.899
3	EMPLOYEE TRAINING	8.354	9.671	8.808	13.855	9.653	9.753
4	LESS: EXPENSES RELATED TO WORK	11.858	6.122	9.301	8.336	12.246	9.378
5	CAPITAL INCOME	22.944	-.259	-11.931	-15.317	32.044	5.768
6	SURPLUSES	5.210	6.561	6.698	8.216	9.002	6.772
7	BEA SURPLUS	-16.268	31.025	8.709	15.619	3.647	6.637
8	SUM OF ABSOLUTE VALUES OF NEGATIVE SURPLUSES	12.155	1.750	5.256	.483	15.826	6.900
9	NET REVALUATIONS	-3.469	N.A.	N.A.	N.A.	N.A.	-5.537
10	NET SURPLUS (6 + 9)	4.019	4.688	9.386	6.632	9.820	6.154
11	CHARGES AGAINST GOVERNMENT ENTERPRISE PRODUCT	6.610	6.543	9.916	9.433	10.090	7.952

		CREDITS					
		1946	1947	1948	1949	1950	1951
12	SALES MINUS PURCHASES OF INT GOODS	2.517	2.570	2.780	3.058	2.955	3.419
13	TRANSFERS	1.651	1.236	1.451	1.359	1.670	1.631
14	CAP INC + NEG SURP + INT PROD FROM GOVT - INDIR TAXES	1.612	1.188	1.390	1.314	1.599	1.555
15	CONSUMPTION	1.133	.829	.935	.887	1.020	.968
16	INVESTMENT	.478	.360	.455	.427	.579	.587
17	EMPLOYEE TRAINING	.039	.048	.061	.045	.071	.076
18	NET REVALUATIONS	.279	.160	.327	-.739	.329	.030
19	LESS: INT PRODUCT FROM GOVT	.981	.564	.588	.419	.408	.440
20	LESS: EXPENSES RELATED TO WORK	.045	.048	.059	.069	.073	.080
21	GROSS GOVERNMENT ENTERPRISE PRODUCT	3.421	3.355	3.911	3.190	4.473	4.560

		1952	1953	1954	1955	1956	1957
12	SALES MINUS PURCHASES OF INT GOODS	4.208	4.443	4.481	4.416	4.195	4.939
13	TRANSFERS	1.438	1.444	1.682	2.195	2.833	2.610
14	CAP INC + NEG SURP + INT PROD FROM GOVT - INDIR TAXES	1.372	1.372	1.612	2.117	2.746	2.549
15	CONSUMPTION	.861	.858	1.035	1.333	1.733	1.627
16	INVESTMENT	.511	.515	.577	.785	1.013	.922
17	EMPLOYEE TRAINING	.066	.072	.070	.078	.087	.061
18	NET REVALUATIONS	-.365	-.130	-.498	-1.199	.196	.807
19	LESS: INT PRODUCT FROM GOVT	.512	.531	.500	.478	.599	.762
20	LESS: EXPENSES RELATED TO WORK	.097	.106	.118	.126	.138	.150
21	GROSS GOVERNMENT ENTERPRISE PRODUCT	4.673	5.120	5.048	4.808	6.488	7.444

188

TABLE 4. GOVERNMENT ENTERPRISE INCOME AND PRODUCT, BILLIONS OF DOLLARS, 1946-81

		CREDITS					
		1958	1959	1960	1961	1962	1963
12	SALES MINUS PURCHASES OF INT GOODS	5.094	6.174	6.436	6.357	6.985	8.036
13	TRANSFERS	3.022	2.509	3.164	3.648	3.676	3.519
14	CAP INC + NEG SURP + INT PROD FROM GOVT - INDIR TAXES	2.957	2.417	3.044	3.528	3.551	3.391
15	CONSUMPTION	1.915	1.536	1.960	2.291	2.245	2.123
16	INVESTMENT	1.042	.882	1.084	1.237	1.306	1.267
17	EMPLOYEE TRAINING	.065	.092	.120	.120	.125	.128
18	NET REVALUATIONS	.997	-.726	.263	-.190	.051	-.277
19	LESS: INT PRODUCT FROM GOVT	.823	.710	.864	.882	.941	.958
20	LESS: EXPENSES RELATED TO WORK	.160	.177	.189	.197	.204	.214
21	GROSS GOVERNMENT ENTERPRISE PRODUCT	8.130	7.071	8.810	8.737	9.567	10.106

		1964	1965	1966	1967	1968	1969
12	SALES MINUS PURCHASES OF INT GOODS	8.494	9.345	10.103	11.452	13.222	14.102
13	TRANSFERS	3.764	3.823	3.786	3.335	3.091	3.807
14	CAP INC + NEG SURP + INT PROD FROM GOVT - INDIR TAXES	3.628	3.655	3.567	3.106	2.824	3.498
15	CONSUMPTION	2.256	2.246	2.155	1.865	1.690	2.078
16	INVESTMENT	1.372	1.409	1.412	1.241	1.135	1.420
17	EMPLOYEE TRAINING	.136	.168	.219	.229	.267	.309
18	NET REVALUATIONS	-.311	.582	-.311	-.132	-.081	.112
19	LESS: INT PRODUCT FROM GOVT	.976	1.111	1.101	1.268	1.420	1.420
20	LESS: EXPENSES RELATED TO WORK	.223	.236	.250	.270	.290	.318
21	GROSS GOVERNMENT ENTERPRISE PRODUCT	10.749	12.403	12.227	13.117	14.522	16.283

		1970	1971	1972	1973	1974	1975
12	SALES MINUS PURCHASES OF INT GOODS	15.144	16.441	18.545	19.156	21.841	24.093
13	TRANSFERS	4.945	5.119	4.876	6.183	6.251	7.560
14	CAP INC + NEG SURP + INT PROD FROM GOVT - INDIR TAXES	4.632	4.785	4.452	5.654	5.686	7.056
15	CONSUMPTION	2.818	2.865	2.622	3.283	3.372	4.283
16	INVESTMENT	1.814	1.920	1.830	2.371	2.315	2.772
17	EMPLOYEE TRAINING	.313	.334	.424	.529	.565	.504
18	NET REVALUATIONS	-.498	.213	.596	.883	-.158	-.069
19	LESS: INT PRODUCT FROM GOVT	1.651	1.766	1.700	1.614	1.594	2.326
20	LESS: EXPENSES RELATED TO WORK	.357	.390	.395	.421	.487	.541
21	GROSS GOVERNMENT ENTERPRISE PRODUCT	17.583	19.617	21.922	24.187	25.853	28.716

189

TABLE 4. GOVERNMENT ENTERPRISE INCOME AND PRODUCT, BILLIONS OF DOLLARS, 1946-81

		CREDITS					
		1976	1977	1978	1979	1980	1981
12	SALES MINUS PURCHASES OF INT GOODS	27.985	29.331	32.795	35.917	38.792	43.426
13	TRANSFERS	5.529	6.493	6.931	7.723	10.037	10.889
14	CAP INC + NEG SURP + INT PROD FROM GOVT - INDIR TAXES	4.890	5.765	6.060	6.765	9.095	9.876
15	CONSUMPTION	2.951	3.432	3.575	4.036	5.581	6.017
16	INVESTMENT	1.938	2.334	2.486	2.729	3.514	3.859
17	EMPLOYEE TRAINING	.639	.728	.871	.958	.942	1.013
18	NET REVALUATIONS	-.264	.033	.837	-.201	-.069	.038
19	LESS: INT PRODUCT FROM GOVT	1.880	2.040	2.122	2.245	2.942	3.528
20	LESS: EXPENSES RELATED TO WORK	.582	.642	.703	.823	.982	1.037
21	GROSS GOVERNMENT ENTERPRISE PRODUCT	30.788	33.175	37.738	40.371	44.837	49.788

		PERCENT PER ANNUM RATES OF GROWTH CURRENT DOLLARS					
		1946-56	1956-66	1966-71	1971-76	1976-81	1946-81
12	SALES MINUS PURCHASES OF INT GOODS	5.241	9.187	10.229	11.224	9.185	8.477
13	TRANSFERS	5.550	2.942	6.219	1.552	14.517	5.538
14	CAP INC + NEG SURP + INT PROD FROM GOVT - INDIR TAXES	5.473	2.650	6.051	.434	15.095	5.316
15	CONSUMPTION	4.337	2.203	5.866	.594	15.311	4.885
16	INVESTMENT	7.796	3.376	6.331	.194	14.763	6.147
17	EMPLOYEE TRAINING	8.354	9.671	8.808	13.855	9.653	9.753
18	NET REVALUATIONS	-3.469	N.A.	N.A.	N.A.	N.A.	-5.537
19	LESS: INT PRODUCT FROM GOVT	-4.823	6.287	9.912	1.258	13.413	3.724
20	LESS: EXPENSES RELATED TO WORK	11.858	6.122	9.301	8.336	12.246	9.378
21	GROSS GOVERNMENT ENTERPRISE PRODUCT	6.610	6.542	9.916	9.433	10.090	7.952

TABLE 5. GOVERNMENT INCOME AND PRODUCT, BILLIONS OF DOLLARS, 1946-81

		DEBITS					
		1946	1947	1948	1949	1950	1951
1	LABOR INCOME	25.662	19.308	19.969	21.961	24.050	32.846
2	COMPENSATION OF EMPLOYEES	20.793	16.715	17.431	19.441	20.879	27.397
3	EMPLOYEE TRAINING	5.368	3.044	3.063	3.158	3.866	6.326
4	LESS: EXPENSES RELATED TO WORK	.499	.451	.525	.638	.695	.877
5	CAPITAL INCOME	7.879	7.881	9.418	9.021	7.854	7.386
6	INTEREST PAID	4.092	4.184	4.218	4.338	4.419	4.466
7	NET IMPUTED INTEREST	3.787	3.697	5.200	4.683	3.435	2.920
8	GROSS IMPUTED INTEREST	7.879	7.881	9.418	9.021	7.854	7.386
9	LAND	.348	.390	.525	.557	.508	.501
10	STRUCTURES AND EQUIPMENT	5.687	5.848	7.190	7.009	6.166	5.859
11	INVENTORIES	1.771	1.556	1.581	1.318	1.047	.897
12	R & D	.073	.086	.122	.138	.133	.130
13	LESS: INTEREST PAID	4.092	4.184	4.218	4.338	4.419	4.466
14	NET REVALUATIONS	-25.491	2.916	2.888	.749	-2.394	8.107
15	LAND	-3.155	-.413	.291	1.227	1.265	1.512
16	STRUCTURES AND EQUIPMENT	-11.660	5.985	4.437	-.023	-2.322	8.762
17	INVENTORIES	-10.676	-2.656	-1.840	-.455	-1.337	-2.167
18	INCOME ORIGINATING (1+5+14)	8.050	30.105	32.275	31.731	29.510	48.339
19	UNCOMPENSATED FACTOR SERVICES	1.317	.816	.960	1.186	1.263	2.955
20	DRAFTEES	1.281	.784	.924	1.142	1.212	2.901
21	JURORS	.036	.032	.036	.044	.051	.054
22	CHARGES AGAINST NET GOVERNMENT PRODUCT	9.367	30.921	33.234	32.916	30.773	51.294
23	CAPITAL CONSUMPTION ALLOWANCES	32.263	27.924	22.551	16.413	12.385	12.529
24	ORIGINAL COST	26.010	19.744	14.791	10.526	7.986	7.610
25	REVALUATIONS	6.253	8.180	7.760	5.887	4.399	4.919
26	CHARGES AGAINST GROSS GOVERNMENT PRODUCT	41.630	58.845	55.785	49.329	43.158	63.823
		1952	1953	1954	1955	1956	1957
1	LABOR INCOME	37.479	38.144	38.314	39.944	42.283	44.462
2	COMPENSATION OF EMPLOYEES	31.161	31.942	32.478	34.194	36.596	39.125
3	EMPLOYEE TRAINING	7.357	7.349	7.109	7.111	7.205	6.995
4	LESS: EXPENSES RELATED TO WORK	1.039	1.147	1.273	1.361	1.518	1.658
5	CAPITAL INCOME	8.717	9.610	11.691	13.844	13.156	14.013
6	INTEREST PAID	4.470	4.561	4.704	4.692	5.154	5.616
7	NET IMPUTED INTEREST	4.247	5.049	6.987	9.152	8.002	8.397
8	GROSS IMPUTED INTEREST	8.717	9.610	11.691	13.844	13.156	14.013
9	LAND	1.116	1.221	1.491	1.805	1.783	2.001
10	STRUCTURES AND EQUIPMENT	6.469	6.953	8.127	9.412	8.941	9.548
11	INVENTORIES	.986	1.272	1.867	2.373	2.178	2.174
12	R & D	.146	.164	.206	.254	.253	.290
13	LESS: INTEREST PAID	4.470	4.561	4.704	4.692	5.154	5.616

TABLE 5. GOVERNMENT INCOME AND PRODUCT, BILLIONS OF DOLLARS, 1946-81

		DEBITS					
		1952	1953	1954	1955	1956	1957
14	NET REVALUATIONS	-1.617	3.457	1.422	11.696	10.010	3.653
15	LAND	1.014	4.271	2.066	5.264	4.035	5.673
16	STRUCTURES AND EQUIPMENT	-.011	-1.931	-4.952	4.448	7.695	-.946
17	INVENTORIES	-2.620	1.117	4.308	1.984	-1.720	-1.074
18	INCOME ORIGINATING (1+5+14)	44.579	51.211	51.427	65.484	65.449	62.128
19	UNCOMPENSATED FACTOR SERVICES	4.100	4.479	4.727	5.459	6.141	7.147
20	DRAFTEES	4.036	4.402	4.634	5.356	6.025	7.034
21	JURORS	.064	.077	.093	.103	.116	.113
22	CHARGES AGAINST NET GOVERNMENT PRODUCT	48.680	55.690	56.154	70.944	71.590	69.275
23	CAPITAL CONSUMPTION ALLOWANCES	13.320	14.103	14.373	15.084	16.559	17.221
24	ORIGINAL COST	8.668	9.732	10.521	11.392	11.935	12.118
25	REVALUATIONS	4.652	4.371	3.852	3.692	4.624	5.103
26	CHARGES AGAINST GROSS GOVERNMENT PRODUCT	62.000	69.793	70.527	86.028	88.149	86.496
		1958	1959	1960	1961	1962	1963
1	LABOR INCOME	47.480	49.469	52.777	56.197	60.362	64.156
2	COMPENSATION OF EMPLOYEES	42.123	43.995	47.146	50.528	54.307	58.021
3	EMPLOYEE TRAINING	7.104	7.335	7.589	7.713	8.189	8.358
4	LESS: EXPENSES RELATED TO WORK	1.747	1.861	1.958	2.044	2.134	2.223
5	CAPITAL INCOME	14.260	16.620	16.707	17.641	20.771	23.047
6	INTEREST PAID	5.336	6.291	6.869	6.361	6.904	7.392
7	NET IMPUTED INTEREST	8.924	10.329	9.838	11.280	13.867	15.655
8	GROSS IMPUTED INTEREST	14.260	16.620	16.707	17.641	20.771	23.047
9	LAND	2.166	2.667	2.823	3.130	3.826	4.349
10	STRUCTURES AND EQUIPMENT	9.650	11.176	11.200	11.834	13.969	15.474
11	INVENTORIES	2.120	2.362	2.228	2.160	2.330	2.464
12	R & D	.324	.415	.455	.517	.647	.760
13	LESS: INTEREST PAID	5.336	6.291	6.869	6.361	6.904	7.392
14	NET REVALUATIONS	-.761	-2.963	.853	4.510	2.731	5.022
15	LAND	4.533	4.938	5.251	6.731	5.479	6.554
16	STRUCTURES AND EQUIPMENT	-5.024	-6.441	-3.639	-1.352	-.841	-.526
17	INVENTORIES	-.270	-1.460	-.759	-.869	-1.907	-1.006
18	INCOME ORIGINATING (1+5+14)	60.979	63.126	70.337	78.348	83.864	92.225
19	UNCOMPENSATED FACTOR SERVICES	7.002	7.999	8.128	8.956	9.995	9.938
20	DRAFTEES	6.877	7.871	7.997	8.824	9.850	9.778
21	JURORS	.125	.128	.131	.132	.145	.160
22	CHARGES AGAINST NET GOVERNMENT PRODUCT	67.980	71.125	78.465	87.304	93.859	102.163
23	CAPITAL CONSUMPTION ALLOWANCES	17.213	17.435	17.614	17.855	18.374	19.078
24	ORIGINAL COST	12.334	12.673	13.114	13.608	14.158	14.815
25	REVALUATIONS	4.879	4.762	4.500	4.247	4.216	4.263
26	CHARGES AGAINST GROSS GOVERNMENT PRODUCT	85.193	88.560	96.079	105.159	112.233	121.241

TABLE 5. GOVERNMENT INCOME AND PRODUCT, BILLIONS OF DOLLARS, 1946-81

		DEBITS					
		1964	1965	1966	1967	1968	1969
1	LABOR INCOME	69.524	74.711	85.513	95.018	106.285	116.360
2	COMPENSATION OF EMPLOYEES	62.876	67.592	76.546	85.142	95.171	104.455
3	EMPLOYEE TRAINING	9.002	9.616	11.706	12.908	14.373	15.482
4	LESS: EXPENSES RELATED TO WORK	2.354	2.497	2.739	3.032	3.259	3.577
5	CAPITAL INCOME	25.728	29.377	30.758	31.147	30.236	28.984
6	INTEREST PAID	7.879	8.084	8.500	8.908	10.310	11.468
7	NET IMPUTED INTEREST	17.849	21.293	22.258	22.239	19.926	17.516
8	GROSS IMPUTED INTEREST	25.728	29.377	30.758	31.147	30.236	28.984
9	LAND	4.963	5.734	6.062	6.159	5.890	5.446
10	STRUCTURES AND EQUIPMENT	17.233	19.725	20.803	21.191	20.712	20.041
11	INVENTORIES	2.631	2.829	2.696	2.543	2.393	2.294
12	R & D	.900	1.089	1.196	1.254	1.242	1.202
13	LESS: INTEREST PAID	7.879	8.084	8.500	8.908	10.310	11.468
14	NET REVALUATIONS	8.239	7.319	5.021	5.744	5.064	4.789
15	LAND	6.508	4.497	5.847	4.088	1.933	-2.151
16	STRUCTURES AND EQUIPMENT	.565	1.533	.098	2.478	4.536	8.137
17	INVENTORIES	1.166	1.289	-.924	-.822	-1.405	-1.197
18	INCOME ORIGINATING (1+5+14)	103.491	111.407	121.292	131.909	141.585	150.133
19	UNCOMPENSATED FACTOR SERVICES	10.596	10.354	10.247	12.942	13.616	15.034
20	DRAFTEES	10.426	10.179	10.061	12.771	13.408	14.752
21	JURORS	.170	.175	.186	.171	.208	.282
22	CHARGES AGAINST NET GOVERNMENT PRODUCT	114.086	121.761	131.539	144.851	155.200	165.167
23	CAPITAL CONSUMPTION ALLOWANCES	19.688	20.745	22.106	23.696	25.510	27.668
24	ORIGINAL COST	15.566	16.432	17.420	18.511	19.608	20.676
25	REVALUATIONS	4.122	4.313	4.686	5.185	5.902	6.992
26	CHARGES AGAINST GROSS GOVERNMENT PRODUCT	133.774	142.506	153.645	168.547	180.710	192.835
		1970	1971	1972	1973	1974	1975
1	LABOR INCOME	127.758	137.855	151.093	163.630	175.912	192.586
2	COMPENSATION OF EMPLOYEES	115.829	126.009	137.786	149.625	162.193	179.606
3	EMPLOYEE TRAINING	15.826	16.061	17.677	18.633	18.977	18.806
4	LESS: EXPENSES RELATED TO WORK	3.897	4.215	4.370	4.628	5.258	5.826
5	CAPITAL INCOME	28.142	32.606	34.592	35.713	30.781	42.463
6	INTEREST PAID	12.318	12.423	12.860	15.199	16.427	18.851
7	NET IMPUTED INTEREST	15.824	20.183	21.732	20.514	14.354	23.612
8	GROSS IMPUTED INTEREST	28.142	32.606	34.592	35.713	30.781	42.463
9	LAND	5.061	5.647	6.021	6.468	5.627	7.817
10	STRUCTURES AND EQUIPMENT	19.756	23.286	24.884	25.700	22.187	30.607
11	INVENTORIES	2.144	2.284	2.205	2.059	1.747	2.378
12	R & D	1.180	1.389	1.482	1.485	1.219	1.660
13	LESS: INTEREST PAID	12.318	12.423	12.860	15.199	16.427	18.851

193

TABLE 5. GOVERNMENT INCOME AND PRODUCT, BILLIONS OF DOLLARS, 1946-81

		DEBITS					
		1970	1971	1972	1973	1974	1975
14	NET REVALUATIONS	14.678	7.455	27.859	59.397	33.465	2.324
15	LAND	-1.156	-2.048	14.714	20.196	6.787	10.410
16	STRUCTURES AND EQUIPMENT	16.859	10.570	12.907	33.838	22.865	-6.974
17	INVENTORIES	-1.025	-1.067	.238	5.363	3.813	-1.112
18	INCOME ORIGINATING (1+5+14)	170.578	177.916	213.544	258.740	240.158	237.373
19	UNCOMPENSATED FACTOR SERVICES	16.337	14.696	10.652	10.373	7.082	3.818
20	DRAFTEES	15.992	14.313	10.249	9.856	6.596	3.302
21	JURORS	.345	.383	.403	.517	.486	.516
22	CHARGES AGAINST NET GOVERNMENT PRODUCT	186.915	192.612	224.196	269.112	247.240	241.191
23	CAPITAL CONSUMPTION ALLOWANCES	30.352	33.100	35.297	38.002	43.438	48.851
24	ORIGINAL COST	21.766	22.922	24.136	25.380	26.751	28.354
25	REVALUATIONS	8.586	10.178	11.161	12.622	16.687	20.497
26	CHARGES AGAINST GROSS GOVERNMENT PRODUCT	217.267	225.712	259.493	307.114	290.678	290.042

		1976	1977	1978	1979	1980	1981
1	LABOR INCOME	208.434	224.736	245.079	263.403	288.645	318.151
2	COMPENSATION OF EMPLOYEES	194.628	210.337	229.280	247.444	272.962	299.267
3	EMPLOYEE TRAINING	20.190	21.558	23.618	25.010	26.490	30.283
4	LESS: EXPENSES RELATED TO WORK	6.384	7.159	7.819	9.051	10.807	11.399
5	CAPITAL INCOME	43.496	50.375	54.986	55.294	56.923	69.380
6	INTEREST PAID	23.138	25.094	28.982	30.562	36.296	53.896
7	NET IMPUTED INTEREST	20.358	25.281	26.004	24.732	20.627	15.484
8	GROSS IMPUTED INTEREST	43.496	50.375	54.986	55.294	56.923	69.380
9	LAND	8.404	10.133	11.391	11.663	12.029	14.210
10	STRUCTURES AND EQUIPMENT	31.073	35.687	38.687	38.716	39.870	49.097
11	INVENTORIES	2.315	2.629	2.900	2.999	3.138	3.831
12	R & D	1.705	1.925	2.007	1.916	1.886	2.241
13	LESS: INTEREST PAID	23.138	25.094	28.982	30.562	36.296	53.896
14	NET REVALUATIONS	21.762	52.551	51.915	93.696	29.844	24.741
15	LAND	28.399	18.750	32.784	22.880	14.290	-29.411
16	STRUCTURES AND EQUIPMENT	-4.295	33.314	18.139	59.056	14.906	51.414
17	INVENTORIES	-2.342	.487	.992	11.760	.648	2.738
18	INCOME ORIGINATING (1+5+14)	273.692	327.662	351.980	412.393	375.412	412.272
19	UNCOMPENSATED FACTOR SERVICES	.559	.545	.513	.497	.548	.659
20	DRAFTEES	.000	.000	.000	.000	.000	.000
21	JURORS	.559	.545	.513	.497	.548	.659
22	CHARGES AGAINST NET GOVERNMENT PRODUCT	274.252	328.206	352.493	412.890	375.960	412.931
23	CAPITAL CONSUMPTION ALLOWANCES	52.135	56.886	64.009	73.417	83.454	91.326
24	ORIGINAL COST	30.159	32.027	34.114	36.735	39.865	43.228
25	REVALUATIONS	21.976	24.859	29.895	36.682	43.589	48.098
26	CHARGES AGAINST GROSS GOVERNMENT PRODUCT	326.387	385.092	416.502	486.307	459.414	504.257

194

TABLE 5.   GOVERNMENT INCOME AND PRODUCT, BILLIONS OF DOLLARS, 1946-81

			DEBITS			
			PERCENT PER ANNUM RATES OF GROWTH CURRENT DOLLARS			
		1946-56	1956-66	1966-71	1971-76	1976-81	1946-81

#		1946-56	1956-66	1966-71	1971-76	1976-81	1946-81
1	LABOR INCOME	5.121	7.297	10.022	8.620	8.826	7.458
2	COMPENSATION OF EMPLOYEES	5.816	7.659	10.483	9.084	8.986	7.917
3	EMPLOYEE TRAINING	2.987	4.973	6.530	4.682	8.446	5.067
4	LESS: EXPENSES RELATED TO WORK	11.768	6.080	9.004	8.657	12.294	9.351
5	CAPITAL INCOME	5.260	8.864	1.173	5.933	9.788	6.413
6	INTEREST PAID	2.334	5.130	7.885	13.245	18.426	7.644
7	NET IMPUTED INTEREST	7.767	10.772	-1.939	.173	-5.327	4.105
8	GROSS IMPUTED INTEREST	5.260	8.864	1.173	5.933	9.788	6.413
9	LAND	17.743	13.017	-1.411	8.277	11.077	11.179
10	STRUCTURES AND EQUIPMENT	4.629	8.811	2.281	5.940	9.581	6.353
11	INVENTORIES	2.090	2.156	-3.269	.271	10.603	2.229
12	R & D	13.253	16.804	3.035	4.175	5.627	10.282
13	LESS: INTEREST PAID	2.334	5.130	7.885	13.245	18.426	7.644
14	NET REVALUATIONS	N.A.	-6.667	8.226	23.894	2.599	N.A.
15	LAND	N.A.	3.779	N.A.	N.A.	N.A.	N.A.
16	STRUCTURES AND EQUIPMENT	N.A.	-35.360	155.017	N.A.	N.A.	N.A.
17	INVENTORIES	N.A.	N.A.	N.A.	N.A.	N.A.	N.A.
18	INCOME ORIGINATING (1+5+14)	23.313	6.364	7.963	8.996	8.539	11.902
19	UNCOMPENSATED FACTOR SERVICES	16.649	5.253	7.478	-47.991	3.338	-1.958
20	DRAFTEES	16.746	5.261	7.304	N.A.	N.A.	N.A.
21	JURORS	12.562	4.824	15.546	7.867	3.338	8.700
22	CHARGES AGAINST NET GOVERNMENT PRODUCT	22.554	6.272	7.926	7.323	8.529	11.424
23	CAPITAL CONSUMPTION ALLOWANCES	-6.452	2.931	8.409	9.512	11.865	3.018
24	ORIGINAL COST	-7.494	3.854	5.643	5.641	7.466	1.462
25	REVALUATIONS	-2.973	.133	16.781	16.643	16.960	6.002
26	CHARGES AGAINST GROSS GOVERNMENT PRODUCT	7.791	5.713	7.996	7.655	9.090	7.387

			CREDITS			
		1946	1947	1948	1949	1950	1951

#		1946	1947	1948	1949	1950	1951
27	CONSUMPTION (TO HOUSEHOLDS)	7.859	6.831	6.311	6.147	6.355	6.223
28	CAPITAL ACCUMULATION	16.208	14.678	14.778	14.914	16.011	18.572
29	TO BUSINESS (R & D)	.569	.710	.920	1.019	1.082	1.300
30	TO HOUSEHOLDS	12.881	11.498	11.605	11.896	13.150	15.372
31	EDUCATION AND TRAINING	11.755	10.198	10.152	10.490	11.820	14.027
32	PUBLIC SCHOOLS	6.387	7.154	7.089	7.332	7.954	7.701
33	EMPLOYEE TRAINING	5.368	3.044	3.063	3.158	3.866	6.326
34	MILITARY	4.941	2.631	2.606	2.814	3.313	5.634
35	NONMILITARY	.427	.413	.457	.344	.553	.692
36	HEALTH	1.126	1.300	1.453	1.406	1.329	1.345
37	TO GOVERNMENT	2.758	2.470	2.253	1.999	1.779	1.901
38	RESEARCH AND DEVELOPMENT	.241	.300	.390	.431	.458	.550
39	NATURAL RESOURCES	2.517	2.170	1.863	1.568	1.321	1.351
40	INTERMEDIATE PRODUCT	56.509	48.795	48.151	39.610	32.186	40.088
41	TO BUSINESS	35.622	31.026	30.409	24.680	19.504	24.109
42	TO NONPROFIT	.771	.702	.609	.582	.424	.550
43	TO GOVT ENTERPRISE	.981	.564	.588	.419	.408	.440
44	TO HOUSEHOLD	19.134	16.504	16.546	13.929	11.849	14.989

195

TABLE 5. GOVERNMENT INCOME AND PRODUCT, BILLIONS OF DOLLARS, 1946-81

		CREDITS					
		1946	1947	1948	1949	1950	1951
45	GROSS CREDITS EXCLUSIVE OF CHANGE IN INVENTORIES AND NET REVALUATIONS	80.576	70.304	69.240	60.671	54.552	64.883
46	CHANGE IN INVENTORIES	-10.189	-9.779	-9.014	-3.506	-2.608	1.790
47	LESS: INTERMEDIATE PURCHASES FROM OTHER SECTORS	2.767	4.145	6.804	7.947	5.697	10.080
48	LESS: EXPENSES RELATED TO WORK	.499	.451	.525	.638	.695	.877
49	GROSS GOVERNMENT PRODUCT EXCLUSIVE OF NET REVALUATIONS	67.121	55.929	52.897	48.580	45.552	55.716
50	NET REVALUATIONS	-25.491	2.916	2.888	.749	-2.394	8.107
51	GROSS GOVERNMENT PRODUCT	41.630	58.845	55.785	49.329	43.158	63.823
		1952	1953	1954	1955	1956	1957
27	CONSUMPTION (TO HOUSEHOLDS)	6.388	6.997	8.587	9.399	9.490	11.092
28	CAPITAL ACCUMULATION	20.779	23.364	26.473	29.133	31.035	34.107
29	TO BUSINESS (R & D)	1.651	1.782	2.155	2.645	3.864	4.949
30	TO HOUSEHOLDS	16.874	18.898	20.838	22.714	23.289	24.766
31	EDUCATION AND TRAINING	15.302	17.036	18.852	20.528	21.028	22.283
32	PUBLIC SCHOOLS	7.945	9.687	11.743	13.417	13.823	15.288
33	EMPLOYEE TRAINING	7.357	7.349	7.109	7.111	7.205	6.995
34	MILITARY	6.768	6.701	6.479	6.422	6.415	6.436
35	NONMILITARY	.589	.648	.630	.689	.790	.559
36	HEALTH	1.572	1.862	1.986	2.186	2.261	2.483
37	TO GOVERNMENT	2.254	2.684	3.479	3.774	3.883	4.392
38	RESEARCH AND DEVELOPMENT	.699	.754	.853	.973	1.131	1.297
39	NATURAL RESOURCES	1.555	1.930	2.626	2.801	2.752	3.095
40	INTERMEDIATE PRODUCT	44.084	45.273	43.246	50.427	51.664	57.690
41	TO BUSINESS	26.174	26.512	24.806	28.544	28.444	31.286
42	TO NONPROFIT	.609	.587	.697	.791	.803	1.231
43	TO GOVT ENTERPRISE	.512	.531	.500	.478	.598	.762
44	TO HOUSEHOLD	16.789	17.643	17.243	20.614	21.819	24.411
45	GROSS CREDITS EXCLUSIVE OF CHANGE IN INVENTORIES AND NET REVALUATIONS	71.251	75.635	78.306	88.959	92.190	102.889
46	CHANGE IN INVENTORIES	6.831	10.827	6.537	1.436	.966	-1.889
47	LESS: INTERMEDIATE PURCHASES FROM OTHER SECTORS	13.426	18.979	14.465	14.702	13.499	16.499
48	LESS: EXPENSES RELATED TO WORK	1.039	1.147	1.273	1.361	1.518	1.658
49	GROSS GOVERNMENT PRODUCT EXCLUSIVE OF NET REVALUATIONS	63.617	66.336	69.105	74.332	78.139	82.843
50	NET REVALUATIONS	-1.617	3.457	1.422	11.696	10.010	3.653
51	GROSS GOVERNMENT PRODUCT	62.000	69.793	70.527	86.028	88.149	86.496

TABLE 5. GOVERNMENT INCOME AND PRODUCT, BILLIONS OF DOLLARS, 1946-81

		CREDITS					
		1958	1959	1960	1961	1962	1963
27	CONSUMPTION (TO HOUSEHOLDS)	11.151	13.602	13.650	16.448	17.311	19.484
28	CAPITAL ACCUMULATION	36.840	41.193	44.465	48.922	51.713	57.113
29	TO BUSINESS (R & D)	5.470	6.477	7.090	7.462	7.908	9.030
30	TO HOUSEHOLDS	26.638	29.493	32.020	35.297	37.506	40.954
31	EDUCATION AND TRAINING	23.995	26.537	28.832	31.794	33.845	36.965
32	PUBLIC SCHOOLS	16.891	19.202	21.243	24.081	25.656	28.607
33	EMPLOYEE TRAINING	7.104	7.335	7.589	7.713	8.189	8.358
34	MILITARY	6.522	6.538	6.569	6.671	7.100	7.256
35	NONMILITARY	.582	.797	1.020	1.042	1.089	1.102
36	HEALTH	2.643	2.956	3.188	3.503	3.662	3.990
37	TO GOVERNMENT	4.732	5.223	5.355	6.163	6.299	7.128
38	RESEARCH AND DEVELOPMENT	1.507	1.681	1.801	1.987	2.188	2.559
39	NATURAL RESOURCES	3.225	3.542	3.554	4.176	4.111	4.569
40	INTERMEDIATE PRODUCT	58.166	61.591	62.075	65.702	68.837	69.122
41	TO BUSINESS	31.532	33.345	33.363	34.913	36.678	36.809
42	TO NONPROFIT	.879	.973	.793	1.303	1.425	1.412
43	TO GOVT ENTERPRISE	.823	.709	.864	.882	.941	.958
44	TO HOUSEHOLD	24.932	26.564	27.055	28.604	29.793	29.943
45	GROSS CREDITS EXCLUSIVE OF CHANGE IN INVENTORIES AND NET REVALUATIONS	106.156	116.386	120.190	131.072	137.861	145.719
46	CHANGE IN INVENTORIES	.554	-2.497	-.946	-4.293	.833	1.101
47	LESS: INTERMEDIATE PURCHASES FROM OTHER SECTORS	19.009	20.505	22.060	24.086	27.058	28.378
48	LESS: EXPENSES RELATED TO WORK	1.747	1.861	1.958	2.044	2.134	2.223
49	GROSS GOVERNMENT PRODUCT EXCLUSIVE OF NET REVALUATIONS	85.954	91.523	95.226	100.649	109.502	116.219
50	NET REVALUATIONS	-.761	-2.963	.853	4.510	2.731	5.022
51	GROSS GOVERNMENT PRODUCT	85.193	88.560	96.079	105.159	112.233	121.241

		1964	1965	1966	1967	1968	1969
27	CONSUMPTION (TO HOUSEHOLDS)	21.971	24.500	27.762	28.773	31.189	34.667
28	CAPITAL ACCUMULATION	63.789	69.197	77.914	84.058	91.019	100.048
29	TO BUSINESS (R&D)	9.817	10.054	10.904	11.185	11.658	11.640
30	TO HOUSEHOLDS	45.692	50.292	57.475	62.975	69.941	78.076
31	EDUCATION AND TRAINING	41.326	45.587	52.371	57.435	63.564	70.970
32	PUBLIC SCHOOLS	32.324	35.971	40.665	44.527	49.191	55.488
33	EMPLOYEE TRAINING	9.002	9.616	11.706	12.908	14.373	15.482
34	MILITARY	7.826	8.156	9.729	10.766	11.886	12.621
35	NONMILITARY	1.176	1.460	1.977	2.142	2.487	2.861
36	HEALTH	4.366	4.705	5.104	5.540	6.377	7.106
37	TO GOVERNMENT	8.279	8.851	9.535	9.898	9.421	10.332
38	RESEARCH AND DEVELOPMENT	2.966	3.157	3.308	3.445	3.497	3.790
39	NATURAL RESOURCES	5.313	5.694	6.227	6.453	5.924	6.542
40	INTERMEDIATE PRODUCT	73.041	78.796	85.959	95.619	105.020	103.154
41	TO BUSINESS	38.760	42.178	45.994	50.844	55.199	53.265
42	TO NONPROFIT	1.517	1.708	1.890	2.229	2.321	2.677
43	TO GOVT ENTERPRISE	.975	1.111	1.101	1.268	1.420	1.420
44	TO HOUSEHOLD	31.788	33.799	36.973	41.278	46.080	45.792

TABLE 5. GOVERNMENT INCOME AND PRODUCT, BILLIONS OF DOLLARS, 1946-81

				CREDITS			
		1964	1965	1966	1967	1968	1969
45	GROSS CREDITS EXCLUSIVE OF CHANGE IN INVENTORIES AND NET REVALUATIONS	158.800	172.493	191.635	208.451	227.228	237.869
46	CHANGE IN INVENTORIES	-1.535	-3.275	-3.622	1.453	1.296	5.333
47	LESS: INTERMEDIATE PURCHASES FROM OTHER SECTORS	29.376	31.534	36.650	44.069	49.619	51.579
48	LESS: EXPENSES RELATED TO WORK	2.354	2.497	2.739	3.032	3.259	3.577
49	GROSS GOVERNMENT PRODUCT EXCLUSIVE OF NET REVALUATIONS	125.535	135.187	148.624	162.803	175.646	188.046
50	NET REVALUATIONS	8.239	7.319	5.021	5.744	5.064	4.789
51	GROSS GOVERNMENT PRODUCT	133.774	142.506	153.645	168.547	180.710	192.835
		1970	1971	1972	1973	1974	1975
27	CONSUMPTION (TO HOUSEHOLDS)	39.595	45.179	51.747	57.779	65.403	74.895
28	CAPITAL ACCUMULATION	110.379	121.632	135.240	145.843	157.623	176.107
29	TO BUSINESS (R & D)	11.087	11.051	11.569	12.025	12.378	13.187
30	TO HOUSEHOLDS	88.035	98.537	110.236	120.224	130.635	145.739
31	EDUCATION AND TRAINING	79.890	89.147	99.313	107.862	116.717	130.249
32	PUBLIC SCHOOLS	64.064	73.086	81.636	89.229	97.740	111.443
33	EMPLOYEE TRAINING	15.826	16.061	17.677	18.633	18.977	18.806
34	MILITARY	13.045	13.068	13.853	13.953	14.191	14.568
35	NONMILITARY	2.781	2.993	3.824	4.680	4.786	4.238
36	HEALTH	8.144	9.390	10.923	12.362	13.918	15.491
37	TO GOVERNMENT	11.257	12.044	13.435	13.594	14.609	17.180
38	RESEARCH AND DEVELOPMENT	4.154	4.409	4.676	4.837	5.133	5.562
39	NATURAL RESOURCES	7.103	7.635	8.759	8.757	9.476	11.618
40	INTERMEDIATE PRODUCT	112.516	114.728	118.234	120.945	118.784	138.076
41	TO BUSINESS	58.529	59.845	61.523	63.108	62.189	73.504
42	TO NONPROFIT	2.965	2.922	3.057	2.924	3.276	3.123
43	TO GOVT ENTERPRISE	1.651	1.766	1.700	1.614	1.594	2.326
44	TO HOUSEHOLD	49.371	50.195	51.954	53.299	51.725	59.123
45	GROSS CREDITS EXCLUSIVE OF CHANGE IN INVENTORIES AND NET REVALUATIONS	262.489	281.539	305.220	324.566	341.809	389.077
46	CHANGE IN INVENTORIES	-3.852	-1.335	-5.592	-5.316	1.597	-2.234
47	LESS: INTERMEDIATE PURCHASES FROM OTHER SECTORS	52.151	57.732	63.624	66.905	80.935	93.299
48	LESS: EXPENSES RELATED TO WORK	3.897	4.215	4.370	4.628	5.258	5.826
49	GROSS GOVERNMENT PRODUCT EXCLUSIVE OF NET REVALUATIONS	202.589	218.257	231.634	247.717	257.213	287.718
50	NET REVALUATIONS	14.678	7.455	27.859	59.397	33.465	2.324
51	GROSS GOVERNMENT PRODUCT	217.267	225.712	259.493	307.114	290.678	290.042

198

TABLE 5. GOVERNMENT INCOME AND PRODUCT, BILLIONS OF DOLLARS, 1946-81

		CREDITS					
		1976	1977	1978	1979	1980	1981
27	CONSUMPTION (TO HOUSEHOLDS)	79.726	87.877	98.473	109.497	121.846	129.516
28	CAPITAL ACCUMULATION	191.145	209.841	232.182	254.352	276.460	314.950
29	TO BUSINESS (R & D)	14.674	16.204	17.767	20.165	22.529	24.914
30	TO HOUSEHOLDS	158.676	173.718	190.673	208.057	227.257	255.144
31	EDUCATION AND TRAINING	142.019	155.149	169.441	184.627	200.701	225.181
32	PUBLIC SCHOOLS	121.829	133.591	145.823	159.617	174.211	194.898
33	EMPLOYEE TRAINING	20.190	21.558	23.618	25.010	26.490	30.283
34	MILITARY	14.808	15.329	16.201	17.005	18.788	21.915
35	NONMILITARY	5.382	6.229	7.417	8.005	7.702	8.368
36	HEALTH	16.657	18.569	21.232	23.431	26.556	29.963
37	TO GOVERNMENT	17.795	19.919	23.743	26.130	26.674	34.891
38	RESEARCH AND DEVELOPMENT	5.850	5.951	6.611	7.268	7.579	8.228
39	NATURAL RESOURCES	11.945	13.968	17.132	18.862	19.095	26.663
40	INTERMEDIATE PRODUCT	140.803	153.483	162.016	176.244	202.604	233.566
41	TO BUSINESS	74.265	80.347	84.213	93.242	107.142	121.323
42	TO NONPROFIT	3.114	3.902	3.960	4.350	5.186	6.171
43	TO GOVT ENTERPRISE	1.880	2.040	2.122	2.245	2.942	3.528
44	TO HOUSEHOLD	61.543	67.194	71.722	76.406	87.335	102.544
45	GROSS CREDITS EXCLUSIVE OF CHANGE IN INVENTORIES AND NET REVALUATIONS	411.674	451.201	492.671	540.093	600.910	678.032
46	CHANGE IN INVENTORIES	.549	3.398	4.138	-.768	1.594	.411
47	LESS: INTERMEDIATE PURCHASES FROM OTHER SECTORS	101.214	114.899	124.403	137.663	162.127	187.528
48	LESS: EXPENSES RELATED TO WORK	6.384	7.159	7.819	9.051	10.807	11.399
49	GROSS GOVERNMENT PRODUCT EXCLUSIVE OF NET REVALUATIONS	304.625	332.541	364.587	392.611	429.570	479.516
50	NET REVALUATIONS	21.762	52.551	51.915	93.696	29.844	24.741
51	GROSS GOVERNMENT PRODUCT	326.387	385.092	416.502	486.307	459.414	504.257

TABLE 5. GOVERNMENT INCOME AND PRODUCT, BILLIONS OF DOLLARS, 1946-81

		CREDITS					
		PERCENT PER ANNUM RATES OF GROWTH CURRENT DOLLARS					
		1946-56	1956-66	1966-71	1971-76	1976-81	1946-81
27	CONSUMPTION (TO HOUSEHOLDS)	1.903	11.332	10.229	12.030	10.191	8.335
28	CAPITAL ACCUMULATION	6.712	9.642	9.317	9.462	10.503	8.847
29	TO BUSINESS (R & D)	21.109	10.933	.267	5.835	11.169	11.402
30	TO HOUSEHOLDS	6.101	9.454	11.384	9.997	9.965	8.906
31	EDUCATION AND TRAINING	5.989	9.554	11.225	9.761	9.657	8.802
32	PUBLIC SCHOOLS	8.027	11.394	12.441	10.760	9.853	10.259
33	EMPLOYEE TRAINING	2.987	4.973	6.530	4.682	8.446	5.067
34	MILITARY	2.645	4.253	6.079	2.532	8.156	4.348
35	NONMILITARY	6.346	9.607	8.648	12.452	9.228	8.873
36	HEALTH	7.218	8.482	12.968	12.146	12.460	9.828
37	TO GOVERNMENT	3.480	9.401	4.782	8.120	14.415	7.520
38	RESEARCH AND DEVELOPMENT	16.727	11.330	5.914	5.819	7.060	10.615
39	NATURAL RESOURCES	.896	8.511	4.161	9.364	17.420	6.976
40	INTERMEDIATE PRODUCT	-.892	5.223	5.944	4.181	10.652	4.138
41	TO BUSINESS	-2.225	4.923	5.406	4.412	10.314	3.563
42	TO NONPROFIT	.406	8.932	9.103	1.285	14.658	6.121
43	TO GOVT ENTERPRISE	-4.824	6.288	9.911	1.258	13.413	3.724
44	TO HOUSEHOLD	1.322	5.416	6.305	4.161	10.751	4.914
45	GROSS CREDITS EXCLUSIVE OF CHANGE IN INVENTORIES AND NET REVALUATIONS	1.356	7.592	7.997	7.895	10.494	6.275
46	CHANGE IN INVENTORIES	N.A.	N.A.	N.A.	N.A.	-5.626	N.A.
47	LESS: INTERMEDIATE PURCHASES FROM OTHER SECTORS	17.173	10.504	9.514	11.883	13.127	12.802
48	LESS: EXPENSES RELATED TO WORK	11.768	6.080	9.004	8.657	12.294	9.351
49	GROSS GOVERNMENT PRODUCT EXCLUSIVE OF NET REVALUATIONS	1.532	6.641	7.988	6.896	9.498	5.779
50	NET REVALUATIONS	N.A.	-6.667	8.226	23.894	2.599	N.A.
51	GROSS GOVERNMENT PRODUCT	7.791	5.713	7.996	7.655	9.090	7.387

TABLE 6. HOUSEHOLD INCOME AND PRODUCT, BILLIONS OF DOLLARS, 1946-81

		DEBITS					
		1946	1947	1948	1949	1950	1951
1	LABOR INCOME	109.031	122.172	129.014	127.731	131.547	141.883
2	COMPENSATION OF EMPLOYEES	2.120	2.348	2.363	2.356	2.572	2.661
3	IMPUTATIONS	107.013	119.949	126.789	125.533	129.159	139.419
4	EMPLOYEE TRAINING	.081	.078	.071	.049	.066	.081
5	OPPORTUNITY COSTS OF STUDENTS	11.640	14.380	15.660	15.570	16.420	18.240
6	UNPAID HOUSEHOLD WORK	95.292	105.491	111.058	109.914	112.673	121.098
7	LESS: EXPENSES RELATED TO WORK	.102	.125	.138	.158	.184	.197
8	CAPITAL INCOME	5.108	4.640	5.175	6.506	7.692	9.006
9	OWNER-OCCUPIED HOUSING	2.726	2.595	2.900	3.566	4.307	5.033
10	INTEREST PAID	.972	1.159	1.378	1.547	1.766	2.093
11	NET IMPUTED INTEREST	1.613	1.187	1.334	1.889	2.187	2.635
12	GROSS IMPUTED INTEREST	2.585	2.346	2.712	3.436	3.953	4.728
13	LAND	.360	.304	.334	.414	.485	.576
14	OWNER-OCCUPIED DWELLINGS	2.225	2.042	2.378	3.022	3.468	4.152
15	LESS: INTEREST PAID	.972	1.159	1.378	1.547	1.766	2.093
16	NET RENTAL INCOME	.141	.249	.188	.130	.354	.305
17	RENTAL INCOME ON NONFARM OWN-OCC. DWELLINGS AND LAND	1.754	1.436	1.522	2.019	2.541	2.940
18	LESS: NET IMPUTED INTEREST	1.613	1.187	1.334	1.889	2.187	2.635
19	CONSUMER GOODS	2.382	2.045	2.275	2.940	3.385	3.973
20	CONSUMER INTEREST	.727	1.046	1.423	1.748	2.269	2.508
21	NET IMPUTED INTEREST	1.655	.999	.852	1.192	1.116	1.465
22	GROSS IMPUTED INTEREST	2.382	2.045	2.275	2.940	3.385	3.973
23	DURABLES	1.545	1.345	1.537	2.048	2.463	2.994
24	SEMIDURABLES	.770	.644	.678	.820	.847	.896
25	INVENTORIES	.068	.057	.060	.071	.075	.083
26	LESS: CONSUMER INTEREST	.727	1.046	1.423	1.748	2.269	2.508
27	NET REVALUATIONS	-22.193	5.006	6.096	1.927	-2.605	6.061
28	LAND	-1.859	1.226	.854	1.022	2.560	1.155
29	OWNER-OCCUPIED DWELLINGS	-6.111	6.228	4.013	-1.476	1.395	3.337
30	CONSUMER GOODS	-14.223	-2.448	1.229	2.381	-6.560	1.569
31	DURABLES	-9.689	-2.228	.171	1.154	-3.161	2.075
32	SEMIDURABLES	-4.206	-.340	.971	1.258	-3.233	-.663
33	INVENTORIES	-.328	.120	.087	-.031	-.166	.157
34	INCOME ORIGINATING (1+8+27)	91.946	131.818	140.285	136.164	136.634	156.950
35	LESS: INTANGIBLE (HUMAN) CAPITAL CONSUMPTION	18.641	19.528	20.575	21.808	20.294	21.695
36	NET INCOME ORIGINATING AND CHARGES AGAINST NET HOUSEHOLD PRODUCT (34-35)	73.305	112.290	119.710	114.356	116.340	135.255
37	CAPITAL CONSUMPTION ALLOWANCES	48.001	53.376	58.110	60.905	60.651	66.278
38	TANGIBLE (NONHUMAN)	29.360	33.848	37.535	39.097	40.357	44.583
39	ORIGINAL COST	23.964	27.496	30.998	34.032	36.740	39.503
40	REVALUATIONS	5.396	6.352	6.537	5.065	3.617	5.080
41	INTANGIBLE (HUMAN)	18.641	19.528	20.575	21.808	20.294	21.695
42	ORIGINAL COST	15.243	14.995	14.322	14.065	14.495	15.415
43	REVALUATIONS	3.398	4.533	6.253	7.743	5.799	6.280
44	CHARGES AGAINST GROSS HOUSEHOLD PRODUCT (36 + 37)	121.306	165.666	177.820	175.261	176.991	201.533

201

TABLE 6. HOUSEHOLD INCOME AND PRODUCT, BILLIONS OF DOLLARS, 1946-81

		DEBITS					
		1952	1953	1954	1955	1956	1957
1	LABOR INCOME	153.773	166.116	175.112	184.372	192.431	203.310
2	COMPENSATION OF EMPLOYEES	2.614	2.690	2.570	3.051	3.266	3.322
3	IMPUTATIONS	151.367	163.657	172.788	181.622	189.517	200.362
4	EMPLOYEE TRAINING	.076	.070	.057	.081	.056	.055
5	OPPORTUNITY COSTS OF STUDENTS	18.780	20.640	20.340	22.940	25.370	28.300
6	UNPAID HOUSEHOLD WORK	132.511	142.947	152.391	158.601	164.091	172.007
7	LESS: EXPENSES RELATED TO WORK	.208	.231	.246	.301	.352	.374
8	CAPITAL INCOME	11.197	13.587	15.757	16.530	17.614	19.348
9	OWNER-OCCUPIED HOUSING	6.204	7.567	8.893	9.611	10.347	11.318
10	INTEREST PAID	2.407	2.718	3.134	3.573	4.226	4.911
11	NET IMPUTED INTEREST	3.553	4.542	5.419	5.528	5.641	6.089
12	GROSS IMPUTED INTEREST	5.960	7.260	8.553	9.101	9.867	11.000
13	LAND	.728	.919	1.121	1.268	1.487	1.756
14	OWNER-OCCUPIED DWELLINGS	5.232	6.341	7.432	7.833	8.380	9.244
15	LESS: INTEREST PAID	2.407	2.718	3.134	3.573	4.226	4.911
16	NET RENTAL INCOME	.244	.307	.340	.510	.480	.318
17	RENTAL INCOME ON NONFARM OWN-OCC. DWELLINGS AND LAND	3.797	4.849	5.759	6.038	6.121	6.407
18	LESS: NET IMPUTED INTEREST	3.553	4.542	5.419	5.528	5.641	6.089
19	CONSUMER GOODS	4.993	6.020	6.864	6.919	7.267	8.030
20	CONSUMER INTEREST	2.863	3.569	3.807	4.437	5.091	5.450
21	NET IMPUTED INTEREST	2.130	2.451	3.057	2.482	2.176	2.580
22	GROSS IMPUTED INTEREST	4.993	6.020	6.864	6.919	7.267	8.030
23	DURABLES	3.812	4.639	5.340	5.419	5.743	6.394
24	SEMIDURABLES	1.078	1.260	1.388	1.364	1.385	1.485
25	INVENTORIES	.103	.122	.136	.135	.139	.152
26	LESS: CONSUMER INTEREST	2.863	3.569	3.807	4.437	5.091	5.450
27	NET REVALUATIONS	.825	-.726	-4.167	-1.934	-2.050	-4.776
28	LAND	2.265	2.627	2.835	5.888	5.141	3.593
29	OWNER-OCCUPIED DWELLINGS	-.525	-.836	-.068	-.273	-4.522	-5.567
30	CONSUMER GOODS	-.915	-2.517	-6.934	-7.549	-2.669	-2.802
31	DURABLES	-1.607	-1.902	-6.332	-6.468	-1.124	-2.360
32	SEMIDURABLES	.693	-.579	-.564	-.960	-1.450	-.490
33	INVENTORIES	-.001	-.036	-.038	-.121	-.095	.048
34	INCOME ORIGINATING (1+8+27)	165.795	178.977	186.702	198.968	207.995	217.882
35	LESS: INTANGIBLE (HUMAN) CAPITAL CONSUMPTION	26.141	28.201	31.982	31.417	35.533	39.038
36	NET INCOME ORIGINATING AND CHARGES AGAINST NET HOUSEHOLD PRODUCT (34-35)	139.654	150.776	154.720	167.551	172.462	178.844
37	CAPITAL CONSUMPTION ALLOWANCES	74.147	78.497	85.279	87.186	95.319	102.418
38	TANGIBLE (NONHUMAN)	48.006	50.296	53.297	55.769	59.786	63.380
39	ORIGINAL COST	42.501	45.749	49.378	52.526	56.143	58.897
40	REVALUATIONS	5.505	4.547	3.919	3.243	3.643	4.483
41	INTANGIBLE (HUMAN)	26.141	28.201	31.982	31.417	35.533	39.038
42	ORIGINAL COST	16.842	18.428	19.692	20.723	21.709	22.775
43	REVALUATIONS	9.299	9.773	12.290	10.694	13.824	16.263
44	CHARGES AGAINST GROSS HOUSEHOLD PRODUCT (36 + 37)	213.801	229.273	239.999	254.737	267.781	281.262

TABLE 6. HOUSEHOLD INCOME AND PRODUCT, BILLIONS OF DOLLARS, 1946-81

		DEBITS					
		1958	1959	1960	1961	1962	1963
1	LABOR INCOME	211.058	223.697	240.126	248.819	260.050	273.021
2	COMPENSATION OF EMPLOYEES	3.503	3.553	3.797	3.734	3.807	3.831
3	IMPUTATIONS	207.964	220.579	236.771	245.551	256.722	269.673
4	EMPLOYEE TRAINING	.062	.068	.066	.065	.072	.065
5	OPPORTUNITY COSTS OF STUDENTS	28.760	32.050	33.220	34.740	39.200	43.660
6	UNPAID HOUSEHOLD WORK	179.142	188.461	203.485	210.746	217.450	225.948
7	LESS: EXPENSES RELATED TO WORK	.409	.435	.442	.466	.479	.483
8	CAPITAL INCOME	20.863	22.860	25.143	26.652	28.862	30.891
9	OWNER-OCCUPIED HOUSING	12.276	13.695	15.117	16.230	17.783	18.921
10	INTEREST PAID	5.579	6.270	6.967	7.629	8.538	9.252
11	NET IMPUTED INTEREST	6.375	6.925	7.903	8.206	8.726	9.447
12	GROSS IMPUTED INTEREST	11.954	13.195	14.870	15.835	17.264	18.699
13	LAND	2.010	2.392	2.803	3.026	3.411	3.816
14	OWNER-OCCUPIED DWELLINGS	9.944	10.802	12.067	12.809	13.853	14.884
15	LESS: INTEREST PAID	5.579	6.270	6.967	7.629	8.538	9.252
16	NET RENTAL INCOME	.322	.500	.247	.395	.519	.222
17	RENTAL INCOME ON NONFARM OWN-OCC. DWELLINGS AND LAND	6.697	7.425	8.150	8.601	9.245	9.669
18	LESS: NET IMPUTED INTEREST	6.375	6.925	7.903	8.206	8.726	9.447
19	CONSUMER GOODS	8.587	9.165	10.026	10.422	11.079	11.970
20	CONSUMER INTEREST	5.560	6.103	6.987	7.311	7.802	8.830
21	NET IMPUTED INTEREST	3.027	3.062	3.039	3.111	3.277	3.140
22	GROSS IMPUTED INTEREST	8.587	9.165	10.026	10.422	11.079	11.970
23	DURABLES	6.869	7.348	8.029	8.324	8.825	9.538
24	SEMIDURABLES	1.554	1.641	1.802	1.893	2.035	2.196
25	INVENTORIES	.164	.176	.194	.204	.219	.236
26	LESS: CONSUMER INTEREST	5.560	6.103	6.987	7.311	7.802	8.830
27	NET REVALUATIONS	-.105	-1.123	-3.751	-4.080	-6.306	-10.950
28	LAND	5.180	8.689	1.928	4.448	5.192	3.905
29	OWNER-OCCUPIED DWELLINGS	-4.501	-5.206	-2.105	-4.121	-4.736	-10.228
30	CONSUMER GOODS	-.784	-4.606	-3.574	-4.407	-6.762	-4.627
31	DURABLES	-.365	-3.717	-3.492	-4.053	-6.066	-4.109
32	SEMIDURABLES	-.465	-.810	-.112	-.331	-.654	-.518
33	INVENTORIES	.046	-.079	.030	-.023	-.042	.000
34	INCOME ORIGINATING (1+8+27)	231.816	245.434	261.518	271.391	282.606	292.962
35	LESS: INTANGIBLE (HUMAN) CAPITAL CONSUMPTION	41.255	43.317	45.728	47.419	50.489	53.608
36	NET INCOME ORIGINATING AND CHARGES AGAINST NET HOUSEHOLD PRODUCT (34-35)	190.561	202.117	215.790	223.972	232.117	239.354
37	CAPITAL CONSUMPTION ALLOWANCES	107.332	111.947	116.403	120.550	125.732	131.533
38	TANGIBLE (NONHUMAN)	66.077	68.630	70.675	73.131	75.243	77.925
39	ORIGINAL COST	61.334	63.769	66.317	69.078	71.683	74.861
40	REVALUATIONS	4.743	4.861	4.358	4.053	3.560	3.064
41	INTANGIBLE (HUMAN)	41.255	43.317	45.728	47.419	50.489	53.608
42	ORIGINAL COST	23.939	25.317	27.018	28.793	30.736	32.896
43	REVALUATIONS	17.316	18.000	18.710	18.626	19.753	20.712
44	CHARGES AGAINST GROSS HOUSEHOLD PRODUCT (36 + 37)	297.893	314.064	332.193	344.522	357.849	370.887

203

TABLE 6. HOUSEHOLD INCOME AND PRODUCT, BILLIONS OF DOLLARS, 1946-81

		DEBITS					
		1964	1965	1966	1967	1968	1969
1	LABOR INCOME	290.432	311.164	332.436	362.775	400.035	427.929
2	COMPENSATION OF EMPLOYEES	3.916	3.969	4.021	4.182	4.377	4.439
3	IMPUTATIONS	287.015	307.693	328.908	359.092	396.172	424.017
4	EMPLOYEE TRAINING	.072	.081	.093	.087	.093	.096
5	OPPORTUNITY COSTS OF STUDENTS	48.480	53.640	60.890	75.760	83.850	92.270
6	UNPAID HOUSEHOLD WORK	238.463	253.972	267.925	283.245	312.229	331.651
7	LESS: EXPENSES RELATED TO WORK	.499	.498	.493	.499	.514	.527
8	CAPITAL INCOME	32.427	34.517	36.821	39.211	39.940	42.550
9	OWNER-OCCUPIED HOUSING	20.047	21.427	22.905	24.143	24.834	26.342
10	INTEREST PAID	10.192	11.147	12.027	12.732	13.809	15.218
11	NET IMPUTED INTEREST	9.208	9.636	10.020	10.697	9.604	10.046
12	GROSS IMPUTED INTEREST	19.400	20.783	22.047	23.429	23.413	25.264
13	LAND	4.056	4.460	4.806	5.144	5.224	5.632
14	OWNER-OCCUPIED DWELLINGS	15.344	16.323	17.241	18.286	18.190	19.632
15	LESS: INTEREST PAID	10.192	11.147	12.027	12.732	13.809	15.218
16	NET RENTAL INCOME	.647	.644	.858	.714	1.421	1.078
17	RENTAL INCOME ON NONFARM OWN-OCC. DWELLINGS AND LAND	9.855	10.280	10.878	11.411	11.025	11.124
18	LESS: NET IMPUTED INTEREST	9.208	9.636	10.020	10.697	9.604	10.046
19	CONSUMER GOODS	12.380	13.090	13.916	15.068	15.106	16.208
20	CONSUMER INTEREST	9.918	11.063	11.965	12.459	13.762	15.625
21	NET IMPUTED INTEREST	2.462	2.027	1.951	2.609	1.344	.583
22	GROSS IMPUTED INTEREST	12.380	13.090	13.916	15.068	15.106	16.208
23	DURABLES	9.869	10.418	11.087	12.067	12.169	13.107
24	SEMIDURABLES	2.268	2.414	2.554	2.711	2.657	2.805
25	INVENTORIES	.242	.258	.275	.290	.281	.296
26	LESS: CONSUMER INTEREST	9.918	11.063	11.965	12.459	13.762	15.625
27	NET REVALUATIONS	3.146	-12.663	1.409	-5.304	16.370	-12.010
28	LAND	6.697	6.582	4.591	4.361	11.638	1.311
29	OWNER-OCCUPIED DWELLINGS	3.016	-5.167	4.122	-4.106	14.082	-.069
30	CONSUMER GOODS	-6.567	-14.078	-7.304	-5.559	-9.350	-13.252
31	DURABLES	-5.953	-12.991	-5.792	-4.573	-8.051	-11.653
32	SEMIDURABLES	-.595	-1.064	-1.528	-.882	-1.225	-1.524
33	INVENTORIES	-.019	-.023	.016	-.104	-.074	-.075
34	INCOME ORIGINATING (1+8+27)	326.005	333.018	370.666	396.682	456.345	458.469
35	LESS: INTANGIBLE (HUMAN) CAPITAL CONSUMPTION	57.171	62.373	68.347	75.238	83.030	91.906
36	NET INCOME ORIGINATING AND CHARGES AGAINST NET HOUSEHOLD PRODUCT (34-35)	268.834	270.645	302.319	321.444	373.315	366.563
37	CAPITAL CONSUMPTION ALLOWANCES	138.698	147.616	158.675	173.327	189.893	209.715
38	TANGIBLE (NONHUMAN)	81.527	85.243	90.328	98.089	106.863	117.809
39	ORIGINAL COST	78.623	83.095	88.259	94.492	100.959	109.412
40	REVALUATIONS	2.904	2.148	2.069	3.597	5.904	8.397
41	INTANGIBLE (HUMAN)	57.171	62.373	68.347	75.238	83.030	91.906
42	ORIGINAL COST	35.361	38.279	41.908	46.180	50.820	55.828
43	REVALUATIONS	21.810	24.094	26.439	29.058	32.210	36.078
44	CHARGES AGAINST GROSS HOUSEHOLD PRODUCT (36 + 37)	407.532	418.261	460.994	494.771	563.208	576.278

TABLE 6. HOUSEHOLD INCOME AND PRODUCT, BILLIONS OF DOLLARS, 1946-81

		DEBITS					
		1970	1971	1972	1973	1974	1975
1	LABOR INCOME	468.437	504.205	541.108	585.097	642.804	700.451
2	COMPENSATION OF EMPLOYEES	4.499	4.552	4.631	4.800	4.560	4.581
3	IMPUTATIONS	464.498	500.248	537.081	580.897	638.854	696.517
4	EMPLOYEE TRAINING	.084	.081	.092	.104	.089	.070
5	OPPORTUNITY COSTS OF STUDENTS	103.857	116.898	131.577	148.100	159.941	174.576
6	UNPAID HOUSEHOLD WORK	360.557	383.269	405.412	432.693	478.824	521.871
7	LESS: EXPENSES RELATED TO WORK	.560	.595	.604	.600	.610	.647
8	CAPITAL INCOME	44.687	48.111	51.110	55.278	60.530	66.253
9	OWNER-OCCUPIED HOUSING	27.517	29.854	32.434	35.988	39.596	42.954
10	INTEREST PAID	16.571	18.681	21.579	25.062	29.034	32.123
11	NET IMPUTED INTEREST	10.027	9.964	8.968	8.301	8.182	9.141
12	GROSS IMPUTED INTEREST	26.598	28.645	30.547	33.363	37.216	41.264
13	LAND	5.864	6.152	6.496	7.227	8.192	9.139
14	OWNER-OCCUPIED DWELLINGS	20.733	22.492	24.051	26.136	29.024	32.125
15	LESS: INTEREST PAID	16.571	18.681	21.579	25.062	29.034	32.123
16	NET RENTAL INCOME	.919	1.209	1.887	2.625	2.380	1.690
17	RENTAL INCOME ON NONFARM OWN-OCC. DWELLINGS AND LAND	10.946	11.173	10.855	10.926	10.562	10.831
18	LESS: NET IMPUTED INTEREST	10.027	9.964	8.968	8.301	8.182	9.141
19	CONSUMER GOODS	17.170	18.257	18.676	19.290	20.934	23.299
20	CONSUMER INTEREST	16.686	17.741	19.549	22.319	24.099	24.428
21	NET IMPUTED INTEREST	.484	.516	-.873	-3.029	-3.165	-1.129
22	GROSS IMPUTED INTEREST	17.170	18.257	18.676	19.290	20.934	23.299
23	DURABLES	13.941	14.863	15.208	15.716	17.164	19.227
24	SEMIDURABLES	2.917	3.064	3.134	3.229	3.395	3.653
25	INVENTORIES	.312	.330	.334	.345	.375	.418
26	LESS: CONSUMER INTEREST	16.686	17.741	19.549	22.319	24.099	24.428
27	NET REVALUATIONS	-9.290	-13.615	23.968	24.725	-1.576	-11.747
28	LAND	2.253	-.669	19.359	21.339	11.561	2.561
29	OWNER-OCCUPIED DWELLINGS	-3.677	7.696	20.265	31.415	-3.148	-4.540
30	CONSUMER GOODS	-7.866	-20.642	-15.656	-28.029	-9.989	-9.768
31	DURABLES	-6.637	-18.803	-13.595	-23.067	-2.888	-7.013
32	SEMIDURABLES	-1.223	-1.709	-2.018	-5.185	-7.617	-2.917
33	INVENTORIES	-.006	-.130	-.043	.223	.516	.162
34	INCOME ORIGINATING (1+8+27)	503.834	538.701	616.186	665.100	701.758	754.957
35	LESS: INTANGIBLE (HUMAN) CAPITAL CONSUMPTION	101.800	111.883	122.626	134.282	153.606	173.777
36	NET INCOME ORIGINATING AND CHARGES AGAINST NET HOUSEHOLD PRODUCT (34-35)	402.034	426.818	493.560	530.818	548.152	581.180
37	CAPITAL CONSUMPTION ALLOWANCES	229.344	249.326	269.606	294.401	332.847	373.921
38	TANGIBLE (NONHUMAN)	127.544	137.443	146.980	160.119	179.241	200.144
39	ORIGINAL COST	117.495	125.525	134.365	146.273	158.093	170.287
40	REVALUATIONS	10.049	11.918	12.615	13.846	21.148	29.857
41	INTANGIBLE (HUMAN)	101.800	111.883	122.626	134.282	153.606	173.777
42	ORIGINAL COST	61.153	66.810	73.119	80.594	89.064	97.750
43	REVALUATIONS	40.647	45.073	49.507	53.688	64.542	76.027
44	CHARGES AGAINST GROSS HOUSEHOLD PRODUCT (36 + 37)	631.378	676.144	763.166	825.219	880.999	955.101

205

TABLE 6. HOUSEHOLD INCOME AND PRODUCT, BILLIONS OF DOLLARS, 1946-81

		DEBITS					
		1976	1977	1978	1979	1980	1981
1	LABOR INCOME	805.637	876.412	948.086	1041.861	1155.367	1271.065
2	COMPENSATION OF EMPLOYEES	5.359	5.930	6.246	6.461	6.585	7.042
3	IMPUTATIONS	800.987	871.300	942.697	1036.304	1149.746	1265.046
4	EMPLOYEE TRAINING	.093	.107	.118	.118	.101	.105
5	OPPORTUNITY COSTS OF STUDENTS	188.640	202.927	218.348	236.874	259.918	284.230
6	UNPAID HOUSEHOLD WORK	612.254	668.266	724.231	799.312	889.727	980.711
7	LESS: EXPENSES RELATED TO WORK	.709	.818	.857	.904	.964	1.023
8	CAPITAL INCOME	71.814	77.306	87.854	102.236	121.252	143.112
9	OWNER-OCCUPIED HOUSING	47.300	51.907	60.543	70.444	83.769	100.503
10	INTEREST PAID	36.641	43.797	52.515	63.192	75.308	87.156
11	NET IMPUTED INTEREST	7.757	4.559	2.820	3.571	4.217	4.060
12	GROSS IMPUTED INTEREST	44.398	48.356	55.335	66.763	79.525	91.216
13	LAND	9.907	10.750	12.265	14.887	18.247	21.131
14	OWNER-OCCUPIED DWELLINGS	34.491	37.605	43.070	51.876	61.278	70.085
15	LESS: INTEREST PAID	36.641	43.797	52.515	63.192	75.308	87.156
16	NET RENTAL INCOME	2.902	3.551	5.208	3.681	4.244	9.287
17	RENTAL INCOME ON NONFARM OWN-OCC. DWELLINGS AND LAND	10.659	8.110	8.028	7.252	8.461	13.347
18	LESS: NET IMPUTED INTEREST	7.757	4.559	2.820	3.571	4.217	4.060
19	CONSUMER GOODS	24.514	25.399	27.311	31.792	37.483	42.609
20	CONSUMER INTEREST	26.680	30.725	37.377	45.468	49.560	54.253
21	NET IMPUTED INTEREST	-2.166	-5.326	-10.066	-13.676	-12.077	-11.644
22	GROSS IMPUTED INTEREST	24.514	25.399	27.311	31.792	37.483	42.609
23	DURABLES	20.277	21.059	22.705	26.512	31.386	35.736
24	SEMIDURABLES	3.795	3.887	4.128	4.720	5.417	6.084
25	INVENTORIES	.441	.453	.477	.560	.680	.789
26	LESS: CONSUMER INTEREST	26.680	30.725	37.377	45.468	49.560	54.253
27	NET REVALUATIONS	70.773	74.646	112.482	-7.445	-29.449	-66.035
28	LAND	30.747	22.840	48.569	15.097	39.006	-17.647
29	OWNER-OCCUPIED DWELLINGS	51.489	69.848	93.339	4.239	-41.052	-13.679
30	CONSUMER GOODS	-11.463	-18.042	-29.426	-26.781	-27.403	-34.709
31	DURABLES	-8.387	-13.043	-20.262	-17.670	-15.157	-25.526
32	SEMIDURABLES	-2.900	-4.827	-9.030	-9.795	-12.654	-9.367
33	INVENTORIES	-.176	-.172	-.134	.684	.408	.184
34	INCOME ORIGINATING (1+8+27)	948.224	1028.364	1148.422	1136.652	1247.170	1348.142
35	LESS: INTANGIBLE (HUMAN) CAPITAL CONSUMPTION	191.104	214.141	239.319	271.108	310.363	351.129
36	NET INCOME ORIGINATING AND CHARGES AGAINST NET HOUSEHOLD PRODUCT (34-35)	757.120	814.223	909.103	865.544	936.807	997.013
37	CAPITAL CONSUMPTION ALLOWANCES	409.292	453.610	505.951	569.338	643.343	711.690
38	TANGIBLE (NONHUMAN)	218.188	239.469	266.632	298.230	332.980	360.561
39	ORIGINAL COST	184.068	200.601	219.793	241.269	263.042	282.863
40	REVALUATIONS	34.120	38.868	46.839	56.961	69.938	77.698
41	INTANGIBLE (HUMAN)	191.104	214.141	239.319	271.108	310.363	351.129
42	ORIGINAL COST	106.839	117.307	129.924	144.446	159.956	176.848
43	REVALUATIONS	84.265	96.834	109.395	126.662	150.407	174.281
44	CHARGES AGAINST GROSS HOUSEHOLD PRODUCT (36 + 37)	1166.412	1267.833	1415.054	1434.882	1580.150	1708.703

206

TABLE 6. HOUSEHOLD INCOME AND PRODUCT, BILLIONS OF DOLLARS, 1946-81

		DEBITS				
		PERCENT PER ANNUM RATES OF GROWTH CURRENT DOLLARS				
		1946-56	1956-66	1966-71	1971-76	1976-81	1946-81
1	LABOR INCOME	5.846	5.619	8.688	9.826	9.548	7.269
2	COMPENSATION OF EMPLOYEES	4.416	2.101	2.512	3.318	5.614	3.489
3	IMPUTATIONS	5.882	5.668	8.748	9.872	9.571	7.312
4	EMPLOYEE TRAINING	-3.624	5.203	-2.725	2.802	2.457	.744
5	OPPORTUNITY COSTS OF STUDENTS	8.103	9.150	13.934	10.044	8.544	9.559
6	UNPAID HOUSEHOLD WORK	5.585	5.025	7.423	9.821	9.881	6.888
7	LESS: EXPENSES RELATED TO WORK	13.186	3.426	3.833	3.568	7.608	6.809
8	CAPITAL INCOME	13.177	7.652	5.495	8.341	14.787	9.990
9	OWNER-OCCUPIED HOUSING	14.269	8.271	5.442	9.641	16.269	10.857
10	INTEREST PAID	15.831	11.026	9.207	14.423	18.923	13.708
11	NET IMPUTED INTEREST	13.336	5.913	-.113	-4.884	-12.143	2.672
12	GROSS IMPUTED INTEREST	14.333	8.371	5.375	9.160	15.489	10.718
13	LAND	15.229	12.444	5.062	9.996	16.359	12.335
14	OWNER-OCCUPIED DWELLINGS	14.181	7.481	5.462	8.927	15.235	10.359
15	LESS: INTEREST PAID	15.831	11.026	9.207	14.423	18.923	13.708
16	NET RENTAL INCOME	13.041	5.989	7.106	19.133	26.192	12.715
17	RENTAL INCOME ON NONFARM OWN-OCC. DWELLINGS AND LAND	13.313	5.919	.537	-.937	4.600	5.970
18	LESS: NET IMPUTED INTEREST	13.336	5.913	-.113	-4.884	-12.143	2.672
19	CONSUMER GOODS	11.799	6.712	5.581	6.070	11.691	8.589
20	CONSUMER INTEREST	21.486	8.921	8.196	8.503	15.252	13.113
21	NET IMPUTED INTEREST	2.774	-1.088	-23.346	N.A.	N.A.	N.A.
22	GROSS IMPUTED INTEREST	11.799	6.712	5.581	6.070	11.691	8.589
23	DURABLES	14.035	6.798	6.038	6.409	12.000	9.391
24	SEMIDURABLES	6.045	6.306	3.712	4.373	9.901	6.083
25	INVENTORIES	7.456	7.098	3.677	5.986	12.322	7.272
26	LESS: CONSUMER INTEREST	21.486	8.921	8.196	8.503	15.252	13.113
27	NET REVALUATIONS	N.A.	N.A.	N.A.	N.A.	N.A.	N.A.
28	LAND	N.A.	-1.125	N.A.	N.A.	N.A.	N.A.
29	OWNER-OCCUPIED DWELLINGS	N.A.	N.A.	13.300	46.248	N.A.	N.A.
30	CONSUMER GOODS	N.A.	N.A.	N.A.	N.A.	N.A.	N.A.
31	DURABLES	N.A.	N.A.	N.A.	N.A.	N.A.	N.A.
32	SEMIDURABLES	N.A.	N.A.	N.A.	N.A.	N.A.	N.A.
33	INVENTORIES	N.A.	N.A.	N.A.	N.A.	N.A.	N.A.
34	INCOME ORIGINATING (1+8+27)	8.506	5.948	7.764	11.973	7.291	7.974
35	LESS: INTANGIBLE (HUMAN) CAPITAL CONSUMPTION	6.664	6.760	10.359	11.302	12.938	8.750
36	NET INCOME ORIGINATING AND CHARGES AGAINST NET HOUSEHOLD PRODUCT (34-35)	8.932	5.774	7.141	12.146	5.659	7.743
37	CAPITAL CONSUMPTION ALLOWANCES	7.101	5.228	9.459	10.421	11.700	8.009
38	TANGIBLE (NONHUMAN)	7.370	4.213	8.758	9.684	10.568	7.429
39	ORIGINAL COST	8.886	4.628	7.299	7.957	8.973	7.307
40	REVALUATIONS	-3.852	-5.500	41.935	23.413	17.891	7.918
41	INTANGIBLE (HUMAN)	6.664	6.760	10.359	11.302	12.938	8.750
42	ORIGINAL COST	3.599	6.799	9.776	9.844	10.605	7.254
43	REVALUATIONS	15.064	6.699	11.259	13.330	15.643	11.907
44	CHARGES AGAINST GROSS HOUSEHOLD PRODUCT (36 + 37)	8.240	5.582	7.961	11.522	7.935	7.851

TABLE 6. HOUSEHOLD INCOME AND PRODUCT, BILLIONS OF DOLLARS, 1946-81

		CREDITS				
		1946	1947	1948	1949	1950	1951
45	CONSUMPTION	143.101	154.339	163.617	162.846	165.962	181.935
46	MARKET (LABOR SERVICES IN HOUSEHOLDS)	2.120	2.348	2.363	2.356	2.572	2.661
47	NONMARKET	125.528	139.150	148.579	150.344	155.271	168.721
48	NET SPACE RENT ON OWNER-OCCUPIED NONFARM DWELLINGS	5.611	6.062	6.861	7.943	9.070	10.468
49	BEA NET SPACE RENT ON OWNER-OCCUPIED NONFARM DWELLINGS	5.611	6.062	6.861	7.943	9.070	10.468
50	SUBSIDIES	.000	.000	.000	.000	.000	.000
51	CAPITAL SERVICES OTHER THAN ON OWNER-OCCUPIED DWELLINGS	28.996	32.436	35.761	37.518	38.692	42.726
52	DURABLES	10.257	11.609	13.182	14.800	16.502	19.270
53	GROSS	11.607	13.237	15.086	17.020	19.049	22.215
54	LESS: SERVICES ALLOCATED TO INVESTMENT	.429	.502	.572	.648	.702	.775
55	LESS: SERVICES TO EXP RELATED TO WORK	.921	1.126	1.332	1.573	1.845	2.170
56	SEMIDURABLES	18.671	20.770	22.519	22.647	22.115	23.373
57	INVENTORIES	.068	.057	.060	.071	.075	.083
58	LABOR SERVICES	90.921	100.652	105.957	104.883	107.509	115.527
59	TOTAL IMPUTED LABOR SERVICES	107.013	119.949	126.789	125.533	129.159	139.419
60	LESS: LABOR SERVICES ALLOCATED TO INVESTMENT	16.092	19.297	20.832	20.650	21.650	23.892
61	INTERMEDIATE PRODUCT OF GOVERNMENT TO CONSUMPTION	15.453	12.841	12.675	10.145	8.119	10.553
62	CAPITAL ACCUMULATION	-3.480	26.830	29.555	24.929	21.216	32.614
63	INTANGIBLE AT ORIGINAL COST	18.713	21.824	23.459	23.002	23.821	26.553
64	EDUCATION	17.461	20.491	22.065	21.648	22.428	25.025
65	TEACHING CHILDREN IN HOME	3.517	3.893	4.104	4.048	4.157	4.490
66	OPPORTUNITY COST OF STUDENTS	11.640	14.380	15.660	15.570	16.420	18.240
67	DURABLE SERVICES ALLOCATED TO EDUCATION	.258	.316	.368	.425	.467	.518
68	INTERMEDIATE PRODUCT OF GOVERNMENT TO EDUCATION	2.046	1.902	1.933	1.605	1.384	1.777
69	HEALTH	1.160	1.247	1.316	1.302	1.323	1.440
70	EMPLOYEE TRAINING	.092	.086	.078	.053	.070	.087
71	NET REVALUATIONS	-22.193	5.006	6.096	1.927	-2.605	6.061
72	SERVICES TO EXP REL TO WORK	.921	1.126	1.332	1.573	1.845	2.170
73	LESS: INTERMEDIATE PRODUCT TRANSFERRED FROM GOVERNMENT	19.134	16.504	16.546	13.929	11.849	14.989
74	LESS: EXPENSES RELATED TO WORK	.102	.125	.138	.158	.18·1	.197
75	GROSS HOUSEHOLD PRODUCT	121.306	165.666	177.820	175.261	176.991	201.533

208

TABLE 6. HOUSEHOLD INCOME AND PRODUCT, BILLIONS OF DOLLARS, 1946-81

		CREDITS					
		1952	1953	1954	1955	1956	1957
45	CONSUMPTION	199.495	214.468	227.737	239.854	250.708	265.402
46	MARKET (LABOR SERVICES IN HOUSEHOLDS)	2.614	2.690	2.570	3.051	3.266	3.322
47	NONMARKET	184.959	199.428	213.382	222.621	232.800	245.789
48	NET SPACE RENT ON OWNER-OCCUPIED NONFARM DWELLINGS	12.192	14.035	15.874	17.355	18.963	20.701
49 50	BEA NET SPACE RENT ON OWNER-OCCUPIED NONFARM DWELLINGS SUBSIDIES	12.192 .000	14.035 .000	15.874 .000	17.355 .000	18.963 .000	20.701 .000
51	CAPITAL SERVICES OTHER THAN ON OWNER-OCCUPIED DWELLINGS	46.353	49.020	52.098	53.941	57.282	60.970
52 53 54	DURABLES GROSS LESS: SERVICES ALLOCATED TO INVESTMENT	21.549 25.045 .840	23.816 27.778 .912	26.367 30.906 .968	27.830 32.753 1.013	30.472 36.054 1.079	33.053 39.042 1.190
55	LESS: SERVICES TO EXP RELATED TO WORK	2.656	3.050	3.572	3.911	4.504	4.799
56 57	SEMIDURABLES INVENTORIES	24.701 .103	25.083 .122	25.595 .136	25.976 .135	26.671 .139	27.765 .152
58 59 60	LABOR SERVICES TOTAL IMPUTED LABOR SERVICES LESS: LABOR SERVICES ALLOCATED TO INVESTMENT	126.414 151.367 24.953	136.373 163.657 27.284	145.410 172.788 27.378	151.325 181.622 30.297	156.555 189.517 32.962	164.118 200.362 36.244
61	INTERMEDIATE PRODUCT OF GOVERNMENT TO CONSUMPTION	11.922	12.350	11.785	14.181	14.642	16.291
62	CAPITAL ACCUMULATION	28.648	29.630	26.179	31.887	34.740	35.846
63	INTANGIBLE AT ORIGINAL COST	27.823	30.356	30.346	33.821	36.790	40.622
64	EDUCATION	26.169	28.597	28.507	31.870	34.800	38.524
65	TEACHING CHILDREN IN HOME	4.915	5.299	5.622	5.865	6.079	6.363
66	OPPORTUNITY COST OF STUDENTS	18.780	20.640	20.340	22.940	25.370	28.300
67	DURABLE SERVICES ALLOCATED TO EDUCATION	.565	.623	.666	.698	.750	.837
68	INTERMEDIATE PRODUCT OF GOVERNMENT TO EDUCATION	1.909	2.035	1.879	2.367	2.601	3.024
69	HEALTH	1.572	1.684	1.778	1.864	1.930	2.039
70	EMPLOYEE TRAINING	.082	.075	.061	.087	.061	.060
71	NET REVALUATIONS	.825	-.726	-4.167	-1.934	-2.050	-4.776
72	SERVICES TO EXP REL TO WORK	2.656	3.050	3.572	3.911	4.504	4.799
73	LESS: INTERMEDIATE PRODUCT TRANSFERRED FROM GOVERNMENT	16.789	17.644	17.243	20.614	21.819	24.411
74	LESS: EXPENSES RELATED TO WORK	.208	.231	.246	.301	.352	.374
75	GROSS HOUSEHOLD PRODUCT	213.801	229.273	239.999	254.737	267.781	281.262

TABLE 6. HOUSEHOLD INCOME AND PRODUCT, BILLIONS OF DOLLARS, 1946-81

				CREDITS			
		1958	1959	1960	1961	1962	1963
45	CONSUMPTION	276.991	291.413	310.755	322.861	334.363	346.931
46	MARKET (LABOR SERVICES IN HOUSEHOLDS)	3.503	3.553	3.797	3.734	3.807	3.831
47	NONMARKET	257.206	270.979	290.133	301.579	312.786	326.100
48	NET SPACE RENT ON OWNER-OCCUPIED NONFARM DWELLINGS	22.570	24.530	26.640	28.588	30.936	32.943
49	BEA NET SPACE RENT ON OWNER-OCCUPIED NONFARM DWELLINGS	22.570	24.530	26.640	28.588	30.936	32.943
50	SUBSIDIES	.000	.000	.000	.000	.000	.000
51	CAPITAL SERVICES OTHER THAN ON OWNER-OCCUPIED DWELLINGS	63.677	66.608	69.310	71.863	74.328	77.517
52	DURABLES	35.050	37.374	39.043	40.538	41.915	43.909
53	GROSS	41.201	43.880	45.619	47.188	48.666	50.888
54	LESS: SERVICES ALLOCATED TO INVESTMENT	1.269	1.329	1.401	1.456	1.510	1.587
55	LESS: SERVICES TO EXP RELATED TO WORK	4.882	5.177	5.175	5.195	5.241	5.392
56	SEMIDURABLES	28.463	29.058	30.072	31.121	32.194	33.372
57	INVENTORIES	.164	.176	.194	.204	.219	.236
58	LABOR SERVICES	170.959	179.841	194.183	201.128	207.522	215.640
59	TOTAL IMPUTED LABOR SERVICES	207.964	220.579	236.771	245.551	256.722	269.673
60	LESS: LABOR SERVICES ALLOCATED TO INVESTMENT	37.005	40.738	42.588	44.423	49.200	54.033
61	INTERMEDIATE PRODUCT OF GOVERNMENT TO CONSUMPTION	16.283	16.880	16.825	17.548	17.770	17.000
62	CAPITAL ACCUMULATION	41.361	44.474	43.760	45.535	48.517	48.990
63	INTANGIBLE AT ORIGINAL COST	41.466	45.597	47.511	49.615	54.823	59.940
64	EDUCATION	39.284	43.300	45.057	47.067	52.180	57.202
65	TEACHING CHILDREN IN HOME	6.594	6.949	7.501	7.753	8.004	8.311
66	OPPORTUNITY COST OF STUDENTS	28.760	32.050	33.220	34.740	39.200	43.660
67	DURABLE SERVICES ALLOCATED TO EDUCATION	.906	.949	.996	1.029	1.061	1.109
68	INTERMEDIATE PRODUCT OF GOVERNMENT TO EDUCATION	3.024	3.352	3.340	3.545	3.915	4.122
69	HEALTH	2.115	2.223	2.383	2.478	2.565	2.667
70	EMPLOYEE TRAINING	.067	.074	.071	.070	.078	.070
71	NET REVALUATIONS	-.105	-1.123	-3.751	-4.080	-6.306	-10.950
72	SERVICES TO EXP REL TO WORK	4.882	5.177	5.175	5.195	5.241	5.392
73	LESS: INTERMEDIATE PRODUCT TRANSFERRED FROM GOVERNMENT	24.932	26.564	27.055	28.604	29.793	29.943
74	LESS: EXPENSES RELATED TO WORK	.409	.435	.442	.466	.479	.483
75	GROSS HOUSEHOLD PRODUCT	297.893	314.064	332.193	344.522	357.849	370.887

TABLE 6. HOUSEHOLD INCOME AND PRODUCT, BILLIONS OF DOLLARS, 1946-81

		CREDITS					
		1964	1965	1966	1967	1968	1969
45	CONSUMPTION	365.270	387.274	409.985	436.969	477.485	508.115
46	MARKET (LABOR SERVICES IN HOUSEHOLDS)	3.916	3.969	4.021	4.182	4.377	4.439
47	NONMARKET	343.655	364.829	385.866	410.996	448.977	481.470
48	NET SPACE RENT ON OWNER-OCCUPIED NONFARM DWELLINGS	35.060	37.586	40.294	43.224	46.019	50.181
49	BEA NET SPACE RENT ON OWNER-OCCUPIED NONFARM DWELLINGS	35.060	37.586	40.294	43.224	46.019	50.174
50	SUBSIDIES	.000	.000	.000	.000	.000	.007
51	CAPITAL SERVICES OTHER THAN ON OWNER-OCCUPIED DWELLINGS	81.015	84.868	90.039	97.787	105.513	115.517
52	DURABLES	45.867	47.725	50.270	54.786	59.154	65.331
53	GROSS	53.081	55.151	57.975	63.125	67.975	75.074
54	LESS: SERVICES ALLOCATED TO INVESTMENT	1.679	1.790	1.935	2.135	2.325	2.566
55	LESS: SERVICES TO EXP RELATED TO WORK	5.536	5.636	5.771	6.204	6.496	7.177
56	SEMIDURABLES	34.905	36.884	39.495	42.711	46.079	49.890
57	INVENTORIES	.242	.258	.275	.290	.281	.296
58	LABOR SERVICES	227.580	242.375	255.533	269.985	297.445	315.772
59	TOTAL IMPUTED LABOR SERVICES	287.015	307.693	328.908	359.092	396.172	424.017
60	LESS: LABOR SERVICES ALLOCATED TO INVESTMENT	59.435	65.318	73.375	89.107	98.727	108.245
61	INTERMEDIATE PRODUCT OF GOVERNMENT TO CONSUMPTION	17.699	18.476	20.098	21.791	24.131	22.207
62	CAPITAL ACCUMULATION	69.013	59.648	82.704	93.375	125.821	107.305
63	INTANGIBLE AT ORIGINAL COST	65.867	72.311	81.295	98.679	109.451	119.315
64	EDUCATION	62.969	69.213	77.964	95.112	105.517	115.111
65	TEACHING CHILDREN IN HOME	8.777	9.358	10.008	10.714	11.950	12.843
66	OPPORTUNITY COST OF STUDENTS	48.480	53.640	60.890	75.760	83.850	92.270
67	DURABLE SERVICES ALLOCATED TO EDUCATION	1.168	1.235	1.326	1.470	1.620	1.794
68	INTERMEDIATE PRODUCT OF GOVERNMENT TO EDUCATION	4.544	4.980	5.740	7.168	8.097	8.204
69	HEALTH	2.820	3.010	3.230	3.473	3.833	4.100
70	EMPLOYEE TRAINING	.078	.087	.100	.094	.101	.103
71	NET REVALUATIONS	3.146	-12.663	1.409	-5.304	16.370	-12.010
72	SERVICES TO EXP REL TO WORK	5.536	5.636	5.771	6.204	6.496	7.177
73	LESS: INTERMEDIATE PRODUCT TRANSFERRED FROM GOVERNMENT	31.788	33.799	36.973	41.278	46.080	45.792
74	LESS: EXPENSES RELATED TO WORK	.499	.498	.493	.499	.514	.527
75	GROSS HOUSEHOLD PRODUCT	407.532	418.261	460.994	494.771	563.208	576.278

211

TABLE 6. HOUSEHOLD INCOME AND PRODUCT, BILLIONS OF DOLLARS, 1946-81

		CREDITS					
		1970	1971	1972	1973	1974	1975
45	CONSUMPTION	549.256	583.547	617.461	660.378	725.899	797.951
46	MARKET (LABOR SERVICES IN HOUSEHOLDS)	4.499	4.552	4.631	4.800	4.560	4.581
47	NONMARKET	521.782	557.239	591.520	635.083	703.053	771.159
48	NET SPACE RENT ON OWNER-OCCUPIED NONFARM DWELLINGS	53.918	58.897	64.825	71.444	78.747	86.251
49	BEA NET SPACE RENT ON OWNER-OCCUPIED NONFARM DWELLINGS	53.863	58.722	64.265	71.064	78.522	86.074
50	SUBSIDIES	.055	.175	.560	.380	.225	.177
51	CAPITAL SERVICES OTHER THAN ON OWNER-OCCUPIED DWELLINGS	124.715	133.729	141.227	152.467	169.496	189.281
52	DURABLES	71.286	77.525	82.141	88.927	99.430	112.960
53	GROSS	81.854	88.947	94.100	101.851	113.530	128.351
54	LESS: SERVICES ALLOCATED TO INVESTMENT	2.852	3.177	3.446	3.722	4.154	4.686
55	LESS: SERVICES TO EXP RELATED TO WORK	7.716	8.245	8.513	9.202	9.946	10.705
56	SEMIDURABLES	53.116	55.874	58.751	63.195	69.691	75.902
57	INVENTORIES	.312	.330	.334	.345	.375	.418
58	LABOR SERVICES	343.149	364.613	385.468	411.172	454.810	495.627
59	TOTAL IMPUTED LABOR SERVICES	464.498	500.248	537.081	580.897	638.854	696.517
60	LESS: LABOR SERVICES ALLOCATED TO INVESTMENT	121.349	135.635	151.613	169.725	184.044	200.890
61	INTERMEDIATE PRODUCT OF GOVERNMENT TO CONSUMPTION	22.976	21.756	21.310	20.495	18.286	22.211
62	CAPITAL ACCUMULATION	124.337	135.142	189.750	209.538	197.489	206.215
63	INTANGIBLE AT ORIGINAL COST	133.627	148.757	165.782	184.813	199.065	217.962
64	EDUCATION	129.025	143.806	160.490	179.121	192.780	211.030
65	TEACHING CHILDREN IN HOME	14.076	15.077	16.124	17.412	19.433	21.217
66	OPPORTUNITY COST OF STUDENTS	103.857	116.898	131.577	148.100	159.941	174.576
67	DURABLE SERVICES ALLOCATED TO EDUCATION	1.990	2.217	2.407	2.593	2.882	3.245
68	INTERMEDIATE PRODUCT OF GOVERNMENT TO EDUCATION	9.102	9.614	10.382	11.016	10.524	11.992
69	HEALTH	4.512	4.864	5.195	5.581	6.191	6.858
70	EMPLOYEE TRAINING	.090	.087	.098	.111	.094	.074
71	NET REVALUATIONS	-9.290	-13.615	23.968	24.725	-1.576	-11.747
72	SERVICES TO EXP REL TO WORK	7.716	8.245	8.513	9.202	9.946	10.705
73	LESS: INTERMEDIATE PRODUCT TRANSFERRED FROM GOVERNMENT	49.371	50.195	51.954	53.299	51.725	59.123
74	LESS: EXPENSES RELATED TO WORK	.560	.595	.604	.600	.610	.647
75	GROSS HOUSEHOLD PRODUCT	631.378	676.144	763.166	825.219	880.999	955.101

TABLE 6. HOUSEHOLD INCOME AND PRODUCT, BILLIONS OF DOLLARS, 1946-81

		CREDITS					
		1976	1977	1978	1979	1980	1981
45	CONSUMPTION	910.610	995.816	1090.339	1211.594	1360.846	1511.139
46	MARKET (LABOR SERVICES IN HOUSEHOLDS)	5.359	5.930	6.246	6.461	6.585	7.042
47	NONMARKET	882.757	965.016	1056.027	1173.404	1315.262	1455.413
48	NET SPACE RENT ON OWNER-OCCUPIED NONFARM DWELLINGS	94.890	105.853	119.660	135.528	155.324	178.872
49	BEA NET SPACE RENT ON OWNER-OCCUPIED NONFARM DWELLINGS	94.727	105.718	119.549	135.423	155.187	178.649
50	SUBSIDIES	.163	.135	.111	.105	.137	.223
51	CAPITAL SERVICES OTHER THAN ON OWNER-OCCUPIED DWELLINGS	204.832	221.225	243.432	271.429	304.924	332.285
52	DURABLES	123.863	134.707	149.296	168.170	191.873	209.489
53	GROSS	140.836	153.458	170.418	191.835	217.920	237.001
54	LESS: SERVICES ALLOCATED TO INVESTMENT	5.136	5.571	6.243	7.013	7.952	8.904
55	LESS: SERVICES TO EXP RELATED TO WORK	11.837	13.180	14.879	16.652	18.095	18.608
56	SEMIDURABLES	80.527	86.065	93.658	102.699	112.371	122.006
57	INVENTORIES	.441	.453	.477	.560	.680	.789
58	LABOR SERVICES	583.035	637.938	692.935	766.447	855.014	944.256
59	TOTAL IMPUTED LABOR SERVICES	800.987	871.300	942.697	1036.304	1149.746	1265.046
60	LESS: LABOR SERVICES ALLOCATED TO INVESTMENT	217.952	233.362	249.762	269.857	294.732	320.790
61	INTERMEDIATE PRODUCT OF GOVERNMENT TO CONSUMPTION	22.494	24.870	28.066	31.728	38.999	48.684
62	CAPITAL ACCUMULATION	306.216	326.848	382.415	283.947	289.507	282.523
63	INTANGIBLE AT ORIGINAL COST	235.443	252.202	269.933	291.392	318.956	348.558
64	EDUCATION	227.420	243.411	260.402	280.881	307.168	335.455
65	TEACHING CHILDREN IN HOME	23.300	23.844	24.262	25.080	25.993	26.771
66	OPPORTUNITY COST OF STUDENTS	188.640	202.927	218.348	236.874	259.918	284.230
67	DURABLE SERVICES ALLOCATED TO EDUCATION	3.546	3.833	4.356	4.929	5.586	6.299
68	INTERMEDIATE PRODUCT OF GOVERNMENT TO EDUCATION	11.934	12.807	13.436	13.998	15.671	18.155
69	HEALTH	7.925	8.678	9.406	10.387	11.682	12.992
70	EMPLOYEE TRAINING	.098	.113	.124	.124	.106	.111
71	NET REVALUATIONS	70.773	74.646	112.482	-7.445	-29.449	-66.035
72	SERVICES TO EXP REL TO WORK	11.837	13.180	14.879	16.652	18.095	18.608
73	LESS: INTERMEDIATE PRODUCT TRANSFERRED FROM GOVERNMENT	61.543	67.194	71.722	76.406	87.334	102.544
74	LESS: EXPENSES RELATED TO WORK	.709	.818	.857	.904	.964	1.023
75	GROSS HOUSEHOLD PRODUCT	1166.412	1267.833	1415.054	1434.882	1580.150	1708.703

213

TABLE 6. HOUSEHOLD INCOME AND PRODUCT, BILLIONS OF DOLLARS, 1946-81

		CREDITS				
		PERCENT PER ANNUM RATES OF GROWTH CURRENT DOLLARS				
		1946-56	1956-66	1966-71	1971-76	1976-81	1946-81
45	CONSUMPTION	5.768	5.041	7.315	9.308	10.661	6.966
46	MARKET (LABOR SERVICES IN HOUSEHOLDS)	4.416	2.101	2.512	3.318	5.614	3.489
47	NONMARKET	6.371	5.183	7.627	9.638	10.517	7.252
48	NET SPACE RENT ON OWNER-OCCUPIED NONFARM DWELLINGS	12.950	7.828	7.887	10.008	13.518	10.397
49	BEA NET SPACE RENT ON OWNER-OCCUPIED NONFARM DWELLINGS	12.950	7.828	7.823	10.036	13.529	10.393
50	SUBSIDIES	N.A.	N.A.	N.A.	-1.411	6.469	N.A.
51	CAPITAL SERVICES OTHER THAN ON OWNER-OCCUPIED DWELLINGS	7.045	4.626	8.233	8.902	10.160	7.217
52	DURABLES	11.503	5.133	9.051	9.825	11.082	9.002
53	GROSS	12.002	4.864	8.938	9.627	10.970	9.001
54	LESS: SERVICES ALLOCATED TO INVESTMENT	9.670	6.017	10.431	10.083	11.632	9.055
55	LESS: SERVICES TO EXP RELATED TO WORK	17.202	2.510	7.396	7.500	9.469	8.968
56	SEMIDURABLES	3.630	4.004	7.185	7.584	8.665	5.510
57	INVENTORIES	7.456	7.098	3.677	5.986	12.322	7.272
58	LABOR SERVICES	5.585	5.021	7.369	9.843	10.123	6.916
59	TOTAL IMPUTED LABOR SERVICES	5.882	5.668	8.748	9.872	9.571	7.312
60	LESS: LABOR SERVICES ALLOCATED TO INVESTMENT	7.434	8.331	13.075	9.951	8.037	8.926
61	INTERMEDIATE PRODUCT OF GOVERNMENT TO CONSUMPTION	-.538	3.218	1.598	.670	16.698	3.333
62	CAPITAL ACCUMULATION	N.A.	9.061	10.320	17.773	-1.598	N.A.
63	INTANGIBLE AT ORIGINAL COST	6.994	8.251	12.845	9.618	8.163	8.715
64	EDUCATION	7.140	8.401	13.025	9.600	8.084	8.811
65	TEACHING CHILDREN IN HOME	5.625	5.112	8.541	9.096	2.816	5.971
66	OPPORTUNITY COST OF STUDENTS	8.103	9.150	13.934	10.044	8.544	9.559
67	DURABLE SERVICES ALLOCATED TO EDUCATION	11.261	5.864	10.827	9.849	12.178	9.559
68	INTERMEDIATE PRODUCT OF GOVERNMENT TO EDUCATION	2.430	8.238	10.865	4.419	8.753	6.436
69	HEALTH	5.217	5.287	8.531	10.254	10.391	7.145
70	EMPLOYEE TRAINING	-4.075	5.191	-2.867	2.488	2.493	.546
71	NET REVALUATIONS	N.A.	N.A.	N.A.	N.A.	N.A.	N.A.
72	SERVICES TO EXP REL TO WORK	17.202	2.510	7.396	7.500	9.469	8.968
73	LESS: INTERMEDIATE PRODUCT TRANSFERRED FROM GOVERNMENT	1.322	5.416	6.305	4.161	10.751	4.914
74	LESS: EXPENSES RELATED TO WORK	13.186	3.426	3.833	3.568	7.608	6.809
75	GROSS HOUSEHOLD PRODUCT	8.240	5.582	7.961	11.522	7.935	7.851

TABLE 7. GROSS NATIONAL PRODUCT ACCOUNT, BILLIONS OF 1972 DOLLARS, 1946-1981

		CREDITS					
		1946	1947	1948	1949	1950	1951
1	CONSUMPTION	667.596	648.355	660.219	649.308	659.447	672.529
2	HOUSEHOLD EXPENDITURES FOR SERVICES AND NONDURABLES	194.580	197.748	200.517	202.930	210.614	216.316
3	GROSS EXPENDITURES INCLUDED FROM BEA PERSONAL CONSUMPTION EXPENDITURES	199.520	202.643	205.394	207.725	215.394	221.352
4	LESS: PCE EXPENSES RELATED TO WORK	4.940	4.894	4.876	4.795	4.780	5.036
5	EXPENSE ACCOUNT ITEMS OF CONSUMPTION	3.868	3.943	4.088	3.985	4.238	4.483
6	BEA IMPUTATIONS OTHER THAN HOUSING	10.765	9.706	9.109	8.538	8.457	9.092
7	SUBSIDIES ALLOCATED TO CONSUMPTION	2.580	.598	.440	.319	.479	.378
8	SUBSIDIES INCLUDED IN BUSINESS INCOME	3.585	.829	.619	.448	.703	.565
9	LESS: AMT. ALLOCATED TO INVESTMENT	1.005	.231	.179	.129	.224	.187
10	TRANSFERS	96.776	74.780	68.028	59.029	55.424	56.501
11	FROM BUSINESS	1.279	1.356	1.428	1.504	1.662	1.826
12	MEDIA SUPPORT	.860	.904	.952	1.030	1.152	1.251
13	TOTAL MEDIA SUPPORT	1.328	1.405	1.477	1.583	1.737	1.846
14	LESS: MEDIA SUPPORT ALLOCATED TO INVESTMENT	.468	.501	.525	.552	.585	.596
15	HEALTH AND SAFETY	.419	.452	.476	.474	.510	.575
16	FROM NONPROFIT INSTITUTIONS	17.239	15.348	15.287	15.250	15.058	15.115
17	FROM GOVERNMENT ENTERPRISES	2.427	1.620	1.765	1.676	1.915	1.717
18	FROM GOVERNMENT	75.832	56.456	49.548	40.599	36.790	37.843
19	NONMARKET SERVICES PRODUCED IN HOUSEHOLDS	359.027	361.581	378.036	374.507	380.236	385.760
20	NET SPACE RENT OF OWNER-OCCUPIED NONFARM DWELLINGS	11.290	11.817	12.543	13.911	15.347	17.021
21	OTHER CAPITAL SERVICES	47.608	49.631	51.443	53.877	55.970	58.890
22	DURABLES	14.072	16.140	17.883	20.253	22.081	24.390
23	TOTAL DURABLES	17.195	19.523	21.460	24.142	26.383	29.115
24	LESS: DURABLES ALLOCATED TO INVESTMENT	.809	.853	.904	.963	1.020	1.086
25	LESS: SERVICES OF DURABLES TO EXP REL TO WORK	2.314	2.531	2.673	2.926	3.283	3.640
26	SEMIDURABLES	33.401	33.392	33.460	33.502	33.764	34.372
27	INVENTORIES	.135	.100	.100	.122	.125	.129
28	LABOR SERVICES	339.086	341.895	357.260	349.424	352.728	355.023
29	LESS: LABOR SERVICES ALLOC. TO INVEST	38.957	41.762	43.210	42.704	43.810	45.175
30	GROSS DOMESTIC CAPITAL ACCUMULATION	77.902	295.449	300.089	274.991	314.963	381.444
31	ORIGINAL COST	258.051	249.772	267.157	262.226	307.109	331.529
32	TANGIBLE	135.095	135.536	154.631	153.779	192.396	210.817

215

				CREDITS			
		1946	1947	1948	1949	1950	1951
33	STRUCTURES AND EQUIPMENT AND HOUSE-HOLD DURABLES AND SEMIDURABLES	137.467	149.632	161.790	163.140	185.475	194.321
34	BUSINESS	50.937	60.389	56.485	47.272	51.161	52.944
35	NONRESIDENTIAL	48.301	56.873	51.912	42.630	45.477	48.710
36	STRUCTURES	19.015	17.529	17.368	15.350	15.559	16.666
37	EQUIPMENT	29.286	39.344	34.544	27.280	29.918	32.044
38	RESIDENTIAL OTHER THAN OWNER-OCCUPIED NONFARM DWELLINGS	2.636	3.516	4.573	4.642	5.684	4.234
39	NONPROFIT INSTITUTIONS	1.144	1.275	1.794	2.327	2.822	2.757
40	STRUCTURES	1.089	1.171	1.637	2.128	2.589	2.523
41	EQUIPMENT	.055	.104	.157	.199	.233	.234
42	GOVERNMENT ENTERPRISES	1.879	4.938	4.074	3.544	3.708	4.531
43	STRUCTURES	1.773	4.636	3.875	3.341	3.487	4.230
44	EQUIPMENT	.106	.302	.199	.203	.221	.301
45	GOVERNMENT	21.812	16.948	17.021	20.582	21.724	29.284
46	STRUCTURES	4.374	4.781	6.370	9.083	10.876	12.193
47	EQUIPMENT	6.302	3.625	4.291	6.472	6.904	13.059
48	PRODUCT ACCUMULATED	11.136	8.542	6.360	5.027	3.944	4.032
49	HOUSEHOLDS	71.698	78.972	85.660	86.408	102.569	94.697
50	OWNER-OCC. NONFARM DWELLINGS	13.327	17.503	21.340	18.609	26.602	22.892
51	DURABLES	25.377	30.121	32.503	35.524	42.584	39.085
52	SEMIDURABLES	32.994	31.348	31.817	32.275	33.383	32.720
53	FIXED GPDI RECONCILIATION	-6.674	-8.938	-2.975	1.599	2.401	1.623
54	NIPA FIXED GPDI	58.734	70.229	76.644	69.807	82.986	80.216
55	LESS: CORRESP. SECTOR TOTALS	65.408	79.167	79.619	68.208	80.585	78.593
56	GOVERNMENT CAPITAL ACCUMULATION RECONCILIATION	-3.329	-3.952	-.269	1.408	1.090	8.485
57	NIPA GOVERNMENT INVESTMENT	9.226	9.392	14.466	20.507	22.578	38.268
58	LESS: GOVERNMENT AND GOVT ENTERPRISE TOTALS	12.555	13.344	14.735	19.099	21.488	29.783
59	CHANGE IN INVENTORIES	-2.372	-14.096	-7.159	-9.361	6.921	16.496
60	BUSINESS	12.160	-.244	5.460	-4.415	10.551	13.726
61	GOVERNMENT	-14.805	-13.767	-12.611	-5.019	-3.753	2.616
62	HOUSEHOLDS	.273	-.085	-.008	.073	.123	.154
63	INTANGIBLE	122.955	114.236	112.526	108.447	114.713	120.713
64	RESEARCH AND DEVELOPMENT	4.527	4.981	5.482	5.374	6.033	6.364
65	BUSINESS	1.709	1.917	1.944	1.657	1.998	2.172
66	NONPROFIT INSTITUTIONS	.098	.094	.098	.109	.119	.123
67	GOVERNMENT	2.720	2.970	3.440	3.608	3.917	4.069
68	EDUCATION AND TRAINING	99.354	90.872	87.947	84.091	89.639	95.278
69	HEALTH	19.074	18.383	19.097	18.982	19.041	19.070
70	SUBSIDIES AND GOVERNMENT ENTERPRISE TRANSFERS ALLOCATED TO INVESTMENT	2.099	.907	.926	.819	1.122	1.032

TABLE 7. GROSS NATIONAL PRODUCT ACCOUNT, BILLIONS OF 1972 DOLLARS, 1946-1981

		CREDITS					
		1946	1947	1948	1949	1950	1951
71	NET REVALUATIONS	-182.247	44.769	32.006	11.946	6.732	48.883
72	LAND	-52.746	-5.818	3.730	15.439	15.411	17.144
73	BUSINESS	-40.060	-7.682	1.587	11.029	8.432	12.266
74	NONPROFIT	-.545	.205	.010	.313	.233	.499
75	GOVERNMENT AND GOVT ENTERPRISES	-7.639	-.843	.542	2.235	2.231	2.483
76	HOUSEHOLDS	-4.501	2.502	1.590	1.862	4.515	1.897
77	STRUCTURES AND EQUIPMENT	-69.889	47.271	32.278	3.168	-2.116	34.144
78	BUSINESS	-27.161	20.739	16.308	5.874	-.480	13.453
79	NONPROFIT INSTITUTIONS	.301	1.608	.234	.024	-.002	.824
80	GOVERNMENT	-28.232	12.214	8.263	-.042	-4.095	14.388
81	HOUSEHOLDS (OWNER-OCC. DWELLINGS)	-14.797	12.710	7.473	-2.689	2.460	5.479
82	HOUSEHOLD DURABLES AND SEMIDURABLES	-33.644	-5.241	2.127	4.393	-11.277	2.319
83	DURABLES	-23.460	-4.547	.318	2.102	-5.575	3.407
84	SEMIDURABLES	-10.184	-.694	1.808	2.291	-5.702	-1.089
85	INVENTORIES	-25.969	8.557	-6.128	-11.055	4.714	-4.724
86	BUSINESS (INCLUDING NONPROFIT)	.000	13.406	-3.473	-8.823	6.785	-1.473
87	GOVERNMENT ENTERPRISES	.676	.327	.609	-1.346	.580	.049
88	GOVERNMENT	-25.850	-5.420	-3.426	-.829	-2.358	-3.558
89	HOUSEHOLDS	-.794	.245	.162	-.056	-.293	.258
90	NET EXPORTS	17.864	24.030	13.091	12.407	4.075	7.742
91	NET BEA EXPORTS	13.215	18.873	10.752	10.653	5.867	10.148
92	EXPORTS	27.264	32.215	26.275	25.806	23.601	28.616
93	IMPORTS	14.049	13.342	15.523	15.153	17.734	18.468
94	TERMS OF TRADE EFFECT	4.649	5.157	2.339	1.754	-1.792	-2.406
95	NET EXPORTS IN CURRENT DOLLARS, DEFLATED	17.864	24.030	13.091	12.407	4.075	7.742
96	LESS: NET EXPORTS IN CONSTANT DOLLARS WITHOUT TERMS OF TRADE EFFECT	13.215	18.873	10.752	10.653	5.867	10.148
97	GROSS NATIONAL PRODUCT	763.362	967.834	973.399	936.706	978.485	1061.715
	ADDENDA:						
98	GNP MINUS NET REVALUATIONS (NR)	945.609	923.065	941.393	924.760	971.754	1012.832
99	NNP MINUS NR	714.082	710.953	743.718	737.502	789.150	826.679
100	NNI MINUS NR	748.965	726.737	759.428	734.276	769.736	806.131
101	GDCA MINUS NR	260.149	250.680	268.083	263.045	308.231	332.561
102	NDCA MINUS NR	28.622	38.568	70.408	75.787	125.628	146.408
103	NDCA	-153.625	83.337	102.414	87.733	132.359	195.291
104	NDCA AT ORIGINAL COST	26.524	37.661	69.482	74.968	124.505	145.376
105	NDCA, TANGIBLE, AT ORIGINAL COST	-43.762	-24.513	6.580	14.756	59.031	76.322
106	NDCA, INTANGIBLE, AT ORIGINAL COST	70.285	62.174	62.902	60.212	65.474	69.054
107	GDCA - NR / GNP - NR, PERCENT	27.511	27.157	28.477	28.445	31.719	32.835
108	NDCA - NR / NNP - NR, PERCENT	4.008	5.425	9.467	10.276	15.919	17.710
109	NDCA, TAN, O.C. / NNP - NR, PERCENT	-6.128	-3.448	.885	2.001	7.480	9.232
110	NDCA, INTAN, O.C. / NNP - NR, PERCENT	9.843	8.745	8.458	8.164	8.297	8.353
111	GROSS BUSINESS PRODUCT	193.882	320.501	335.764	341.458	399.061	435.032
112	GROSS NONPROFIT PRODUCT	22.120	23.215	22.621	23.141	23.156	24.711
113	GROSS GOVT ENTERPRISE PRODUCT	10.830	11.764	12.853	11.051	13.367	12.810
114	GROSS GOVERNMENT PRODUCT	178.301	183.357	156.522	128.447	114.161	138.754
115	GROSS HOUSEHOLD PRODUCT	351.763	421.349	440.306	428.110	427.513	449.102
116	GROSS DOMESTIC PRODUCT	756.897	960.185	968.066	932.207	977.256	1060.409
117	GROSS PRODUCT, REST OF WORLD	6.467	7.649	5.333	4.499	1.231	1.307

217

TABLE 7. GROSS NATIONAL PRODUCT ACCOUNT, BILLIONS OF 1972 DOLLARS, 1946-1981

		CREDITS					
		1946	1947	1948	1949	1950	1951
118	BEA GNP	478.256	470.339	489.795	492.160	534.794	579.357
119	BEA NNP	444.304	434.227	451.268	451.483	491.950	534.098
120	BEA NI	402.141	389.713	410.887	406.759	442.174	479.526
121	BEA GPDI	70.894	69.985	82.104	65.392	93.537	93.942
122	BEA NPDI	36.942	33.873	43.577	24.715	50.693	48.683
123	BEA PCE	301.030	305.794	312.229	319.336	337.294	341.575
124	BEA GPDI / BEA GNP, PERCENT	14.823	14.880	16.763	13.287	17.490	16.215
125	BEA NPDI / BEA NNP, PERCENT	8.315	7.801	9.657	5.474	10.305	9.115
126	TISA GNP / BEA GNP, PERCENT	159.614	205.774	198.736	190.325	182.965	183.257
127	TISA NNP / BEA NNP, PERCENT	119.701	174.039	171.899	165.997	161.781	163.933
128	TISA NNI / BEA NI, PERCENT	140.925	197.968	192.616	183.455	175.602	178.304
129	TISA GNP - NR / BEA GNP, PERCENT	197.720	196.255	192.201	187.898	181.706	174.820
130	TISA NNP - NR / BEA NNP, PERCENT	160.719	163.728	164.806	163.351	160.413	154.780
131	TISA GDCA - NR / BEA GPDI, PERCENT	366.955	358.190	326.516	402.259	329.528	354.007
132	TISA NDCA - NR / BEA NPDI, PERCENT	77.479	113.860	161.571	306.644	247.820	300.737
133	TISA NDCA, TAN, OC / BEA NPDI,PERCENT	-118.461	-72.369	15.099	59.704	116.449	156.774
134	TISA CONSUMPTION / BEA PCE, PERCENT	221.771	212.024	211.453	203.331	195.511	196.891
135	GNP	763.362	967.834	973.399	936.706	978.485	1061.715
136	CAPITAL CONSUMPTION ALLOWANCES (CCA)	231.527	212.112	197.675	187.258	182.603	186.153
137	CCA, TANGIBLE	178.857	160.050	148.051	139.023	133.364	134.494
138	CCA, INTANGIBLE	52.670	52.062	49.624	48.235	49.239	51.659
139	NNP	531.835	755.723	775.724	749.448	795.882	875.562
140	BUS TRANS PAY + UNCOMP FACTOR SERVICES + NET INDIR TAXES + STAT DISCREPANCY	-34.883	-15.784	-15.710	3.226	19.415	20.547
141	NNI	566.718	771.507	791.434	746.221	776.468	855.014
142	GNP LESS SUM OF SECTOR & RW	-.001	.000	.000	-.001	-.002	-.001

		1952	1953	1954	1955	1956	1957
1	CONSUMPTION	689.014	706.073	723.657	746.990	765.553	783.801
2	HOUSEHOLD EXPENDITURES FOR SERVICES AND NONDURABLES	220.564	226.449	230.236	240.294	249.290	255.095
3	GROSS EXPENDITURES INCLUDED FROM BEA PERSONAL CONSUMPTION EXPENDITURES	225.591	231.697	235.350	245.874	255.246	261.211
4	LESS: PCE EXPENSES RELATED TO WORK	5.027	5.248	5.113	5.580	5.956	6.116
5	EXPENSE ACCOUNT ITEMS OF CONSUMPTION	4.643	4.987	4.921	5.353	5.611	5.744
6	BEA IMPUTATIONS OTHER THAN HOUSING	9.374	9.408	9.060	9.307	9.150	8.880
7	SUBSIDIES ALLOCATED TO CONSUMPTION	.443	.435	.603	.564	.927	1.392
8	SUBSIDIES INCLUDED IN BUSINESS INCOME	.667	.665	.907	.864	1.409	2.100
9	LESS: AMT. ALLOCATED TO INVESTMENT	.224	.230	.304	.300	.482	.708
10	TRANSFERS	58.829	60.119	61.966	68.886	70.064	74.404
11	FROM BUSINESS	1.973	2.136	2.242	2.471	2.651	2.715
12	MEDIA SUPPORT	1.376	1.512	1.637	1.845	2.000	2.049
13	TOTAL MEDIA SUPPORT	2.014	2.187	2.317	2.591	2.778	2.843
14	LESS: MEDIA SUPPORT ALLOCATED TO INVESTMENT	.638	.675	.680	.747	.778	.794
15	HEALTH AND SAFETY	.598	.624	.605	.626	.652	.666
16	FROM NONPROFIT INSTITUTIONS	15.941	16.336	17.021	17.685	18.223	19.186
17	FROM GOVERNMENT ENTERPRISES	1.469	1.419	1.682	2.147	2.753	2.491
18	FROM GOVERNMENT	39.445	40.227	41.021	46.583	46.437	50.013

TABLE 7. GROSS NATIONAL PRODUCT ACCOUNT, BILLINGS OF 1972 DOLLARS, 1946-1981

					CREDITS		
		1952	1953	1954	1955	1956	1957
19	NONMARKET SERVICES PRODUCED IN HOUSEHOLDS	395.161	404.676	416.872	422.585	430.511	438.286
20	NET SPACE RENT OF OWNER-OCCUPIED NONFARM DWELLINGS	19.050	20.793	22.742	24.513	26.301	28.203
21	OTHER CAPITAL SERVICES	62.615	66.427	71.613	73.738	76.838	79.500
22	DURABLES	27.322	30.202	34.737	36.316	38.636	40.338
23	TOTAL DURABLES	32.653	35.981	41.208	43.324	46.402	48.259
24	LESS: DURABLES ALLOCATED TO INVESTMENT	1.168	1.254	1.338	1.393	1.455	1.521
25	LESS: SERVICES OF DURABLES TO EXP REL TO WORK	4.164	4.526	5.133	5.616	6.312	6.400
26	SEMIDURABLES	35.136	36.039	36.669	37.216	37.993	38.941
27	INVENTORIES	.157	.186	.206	.206	.209	.221
28	LABOR SERVICES	359.028	365.530	370.022	375.677	381.888	388.293
29	LESS: LABOR SERVICES ALLOC. TO INVEST	45.532	48.073	47.505	51.342	54.516	57.710
30	GROSS DOMESTIC CAPITAL ACCUMULATION	341.041	379.460	361.236	426.835	438.954	410.279
31	ORIGINAL COST	348.024	373.206	364.301	395.381	396.589	396.839
32	TANGIBLE	222.677	239.756	226.862	245.634	243.219	235.454
33	STRUCTURES AND EQUIPMENT AND HOUSEHOLD DURABLES AND SEMIDURABLES	207.570	220.953	219.403	235.717	235.952	236.242
34	BUSINESS	51.352	54.829	53.276	59.887	62.188	63.023
35	NONRESIDENTIAL	47.376	50.655	48.988	55.237	57.755	58.492
36	STRUCTURES	16.810	18.326	18.327	21.401	23.056	22.534
37	EQUIPMENT	30.566	32.329	30.661	33.836	34.699	35.958
38	RESIDENTIAL OTHER THAN OWNER-OCCUPIED NONFARM DWELLINGS	3.976	4.174	4.288	4.650	4.433	4.531
39	NONPROFIT INSTITUTIONS	2.526	2.735	3.350	3.414	3.648	3.890
40	STRUCTURES	2.307	2.505	3.073	3.144	3.351	3.583
41	EQUIPMENT	.219	.230	.277	.270	.297	.307
42	GOVERNMENT ENTERPRISES	4.792	5.103	5.734	5.823	5.789	5.588
43	STRUCTURES	4.490	4.836	5.448	5.454	5.495	5.297
44	EQUIPMENT	.302	.267	.286	.369	.294	.291
45	GOVERNMENT	44.933	45.748	44.275	40.908	38.632	37.563
46	STRUCTURES	14.646	15.068	15.993	16.079	15.907	17.216
47	EQUIPMENT	25.754	25.228	21.047	17.438	15.688	12.510
48	PRODUCT ACCUMULATED	4.533	5.452	7.235	7.391	7.037	7.837
49	HOUSEHOLDS	94.305	99.562	101.915	116.783	112.358	109.935
50	OWNER-OCC. NONFARM DWELLINGS	21.748	22.580	24.663	29.084	25.957	23.970
51	DURABLES	38.019	42.111	42.465	51.074	48.788	48.647
52	SEMIDURABLES	34.538	34.871	34.787	36.625	37.613	37.318

219

		CREDITS					
		1952	1953	1954	1955	1956	1957
53	FIXED GPDI RECONCILIATION	3.041	3.701	4.047	3.688	5.028	4.576
54	NIPA FIXED GPDI	78.667	83.845	85.336	96.073	96.821	95.459
55	LESS: CORRESP. SECTOR TOTALS	75.626	80.144	81.289	92.385	91.793	90.883
56	GOVERNMENT CAPITAL ACCUMULATION RECONCILIATION	6.621	9.275	6.806	5.214	8.309	11.667
57	NIPA GOVERNMENT INVESTMENT	51.813	54.674	49.580	44.554	45.693	46.981
58	LESS: GOVERNMENT AND GOVT ENTERPRISE TOTALS	45.192	45.399	42.774	39.340	37.384	35.314
59	CHANGE IN INVENTORIES	15.107	18.803	7.459	9.917	7.267	-.788
60	BUSINESS	4.311	1.489	-2.192	7.724	5.808	1.515
61	GOVERNMENT	10.631	17.149	9.593	1.939	1.259	-2.441
62	HOUSEHOLDS	.165	.165	.058	.254	.200	.138
63	INTANGIBLE	125.347	133.451	137.439	149.747	153.370	161.385
64	RESEARCH AND DEVELOPMENT	8.025	9.067	10.201	11.517	15.015	16.963
65	BUSINESS	2.970	3.740	3.896	4.043	5.219	5.230
66	NONPROFIT INSTITUTIONS	.135	.148	.161	.169	.185	.215
67	GOVERNMENT	4.920	5.179	6.144	7.306	9.611	11.518
68	EDUCATION AND TRAINING	97.439	103.467	105.461	115.619	114.927	119.792
69	HEALTH	19.883	20.916	21.777	22.611	23.428	24.630
70	SUBSIDIES AND GOVERNMENT ENTERPRISE TRANSFERS ALLOCATED TO INVESTMENT	.965	.984	1.155	1.430	1.855	1.917
71	NET REVALUATIONS	-7.948	5.270	-4.220	30.024	40.509	11.523
72	LAND	11.238	12.808	17.954	30.171	31.607	26.557
73	BUSINESS	5.500	1.766	8.757	12.157	16.865	7.385
74	NONPROFIT	.475	.111	1.492	.857	1.347	6.140
75	GOVERNMENT AND GOVT ENTERPRISES	1.628	6.769	3.248	8.098	5.891	7.979
76	HOUSEHOLDS	3.636	4.163	4.458	9.058	7.505	5.053
77	STRUCTURES AND EQUIPMENT	-.484	-3.716	-12.821	15.024	13.835	-12.071
78	BUSINESS	.434	.972	-4.596	7.989	8.620	-2.201
79	NONPROFIT INSTITUTIONS	-.058	-.303	-.332	.612	.582	-.709
80	GOVERNMENT	-.018	-3.060	-7.786	6.843	11.234	-1.331
81	HOUSEHOLDS (OWNER-OCC. DWELLINGS)	-.843	-1.325	-.107	-.420	-6.601	-7.830
82	HOUSEHOLD DURABLES AND SEMIDURABLES	-1.467	-3.932	-10.843	-11.428	-3.758	-4.008
83	DURABLES	-2.579	-3.014	-9.956	-9.951	-1.641	-3.319
84	SEMIDURABLES	1.112	-.918	-.887	-1.477	-2.117	-.689
85	INVENTORIES	-17.234	.109	1.489	-3.743	-1.175	1.045
86	BUSINESS (INCLUDING NONPROFIT)	-12.441	-1.398	-4.442	-4.765	1.188	1.353
87	GOVERNMENT ENTERPRISES	-.586	-.206	-.783	-1.845	.286	1.135
88	GOVERNMENT	-4.205	1.770	6.774	3.052	-2.511	-1.511
89	HOUSEHOLDS	-.002	-.057	-.060	-.186	-.139	.068
90	NET EXPORTS	5.496	2.132	4.249	4.919	8.406	11.209
91	NET BEA EXPORTS	7.935	4.803	6.883	7.307	10.087	11.816
92	EXPORTS	27.900	26.608	27.824	30.663	35.276	37.964
93	IMPORTS	19.965	21.805	20.941	23.356	25.189	26.148
94	TERMS OF TRADE EFFECT	-2.439	-2.671	-2.634	-2.388	-1.681	-.607
95	NET EXPORTS IN CURRENT DOLLARS, DEFLATED	5.496	2.132	4.249	4.919	8.406	11.209
96	LESS: NET EXPORTS IN CONSTANT DOLLARS WITHOUT TERMS OF TRADE EFFECT	7.935	4.803	6.883	7.307	10.087	11.816
97	GROSS NATIONAL PRODUCT	1035.550	1087.665	1089.141	1178.744	1212.912	1205.289

TABLE 7. GROSS NATIONAL PRODUCT ACCOUNT, BILLIONS OF 1972 DOLLARS, 1946-1981

		CREDITS					
		1952	1953	1954	1955	1956	1957
	ADDENDA:						
98	GNP MINUS NET REVALUATIONS (NR)	1043.498	1082.395	1093.362	1148.720	1172.403	1193.766
99	NNP MINUS NR	847.712	877.453	879.490	927.818	945.945	961.211
100	NNI MINUS NR	827.624	853.111	852.042	902.187	920.175	934.145
101	GDCA MINUS NR	348.989	374.190	365.456	396.811	398.444	398.756
102	NDCA MINUS NR	153.203	169.248	151.584	175.909	171.986	166.200
103	NDCA	145.255	174.517	147.363	205.932	212.496	177.723
104	NDCA AT ORIGINAL COST	152.238	168.264	150.429	174.479	170.132	164.283
105	NDCA, TANGIBLE, AT ORIGINAL COST	81.792	93.097	74.044	88.260	82.752	71.329
106	NDCA, INTANGIBLE, AT ORIGINAL COST	70.446	75.167	76.385	86.219	87.379	92.954
107	GDCA - NR / GNP - NR, PERCENT	33.444	34.571	33.425	34.544	33.985	33.403
108	NDCA - NR / NNP - NR, PERCENT	18.073	19.289	17.235	18.959	18.181	17.291
109	NDCA, TAN, O.C. / NNP - NR, PERCENT	9.649	10.610	8.419	9.513	8.748	7.421
110	NDCA, INTAN, O.C. / NNP - NR, PERCENT	8.310	8.566	8.685	9.293	9.237	9.671
111	GROSS BUSINESS PRODUCT	415.327	446.134	439.092	487.144	507.518	492.152
112	GROSS NONPROFIT PRODUCT	24.629	24.953	27.119	28.910	29.912	34.697
113	GROSS GOVT ENTERPRISE PRODUCT	12.056	12.376	11.930	11.832	14.669	14.957
114	GROSS GOVERNMENT PRODUCT	132.156	143.739	144.364	169.286	166.399	160.715
115	GROSS HOUSEHOLD PRODUCT	449.894	459.392	465.310	479.415	490.997	497.921
116	GROSS DOMESTIC PRODUCT	1034.062	1086.594	1087.814	1176.587	1209.493	1200.442
117	GROSS PRODUCT, REST OF WORLD	1.489	1.073	1.331	2.160	3.418	4.846
118	BEA GNP	600.787	623.578	616.056	657.518	671.588	683.764
119	BEA NNP	553.240	573.799	564.004	603.269	615.055	625.185
120	BEA NI	499.127	516.748	506.605	543.260	557.966	565.197
121	BEA GPDI	82.978	85.334	83.144	103.797	102.629	96.974
122	BEA NPDI	35.431	35.555	31.092	49.548	46.096	38.395
123	BEA PCE	350.064	363.377	370.002	394.077	405.369	413.800
124	BEA GPDI / BEA GNP, PERCENT	13.812	13.685	13.496	15.786	15.282	14.182
125	BEA NPDI / BEA NNP, PERCENT	6.404	6.196	5.513	8.213	7.495	6.141
126	TISA GNP / BEA GNP, PERCENT	172.366	174.423	176.793	179.272	180.604	176.273
127	TISA NNP / BEA NNP, PERCENT	151.790	153.838	155.188	158.775	160.385	155.591
128	TISA NNI / BEA NI, PERCENT	164.222	166.112	167.353	171.596	172.176	167.317
129	TISA GNP - NR / BEA GNP, PERCENT	173.689	173.578	177.478	174.706	174.572	174.587
130	TISA NNP - NR / BEA NNP, PERCENT	153.227	152.920	155.937	153.798	153.798	153.748
131	TISA GDCA - NR / BEA GPDI, PERCENT	420.580	438.501	439.546	382.296	388.237	411.199
132	TISA NDCA - NR / BEA NPDI, PERCENT	432.399	476.016	487.533	355.027	373.105	432.870
133	TISA NDCA, TAN, OC / BEA NPDI,PERCENT	230.849	261.840	238.145	178.130	179.522	185.778
134	TISA CONSUMPTION / BEA PCE, PERCENT	196.825	194.309	195.582	189.554	188.853	189.415
135	GNP	1035.550	1087.665	1089.141	1178.744	1212.912	1205.289
136	CAPITAL CONSUMPTION ALLOWANCES (CCA)	195.786	204.943	213.872	220.903	226.458	232.555
137	CCA, TANGIBLE	140.885	146.659	152.818	157.375	160.467	164.124
138	CCA, INTANGIBLE	54.901	58.284	61.054	63.528	65.991	68.431
139	NNP	839.764	882.722	875.269	957.841	986.454	972.734
140	BUS TRANS PAY + UNCOMP FACTOR SERVICES + NET INDIR TAXES + STAT DISCREPANCY	20.089	24.342	27.448	25.631	25.770	27.066
141	NNI	819.675	858.381	847.821	932.211	960.684	945.668
142	GNP LESS SUM OF SECTOR & RW	-.001	-.002	-.003	-.003	.001	.001

221

TABLE 7. GROSS NATIONAL PRODUCT ACCOUNT, BILLIONS OF 1972 DOLLARS, 1946-1981

		CREDITS					
		1958	1959	1960	1961	1962	1963
1	CONSUMPTION	797.493	820.707	839.798	862.395	881.790	903.358
2	HOUSEHOLD EXPENDITURES FOR SERVICES AND NONDURABLES	259.145	269.415	275.724	282.711	291.495	299.375
3	GROSS EXPENDITURES INCLUDED FROM BEA PERSONAL CONSUMPTION EXPENDITURES	265.249	275.947	282.746	289.856	299.127	307.352
4	LESS: PCE EXPENSES RELATED TO WORK	6.104	6.532	7.022	7.145	7.632	7.977
5	EXPENSE ACCOUNT ITEMS OF CONSUMPTION	5.810	5.904	6.072	6.112	6.405	6.287
6	BEA IMPUTATIONS OTHER THAN HOUSING	8.754	9.108	9.265	9.390	9.074	9.554
7	SUBSIDIES ALLOCATED TO CONSUMPTION	1.472	1.097	1.175	2.020	2.178	2.022
8	SUBSIDIES INCLUDED IN BUSINESS INCOME	2.204	1.675	1.785	3.062	3.379	3.172
9	LESS: AMT. ALLOCATED TO INVESTMENT	.733	.578	.611	1.041	1.201	1.151
10	TRANSFERS	73.382	78.062	78.989	84.490	86.099	87.948
11	FROM BUSINESS	2.739	2.933	3.374	3.065	3.232	3.405
12	MEDIA SUPPORT	2.097	2.261	2.687	2.366	2.502	2.658
13	TOTAL MEDIA SUPPORT	2.885	3.101	3.611	3.240	3.395	3.594
14	LESS: MEDIA SUPPORT ALLOCATED TO INVESTMENT	.789	.840	.924	.874	.893	.936
15	HEALTH AND SAFETY	.643	.672	.687	.699	.730	.747
16	FROM NONPROFIT INSTITUTIONS	19.312	20.349	20.670	21.527	22.424	23.369
17	FROM GOVERNMENT ENTERPRISES	2.853	2.242	2.785	3.207	3.105	2.889
18	FROM GOVERNMENT	48.478	52.538	52.159	56.691	57.338	58.286
19	NONMARKET SERVICES PRODUCED IN HOUSEHOLDS	448.930	457.122	468.573	477.672	486.539	498.171
20	NET SPACE RENT OF OWNER-OCCUPIED NONFARM DWELLINGS	30.174	32.362	34.597	36.651	39.209	41.334
21	OTHER CAPITAL SERVICES	82.628	84.718	87.711	90.287	92.349	95.486
22	DURABLES	42.809	44.279	46.359	47.895	48.781	50.556
23	TOTAL DURABLES	50.678	52.363	54.438	55.977	56.986	59.035
24	LESS: DURABLES ALLOCATED TO INVESTMENT	1.570	1.622	1.682	1.726	1.793	1.881
25	LESS: SERVICES OF DURABLES TO EXP REL TO WORK	6.299	6.462	6.397	6.356	6.413	6.598
26	SEMIDURABLES	39.587	40.191	41.082	42.112	43.272	44.615
27	INVENTORIES	.231	.248	.269	.279	.297	.315
28	LABOR SERVICES	393.868	401.831	409.149	415.447	425.251	437.082
29	LESS: LABOR SERVICES ALLOC. TO INVEST	57.739	61.790	62.884	64.713	70.271	75.730
30	GROSS DOMESTIC CAPITAL ACCUMULATION	415.539	431.710	434.166	449.690	486.182	504.110
31	ORIGINAL COST	394.863	430.704	434.647	441.747	483.278	511.359
32	TANGIBLE	229.559	252.141	248.925	247.418	276.774	291.862

TABLE 7. GROSS NATIONAL PRODUCT ACCOUNT, BILLIONS OF 1972 DOLLARS, 1946-1981

		CREDITS					
		1958	1959	1960	1961	1962	1963
33	STRUCTURES AND EQUIPMENT AND HOUSE-HOLD DURABLES AND SEMIDURABLES	230.626	248.022	246.478	249.807	267.679	282.772
34	BUSINESS	54.919	60.502	63.334	63.528	69.072	73.610
35	NONRESIDENTIAL	50.011	54.306	57.337	56.406	60.586	63.510
36	STRUCTURES	20.022	20.729	22.404	22.666	23.361	23.334
37	EQUIPMENT	29.989	33.577	34.933	33.740	37.225	40.176
38	RESIDENTIAL OTHER THAN OWNER-OCCUPIED NONFARM DWELLINGS	4.908	6.196	5.997	7.122	8.486	10.100
39	NONPROFIT INSTITUTIONS	4.389	4.553	4.866	5.327	6.278	6.101
40	STRUCTURES	4.041	4.197	4.479	4.915	5.802	5.631
41	EQUIPMENT	.348	.356	.387	.412	.476	.470
42	GOVERNMENT ENTERPRISES	5.578	5.823	5.909	6.780	7.105	7.175
43	STRUCTURES	5.280	5.529	5.565	6.418	6.778	6.756
44	EQUIPMENT	.298	.294	.344	.362	.327	.419
45	GOVERNMENT	39.686	41.589	42.596	46.396	45.600	48.932
46	STRUCTURES	19.887	20.549	20.654	22.084	22.538	24.352
47	EQUIPMENT	12.047	12.686	13.716	14.969	15.126	15.567
48	PRODUCT ACCUMULATED	7.752	8.354	8.226	9.343	7.936	9.013
49	HOUSEHOLDS	107.337	119.555	117.475	115.091	123.643	132.190
50	OWNER-OCC. NONFARM DWELLINGS	24.392	29.476	26.226	25.150	26.453	29.102
51	DURABLES	45.326	50.650	51.415	49.315	54.683	59.673
52	SEMIDURABLES	37.619	39.429	39.834	40.626	42.507	43.415
53	FIXED GPDI RECONCILIATION	5.615	6.417	6.733	6.925	7.912	8.722
54	NIPA FIXED GPDI	89.315	100.948	101.159	100.930	109.715	117.535
55	LESS: CORRESP. SECTOR TOTALS	83.700	94.531	94.426	94.005	101.803	108.813
56	GOVERNMENT CAPITAL ACCUMULATION RECONCILIATION	13.102	9.583	5.565	5.760	8.069	6.042
57	NIPA GOVERNMENT INVESTMENT	50.614	48.641	45.844	49.593	52.838	53.136
58	LESS: GOVERNMENT AND GOVT ENTERPRISE TOTALS	37.512	39.058	40.279	43.833	44.769	47.094
59	CHANGE IN INVENTORIES	-1.067	4.119	2.447	-2.389	9.095	9.090
60	BUSINESS	-1.838	7.046	3.544	2.973	7.843	7.523
61	GOVERNMENT	.709	-3.173	-1.205	-5.474	1.071	1.429
62	HOUSEHOLDS	.062	.246	.108	.112	.181	.138
63	INTANGIBLE	165.303	178.562	185.722	194.329	206.504	219.498
64	RESEARCH AND DEVELOPMENT	18.118	20.326	21.980	22.981	23.969	26.344
65	BUSINESS	5.497	5.892	6.445	6.733	7.122	7.479
66	NONPROFIT INSTITUTIONS	.243	.262	.278	.322	.375	.410
67	GOVERNMENT	12.379	14.172	15.256	15.926	16.472	18.455
68	EDUCATION AND TRAINING	121.901	131.477	136.144	142.503	152.294	161.540
69	HEALTH	25.283	26.759	27.598	28.845	30.242	31.614
70	SUBSIDIES AND GOVERNMENT ENTERPRISE TRANSFERS ALLOCATED TO INVESTMENT	2.117	1.740	2.055	2.712	2.949	2.852

223

TABLE 7. GROSS NATIONAL PRODUCT ACCOUNT, BILLIONS OF 1972 DOLLARS, 1946-1981

		CREDITS					
		1958	1959	1960	1961	1962	1963
71	NET REVALUATIONS	18.559	-.734	-2.536	5.230	-.044	-10.101
72	LAND	34.528	37.859	19.229	31.500	31.342	23.604
73	BUSINESS	20.696	18.635	13.027	14.509	14.764	8.936
74	NONPROFIT	.152	.245	-3.755	1.421	1.798	.202
75	GOVERNMENT AND GOVT ENTERPRISES	6.385	6.877	7.283	9.375	7.589	9.065
76	HOUSEHOLDS	7.296	12.102	2.674	6.195	7.191	5.401
77	STRUCTURES AND EQUIPMENT	-18.069	-24.794	-15.808	-15.236	-16.306	-22.243
78	BUSINESS	-4.063	-7.817	-7.240	-7.584	-8.388	-7.659
79	NONPROFIT INSTITUTIONS	-.591	-.755	-.602	-.030	-.194	.290
80	GOVERNMENT	-7.076	-8.971	-5.047	-1.883	-1.165	-.728
81	HOUSEHOLDS (OWNER-OCC. DWELLINGS)	-6.339	-7.251	-2.920	-5.740	-6.560	-14.147
82	HOUSEHOLD DURABLES AND SEMIDURABLES	-1.169	-6.305	-4.999	-6.106	-9.307	-6.400
83	DURABLES	-.514	-5.177	-4.843	-5.645	-8.402	-5.683
84	SEMIDURABLES	-.655	-1.128	-.155	-.461	-.906	-.716
85	INVENTORIES	3.269	-7.494	-.958	-4.928	-5.773	-5.062
86	BUSINESS (INCLUDING NONPROFIT)	2.180	-4.340	-.312	-3.421	-3.144	-3.288
87	GOVERNMENT ENTERPRISES	1.404	-1.011	.365	-.265	.071	-.383
88	GOVERNMENT	-.380	-2.033	-1.053	-1.210	-2.641	-1.391
89	HOUSEHOLDS	.065	-.110	.042	-.032	-.058	.000
90	NET EXPORTS	4.926	2.093	7.953	9.553	9.015	10.559
91	NET BEA EXPORTS	5.577	2.673	7.659	8.453	7.519	9.395
92	EXPORTS	33.150	33.779	38.396	39.327	41.823	44.820
93	IMPORTS	27.573	31.106	30.737	30.874	34.304	35.425
94	TERMS OF TRADE EFFECT	-.651	-.580	.294	1.100	1.496	1.164
95	NET EXPORTS IN CURRENT DOLLARS, DEFLATED	4.926	2.093	7.953	9.553	9.015	10.559
96	LESS: NET EXPORTS IN CONSTANT DOLLARS WITHOUT TERMS OF TRADE EFFECT	5.577	2.673	7.659	8.453	7.519	9.395
97	GROSS NATIONAL PRODUCT	1217.958	1254.510	1281.916	1321.638	1376.987	1418.027
	ADDENDA:						
98	GNP MINUS NET REVALUATIONS (NR)	1199.398	1255.243	1284.453	1316.408	1377.032	1428.128
99	NNP MINUS NR	960.977	1010.253	1031.936	1055.229	1107.353	1147.930
100	NNI MINUS NR	931.268	980.059	998.804	1017.102	1062.791	1101.230
101	GDCA MINUS NR	396.980	432.443	436.702	444.460	486.227	514.211
102	NDCA MINUS NR	158.559	187.453	184.185	183.281	216.548	234.013
103	NDCA	177.118	186.720	181.649	188.511	216.504	223.912
104	NDCA AT ORIGINAL COST	156.442	185.714	182.130	180.569	213.600	231.162
105	NDCA, TANGIBLE, AT ORIGINAL COST	62.042	80.869	73.507	66.877	91.529	100.202
106	NDCA, INTANGIBLE, AT ORIGINAL COST	94.399	104.844	108.623	113.691	122.070	130.960
107	GDCA - NR / GNP - NR, PERCENT	33.098	34.451	33.999	33.763	35.310	36.006
108	NDCA - NR / NNP - NR, PERCENT	16.500	18.555	17.849	17.369	19.555	20.386
109	NDCA, TAN, O.C. / NNP - NR, PERCENT	6.456	8.005	7.123	6.338	8.266	8.729
110	NDCA, INTAN, O.C. / NNP - NR, PERCENT	9.823	10.378	10.526	10.774	11.024	11.408
111	GROSS BUSINESS PRODUCT	500.667	522.569	530.450	540.531	576.441	597.504
112	GROSS NONPROFIT PRODUCT	29.756	30.780	28.816	35.417	37.629	37.902
113	GROSS GOVT ENTERPRISE PRODUCT	15.791	13.227	15.828	16.172	16.771	16.569
114	GROSS GOVERNMENT PRODUCT	153.169	158.794	168.267	180.187	184.708	194.368
115	GROSS HOUSEHOLD PRODUCT	514.593	524.845	533.036	542.574	553.470	563.600
116	GROSS DOMESTIC PRODUCT	1213.975	1250.215	1276.396	1314.881	1369.018	1409.944
117	GROSS PRODUCT, REST OF WORLD	3.984	4.294	5.520	6.756	7.966	8.083

224

TABLE 7. GROSS NATIONAL PRODUCT ACCOUNT, BILLIONS OF 1972 DOLLARS, 1946-1981

		CREDITS					
		1958	1959	1960	1961	1962	1963
118	BEA GNP	680.878	721.720	737.246	756.640	800.281	832.529
119	BEA NNP	620.606	660.097	673.948	691.601	733.427	763.504
120	BEA NI	558.265	596.168	609.661	622.467	657.372	684.853
121	BEA GPDI	87.477	107.994	104.703	103.903	117.558	125.058
122	BEA NPDI	27.205	46.371	41.405	38.864	50.704	56.033
123	BEA PCE	418.009	440.449	452.041	461.407	482.011	500.502
124	BEA GPDI / BEA GNP, PERCENT	12.848	14.963	14.202	13.732	14.690	15.021
125	BEA NPDI / BEA NNP, PERCENT	4.384	7.025	6.144	5.619	6.913	7.339
126	TISA GNP / BEA GNP, PERCENT	178.880	173.822	173.879	174.672	172.063	170.328
127	TISA NNP / BEA NNP, PERCENT	157.836	152.935	152.742	153.334	150.977	149.027
128	TISA NNI / BEA NI, PERCENT	170.139	164.270	163.413	164.239	161.666	159.323
129	TISA GNP - NR / BEA GNP, PERCENT	176.155	173.924	174.223	173.981	172.069	171.541
130	TISA NNP - NR / BEA NNP, PERCENT	154.845	153.046	153.118	152.578	150.983	150.350
131	TISA GDCA - NR / BEA GPDI, PERCENT	453.810	400.433	417.087	427.764	413.606	411.178
132	TISA NDCA - NR / BEA NPDI, PERCENT	582.829	404.247	444.839	471.596	427.083	417.635
133	TISA NDCA, TAN, OC / BEA NPDI,PERCENT	228.055	174.396	177.533	172.080	180.517	178.826
134	TISA CONSUMPTION / BEA PCE, PERCENT	190.784	186.334	185.779	186.905	182.940	180.490
135	GNP	1217.958	1254.510	1281.916	1321.638	1376.987	1418.027
136	CAPITAL CONSUMPTION ALLOWANCES (CCA)	238.421	244.990	252.517	261.178	269.679	280.198
137	CCA, TANGIBLE	167.517	171.272	175.418	180.540	185.245	191.660
138	CCA, INTANGIBLE	70.904	73.718	77.099	80.638	84.434	88.538
139	NNP	979.537	1009.520	1029.399	1060.460	1107.309	1137.829
140	BUS TRANS PAY + UNCOMP FACTOR SERVICES + NET INDIR TAXES + STAT DISCREPANCY	29.709	30.194	33.132	38.128	44.562	46.700
141	NNI	949.827	979.326	996.267	1022.332	1062.747	1091.129
142	GNP LESS SUM OF SECTOR & RW	-.001	.000	.000	.001	.003	.000

		1964	1965	1966	1967	1968	1969
1	CONSUMPTION	934.987	967.451	993.620	1016.222	1044.075	1065.163
2	HOUSEHOLD EXPENDITURES FOR SERVICES AND NONDURABLES	312.455	328.582	340.291	351.520	365.068	376.632
3	GROSS EXPENDITURES INCLUDED FROM BEA PERSONAL CONSUMPTION EXPENDITURES	320.962	337.825	350.298	362.024	376.262	388.655
4	LESS: PCE EXPENSES RELATED TO WORK	8.507	9.243	10.008	10.504	11.194	12.022
5	EXPENSE ACCOUNT ITEMS OF CONSUMPTION	6.911	7.308	7.795	8.071	8.433	8.886
6	BEA IMPUTATIONS OTHER THAN HOUSING	9.818	9.822	10.632	11.956	12.548	13.088
7	SUBSIDIES ALLOCATED TO CONSUMPTION	2.388	2.565	3.294	3.042	3.114	3.151
8	SUBSIDIES INCLUDED IN BUSINESS INCOME	3.782	4.128	5.412	5.027	5.188	5.288
9	LESS: AMT. ALLOCATED TO INVESTMENT	1.394	1.563	2.118	1.985	2.074	2.137
10	TRANSFERS	93.120	97.766	102.760	103.190	108.075	107.168
11	FROM BUSINESS	3.660	4.398	4.709	4.719	4.969	5.175
12	MEDIA SUPPORT	2.878	3.578	3.845	3.850	4.055	4.232
13	TOTAL MEDIA SUPPORT	3.878	4.718	5.040	5.041	5.280	5.496
14	LESS: MEDIA SUPPORT ALLOCATED TO INVESTMENT	1.000	1.140	1.196	1.192	1.225	1.264
15	HEALTH AND SAFETY	.783	.821	.864	.870	.914	.944
16	FROM NONPROFIT INSTITUTIONS	24.577	25.659	26.575	26.198	28.131	28.779
17	FROM GOVERNMENT ENTERPRISES	3.018	2.942	2.735	2.309	2.004	2.358
18	FROM GOVERNMENT	61.865	64.767	68.742	69.964	72.971	70.856

225

TABLE 7. GROSS NATIONAL PRODUCT ACCOUNT, BILLIONS OF 1972 DOLLARS, 1946-1981

		CREDITS					
		1964	1965	1966	1967	1968	1969
19	NONMARKET SERVICES PRODUCED IN HOUSEHOLDS	510.295	521.408	528.848	538.444	546.838	556.239
20	NET SPACE RENT OF OWNER-OCCUPIED NONFARM DWELLINGS	43.553	46.231	48.901	51.519	53.573	56.574
21	OTHER CAPITAL SERVICES	98.812	103.425	109.050	115.531	119.755	126.411
22	DURABLES	52.198	54.624	57.682	61.854	64.569	69.706
23	TOTAL DURABLES	60.943	63.538	66.869	71.570	74.615	80.465
24	LESS: DURABLES ALLOCATED TO INVESTMENT	1.977	2.107	2.273	2.452	2.599	2.793
25	LESS: SERVICES OF DURABLES TO EXP REL TO WORK	6.768	6.807	6.914	7.264	7.447	7.967
26	SEMIDURABLES	46.294	48.468	51.027	53.323	54.855	56.373
27	INVENTORIES	.320	.333	.342	.354	.330	.332
28	LABOR SERVICES	449.495	459.127	465.689	482.814	491.300	496.509
29	LESS: LABOR SERVICES ALLOC. TO INVEST	81.565	87.376	94.792	111.419	117.790	123.256
30	GROSS DOMESTIC CAPITAL ACCUMULATION	572.903	599.059	654.504	664.245	710.375	711.690
31	ORIGINAL COST	542.911	585.980	634.872	659.749	692.242	718.581
32	TANGIBLE	305.431	333.630	360.053	363.512	381.391	394.766
33	STRUCTURES AND EQUIPMENT AND HOUSE-HOLD DURABLES AND SEMIDURABLES	300.032	325.517	347.223	349.470	370.572	377.578
34	BUSINESS	80.878	92.801	100.991	98.171	103.879	112.348
35	NONRESIDENTIAL	70.924	83.433	92.922	90.703	94.900	101.890
36	STRUCTURES	25.084	30.221	31.905	31.357	32.198	34.258
37	EQUIPMENT	45.840	53.212	61.017	59.346	62.702	67.632
38	RESIDENTIAL OTHER THAN OWNER-OCCUPIED NONFARM DWELLINGS	9.954	9.368	8.069	7.468	8.979	10.458
39	NONPROFIT INSTITUTIONS	6.611	7.245	7.211	6.568	6.450	6.540
40	STRUCTURES	6.100	6.664	6.600	5.988	6.002	6.016
41	EQUIPMENT	.511	.581	.611	.580	.448	.524
42	GOVERNMENT ENTERPRISES	7.838	7.893	8.084	8.694	9.911	9.470
43	STRUCTURES	7.495	7.547	7.642	8.239	9.368	8.898
44	EQUIPMENT	.343	.346	.442	.455	.543	.572
45	GOVERNMENT	48.665	49.824	53.453	52.417	51.393	48.832
46	STRUCTURES	24.337	25.740	27.674	27.865	28.293	26.098
47	EQUIPMENT	15.183	14.780	16.184	15.227	15.377	15.029
48	PRODUCT ACCUMULATED	9.145	9.304	9.595	9.325	7.723	7.705
49	HOUSEHOLDS	141.815	151.814	157.810	158.883	174.193	177.653
50	OWNER-OCC. NONFARM DWELLINGS	30.287	30.615	27.823	27.741	31.893	30.907
51	DURABLES	64.812	72.597	78.394	79.476	88.335	91.835
52	SEMIDURABLES	46.716	48.602	51.593	51.666	53.965	54.911

TABLE 7. GROSS NATIONAL PRODUCT ACCOUNT, BILLIONS OF 1972 DOLLARS, 1946-1981

		CREDITS					
		1964	1965	1966	1967	1968	1969
53	FIXED GPDI RECONCILIATION	8.084	9.485	10.185	10.197	10.362	10.585
54	NIPA FIXED GPDI	125.860	140.146	146.210	142.677	152.584	160.380
55	LESS: CORRESP. SECTOR TOTALS	117.776	130.661	136.025	132.480	142.222	149.795
56	GOVERNMENT CAPITAL ACCUMULATION RECONCILIATION	6.141	6.455	9.489	14.540	14.384	12.150
57	NIPA GOVERNMENT INVESTMENT	53.499	54.868	61.431	66.326	67.965	62.747
58	LESS: GOVERNMENT AND GOVT ENTERPRISE TOTALS	47.358	48.413	51.942	51.786	53.581	50.597
59	CHANGE IN INVENTORIES	5.399	8.113	12.830	14.042	10.819	17.188
60	BUSINESS	7.090	11.787	16.805	12.199	9.005	11.056
61	GOVERNMENT	-1.960	-4.012	-4.298	1.693	1.479	5.905
62	HOUSEHOLDS	.269	.338	.323	.150	.335	.227
63	INTANGIBLE	237.480	252.350	274.818	296.237	310.851	323.815
64	RESEARCH AND DEVELOPMENT	28.258	29.075	30.420	30.846	31.098	30.992
65	BUSINESS	7.959	8.667	9.401	10.144	10.745	11.357
66	NONPROFIT INSTITUTIONS	.428	.470	.513	.535	.543	.551
67	GOVERNMENT	19.871	19.938	20.506	20.167	19.810	19.085
68	EDUCATION AND TRAINING	175.545	188.392	208.250	228.792	241.719	252.589
69	HEALTH	33.677	34.884	36.149	36.599	38.034	40.233
70	SUBSIDIES AND GOVERNMENT ENTERPRISE TRANSFERS ALLOCATED TO INVESTMENT	3.229	3.433	3.947	3.542	3.448	3.762
71	NET REVALUATIONS	26.763	9.646	15.685	.955	14.685	-10.652
72	LAND	33.169	34.335	21.514	17.294	4.071	-11.966
73	BUSINESS	14.121	18.005	7.078	5.839	-11.233	-11.468
74	NONPROFIT	.934	1.359	.756	.733	-1.206	.468
75	GOVERNMENT AND GOVT ENTERPRISES	8.927	6.077	7.663	5.188	2.352	-2.472
76	HOUSEHOLDS	9.187	8.895	6.017	5.534	14.158	1.507
77	STRUCTURES AND EQUIPMENT	4.736	-8.771	9.976	-1.912	28.064	19.436
78	BUSINESS	-.300	-4.269	3.792	-.388	4.974	7.001
79	NONPROFIT INSTITUTIONS	.125	.409	.653	.542	.441	3.162
80	GOVERNMENT	.775	2.072	.128	3.145	5.518	9.353
81	HOUSEHOLDS (OWNER-OCC. DWELLINGS)	4.137	-6.982	5.402	-5.211	17.131	-.079
82	HOUSEHOLD DURABLES AND SEMIDURABLES	-8.982	-18.993	-9.594	-6.923	-11.285	-15.146
83	DURABLES	-8.166	-17.555	-7.591	-5.803	-9.794	-13.394
84	SEMIDURABLES	-.816	-1.438	-2.003	-1.119	-1.490	-1.752
85	INVENTORIES	-2.160	3.076	-6.211	-7.505	-6.165	-2.977
86	BUSINESS (INCLUDING NONPROFIT)	-3.307	.578	-4.613	-6.162	-4.268	-1.644
87	GOVERNMENT ENTERPRISES	-.427	.786	-.408	-.168	-.099	.129
88	GOVERNMENT	1.599	1.742	-1.211	-1.043	-1.709	-1.376
89	HOUSEHOLDS	-.026	-.031	.021	-.132	-.090	-.086
90	NET EXPORTS	13.820	11.799	8.481	7.980	5.157	4.805
91	NET BEA EXPORTS	12.848	10.136	6.465	5.372	1.915	.915
92	EXPORTS	50.323	51.739	54.396	56.691	61.238	65.000
93	IMPORTS	37.475	41.603	47.931	51.319	59.323	64.085
94	TERMS OF TRADE EFFECT	.972	1.663	2.016	2.608	3.242	3.890
95	NET EXPORTS IN CURRENT DOLLARS, DEFLATED	13.820	11.799	8.481	7.980	5.157	4.805
96	LESS: NET EXPORTS IN CONSTANT DOLLARS WITHOUT TERMS OF TRADE EFFECT	12.848	10.136	6.465	5.372	1.915	.915
97	GROSS NATIONAL PRODUCT	1521.710	1578.309	1656.605	1688.448	1759.608	1781.658

TABLE 7. GROSS NATIONAL PRODUCT ACCOUNT, BILLIONS OF 1972 DOLLARS, 1946-1981

		CREDITS					
		1964	1965	1966	1967	1968	1969
	ADDENDA:						
98	GNP MINUS NET REVALUATIONS (NR)	1494.947	1568.662	1640.920	1687.493	1744.923	1792.310
99	NNP MINUS NR	1203.446	1264.938	1323.586	1352.930	1393.336	1423.904
100	NNI MINUS NR	1155.386	1217.937	1273.886	1304.015	1344.585	1366.110
101	GDCA MINUS NR	546.141	589.413	638.819	663.291	695.691	722.342
102	NDCA MINUS NR	254.640	285.689	321.486	328.727	344.104	353.937
103	NDCA	281.402	295.335	337.170	329.682	358.788	343.285
104	NDCA AT ORIGINAL COST	251.410	282.256	317.539	325.185	340.655	350.175
105	NDCA, TANGIBLE, AT ORIGINAL COST	106.987	127.995	146.587	139.165	146.464	149.447
106	NDCA, INTANGIBLE, AT ORIGINAL COST	144.424	154.261	170.951	186.021	194.191	200.729
107	GDCA - NR / GNP - NR, PERCENT	36.532	37.574	38.931	39.306	39.869	40.302
108	NDCA - NR / NNP - NR, PERCENT	21.159	22.585	24.289	24.297	24.696	24.857
109	NDCA, TAN, O.C. / NNP - NR, PERCENT	8.890	10.119	11.075	10.286	10.512	10.496
110	NDCA, INTAN, O.C. / NNP - NR, PERCENT	12.001	12.195	12.916	13.749	13.937	14.097
111	GROSS BUSINESS PRODUCT	647.085	695.566	732.122	734.111	761.750	794.927
112	GROSS NONPROFIT PRODUCT	40.078	43.139	45.311	46.589	45.605	51.349
113	GROSS GOVT ENTERPRISE PRODUCT	17.517	19.443	19.089	18.803	18.383	19.712
114	GROSS GOVERNMENT PRODUCT	208.094	215.682	222.850	233.889	237.491	238.675
115	GROSS HOUSEHOLD PRODUCT	600.458	594.929	627.868	644.947	684.980	665.178
116	GROSS DOMESTIC PRODUCT	1513.232	1568.758	1647.239	1678.339	1748.208	1769.841
117	GROSS PRODUCT, REST OF WORLD	8.477	9.552	9.368	10.109	11.402	11.820
118	BEA GNP	876.404	929.311	984.834	1011.423	1058.116	1087.644
119	BEA NNP	804.831	854.528	906.155	928.661	971.059	996.027
120	BEA NI	724.196	770.880	816.024	836.411	877.414	899.523
121	BEA GPDI	132.950	151.933	163.015	154.876	161.589	171.436
122	BEA NPDI	61.377	77.150	84.336	72.114	74.532	79.819
123	BEA PCE	527.977	557.481	585.683	602.655	634.421	657.897
124	BEA GPDI / BEA GNP, PERCENT	15.170	16.349	16.553	15.313	15.271	15.762
125	BEA NPDI / BEA NNP, PERCENT	7.626	9.028	9.307	7.765	7.675	8.014
126	TISA GNP / BEA GNP, PERCENT	173.631	169.836	168.212	166.938	166.296	163.809
127	TISA NNP / BEA NNP, PERCENT	152.853	149.157	147.797	145.789	144.999	141.889
128	TISA NNI / BEA NI, PERCENT	163.236	159.244	158.031	156.020	154.918	150.686
129	TISA GNP - NR / BEA GNP, PERCENT	170.577	168.798	166.619	166.843	164.909	164.788
130	TISA NNP - NR / BEA NNP, PERCENT	149.528	148.028	146.066	145.686	143.486	142.958
131	TISA GDCA - NR / BEA GPDI, PERCENT	410.786	387.943	391.877	428.272	430.531	421.348
132	TISA NDCA - NR / BEA NPDI, PERCENT	414.878	370.303	381.196	455.844	461.686	443.424
133	TISA NDCA, TAN, OC / BEA NPDI, PERCENT	174.310	165.904	173.813	192.979	196.512	187.232
134	TISA CONSUMPTION / BEA PCE, PERCENT	177.089	173.540	169.652	168.624	164.571	161.904
135	GNP	1521.710	1578.309	1656.605	1688.448	1759.608	1781.658
136	CAPITAL CONSUMPTION ALLOWANCES (CCA)	291.501	303.724	317.333	334.563	351.587	368.406
137	CCA, TANGIBLE	198.445	205.635	213.466	224.347	234.927	245.320
138	CCA, INTANGIBLE	93.056	98.089	103.867	110.216	116.660	123.086
139	NNP	1230.209	1274.585	1339.271	1353.885	1408.021	1413.252
140	BUS TRANS PAY + UNCOMP FACTOR SERVICES + NET INDIR TAXES + STAT DISCREPANCY	48.061	47.001	49.701	48.915	48.752	57.794
141	NNI	1182.148	1227.584	1289.571	1304.970	1359.269	1355.458
142	GNP LESS SUM OF SECTOR & RW	.001	-.002	-.002	-.001	-.002	-.003

TABLE 7. GROSS NATIONAL PRODUCT ACCOUNT, BILLIONS OF 1972 DOLLARS, 1946-1981

		CREDITS					
		1970	1971	1972	1973	1974	1975
1	CONSUMPTION	1091.135	1110.195	1143.726	1167.006	1176.521	1207.813
2	HOUSEHOLD EXPENDITURES FOR SERVICES AND NONDURABLES	388.152	394.748	410.026	418.568	416.608	423.971
3	GROSS EXPENDITURES INCLUDED FROM BEA PERSONAL CONSUMPTION EXPENDITURES	400.713	407.782	423.914	433.268	431.655	438.900
4	LESS: PCE EXPENSES RELATED TO WORK	12.561	13.033	13.888	14.700	15.047	14.930
5	EXPENSE ACCOUNT ITEMS OF CONSUMPTION	8.979	9.149	9.782	10.420	10.449	10.212
6	BEA IMPUTATIONS OTHER THAN HOUSING	14.043	14.282	14.559	15.612	17.402	19.668
7	SUBSIDIES ALLOCATED TO CONSUMPTION	3.192	2.884	3.773	2.947	1.846	2.458
8	SUBSIDIES INCLUDED IN BUSINESS INCOME	5.247	4.812	6.406	5.096	3.129	4.042
9	LESS: AMT. ALLOCATED TO INVESTMENT	2.055	1.928	2.633	2.149	1.283	1.584
10	TRANSFERS	110.136	111.145	114.066	115.554	112.588	118.996
11	FROM BUSINESS	5.024	4.927	5.346	5.480	5.401	5.269
12	MEDIA SUPPORT	4.093	3.989	4.333	4.406	4.336	4.270
13	TOTAL MEDIA SUPPORT	5.314	5.203	5.607	5.676	5.569	5.465
14	LESS: MEDIA SUPPORT ALLOCATED TO INVESTMENT	1.222	1.214	1.274	1.270	1.234	1.195
15	HEALTH AND SAFETY	.931	.938	1.013	1.075	1.065	.999
16	FROM NONPROFIT INSTITUTIONS	30.119	31.758	33.042	33.506	33.227	34.367
17	FROM GOVERNMENT ENTERPRISES	3.046	2.972	2.622	3.093	2.882	3.424
18	FROM GOVERNMENT	71.947	71.489	73.057	73.476	71.078	75.936
19	NONMARKET SERVICES PRODUCED IN HOUSEHOLDS	566.634	577.987	591.520	603.906	617.628	632.508
20	NET SPACE RENT OF OWNER-OCCUPIED NONFARM DWELLINGS	58.353	60.970	64.825	68.433	71.850	74.806
21	OTHER CAPITAL SERVICES	131.959	136.803	141.227	150.073	157.964	164.311
22	DURABLES	74.326	78.259	82.142	87.558	92.537	96.717
23	TOTAL DURABLES	85.532	89.846	94.100	100.148	104.926	109.421
24	LESS: DURABLES ALLOCATED TO INVESTMENT	3.014	3.244	3.446	3.658	3.892	4.149
25	LESS: SERVICES OF DURABLES TO EXP REL TO WORK	8.192	8.343	8.513	8.932	8.497	8.556
26	SEMIDURABLES	57.299	58.202	58.751	62.200	65.132	67.289
27	INVENTORIES	.334	.343	.334	.314	.296	.305
28	LABOR SERVICES	507.782	520.889	537.081	545.784	545.774	553.604
29	LESS: LABOR SERVICES ALLOC. TO INVEST	131.460	140.676	151.613	160.384	157.959	160.212
30	GROSS DOMESTIC CAPITAL ACCUMULATION	704.514	729.590	902.324	1030.276	951.969	736.244
31	ORIGINAL COST	698.557	738.200	793.839	846.805	814.680	774.668
32	TANGIBLE	364.113	388.777	421.833	458.189	432.476	392.071

229

		CREDITS					
		1970	1971	1972	1973	1974	1975
33	STRUCTURES AND EQUIPMENT AND HOUSE-HOLD DURABLES AND SEMIDURABLES	364.194	381.999	416.888	445.740	419.781	400.264
34	BUSINESS	107.839	106.037	118.091	136.023	131.310	114.917
35	NONRESIDENTIAL	98.791	95.667	105.132	123.225	123.085	107.481
36	STRUCTURES	33.334	31.942	33.267	37.479	36.242	31.732
37	EQUIPMENT	65.457	63.725	71.865	85.746	86.843	75.749
38	RESIDENTIAL OTHER THAN OWNER-OCCUPIED NONFARM DWELLINGS	9.048	10.370	12.959	12.798	8.225	7.436
39	NONPROFIT INSTITUTIONS	6.048	5.932	6.165	5.768	4.811	4.293
40	STRUCTURES	5.526	5.429	5.557	5.072	4.117	3.722
41	EQUIPMENT	.522	.503	.608	.696	.694	.571
42	GOVERNMENT ENTERPRISES	9.320	8.985	9.385	9.587	10.190	9.513
43	STRUCTURES	8.724	8.302	8.500	8.673	9.343	8.630
44	EQUIPMENT	.596	.683	.885	.914	.847	.883
45	GOVERNMENT	47.079	46.933	48.715	47.522	46.890	46.989
46	STRUCTURES	23.911	24.196	23.288	23.271	22.406	20.413
47	EQUIPMENT	15.087	14.817	16.668	16.059	15.806	17.528
48	PRODUCT ACCUMULATED	8.081	7.920	8.759	8.192	8.678	9.048
49	HOUSEHOLDS	172.912	194.933	218.507	231.421	212.711	209.732
50	OWNER-OCC. NONFARM DWELLINGS	29.608	40.057	46.873	45.274	36.435	31.138
51	DURABLES	89.072	98.196	111.108	121.323	112.348	112.669
52	SEMIDURABLES	54.232	56.680	60.526	64.824	63.928	65.925
53	FIXED GPDI RECONCILIATION	11.282	13.798	13.676	13.288	11.299	11.163
54	NIPA FIXED GPDI	154.777	165.824	184.805	200.353	183.855	161.511
55	LESS: CORRESP. SECTOR TOTALS	143.495	152.026	171.129	187.065	172.556	150.348
56	GOVERNMENT CAPITAL ACCUMULATION RECONCILIATION	9.714	5.381	2.349	2.131	2.570	3.657
57	NIPA GOVERNMENT INVESTMENT	58.032	53.379	51.690	51.048	50.972	51.111
58	LESS: GOVERNMENT AND GOVT ENTERPRISE TOTALS	48.318	47.998	49.341	48.917	48.402	47.454
59	CHANGE IN INVENTORIES	-.081	6.778	4.945	12.449	12.695	-8.193
60	BUSINESS	3.764	8.062	10.225	17.178	11.601	-6.727
61	GOVERNMENT	-4.118	-1.384	-5.592	-4.825	1.248	-1.581
62	HOUSEHOLDS	.273	.100	.312	.096	-.154	.115
63	INTANGIBLE	334.445	349.423	372.006	388.617	382.204	382.597
64	RESEARCH AND DEVELOPMENT	29.262	28.221	28.388	28.815	28.407	27.696
65	BUSINESS	11.250	11.097	11.535	12.391	12.745	12.387
66	NONPROFIT INSTITUTIONS	.573	.599	.608	.603	.597	.608
67	GOVERNMENT	17.439	16.525	16.245	15.820	15.065	14.701
68	EDUCATION AND TRAINING	263.018	276.191	295.680	309.361	302.093	302.286
69	HEALTH	42.166	45.012	47.938	50.441	51.704	52.614
70	SUBSIDIES AND GOVERNMENT ENTERPRISE TRANSFERS ALLOCATED TO INVESTMENT	4.047	3.931	4.463	4.409	3.281	3.681

TABLE 7. GROSS NATIONAL PRODUCT ACCOUNT, BILLIONS OF 1972 DOLLARS, 1946-1981

		CREDITS					
		1970	1971	1972	1973	1974	1975
71	NET REVALUATIONS	1.910	-12.541	104.022	179.062	134.007	-42.105
72	LAND	-6.144	-10.359	71.217	92.653	28.149	38.199
73	BUSINESS	-7.371	-5.989	36.210	53.032	11.252	30.710
74	NONPROFIT	.023	-1.531	.934	.251	1.175	-2.345
75	GOVERNMENT AND GOVT ENTERPRISES	-1.269	-2.140	14.714	19.143	5.816	7.892
76	HOUSEHOLDS	2.473	-.699	19.359	20.227	9.907	1.942
77	STRUCTURES AND EQUIPMENT	24.916	22.908	41.721	82.206	94.578	-17.978
78	BUSINESS	8.889	3.438	7.032	17.372	70.739	-3.475
79	NONPROFIT INSTITUTIONS	1.558	.383	1.517	2.983	6.944	-5.774
80	GOVERNMENT	18.506	11.045	12.907	32.074	19.593	-5.287
81	HOUSEHOLDS (OWNER-OCC. DWELLINGS)	-4.036	8.042	20.265	29.777	-2.698	-3.442
82	HOUSEHOLD DURABLES AND SEMIDURABLES	-8.628	-21.434	-15.613	-26.779	-9.002	-7.528
83	DURABLES	-7.285	-19.648	-13.595	-21.864	-2.475	-5.317
84	SEMIDURABLES	-1.342	-1.786	-2.018	-4.915	-6.527	-2.212
85	INVENTORIES	-8.235	-3.657	6.697	30.982	20.282	-54.797
86	BUSINESS (INCLUDING NONPROFIT)	-6.557	-2.629	5.906	24.850	16.708	-54.024
87	GOVERNMENT ENTERPRISES	-.547	.223	.596	.837	-.135	-.052
88	GOVERNMENT	-1.125	-1.115	.238	5.083	3.267	-.843
89	HOUSEHOLDS	-.007	-.136	-.043	.211	.442	.123
90	NET EXPORTS	7.280	4.273	.739	13.437	11.634	21.292
91	NET BEA EXPORTS	3.906	1.614	.738	15.513	27.781	32.167
92	EXPORTS	70.476	70.959	77.464	97.271	108.471	103.531
93	IMPORTS	66.570	69.345	76.726	81.758	80.690	71.364
94	TERMS OF TRADE EFFECT	3.374	2.659	.001	-2.076	-16.147	-10.875
95	NET EXPORTS IN CURRENT DOLLARS, DEFLATED	7.280	4.273	.739	13.437	11.634	21.292
96	LESS: NET EXPORTS IN CONSTANT DOLLARS WITHOUT TERMS OF TRADE EFFECT	3.906	1.614	.738	15.513	27.781	32.167
97	GROSS NATIONAL PRODUCT	1802.929	1844.058	2046.789	2210.720	2140.123	1965.348
	ADDENDA:						
98	GNP MINUS NET REVALUATIONS (NR)	1801.019	1856.600	1942.767	2031.658	2006.116	2007.453
99	NNP MINUS NR	1416.472	1457.672	1527.851	1600.273	1561.028	1552.611
100	NNI MINUS NR	1356.171	1388.821	1457.284	1526.031	1484.491	1481.692
101	GDCA MINUS NR	702.604	742.131	798.302	851.215	817.961	778.349
102	NDCA MINUS NR	318.057	343.204	383.386	419.829	372.874	323.506
103	NDCA	319.966	330.663	487.408	598.891	506.881	281.401
104	NDCA AT ORIGINAL COST	314.010	339.273	378.923	415.420	369.592	319.826
105	NDCA, TANGIBLE, AT ORIGINAL COST	108.915	125.295	148.607	175.422	143.171	99.363
106	NDCA, INTANGIBLE, AT ORIGINAL COST	205.095	213.978	230.316	239.998	226.421	220.463
107	GDCA - NR / GNP - NR, PERCENT	39.011	39.973	41.091	41.898	40.773	38.773
108	NDCA - NR / NNP - NR, PERCENT	22.454	23.545	25.093	26.235	23.886	20.836
109	NDCA, TAN, O.C. / NNP - NR, PERCENT	7.689	8.596	9.727	10.962	9.172	6.400
110	NDCA, INTAN, O.C. / NNP - NR, PERCENT	14.479	14.679	15.075	14.997	14.505	14.199
111	GROSS BUSINESS PRODUCT	787.686	819.924	937.507	1045.135	1032.801	879.479
112	GROSS NONPROFIT PRODUCT	49.160	48.466	53.808	55.851	60.110	46.044
113	GROSS GOVT ENTERPRISE PRODUCT	20.011	21.198	21.922	23.872	23.520	24.429
114	GROSS GOVERNMENT PRODUCT	248.904	240.756	259.493	289.649	253.318	233.547
115	GROSS HOUSEHOLD PRODUCT	685.798	701.513	763.166	783.182	769.272	778.900
116	GROSS DOMESTIC PRODUCT	1791.559	1831.856	2035.896	2197.690	2139.019	1962.398
117	GROSS PRODUCT, REST OF WORLD	11.370	12.203	10.901	13.031	1.105	2.951

231

TABLE 7. GROSS NATIONAL PRODUCT ACCOUNT, BILLIONS OF 1972 DOLLARS, 1946-1981

		CREDITS					
		1970	1971	1972	1973	1974	1975
118	BEA GNP	1085.592	1122.393	1185.922	1254.258	1246.300	1231.624
119	BEA NNP	989.482	1022.156	1079.505	1143.506	1130.182	1110.868
120	BEA NI	888.839	911.766	963.657	1023.473	1008.182	986.658
121	BEA GPDI	158.541	173.886	195.030	217.531	195.456	154.784
122	BEA NPDI	62.431	73.649	88.613	106.779	79.338	34.028
123	BEA PCE	672.089	696.789	737.054	767.873	762.810	779.444
124	BEA GPDI / BEA GNP, PERCENT	14.604	15.492	16.445	17.343	15.683	12.567
125	BEA NPDI / BEA NNP, PERCENT	6.309	7.205	8.209	9.338	7.020	3.063
126	TISA GNP / BEA GNP, PERCENT	166.078	164.297	172.591	176.257	171.718	159.574
127	TISA NNP / BEA NNP, PERCENT	143.346	141.381	151.169	155.603	149.979	135.975
128	TISA NNI / BEA NI, PERCENT	152.793	150.947	162.019	166.599	160.536	145.905
129	TISA GNP - NR / BEA GNP, PERCENT	165.902	165.414	163.819	161.981	160.966	162.992
130	TISA NNP - NR / BEA NNP, PERCENT	143.153	142.608	141.533	139.944	138.122	139.766
131	TISA GDCA - NR / BEA GPDI, PERCENT	443.169	426.792	409.323	391.307	418.489	502.861
132	TISA NDCA - NR / BEA NPDI, PERCENT	509.453	466.000	432.652	393.176	469.981	950.706
133	TISA NDCA, TAN, OC / BEA NPDI,PERCENT	174.457	170.125	167.703	164.285	180.457	292.003
134	TISA CONSUMPTION / BEA PCE, PERCENT	162.350	159.330	155.175	151.979	154.235	154.958
135	GNP	1802.929	1844.058	2046.789	2210.720	2140.123	1965.348
136	CAPITAL CONSUMPTION ALLOWANCES (CCA)	384.547	398.927	414.916	431.386	445.088	454.843
137	CCA, TANGIBLE	255.197	263.482	273.226	282.767	289.305	292.709
138	CCA, INTANGIBLE	129.350	135.445	141.690	148.619	155.783	162.134
139	NNP	1418.381	1445.131	1631.873	1779.335	1695.036	1510.506
140	BUS TRANS PAY + UNCOMP FACTOR SERVICES + NET INDIR TAXES + STAT DISCREPANCY	60.301	68.851	70.567	74.242	76.537	70.919
141	NNI	1358.080	1376.280	1561.306	1705.093	1618.499	1439.587
142	GNP LESS SUM OF SECTOR & RW	.000	-.001	-.008	-.001	-.001	-.001

		1976	1977	1978	1979	1980	1981
1	CONSUMPTION	1249.146	1286.775	1327.921	1367.339	1403.045	1430.046
2	HOUSEHOLD EXPENDITURES FOR SERVICES AND NONDURABLES	443.183	459.297	473.792	485.297	491.060	500.092
3	GROSS EXPENDITURES INCLUDED FROM BEA PERSONAL CONSUMPTION EXPENDITURES	458.999	476.439	491.824	504.354	510.612	519.505
4	LESS: PCE EXPENSES RELATED TO WORK	15.816	17.142	18.033	19.057	19.553	19.413
5	EXPENSE ACCOUNT ITEMS OF CONSUMPTION	10.825	11.483	12.194	12.857	12.895	13.280
6	BEA IMPUTATIONS OTHER THAN HOUSING	20.011	21.431	22.896	24.085	24.308	22.986
7	SUBSIDIES ALLOCATED TO CONSUMPTION	2.684	3.493	4.193	4.056	4.255	4.135
8	SUBSIDIES INCLUDED IN BUSINESS INCOME	4.477	5.909	7.159	6.854	6.998	6.856
9	LESS: AMT. ALLOCATED TO INVESTMENT	1.793	2.417	2.966	2.797	2.743	2.721
10	TRANSFERS	117.458	119.244	123.062	124.470	125.492	125.652
11	FROM BUSINESS	6.029	6.453	7.019	7.201	7.328	7.476
12	MEDIA SUPPORT	5.046	5.428	5.936	6.101	6.239	6.391
13	TOTAL MEDIA SUPPORT	6.426	6.919	7.515	7.758	7.922	8.114
14	LESS: MEDIA SUPPORT ALLOCATED TO INVESTMENT	1.380	1.491	1.579	1.657	1.683	1.723
15	HEALTH AND SAFETY	.984	1.025	1.083	1.100	1.089	1.085
16	FROM NONPROFIT INSTITUTIONS	35.181	35.557	35.975	35.756	35.596	35.754
17	FROM GOVERNMENT ENTERPRISES	2.226	2.446	2.380	2.464	3.086	3.063
18	FROM GOVERNMENT	74.021	74.788	77.689	79.048	79.482	79.360

TABLE 7. GROSS NATIONAL PRODUCT ACCOUNT, BILLIONS OF 1972 DOLLARS, 1946-1981

		CREDITS					
		1976	1977	1978	1979	1980	1981
19	NONMARKET SERVICES PRODUCED IN HOUSEHOLDS	654.985	671.829	691.785	716.574	745.036	763.901
20	NET SPACE RENT OF OWNER-OCCUPIED NONFARM DWELLINGS	78.035	82.184	86.899	91.697	96.535	102.330
21	OTHER CAPITAL SERVICES	169.694	176.357	185.429	197.486	209.429	215.327
22	DURABLES	100.439	104.984	110.266	117.504	125.056	127.286
23	TOTAL DURABLES	113.669	118.775	124.940	132.300	139.424	141.493
24	LESS: DURABLES ALLOCATED TO INVESTMENT	4.393	4.637	4.914	5.261	5.633	5.981
25	LESS: SERVICES OF DURABLES TO EXP REL TO WORK	8.838	9.154	9.760	9.536	8.735	8.227
26	SEMIDURABLES	68.944	71.070	74.867	79.674	84.040	87.687
27	INVENTORIES	.310	.303	.296	.308	.333	.355
28	LABOR SERVICES	570.973	578.687	584.923	591.557	601.997	609.659
29	LESS: LABOR SERVICES ALLOC. TO INVEST	163.716	165.399	165.466	164.166	162.925	163.415
30	GROSS DOMESTIC CAPITAL ACCUMULATION	1012.641	1048.825	1119.534	1075.528	909.007	866.846
31	ORIGINAL COST	830.969	886.219	934.830	938.303	899.596	936.117
32	TANGIBLE	437.767	484.374	526.007	526.570	492.114	521.513
33	STRUCTURES AND EQUIPMENT AND HOUSE- HOLD DURABLES AND SEMIDURABLES	429.186	468.586	507.320	519.472	495.689	512.780
34	BUSINESS	119.772	135.281	154.382	164.019	161.361	166.275
35	NONRESIDENTIAL	111.952	125.817	144.245	153.494	151.679	156.692
36	STRUCTURES	31.098	33.222	36.967	40.132	41.583	44.664
37	EQUIPMENT	80.854	92.595	107.278	113.362	110.096	112.028
38	RESIDENTIAL OTHER THAN OWNER- OCCUPIED NONFARM DWELLINGS	7.820	9.464	10.137	10.525	9.682	9.583
39	NONPROFIT INSTITUTIONS	4.663	4.576	4.825	5.009	4.961	5.245
40	STRUCTURES	3.971	3.768	3.773	3.884	3.898	4.039
41	EQUIPMENT	.692	.808	1.052	1.125	1.063	1.206
42	GOVERNMENT ENTERPRISES	9.146	9.375	11.013	10.235	10.509	9.936
43	STRUCTURES	8.320	8.416	10.116	9.268	9.566	8.782
44	EQUIPMENT	.826	.959	.897	.967	.943	1.154
45	GOVERNMENT	44.897	42.563	47.519	49.314	48.301	48.688
46	STRUCTURES	18.521	16.729	16.933	15.707	15.859	14.289
47	EQUIPMENT	18.046	17.288	20.175	22.557	21.852	20.772
48	PRODUCT ACCUMULATED	8.330	8.546	10.411	11.050	10.590	13.627
49	HOUSEHOLDS	234.546	256.721	272.252	272.095	257.881	264.457
50	OWNER-OCC. NONFARM DWELLINGS	38.965	45.796	46.205	42.558	36.918	34.875
51	DURABLES	126.551	137.989	146.808	147.208	137.453	141.158
52	SEMIDURABLES	69.030	72.936	79.239	82.329	83.510	88.424

233

TABLE 7. GROSS NATIONAL PRODUCT ACCOUNT, BILLIONS OF 1972 DOLLARS, 1946-1981

		CREDITS					
		1976	1977	1978	1979	1980	1981
53	FIXED GPDI RECONCILIATION	13.344	15.263	15.281	17.474	9.654	12.658
54	NIPA FIXED GPDI	176.744	200.916	220.693	229.060	212.894	219.053
55	LESS: CORRESP SECTOR TOTALS	163.400	185.653	205.412	211.586	203.240	206.395
56	GOVERNMENT CAPITAL ACCUMULATION RECONCILIATION	2.818	4.807	2.048	1.326	3.022	5.521
57	NIPA GOVERNMENT INVESTMENT	48.531	48.199	50.169	49.825	51.242	50.518
58	LESS: GOVERNMENT AND GOVT ENTERPRISE TOTALS	45.713	43.392	48.121	48.499	48.220	44.997
59	CHANGE IN INVENTORIES	8.581	15.788	18.687	7.098	-3.575	8.733
60	BUSINESS	7.771	13.273	16.012	7.285	-4.360	8.498
61	GOVERNMENT	.375	2.223	2.494	-.402	.727	.170
62	HOUSEHOLDS	.435	.292	.181	.215	.058	.065
63	INTANGIBLE	393.202	401.846	408.823	411.733	407.482	414.604
64	RESEARCH AND DEVELOPMENT	28.964	29.798	31.085	32.700	33.523	34.027
65	BUSINESS	13.175	13.857	14.729	15.699	16.760	17.314
66	NONPROFIT INSTITUTIONS	.665	.698	.743	.757	.764	.763
67	GOVERNMENT	15.124	15.243	15.613	16.244	16.000	15.951
68	EDUCATION AND TRAINING	310.375	315.751	320.181	319.900	313.621	318.028
69	HEALTH	53.864	56.296	57.557	59.133	60.338	62.549
70	SUBSIDIES AND GOVERNMENT ENTERPRISE TRANSFERS ALLOCATED TO INVESTMENT	3.199	3.990	4.505	4.344	4.587	4.605
71	NET REVALUATIONS	178.473	158.615	180.200	132.881	4.824	-73.876
72	LAND	98.746	60.585	97.227	62.040	35.782	-68.438
73	BUSINESS	56.266	32.472	46.680	40.509	8.869	-45.238
74	NONPROFIT	-.010	.349	.698	.256	-.659	-.575
75	GOVERNMENT AND GOVT ENTERPRISES	20.402	12.517	20.088	12.818	7.393	-14.140
76	HOUSEHOLDS	22.088	15.247	29.760	8.458	20.179	-8.484
77	STRUCTURES AND EQUIPMENT	45.947	111.279	95.570	58.469	-22.103	24.634
78	BUSINESS	13.687	39.167	24.843	20.054	-8.062	8.532
79	NONPROFIT INSTITUTIONS	-1.643	3.245	2.419	2.956	-.515	-2.041
80	GOVERNMENT	-3.085	22.239	11.115	33.085	7.711	24.718
81	HOUSEHOLDS (OWNER-OCC. DWELLINGS)	36.989	46.628	57.193	2.375	-21.237	-6.576
82	HOUSEHOLD DURABLES AND SEMIDURABLES	-8.108	-11.929	-17.949	-15.387	-14.387	-16.775
83	DURABLES	-6.025	-8.707	-12.415	-9.899	-7.841	-12.272
84	SEMIDURABLES	-2.083	-3.222	-5.533	-5.487	-6.546	-4.503
85	INVENTORIES	41.888	-1.320	5.351	27.759	5.533	-13.296
86	BUSINESS (INCLUDING NONPROFIT)	43.886	-1.552	4.313	20.900	5.022	-14.719
87	GOVERNMENT ENTERPRISES	-.190	.022	.513	-.113	-.036	.018
88	GOVERNMENT	-1.682	.325	.608	6.588	.335	1.316
89	HOUSEHOLDS	-.126	-.115	-.082	.383	.211	.088
90	NET EXPORTS	10.413	-2.846	-.742	8.085	13.423	13.458
91	NET BEA EXPORTS	25.404	22.007	24.033	37.208	50.333	43.024
92	EXPORTS	110.062	112.882	126.707	146.177	159.114	159.745
93	IMPORTS	84.658	90.875	102.674	108.969	108.781	116.721
94	TERMS OF TRADE EFFECT	-14.991	-24.853	-24.775	-29.123	-36.910	-29.566
95	NET EXPORTS IN CURRENT DOLLARS, DEFLATED	10.413	-2.846	-.742	8.085	13.423	13.458
96	LESS: NET EXPORTS IN CONSTANT DOLLARS WITHOUT TERMS OF TRADE EFFECT	25.404	22.007	24.033	37.208	50.333	43.024
97	GROSS NATIONAL PRODUCT	2272.200	2332.754	2446.713	2450.952	2325.475	2310.351

234

TABLE 7. GROSS NATIONAL PRODUCT ACCOUNT, BILLIONS OF 1972 DOLLARS, 1946-1981

		CREDITS					
		1976	1977	1978	1979	1980	1981
	ADDENDA:						
98	GNP MINUS NET REVALUATIONS (NR)	2093.728	2174.139	2266.513	2318.071	2320.651	2384.226
99	NNP MINUS NR	1625.061	1692.195	1768.396	1801.186	1785.817	1836.560
100	NNI MINUS NR	1550.302	1615.494	1688.002	1719.785	1700.329	1752.720
101	GDCA MINUS NR	834.168	890.210	939.334	942.647	904.182	940.722
102	NDCA MINUS NR	365.502	408.266	441.217	425.762	369.349	393.055
103	NDCA	543.975	566.880	621.417	558.643	374.173	319.180
104	NDCA AT ORIGINAL COST	362.303	404.275	436.713	421.418	364.762	388.451
105	NDCA, TANGIBLE, AT ORIGINAL COST	137.015	176.435	208.812	197.851	152.034	174.614
106	NDCA, INTANGIBLE, AT ORIGINAL COST	225.288	227.840	227.901	223.567	212.728	213.836
107	GDCA - NR / GNP - NR, PERCENT	39.841	40.945	41.444	40.665	38.962	39.456
108	NDCA - NR / NNP - NR, PERCENT	22.492	24.126	24.950	23.638	20.682	21.402
109	NDCA, TAN, O.C. / NNP - NR, PERCENT	8.431	10.426	11.808	10.984	8.513	9.508
110	NDCA, INTAN, O.C. / NNP - NR, PERCENT	13.863	13.464	12.887	12.412	11.912	11.643
111	GROSS BUSINESS PRODUCT	1087.721	1111.135	1178.219	1209.702	1119.203	1093.535
112	GROSS NONPROFIT PRODUCT	51.836	56.582	57.059	57.232	52.690	51.457
113	GROSS GOVT ENTERPRISE PRODUCT	23.126	24.301	25.778	26.360	27.647	28.181
114	GROSS GOVERNMENT PRODUCT	244.637	267.259	268.453	286.900	247.672	249.409
115	GROSS HOUSEHOLD PRODUCT	864.304	881.437	922.128	873.605	889.443	891.698
116	GROSS DOMESTIC PRODUCT	2271.625	2340.715	2451.636	2453.799	2336.655	2314.280
117	GROSS PRODUCT, REST OF WORLD	.575	-7.961	-4.923	-2.846	-11.179	-3.930
118	BEA GNP	1298.215	1369.718	1438.570	1479.443	1475.012	1513.843
119	BEA NNP	1173.112	1239.868	1302.746	1336.394	1325.189	1357.927
120	BEA NI	1042.953	1105.383	1165.016	1194.811	1181.625	1212.589
121	BEA GPDI	184.515	214.189	236.705	236.345	208.534	227.551
122	BEA NPDI	59.412	84.339	100.881	93.296	58.711	71.635
123	BEA PCE	823.127	864.343	903.196	927.591	931.840	956.754
124	BEA GPDI / BEA GNP, PERCENT	14.213	15.637	16.454	15.975	14.138	15.031
125	BEA NPDI / BEA NNP, PERCENT	5.064	6.802	7.744	6.981	4.430	5.275
126	TISA GNP / BEA GNP, PERCENT	175.025	170.309	170.080	165.667	157.658	152.615
127	TISA NNP / BEA NNP, PERCENT	153.739	149.275	149.576	144.723	135.123	129.807
128	TISA NNI / BEA NI, PERCENT	165.758	160.497	160.358	155.059	144.306	138.451
129	TISA GNP - NR / BEA GNP, PERCENT	161.277	158.729	157.553	156.685	157.331	157.495
130	TISA NNP - NR / BEA NNP, PERCENT	138.526	136.482	135.744	134.780	134.759	135.247
131	TISA GDCA - NR / BEA GPDI, PERCENT	452.087	415.619	396.838	398.843	433.590	413.411
132	TISA NDCA - NR / BEA NPDI, PERCENT	615.199	484.077	437.364	456.356	629.096	548.692
133	TISA NDCA, TAN, OC / BEA NPDI, PERCENT	230.618	209.198	206.988	212.068	258.953	243.756
134	TISA CONSUMPTION / BEA PCE, PERCENT	151.756	148.873	147.025	147.408	150.567	149.469
135	GNP	2272.200	2332.754	2446.713	2450.952	2325.475	2310.351
136	CAPITAL CONSUMPTION ALLOWANCES (CCA)	468.666	481.944	498.117	516.885	534.834	547.666
137	CCA, TANGIBLE	300.752	307.938	317.195	328.719	340.080	346.898
138	CCA, INTANGIBLE	167.914	174.006	180.922	188.166	194.754	200.768
139	NNP	1803.534	1850.809	1948.596	1934.067	1790.641	1762.684
140	BUS TRANS PAY + UNCOMP FACTOR SERVICES + NET INDIR TAXES + STAT DISCREPANCY	74.759	76.701	80.394	81.401	85.489	83.840
141	NNI	1728.775	1774.109	1868.202	1852.666	1705.153	1678.844
142	GNP LESS SUM OF SECTOR & RW	.000	.000	-.001	-.001	-.001	.000

TABLE 7. GROSS NATIONAL PRODUCT ACCOUNT, BILLIONS OF 1972 DOLLARS, 1946-1981

		CREDITS					
		PERCENT PER ANNUM RATES OF GROWTH 1972 DOLLARS					
		1946-56	1956-66	1966-71	1971-76	1976-81	1946-81
1	CONSUMPTION	1.379	2.642	2.244	2.387	2.742	2.200
2	HOUSEHOLD EXPENDITURES FOR SERVICES AND NONDURABLES	2.509	3.161	3.013	2.342	2.446	2.734
3	GROSS EXPENDITURES INCLUDED FROM BEA PERSONAL CONSUMPTION EXPENDITURES	2.494	3.216	3.086	2.395	2.507	2.772
4	LESS: PCE EXPENSES RELATED TO WORK	1.887	5.327	5.426	3.946	4.183	3.988
5	EXPENSE ACCOUNT ITEMS OF CONSUMPTION	3.789	3.343	3.254	3.421	4.174	3.587
6	BEA IMPUTATIONS OTHER THAN HOUSING	-1.612	1.512	6.080	6.978	2.811	2.191
7	SUBSIDIES ALLOCATED TO CONSUMPTION	-9.732	13.523	-2.626	-1.426	9.028	1.357
8	SUBSIDIES INCLUDED IN BUSINESS INCOME	-8.915	14.404	-2.324	-1.433	8.898	1.870
9	LESS: AMT. ALLOCATED TO INVESTMENT	-7.075	15.944	-1.862	-1.444	8.702	2.887
10	TRANSFERS	-3.178	3.904	1.581	1.111	1.358	.749
11	FROM BUSINESS	7.564	5.911	.909	4.123	4.394	5.174
12	MEDIA SUPPORT	8.802	6.754	.741	4.813	4.839	5.897
13	TOTAL MEDIA SUPPORT	7.663	6.137	.639	4.311	4.775	5.308
14	LESS: MEDIA SUPPORT ALLOCATED TO INVESTMENT	5.231	4.385	.309	2.592	4.538	3.797
15	HEALTH AND SAFETY	4.525	2.863	1.646	.963	1.984	2.759
16	FROM NONPROFIT INSTITUTIONS	.556	3.845	3.628	2.069	.323	2.106
17	FROM GOVERNMENT ENTERPRISES	1.270	-.067	1.679	-5.615	6.588	.667
18	FROM GOVERNMENT	-4.786	4.001	.787	.699	1.403	.130
19	NONMARKET SERVICES PRODUCED IN HOUSEHOLDS	1.832	2.079	1.793	2.533	3.124	2.181
20	NET SPACE RENT OF OWNER-OCCUPIED NONFARM DWELLINGS	8.825	6.398	4.511	5.059	5.571	6.501
21	OTHER CAPITAL SERVICES	4.903	3.563	4.639	4.403	4.879	4.406
22	DURABLES	10.627	4.089	6.292	5.117	4.852	6.494
23	TOTAL DURABLES	10.437	3.721	6.085	4.816	4.476	6.207
24	LESS: DURABLES ALLOCATED TO INVESTMENT	6.048	4.566	7.373	6.249	6.367	5.884
25	LESS: SERVICES OF DURABLES TO EXP REL TO WORK	10.554	.916	3.829	1.158	-1.423	3.690
26	SEMIDURABLES	1.297	2.993	2.666	3.446	4.927	2.796
27	INVENTORIES	4.478	5.053	.029	-1.962	2.706	2.801
28	LABOR SERVICES	1.196	2.004	2.266	1.853	1.320	1.690
29	LESS: LABOR SERVICES ALLOC. TO INVEST	3.418	5.688	8.216	3.080	-.037	4.182
30	GROSS DOMESTIC CAPITAL ACCUMULATION	18.874	4.076	2.196	6.776	-3.061	7.127
31	ORIGINAL COST	4.391	4.818	3.062	2.396	2.412	3.750
32	TANGIBLE	6.056	4.001	1.547	2.402	3.563	3.935

TABLE 7. GROSS NATIONAL PRODUCT ACCOUNT, BILLIONS OF 1972 DOLLARS, 1946-1981

				CREDITS			
		PERCENT PER ANNUM RATES OF GROWTH 1972 DOLLARS					
		1946-56	1956-66	1966-71	1971-76	1976-81	1946-81
33	STRUCTURES AND EQUIPMENT AND HOUSE-HOLD DURABLES AND SEMIDURABLES	5.551	3.939	1.927	2.357	3.623	3.833
34	BUSINESS	2.016	4.968	.980	2.466	6.781	3.438
35	NONRESIDENTIAL	1.804	4.870	.584	3.194	6.955	3.420
36	STRUCTURES	1.946	3.302	.023	-.534	7.509	2.470
37	EQUIPMENT	1.710	5.807	.872	4.877	6.739	3.908
38	RESIDENTIAL OTHER THAN OWNER-OCCUPIED NONFARM DWELLINGS	5.336	6.173	5.146	-5.488	4.150	3.757
39	NONPROFIT INSTITUTIONS	12.296	7.052	-3.830	-4.700	2.380	4.447
40	STRUCTURES	11.896	7.013	-3.831	-6.063	.340	3.816
41	EQUIPMENT	18.369	7.480	-3.815	6.588	11.750	9.223
42	GOVERNMENT ENTERPRISES	11.910	3.396	2.136	.356	1.671	4.873
43	STRUCTURES	11.976	3.353	1.671	.043	1.087	4.678
44	EQUIPMENT	10.740	4.162	9.094	3.875	6.917	7.060
45	GOVERNMENT	5.883	3.301	-2.568	-.883	1.634	2.321
46	STRUCTURES	13.781	5.694	-2.650	-5.205	-5.056	3.440
47	EQUIPMENT	9.549	.312	-1.749	4.022	2.854	3.467
48	PRODUCT ACCUMULATED	-4.486	3.149	-3.764	1.014	10.344	.578
49	HOUSEHOLDS	4.595	3.455	4.316	3.769	2.430	3.800
50	OWNER-OCC. NONFARM DWELLINGS	6.894	.697	7.561	-.551	-2.193	2.787
51	DURABLES	6.755	4.857	4.607	5.205	2.209	5.025
52	SEMIDURABLES	1.319	3.211	1.899	4.021	5.077	2.857
53	FIXED GPDI RECONCILIATION	N.A.	7.314	6.260	-.667	-1.050	N.A.
54	NIPA FIXED GPDI	5.125	4.208	2.550	1.284	4.386	3.832
55	LESS: CORRESP. SECTOR TOTALS	3.447	4.011	2.249	1.453	4.783	3.338
56	GOVERNMENT CAPITAL ACCUMULATION RECONCILIATION	N.A.	1.337	-10.725	-12.135	14.397	N.A.
57	NIPA GOVERNMENT INVESTMENT	17.350	3.004	-2.771	-1.886	.806	4.978
58	LESS: GOVERNMENT AND GOVT ENTERPRISE TOTALS	11.529	3.344	-1.567	-.971	-.315	3.714
59	CHANGE IN INVENTORIES	N.A.	5.849	-11.981	4.830	.352	N.A.
60	BUSINESS	-7.123	11.209	-13.662	-.733	1.805	-1.019
61	GOVERNMENT	N.A.	N.A.	N.A.	N.A.	-14.634	N.A.
62	HOUSEHOLDS	-3.064	4.910	-20.903	34.183	-31.627	-4.017
63	INTANGIBLE	2.235	6.006	4.921	2.389	1.066	3.534
64	RESEARCH AND DEVELOPMENT	12.738	7.315	-1.490	.521	3.275	5.932
65	BUSINESS	11.810	6.061	3.373	3.493	5.615	6.839
66	NONPROFIT INSTITUTIONS	6.599	10.729	3.163	2.087	2.790	6.046
67	GOVERNMENT	13.453	7.872	-4.226	-1.756	1.071	5.184
68	EDUCATION AND TRAINING	1.467	6.125	5.810	2.361	.488	3.380
69	HEALTH	2.077	4.432	4.483	3.656	3.035	3.451
70	SUBSIDIES AND GOVERNMENT ENTERPRISE TRANSFERS ALLOCATED TO INVESTMENT	-1.227	7.844	-.081	-4.036	7.556	2.271

TABLE 7. GROSS NATIONAL PRODUCT ACCOUNT, BILLIONS OF 1972 DOLLARS, 1946-1981

| | | CREDITS | | | | | |
| | | PERCENT PER ANNUM RATES OF GROWTH 1972 DOLLARS | | | | | |
		1946-56	1956-66	1966-71	1971-76	1976-81	1946-81
71	NET REVALUATIONS	N.A.	-9.052	N.A.	N.A.	N.A.	N.A.
72	LAND	N.A.	-3.774	N.A.	N.A.	N.A.	N.A.
73	BUSINESS	N.A.	-8.316	N.A.	N.A.	N.A.	N.A.
74	NONPROFIT	N.A.	-5.615	N.A.	N.A.	N.A.	N.A.
75	GOVERNMENT AND GOVT ENTERPRISES	N.A.	2.666	N.A.	N.A.	N.A.	N.A.
76	HOUSEHOLDS	N.A.	-2.186	N.A.	N.A.	N.A.	N.A.
77	STRUCTURES AND EQUIPMENT	N.A.	-3.217	18.089	14.935	-11.722	N.A.
78	BUSINESS	N.A.	-7.883	-1.942	31.825	-9.019	N.A.
79	NONPROFIT INSTITUTIONS	6.817	1.142	-10.091	N.A.	N.A.	N.A.
80	GOVERNMENT	N.A.	-36.053	143.721	N.A.	N.A.	N.A.
81	HOUSEHOLDS (OWNER-OCC. DWELLINGS)	N.A.	N.A.	8.281	35.689	N.A.	N.A.
82	HOUSEHOLD DURABLES AND SEMIDURABLES	N.A.	N.A.	N.A.	N.A.	N.A.	N.A.
83	DURABLES	N.A.	N.A.	N.A.	N.A.	N.A.	N.A.
84	SEMIDURABLES	N.A.	N.A.	N.A.	N.A.	N.A.	N.A.
85	INVENTORIES	N.A.	N.A.	N.A.	N.A.	N.A.	N.A.
86	BUSINESS (INCLUDING NONPROFIT)	N.A.	N.A.	N.A.	N.A.	N.A.	N.A.
87	GOVERNMENT ENTERPRISES	-8.232	N.A.	N.A.	N.A.	N.A.	-9.801
88	GOVERNMENT	N.A.	N.A.	N.A.	N.A.	N.A.	N.A.
89	HOUSEHOLDS	N.A.	N.A.	N.A.	N.A.	N.A.	N.A.
90	NET EXPORTS	-7.261	.089	-12.809	19.497	5.265	-.806
91	NET BEA EXPORTS	-2.665	-4.351	-24.235	73.540	11.112	3.430
92	EXPORTS	2.610	4.426	5.460	9.176	7.735	5.181
93	IMPORTS	6.012	6.645	7.666	4.071	6.634	6.236
94	TERMS OF TRADE EFFECT	N.A.	N.A.	5.699	N.A.	N.A.	N.A.
95	NET EXPORTS IN CURRENT DOLLARS, DEFLATED	-7.261	.089	-12.809	19.497	5.265	-.806
96	LESS: NET EXPORTS IN CONSTANT DOLLARS WITHOUT TERMS OF TRADE EFFECT	-2.665	-4.351	-24.235	73.540	11.112	3.430
97	GROSS NATIONAL PRODUCT	4.739	3.167	2.167	4.264	.334	3.215
	ADDENDA:						
98	GNP MINUS NET REVALUATIONS (NR)	2.173	3.419	2.501	2.433	2.633	2.678
99	NNP MINUS NR	2.852	3.416	1.949	2.198	2.477	2.736
100	NNI MINUS NR	2.080	3.306	1.743	2.224	2.485	2.459
101	GDCA MINUS NR	4.355	4.834	3.044	2.366	2.433	3.741
102	NDCA MINUS NR	19.641	6.455	1.316	1.267	1.464	7.772
103	NDCA	N.A.	4.725	-.389	10.469	-10.114	N.A.
104	NDCA AT ORIGINAL COST	20.425	6.439	1.333	1.322	1.403	7.971
105	NDCA, TANGIBLE, AT ORIGINAL COST	N.A.	5.884	-3.090	1.804	4.969	N.A.
106	NDCA, INTANGIBLE, AT ORIGINAL COST	2.201	6.942	4.592	1.035	-1.038	3.230
107	GDCA - NR / GNP - NR, PERCENT	2.136	1.368	.530	-.066	-.194	1.036
108	NDCA - NR / NNP - NR, PERCENT	16.323	2.939	-.621	-.911	-.988	4.902
109	NDCA, TAN, O.C. / NNP - NR, PERCENT	N.A.	2.387	-4.943	-.385	2.432	N.A.
110	NDCA, INTAN, O.C. / NNP - NR, PERCENT	-.633	3.409	2.593	-1.137	-3.430	.481
111	GROSS BUSINESS PRODUCT	10.101	3.732	2.291	5.815	.107	5.067
112	GROSS NONPROFIT PRODUCT	3.063	4.240	1.355	1.354	-.147	2.442
113	GROSS GOVT ENTERPRISE PRODUCT	3.081	2.669	2.118	1.757	4.033	2.770
114	GROSS GOVERNMENT PRODUCT	-.689	2.964	1.558	.320	.387	.964
115	GROSS HOUSEHOLD PRODUCT	3.391	2.489	2.243	4.262	.626	2.693
116	GROSS DOMESTIC PRODUCT	4.799	3.137	2.147	4.397	.373	3.245
117	GROSS PRODUCT, REST OF WORLD	-6.178	10.609	5.431	-45.724	N.A.	N.A.

238

TABLE 7. GROSS NATIONAL PRODUCT ACCOUNT, BILLIONS OF 1972 DOLLARS, 1946-1981

			CREDITS			
			PERCENT PER ANNUM RATES OF GROWTH 1972 DOLLARS			
		1946-56	1956-66	1966-71	1971-76	1976-81	1946-81

		1946-56	1956-66	1966-71	1971-76	1976-81	1946-81
18	BEA GNP	3.453	3.903	2.649	2.953	3.121	3.347
19	BEA NNP	3.305	3.951	2.438	2.793	2.969	3.244
20	BEA NI	3.329	3.875	2.244	2.725	3.060	3.204
21	BEA GPDI	3.769	4.736	1.300	1.194	4.282	3.388
22	BEA NPDI	2.238	6.227	-2.674	-4.205	3.813	1.910
23	BEA PCE	3.021	3.748	3.535	3.389	3.054	3.359
24	BEA GPDI / BEA GNP, PERCENT	.305	.802	-1.315	-1.709	1.126	.040
25	BEA NPDI / BEA NNP, PERCENT	-1.033	2.189	-4.990	-6.808	.819	-1.292
26	TISA GNP / BEA GNP, PERCENT	1.243	-.708	-.470	1.273	-2.703	-.128
27	TISA NNP / BEA NNP, PERCENT	2.969	-.814	-.884	1.690	-3.328	.232
28	TISA NNI / BEA NI, PERCENT	2.023	-.854	-.913	1.890	-3.536	-.051
29	TISA GNP - NR / BEA GNP, PERCENT	-1.237	-.465	-.145	-.505	-.474	-.648
30	TISA NNP - NR / BEA NNP, PERCENT	-.439	-.514	-.478	-.579	-.478	-.492
31	TISA GDCA - NR / BEA GPDI, PERCENT	.565	.093	1.722	1.158	-1.773	.341
32	TISA NDCA - NR / BEA NPDI, PERCENT	17.021	.215	4.099	5.712	-2.262	5.752
33	TISA NDCA, TAN, OC / BEA NPDI,PERCENT	N.A.	-.323	-.428	6.274	1.114	N.A.
34	TISA CONSUMPTION / BEA PCE, PERCENT	-1.594	-1.067	-1.248	-.969	-.303	-1.121
35	GNP	4.739	3.167	2.167	4.264	.334	3.215
36	CAPITAL CONSUMPTION ALLOWANCES (CCA)	-.221	3.432	4.683	3.275	3.165	2.490
37	CCA, TANGIBLE	-1.079	2.895	4.300	2.681	2.896	1.911
38	CCA, INTANGIBLE	2.280	4.640	5.453	4.391	3.639	3.897
39	NNP	6.373	3.105	1.533	4.531	-.457	3.483
40	BUS TRANS PAY + UNCOMP FACTOR SERVICES + NET INDIR TAXES + STAT DISCREPANCY	N.A.	6.788	6.736	1.660	2.319	N.A.
41	NNI	5.420	2.988	1.310	4.666	-.584	3.151
42	GNP LESS SUM OF SECTOR & RW	N.A.	N.A.	N.A.	N.A.	2.557	N.A.

239

TABLE 8. GROSS BUSINESS PRODUCT, BILLIONS OF 1972 DOLLARS, 1946-81

		CREDITS					
		1946	1947	1948	1949	1950	1951
1	BEA GROSS DOMESTIC PRODUCT, BUSINESS	385.471	393.838	411.981	409.845	448.725	477.983
2	LESS: NET SPACE RENT OF OWNER-OCC. NONFARM DWELLINGS	11.290	11.817	12.543	13.911	15.347	17.021
3	LESS: BEA GOVT ENTERPRISE PRODUCT	9.834	10.696	11.172	11.044	10.921	11.096
4	LESS: RENTAL VALUE OF BLDGS. OWNED AND USED BY NONPROFIT INSTITUTIONS	1.104	1.283	1.348	1.331	1.358	1.461
5	BEA-TYPE GROSS DOMESTIC PRODUCT OF TISA BUSINESS SECTOR	363.243	370.042	386.918	383.559	421.099	448.405
6	SUBSIDIES INCLUDED IN BUSINESS INCOME	3.585	.829	.619	.448	.703	.565
7	EXPENSE ACCOUNT ITEMS OF CONSUMPTION	3.868	3.943	4.088	3.985	4.238	4.483
8	LESS: EXPENSES RELATED TO WORK	5.435	5.811	5.863	5.854	6.099	6.459
9	BUSINESS INVESTMENT IN RESEARCH AND DEVELOPMENT	1.709	1.917	1.944	1.657	1.998	2.172
10	TRAINING PRODUCED IN BUSINESS SECTOR	8.814	8.318	7.947	5.807	7.465	9.592
11	MEDIA SUPPORT PLUS HEALTH AND SAFETY	2.165	2.308	2.428	2.531	2.757	2.996
12	NET REVALUATIONS	-67.221	26.462	14.422	8.080	14.737	24.246
13	LESS: INT PRODUCT FROM GOVT	116.846	87.508	76.739	58.755	47.837	50.969
14	GROSS BUSINESS PRODUCT	193.882	320.500	335.764	341.458	399.061	435.032

		1952	1953	1954	1955	1956	1957
1	BEA GROSS DOMESTIC PRODUCT, BUSINESS	492.755	515.619	508.524	547.040	557.351	566.074
2	LESS: NET SPACE RENT OF OWNER-OCC. NONFARM DWELLINGS	19.050	20.793	22.742	24.513	26.301	28.203
3	LESS: BEA GOVT ENTERPRISE PRODUCT	11.484	11.465	11.178	11.335	11.380	11.544
4	LESS: RENTAL VALUE OF BLDGS. OWNED AND USED BY NONPROFIT INSTITUTIONS	1.493	1.493	1.492	1.548	1.662	1.726
5	BEA-TYPE GROSS DOMESTIC PRODUCT OF TISA BUSINESS SECTOR	460.728	481.869	473.112	509.644	518.008	524.601
6	SUBSIDIES INCLUDED IN BUSINESS INCOME	.667	.665	.907	.864	1.409	2.100
7	EXPENSE ACCOUNT ITEMS OF CONSUMPTION	4.643	4.987	4.921	5.353	5.611	5.744
8	LESS: EXPENSES RELATED TO WORK	6.780	7.238	7.521	8.206	8.978	9.102
9	BUSINESS INVESTMENT IN RESEARCH AND DEVELOPMENT	2.970	3.740	3.896	4.043	5.219	5.230
10	TRAINING PRODUCED IN BUSINESS SECTOR	9.554	9.575	8.756	10.793	7.683	7.664
11	MEDIA SUPPORT PLUS HEALTH AND SAFETY	3.209	3.435	3.526	3.843	4.081	4.174
12	NET REVALUATIONS	-6.508	1.340	-.281	15.381	26.673	6.537
13	LESS: INT PRODUCT FROM GOVT	53.156	52.239	48.225	54.572	52.188	54.796
14	GROSS BUSINESS PRODUCT	415.326	446.134	439.092	487.144	507.518	492.152

240

TABLE 8. GROSS BUSINESS PRODUCT, BILLIONS OF 1972 DOLLARS, 1946-81

		CREDITS					
		1958	1959	1960	1961	1962	1963
1	BEA GROSS DOMESTIC PRODUCT, BUSINESS	561.688	599.962	610.089	625.090	663.177	691.575
2	LESS: NET SPACE RENT OF OWNER-OCC. NONFARM DWELLINGS	30.174	32.361	34.597	36.651	39.209	41.334
3	LESS: BEA GOVT ENTERPRISE PRODUCT	11.621	12.066	12.679	13.017	13.371	13.888
4	LESS: RENTAL VALUE OF BLDGS. OWNED AND USED BY NONPROFIT INSTITUTIONS	1.734	1.772	1.851	1.937	2.055	2.211
5	BEA-TYPE GROSS DOMESTIC PRODUCT OF TISA BUSINESS SECTOR	518.159	553.763	560.962	573.486	608.542	634.143
6	SUBSIDIES INCLUDED IN BUSINESS INCOME	2.204	1.675	1.785	3.062	3.379	3.172
7	EXPENSE ACCOUNT ITEMS OF CONSUMPTION	5.810	5.903	6.072	6.112	6.405	6.287
8	LESS: EXPENSES RELATED TO WORK	8.873	9.323	9.568	9.518	9.883	10.245
9	BUSINESS INVESTMENT IN RESEARCH AND DEVELOPMENT	5.497	5.892	6.445	6.733	7.122	7.479
10	TRAINING PRODUCED IN BUSINESS SECTOR	7.869	8.816	9.040	8.753	10.436	9.970
11	MEDIA SUPPORT PLUS HEALTH AND SAFETY	4.170	4.444	4.985	4.637	4.854	5.087
12	NET REVALUATIONS	18.814	6.478	5.475	3.505	3.233	-2.011
13	LESS: INT PRODUCT FROM GOVT	52.983	55.080	54.747	56.238	57.647	56.379
14	GROSS BUSINESS PRODUCT	500.667	522.569	530.450	540.531	576.441	597.504

		1964	1965	1966	1967	1968	1969
1	BEA GROSS DOMESTIC PRODUCT, BUSINESS	730.297	777.747	824.025	841.968	882.112	907.096
2	LESS: NET SPACE RENT OF OWNER-OCC. NONFARM DWELLINGS	43.553	46.231	48.900	51.518	53.573	56.566
3	LESS: BEA GOVT ENTERPRISE PRODUCT	14.612	15.485	16.449	16.820	16.920	17.323
4	LESS: RENTAL VALUE OF BLDGS. OWNED AND USED BY NONPROFIT INSTITUTIONS	2.394	2.594	2.870	3.083	3.264	3.486
5	BEA-TYPE GROSS DOMESTIC PRODUCT OF TISA BUSINESS SECTOR	669.738	713.437	755.806	770.546	808.355	829.721
6	SUBSIDIES INCLUDED IN BUSINESS INCOME	3.782	4.128	5.412	5.027	5.188	5.288
7	EXPENSE ACCOUNT ITEMS OF CONSUMPTION	6.911	7.308	7.795	8.071	8.433	8.886
8	LESS: EXPENSES RELATED TO WORK	10.704	11.278	11.818	12.306	12.889	13.895
9	BUSINESS INVESTMENT IN RESEARCH AND DEVELOPMENT	7.959	8.667	9.401	10.144	10.745	11.357
10	TRAINING PRODUCED IN BUSINESS SECTOR	11.469	13.782	16.526	15.309	16.603	17.959
11	MEDIA SUPPORT PLUS HEALTH AND SAFETY	5.443	6.359	6.768	6.780	7.108	7.383
12	NET REVALUATIONS	10.514	14.314	6.257	-.711	-10.527	-6.111
13	LESS: INT PRODUCT FROM GOVT	58.027	61.152	64.026	68.750	71.266	65.662
14	GROSS BUSINESS PRODUCT	647.085	695.566	732.122	734.111	761.750	794.927

241

TABLE 8. GROSS BUSINESS PRODUCT, BILLIONS OF 1972 DOLLARS, 1946-81

		CREDITS					
		1970	1971	1972	1973	1974	1975
1	BEA GROSS DOMESTIC PRODUCT, BUSINESS	904.816	938.550	998.613	1060.673	1047.408	1032.446
2	LESS: NET SPACE RENT OF OWNER-OCC. NONFARM DWELLINGS	58.293	60.789	64.265	68.069	71.644	74.652
3	LESS: BEA GOVT ENTERPRISE PRODUCT	17.433	17.926	18.545	19.120	20.092	20.869
4	LESS: RENTAL VALUE OF BLDGS. OWNED AND USED BY NONPROFIT INSTITUTIONS	3.656	3.844	4.069	4.316	4.725	4.883
5	BEA-TYPE GROSS DOMESTIC PRODUCT OF TISA BUSINESS SECTOR	825.434	855.991	911.734	969.168	950.947	932.042
6	SUBSIDIES INCLUDED IN BUSINESS INCOME	5.247	4.812	6.406	5.096	3.129	4.042
7	EXPENSE ACCOUNT ITEMS OF CONSUMPTION	8.979	9.149	9.782	10.420	10.449	10.212
8	LESS: EXPENSES RELATED TO WORK	14.397	14.797	15.643	16.709	16.663	16.340
9	BUSINESS INVESTMENT IN RESEARCH AND DEVELOPMENT	11.250	11.097	11.535	12.391	12.745	12.387
10	TRAINING PRODUCED IN BUSINESS SECTOR	16.080	15.694	18.435	21.318	19.790	15.514
11	MEDIA SUPPORT PLUS HEALTH AND SAFETY	7.176	7.078	7.633	7.825	7.699	7.463
12	NET REVALUATIONS	-5.039	-5.180	49.148	95.254	98.699	-26.789
13	LESS: INT PRODUCT FROM GOVT	67.044	63.920	61.523	59.629	53.995	59.053
14	GROSS BUSINESS PRODUCT	787.686	819.924	937.507	1045.135	1032.801	879.479

		1976	1977	1978	1979	1980	1981
1	BEA GROSS DOMESTIC PRODUCT, BUSINESS	1095.427	1163.683	1224.304	1255.570	1248.220	1285.845
2	LESS: NET SPACE RENT OF OWNER-OCC. NONFARM DWELLINGS	77.900	82.079	86.818	91.626	96.449	102.202
3	LESS: BEA GOVT ENTERPRISE PRODUCT	21.065	21.629	22.624	23.702	24.267	24.850
4	LESS: RENTAL VALUE OF BLDGS. OWNED AND USED BY NONPROFIT INSTITUTIONS	4.733	4.823	4.862	4.970	5.101	5.196
5	BEA-TYPE GROSS DOMESTIC PRODUCT OF TISA BUSINESS SECTOR	991.729	1055.151	1109.999	1135.272	1122.403	1153.597
6	SUBSIDIES INCLUDED IN BUSINESS INCOME	4.477	5.909	7.159	6.854	6.997	6.856
7	EXPENSE ACCOUNT ITEMS OF CONSUMPTION	10.825	11.482	12.194	12.857	12.895	13.280
8	LESS: EXPENSES RELATED TO WORK	17.313	18.625	19.853	20.572	20.238	19.798
9	BUSINESS INVESTMENT IN RESEARCH AND DEVELOPMENT	13.175	13.857	14.729	15.699	16.760	17.314
10	TRAINING PRODUCED IN BUSINESS SECTOR	18.469	20.342	22.908	23.445	20.491	20.585
11	MEDIA SUPPORT PLUS HEALTH AND SAFETY	8.393	8.969	9.680	9.958	10.099	10.284
12	NET REVALUATIONS	113.839	70.088	75.836	81.463	5.830	-51.425
13	LESS: INT PRODUCT FROM GOVT	55.873	56.039	54.433	55.274	56.035	57.157
14	GROSS BUSINESS PRODUCT	1087.721	1111.135	1178.218	1209.702	1119.203	1093.535

TABLE 8.   GROSS BUSINESS PRODUCT, BILLINGS OF 1972 DOLLARS, 1946-81

		CREDITS					
		PERCENT PER ANNUM RATES OF GROWTH CURRENT DOLLARS					
		1946-56	1956-66	1966-71	1971-76	1976-81	1946-81
1	BEA GROSS DOMESTIC PRODUCT, BUSINESS	3.756	3.988	2.637	3.140	3.257	3.502
2	LESS: NET SPACE RENT OF OWNER-OCC. NONFARM DWELLINGS	8.825	6.398	4.448	5.086	5.581	6.497
3	LESS: BEA GOVT ENTERPRISE PRODUCT	1.471	3.752	1.735	3.280	3.360	2.684
4	LESS: RENTAL VALUE OF BLDGS. OWNED AND USED BY NONPROFIT INSTITUTIONS	4.179	5.615	6.020	4.247	1.883	4.526
5	BEA-TYPE GROSS DOMESTIC PRODUCT OF TISA BUSINESS SECTOR	3.613	3.850	2.521	2.988	3.070	3.357
6	SUBSIDIES INCLUDED IN BUSINESS INCOME	-8.915	14.404	-2.324	-1.433	8.898	1.870
7	EXPENSE ACCOUNT ITEMS OF CONSUMPTION	3.789	3.343	3.254	3.421	4.173	3.587
8	LESS: EXPENSES RELATED TO WORK	5.148	2.786	4.599	3.190	2.720	3.763
9	BUSINESS INVESTMENT IN RESEARCH AND DEVELOPMENT	11.810	6.061	3.373	3.493	5.615	6.839
10	TRAINING PRODUCED IN BUSINESS SECTOR	-1.364	7.960	-1.028	3.310	2.193	2.453
11	MEDIA SUPPORT PLUS HEALTH AND SAFETY	6.546	5.188	.900	3.465	4.147	4.553
12	NET REVALUATIONS	N.A.	-13.498	N.A.	N.A.	N.A.	N.A.
13	LESS: INT PRODUCT FROM GOVT	-7.744	2.065	-.033	-2.655	.456	-2.022
14	GROSS BUSINESS PRODUCT	10.101	3.732	2.291	5.815	.107	5.067

TABLE 9. GROSS NONPROFIT PRODUCT, BILLIONS OF 1972 DOLLARS, 1946-81

		CREDITS					
		1946	1947	1948	1949	1950	1951
1	CONSUMPTION	17.239	15.348	15.287	15.250	15.058	15.115
2	CONSUMPTION IN BEA PCE	7.780	7.384	7.527	7.631	7.898	7.973
3	ADDITIONAL IMPUTED CONSUMPTION	9.459	7.964	7.760	7.619	7.160	7.142
4	CAPITAL ACCUMULATION	9.860	11.483	9.982	10.219	10.072	11.321
5	RESEARCH AND DEVELOPMENT	.098	.094	.097	.109	.119	.123
6	EDUCATION AND TRAINING	6.396	6.274	6.281	6.344	6.257	6.408
7	INVESTMENT IN BEA PCE	3.039	3.283	3.391	3.542	3.615	3.719
8	ADDITIONAL IMPUTED INVESTMENT	3.159	2.812	2.714	2.669	2.468	2.475
9	EMPLOYEE TRAINING	.198	.179	.176	.133	.174	.214
10	HEALTH	3.610	3.302	3.359	3.429	3.465	3.466
11	INVESTMENT IN BEA PCE	1.708	1.725	1.816	1.926	2.093	2.125
12	ADDITIONAL IMPUTED INVESTMENT	1.902	1.577	1.543	1.503	1.372	1.341
13	NET REVALUATIONS	-.244	1.813	.245	.337	.231	1.324
14	LESS: INTERMEDIATE PRODUCT TRANSFERRED FROM GOVERNMENT	2.531	1.981	1.537	1.386	1.041	1.164
15	LESS: INTERMEDIATE PRODUCT PURCHASED	2.252	1.424	.875	.683	.663	.280
16	LESS: EXPENSES RELATED TO WORK	.196	.211	.237	.259	.270	.282
17	GROSS NONPROFIT PRODUCT	22.120	23.215	22.621	23.141	23.156	24.711

		1952	1953	1954	1955	1956	1957
1	CONSUMPTION	15.941	16.336	17.021	17.685	18.223	19.186
2	CONSUMPTION IN BEA PCE	8.531	8.831	9.203	9.471	10.122	10.437
3	ADDITIONAL IMPUTED CONSUMPTION	7.410	7.505	7.818	8.214	8.101	8.749
4	CAPITAL ACCUMULATION	10.986	10.742	12.640	13.655	14.316	18.760
5	RESEARCH AND DEVELOPMENT	.135	.148	.161	.168	.185	.215
6	EDUCATION AND TRAINING	6.812	7.029	7.351	7.832	7.901	8.484
7	INVESTMENT IN BEA PCE	3.982	4.153	4.327	4.568	4.817	5.094
8	ADDITIONAL IMPUTED INVESTMENT	2.614	2.666	2.831	3.017	2.915	3.219
9	EMPLOYEE TRAINING	.215	.210	.193	.247	.169	.171
10	HEALTH	3.622	3.758	3.969	4.185	4.301	4.630
11	INVESTMENT IN BEA PCE	2.248	2.385	2.517	2.654	2.818	2.984
12	ADDITIONAL IMPUTED INVESTMENT	1.375	1.373	1.451	1.532	1.483	1.647
13	NET REVALUATIONS	.417	-.193	1.159	1.469	1.929	5.431
14	LESS: INTERMEDIATE PRODUCT TRANSFERRED FROM GOVERNMENT	1.236	1.157	1.356	1.511	1.474	2.157
15	LESS: INTERMEDIATE PRODUCT PURCHASED	.758	.634	.813	.496	.678	.589
16	LESS: EXPENSES RELATED TO WORK	.304	.334	.374	.422	.475	.504
17	GROSS NONPROFIT PRODUCT	24.629	24.953	27.119	28.910	29.912	34.697

TABLE 9. GROSS NONPROFIT PRODUCT, BILLIONS OF 1972 DOLLARS, 1946-81

		CREDITS					
		1958	1959	1960	1961	1962	1963
1	CONSUMPTION	19.312	20.349	20.670	21.527	22.424	23.369
2	CONSUMPTION IN BEA PCE	10.935	11.624	12.092	12.375	12.730	13.397
3	ADDITIONAL IMPUTED CONSUMPTION	8.377	8.725	8.578	9.152	9.694	9.972
4	CAPITAL ACCUMULATION	13.138	13.846	10.343	17.154	18.297	18.012
5	RESEARCH AND DEVELOPMENT	.243	.262	.278	.322	.375	.410
6	EDUCATION AND TRAINING	8.621	9.053	9.247	9.942	10.475	10.815
7	INVESTMENT IN BEA PCE	5.380	5.667	5.948	6.351	6.631	6.917
8	ADDITIONAL IMPUTED INVESTMENT	3.040	3.151	3.057	3.336	3.540	3.606
9	EMPLOYEE TRAINING	.200	.236	.242	.256	.304	.292
10	HEALTH	4.713	5.040	5.175	5.498	5.843	6.295
11	INVESTMENT IN BEA PCE	3.194	3.441	3.667	3.843	4.066	4.464
12	ADDITIONAL IMPUTED INVESTMENT	1.520	1.600	1.508	1.656	1.777	1.830
13	NET REVALUATIONS	-.439	-.510	-4.357	1.391	1.604	.492
14	LESS: INTERMEDIATE PRODUCT TRANSFERRED FROM GOVERNMENT	1.477	1.607	1.301	2.099	2.239	2.163
15	LESS: INTERMEDIATE PRODUCT PURCHASED	.675	1.224	.245	.494	.138	.558
16	LESS: EXPENSES RELATED TO WORK	.542	.584	.651	.670	.715	.757
17	GROSS NONPROFIT PRODUCT	29.756	30.780	28.816	35.417	37.629	37.902
		1964	1965	1966	1967	1968	1969
1	CONSUMPTION	24.576	25.659	26.575	26.198	28.131	28.779
2	CONSUMPTION IN BEA PCE	14.257	14.649	15.367	14.963	17.221	18.135
3	ADDITIONAL IMPUTED CONSUMPTION	10.319	11.010	11.208	11.235	10.910	10.644
4	CAPITAL ACCUMULATION	19.617	20.102	22.340	21.640	21.553	27.203
5	RESEARCH AND DEVELOPMENT	.427	.469	.513	.535	.543	.551
6	EDUCATION AND TRAINING	11.462	10.811	12.944	13.422	13.890	14.318
7	INVESTMENT IN BEA PCE	7.390	6.544	8.399	8.766	9.358	9.830
8	ADDITIONAL IMPUTED INVESTMENT	3.731	3.858	4.041	4.160	3.983	3.874
9	EMPLOYEE TRAINING	.341	.409	.504	.497	.549	.613
10	HEALTH	6.669	7.055	7.475	6.408	7.885	8.705
11	INVESTMENT IN BEA PCE	4.772	4.996	5.370	4.397	5.910	6.746
12	ADDITIONAL IMPUTED INVESTMENT	1.897	2.059	2.105	2.011	1.975	1.960
13	NET REVALUATIONS	1.058	1.767	1.408	1.275	-.765	3.630
14	LESS: INTERMEDIATE PRODUCT TRANSFERRED FROM GOVERNMENT	2.272	2.477	2.631	3.014	2.997	3.300
15	LESS: INTERMEDIATE PRODUCT PURCHASED	1.033	-.724	.041	-2.777	-.010	.147
16	LESS: EXPENSES RELATED TO WORK	.810	.870	.932	1.012	1.094	1.185
17	GROSS NONPROFIT PRODUCT	40.078	43.139	45.311	46.589	45.604	51.349

TABLE 9. GROSS NONPROFIT PRODUCT, BILLIONS OF 1972 DOLLARS, 1946-81

		CREDITS					
		1970	1971	1972	1973	1974	1975
1	CONSUMPTION	30.119	31.758	33.042	33.506	33.227	34.367
2	CONSUMPTION IN BEA PCE	19.487	20.754	21.884	22.414	22.951	23.769
3	ADDITIONAL IMPUTED CONSUMPTION	10.632	11.004	11.158	11.092	10.276	10.598
4	CAPITAL ACCUMULATION	25.861	24.592	29.393	30.856	35.694	20.101
5	RESEARCH AND DEVELOPMENT	.573	.599	.608	.603	.597	.608
6	EDUCATION AND TRAINING	14.497	14.965	15.647	15.888	15.395	15.446
7	INVESTMENT IN BEA PCE	10.165	10.558	11.099	11.376	11.344	11.459
8	ADDITIONAL IMPUTED INVESTMENT	3.771	3.839	3.870	3.750	3.359	3.432
9	EMPLOYEE TRAINING	.561	.569	.677	.762	.692	.555
10	HEALTH	9.211	10.174	10.687	11.130	11.583	12.166
11	INVESTMENT IN BEA PCE	7.303	8.173	8.659	9.139	9.769	10.288
12	ADDITIONAL IMPUTED INVESTMENT	1.908	2.001	2.028	1.991	1.814	1.878
13	NET REVALUATIONS	1.581	-1.147	2.451	3.234	8.118	-8.119
14	LESS: INTERMEDIATE PRODUCT TRANSFERRED FROM GOVERNMENT	3.396	3.121	3.057	2.763	2.844	2.509
15	LESS: INTERMEDIATE PRODUCT PURCHASED	2.179	3.446	4.181	4.306	4.514	4.374
16	LESS: EXPENSES RELATED TO WORK	1.245	1.318	1.389	1.440	1.452	1.540
17	GROSS NONPROFIT PRODUCT	49.160	48.466	53.808	55.851	60.110	46.044

		1976	1977	1978	1979	1980	1981
1	CONSUMPTION	35.181	35.557	35.975	35.756	35.596	35.754
2	CONSUMPTION IN BEA PCE	25.190	26.055	27.191	27.882	28.569	29.234
3	ADDITIONAL IMPUTED CONSUMPTION	9.991	9.502	8.784	7.874	7.027	6.520
4	CAPITAL ACCUMULATION	26.979	32.817	33.003	33.226	28.751	28.155
5	RESEARCH AND DEVELOPMENT	.665	.698	.743	.757	.764	.762
6	EDUCATION AND TRAINING	15.254	15.168	15.446	15.288	14.931	15.014
7	INVESTMENT IN BEA PCE	11.434	11.430	11.867	12.038	12.055	12.257
8	ADDITIONAL IMPUTED INVESTMENT	3.167	3.047	2.823	2.500	2.216	2.088
9	EMPLOYEE TRAINING	.653	.690	.756	.750	.659	.669
10	HEALTH	12.714	13.358	13.697	13.969	14.231	14.995
11	INVESTMENT IN BEA PCE	11.001	11.663	12.124	12.587	13.027	13.868
12	ADDITIONAL IMPUTED INVESTMENT	1.713	1.696	1.573	1.382	1.203	1.126
13	NET REVALUATIONS	-1.653	3.594	3.117	3.211	-1.174	-2.616
14	LESS: INTERMEDIATE PRODUCT TRANSFERRED FROM GOVERNMENT	2.343	2.722	2.559	2.579	2.712	2.907
15	LESS: INTERMEDIATE PRODUCT PURCHASED	6.370	7.386	7.572	7.322	7.052	7.654
16	LESS: EXPENSES RELATED TO WORK	1.611	1.685	1.787	1.849	1.893	1.890
17	GROSS NONPROFIT PRODUCT	51.836	56.582	57.059	57.232	52.690	51.457

246

TABLE 9. GROSS NONPROFIT PRODUCT, BILLIONS OF 1972 DOLLARS, 1946-81

		CREDITS					
		PERCENT PER ANNUM RATES OF GROWTH					
		1946-56	1956-66	1966-71	1971-76	1976-81	1946-81
1	CONSUMPTION	.556	3.845	3.628	2.069	.323	2.106
2	CONSUMPTION IN BEA PCE	2.666	4.263	6.195	3.950	3.022	3.855
3	ADDITIONAL IMPUTED CONSUMPTION	-1.538	3.300	-.366	-1.912	-8.184	-1.058
4	CAPITAL ACCUMULATION	3.800	4.551	1.939	1.870	.857	3.043
5	RESEARCH AND DEVELOPMENT	6.601	10.727	3.162	2.088	2.787	6.046
6	EDUCATION AND TRAINING	2.136	5.061	2.944	.383	-.317	2.468
7	INVESTMENT IN BEA PCE	4.715	5.717	4.681	1.607	1.400	4.065
8	ADDITIONAL IMPUTED INVESTMENT	-.801	3.320	-1.024	-3.770	-7.998	-1.177
9	EMPLOYEE TRAINING	-1.571	11.546	2.456	2.792	.485	3.540
10	HEALTH	1.767	5.683	6.361	4.557	3.355	4.153
11	INVESTMENT IN BEA PCE	5.133	6.661	8.762	6.123	4.741	6.166
12	ADDITIONAL IMPUTED INVESTMENT	-2.457	3.565	-1.001	-3.068	-8.038	-1.485
13	NET REVALUATIONS	N.A.	-3.099	N.A.	N.A.	N.A.	N.A.
14	LESS: INTERMEDIATE PRODUCT TRANSFERRED FROM GOVERNMENT	-5.261	5.965	3.473	-5.571	4.412	.397
15	LESS: INTERMEDIATE PRODUCT PURCHASED	-11.310	-24.441	142.451	13.078	3.739	3.557
16	LESS: EXPENSES RELATED TO WORK	9.257	6.973	7.166	4.107	3.248	6.690
17	GROSS NONPROFIT PRODUCT	3.063	4.240	1.355	1.354	-.147	2.441

TABLE 10. GROSS GOVERNMENT ENTERPRISE PRODUCT, BILLIONS OF 1972 DOLLARS, 1946-81

		CREDITS					
		1946	1947	1948	1949	1950	1951
1	SALES MINUS PURCHASES OF INT. GOODS	9.834	10.696	11.172	11.044	10.921	11.096
2	TRANSFERS	3.653	2.440	2.673	2.479	2.996	2.729
3	CAP INC + NEG SURP + INT PROD FROM GOVT - INDIR TAXES	3.521	2.296	2.512	2.365	2.814	2.561
4	CONSUMPTION	2.427	1.620	1.765	1.676	1.915	1.717
5	INVESTMENT	1.094	.676	.747	.690	.898	.845
6	EMPLOYEE TRAINING	.132	.144	.161	.114	.182	.168
7	NET REVALUATIONS	.676	.327	.609	-1.346	.580	.049
8	LESS: INT PRODUCT FROM GOVT	3.219	1.590	1.485	.998	1.001	.930
9	LESS: EXPENSES RELATED TO WORK	.114	.109	.117	.129	.129	.134
10	GROSS GOVERNMENT ENTERPRISE PRODUCT	10.830	11.764	12.853	11.051	13.367	12.810

		1952	1953	1954	1955	1956	1957
1	SALES MINUS PURCHASES OF INT. GOODS	11.484	11.465	11.178	11.335	11.380	11.544
2	TRANSFERS	2.349	2.321	2.677	3.435	4.294	3.813
3	CAP INC + NEG SURP + INT PROD FROM GOVT - INDIR TAXES	2.210	2.173	2.533	3.277	4.125	3.700
4	CONSUMPTION	1.469	1.419	1.682	2.147	2.753	2.491
5	INVESTMENT	.741	.753	.851	1.130	1.372	1.209
6	EMPLOYEE TRAINING	.139	.148	.144	.158	.169	.113
7	NET REVALUATIONS	-.586	-.206	-.783	-1.845	.286	1.135
8	LESS: INT PRODUCT FROM GOVT	1.039	1.046	.972	.914	1.098	1.335
9	LESS: EXPENSES RELATED TO WORK	.152	.157	.169	.180	.194	.201
10	GROSS GOVERNMENT ENTERPRISE PRODUCT	12.056	12.376	11.930	11.832	14.669	14.957

		1958	1959	1960	1961	1962	1963
1	SALES MINUS PURCHASES OF INT. GOODS	11.621	12.066	12.679	13.017	13.371	13.888
2	TRANSFERS	4.354	3.565	4.437	5.082	5.058	4.794
3	CAP INC + NEG SURP + INT PROD FROM GOVT - INDIR TAXES	4.237	3.404	4.230	4.879	4.853	4.590
4	CONSUMPTION	2.853	2.242	2.786	3.207	3.106	2.889
5	INVESTMENT	1.384	1.162	1.445	1.671	1.748	1.701
6	EMPLOYEE TRAINING	.117	.161	.207	.203	.205	.204
7	NET REVALUATIONS	1.404	-1.011	.365	-.265	.071	-.383
8	LESS: INT PRODUCT FROM GOVT	1.383	1.172	1.418	1.420	1.479	1.467
9	LESS: EXPENSES RELATED TO WORK	.206	.221	.234	.241	.250	.262
10	GROSS GOVERNMENT ENTERPRISE PRODUCT	15.790	13.227	15.828	16.172	16.771	16.569

248

TABLE 10. GROSS GOVERNMENT ENTERPRISE PRODUCT, BILLIONS OF 1972 DOLLARS, 1946-81

		CREDITS					
		1964	1965	1966	1967	1968	1969
1	SALES MINUS PURCHASES OF INT. GOODS	14.612	15.485	16.449	16.820	16.920	17.323
2	TRANSFERS	5.065	5.067	4.881	4.181	3.727	4.364
3	CAP INC + NEG SURP + INT PROD FROM GOVT - INDIR TAXES	4.853	4.812	4.564	3.865	3.378	3.983
4	CONSUMPTION	3.018	2.942	2.735	2.309	2.004	2.358
5	INVESTMENT	1.835	1.870	1.829	1.557	1.374	1.625
6	EMPLOYEE TRAINING	.212	.255	.317	.316	.349	.381
7	NET REVALUATIONS	-.427	.786	-.408	-.168	-.099	.129
8	LESS: INT PRODUCT FROM GOVT	1.460	1.610	1.533	1.715	1.834	1.751
9	LESS: EXPENSES RELATED TO WORK	.273	.285	.300	.316	.332	.353
10	GROSS GOVERNMENT ENTERPRISE PRODUCT	17.517	19.443	19.089	18.803	18.383	19.712

		1970	1971	1972	1973	1974	1975
1	SALES MINUS PURCHASES OF INT. GOODS	17.433	17.926	18.545	19.120	20.092	20.869
2	TRANSFERS	5.395	5.330	4.876	5.848	5.363	5.914
3	CAP INC + NEG SURP + INT PROD FROM GOVT - INDIR TAXES	5.038	4.975	4.452	5.353	4.880	5.521
4	CONSUMPTION	3.046	2.972	2.622	3.093	2.882	3.424
5	INVESTMENT	1.992	2.003	1.830	2.260	1.998	2.097
6	EMPLOYEE TRAINING	.357	.355	.424	.495	.483	.393
7	NET REVALUATIONS	-.547	.223	.596	.837	-.135	-.052
8	LESS: INT PRODUCT FROM GOVT	1.891	1.887	1.700	1.525	1.384	1.869
9	LESS: EXPENSES RELATED TO WORK	.379	.394	.395	.408	.416	.432
10	GROSS GOVERNMENT ENTERPRISE PRODUCT	20.011	21.198	21.922	23.872	23.520	24.429

		1976	1977	1978	1979	1980	1981
1	SALES MINUS PURCHASES OF INT. GOODS	21.065	21.629	22.624	23.702	24.267	24.850
2	TRANSFERS	4.101	4.518	4.473	4.573	5.428	5.434
3	CAP INC + NEG SURP + INT PROD FROM GOVT - INDIR TAXES	3.633	4.020	3.919	4.011	4.930	4.947
4	CONSUMPTION	2.226	2.446	2.380	2.464	3.086	3.063
5	INVESTMENT	1.407	1.574	1.539	1.547	1.844	1.884
6	EMPLOYEE TRAINING	.468	.498	.554	.562	.498	.487
7	NET REVALUATIONS	-.190	.022	.513	-.113	-.036	.018
8	LESS: INT PRODUCT FROM GOVT	1.415	1.423	1.371	1.331	1.539	1.662
9	LESS: EXPENSES RELATED TO WORK	.435	.446	.461	.471	.474	.459
10	GROSS GOVERNMENT ENTERPRISE PRODUCT	23.126	24.301	25.778	26.360	27.647	28.181

249

TABLE 10.   GROSS GOVERNMENT ENTERPRISE PRODUCT, BILLIONS OF 1972 DOLLARS, 1946-81

		CREDITS					
		PERCENT PER ANNUM RATES OF GROWTH CURRENT DOLLARS					
		1946-56	1956-66	1966-71	1971-76	1976-81	1946-81
1	SALES MINUS PURCHASES OF INT. GOODS	1.471	3.752	1.735	3.280	3.360	2.684
2	TRANSFERS	1.632	1.288	1.777	-5.109	5.791	1.141
3	CAP INC + NEG SURP + INT PROD FROM GOVT - INDIR TAXES	1.598	1.015	1.741	-6.096	6.370	.977
4	CONSUMPTION	1.270	-.067	1.679	-5.615	6.588	.667
5	INVESTMENT	2.295	2.915	1.833	-6.827	6.021	1.566
6	EMPLOYEE TRAINING	2.502	6.492	2.290	5.683	.799	3.800
7	NET REVALUATIONS	-8.232	N.A.	N.A.	N.A.	N.A.	-9.801
8	LESS: INT PRODUCT FROM GOVT	-10.195	3.393	4.239	-5.597	3.279	-1.870
9	LESS: EXPENSES RELATED TO WORK	5.460	4.456	5.603	2.000	1.080	4.060
10	GROSS GOVERNMENT ENTERPRISE PRODUCT	3.081	2.669	2.118	1.757	4.033	2.770

TABLE 11. GROSS GOVERNMENT PRODUCT, BILLIONS OF 1972 DOLLARS, 1946-81

		CREDITS					
		1946	1947	1948	1949	1950	1951
1	CONSUMPTION (TO HOUSEHOLDS)	21.662	17.345	14.866	13.993	14.009	13.067
2	CAPITAL ACCUMULATION	57.297	45.688	40.756	39.184	41.360	43.198
3	TO BUSINESS (R & D)	1.923	2.112	2.442	2.566	2.760	2.889
4	TO HOUSEHOLDS	43.440	34.176	30.956	30.549	33.500	35.097
5	EDUCATION AND TRAINING	40.213	30.824	27.369	27.061	30.226	31.832
6	PUBLIC SCHOOLS	22.409	22.079	19.475	19.396	20.448	18.205
7	EMPLOYEE TRAINING	17.804	8.745	7.894	7.664	9.777	13.627
8	MILITARY	16.361	7.517	6.682	6.797	8.366	12.090
9	NONMILITARY	1.443	1.228	1.212	.867	1.411	1.537
10	HEALTH	3.227	3.352	3.587	3.489	3.274	3.265
11	TO GOVERNMENT	11.934	9.400	7.358	6.068	5.100	5.212
12	RESEARCH AND DEVELOPMENT	.798	.858	.999	1.041	1.156	1.180
13	NATURAL RESOURCES	11.136	8.542	6.360	5.027	3.944	4.032
14	INTERMEDIATE PRODUCT	185.114	137.416	121.306	94.085	78.792	84.497
15	TO BUSINESS	116.846	87.507	76.739	58.755	47.837	50.968
16	TO NONPROFIT	2.530	1.980	1.537	1.386	1.041	1.164
17	TO GOVT ENTERPRISE	3.219	1.590	1.485	.998	1.001	.930
18	TO HOUSEHOLD	62.519	46.338	41.545	32.946	28.914	31.435
19	GROSS CREDITS EXCLUSIVE OF CHANGE IN INVENTORIES AND NET REVALUATIONS	264.072	200.449	176.927	147.262	134.161	140.762
20	CHANGE IN INVENTORIES	-14.805	-13.767	-12.611	-5.019	-3.753	2.616
21	LESS: INTERMEDIATE PURCHASES FROM OTHER SECTORS	7.993	8.264	12.118	13.974	10.790	16.464
22	LESS: EXPENSES RELATED TO WORK	1.254	1.014	1.053	1.187	1.236	1.471
23	GROSS GOVERNMENT PRODUCT EXCLUSIVE OF NET REVALUATIONS	240.020	177.405	151.145	127.082	118.382	125.442
24	NET REVALUATIONS	-61.719	5.952	5.377	1.365	-4.221	13.312
25	GROSS GOVERNMENT PRODUCT	178.301	183.357	156.522	128.447	114.161	138.754

		1952	1953	1954	1955	1956	1957
1	CONSUMPTION (TO HOUSEHOLDS)	12.753	13.325	15.564	16.505	16.460	18.114
2	CAPITAL ACCUMULATION	46.160	50.797	57.026	61.435	62.325	65.872
3	TO BUSINESS (R & D)	3.491	3.674	4.435	5.375	7.473	9.164
4	TO HOUSEHOLDS	36.707	40.166	43.647	46.738	45.677	46.517
5	EDUCATION AND TRAINING	33.101	36.144	39.535	42.331	41.190	41.780
6	PUBLIC SCHOOLS	18.016	21.432	25.254	28.188	27.536	29.065
7	EMPLOYEE TRAINING	15.085	14.712	14.281	14.143	13.655	12.715
8	MILITARY	13.840	13.375	12.984	12.742	12.127	11.681
9	NONMILITARY	1.245	1.337	1.297	1.401	1.528	1.034
10	HEALTH	3.606	4.022	4.112	4.407	4.486	4.738
11	TO GOVERNMENT	5.962	6.957	8.945	9.322	9.175	10.191
12	RESEARCH AND DEVELOPMENT	1.429	1.505	1.709	1.931	2.138	2.354
13	NATURAL RESOURCES	4.533	5.452	7.235	7.391	7.037	7.837
14	INTERMEDIATE PRODUCT	89.362	89.125	84.095	96.595	95.001	101.337
15	TO BUSINESS	53.156	52.239	48.225	54.572	52.188	54.796
16	TO NONPROFIT	1.236	1.157	1.356	1.511	1.474	2.157
17	TO GOVT ENTERPRISE	1.039	1.046	.972	.914	1.098	1.335
18	TO HOUSEHOLD	33.931	34.682	33.543	39.597	40.241	43.051

251

TABLE 11. GROSS GOVERNMENT PRODUCT, BILLIONS OF 1972 DOLLARS, 1946-81

		CREDITS					
		1952	1953	1954	1955	1956	1957
19	GROSS CREDITS EXCLUSIVE OF CHANGE IN INVENTORIES AND NET REVALUATIONS	148.274	153.246	156.686	174.535	173.786	185.323
20	CHANGE IN INVENTORIES	10.631	17.149	9.593	1.939	1.259	-2.441
21	LESS: INTERMEDIATE PURCHASES FROM OTHER SECTORS	22.524	30.434	22.323	23.230	21.132	25.094
22	LESS: EXPENSES RELATED TO WORK	1.629	1.702	1.829	1.954	2.127	2.211
23	GROSS GOVERNMENT PRODUCT EXCLUSIVE OF NET REVALUATIONS	134.752	138.259	142.126	151.290	151.786	155.577
24	NET REVALUATIONS	-2.596	5.480	2.237	17.996	14.613	5.138
25	GROSS GOVERNMENT PRODUCT	132.156	143.739	144.363	169.286	166.399	160.715

		1958	1959	1960	1961	1962	1963
1	CONSUMPTION (TO HOUSEHOLDS)	17.770	20.879	20.648	24.376	25.356	28.106
2	CAPITAL ACCUMULATION	68.746	75.139	79.424	85.530	86.322	93.488
3	TO BUSINESS (R & D)	9.767	11.323	12.224	12.625	12.943	14.425
4	TO HOUSEHOLDS	48.615	52.612	55.941	60.261	61.915	66.020
5	EDUCATION AND TRAINING	43.739	47.324	50.417	54.364	55.922	59.626
6	PUBLIC SCHOOLS	31.396	34.849	37.599	41.519	42.688	46.439
7	EMPLOYEE TRAINING	12.342	12.475	12.818	12.844	13.234	13.187
8	MILITARY	11.303	11.081	11.059	11.081	11.452	11.427
9	NONMILITARY	1.039	1.394	1.759	1.763	1.782	1.760
10	HEALTH	4.876	5.289	5.524	5.898	5.993	6.394
11	TO GOVERNMENT	10.364	11.204	11.258	12.643	11.465	13.043
12	RESEARCH AND DEVELOPMENT	2.612	2.849	3.032	3.301	3.529	4.030
13	NATURAL RESOURCES	7.752	8.354	8.226	9.343	7.936	9.013
14	INTERMEDIATE PRODUCT	98.133	102.193	102.350	106.380	108.637	106.373
15	TO BUSINESS	52.983	55.080	54.747	56.238	57.647	56.379
16	TO NONPROFIT	1.477	1.607	1.301	2.099	2.239	2.162
17	TO GOVT ENTERPRISE	1.383	1.172	1.418	1.420	1.479	1.467
18	TO HOUSEHOLD	42.290	44.334	44.884	46.622	47.272	46.364
19	GROSS CREDITS EXCLUSIVE OF CHANGE IN INVENTORIES AND NET REVALUATIONS	184.650	198.211	202.422	216.286	220.316	227.966
20	CHANGE IN INVENTORIES	.709	-3.173	-1.205	-5.474	1.071	1.429
21	LESS: INTERMEDIATE PURCHASES FROM OTHER SECTORS	28.865	29.795	31.713	34.405	37.847	39.253
22	LESS: EXPENSES RELATED TO WORK	2.254	2.323	2.420	2.501	2.611	2.720
23	GROSS GOVERNMENT PRODUCT EXCLUSIVE OF NET REVALUATIONS	154.240	162.920	167.084	173.906	180.928	187.422
24	NET REVALUATIONS	-1.071	-4.126	1.183	6.281	3.780	6.946
25	GROSS GOVERNMENT PRODUCT	153.169	158.794	168.267	180.187	184.708	194.368

TABLE 11. GROSS GOVERNMENT PRODUCT, BILLIONS OF 1972 DOLLARS, 1946-81

		CREDITS					
		1964	1965	1966	1967	1968	1969
1	CONSUMPTION (TO HOUSEHOLDS)	31.175	34.064	37.352	37.246	38.829	40.804
2	CAPITAL ACCUMULATION	100.889	106.119	113.799	116.173	118.769	122.122
3	TO BUSINESS (R & D)	15.315	15.233	15.780	15.428	15.239	14.353
4	TO HOUSEHOLDS	71.873	76.877	83.697	86.682	91.236	95.332
5	EDUCATION AND TRAINING	65.082	69.792	76.385	79.266	83.175	86.953
6	PUBLIC SCHOOLS	51.227	55.426	59.626	61.502	64.386	67.668
7	EMPLOYEE TRAINING	13.856	14.366	16.760	17.764	18.788	19.285
8	MILITARY	12.022	12.155	13.899	14.809	15.537	15.757
9	NONMILITARY	1.834	2.211	2.861	2.955	3.251	3.528
10	HEALTH	6.790	7.086	7.312	7.416	8.061	8.379
11	TO GOVERNMENT	13.701	14.009	14.321	14.064	12.294	12.437
12	RESEARCH AND DEVELOPMENT	4.556	4.705	4.726	4.739	4.571	4.732
13	NATURAL RESOURCES	9.145	9.304	9.595	9.325	7.723	7.705
14	INTERMEDIATE PRODUCT	109.863	114.784	120.118	129.560	135.792	127.302
15	TO BUSINESS	58.027	61.152	64.026	68.750	71.266	65.662
16	TO NONPROFIT	2.272	2.477	2.631	3.014	2.997	3.300
17	TO GOVT ENTERPRISE	1.460	1.610	1.533	1.715	1.834	1.751
18	TO HOUSEHOLD	48.104	49.545	51.929	56.081	59.696	56.590
19	GROSS CREDITS EXCLUSIVE OF CHANGE IN INVENTORIES AND NET REVALUATIONS	241.927	254.968	271.269	282.980	293.391	290.228
20	CHANGE IN INVENTORIES	-1.960	-4.012	-4.298	1.693	1.479	5.905
21	LESS: INTERMEDIATE PURCHASES FROM OTHER SECTORS	40.297	42.150	47.422	54.524	59.805	58.994
22	LESS: EXPENSES RELATED TO WORK	2.878	3.016	3.282	3.550	3.736	3.970
23	GROSS GOVERNMENT PRODUCT EXCLUSIVE OF NET REVALUATIONS	196.792	205.790	216.268	226.599	231.328	233.169
24	NET REVALUATIONS	11.302	9.892	6.582	7.290	6.162	5.506
25	GROSS GOVERNMENT PRODUCT	208.094	215.682	222.850	233.889	237.490	238.675

		1970	1971	1972	1973	1974	1975
1	CONSUMPTION (TO HOUSEHOLDS)	43.844	47.040	51.747	55.017	56.436	59.338
2	CAPITAL ACCUMULATION	125.182	128.853	135.240	136.745	135.416	137.303
3	TO BUSINESS (R & D)	12.642	11.768	11.569	11.270	10.598	10.287
4	TO HOUSEHOLDS	99.662	104.408	110.236	112.733	111.673	113.554
5	EDUCATION AND TRAINING	90.542	94.461	99.313	100.904	99.279	100.990
6	PUBLIC SCHOOLS	72.308	77.176	81.636	83.392	82.830	86.123
7	EMPLOYEE TRAINING	18.235	17.285	17.677	17.512	16.449	14.868
8	MILITARY	15.064	14.097	13.853	13.126	12.351	11.562
9	NONMILITARY	3.171	3.188	3.824	4.386	4.098	3.306
10	HEALTH	9.120	9.947	10.923	11.829	12.394	12.563
11	TO GOVERNMENT	12.877	12.677	13.435	12.742	13.145	13.463
12	RESEARCH AND DEVELOPMENT	4.797	4.756	4.676	4.550	4.467	4.414
13	NATURAL RESOURCES	8.081	7.920	8.759	8.192	8.678	9.048
14	INTERMEDIATE PRODUCT	128.948	122.708	118.234	114.116	102.973	110.629
15	TO BUSINESS	67.044	63.920	61.523	59.629	53.995	59.053
16	TO NONPROFIT	3.396	3.121	3.057	2.763	2.844	2.509
17	TO GOVT ENTERPRISE	1.891	1.887	1.700	1.525	1.384	1.869
18	TO HOUSEHOLD	56.617	53.781	51.954	50.199	44.750	47.198

253

TABLE 11. GROSS GOVERNMENT PRODUCT, BILLIONS OF 1972 DOLLARS, 1946-81

		CREDITS					
		1970	1971	1972	1973	1974	1975
19	GROSS CREDITS EXCLUSIVE OF CHANGE IN INVENTORIES AND NET REVALUATIONS	297.974	298.602	305.220	305.878	294.825	307.270
20	CHANGE IN INVENTORIES	-4.118	-1.384	-5.592	-4.825	1.248	-1.581
21	LESS: INTERMEDIATE PURCHASES FROM OTHER SECTORS	56.927	59.987	63.624	63.212	66.940	69.248
22	LESS: EXPENSES RELATED TO WORK	4.137	4.265	4.370	4.492	4.492	4.656
23	GROSS GOVERNMENT PRODUCT EXCLUSIVE OF NET REVALUATIONS	232.792	232.966	231.634	233.349	224.641	231.785
24	NET REVALUATIONS	16.112	7.790	27.859	56.300	28.677	1.762
25	GROSS GOVERNMENT PRODUCT	248.904	240.756	259.493	289.649	253.318	233.547

		1976	1977	1978	1979	1980	1981
1	CONSUMPTION (TO HOUSEHOLDS)	58.787	59.813	62.126	62.985	62.444	60.325
2	CAPITAL ACCUMULATION	139.148	141.341	145.593	147.731	145.479	151.629
3	TO BUSINESS (R & D)	10.742	11.076	11.295	11.834	11.907	11.984
4	TO HOUSEHOLDS	115.694	117.552	119.570	120.437	118.890	122.051
5	EDUCATION AND TRAINING	103.123	104.763	106.186	106.909	105.131	108.265
6	PUBLIC SCHOOLS	88.091	89.771	90.889	91.892	90.915	93.674
7	EMPLOYEE TRAINING	15.032	14.993	15.297	15.017	14.216	14.592
8	MILITARY	11.092	10.735	10.582	10.319	10.145	10.567
9	NONMILITARY	3.940	4.258	4.715	4.698	4.071	4.025
10	HEALTH	12.571	12.788	13.384	13.528	13.758	13.786
11	TO GOVERNMENT	12.712	12.713	14.729	15.460	14.682	17.594
12	RESEARCH AND DEVELOPMENT	4.382	4.167	4.318	4.410	4.092	3.967
13	NATURAL RESOURCES	8.330	8.546	10.411	11.050	10.590	13.627
14	INTERMEDIATE PRODUCT	105.794	107.073	104.872	104.716	106.297	110.471
15	TO BUSINESS	55.873	56.038	54.433	55.274	56.035	57.157
16	TO NONPROFIT	2.343	2.722	2.559	2.579	2.712	2.907
17	TO GOVT ENTERPRISE	1.415	1.423	1.371	1.331	1.538	1.662
18	TO HOUSEHOLD	46.164	46.891	46.508	45.532	46.011	48.745
19	GROSS CREDITS EXCLUSIVE OF CHANGE IN INVENTORIES AND NET REVALUATIONS	303.730	308.227	312.591	315.432	314.219	322.425
20	CHANGE IN INVENTORIES	.375	2.223	2.494	-.402	.727	.170
21	LESS: INTERMEDIATE PURCHASES FROM OTHER SECTORS	70.335	73.299	73.313	75.438	77.497	80.042
22	LESS: EXPENSES RELATED TO WORK	4.766	4.972	5.129	5.183	5.217	5.039
23	GROSS GOVERNMENT PRODUCT EXCLUSIVE OF NET REVALUATIONS	229.003	232.178	236.643	234.409	232.232	237.514
24	NET REVALUATIONS	15.634	35.081	31.810	52.491	15.440	11.895
25	GROSS GOVERNMENT PRODUCT	244.637	267.259	268.453	286.900	247.672	249.409

TABLE 11. GROSS GOVERNMENT PRODUCT, BILLIONS OF 1972 DOLLARS, 1946-81

		CREDITS					
		PERCENT PER ANNUM RATES OF GROWTH CONSTANT DOLLARS					
		1946-56	1956-66	1966-71	1971-76	1976-81	1946-81
1	CONSUMPTION (TO HOUSEHOLDS)	-2.709	8.540	4.720	4.559	.518	2.970
2	CAPITAL ACCUMULATION	.845	6.206	2.516	1.549	1.733	2.820
3	TO BUSINESS (R & D)	14.540	7.761	-5.698	-1.809	2.212	5.367
4	TO HOUSEHOLDS	.503	6.243	4.521	2.074	1.075	2.996
5	EDUCATION AND TRAINING	.240	6.371	4.339	1.770	.978	2.870
6	PUBLIC SCHOOLS	2.082	8.032	5.295	2.681	1.237	4.171
7	EMPLOYEE TRAINING	-2.618	2.070	.619	-2.754	-.593	-.567
8	MILITARY	-2.950	1.373	.284	-4.682	-.966	-1.241
9	NONMILITARY	.574	6.473	2.188	4.327	.428	2.974
10	HEALTH	3.349	5.007	6.349	4.794	1.861	4.236
11	TO GOVERNMENT	-2.594	4.553	-2.410	.056	6.716	1.115
12	RESEARCH AND DEVELOPMENT	10.364	8.255	.129	-1.625	-1.969	4.690
13	NATURAL RESOURCES	-4.486	3.149	-3.764	1.014	10.344	.578
14	INTERMEDIATE PRODUCT	-6.453	2.374	.428	-2.923	.869	-1.464
15	TO BUSINESS	-7.744	2.065	-.033	-2.655	.456	-2.022
16	TO NONPROFIT	-5.261	5.965	3.473	-5.571	4.412	.397
17	TO GOVT ENTERPRISE	-10.195	3.393	4.240	-5.596	3.278	-1.870
18	TO HOUSEHOLD	-4.310	2.583	.703	-3.008	1.094	-.709
19	GROSS CREDITS EXCLUSIVE OF CHANGE IN INVENTORIES AND NET REVALUATIONS	-4.098	4.554	1.939	.341	1.202	.572
20	CHANGE IN INVENTORIES	N.A.	N.A.	N.A.	N.A.	-14.634	N.A.
21	LESS: INTERMEDIATE PURCHASES FROM OTHER SECTORS	10.211	8.419	4.813	3.234	2.619	6.804
22	LESS: EXPENSES RELATED TO WORK	5.428	4.430	5.384	2.247	1.120	4.055
23	GROSS GOVERNMENT PRODUCT EXCLUSIVE OF NET REVALUATIONS	-4.479	3.604	1.499	-.343	.732	-.030
24	NET REVALUATIONS	N.A.	-7.666	3.427	14.949	-5.320	N.A.
25	GROSS GOVERNMENT PRODUCT	-.688	2.964	1.558	.320	.387	.964

255

TABLE 12. GROSS HOUSEHOLD PRODUCT, BILLIONS OF 1972 DOLLARS, 1946-81

		CREDITS					
		1946	1947	1948	1949	1950	1951
1	CONSUMPTION	418.997	406.891	418.803	407.192	409.632	417.039
2	MARKET (LABOR SERVICES IN HOUSEHOLDS)	5.800	6.199	6.085	6.079	6.615	6.503
3	NONMARKET	359.027	361.581	378.036	374.507	380.236	385.760
4	NET SPACE RENT ON OWNER-OCCUPIED NONFARM DWELLINGS	11.290	11.817	12.543	13.911	15.347	17.021
5	BEA NET SPACE RENT ON OWNER-OCCUPIED NONFARM DWELLINGS	11.290	11.817	12.543	13.911	15.347	17.021
6	SUBSIDIES	.000	.000	.000	.000	.000	.000
7	CAPITAL SERVICES OTHER THAN ON OWNER-OCCUPIED DWELLINGS	47.608	49.631	51.443	53.877	55.970	58.890
8	DURABLES	14.072	16.140	17.883	20.253	22.081	24.389
9	GROSS	17.195	19.523	21.459	24.142	26.383	29.115
10	LESS: SERVICES ALLOCATED TO INVESTMENT	.809	.853	.904	.963	1.020	1.086
11	LESS: SERVICES TO EXP RELATED TO WORK	2.314	2.530	2.673	2.926	3.282	3.640
12	SEMIDURABLES	33.401	33.391	33.460	33.502	33.764	34.372
13	INVENTORIES	.135	.100	.099	.122	.125	.129
14	LABOR SERVICES	300.129	300.132	314.050	306.720	308.918	309.848
15	TOTAL IMPUTED LABOR SERVICES	339.086	341.895	357.260	349.424	352.728	355.023
16	LESS: LABOR SERVICES ALLOCATED TO INVESTMENT	38.956	41.762	43.210	42.704	43.810	45.175
17	INTERMEDIATE PRODUCT OF GOVERNMENT TO CONSUMPTION	54.170	39.112	34.682	26.606	22.781	24.777
18	CAPITAL ACCUMULATION	-6.773	58.546	60.653	51.232	43.840	60.188
19	INTANGIBLE AT ORIGINAL COST	46.963	48.330	49.301	47.722	48.434	50.235
20	EDUCATION	43.127	44.643	45.524	44.118	44.800	46.540
21	TEACHING CHILDREN IN HOME	11.608	11.608	12.164	11.838	11.944	12.044
22	OPPORTUNITY COST OF STUDENTS	24.351	27.183	27.964	27.903	28.858	30.099
23	DURABLE SERVICES ALLOCATED TO EDUCATION	.483	.511	.543	.582	.622	.669
24	INTERMEDIATE PRODUCT OF GOVERNMENT TO EDUCATION	5.631	4.438	3.946	3.131	2.775	3.069
25	HEALTH	3.632	3.519	3.636	3.509	3.510	3.552
26	EMPLOYEE TRAINING	.204	.168	.140	.095	.124	.144
27	NET REVALUATIONS	-53.736	10.216	11.352	3.510	-4.594	9.952
28	SERVICES TO EXP REL TO WORK	2.314	2.530	2.673	2.926	3.282	3.640
29	LESS: INTERMEDIATE PRODUCT TRANSFERRED FROM GOVERNMENT	62.519	46.338	41.545	32.946	28.914	31.435
30	LESS: EXPENSES RELATED TO WORK	.256	.281	.277	.294	.327	.330
31	GROSS HOUSEHOLD PRODUCT	351.763	421.349	440.306	428.110	427.513	449.102

TABLE 12. GROSS HOUSEHOLD PRODUCT, BILLIONS OF 1972 DOLLARS, 1946-81

		CREDITS					
		1952	1953	1954	1955	1956	1957
1	CONSUMPTION	427.840	437.448	447.869	459.223	467.347	476.907
2	MARKET (LABOR SERVICES IN HOUSEHOLDS)	5.987	5.869	5.541	6.560	6.858	6.723
3	NONMARKET	395.161	404.677	416.872	422.585	430.511	438.286
4	NET SPACE RENT ON OWNER-OCCUPIED NONFARM DWELLINGS	19.050	20.793	22.742	24.513	26.301	28.203
5	BEA NET SPACE RENT ON OWNER-OCCUPIED NONFARM DWELLINGS	19.050	20.793	22.742	24.513	26.301	28.203
6	SUBSIDIES	.000	.000	.000	.000	.000	.000
7	CAPITAL SERVICES OTHER THAN ON OWNER-OCCUPIED DWELLINGS	62.615	66.427	71.613	73.738	76.838	79.500
8	DURABLES	27.322	30.202	34.737	36.316	38.636	40.338
9	GROSS	32.653	35.981	41.208	43.324	46.402	48.259
10	LESS: SERVICES ALLOCATED TO INVESTMENT	1.168	1.254	1.338	1.393	1.455	1.521
11	LESS: SERVICES TO EXP RELATED TO WORK	4.164	4.526	5.133	5.616	6.312	6.400
12	SEMIDURABLES	35.136	36.039	36.669	37.215	37.993	38.941
13	INVENTORIES	.157	.186	.206	.206	.209	.221
14	LABOR SERVICES	313.496	317.457	322.517	324.335	327.372	330.583
15	TOTAL IMPUTED LABOR SERVICES	359.028	365.530	370.022	375.677	381.887	388.293
16	LESS: LABOR SERVICES ALLOCATED TO INVESTMENT	45.532	48.073	47.505	51.342	54.516	57.710
17	INTERMEDIATE PRODUCT OF GOVERNMENT TO CONSUMPTION	26.693	26.903	25.457	30.078	29.978	31.898
18	CAPITAL ACCUMULATION	52.147	52.444	46.203	54.606	58.073	58.163
19	INTANGIBLE AT ORIGINAL COST	50.823	53.594	52.755	57.581	61.065	64.880
20	EDUCATION	47.064	49.777	48.898	53.622	57.113	60.871
21	TEACHING CHILDREN IN HOME	12.190	12.335	12.469	12.571	12.711	12.817
22	OPPORTUNITY COST OF STUDENTS	30.290	32.658	31.931	35.621	38.674	41.740
23	DURABLE SERVICES ALLOCATED TO EDUCATION	.726	.784	.842	.884	.931	.980
24	INTERMEDIATE PRODUCT OF GOVERNMENT TO EDUCATION	3.274	3.452	3.220	4.033	4.267	4.742
25	HEALTH	3.627	3.697	3.760	3.823	3.861	3.924
26	EMPLOYEE TRAINING	.131	.120	.096	.136	.092	.086
27	NET REVALUATIONS	1.324	-1.151	-6.552	-2.975	-2.993	-6.717
28	SERVICES TO EXP REL TO WORK	4.164	4.526	5.133	5.616	6.312	6.400
29	LESS: INTERMEDIATE PRODUCT TRANSFERRED FROM GOVERNMENT	33.931	34.682	33.543	39.598	40.241	43.051
30	LESS: EXPENSES RELATED TO WORK	.326	.343	.354	.432	.493	.499
31	GROSS HOUSEHOLD PRODUCT	449.894	459.392	465.310	479.415	490.997	497.921

257

TABLE 12. GROSS HOUSEHOLD PRODUCT, BILLIONS OF 1972 DOLLARS, 1946-81

		CREDITS					
		1958	1959	1960	1961	1962	1963
1	CONSUMPTION	486.514	495.497	506.841	516.542	525.038	534.782
2	MARKET (LABOR SERVICES IN HOUSEHOLDS)	6.876	6.717	6.756	6.555	6.517	6.431
3	NONMARKET	448.930	457.122	468.573	477.672	486.539	498.171
4	NET SPACE RENT ON OWNER-OCCUPIED NONFARM DWELLINGS	30.174	32.361	34.597	36.651	39.209	41.334
5	BEA NET SPACE RENT ON OWNER-OCCUPIED NONFARM DWELLINGS	30.174	32.361	34.597	36.651	39.209	41.334
6	SUBSIDIES	.000	.000	.000	.000	.000	.000
7	CAPITAL SERVICES OTHER THAN ON OWNER-OCCUPIED DWELLINGS	82.628	84.718	87.711	90.287	92.349	95.486
8	DURABLES	42.809	44.279	46.359	47.895	48.781	50.556
9	GROSS	50.678	52.363	54.438	55.977	56.986	59.035
10	LESS: SERVICES ALLOCATED TO INVESTMENT	1.570	1.622	1.682	1.726	1.793	1.881
11	LESS: SERVICES TO EXP RELATED TO WORK	6.299	6.462	6.397	6.356	6.413	6.598
12	SEMIDURABLES	39.587	40.191	41.082	42.112	43.272	44.615
13	INVENTORIES	.231	.248	.269	.279	.297	.315
14	LABOR SERVICES	336.129	340.042	346.265	350.733	354.981	361.352
15	TOTAL IMPUTED LABOR SERVICES	393.867	401.831	409.149	415.447	425.251	437.082
16	LESS: LABOR SERVICES ALLOCATED TO INVESTMENT	57.739	61.790	62.884	64.713	70.271	75.730
17	INTERMEDIATE PRODUCT OF GOVERNMENT TO CONSUMPTION	30.708	31.658	31.511	32.315	31.982	30.180
18	CAPITAL ACCUMULATION	64.598	67.763	65.229	66.869	69.877	69.175
19	INTANGIBLE AT ORIGINAL COST	64.746	69.327	70.431	72.551	78.611	84.321
20	EDUCATION	60.673	65.180	66.210	68.270	74.255	79.894
21	TEACHING CHILDREN IN HOME	12.966	13.139	13.377	13.520	13.692	13.926
22	OPPORTUNITY COST OF STUDENTS	41.561	45.397	46.203	47.851	53.189	58.369
23	DURABLE SERVICES ALLOCATED TO EDUCATION	1.017	1.050	1.089	1.121	1.163	1.216
24	INTERMEDIATE PRODUCT OF GOVERNMENT TO EDUCATION	4.560	5.010	5.044	5.291	5.692	5.854
25	HEALTH	3.978	4.044	4.121	4.184	4.248	4.331
26	EMPLOYEE TRAINING	.095	.103	.100	.098	.107	.095
27	NET REVALUATIONS	-.148	-1.564	-5.202	-5.682	-8.734	-15.145
28	SERVICES TO EXP REL TO WORK	6.299	6.462	6.397	6.356	6.413	6.598
29	LESS: INTERMEDIATE PRODUCT TRANSFERRED FROM GOVERNMENT	42.290	44.334	44.884	46.622	47.272	46.364
30	LESS: EXPENSES RELATED TO WORK	.528	.543	.546	.570	.586	.591
31	GROSS HOUSEHOLD PRODUCT	514.593	524.845	533.036	542.574	553.470	563.600

TABLE 12. GROSS HOUSEHOLD PRODUCT, BILLIONS OF 1972 DOLLARS, 1946-81

				CREDITS			
		1964	1965	1966	1967	1968	1969
1	CONSUMPTION	547.333	558.253	566.140	577.092	586.623	591.626
2	MARKET (LABOR SERVICES IN HOUSEHOLDS)	6.348	6.143	5.902	5.930	5.644	5.336
3	NONMARKET	510.295	521.408	528.848	538.444	546.838	556.239
4	NET SPACE RENT ON OWNER-OCCUPIED NONFARM DWELLINGS	43.553	46.231	48.900	51.518	53.573	56.574
5	BEA NET SPACE RENT ON OWNER-OCCUPIED NONFARM DWELLINGS	43.553	46.231	48.900	51.518	53.573	56.566
6	SUBSIDIES	.000	.000	.000	.000	.000	.008
7	CAPITAL SERVICES OTHER THAN ON OWNER-OCCUPIED DWELLINGS	98.812	103.425	109.050	115.531	119.755	126.411
8	DURABLES	52.198	54.624	57.681	61.854	64.569	69.706
9	GROSS	60.943	63.538	66.869	71.570	74.615	80.465
10	LESS: SERVICES ALLOCATED TO INVESTMENT	1.977	2.107	2.273	2.452	2.599	2.793
11	LESS: SERVICES TO EXP RELATED TO WORK	6.767	6.807	6.914	7.264	7.447	7.966
12	SEMIDURABLES	46.294	48.468	51.026	53.322	54.855	56.373
13	INVENTORIES	.320	.333	.342	.354	.330	.332
14	LABOR SERVICES	367.931	371.752	370.897	371.395	373.510	373.253
15	TOTAL IMPUTED LABOR SERVICES	449.495	459.127	465.689	482.814	491.300	496.509
16	LESS: LABOR SERVICES ALLOCATED TO INVESTMENT	81.565	87.376	94.792	111.419	117.789	123.256
17	INTERMEDIATE PRODUCT OF GOVERNMENT TO CONSUMPTION	30.690	30.702	31.391	32.718	34.142	30.051
18	CAPITAL ACCUMULATION	95.071	80.016	107.333	117.257	151.194	122.760
19	INTANGIBLE AT ORIGINAL COST	90.755	97.128	105.486	123.988	131.279	136.565
20	EDUCATION	86.216	92.498	100.754	119.170	126.356	131.596
21	TEACHING CHILDREN IN HOME	14.191	14.354	14.526	14.738	15.006	15.180
22	OPPORTUNITY COST OF STUDENTS	63.874	69.482	76.688	93.071	99.113	104.378
23	DURABLE SERVICES ALLOCATED TO EDUCATION	1.275	1.361	1.478	1.622	1.747	1.900
24	INTERMEDIATE PRODUCT OF GOVERNMENT TO EDUCATION	6.359	6.841	7.618	9.323	10.280	9.996
25	HEALTH	4.435	4.516	4.605	4.701	4.802	4.850
26	EMPLOYEE TRAINING	.104	.115	.128	.117	.121	.118
27	NET REVALUATIONS	4.316	-17.112	1.847	-6.731	19.915	-13.805
28	SERVICES TO EXP REL TO WORK	6.767	6.807	6.914	7.264	7.447	7.966
29	LESS: INTERMEDIATE PRODUCT TRANSFERRED FROM GOVERNMENT	48.104	49.545	51.929	56.081	59.696	56.590
30	LESS: EXPENSES RELATED TO WORK	.610	.601	.591	.584	.589	.585
31	GROSS HOUSEHOLD PRODUCT	600.458	594.929	627.868	644.947	684.979	665.178

TABLE 12. GROSS HOUSEHOLD PRODUCT, BILLIONS OF 1972 DOLLARS, 1946-81

		CREDITS					
		1970	1971	1972	1973	1974	1975
1	CONSUMPTION	599.728	607.202	617.461	626.851	636.147	652.722
2	MARKET (LABOR SERVICES IN HOUSEHOLDS)	4.991	4.767	4.631	4.487	3.877	3.615
3	NONMARKET	566.634	577.986	591.520	603.906	617.628	632.508
4	NET SPACE RENT ON OWNER-OCCUPIED NONFARM DWELLINGS	58.353	60.970	64.825	68.433	71.849	74.806
5	BEA NET SPACE RENT ON OWNER-OCCUPIED NONFARM DWELLINGS	58.293	60.789	64.265	68.069	71.644	74.652
6	SUBSIDIES	.060	.181	.560	.364	.205	.154
7	CAPITAL SERVICES OTHER THAN ON OWNER-OCCUPIED DWELLINGS	131.959	136.803	141.227	150.073	157.964	164.311
8	DURABLES	74.326	78.259	82.141	87.558	92.537	96.717
9	GROSS	85.532	89.846	94.100	100.148	104.926	109.421
10	LESS: SERVICES ALLOCATED TO INVESTMENT	3.014	3.244	3.446	3.658	3.892	4.149
11	LESS: SERVICES TO EXP RELATED TO WORK	8.192	8.343	8.513	8.932	8.497	8.556
12	SEMIDURABLES	57.299	58.202	58.751	62.200	65.131	67.289
13	INVENTORIES	.334	.343	.334	.314	.296	.305
14	LABOR SERVICES	376.322	380.213	385.468	385.400	387.815	393.392
15	TOTAL IMPUTED LABOR SERVICES	507.781	520.889	537.081	545.784	545.774	553.604
16	LESS: LABOR SERVICES ALLOCATED TO INVESTMENT	131.460	140.676	151.613	160.384	157.959	160.212
17	INTERMEDIATE PRODUCT OF GOVERNMENT TO CONSUMPTION	28.103	24.449	21.310	18.459	14.642	16.598
18	CAPITAL ACCUMULATION	135.090	140.350	189.750	198.180	169.898	165.337
19	INTANGIBLE AT ORIGINAL COST	145.288	154.577	165.782	174.744	171.249	174.243
20	EDUCATION	140.222	149.411	160.490	169.381	165.832	168.690
21	TEACHING CHILDREN IN HOME	15.437	15.722	16.124	16.321	16.571	16.841
22	OPPORTUNITY COST OF STUDENTS	112.278	121.138	131.577	140.114	137.406	139.326
23	DURABLE SERVICES ALLOCATED TO EDUCATION	2.069	2.250	2.407	2.571	2.750	2.949
24	INTERMEDIATE PRODUCT OF GOVERNMENT TO EDUCATION	10.406	10.295	10.382	10.333	8.953	9.382
25	HEALTH	4.968	5.076	5.195	5.259	5.336	5.495
26	EMPLOYEE TRAINING	.098	.090	.098	.104	.080	.058
27	NET REVALUATIONS	-10.198	-14.227	23.968	23.436	-1.350	-8.906
28	SERVICES TO EXP REL TO WORK	8.192	8.343	8.513	8.932	8.497	8.556
29	LESS: INTERMEDIATE PRODUCT TRANSFERRED FROM GOVERNMENT	56.617	53.781	51.954	50.199	44.750	47.198
30	LESS: EXPENSES RELATED TO WORK	.595	.602	.604	.582	.521	.517
31	GROSS HOUSEHOLD PRODUCT	685.798	701.513	763.166	783.182	769.272	778.900

TABLE 12. GROSS HOUSEHOLD PRODUCT, BILLIONS OF 1972 DOLLARS, 1946-81

		CREDITS					
		1976	1977	1978	1979	1980	1981
1	CONSUMPTION	673.953	690.629	711.119	736.225	765.306	786.071
2	MARKET (LABOR SERVICES IN HOUSEHOLDS)	3.733	3.826	3.771	3.588	3.232	3.136
3	NONMARKET	654.985	671.828	691.785	716.574	745.036	763.901
4	NET SPACE RENT ON OWNER-OCCUPIED NONFARM DWELLINGS	78.035	82.184	86.899	91.697	96.534	102.330
5	BEA NET SPACE RENT ON OWNER-OCCUPIED NONFARM DWELLINGS	77.900	82.079	86.818	91.626	96.449	102.202
6	SUBSIDIES	.134	.105	.081	.071	.085	.128
7	CAPITAL SERVICES OTHER THAN ON OWNER-OCCUPIED DWELLINGS	169.694	176.357	185.429	197.486	209.429	215.327
8	DURABLES	100.439	104.984	110.266	117.504	125.056	127.286
9	GROSS	113.669	118.775	124.940	132.300	139.424	141.493
10	LESS: SERVICES ALLOCATED TO INVESTMENT	4.393	4.637	4.914	5.261	5.633	5.981
11	LESS: SERVICES TO EXP RELATED TO WORK	8.838	9.154	9.760	9.536	8.735	8.227
12	SEMIDURABLES	68.944	71.070	74.867	79.674	84.040	87.687
13	INVENTORIES	.310	.303	.296	.308	.333	.355
14	LABOR SERVICES	407.257	413.287	419.457	427.392	439.072	446.244
15	TOTAL IMPUTED LABOR SERVICES	570.973	578.687	584.923	591.557	601.997	609.658
16	LESS: LABOR SERVICES ALLOCATED TO INVESTMENT	163.716	165.399	165.466	164.166	162.925	163.415
17	INTERMEDIATE PRODUCT OF GOVERNMENT TO CONSUMPTION	15.234	14.975	15.563	16.063	17.038	19.035
18	CAPITAL ACCUMULATION	228.208	229.113	248.320	173.894	161.878	146.598
19	INTANGIBLE AT ORIGINAL COST	177.365	179.282	179.397	178.065	177.113	178.346
20	EDUCATION	171.607	173.410	173.427	171.966	170.829	171.898
21	TEACHING CHILDREN IN HOME	16.276	15.447	14.687	13.986	13.348	12.651
22	OPPORTUNITY COST OF STUDENTS	143.235	145.676	146.444	145.769	145.044	146.134
23	DURABLE SERVICES ALLOCATED TO EDUCATION	3.144	3.349	3.583	3.870	4.182	4.482
24	INTERMEDIATE PRODUCT OF GOVERNMENT TO EDUCATION	9.082	9.119	8.847	8.375	8.159	8.499
25	HEALTH	5.684	5.793	5.889	6.025	6.226	6.392
26	EMPLOYEE TRAINING	.074	.079	.081	.074	.058	.056
27	NET REVALUATIONS	50.843	49.830	68.923	-4.171	-15.235	-31.748
28	SERVICES TO EXP REL TO WORK	8.838	9.154	9.760	9.536	8.735	8.227
29	LESS: INTERMEDIATE PRODUCT TRANSFERRED FROM GOVERNMENT	46.164	46.891	46.509	45.532	46.011	48.745
30	LESS: EXPENSES RELATED TO WORK	.529	.568	.562	.518	.465	.452
31	GROSS HOUSEHOLD PRODUCT	864.304	881.437	922.128	873.605	889.443	891.698

261

TABLE 12. GROSS HOUSEHOLD PRODUCT, BILLIONS OF 1972 DOLLARS, 1946-81

		CREDITS					
		PERCENT PER ANNUM RATES OF GROWTH CONSTANT DOLLARS					
		1946-56	1956-66	1966-71	1971-76	1976-81	1946-81
1	CONSUMPTION	1.098	1.936	1.410	2.108	3.126	1.814
2	MARKET (LABOR SERVICES IN HOUSEHOLDS)	1.690	-1.490	-4.182	-4.772	-3.425	-1.742
3	NONMARKET	1.832	2.079	1.793	2.533	3.124	2.181
4	NET SPACE RENT ON OWNER-OCCUPIED NONFARM DWELLINGS	8.825	6.398	4.511	5.059	5.571	6.501
5	BEA NET SPACE RENT ON OWNER-OCCUPIED NONFARM DWELLINGS	8.825	6.398	4.448	5.086	5.581	6.497
6	SUBSIDIES	N.A.	N.A.	N.A.	-5.846	-.985	N.A.
7	CAPITAL SERVICES OTHER THAN ON OWNER-OCCUPIED DWELLINGS	4.903	3.563	4.639	4.403	4.879	4.406
8	DURABLES	10.627	4.089	6.292	5.117	4.852	6.494
9	GROSS	10.437	3.721	6.085	4.816	4.476	6.207
10	LESS: SERVICES ALLOCATED TO INVESTMENT	6.048	4.566	7.373	6.249	6.367	5.884
11	LESS: SERVICES TO EXP RELATED TO WORK	10.554	.916	3.829	1.158	-1.423	3.690
12	SEMIDURABLES	1.297	2.993	2.666	3.446	4.927	2.796
13	INVENTORIES	4.481	5.053	.029	-1.964	2.709	2.802
14	LABOR SERVICES	.873	1.256	.497	1.384	1.845	1.140
15	TOTAL IMPUTED LABOR SERVICES	1.196	2.004	2.266	1.853	1.320	1.690
16	LESS: LABOR SERVICES ALLOCATED TO INVESTMENT	3.418	5.688	8.216	3.080	-.037	4.182
17	INTERMEDIATE PRODUCT OF GOVERNMENT TO CONSUMPTION	-5.745	.462	-4.876	-9.027	4.555	-2.944
18	CAPITAL ACCUMULATION	N.A.	6.335	5.511	10.211	-8.471	N.A.
19	INTANGIBLE AT ORIGINAL COST	2.661	5.619	7.942	2.789	.110	3.886
20	EDUCATION	2.849	5.841	8.199	2.809	.034	4.030
21	TEACHING CHILDREN IN HOME	.912	1.344	1.595	.695	-4.914	.246
22	OPPORTUNITY COST OF STUDENTS	4.734	7.086	9.575	3.408	.402	5.253
23	DURABLE SERVICES ALLOCATED TO EDUCATION	6.783	4.730	8.768	6.920	7.349	6.572
24	INTERMEDIATE PRODUCT OF GOVERNMENT TO EDUCATION	-2.735	5.967	6.208	-2.478	-1.318	1.183
25	HEALTH	.614	1.778	1.967	2.290	2.375	1.628
26	EMPLOYEE TRAINING	-7.677	3.341	-6.713	-3.909	-5.480	-3.643
27	NET REVALUATIONS	N.A.	N.A.	N.A.	N.A.	N.A.	N.A.
28	SERVICES TO EXP REL TO WORK	10.554	.916	3.829	1.158	-1.423	3.690
29	LESS: INTERMEDIATE PRODUCT TRANSFERRED FROM GOVERNMENT	-4.310	2.583	.703	-3.008	1.094	-.709
30	LESS: EXPENSES RELATED TO WORK	6.766	1.818	.384	-2.542	-3.099	1.636
31	GROSS HOUSEHOLD PRODUCT	3.391	2.489	2.243	4.262	.626	2.693

TABLE 13. TOTAL CAPITAL, BILLIONS OF DOLLARS, YEAR-END TOTALS, 1945-81

		1945	1946	1947	1948	1949	1950
1	TOTAL CAPITAL	1195.830	1281.461	1402.922	1526.335	1608.593	1686.491
2	BUSINESS	331.055	393.718	455.805	494.077	497.256	559.925
3	TANGIBLE	319.671	381.521	441.744	478.219	479.984	540.497
4	LAND	115.207	124.926	132.219	136.714	140.518	155.112
5	STRUCTURES AND EQUIPMENT	90.072	114.476	143.398	165.487	174.894	195.232
6	RESIDENTIAL	63.337	71.427	82.792	88.300	86.087	94.050
7	INVENTORIES	51.055	70.692	83.335	87.718	78.485	96.102
8	INTANGIBLE (R&D)	11.384	12.197	14.061	15.858	17.272	19.428
9	NONPROFIT	11.789	14.050	16.542	17.583	17.914	20.092
10	LAND	2.728	3.125	3.501	3.604	3.716	4.108
11	STRUCTURES AND EQUIPMENT	5.036	6.406	7.855	8.518	8.932	10.302
12	RESIDENTIAL	4.025	4.519	5.186	5.461	5.266	5.683
13	GOVERNMENT	245.937	237.477	225.499	207.630	192.395	198.623
14	LAND	21.949	23.798	25.491	26.484	27.275	30.445
15	STRUCTURES AND EQUIPMENT	161.077	157.945	152.324	143.982	133.720	138.679
16	RESIDENTIAL	2.085	2.426	2.492	2.100	1.904	1.997
17	INVENTORIES	58.686	50.852	42.392	31.923	26.092	23.771
18	INTANGIBLE (R&D)	2.140	2.456	2.800	3.141	3.404	3.731
19	GOVERNMENT ENTERPRISE	17.537	19.494	23.693	27.168	29.329	31.694
20	STRUCTURES AND EQUIPMENT	15.191	17.318	21.137	23.606	24.177	25.803
21	RESIDENTIAL	1.073	1.335	1.718	1.900	2.116	2.595
22	INVENTORIES	1.273	.841	.838	1.662	3.036	3.296
23	HOUSEHOLD	589.512	616.722	681.383	779.877	871.699	876.157
24	TANGIBLE	154.280	178.784	215.267	245.615	261.193	304.993
25	LAND	11.681	12.485	14.816	16.078	16.835	20.571
26	RESIDENTIAL	67.779	81.386	101.844	117.907	122.297	145.322
27	DURABLES	48.600	54.956	65.706	76.346	86.465	103.553
28	SEMIDURABLES	24.105	27.540	30.200	32.426	32.773	32.616
29	INVENTORIES	2.115	2.417	2.701	2.858	2.823	2.931
30	INTANGIBLE (HUMAN CAPITAL)	435.232	437.938	466.116	534.262	610.506	571.164

		1951	1952	1953	1954	1955	1956
1	TOTAL CAPITAL	1829.048	2019.773	2133.024	2313.184	2411.188	2681.545
2	BUSINESS	614.352	635.966	655.991	676.031	724.778	792.898
3	TANGIBLE	592.155	610.683	626.374	642.470	685.994	747.389
4	LAND	167.201	173.793	176.063	184.494	197.422	216.627
5	STRUCTURES AND EQUIPMENT	217.464	230.576	243.004	251.945	274.503	305.271
6	RESIDENTIAL	98.783	100.119	100.201	101.600	104.265	106.157
7	INVENTORIES	108.706	106.195	107.106	104.431	109.805	119.334
8	INTANGIBLE (R&D)	22.197	25.283	29.617	33.561	38.784	45.509
9	NONPROFIT	22.349	23.624	24.325	26.418	29.075	32.580
10	LAND	4.535	4.916	5.018	6.049	6.770	7.955
11	STRUCTURES AND EQUIPMENT	11.881	12.725	13.325	14.290	16.031	18.175
12	RESIDENTIAL	5.934	5.983	5.982	6.079	6.273	6.450
13	GOVERNMENT	217.858	238.012	262.216	283.526	310.744	338.097
14	LAND	32.864	34.500	39.000	41.700	48.100	54.000
15	STRUCTURES AND EQUIPMENT	153.548	166.961	176.917	184.073	199.443	219.471
16	RESIDENTIAL	1.762	1.785	1.800	1.814	1.853	1.903
17	INVENTORIES	25.492	30.116	39.257	50.046	54.608	54.970
18	INTANGIBLE (R&D)	4.192	4.650	5.242	5.893	6.740	7.753
19	GOVERNMENT ENTERPRISE	33.850	36.537	41.810	45.085	49.253	55.165
20	STRUCTURES AND EQUIPMENT	28.598	30.704	32.233	34.028	37.475	41.817
21	RESIDENTIAL	3.273	3.902	4.324	4.596	4.851	5.124
22	INVENTORIES	1.979	1.931	5.253	6.461	6.927	8.224
23	HOUSEHOLD	940.639	1085.634	1148.682	1282.124	1297.338	1462.805
24	TANGIBLE	342.890	370.169	393.526	416.820	454.267	493.720
25	LAND	22.339	25.027	27.820	31.107	37.842	44.450
26	RESIDENTIAL	163.819	176.806	187.842	202.783	223.137	240.487
27	DURABLES	119.379	128.795	137.944	142.741	151.940	165.812
28	SEMIDURABLES	34.078	36.095	36.378	36.590	37.603	39.040
29	INVENTORIES	3.275	3.446	3.542	3.599	3.745	3.931
30	INTANGIBLE (HUMAN CAPITAL)	597.749	715.465	755.156	865.304	843.071	969.085

263

TABLE 13. TOTAL CAPITAL, BILLIONS OF DOLLARS, YEAR-END TOTALS, 1945-81

		1957	1958	1959	1960	1961	1962
1	TOTAL CAPITAL	2885.104	3041.673	3206.406	3350.249	3480.226	3679.164
2	BUSINESS	835.273	875.860	922.187	957.156	994.050	1043.391
3	TANGIBLE	782.577	815.301	852.859	878.974	906.586	945.662
4	LAND	226.799	245.839	264.615	276.722	291.235	307.328
5	STRUCTURES AND EQUIPMENT	325.328	336.192	348.185	356.992	366.312	379.626
6	RESIDENTIAL	106.257	106.636	108.086	109.294	111.110	114.105
7	INVENTORIES	124.193	126.634	131.974	135.966	137.930	144.603
8	INTANGIBLE (R&D)	52.696	60.559	69.328	78.182	87.464	97.729
9	NONPROFIT	38.350	40.152	42.078	40.957	44.284	48.469
10	LAND	12.501	12.849	13.306	10.736	11.915	13.436
11	STRUCTURES AND EQUIPMENT	19.327	20.648	21.930	23.225	25.170	27.402
12	RESIDENTIAL	6.522	6.655	6.841	6.996	7.198	7.631
13	GOVERNMENT	353.693	365.709	378.570	390.731	410.026	432.653
14	LAND	60.900	66.600	73.000	79.000	86.900	94.000
15	STRUCTURES AND EQUIPMENT	227.777	232.962	238.920	245.600	257.450	271.588
16	RESIDENTIAL	2.016	2.348	2.796	3.082	3.438	3.751
17	INVENTORIES	54.092	53.647	52.303	50.087	47.799	47.183
18	INTANGIBLE (R&D)	8.908	10.152	11.551	12.962	14.439	16.131
19	GOVERNMENT ENTERPRISE	57.674	62.222	63.426	66.683	67.667	71.753
20	STRUCTURES AND EQUIPMENT	44.756	46.966	49.015	50.775	53.283	56.015
21	RESIDENTIAL	5.371	5.787	6.198	6.568	7.089	7.870
22	INVENTORIES	7.547	9.469	8.213	9.340	7.295	7.868
23	HOUSEHOLD	1600.114	1697.730	1800.145	1894.722	1964.199	2082.898
24	TANGIBLE	519.872	545.244	578.665	600.406	621.383	648.184
25	LAND	49.053	55.173	65.073	67.669	73.118	79.674
26	RESIDENTIAL	251.885	263.744	279.227	292.272	303.780	316.715
27	DURABLES	174.736	181.449	187.882	192.384	194.982	200.319
28	SEMIDURABLES	40.033	40.544	41.956	43.399	44.692	46.483
29	INVENTORIES	4.165	4.334	4.527	4.682	4.811	4.993
30	INTANGIBLE (HUMAN CAPITAL)	1080.242	1152.486	1221.480	1294.316	1342.816	1434.714

		1963	1964	1965	1966	1967	1968
1	TOTAL CAPITAL	3875.471	4126.391	4454.742	4845.671	5252.536	5759.475
2	BUSINESS	1088.320	1150.181	1238.686	1344.103	1439.194	1548.444
3	TANGIBLE	979.514	1029.303	1104.265	1195.273	1274.611	1366.597
4	LAND	318.189	333.766	355.586	373.565	390.811	400.187
5	STRUCTURES AND EQUIPMENT	395.070	416.949	451.454	499.659	544.926	599.256
6	RESIDENTIAL	115.864	122.355	126.705	134.659	139.442	153.671
7	INVENTORIES	150.391	156.233	170.520	187.390	199.433	213.483
8	INTANGIBLE (R&D)	108.806	120.878	134.421	148.830	164.583	181.847
9	NONPROFIT	51.428	55.509	60.876	66.969	72.567	77.892
10	LAND	13.774	14.684	16.063	17.208	18.368	18.250
11	STRUCTURES AND EQUIPMENT	29.817	32.353	35.779	39.893	43.797	48.271
12	RESIDENTIAL	7.837	8.472	9.034	9.868	10.402	11.371
13	GOVERNMENT	459.395	487.212	516.884	555.726	597.595	645.180
14	LAND	101.900	110.100	117.400	127.400	135.800	144.200
15	STRUCTURES AND EQUIPMENT	286.877	302.842	323.567	349.245	376.548	411.467
16	RESIDENTIAL	3.836	3.921	4.003	4.215	4.287	4.647
17	INVENTORIES	48.693	49.975	49.082	49.386	52.854	53.943
18	INTANGIBLE (R&D)	18.089	20.374	22.832	25.480	28.106	30.923
19	GOVERNMENT ENTERPRISE	74.339	78.062	83.349	86.040	91.699	102.923
20	STRUCTURES AND EQUIPMENT	58.983	62.983	67.685	72.511	78.516	86.990
21	RESIDENTIAL	8.105	8.598	8.969	9.813	10.459	11.711
22	INVENTORIES	7.251	6.481	6.695	3.716	2.724	4.222
23	HOUSEHOLD	2201.989	2355.427	2554.947	2792.833	3051.481	3385.036
24	TANGIBLE	673.195	717.920	759.975	824.299	882.145	985.917
25	LAND	84.720	92.824	101.769	109.960	118.043	135.302
26	RESIDENTIAL	324.555	347.102	365.063	394.443	416.089	466.041
27	DURABLES	210.616	221.392	233.137	255.279	279.593	310.542
28	SEMIDURABLES	48.135	51.160	54.182	58.307	61.875	66.959
29	INVENTORIES	5.169	5.442	5.824	6.310	6.545	7.073
30	INTANGIBLE (HUMAN CAPITAL)	1528.794	1637.507	1794.972	1968.534	2169.336	2399.119

264

TABLE 13. TOTAL CAPITAL, BILLIONS OF DOLLARS, YEAR-END TOTALS, 1945-81

		1969	1970	1971	1972	1973	1974
1	TOTAL CAPITAL	6334.720	6917.751	7526.113	8304.684	9374.826	10824.621
2	BUSINESS	1686.605	1809.021	1931.197	2120.633	2458.008	2899.389
3	TANGIBLE	1487.119	1592.648	1698.876	1871.071	2186.437	2601.356
4	LAND	412.829	426.743	440.775	495.820	588.066	663.391
5	STRUCTURES AND EQUIPMENT	672.987	744.842	804.846	872.056	993.089	1230.692
6	RESIDENTIAL	166.729	177.108	192.475	214.475	247.546	274.922
7	INVENTORIES	234.574	243.955	260.780	288.720	357.736	432.351
8	INTANGIBLE (R&D)	199.486	216.373	232.321	249.562	271.571	298.033
9	NONPROFIT	87.775	95.571	101.034	110.339	124.210	147.804
10	LAND	19.689	20.694	20.188	21.985	23.860	27.754
11	STRUCTURES AND EQUIPMENT	56.049	62.443	67.864	74.662	85.334	103.967
12	RESIDENTIAL	12.037	12.434	12.982	13.692	15.016	16.083
13	GOVERNMENT	702.951	759.425	808.832	875.901	999.268	1146.218
14	LAND	150.200	156.549	161.751	183.377	216.997	246.734
15	STRUCTURES AND EQUIPMENT	453.181	499.605	539.940	583.158	661.835	759.401
16	RESIDENTIAL	4.881	5.201	5.869	6.987	8.857	10.350
17	INVENTORIES	60.631	60.610	60.413	58.267	63.757	77.087
18	INTANGIBLE (R&D)	34.058	37.460	40.859	44.112	47.822	52.646
19	GOVERNMENT ENTERPRISE	115.673	127.527	142.192	156.002	179.351	211.624
20	STRUCTURES AND EQUIPMENT	97.441	109.667	121.753	134.247	156.101	186.554
21	RESIDENTIAL	13.002	14.366	16.233	18.263	21.298	23.868
22	INVENTORIES	5.230	3.494	4.206	3.492	1.952	1.202
23	HOUSEHOLD	3741.716	4126.207	4542.858	5041.809	5613.989	6419.586
24	TANGIBLE	1072.749	1151.229	1241.732	1384.195	1586.372	1804.297
25	LAND	144.261	153.723	163.776	186.376	221.359	256.331
26	RESIDENTIAL	508.505	545.016	602.553	680.490	794.051	898.312
27	DURABLES	340.076	368.307	390.032	421.276	465.364	535.434
28	SEMIDURABLES	72.301	75.941	80.382	86.818	95.355	102.584
29	INVENTORIES	7.606	8.242	8.592	9.235	10.243	11.636
30	INTANGIBLE (HUMAN CAPITAL)	2668.967	2974.978	3301.126	3657.614	4027.617	4615.289

		1975	1976	1977	1978	1979	1980
1	TOTAL CAPITAL	11901.351	13193.049	14821.115	16845.460	19064.608	21503.239
2	BUSINESS	3082.331	3441.140	3833.156	4391.504	5024.978	5625.531
3	TANGIBLE	2759.895	3095.112	3458.232	3980.564	4571.023	5121.779
4	LAND	748.840	863.807	965.113	1127.043	1294.044	1443.535
5	STRUCTURES AND EQUIPMENT	1336.632	1434.605	1606.208	1823.916	2094.131	2377.514
6	RESIDENTIAL	292.875	323.080	366.007	429.140	472.706	515.349
7	INVENTORIES	381.549	473.620	520.904	600.464	710.142	785.381
8	INTANGIBLE (R&D)	322.436	346.028	374.924	410.940	453.955	503.752
9	NONPROFIT	147.509	154.004	170.329	192.471	214.707	234.242
10	LAND	26.541	27.827	30.046	33.854	37.154	39.680
11	STRUCTURES AND EQUIPMENT	104.193	108.172	120.618	136.383	154.087	169.951
12	RESIDENTIAL	16.774	18.005	19.665	22.234	23.466	24.611
13	GOVERNMENT	1235.185	1326.604	1459.170	1650.819	1883.519	2115.934
14	LAND	273.859	315.660	353.655	417.860	475.848	538.805
15	STRUCTURES AND EQUIPMENT	814.024	857.343	941.783	1049.991	1196.333	1344.735
16	RESIDENTIAL	11.019	12.095	13.692	16.217	17.445	18.832
17	INVENTORIES	78.358	79.846	84.536	96.303	117.495	130.867
18	INTANGIBLE (R&D)	57.925	61.660	65.504	70.448	76.398	82.695
19	GOVERNMENT ENTERPRISE	234.995	254.521	286.952	327.160	375.598	426.559
20	STRUCTURES AND EQUIPMENT	208.474	225.532	250.376	283.613	330.376	375.917
21	RESIDENTIAL	24.765	26.572	29.722	34.806	37.961	41.581
22	INVENTORIES	1.756	2.417	6.854	8.741	7.261	9.061
23	HOUSEHOLD	7201.331	8016.780	9071.508	10283.507	11565.806	13100.973
24	TANGIBLE	1958.113	2193.184	2495.593	2939.876	3282.034	3655.961
25	LAND	276.257	320.523	362.904	443.716	496.093	585.836
26	RESIDENTIAL	973.777	1104.022	1286.657	1545.989	1729.014	1904.433
27	DURABLES	585.020	636.500	702.268	791.020	882.712	978.295
28	SEMIDURABLES	110.310	118.307	128.812	142.700	155.289	166.005
29	INVENTORIES	12.749	13.832	14.952	16.451	18.926	21.392
30	INTANGIBLE (HUMAN CAPITAL)	5243.218	5823.596	6575.915	7343.631	8283.772	9445.012

265

TABLE 13. TOTAL CAPITAL, BILLIONS OF DOLLARS, YEAR-END TOTALS, 1945-81

		1981
1	TOTAL CAPITAL	23746.352
2	BUSINESS	6085.898
3	TANGIBLE	5528.925
4	LAND	1465.100
5	STRUCTURES AND EQUIPMENT	2668.378
6	RESIDENTIAL	557.659
7	INVENTORIES	837.788
8	INTANGIBLE (R&D)	556.973
9	NONPROFIT	248.232
10	LAND	41.664
11	STRUCTURES AND EQUIPMENT	180.823
12	RESIDENTIAL	25.745
13	GOVERNMENT	2309.899
14	LAND	552.565
15	STRUCTURES AND EQUIPMENT	1502.788
16	RESIDENTIAL	20.040
17	INVENTORIES	145.047
18	INTANGIBLE (R&D)	89.459
19	GOVERNMENT ENTERPRISE	476.314
20	STRUCTURES AND EQUIPMENT	421.803
21	RESIDENTIAL	45.232
22	INVENTORIES	9.279
23	HOUSEHOLD	14626.009
24	TANGIBLE	3949.716
25	LAND	615.128
26	RESIDENTIAL	2078.827
27	DURABLES	1052.730
28	SEMIDURABLES	179.589
29	INVENTORIES	23.442
30	INTANGIBLE (HUMAN CAPITAL)	10676.293

		PERCENT PER ANNUM RATES OF GROWTH CURRENT DOLLARS					
		1945-55	1955-65	1965-70	1970-75	1975-81	1945-81
1	TOTAL CAPITAL	7.265	6.331	9.201	11.462	12.202	8.656
2	BUSINESS	8.151	5.506	7.869	11.247	12.006	8.423
3	TANGIBLE	7.935	4.876	7.599	11.623	12.277	8.240
4	LAND	5.534	6.061	3.716	11.904	11.836	7.319
5	STRUCTURES AND EQUIPMENT	11.788	5.101	10.533	12.406	12.212	9.870
6	RESIDENTIAL	5.111	1.968	6.927	10.583	11.331	6.229
7	INVENTORIES	7.959	4.500	7.425	9.357	14.007	8.082
8	INTANGIBLE (R&D)	13.041	13.235	9.988	8.305	9.538	11.412
9	NONPROFIT	9.447	7.670	9.440	9.068	9.062	8.833
10	LAND	9.517	9.024	5.197	5.103	7.805	7.867
11	STRUCTURES AND EQUIPMENT	12.276	8.359	11.782	10.783	9.623	10.459
12	RESIDENTIAL	4.537	3.715	6.597	6.171	7.401	5.290
13	GOVERNMENT	2.367	5.220	7.999	10.217	10.997	6.420
14	LAND	8.162	9.333	5.925	11.834	12.411	9.374
15	STRUCTURES AND EQUIPMENT	2.159	4.958	9.077	10.256	10.758	6.400
16	RESIDENTIAL	-1.173	8.007	5.376	16.201	10.482	6.488
17	INVENTORIES	-.718	-1.061	4.310	5.271	10.808	2.545
18	INTANGIBLE (R&D)	12.157	12.977	10.409	9.109	7.513	10.926
19	GOVERNMENT ENTERPRISE	10.879	5.401	8.878	13.003	12.497	9.605
20	STRUCTURES AND EQUIPMENT	9.450	6.090	10.133	13.709	12.463	9.673
21	RESIDENTIAL	16.285	6.339	9.880	11.507	10.561	10.952
22	INVENTORIES	18.460	-.340	-12.196	-12.855	31.976	5.673
23	HOUSEHOLD	8.207	7.012	10.061	11.782	12.534	9.330
24	TANGIBLE	11.404	5.281	8.661	11.208	12.406	9.425
25	LAND	12.473	10.399	8.599	12.438	14.273	11.640
26	RESIDENTIAL	12.654	5.046	8.345	12.308	13.473	9.976
27	DURABLES	12.074	4.374	9.577	9.696	10.287	8.919
28	SEMIDURABLES	4.547	3.720	6.985	7.753	8.462	5.737
29	INVENTORIES	5.880	4.515	7.192	9.116	10.684	6.910
30	INTANGIBLE (HUMAN CAPITAL)	6.835	7.850	10.633	12.001	12.582	9.296

266

TABLE 14. TOTAL CAPITAL, BILLIONS OF 1972 DOLLARS, YEAR-END TOTALS, 1945-81

		1945	1946	1947	1948	1949	1950
1	TOTAL CAPITAL	2941.658	2907.986	2933.743	2998.310	3072.465	3211.690
2	BUSINESS	805.285	825.286	846.027	880.644	899.552	945.607
3	TANGIBLE	786.132	804.133	822.483	854.433	871.173	914.845
4	LAND	281.715	267.422	257.912	259.248	265.003	280.365
5	STRUCTURES AND EQUIPMENT	249.264	270.689	299.251	323.860	338.717	354.990
6	RESIDENTIAL	150.953	149.662	149.204	149.749	150.292	151.778
7	INVENTORIES	104.200	116.360	116.116	121.576	117.161	127.712
8	INTANGIBLE (R&D)	19.153	21.153	23.544	26.211	28.379	30.762
9	NONPROFIT	32.528	32.574	32.854	33.462	34.697	36.608
10	LAND	6.670	6.689	6.830	6.834	7.009	7.425
11	STRUCTURES AND EQUIPMENT	16.234	16.378	16.637	17.318	18.443	19.952
12	RESIDENTIAL	9.624	9.507	9.387	9.311	9.246	9.231
13	GOVERNMENT	598.009	508.378	439.253	390.705	368.520	363.766
14	LAND	53.672	50.943	49.724	50.221	51.438	55.029
15	STRUCTURES AND EQUIPMENT	450.233	376.531	322.441	287.639	271.295	266.109
16	RESIDENTIAL	5.189	5.289	4.663	3.705	3.461	3.352
17	INVENTORIES	86.129	72.515	58.979	45.310	38.123	34.678
18	INTANGIBLE (R&D)	2.786	3.100	3.446	3.830	4.203	4.598
19	GOVERNMENT ENTERPRISE	51.025	50.148	52.992	56.260	60.231	61.837
20	STRUCTURES AND EQUIPMENT	46.183	46.255	49.030	51.110	52.438	53.849
21	RESIDENTIAL	2.568	2.810	3.110	3.240	3.715	4.218
22	INVENTORIES	2.274	1.083	.852	1.910	4.078	3.770
23	HOUSEHOLD	1454.811	1491.600	1562.617	1637.238	1709.465	1803.871
24	TANGIBLE	320.047	335.883	360.435	389.040	416.525	461.590
25	LAND	28.563	26.726	28.901	30.488	31.749	37.182
26	RESIDENTIAL	161.948	171.059	184.123	200.705	214.343	235.680
27	DURABLES	77.357	84.046	94.109	104.919	117.133	133.989
28	SEMIDURABLES	47.633	49.233	48.567	48.201	48.500	49.816
29	INVENTORIES	4.546	4.819	4.735	4.727	4.800	4.923
30	INTANGIBLE (HUMAN CAPITAL)	1134.764	1155.717	1202.182	1248.198	1292.940	1342.281

		1951	1952	1953	1954	1955	1956
1	TOTAL CAPITAL	3355.596	3503.788	3660.339	3806.806	3989.205	4165.896
2	BUSINESS	989.791	1018.557	1040.923	1065.553	1109.889	1162.404
3	TANGIBLE	956.224	981.233	998.651	1018.094	1055.972	1100.206
4	LAND	290.760	297.744	297.479	306.494	319.375	339.221
5	STRUCTURES AND EQUIPMENT	372.298	386.359	402.748	415.496	432.592	451.253
6	RESIDENTIAL	151.729	151.381	151.186	151.058	151.235	151.154
7	INVENTORIES	141.437	145.749	147.238	145.046	152.770	158.578
8	INTANGIBLE (R&D)	33.567	37.324	42.272	47.459	53.917	62.198
9	NONPROFIT	38.452	40.106	41.433	44.794	47.499	50.952
10	LAND	7.886	8.422	8.479	10.049	10.953	12.457
11	STRUCTURES AND EQUIPMENT	21.390	22.575	23.861	25.643	27.386	29.249
12	RESIDENTIAL	9.176	9.109	9.093	9.103	9.161	9.246
13	GOVERNMENT	375.559	407.581	445.865	472.102	491.886	508.535
14	LAND	57.150	59.106	65.895	69.275	77.813	84.560
15	STRUCTURES AND EQUIPMENT	271.613	290.843	309.197	324.085	334.963	343.717
16	RESIDENTIAL	2.827	2.816	2.811	2.765	2.734	2.754
17	INVENTORIES	38.877	49.144	61.512	68.675	67.985	67.878
18	INTANGIBLE (R&D)	5.092	5.672	6.450	7.302	8.391	9.626
19	GOVERNMENT ENTERPRISE	62.918	66.119	73.968	80.016	86.249	91.079
20	STRUCTURES AND EQUIPMENT	55.667	57.623	60.059	63.368	66.772	69.975
21	RESIDENTIAL	5.064	5.945	6.577	6.886	7.086	7.347
22	INVENTORIES	2.187	2.551	7.332	9.762	12.391	13.757
23	HOUSEHOLD	1888.877	1971.425	2058.150	2144.340	2253.681	2352.926
24	TANGIBLE	493.029	523.226	555.631	587.327	633.608	671.389
25	LAND	38.847	42.876	47.005	51.677	61.218	69.605
26	RESIDENTIAL	252.932	268.766	285.112	303.204	325.327	343.918
27	DURABLES	146.090	154.976	165.857	174.531	187.461	196.365
28	SEMIDURABLES	50.083	51.366	52.249	52.450	53.883	55.582
29	INVENTORIES	5.077	5.242	5.408	5.465	5.719	5.919
30	INTANGIBLE (HUMAN CAPITAL)	1395.848	1448.199	1502.519	1557.013	1620.073	1681.537

267

TABLE 14. TOTAL CAPITAL, BILLIONS OF 1972 DOLLARS, YEAR-END TOTALS, 1945-81

		1957	1958	1959	1960	1961	1962
1	TOTAL CAPITAL	4323.016	4479.721	4671.504	4841.558	5023.345	5238.914
2	BUSINESS	1197.954	1236.800	1288.498	1331.159	1375.158	1430.262
3	TANGIBLE	1126.744	1155.942	1197.116	1229.010	1262.237	1305.899
4	LAND	346.337	367.912	388.283	400.959	416.228	432.005
5	STRUCTURES AND EQUIPMENT	469.183	478.296	490.501	504.889	517.455	533.779
6	RESIDENTIAL	151.131	151.478	153.032	154.317	156.735	160.454
7	INVENTORIES	160.093	158.255	165.301	168.845	171.818	179.661
8	INTANGIBLE (R&D)	71.210	80.858	91.382	102.149	112.921	124.363
9	NONPROFIT	59.678	62.264	65.089	63.841	68.289	73.878
10	LAND	19.090	19.229	19.525	15.556	17.029	18.886
11	STRUCTURES AND EQUIPMENT	31.241	33.511	35.801	38.329	41.033	44.192
12	RESIDENTIAL	9.347	9.524	9.762	9.956	10.228	10.800
13	GOVERNMENT	525.621	543.264	561.315	580.288	603.711	629.364
14	LAND	92.998	99.671	107.117	114.468	124.196	132.134
15	STRUCTURES AND EQUIPMENT	350.812	360.075	370.568	382.349	396.590	411.334
16	RESIDENTIAL	2.915	3.397	4.042	4.458	4.997	5.479
17	INVENTORIES	67.913	67.621	65.452	63.223	60.371	60.948
18	INTANGIBLE (R&D)	10.983	12.500	14.136	15.790	17.557	19.469
19	GOVERNMENT ENTERPRISE	91.760	95.822	98.009	102.194	103.464	108.090
20	STRUCTURES AND EQUIPMENT	72.780	75.255	77.882	80.542	83.706	86.774
21	RESIDENTIAL	7.699	8.285	8.849	9.350	10.078	11.142
22	INVENTORIES	11.281	12.282	11.278	12.302	9.680	10.174
23	HOUSEHOLD	2448.002	2541.572	2658.594	2764.076	2872.723	2997.320
24	TANGIBLE	700.534	727.303	768.749	795.508	821.886	855.211
25	LAND	74.907	82.570	95.485	98.050	104.499	111.996
26	RESIDENTIAL	360.151	376.446	397.431	414.751	430.620	447.412
27	DURABLES	203.285	205.768	211.469	216.951	219.732	226.539
28	SEMIDURABLES	56.133	56.400	57.999	59.283	60.450	62.499
29	INVENTORIES	6.058	6.119	6.365	6.473	6.585	6.765
30	INTANGIBLE (HUMAN CAPITAL)	1747.468	1814.269	1889.845	1968.568	2050.837	2142.109

		1963	1964	1965	1966	1967	1968
1	TOTAL CAPITAL	5462.480	5714.704	5996.954	6299.961	6596.460	6899.748
2	BUSINESS	1481.426	1542.452	1622.357	1704.931	1771.479	1821.784
3	TANGIBLE	1344.888	1393.538	1460.697	1530.027	1583.490	1620.726
4	LAND	440.583	453.702	470.601	479.483	483.676	472.671
5	STRUCTURES AND EQUIPMENT	551.423	574.891	609.116	649.951	684.993	720.586
6	RESIDENTIAL	165.699	170.671	174.919	177.727	179.755	183.399
7	INVENTORIES	187.184	194.274	206.061	222.866	235.065	244.070
8	INTANGIBLE (R&D)	136.538	148.914	161.660	174.904	187.989	201.058
9	NONPROFIT	77.463	82.090	87.581	92.431	96.415	98.121
10	LAND	19.073	19.960	21.259	22.087	22.732	21.556
11	STRUCTURES AND EQUIPMENT	47.107	50.240	53.785	57.263	60.216	62.954
12	RESIDENTIAL	11.283	11.889	12.538	13.081	13.467	13.612
13	GOVERNMENT	659.797	686.108	707.785	737.047	764.679	786.546
14	LAND	141.097	149.664	155.373	163.522	168.069	170.318
15	STRUCTURES AND EQUIPMENT	428.263	444.635	461.288	480.523	498.272	515.839
16	RESIDENTIAL	5.760	5.717	5.758	5.773	5.700	5.654
17	INVENTORIES	62.970	61.790	58.419	57.669	60.570	60.331
18	INTANGIBLE (R&D)	21.707	24.302	26.947	29.560	32.068	34.404
19	GOVERNMENT ENTERPRISE	111.539	115.331	119.278	120.273	124.058	131.787
20	STRUCTURES AND EQUIPMENT	90.285	94.461	98.669	102.654	107.114	112.648
21	RESIDENTIAL	11.673	12.069	12.449	13.007	13.540	14.017
22	INVENTORIES	9.581	8.801	8.160	4.612	3.404	5.122
23	HOUSEHOLD	3132.255	3288.724	3459.952	3645.279	3839.829	4061.509
24	TANGIBLE	891.519	937.016	987.511	1036.338	1078.646	1139.286
25	LAND	117.308	126.180	134.686	141.137	146.093	159.809
26	RESIDENTIAL	466.430	486.165	505.755	522.103	537.934	557.436
27	DURABLES	236.545	249.649	268.326	289.948	309.368	333.973
28	SEMIDURABLES	64.332	67.849	71.232	75.315	77.266	79.749
29	INVENTORIES	6.904	7.173	7.512	7.835	7.985	8.319
30	INTANGIBLE (HUMAN CAPITAL)	2240.736	2351.708	2472.441	2608.941	2761.183	2922.223

TABLE 14. TOTAL CAPITAL, BILLIONS OF 1972 DOLLARS, YEAR-END TOTALS, 1945-81

		1969	1970	1971	1972	1973	1974
1	TOTAL CAPITAL	7201.638	7471.424	7765.201	8170.308	8634.080	8999.918
2	BUSINESS	1879.567	1921.751	1965.600	2057.848	2189.673	2274.279
3	TANGIBLE	1666.500	1698.106	1732.038	1814.515	1935.807	2008.518
4	LAND	463.228	455.289	449.747	482.104	533.127	551.722
5	STRUCTURES AND EQUIPMENT	759.734	791.936	818.312	850.634	896.512	936.724
6	RESIDENTIAL	188.412	191.993	197.029	204.601	211.814	214.118
7	INVENTORIES	255.126	258.888	266.950	277.176	294.354	305.954
8	INTANGIBLE (R&D)	213.067	223.645	233.562	243.333	253.866	265.761
9	NONPROFIT	101.463	103.721	104.262	107.114	108.980	111.226
10	LAND	22.093	22.079	20.599	21.377	21.631	23.082
11	STRUCTURES AND EQUIPMENT	65.728	68.131	70.365	72.698	74.554	75.671
12	RESIDENTIAL	13.643	13.511	13.298	13.039	12.795	12.473
13	GOVERNMENT	806.702	816.983	826.844	849.804	878.088	899.950
14	LAND	168.537	167.021	165.044	178.304	196.725	205.201
15	STRUCTURES AND EQUIPMENT	530.237	541.815	552.611	563.678	573.558	582.318
16	RESIDENTIAL	5.595	5.700	6.035	6.595	7.271	7.555
17	INVENTORIES	65.523	63.127	61.393	57.115	54.083	55.855
18	INTANGIBLE (R&D)	36.810	39.320	41.761	44.112	46.451	49.021
19	GOVERNMENT ENTERPRISE	138.045	141.508	146.655	150.241	153.565	158.664
20	STRUCTURES AND EQUIPMENT	117.480	121.791	125.571	129.710	134.078	139.340
21	RESIDENTIAL	14.730	15.604	16.621	17.382	18.131	18.492
22	INVENTORIES	5.835	4.113	4.463	3.149	1.356	.832
23	HOUSEHOLD	4275.861	4487.461	4721.839	5005.301	5303.774	5555.798
24	TANGIBLE	1184.363	1219.031	1266.482	1347.686	1434.469	1487.366
25	LAND	161.873	164.006	163.433	181.220	200.679	213.183
26	RESIDENTIAL	575.423	591.416	617.010	648.564	677.641	697.105
27	DURABLES	356.855	372.873	393.404	420.765	452.989	472.004
28	SEMIDURABLES	81.666	81.917	83.716	87.903	93.810	95.870
29	INVENTORIES	8.546	8.819	8.919	9.234	9.350	9.204
30	INTANGIBLE (HUMAN CAPITAL)	3091.498	3268.430	3455.357	3657.615	3869.305	4068.432

		1975	1976	1977	1978	1979	1980
1	TOTAL CAPITAL	9301.933	9697.217	10083.719	10542.788	10932.644	11264.174
2	BUSINESS	2331.498	2428.504	2519.932	2648.598	2765.380	2854.459
3	TANGIBLE	2052.664	2137.758	2214.976	2326.002	2421.402	2485.675
4	LAND	581.239	635.293	665.871	720.570	758.058	771.634
5	STRUCTURES AND EQUIPMENT	957.451	979.807	1011.664	1051.032	1095.596	1146.592
6	RESIDENTIAL	214.746	215.661	218.097	221.101	224.265	226.898
7	INVENTORIES	299.227	306.997	319.344	333.300	343.482	340.551
8	INTANGIBLE (R&D)	278.834	290.746	304.956	322.596	343.978	368.784
9	NONPROFIT	109.065	109.494	110.141	111.403	111.733	111.649
10	LAND	20.601	20.465	20.730	21.644	21.765	21.211
11	STRUCTURES AND EQUIPMENT	76.223	77.088	77.800	78.448	78.975	79.751
12	RESIDENTIAL	12.241	11.941	11.611	11.310	10.993	10.687
13	GOVERNMENT	916.416	944.398	961.360	993.466	1017.586	1035.968
14	LAND	212.566	232.154	244.001	267.157	278.755	288.016
15	STRUCTURES AND EQUIPMENT	590.632	597.092	600.602	604.695	613.587	619.233
16	RESIDENTIAL	7.594	7.606	7.587	7.505	7.374	7.260
17	INVENTORIES	53.918	53.686	53.179	55.443	56.041	56.264
18	INTANGIBLE (R&D)	51.706	53.860	55.991	58.666	61.829	65.195
19	GOVERNMENT ENTERPRISE	163.812	168.702	175.746	181.906	185.166	190.494
20	STRUCTURES AND EQUIPMENT	144.572	149.310	153.709	159.497	163.673	168.234
21	RESIDENTIAL	18.052	17.597	17.512	17.654	17.738	18.001
22	INVENTORIES	1.188	1.795	4.525	4.755	3.755	4.259
23	HOUSEHOLD	5781.143	6046.119	6316.540	6607.415	6852.780	7071.605
24	TANGIBLE	1520.532	1591.003	1668.024	1768.127	1832.900	1888.208
25	LAND	214.427	235.731	250.382	283.688	290.614	313.156
26	RESIDENTIAL	711.392	732.966	760.715	788.092	811.255	828.129
27	DURABLES	487.582	511.312	540.904	572.492	600.139	612.372
28	SEMIDURABLES	97.816	101.248	105.965	113.597	120.480	124.082
29	INVENTORIES	9.315	9.746	10.058	10.258	10.412	10.469
30	INTANGIBLE (HUMAN CAPITAL)	4260.611	4455.116	4648.516	4839.288	5019.880	5183.397

TABLE 14. TOTAL CAPITAL, BILLIONS OF 1972 DOLLARS, YEAR-END TOTALS, 1945-81

		1981
1	TOTAL CAPITAL	11487.760
2	BUSINESS	2893.147
3	TANGIBLE	2496.643
4	LAND	731.070
5	STRUCTURES AND EQUIPMENT	1188.035
6	RESIDENTIAL	228.918
7	INVENTORIES	348.620
8	INTANGIBLE (R&D)	396.504
9	NONPROFIT	111.717
10	LAND	20.790
11	STRUCTURES AND EQUIPMENT	80.511
12	RESIDENTIAL	10.416
13	GOVERNMENT	1030.129
14	LAND	275.724
15	STRUCTURES AND EQUIPMENT	621.679
16	RESIDENTIAL	7.120
17	INVENTORIES	56.663
18	INTANGIBLE (R&D)	68.943
19	GOVERNMENT ENTERPRISE	194.321
20	STRUCTURES AND EQUIPMENT	172.052
21	RESIDENTIAL	18.239
22	INVENTORIES	4.030
23	HOUSEHOLD	7258.446
24	TANGIBLE	1914.587
25	LAND	306.942
26	RESIDENTIAL	842.443
27	DURABLES	625.386
28	SEMIDURABLES	129.281
29	INVENTORIES	10.535
30	INTANGIBLE (HUMAN CAPITAL)	5343.859

		PERCENT PER ANNUM RATES OF GROWTH CONSTANT DOLLARS					
		1945-55	1955-65	1965-70	1970-75	1975-81	1945-81
1	TOTAL CAPITAL	3.093	4.161	4.495	4.480	3.580	3.857
2	BUSINESS	3.260	3.869	3.445	3.941	3.663	3.616
3	TANGIBLE	2.995	3.298	3.058	3.865	3.317	3.262
4	LAND	1.263	3.953	-.659	5.006	3.896	2.684
5	STRUCTURES AND EQUIPMENT	5.668	3.481	5.390	3.869	3.662	4.433
6	RESIDENTIAL	.019	1.466	1.880	2.265	1.071	1.163
7	INVENTORIES	3.900	3.038	4.670	2.938	2.579	3.412
8	INTANGIBLE (R&D)	10.904	11.606	6.707	4.510	6.043	8.782
9	NONPROFIT	3.859	6.310	3.441	1.010	.401	3.487
10	LAND	5.085	6.857	.760	-1.376	.152	3.208
11	STRUCTURES AND EQUIPMENT	5.368	6.983	4.842	2.270	.916	4.548
12	RESIDENTIAL	-.492	3.188	1.506	-1.955	-2.655	.220
13	GOVERNMENT	-1.935	3.706	2.911	2.324	1.969	1.522
14	LAND	3.784	7.160	1.456	4.941	4.431	4.651
15	STRUCTURES AND EQUIPMENT	-2.914	3.252	3.270	1.740	.858	.900
16	RESIDENTIAL	-6.207	7.733	-.202	5.906	-1.068	.883
17	INVENTORIES	-2.338	-1.505	1.562	-3.104	.831	-1.156
18	INTANGIBLE (R&D)	11.656	12.375	7.850	5.630	4.912	9.322
19	GOVERNMENT ENTERPRISE	5.389	3.295	3.477	2.971	2.887	3.784
20	STRUCTURES AND EQUIPMENT	3.756	3.982	4.301	3.489	2.943	3.721
21	RESIDENTIAL	10.683	5.797	4.621	2.957	.172	5.597
22	INVENTORIES	18.476	-4.091	-12.805	-21.993	22.579	1.602
23	HOUSEHOLD	4.474	4.380	5.338	5.197	3.866	4.566
24	TANGIBLE	7.068	4.538	4.302	4.519	3.915	5.094
25	LAND	7.921	8.204	4.018	5.508	6.160	6.818
26	RESIDENTIAL	7.225	4.511	3.179	3.763	2.858	4.687
27	DURABLES	9.255	3.651	6.802	5.511	4.236	5.977
28	SEMIDURABLES	1.241	2.831	2.835	3.611	4.758	2.812
29	INVENTORIES	2.322	2.765	3.260	1.100	2.072	2.362
30	INTANGIBLE (HUMAN CAPITAL)	3.625	4.318	5.741	5.445	3.848	4.398

TABLE 15. YEAR-END IMPLICIT DEFLATORS FOR CAPITAL, MID-1972=100

		1945	1946	1947	1948	1949	1950
1	TOTAL CAPITAL	40.652	44.067	47.820	50.907	52.355	52.511
2	BUSINESS	41.110	47.707	53.876	56.104	55.278	59.213
3	TANGIBLE	40.664	47.445	53.709	55.969	55.096	59.081
4	LAND	40.895	46.715	51.265	52.735	53.025	55.325
5	STRUCTURES AND EQUIPMENT	36.135	42.291	47.919	51.098	51.634	54.997
6	RESIDENTIAL	41.958	47.726	55.489	58.965	57.280	61.966
7	INVENTORIES	48.997	60.753	71.769	72.151	66.989	75.249
8	INTANGIBLE (R&D)	59.437	57.661	59.722	60.501	60.862	63.156
9	NONPROFIT	36.241	43.131	50.351	52.545	51.629	54.885
10	LAND	40.895	46.715	51.266	52.736	53.026	55.325
11	STRUCTURES AND EQUIPMENT	31.021	39.112	47.213	49.187	48.429	51.631
12	RESIDENTIAL	41.823	47.533	55.247	58.651	56.954	61.564
13	GOVERNMENT	41.126	46.713	51.337	53.142	52.207	54.602
14	LAND	40.895	46.715	51.265	52.735	53.025	55.325
15	STRUCTURES AND EQUIPMENT	35.776	41.947	47.241	50.056	49.290	52.114
16	RESIDENTIAL	40.181	45.869	53.442	56.680	55.013	59.576
17	INVENTORIES	68.137	70.126	71.876	70.455	68.442	68.548
18	INTANGIBLE (R&D)	76.813	79.226	81.254	82.010	80.990	81.144
19	GOVERNMENT ENTERPRISE	34.369	38.873	44.711	48.290	48.694	51.254
20	STRUCTURES AND EQUIPMENT	32.893	37.440	43.110	46.187	46.106	47.917
21	RESIDENTIAL	41.783	47.509	55.241	58.642	56.958	61.522
22	INVENTORIES	55.981	77.655	98.357	87.016	74.448	87.427
23	HOUSEHOLD	40.522	41.346	43.605	47.634	50.992	48.571
24	TANGIBLE	48.205	53.228	59.724	63.134	62.708	66.074
25	LAND	40.895	46.715	51.265	52.735	53.025	55.325
26	RESIDENTIAL	41.852	47.578	55.313	58.746	57.057	61.661
27	DURABLES	62.826	65.388	69.819	72.767	73.818	77.285
28	SEMIDURABLES	50.606	55.938	62.182	67.272	67.573	65.473
29	INVENTORIES	46.524	50.156	57.043	60.461	58.812	59.537
30	INTANGIBLE (HUMAN CAPITAL)	38.354	37.893	38.772	42.803	47.218	42.552

		1951	1952	1953	1954	1955	1956
1	TOTAL CAPITAL	54.507	57.645	58.274	60.764	60.443	64.369
2	BUSINESS	62.069	62.438	63.020	63.444	65.302	68.212
3	TANGIBLE	61.926	62.236	62.722	63.105	64.963	67.932
4	LAND	57.505	58.370	59.185	60.195	61.815	63.860
5	STRUCTURES AND EQUIPMENT	58.411	59.679	60.336	60.637	63.455	67.650
6	RESIDENTIAL	65.105	66.137	66.277	67.259	68.942	70.231
7	INVENTORIES	76.858	72.862	72.743	71.999	71.876	75.253
8	INTANGIBLE (R&D)	66.127	67.739	70.063	70.716	71.933	73.168
9	NONPROFIT	58.123	58.905	58.710	58.976	61.211	63.943
10	LAND	57.505	58.370	59.185	60.195	61.815	63.860
11	STRUCTURES AND EQUIPMENT	55.544	56.369	55.844	55.728	58.539	62.140
12	RESIDENTIAL	64.669	65.682	65.787	66.780	68.475	69.760
13	GOVERNMENT	58.009	58.396	58.811	60.056	63.174	66.485
14	LAND	57.505	58.370	59.185	60.195	61.815	63.860
15	STRUCTURES AND EQUIPMENT	56.532	57.406	57.218	56.798	59.542	63.852
16	RESIDENTIAL	62.328	63.388	64.034	65.606	67.776	69.099
17	INVENTORIES	65.571	61.281	63.820	72.874	80.324	80.984
18	INTANGIBLE (R&D)	82.325	81.982	81.271	80.704	80.324	80.542
19	GOVERNMENT ENTERPRISE	53.800	55.259	56.524	56.345	57.106	60.568
20	STRUCTURES AND EQUIPMENT	51.373	53.284	53.669	53.699	56.124	59.760
21	RESIDENTIAL	64.633	65.635	65.744	66.744	68.459	69.743
22	INVENTORIES	90.489	75.696	71.645	66.185	55.903	59.780
23	HOUSEHOLD	49.799	55.068	55.811	59.791	57.565	62.170
24	TANGIBLE	69.548	70.747	70.825	70.969	71.695	73.537
25	LAND	57.505	58.370	59.185	60.195	61.815	63.860
26	RESIDENTIAL	64.768	65.784	65.884	66.880	68.589	69.926
27	DURABLES	81.716	83.106	83.170	81.785	81.052	84.441
28	SEMIDURABLES	68.043	70.270	69.624	69.762	69.786	70.239
29	INVENTORIES	64.507	65.738	65.496	65.855	65.483	66.413
30	INTANGIBLE (HUMAN CAPITAL)	42.823	49.404	50.259	55.575	52.039	57.631

271

TABLE 15. YEAR-END IMPLICIT DEFLATORS FOR CAPITAL, MID-1972=100

		1957	1958	1959	1960	1961	1962
1	TOTAL CAPITAL	66.738	67.899	68.638	69.198	69.281	70.228
2	BUSINESS	69.725	70.817	71.571	71.904	72.286	72.951
3	TANGIBLE	69.455	70.531	71.243	71.519	71.824	72.415
4	LAND	65.485	66.820	68.150	69.015	69.970	71.140
5	STRUCTURES AND EQUIPMENT	69.339	70.290	70.986	70.707	70.791	71.120
6	RESIDENTIAL	70.308	70.397	70.630	70.824	70.890	71.114
7	INVENTORIES	77.576	80.019	79.839	80.527	80.277	80.487
8	INTANGIBLE (R&D)	74.001	74.895	75.866	76.537	77.456	78.584
9	NONPROFIT	64.262	64.486	64.647	64.154	64.847	65.607
10	LAND	65.485	66.820	68.150	69.015	69.970	71.140
11	STRUCTURES AND EQUIPMENT	61.864	61.616	61.256	60.594	61.343	62.008
12	RESIDENTIAL	69.776	69.876	70.078	70.269	70.375	70.657
13	GOVERNMENT	67.290	67.317	67.443	67.334	67.918	68.745
14	LAND	65.485	66.820	68.150	69.015	69.970	71.140
15	STRUCTURES AND EQUIPMENT	64.929	64.698	64.474	64.235	64.916	66.026
16	RESIDENTIAL	69.160	69.120	69.174	69.134	68.801	68.461
17	INVENTORIES	79.649	79.335	79.910	79.223	79.175	77.415
18	INTANGIBLE (R&D)	81.107	81.216	81.713	82.090	82.241	82.855
19	GOVERNMENT ENTERPRISE	62.853	64.935	64.714	65.251	65.401	66.383
20	STRUCTURES AND EQUIPMENT	61.495	62.409	62.935	63.042	63.655	64.553
21	RESIDENTIAL	69.762	69.849	70.042	70.246	70.341	70.634
22	INVENTORIES	66.900	77.097	72.823	75.923	75.362	77.334
23	HOUSEHOLD	65.364	66.798	67.710	68.548	68.374	69.492
24	TANGIBLE	74.211	74.968	75.274	75.475	75.605	75.792
25	LAND	65.485	66.820	68.150	69.015	69.970	71.140
26	RESIDENTIAL	69.939	70.062	70.258	70.469	70.545	70.788
27	DURABLES	85.956	88.181	88.846	88.676	88.736	88.426
28	SEMIDURABLES	71.318	71.887	72.339	73.206	73.932	74.374
29	INVENTORIES	68.752	70.829	71.123	72.331	73.060	73.806
30	INTANGIBLE (HUMAN CAPITAL)	61.818	63.523	64.634	65.749	65.476	66.977

		1963	1964	1965	1966	1967	1968
1	TOTAL CAPITAL	70.947	72.207	74.283	76.916	79.627	83.474
2	BUSINESS	73.464	74.568	76.351	78.836	81.243	84.996
3	TANGIBLE	72.832	73.863	75.598	78.121	80.494	84.320
4	LAND	72.220	73.565	75.560	77.910	80.800	84.665
5	STRUCTURES AND EQUIPMENT	71.646	72.527	74.116	76.876	79.552	83.162
6	RESIDENTIAL	69.924	71.691	72.436	75.767	77.573	83.791
7	INVENTORIES	80.344	80.419	82.752	84.082	84.842	87.468
8	INTANGIBLE (R&D)	79.689	81.173	83.150	85.092	87.549	90.445
9	NONPROFIT	66.390	67.619	69.508	72.453	75.265	79.383
10	LAND	72.220	73.565	75.560	77.910	80.800	84.665
11	STRUCTURES AND EQUIPMENT	63.295	64.396	66.523	69.667	72.734	76.677
12	RESIDENTIAL	69.458	71.259	72.053	75.438	77.241	83.537
13	GOVERNMENT	69.627	71.011	73.028	75.399	78.150	82.027
14	LAND	72.220	73.565	75.560	77.910	80.800	84.665
15	STRUCTURES AND EQUIPMENT	66.986	68.110	70.144	72.680	75.571	79.767
16	RESIDENTIAL	66.597	68.585	69.521	73.012	75.211	82.190
17	INVENTORIES	77.327	80.879	84.017	85.637	87.261	89.412
18	INTANGIBLE (R&D)	83.333	83.837	84.729	86.198	87.645	89.882
19	GOVERNMENT ENTERPRISE	66.648	67.685	69.878	71.537	73.916	78.098
20	STRUCTURES AND EQUIPMENT	65.330	66.676	68.598	70.636	73.301	77.223
21	RESIDENTIAL	69.434	71.240	72.046	75.444	77.245	83.549
22	INVENTORIES	75.681	73.639	82.047	80.572	80.024	82.429
23	HOUSEHOLD	70.300	71.621	73.843	76.615	79.469	83.344
24	TANGIBLE	75.511	76.618	76.959	79.540	81.783	86.538
25	LAND	72.220	73.565	75.560	77.910	80.800	84.665
26	RESIDENTIAL	69.583	71.396	72.182	75.549	77.349	83.604
27	DURABLES	89.038	88.681	86.886	88.043	90.376	92.984
28	SEMIDURABLES	74.823	75.403	76.064	77.418	80.081	83.962
29	INVENTORIES	74.870	75.868	77.529	80.536	81.966	85.022
30	INTANGIBLE (HUMAN CAPITAL)	68.227	69.631	72.599	75.453	78.565	82.099

272

TABLE 15. YEAR-END IMPLICIT DEFLATORS FOR CAPITAL, MID-1972=100

		1969	1970	1971	1972	1973	1974
1	TOTAL CAPITAL	87.962	92.589	96.921	101.645	108.579	120.275
2	BUSINESS	89.734	94.134	98.250	103.051	112.255	127.486
3	TANGIBLE	89.236	93.790	98.085	103.117	112.947	129.516
4	LAND	89.120	93.730	98.005	102.845	110.305	120.240
5	STRUCTURES AND EQUIPMENT	88.582	94.053	98.354	102.518	110.773	131.383
6	RESIDENTIAL	88.492	92.247	97.689	104.826	116.870	128.397
7	INVENTORIES	91.944	94.232	97.689	104.165	121.533	141.312
8	INTANGIBLE (R&D)	93.626	96.748	99.469	102.560	106.974	112.143
9	NONPROFIT	86.509	92.143	96.904	103.011	113.975	132.885
10	LAND	89.120	93.730	98.005	102.845	110.305	120.240
11	STRUCTURES AND EQUIPMENT	85.275	91.652	96.446	102.702	114.459	137.392
12	RESIDENTIAL	88.228	92.029	97.624	105.008	117.358	128.943
13	GOVERNMENT	87.139	92.955	97.822	103.071	113.801	127.365
14	LAND	89.120	93.730	98.005	102.845	110.305	120.240
15	STRUCTURES AND EQUIPMENT	85.468	92.210	97.707	103.456	115.391	130.410
16	RESIDENTIAL	87.239	91.246	97.249	105.944	121.813	136.995
17	INVENTORIES	92.534	96.013	98.404	102.017	117.887	138.013
18	INTANGIBLE (R&D)	92.524	95.270	97.840	100.000	102.951	107.395
19	GOVERNMENT ENTERPRISE	83.794	90.120	96.957	103.835	116.792	133.379
20	STRUCTURES AND EQUIPMENT	82.943	90.045	96.959	103.498	116.426	133.884
21	RESIDENTIAL	88.269	92.067	97.666	105.068	117.467	129.072
22	INVENTORIES	89.632	84.950	94.242	110.892	143.953	144.471
23	HOUSEHOLD	87.508	91.950	96.209	100.729	105.849	115.548
24	TANGIBLE	90.576	94.438	98.046	102.709	110.589	121.308
25	LAND	89.120	93.730	98.005	102.845	110.305	120.240
26	RESIDENTIAL	88.371	92.154	97.657	104.923	117.179	128.863
27	DURABLES	95.298	98.775	99.143	100.121	102.732	113.438
28	SEMIDURABLES	88.533	92.705	96.017	98.766	101.647	107.003
29	INVENTORIES	89.001	93.457	96.334	100.011	109.551	126.423
30	INTANGIBLE (HUMAN CAPITAL)	86.332	91.022	95.536	100.000	104.091	113.441

		1975	1976	1977	1978	1979	1980
1	TOTAL CAPITAL	127.945	136.050	146.981	159.782	174.382	190.899
2	BUSINESS	132.204	141.698	152.113	165.805	181.710	197.079
3	TANGIBLE	134.454	144.783	156.130	171.133	188.776	206.052
4	LAND	128.835	135.970	144.940	156.410	170.705	187.075
5	STRUCTURES AND EQUIPMENT	139.603	146.417	158.769	173.536	191.141	207.355
6	RESIDENTIAL	136.382	149.809	167.818	194.092	210.780	227.128
7	INVENTORIES	127.512	154.275	163.117	180.157	206.748	230.621
8	INTANGIBLE (R&D)	115.637	119.014	122.944	127.385	131.972	136.598
9	NONPROFIT	135.249	140.650	154.646	172.770	192.161	209.802
10	LAND	128.835	135.970	144.940	156.410	170.705	187.075
11	STRUCTURES AND EQUIPMENT	136.696	140.323	155.036	173.850	195.109	213.101
12	RESIDENTIAL	137.031	150.783	169.365	196.587	213.463	230.289
13	GOVERNMENT	134.784	140.471	151.782	166.168	185.097	204.247
14	LAND	128.835	135.970	144.940	156.410	170.705	187.075
15	STRUCTURES AND EQUIPMENT	137.823	143.586	156.807	173.640	194.974	217.161
16	RESIDENTIAL	145.101	159.019	180.467	216.083	236.574	259.394
17	INVENTORIES	145.328	148.728	158.965	173.697	209.659	232.595
18	INTANGIBLE (R&D)	112.028	114.482	116.990	120.083	123.563	126.843
19	GOVERNMENT ENTERPRISE	143.454	150.870	163.277	179.851	202.844	223.923
20	STRUCTURES AND EQUIPMENT	144.201	151.049	162.890	177.817	201.851	223.449
21	RESIDENTIAL	137.187	151.003	169.724	197.156	214.009	230.993
22	INVENTORIES	147.811	134.652	151.470	183.828	193.369	212.749
23	HOUSEHOLD	124.566	132.594	143.615	155.636	168.775	185.262
24	TANGIBLE	128.778	137.849	149.614	166.271	179.062	193.621
25	LAND	128.835	135.970	144.940	156.410	170.705	187.075
26	RESIDENTIAL	136.883	150.624	169.138	196.169	213.128	229.968
27	DURABLES	119.984	124.484	129.832	138.171	147.085	159.755
28	SEMIDURABLES	112.773	116.849	121.561	125.620	128.892	133.787
29	INVENTORIES	136.865	141.925	148.658	160.372	181.771	204.337
30	INTANGIBLE (HUMAN CAPITAL)	123.063	130.717	141.463	151.750	165.019	182.217

273

TABLE 15. YEAR-END IMPLICIT DEFLATORS FOR CAPITAL, MID-1972=100

		1981
1	TOTAL CAPITAL	206.710
2	BUSINESS	210.356
3	TANGIBLE	221.454
4	LAND	200.405
5	STRUCTURES AND EQUIPMENT	224.604
6	RESIDENTIAL	243.606
7	INVENTORIES	240.316
8	INTANGIBLE (R&D)	140.471
9	NONPROFIT	222.197
10	LAND	200.405
11	STRUCTURES AND EQUIPMENT	224.594
12	RESIDENTIAL	247.168
13	GOVERNMENT	224.294
14	LAND	200.405
15	STRUCTURES AND EQUIPMENT	241.731
16	RESIDENTIAL	281.461
17	INVENTORIES	255.982
18	INTANGIBLE (R&D)	129.758
19	GOVERNMENT ENTERPRISE	245.117
20	STRUCTURES AND EQUIPMENT	245.160
21	RESIDENTIAL	247.996
22	INVENTORIES	230.248
23	HOUSEHOLD	201.503
24	TANGIBLE	206.296
25	LAND	200.405
26	RESIDENTIAL	246.762
27	DURABLES	168.333
28	SEMIDURABLES	138.914
29	INVENTORIES	222.515
30	INTANGIBLE (HUMAN CAPITAL)	199.786

		PERCENT PER ANNUM RATES OF GROWTH					
		1945-55	1955-65	1965-70	1970-75	1975-81	1945-81
1	TOTAL CAPITAL	4.046	2.083	4.504	6.682	8.324	4.621
2	BUSINESS	4.736	1.575	4.276	7.029	8.048	4.639
3	TANGIBLE	4.796	1.528	4.407	7.469	8.672	4.821
4	LAND	4.218	2.028	4.404	6.569	7.641	4.514
5	STRUCTURES AND EQUIPMENT	5.792	1.565	4.880	8.219	8.248	5.206
6	RESIDENTIAL	5.091	.496	4.954	8.134	10.151	5.007
7	INVENTORIES	3.906	1.419	2.632	6.236	11.140	4.516
8	INTANGIBLE (R&D)	1.926	1.460	3.076	3.631	3.296	2.418
9	NONPROFIT	5.381	1.279	5.800	7.978	8.626	5.166
10	LAND	4.218	2.028	4.404	6.569	7.641	4.514
11	STRUCTURES AND EQUIPMENT	6.556	1.287	6.619	8.324	8.628	5.653
12	RESIDENTIAL	5.054	.511	5.016	8.288	10.330	5.059
13	GOVERNMENT	4.386	1.460	4.944	7.714	8.854	4.824
14	LAND	4.218	2.028	4.404	6.569	7.641	4.514
15	STRUCTURES AND EQUIPMENT	5.226	1.652	5.623	8.370	9.817	5.450
16	RESIDENTIAL	5.367	.254	5.589	9.722	11.675	5.556
17	INVENTORIES	1.659	.451	2.705	8.644	9.895	3.745
18	INTANGIBLE (R&D)	.448	.535	2.373	3.294	2.479	1.467
19	GOVERNMENT ENTERPRISE	5.208	2.039	5.219	9.743	9.339	5.609
20	STRUCTURES AND EQUIPMENT	5.488	2.027	5.592	9.876	9.248	5.738
21	RESIDENTIAL	5.061	.512	5.026	8.304	10.371	5.071
22	INVENTORIES	-.014	3.911	.698	11.714	7.667	4.006
23	HOUSEHOLD	3.573	2.522	4.483	6.260	8.346	4.556
24	TANGIBLE	4.049	.711	4.178	6.399	8.170	4.121
25	LAND	4.218	2.028	4.404	6.569	7.641	4.514
26	RESIDENTIAL	5.064	.512	5.007	8.235	10.320	5.052
27	DURABLES	2.580	.698	2.598	3.967	5.805	2.776
28	SEMIDURABLES	3.266	.865	4.036	3.997	3.536	2.845
29	INVENTORIES	3.477	1.703	3.808	7.928	8.437	4.443
30	INTANGIBLE (HUMAN CAPITAL)	3.098	3.386	4.627	6.218	8.411	4.691

Table 16 National Income and Product Account, Billions of Dollars, 1946–81 (Summary Statistics)

Year	GNP	Consumption	Gross Domestic Capital Accumulation Total	Original Cost Tangible	Original Cost Intangible	Net Exports	Net National Income	Net Domestic Capital Accumulation
				Current Dollars				
1946	291.1	252.1	31.1	62.7	42.7	7.8	212.1	−62.0
1951	559.9	327.2	228.3	138.5	59.4	4.4	445.1	124.5
1956	726.5	437.6	283.6	168.7	85.8	5.3	563.0	135.3
1961	882.0	566.0	309.3	180.1	123.5	6.6	670.4	124.3
1966	1246.8	742.0	498.3	282.6	200.7	6.5	966.7	255.3
1971	1771.2	1065.3	701.8	376.6	333.4	4.1	1319.5	318.4
1976	3067.2	1693.0	1360.4	576.2	531.6	13.8	2331.0	718.3
1981	4560.1	2856.0	1677.9	972.8	850.2	26.3	3279.5	542.4
				1972 Dollars				
1946	763.4	667.6	77.9	135.1	123.0	17.9	566.7	−153.6
1947	967.8	648.4	295.4	135.5	114.2	24.0	771.5	83.3
1948	973.4	660.2	300.1	154.6	112.5	13.1	791.4	102.4
1949	936.7	649.3	275.0	153.8	108.4	12.4	746.2	87.7
1950	978.5	659.4	315.0	192.4	114.7	4.1	776.5	132.4
1951	1061.7	672.5	381.4	210.8	120.7	7.7	855.0	195.3
1952	1035.6	689.0	341.0	222.7	125.3	5.5	819.7	145.3
1953	1087.7	706.1	379.5	239.8	133.5	2.1	858.4	174.5
1954	1089.1	723.7	361.2	226.9	137.4	4.2	847.8	147.4
1955	1178.7	747.0	426.8	245.6	149.7	4.9	932.2	205.9

(continued on next page)

Table 16 *(Continued)*

Year	GNP	Consumption	Gross Domestic Capital Accumulation				Net Exports	Net National Income	Net Domestic Capital Accumulation
			Total	Original					
				Tangible	Intangible				
				1972 Dollars					
1956	1212.9	765.6	439.0	243.2	153.4		8.4	960.7	212.5
1957	1205.3	783.8	410.3	235.5	161.4		11.2	945.7	177.7
1958	1218.0	797.5	415.5	229.6	165.3		4.9	949.8	177.1
1959	1254.5	820.7	431.7	252.1	178.6		2.1	979.3	186.7
1960	1281.9	839.8	434.2	248.9	185.7		8.0	996.3	181.6
1961	1321.6	862.4	449.7	247.4	194.3		9.6	1022.3	188.5
1962	1377.0	881.8	486.2	276.8	206.5		9.0	1062.7	216.5
1963	1418.0	903.4	504.1	291.9	219.5		10.6	1091.1	223.9
1964	1521.7	935.0	572.9	305.4	237.5		13.8	1182.1	281.4

1965	1578.3	967.5	599.1	333.6	252.4	11.8	1227.6	295.3
1966	1656.6	993.6	654.5	360.1	274.8	8.5	1289.6	337.2
1967	1688.4	1016.2	664.2	363.5	296.2	8.0	1305.0	329.7
1968	1759.6	1044.1	710.4	381.4	310.9	5.2	1359.3	358.8
1969	1781.7	1065.2	711.7	394.8	323.8	4.8	1355.5	343.3
1970	1802.9	1091.1	704.5	364.1	334.4	7.3	1358.1	320.0
1971	1844.1	1110.2	729.6	388.8	349.4	4.3	1376.3	330.7
1972	2046.8	1143.7	902.3	421.8	372.0	.7	1561.3	487.4
1973	2210.7	1167.0	1030.3	458.2	388.6	13.4	1705.1	598.9
1974	2140.1	1176.5	952.0	432.5	382.2	11.6	1618.5	506.9
1975	1965.3	1207.8	736.2	392.1	382.6	21.3	1439.6	281.4
1976	2272.2	1249.1	1012.6	437.8	393.2	10.4	1728.8	544.0
1977	2332.8	1286.8	1048.8	484.4	401.8	−2.8	1774.1	566.9
1978	2446.7	1327.9	1119.5	526.0	408.8	−.7	1868.2	621.4
1979	2451.0	1367.3	1075.5	526.6	411.7	8.1	1852.7	558.6
1980	2325.5	1403.0	909.0	492.1	407.5	13.4	1705.2	374.2
1981	2310.4	1430.0	866.8	521.5	414.6	13.5	1678.8	319.2

Table 17   National Income and Product Account (TISA as Percent of BEA, Current Dollars)

Year	GNP	Consumption	GDCA/GPDI	NNI/NI	NDCA/NPDI
			Selected Years		
1946	138.70	175.29	101.56	118.80	−373.12
1951	169.29	158.01	385.84	162.35	389.02
1956	172.28	164.51	399.35	161.14	419.01
1961	168.14	168.97	413.66	156.34	455.93
1966	164.93	159.53	396.49	153.92	392.61
1971	164.37	158.48	421.70	151.41	455.53
1976	178.53	156.15	527.56	169.01	867.02
1981	154.37	153.78	353.30	138.20	373.04
			Multiyear Means		
1946−55	166.72	164.36	360.30	155.87	282.56
1956−65	167.52	165.17	403.38	155.86	429.08
1966−75	167.07	157.41	441.08	155.16	519.49
1976−81	168.89	154.04	436.73	156.35	586.13
1946−81	167.40	160.94	407.44	155.75	439.67

Table 18   National Income and Product Account (TISA as Percent of BEA, 1972 Dollars)

Year	GNP	Consumption	GDCA/GPDI	NNI/NI	NDCA/NPDI
			Selected Years		
1946	159.61	221.77	109.89	140.93	−415.85
1951	183.26	196.89	406.04	178.30	401.15
1956	180.60	188.85	427.71	172.18	460.99
1961	174.67	186.91	432.80	164.24	485.05
1966	168.21	169.65	401.50	158.03	399.79
1971	164.30	159.33	419.58	150.95	448.97
1976	175.02	151.76	548.81	165.76	915.60
1981	152.61	149.47	380.95	138.45	445.56
			Multiyear Means		
1946−55	182.35	201.72	376.22	173.82	287.28
1956−65	174.40	184.21	421.49	164.50	456.92
1966−75	167.58	160.28	444.81	155.85	530.67
1976−81	165.23	149.18	463.89	154.07	647.57
1946−81	173.18	176.59	422.46	162.95	462.06

Table 19   Current Dollar Sector Products, 1946–81

Year	Total (GNP)	Business	Non-Profit	Government Enterprises	Government	House-hold	Rest of World
			Sector Product in Billions of Dollars				
1946	291.1	118.7	5.2	3.4	41.6	121.3	.8
1951	559.9	278.3	9.6	4.6	63.8	201.5	2.1
1956	726.5	347.1	13.8	6.5	88.1	267.8	3.2
1961	882.0	400.2	19.4	8.7	105.2	344.5	3.9
1966	1246.8	584.7	29.6	12.2	153.6	461.0	5.6
1971	1771.2	795.0	45.6	19.6	225.7	676.1	9.2
1976	3067.2	1452.4	70.8	30.8	326.4	1166.4	20.5
1981	4560.1	2134.5	113.3	49.8	504.3	1708.7	49.6
			Percent of Total Product				
1946	100.0	40.8	1.8	1.2	14.3	41.7	.3
1951	100.0	49.7	1.7	.8	11.4	36.0	.4
1956	100.0	47.8	1.9	.9	12.1	36.9	.4
1961	100.0	45.4	2.2	1.0	11.9	39.1	.4
1966	100.0	46.9	2.4	1.0	12.3	37.0	.5
1971	100.0	44.9	2.6	1.1	12.7	38.2	.5
1976	100.0	47.4	2.3	1.0	10.6	38.0	.7
1981	100.0	46.8	2.5	1.1	11.1	37.5	1.1

Table 20   Constant Dollar Sector Products, 1946–81

Year	Total (GNP)	Business	Non-Profit	Government Enterprises	Government	House-hold	Rest of World
			Sector Product in Billions of 1972 Dollars				
1946	763.4	193.9	22.1	10.8	178.3	351.8	6.5
1951	1061.7	435.0	24.7	12.8	138.8	449.1	1.3
1956	1212.9	507.5	29.9	14.7	166.4	491.0	3.4
1961	1321.6	540.5	35.4	16.2	180.2	542.6	6.8
1966	1656.6	732.1	45.3	19.1	222.8	627.9	9.4
1971	1844.1	819.9	48.5	21.2	240.8	701.5	12.2
1976	2272.2	1087.7	51.8	23.1	244.6	864.3	.6
1981	2310.4	1093.5	51.5	28.2	249.4	891.7	− 3.9
			Percent of Total Product				
1946	100.0	25.4	2.9	1.4	23.4	46.1	.8
1951	100.0	41.0	2.3	1.2	13.1	42.3	.1
1956	100.0	41.8	2.5	1.2	13.7	40.5	.3
1961	100.0	40.9	2.7	1.2	13.6	41.1	.5
1966	100.0	44.2	2.7	1.2	13.5	37.9	.6
1971	100.0	44.5	2.6	1.1	13.1	38.0	.7
1976	100.0	47.9	2.3	1.0	10.8	38.0	.0
1981	100.0	47.3	2.2	1.2	10.8	38.6	− .2

Table 21   Implicit Price Deflator and Inflation Rates, GNP and Components, 1946–81

			Implicit Deflators (1972 = 100)						Annual Inflation Rate		
			Gross Domestic Capital Accumulation								
				Original Cost							
Year	GNP	Consumption	Total	Tangible	Intangible	Net Exports	NNI	NDCA	GNP	Con- sumption	GDCA
1946	38.1	37.8	40.0	46.4	34.8	43.9	37.4	40.4			
1947	43.9	42.1	47.5	53.1	40.2	49.6	43.5	51.8	15.2	11.5	18.9
1948	46.7	43.9	52.7	59.2	43.5	53.0	45.9	57.7	6.4	4.2	11.0
1949	47.1	44.5	53.0	59.1	44.1	52.5	45.9	55.3	.9	1.5	.5
1950	48.5	45.3	55.1	61.0	45.0	53.6	47.6	59.6	2.9	1.7	3.9
1951	52.7	48.6	59.9	65.7	49.2	57.1	52.1	63.8	8.8	7.4	8.7
1952	54.2	51.2	60.0	65.1	51.0	57.9	53.1	62.1	2.7	5.3	.3
1953	55.7	53.2	60.3	64.5	52.4	58.8	54.7	61.5	2.8	3.8	.4
1954	56.5	54.7	60.3	64.8	52.9	59.5	55.4	59.5	1.6	2.8	.0
1955	58.0	55.7	62.0	66.4	54.1	60.8	57.3	63.1	2.6	2.0	2.8
1956	59.9	57.2	64.6	69.4	56.0	62.8	58.6	63.7	3.2	2.5	4.2
1957	61.7	59.3	66.2	71.4	58.2	64.9	60.0	63.3	3.0	3.7	2.5
1958	62.8	60.8	66.7	71.3	59.7	66.0	61.1	62.7	1.8	2.6	.7
1959	64.4	62.4	68.0	72.8	61.2	67.6	62.8	64.8	2.4	2.7	2.1
1960	66.0	64.5	68.7	73.2	62.6	68.7	64.6	65.6	2.5	3.4	.9

1961	66.7	65.6	68.8	72.8	63.6	69.3	65.6	66.0	1.2	1.7	.2
1962	68.1	66.8	70.5	74.3	65.3	70.6	67.1	69.3	2.0	1.7	2.4
1963	69.2	68.0	71.3	74.7	66.7	71.7	68.3	70.6	1.6	1.8	1.1
1964	70.6	69.5	72.4	75.6	68.2	72.8	70.0	72.1	2.1	2.3	1.6
1965	72.6	71.7	73.9	76.6	70.2	74.4	72.1	73.5	2.7	3.2	2.0
1966	75.3	74.7	76.1	78.5	73.0	76.8	75.0	75.7	3.7	4.1	3.1
1967	78.0	77.4	78.9	81.0	76.4	79.1	77.7	78.6	3.6	3.6	3.7
1968	82.3	82.0	82.6	84.5	80.4	82.5	82.1	82.7	5.5	6.0	4.7
1969	86.6	86.4	87.0	88.6	85.0	86.8	86.5	87.0	5.3	5.3	5.3
1970	91.5	91.5	91.5	92.4	90.5	91.4	91.5	91.6	5.7	6.0	5.2
1971	96.1	96.0	96.2	96.9	95.4	96.0	95.9	96.3	4.9	4.8	5.1
1972	100.0	100.0	100.0	100.0	100.0	100.0	100.0	99.9	4.1	4.2	4.0
1973	105.7	106.1	105.2	104.2	106.1	105.8	105.9	105.2	5.7	6.1	5.2
1974	116.1	116.6	115.4	113.9	116.6	115.1	116.2	114.7	9.8	9.9	9.7
1975	125.5	125.5	125.7	125.1	126.9	125.8	124.6	120.0	8.2	7.6	8.9
1976	135.0	135.5	134.3	131.6	135.2	132.3	134.8	132.1	7.5	8.0	6.9
1977	143.9	144.5	143.2	140.1	144.5	140.1	143.7	139.7	6.6	6.6	6.6
1978	154.4	154.7	153.9	149.6	155.4	150.4	153.9	149.2	7.2	7.1	7.4
1979	167.5	168.2	166.6	161.7	169.3	163.4	166.9	159.6	8.5	8.7	8.3
1980	182.3	183.9	179.8	173.6	187.2	178.4	181.1	163.6	8.8	9.4	7.9
1981	197.4	199.7	193.6	186.5	205.1	195.1	195.3	169.9	8.3	8.6	7.7

Sources and Methods

1. National Income and Product Account

Debits

1. Labor income
   2 + 5 − 11

2. Compensation of employees
   3 + 4

3.   Domestic
   Equal to the sum of the compensation of employees in each sector:
   2-2 + 3-2 + 4-2 + 5-2 + 6-2

4.   Rest of world
   N1.12-49

5.   Additional imputations
   6 + 7 + 8 + 9 + 10

This section was prepared jointly with Hilary Lieb, Wilson Lim, and John W. Keating.

The following notation is employed: Single integers indicate lines in table or account currently under discussion. Thus, "2 + 5 − 11" under "Labor income," on this page, denotes line 2 plus line 5 minus line 11 of "1. National Income and Product Account." In references to other accounts than the one under discussion, the account number precedes the line number. Thus, 3-2 refers to account 3, Nonprofit Income and Product, line 2. BEA NIPA tables are designated by the letter "N": N1.12-49 denotes BEA NIPA table 1.12, line 49, as published in the July 1983 *Survey of Current Business*. Table and line numbers may differ for years earlier than those, beginning in 1979, taken from the July 1983 *Survey*, as well as for later issues.

6.   Employee training
      Equal to the sum of the sector employee training items in each
      sector: 2-4 + 3-3 + 4-3 + 5-3 + 6-4. Derivation explained below
      in section 13: Human Capital.

7.   Expense account items of consumption
      2-5

8.   Labor income of self-employed
      2-6

9.   Opportunity costs of students
      6-5

10.   Unpaid household work
      6-6

11.   Less: Expenses related to work
      Equal to the sum of the sectors' expenses related to work: 2-7 +
      3-4 + 4-4 + 5-4 + 6-7; derivation explained above in appendix
      B, Expenses Related to Work.

12.   Rental income on owner-occupied nonfarm dwellings
      6-16

13.   Gross rental income
      6-17

14.   Less: Net imputed interest on owner-occupied nonfarm dwellings and
      land
      6-18

15.   Capital income
      16 + 17 + 26

16.   Interest paid
      Equal to the sum of business, nonprofit, government, and household
      interest paid: 2-9 + 3-6 + 5-13 + 6-10 + 6-20.

17.   Net imputed interest (excluding business)
      Equal to sum of nonprofit, government enterprise, government, and
      household imputed interest: 18 − 25 or 3-7 + 4-5 + 5-7 + 6-11.

18.   Gross imputed interest
      19 + 20 + 21 + 22 + 23 + 24

19.   Land
      Equal to the sum of nonprofit, government, and household
      imputed interest on land: 3-9 + 5-9 + 6-13.

20.   Owner-occupied dwellings
      6-14

21.   Structures and equipment
        Equal to imputed interest on nonprofit and government structures and equipment: 3-10 + 3-11 + 5-10.

22.   Consumer durables and semidurables
        6-23 + 6-24

23.   Inventories
        Equal to imputed interest on government enterprise, government and household inventories: 4-5 + 5-11 + 6-25. Note that the nonprofit sector is assumed not to hold any inventories.

24.   Government research and development
        5-12

25.   Less: Interest paid (excluding business)
        Equals interest paid by nonprofit institutions, government and households: 3-6 + 5-6 + 6-10 + 6-20.

26.   Net interest, rest of world
        N1.12-51

27.   Net operating surplus
        28 + 31 + 34 + 35 + 36

28.   Corporate profits
        29 + 30

29.   Domestic
        2-10

30.   Rest of world
        N1.12-50

31.   Proprietors' capital income
        32-33

32.   Proprietors' income
        2-12

33.   Less: labor income of self-employed
        2-13

34.   Gross business investment in R&D
        2-20

35.   Government enterprise surpluses
        4-6

36.   Net rental income of persons
        2-16

37.   Net revaluations
        38 + 39 + 40 + 41 + 42

38.   Land
Equal to the sum of the sectors' land net revaluations

39.   Owner-occupied dwellings
6-29

40.   Structures and equipment other than owner-occupied dwellings
Equal to the sum of business, nonprofit, and government net revaluations on nonresidential structures and equipment plus business
and nonprofit residential net revaluations: 2-24 + 2-26 + 3-15 +
3-16 + 5-16.

41.   Consumer durables and semidurables
6-31 + 6-32

42.   Inventories
Equal to the sum of sectors' net revaluations on inventories:
2-25 + 4-9 + 5-17 + 6-33.

43. Net surplus
27 + 37

44. National income
1 + 12 + 15 + 43

45. Less: Intangible capital consumption

46.   Capital consumption on all R&D
2-21 + 2-29

47.   Capital consumption on human capital
6-41

48. Net national income
44 − 55

49. Business transfer payments
50 + 51 + 52

50.   Media support
2-32

51.   Health and safety
2-33

52.   Other
2-34

53. Uncompensated factor services
54 + 55 + 56

54.   Volunteers
3-18

55.   Draftees
      5-20

56.   Jurors
      5-21

57. Net indirect business taxes
    58-59

58.   Indirect business taxes
      2-36

59.   Less: Intermediate product transferred from government to business
      (and government enterprises)
      2-37 + 4-19

60. Statistical discrepancy
    61 + 62

61.   BEA statistical discrepancy
      2-39 (N1.7-8)

62.   TISA statistical discrepancy
      2-40 (zero, except for occasional rounding errors)

63. Net national product
    48 + 49 + 53 + 57 + 60

64. Capital consumption allowances
    65 + 68

65.   Tangible
      66 + 67

66.   Original cost
        Equal to the sum of the sectors' tangible original cost depreciation:
        2-44 + 3-21 + 5-24 + 6-39.

67.   Revaluations
        2-45 + 3-22 + 5-25 + 6-40

68.   Intangible
      69 + 72

69.   Original cost
        70 + 71

70.   On research and development
          2-47

71.   On human capital
          6-42

72.   Revaluations
        73 + 74

73.   On research and development
           2-50

74.   On human capital
           6-43

75. Gross national product
    63 + 64

Credits

1. Consumption
   This includes household expenditures for services and nondurables (2),
   the capital services of household durables and semidurables allocated
   to consumption (21), space rent of owner-occupied nonfarm dwellings
   (20), other BEA imputations allocated to consumption (6) household
   labor services, market and nonmarket, allocated to consumption (chiefly
   unpaid housework and opportunity costs of students: 28 minus 29),
   expense account items of consumption (5) and other expenditures and
   imputations considered transfers of consumption services from other
   sectors to households (7 + 10).

2. Household expenditures for services and nondurables
   This is net of expenditures traveling to and from work.

3. Gross expenditures included from BEA personal consumption expenditures (PCE)
   To obtain these expenditures we start with BEA PCE and delete
   imputations and items included elsewhere as investment by households or as investment or consumption by nonprofit institutions.
   They are thus defined as follows:

Item	Source
Gross expenditures from BEA PCE (3)	
= Personal consumption expenditure	N1.1-2
− Investment in durables	N1.1-3
− Investment in semidurables	N2.4-12 + N2.4-13 + N2.4-33
− BEA net space rent on owner-occupied nonfarm housing	N8.8-72
− BEA PCE imputations other than housing services	N8.8-7

- Nonprofit consumption in   3-25
  BEA PCE
- Investment in inventories   62
  (households)
- Nonprofit investment in R&D   3-28
     in education and training   3-30
     in BEA PCE
     in health in BEA PCE   3-34
- Medical care expenditures   N2.4-44 − N2.4-46
                                      − N2.4-53 − N2.4-54
                                      − .5(N2.4-50)

4.   Less: PCE expenses related to work
These are the sum of the sector expenses related to work (2-7 + 3-39 + 4-4 + 5-48 + 6-7) minus the services of household durables included in expenses to work (6-72).

5.   Expense account items of consumption
2-5

6.   BEA imputations other than housing
This is N8.8-7, BEA PCE imputations other than housing services.

7.   Subsidies allocated to consumption

8.   Subsidies included in business income
2-59

9.   Less: Amount allocated to investment
Subsidies included in business income are divided between consumption and investment on the basis of the ratio of consumption to gross domestic capital accumulation at original cost. Thus,

$$SUBI = \frac{GDCA}{CON + GDCA} \times SUB,$$

where

$SUBI$ = subsidies allocated to investment.
$GDCA$ = gross domestic capital accumulation at original cost (31).
CON = 1 − 7 − 18.
SUB = subsidies included in business income (2-59).

10.   Transfers

11.   From business

12.   Media support

13.   Total media support
            2-32

14.   Less: Media support allocated to investment.
            See section 13, Investment in Human Capital.

15.   Health and safety
            Half of 2-33, since we assume that half of the expenditures on
            health and safety are consumption and half are investment. (See
            section 13.)

16.   From nonprofit institutions
        3-24

17.   From government enterprises
        4-15

18.   From government
        5-27 + 6-61

19.   Nonmarket services produced in households

20.   Net space rent of owner-occupied nonfarm dwellings
      6-48

21.   Other capital services

22.   Durables

23.   Total durables
            6-53

24.   Less: Durables allocated to investment
            6-54

25.   Less: Services of durables included in expenses related to work
            6-55

26.   Semidurables
          6-56

27.   Inventories
          6-57

28.   Labor services
        6-59

29.   Less: Labor services allocated to investment
        6-60

30. Gross domestic capital accumulation

31.   Original cost

32.   Tangible

33.   Structures and equipment and household durables and semidurables

34.   Business

35.   Nonresidential

36.   Structures
                    Data for 1946 to 1972 from *Fixed Nonresidential Business Capital in the United States, 1925–1973* (U.S. Dept. of Commerce, BEA, 1974, p. 375). Data for 1973 to 1981 are from unpublished BEA revisions and extensions of these tables.

37.   Equipment
                    Same source as for structures.

38.   Residential other than owner-occupied nonfarm dwellings
                For 1946 to 1972, all private residential capital investment data are from *Fixed Nonresidential Business Capital,* p. 415, and owner-occupied nonfarm dwellings data are from the same source, p. 418. Data for 1973 to 1981 are from unpublished BEA revisions and extensions of these tables. TISA business residential investment is then calculated as the business residential investment minus nonprofit and household residential investment from these sources.

39.   Nonprofit institutions
           Nonprofit structures plus residential investment from unpublished BEA tables.

40.   Structures

41.   Equipment

42.   Government enterprises
           Government enterprise structures plus residential investment from unpublished BEA tables.

43.   Structures

44.   Equipment

45.   Government
           Expenditures for structures and equipment are from BEA unpublished tables and product accumulated is from 5-39.

46.   Structures

47.   Equipment

48.   Product accumulated

49.   Households

50.   Owner-occupied nonfarm dwellings
                From *Fixed Nonresidential Business Capital,* p. 418, for

	1946 to 1972 and from unpublished BEA tables, 1973 to 1982.
51.	Durables N1.1-3
52.	Semidurables N2.4-12 + N2.4-13 + N2.4-33
53.	Fixed GPDI reconciliation Since consumption, other investment, and net exports are taken from NIPA, this item and line 56 below are incorporated in the accounts to reconcile the sector investment data obtained from *Fixed Nonresidential Business and Residential Business and Residential Capital in the United States, 1925–1981* and unpublished BEA tables with the aggregate investment data in NIPA, thus avoiding additions to the statistical discrepancy. These differences stem primarily from the treatment of sales of used equipment as exports and purchases between government and business, where the disinvestment in capital of the disposing sector is not recorded with the same valuation as the investment of the acquiring sector.
54.	NIPA fixed GPDI N1.1-7
55.	Less: Corresponding sector totals 34 + 39 + 50
56.	Government capital accumulation reconciliation The differences between the unpublished BEA tables used above and NIPA government purchases of durables and structures stem primarily from the treatment of sales and purchases between government and business, the treatment of military capital, and construction force account compensation. The latter is excluded from NIPA (see N3.7A) but included in the unpublished tables.
57.	NIPA government investment This is the sum of federal and state and local government expenditures on durables and structures. For pre-1972: N3.7-3 + N3.7-12 + N3.7-14 + N3.7-19. For 1972 and after: N3.7B-4 + N3.7B-11 + N3.7B-20 + N3.7B-25.
58.	Less: Government and government enterprise totals 42 + 46 + 47
59.	Change in inventories

60.   Business
        N1.1-15

61.   Government
        5-46
        The calculation of stocks of inventories is described in the
        government sector. Change in inventories in year t is then
        the difference between stocks in year t and year t-1.

62.   Households
        This is equal to (N1.1-4 − N2.4-12 − N2.4-13 − N2.4-
        33) / 26, where 26 is an integer relating to $1/26$ of a year or
        2 weeks of stocks.

63.   Intangible

64.   Research and development

65.   Business
        2-20

66.   Nonprofit institutions
        3-28

67.   Government
        5-29 + 5-38

68.   Education
        See section 13.

69.   Health
        See section 13.

70.   Subsidies and government enterprise transfers allocated to investment
        This is the sum of business subsidies allocated to investment and
        government enterprise transfers allocated to investment: 9 + 4-16.

71.   Net revaluations

72.   Land

73.   Business
        2-23

74.   Nonprofit
        3-14

75.   Government and government enterprises
        5-15

76.   Households
        6-28

77.   Structures and equipment

78.   Business
        2-24 + 2-26

79.   Nonprofit institutions
         3-15 + 3-16

80.   Government
         5-16

81.   Households (owner-occupied dwellings)
         6-29

82.   Household durables and semidurables

83.   Durables
         6-31

84.   Semidurables
         6-32

85.   Inventories

86.   Business (including nonprofit)
         2-25

87.   Government enterprises
         4-9

88.   Government
         5-17

89.   Households
         6-33

90. Net exports

91.   Exports
       N1.1-19

92.   Imports
       N1.1-20

93. Gross national product
       1 + 30 + 90

2. Business Income and Product

Debits

1. Labor income

2. Compensation of employees
   This was taken from NIPA, and is the sum of compensation of employees in corporate business, sole proprietorships and partnerships, and other private business: N1.12-3 + N1.12-12 + N1.12-25.

3. Additional imputations

4. Employee training
   Kendrick's series on training costs is used for 1946 to 1966 and is extrapolated for the remaining years. The method used is described in section 13, Investment in Human Capital. These costs consist primarily of lost trainee product and the value of supervisor time during the initial employment period.

5. Expense account items of consumption
   This consists of two parts: the value of the service of company-owned cars and expense account items other than the value of the services of company-owned cars. For each part, the total value of services is computed and then fifty percent is considered to be final consumption.

   A. Value of services of company-owned cars

   The total value of the service of automobiles owned by companies and used by reimbursable employees is defined as:

   $$YAR = (RYAKA \times KAR) + GIIAR + DAR,$$

   where

   YAR = value of services of automobiles owned by companies used by reimbursable employees,

   $RYAKA$ = ratio of auto expense to auto stocks of households,

   KAR = stocks of autos owned by business and used by reimbursable employees,

   $GIIAR$ = gross imputed interest on the stock of autos used by reimbursable employees, and

   DAR = depreciation of autos used by reimbursable employees.

RYAKA was calculated from household data since comparable data for businesses are not available. It is hence assumed that ratio of expense to stocks is the same in both sectors. Household auto expenses are from N2.4 and are the sum of: line 68, tires, tubes, accessories, and other parts; line 69, repair, greasing, washing, parking, storage, and rental; line 70, gasoline and oil; and line 72, insurance premiums less claims paid. Household auto stocks were obtained from the BEA.

Depreciation and stocks of autos used by reimbursable employees are calculated from current dollar investment data for "producer durable equipment, autos" from N5.6-20, and deflators for "producer durable equipment, autos" from N7.20-20. The portion of "producer durable equipment, autos" used by reimbursable employees is obtained from U.S. Dept. of Commerce, BEA (1982). Straight-line depreciation was applied with the half-year convention. Gross imputed interest is then obtained by applying a household real rate to net stocks averaged over years t and t-1. The household real rate is explained in 6-20.

B. Expense account items other than the services of company-owned cars.

Expense account expenditures for industry 81: Business Travel, Entertainment, and Gifts were obtained from *Input-Output Structure of the U.S. Economy* (U.S. Dept. of Commerce, BEA 1958, 1963, 1967).

For these three years the ratio of expense account items to compensation of employees in the business sector (line 2) was taken and the average of these three ratios, .03150833, was then multiplied by compensation of employees in the business sector to estimate expenditures on expense account items for the remaining years.*

6.   Labor income of self-employed
This is proprietors' income minus proprietors' capital income: $12 - 11$.

---

*The ratios for the three years, 1958, 1963, 1967, are .03305302, .02978645, and .03168553, respectively. Since the path is not monotonic an average was used rather than a trend.

7. Less: Expenses related to work
    Expenses related to work are the costs incurred in commuting to and
    from work. See above, appendix B, Expenses Related to Work.

8. Capital income and surplus

9. Interest paid
    This consists of interest paid by or in relation to corporate business,
    sole proprietorship and partnerships, and other private business, net
    of interest on owner-occupied nonfarm dwellings and nonprofit build-
    ings and equipment: N1.12-11 + N1.12-24 + N1.12-35 − N8.8-
    78 − N8.8-90.

10. Corporate profits
    This is N1.12-7, corporate profits with inventory valuations and
    capital consumption adjustments.

11. Proprietors' capital income
    This is net of interest paid and is calculated by assuming that the
    after-tax rates of return to corporate and proprietors' capital are equal
    and applying the corporate rate of return to proprietors' capital. It
    is done for two types of capital, farm and nonfarm. In symbols:

$$P_P = \frac{P_{CF} + I_{CF}}{K_{CF}} \times K_{PF} + \frac{P_{CNF} + I_{CNF}}{K_{CNF}} \times K_{PNF} - I_P$$

where

P_P = proprietors' capital income.

P_{CF} = farm corporate profits with inventory valuation and capital
consumption allowance adjustments, less farm corporate
profits taxes: N1.18-23 − N6.22-4.

I_{CF} = interest paid, corporate farm. Equal to total farm net interest
paid minus net interest paid, proprietorship and partnership
farms. Total farm interest paid is from N1.18-24. Net interest paid, proprietorship and partnership farms, is equal
to N8.7-9 − N8.7-45.

P_{CNF} = nonfinancial, nonfarm corporate profits, with inventory valuation and capital consumption allowance adjustments, less
nonfinancial, nonfarm corporate taxes. It is equal to N1.13-
27 − N1.13-29.

I_{CNF} = interest paid by nonfinancial, nonfarm corporations, N1.13-
35.

I_P = interest paid by proprietorships and partnerships, N1.12-
24.

K_{CF} = total current cost corporate farm tangible capital. Structures, equipment, and inventory data from the BEA. Flow of Funds provided total farm land data. They were divided between corporate and noncorporate farms on the basis of their relative shares of total farm structures and equipment.

K_{CNF} = total current cost for nonfinancial, nonfarm corporation, tangible capital.

K_{PF} = farm proprietors' capital.

K_{PNF} = nonfarm proprietors' capital.

12. Proprietors' income
     N1.12-16 + N1.12-29

13. Less: Labor income of self-employed

14.   Opportunity cost of self-employed

We include in the opportunity costs of self-employed, *OPCST,* the opportunity costs of their unpaid family members. We divide both the self-employed and the unpaid family workers into agricultural and nonagricultural workers. For each category, i, the opportunity costs are considered to be the average hourly wage, $AVWAG_i$, times the average hours worked per week, $AVHOUR_i$, times 52.14, except for leap years where we use 52.28, times the number of persons, $SELFEMP_i$. Thus,

$$OPCST = 52.14 \sum_i AVWAG_i$$
$$\times\ AVHOUR_i \times SELFEMP_i\ ,$$

or in leap year,

$$OPCST = 52.28 \sum_i AVWAG_i$$
$$\times\ AVHOUR_i \times SELFEMP_i\ .$$

For each category the average hourly wage, $AVWAG_i$, is computed by dividing total compensation of employees, N6.5A, by total number of hours worked, N6.11. From each table, line 2, domestic industries, is used for agricultural self-employed workers rather than the low-wage agricultural industries; line 5, farms, is used for agricultural unpaid family workers; line 2, domestic industries, minus line 5, farms, minus 75, government and government enterprises, is used for nonagricultural self-employed and unpaid family workers.

The number of self-employed in each category from 1948 to 1981 came from unpublished data provided by John Stenson of the Bureau of Labor Statistics. The data are now available in U.S. Department of Labor (1982), *Employment and Training Report of the President, 1982,* table A-23, page 123. Data for 1946 and 1947 are estimated on the basis of the rate of growth over the previous ten years.

The average number of hours worked per week by each category of workers from 1958 to 1981 is from the Bureau of Labor Statistics. Data for 1948 to 1957 are extrapolated using the following:

$$AVHR_{i,t} = \frac{AVHR_{i,58}}{AVHR_{TOT,58}} \times AVHR_{TOT,t}$$

$$i = NS, AS, NF, AF,$$
$$t = 1948 \text{ to } 1957.$$

NS = denotes nonagricultural self-employed.
AS = denotes agricultural self-employed.
NF = denotes nonagricultural unpaid family.
AF = denotes agricultural unpaid family.
TOT = total for the economy.

15.   Less: Underremuneration of labor
       $14 - 6$

16. Net rental income of persons

17.   Total rental income
       Rental income of persons with capital consumption adjustment: N2.1-12.

18.   Less: Owner-occupied nonfarm rental income
       N8.8-79

19. Net business investment in research and development

20.   Gross Investment
       For 1946–52, we use Kendrick's series, Total Gross Investment in Current Dollars, by type, Business Sector (table 6), Total Non-human Intangibles. For 1953–81, data are taken from *National Patterns of R&D Resources and Manpower in the United States 1953–1977,* table B-1: Industry: Resources—Industry (National Science Foundation 1977). This is an updated version of Kendrick's series.

21.   Less: Capital consumption allowance
       $48 + 51$

22. Net revaluations

Net revaluations of land, residential structures, nonresidential structures and equipment, and inventories are calculated using the formula below. Net investment in land is assumed to be zero. Stocks of land are from the Federal Reserve Board's Flow of Funds section. Stocks and investment in residential structures, nonresidential structures, and equipment and inventories are from BEA capital stock tapes provided by John Musgrave. Net revaluations for wholesale cooperatives are calculated as 7 percent of the net revaluation for nonprofit institutions and are included in business net revaluations.

The general formula for computing net revaluations is as follows:

$$ NR_t = K_t - \frac{P_{t,end}}{P_{t-1,end}} \times K_{t-1} - \frac{P_{t,end}}{\overline{P}_t} \times IN_t, $$

where

NR_t = net revaluations of the year t.
K_t = net value of capital at the end of the year t.
K_{t-1} = net value of capital at the end of the year t-1.
$P_{t,end}$ = general price deflator at the end of the year t.
$P_{t-1,end}$ = general price deflator at the end of the year t-1.
$\overline{P}_t$ = average value of general price deflator in the year t.
IN_t = net investment in the year t.

The general price deflator used is the GNP implicit deflator (N7.1-1).

23. Land

24. Nonresidential structures and equipment

25. Inventories

26. Residential structures

27. Net surplus
    8 + 22

28. Income originating
    1 + 27

29. Less: Capital consumption on R&D transferred to business
    49 + 52

30. Net income originating
    28 − 29

31. Business transfers

32. Media support
     The value of media support from business is considered to be the
     receipts from advertising minus the cost of product promotion. Re-
     ceipts from advertising are from the *Statistical Abstract of the United
     States* (U.S. Dept. of Commerce, Bureau of the Census). Table
     numbers vary each year. In the 1978 volume, table 981 is used for
     television, table 982 for radio, and a combination of table 992 and
     table 1489 for newspapers and magazines. table 994 is also used to
     obtain the percentage of advertising content in newspapers.

     Receipts from advertising in newspapers are available only for 1947,
     1954, 1958, 1963, 1967, and 1972. The ratio of receipts from
     advertising in newspapers to expenditures by business on advertising
     in newspapers and magazines for these years exhibits no trend, and
     the standard deviation equals only .017. Therefore, the average ratio,
     .786, is applied to the expenditure data in table 1489 to obtain an
     estimate of advertising receipts for newspapers from 1946 to 1981.

     Cremeans (1980) estimates that 24 percent of household TV viewing
     time is advertising and that 30 percent of radio and print media
     production costs go to advertising. We took his figure and allocated
     76 percent of TV advertising receipts and 70 percent of radio ad-
     vertising receipts to media support.

     Since we do not know how much time is devoted to the reading of
     advertising in print media, these are treated differently. We take 70
     percent of the receipts from advertising and multiply them by the
     fraction of content that is nonadvertising.
     Total media support, *MEDSUP*, is the sum of the support given to
     the three types of media:

     $$MEDSUP = .76 \times TV + .7 \times RADIO$$
     $$+ .7 \times NONAD \times NEWMAG,$$

     where

     TV   = receipts from advertising on television.
     RADIO   = receipts from advertising on radio.
     NONAD   = portion of content in newspapers which is nonadver-
                  tising; the percent of content of magazines which is
                  nonadvertising was not available and is above as-
                  sumed implicitly to be the same as the nonadvertising
                  portion of the content of newspapers.

NEWMAG = Receipts from advertising and expenditures by business in magazines.*

33. Health and safety
     These are expenditures for in-plant health and safety and are described in section 13.

34. Other
     This is business transfer payments: N1.7-7.

35. Net indirect business taxes

36. Indirect business taxes
     Total indirect business taxes (N1.7-6) less owner-occupied nonfarm housing indirect taxes (N8.8-76) less government enterprise indirect taxes less nonprofit taxes.

37. Less: Intermediate product transferred from government to business
     5-40

38. Statistical discrepancy

39. BEA statistical discrepancy
     N1.7-8

40. TISA statistical discrepancy
     $67 - 30 - 31 - 35 - 39 - 42$

41. Charges against net business product
     $30 + 31 + 35 + 38$

42. Capital consumption allowances

43. Tangible

44. Original cost
     Original cost depreciation for structures and equipment and residential capital are from BEA capital stock tapes.

45. Revaluations
     This is adjustment of consistent accounting at historical cost to current replacement cost. It is calculated as the difference between current cost depreciation and original cost depreciation or business structures and equipment and residential capital.

46. Intangible
     Intangible capital in the business sector consists of the stock of knowledge produced by research and development. Following Kendrick, we assume that basic research and development has an infinite life. Hence, it has no capital consumption. This leaves applied re-

*Receipts from advertising in periodicals exceed expenditures by businesses. Nonprofit and personal advertising in periodicals are assumed to make up the difference. Therefore, expenditures data are used.

search and development to account for all of business intangible capital consumption allowances. It is assumed that stocks of applied research and development produced by other sectors, government and nonprofit, are transferred to the business sector. These stocks are accumulated from the investment series shown in 3-28 and 5-29.

A twenty-year life is assumed for applied research and development. Constant dollar stocks and depreciation are calculated from constant dollar investment data applying straight-line depreciation with the half-year convention. Capital consumption allowance with adjustment is then calculated by applying implicit price deflators to the constant dollar depreciation. The implicit price deflator for applied research and development is

$$PARD = IGRD^{cur\$} / IGRD^{72\$},$$

where

$IGRD$ = gross investment in research and development, and is estimated both for the U.S. domestic economy and for the business sector alone.

Research and development capital consumption allowance with adjustment transferred from government and nonprofit institutions is then the difference between research and development capital consumption adjustment for the U.S. domestic economy and research and development capital consumption adjustment calculated from investment originally undertaken in the business sector.

Research and development investment data, current and constant dollars, are taken from Kendrick, appendix tables 2, 6, 11, and 15 for 1924–1952 and from *National Patterns of Service and Technology Resources 1982*, tables 9 and 11 for 1953–1981 (National Science Foundation 1982a). The NSF data are adjusted by averaging contiguous years to account for the fact that government data are for fiscal years (1 July–30 June) and other data are for calendar years. The NSF publication is an updated version of the source Kendrick used for these years. Note that NSF constant dollar series are based on the GNP implicit price deflator.

47.   Original cost
Original cost capital consumption allowances are calculated with the same twenty-year average service life and the perpetual in-

ventory method but current dollar rather than constant dollar gross investment data were used.

48.   On business R&D investment

49.   On R&D investment transferred from government and nonprofit institutions

50.   Revaluations
Revaluation capital consumption allowances are the difference between total and original cost capital consumption allowances.

51.   On business R&D investment

52.   On R&D investment transferred from government and nonprofit institutions

53. Charges against gross business product
41 + 42

Credits

54. BEA gross domestic product, business
N1.5-3

55. Less: Net space rent of owner-occupied nonfarm dwellings
N8.8-74

56. Less: BEA government enterprise product
This is compensation of employees, (N6.5A-78 + N6.5A-81) plus current surplus of government enterprises (N3.12-9 + N3.12-17) plus indirect business tax paid by government enterprises.

57. Less: Rental value of buildings owned and used by nonprofit institutions
N8.8-87 − N8.8-88 + 3-20

58. BEA-type gross domestic product of TISA business sector
54 − 55 − 56 − 57

59. Subsidies included in business income
This may be written as:

$$SUBIBI = CSUBGE + SUBLSURGE - SUBOOH,$$

where

$CSUBGE$ = current surplus of government enterprise: N3.12-9
+ N3.12-17, for 1952 to 1981.
$CSUBGE$ is from an unpublished version of N6.1 for 1946 to 1951.
$SUBLSURGE$ = subsidies less surplus of government enterprises:
N1.7-9.
$SUBOOH$ = subsidies to owner-occupied housing: N8.8-77.

60. Expense account items of consumption
    5
61. Less: Expenses related to work
    7
62. Business investment in research and development
    20
63. Training produced in the business sector
    4
64. Media support plus health and safety
    32 + 33
65. Net revaluations
    22
66. Less: Intermediate product from government
    37
67. Gross business product
    58 + 59 + 60 + 62 + 63 + 64 + 65 − 61 − 66

3. Nonprofit Income and Product

Debits

1. Labor income
2. Compensation of employees
   N1.12-41 − N6.5A-74
3. Employee training
   See section 13, Investment in Human Capital.
4. Less: Expenses related to work
   See appendix B, Expenses Related to Work.
5. Capital Income
6. Interest paid
   N8.8-90
7. Net imputed interest
8. Gross imputed interest
   The rate of return used in imputing services of nonprofit, government enterprise, and government capital is a weighted average of
   the after-tax rate of return to household and business capital. This
   is obtained by dividing an estimate of total return—the sum of
   after-tax corporate profits, proprietors' capital income, interest paid
   by business and on owner-occupied housing, rental income, and
   imputed interest on household capital, less personal taxes on business capital—by the total stock of business and household tangible
   capital.

$$r = \frac{P_P + P_C + I_B + I_{OOH} + I_{HH} + R - T_{BP} - T_{BE}}{K_B + K_{HH}}$$

where

r = the rate of return applied to nonprofit government enterprise and government capital.

P_P = proprietors' capital income: 2-11.

P_C = domestic corporate profits with inventory valuation and
capital consumption allowance adjustments, less corporate
profits tax: N1.13-9 − N1.13-11.

I_B = business interest paid: 2-9.

I_{OOH} = net interest paid on owner-occupied housing: N8.8-78.

I_{HH} = Net imputed interest on household durables, semidurables and inventories: 6-21 [equal to $r_{HH} \times (DUR + SEMI + INVENT)$].

R = rental income of persons with capital consumption allowance adjustment, N1.12-32.

T_{BP} = personal taxes on business income, derived below.

T_{BE} = estate and gift taxes, derived below.

K_B = business land + structures + equipment + inventories.

K_{HH} = household land + structures + durables + semidurables + inventories.

Since neither the nonprofit nor government sectors is taxed, taxes on business capital income are subtracted in personal taxes, which include personal income taxes and estate and gift taxes, and are subtracted in calculating their rate of return.

Ando and Brown (1968) estimated federal income taxes attributable to wages and salaries by taking for each income bracket the ratio of wage and salary income to adjusted gross income, and applying this ratio to taxes paid. Since the percentage of taxes attributable to wages and salaries varied only slightly, we use the average percentage of 75.5 percent, and assume it to be constant for all years.

IRS data show that approximately 6 percent of the remainder is due to pensions. Thus rent, dividends, interest, capital gains, and proprietors' income account for an estimated 23 percent of federal income taxes. This percentage is assumed to be the same for state and local personal income taxes.

The personal taxes attributable to business capital are then

$$T_{BP} = .23 \frac{P_C + P_K + I_{BM} + R}{P + P_C + I_{HM} + R} \times T_P,$$

where

P_C = corporate profits after tax: N1.12-7.

P_K = proprietors' capital income: 2-11.

R = rental income of persons less rental income of owner-occupied nonfarm dwellings: N1.12-32 − N8.8-79.

I_{BM} = business monetary interest paid: N8.7-2.

I_{HM} = monetary interest received by households: N8.7-28.
P = total proprietors' income: N1.12-16 + N1.12-29.
T_P = personal income taxes, federal plus state and local: N3.2-3 + N3.3-3.

The numerator and denominator differ by proprietors' labor income and the amount of nonbusiness monetary interest received by households.

Estate and gift taxes are estimated by applying the share of business capital in household net worth to estate and gift taxes.

$$T_{BE} = \frac{E_C + E_{NC} + B_C}{E_C + E_{NC} + B_C + B_G + H + DUR - D_H} \times T_E,$$

where

T_{BE} = estate and gift taxes attributable to business capital.
E_C and E_{NC} = corporate and noncorporate equity, respectively, held by households.
B_C and B_G = corporate and government bonds, respectively, held by households, with B_C including open market paper.
H = value of owner-occupied housing and land held by households.
DUR = value of consumer durables.
D_H = household home mortgage and consumer debt.
T_E = estate and gift taxes, federal plus state and local: N3.4-7 + N3.4-11.

The source for the data above, other than T_E, is the Flow of Funds accounts of the Federal Reserve.

9.   Land
     This is taken to be .93 × $AVGLAND$ × r, where $AVGLAND_t$ = .5 (Land $_t$ + Land $_{t-1}$), with end-of-year land values from the Federal Reserve Board *Flow of Funds Accounts*.

The multiplier of .93 is applied to exclude wholesale cooperatives (which we include in the business sector), estimated by the BEA as 7 percent on the nonprofit structures and equipment total. Since the Federal Reserve Board's land data are based on the BEA's structures and equipment, the multiplier of .93 is applied to nonprofit land and corresponding net revaluations and capital consumption allowances.

10.   Structures and equipment
This equals $.93 \times AVESEG \times r$, where $AVGSEQ = .5(SEQ_t + SEQ_{t-1})$ and SEQ are end-of-year net stocks of structures and equipment held by nonprofit institutions. Data are from John Musgrave, BEA, *Fixed Nonresidential Business Capital, Nonprofit Institutions, Current and Constant Cost Valuation* (U.S. Dept. of Commerce, BEA 1980b).

11.   Residential
This equals $AVGRES \times r$ where $AVGRES_t = .5(RES_t + RES_{t-1})$ and *RES* are end-of-year nonprofit residential stocks. Data are from printouts provided by John Musgrave, BEA, "Nonprofit Residential Capital, Current Cost Valuation."

12.   Less: Interest paid
N8.8-90

13. Net revaluations
The general method is as described for the business sector: 2-22. The stock data used here are as described in line 8 above; sources on the investment data are noted below.

14.   Land
Net investment in land is assumed to be zero for all years.

15.   Structures and equipment
Investment data are from John Musgrave, BEA capital stock tapes.

16.   Residential structures
Investment data are the first differences of constant dollar net stocks, converted to current dollars by multiplying by the implicit price deflator for residential structures: N7.1-11.

17. Income originating
$1 + 5 + 13$

18. Imputed value of volunteer services

$$\text{Volunteer Value} = POP15 \times (VTIME) \times (VWAGE),$$

where

$POP15$ = resident population 15 and over. This is considered to be the part of the population performing volunteer services. It is calculated by adding population in the age groups 0–4, 5–9, and 10–14, and subtracting this sum from the total resident population. Data for the three age groups and total population were obtained from the *Current Population Reports, Population Estimates and Projections,* series P-25 (U.S. Dept. of Commerce, Bureau of the Census), as follows:

Years	Publication No.	Table No.
1978–81	917	2
1970–77	721	2
1960–69	519	2
1950–59	310	1
1946–49	98	1

VTIME = average time per capita spent on volunteer activities. We have from Szalai, *The Use of Time* (1972, 576–77), average minutes per day, per adult (aged 19 to 65) spent in

Civic Activities	1.2
Religious Organizations	2.0
	3.2 minutes per day

3.2 × 365 = 1168 minutes per year per person. 1168 minutes ÷ 60 = 19.466 hours per year per person. This is assumed, for lack of data, to be constant for all years, 1946 to 1981.

VWAGE = Hourly value of time spent on volunteer work. This is taken to be average hourly earnings of nonsupervisory workers in service, *WS*. We have data for the years 1964 to 1981. For earlier years this is calculated as

$$WS_t = WM_t \times \frac{WS_{64}}{WM_{64}},$$

where *WM* = average hourly earnings on nonsupervisory workers in manufacturing.

Hourly earnings data for the years 1946–72 are from the *Handbook of Labor Statistics, 1975,* table 98, p. 248 (U.S. Dept of Labor, Bureau of Labor Statistics). Data for 1973–81 are from *Employment and Earnings* (U.S. Dept. of Labor, Bureau of Labor Statistics 1979).

19. Charges against net nonprofit product
    17 + 18

20. Capital consumption allowances
    This is equal to depreciation at replacement cost for structures and equipment and residential capital. Data used are the same as for line 10 and 11 above.

21. Original cost
    Unpublished data are from tables provided by John Musgrave and the BEA, entitled "Residential Capital, Nonprofit Institutions, Historical Cost Valuation" and "Fixed Nonresidential Business Capital, Nonprofit Institutions, Historical Cost Valuation" (U.S. Dept. of Commerce, BEA).

22. Revaluations
    This is the difference in depreciation resulting from valuing the capital stock at current cost instead of historical cost, and equals 20 − 21.

23. Charges against gross nonprofit product
    19 + 20

Credits

The BEA classifies operating expenses of nonprofit institutions as personal consumption expenditures. Our general procedure is to reclassify nonprofit operating expenses as consumption, investment in health, education, research and development, or as intermediate product purchased. In addition, the nonprofit debits include the value of volunteer services and net imputed interest. Thus, volunteer services plus real net imputed interest, along with intermediate product of government, must also be allocated among consumption and investment in health and in education.

We have set up eleven categories of BEA nonprofit operating expenses:*

	NIPA Item	Data from
A. Blue Cross–Blue Shield	Part of 2.4-52	1958
B. Private hospitals and sanitoriums	80% of 2.4-50	1946
C. Fraternal benefit life insurance	Part of 2.4-59	1958
D. Labor union expenses	Part of 2.4-52	1959
E. Professional association dues	Part of 2.4-62	1959
F. Health insurance	Part of 2.4-52	1946

*Numbers for 1967–81 are unpublished figures from Clint McCully, Bureau of Economic Analysis, Department of Commerce, Washington, D.C.

G. Clubs and fraternal organizations	2.4-94	1946
H. Private higher education	2.4-99	1946
I. Private lower education	2.4-100	1946
J. Nonprofit R&D and foundation expenses	2.4-101	1959
K. Religious and welfare activities	2.4-102	1946

The BEA has further broken down religious and welfare activities into five subcategories: political organizations, museums, foundation expenses, social welfare organizations, and religious organizations. We take 30 percent of museums and 25 percent of religious organizations to be investment in education. The rest is classified as consumption.

Data series which are incomplete are extended backwards as follows:

A. Blue Cross-Blue Shield (BC)

$$BC_t = BC_{1958} \times \frac{N2.4\text{-}52,t}{N2.4\text{-}52,1958} \qquad t = 1948\text{-}57$$

$$BC_t = BC_{1948} \times \frac{N2.4\text{-}51,t}{N2.4\text{-}51,1948} \qquad t = 1946\text{-}47$$

C. Fraternal benefit life insurance ($FBLI$)

$$FBLI_t = FBLI_{1958} \times \frac{N2.4\text{-}59,t}{N2.4\text{-}59,1958} \qquad t = 1946\text{-}57$$

D. Labor union expenses and professional association dues (X)

$$X_t = X_{1959} \times \frac{N2.4\text{-}62,t}{N2.4\text{-}62,1959} \qquad t = 1946\text{-}58$$

J. Nonprofit R&D and foundation expenses (Y)

$$Y_t = Y_{1958} \times \frac{N2.4\text{-}101,t}{N2.4\text{-}101,1958} \qquad t = 1946\text{-}57$$

Additional TISA nonprofit debit items not included in BEA operating expenses are

L. Volunteer services

This is broken down according to the percentage of volunteer hours spent in various activities:

Health	17.2%
Education	21.6%
Consumption	61.2%

Data are taken from Weisbrod and Long (1975, 13).

M. Net imputed interest

This is separated according to the proportions of nonprofit structures and equipment that are religious, health, education, and other. Nonprofit investment in these categories comes from the BEA, which takes a fixed percentage of N5.4-8 to N5.4-11. There are series for both structures and equipment. Using these investment series and straight-line depreciation, we formed a stock series for religious, health, education, and other capital. Service lives and early investment data are taken from the BEA's *Fixed Nonresidential Business Capital in the U.S.* (U.S. Dept. of Commerce, BEA 1971).

The data discussed above are used to calculate the following credit items:

24. Consumption

25. Consumption included in BEA personal consumption expenditures

BEAPCE = OPEXNP − HEALTH − EDTRAIN − R&DNP,

where

BEAPCE = consumption included in BEA personal consumption expenditures (PCE).

OPEXNP = total BEA operating expense by nonprofit institutions: A + B + C + . . . + K, above.

HEALTH = health investment in BEA PCE: 34.

EDTRAIN = education and training investment in BEA PCE: 30.

R&DNP = nonprofit investment in research and development: 28.

26. Additional imputed consumption

This is equal to 69.8 percent of volunteer services (consumption plus half of health) plus a portion of real interest minus nominal interest paid. The portion is the percentage on nonprofit structures and equipment which is "other," plus half of health. Additional imputed consumption may thus be written as:

$$\text{AIC} = .698 \text{ VOLVAL}$$
$$+ \frac{\text{NPSEQ}_{\text{OTH}} + .5\text{NPSEQ}_{\text{HLT}}}{\text{NPSEQ}_{\text{TOT}}} \times \text{NETINT},$$

where

VOLVAL = value of volunteer services.

$NPSEQ_{OTH}$, $NPSEQ_{HLT}$, $NPSEQ_{TOT}$ = nonprofit structures and equipment which are other, health, and the total, respectively.

NETINT = net imputed interest.

27. Capital accumulation

28. Research and development

Only basic research expenditures by the nonprofit sector are assumed to be nonprofit capital accumulation; business-financed R&D in non-profit institutions is included in the business sector. There is no depreciation of basic research capital.

Nonprofit R&D is performed either by universities and colleges or other nonprofit institutions. Our data for research in universities include both nonprofit and government-supported institutions. To separate nonprofit from the total, an expenditure survey by HEW is used. This gives a ratio of R&D, nonpublic universities, to R&D, all universities. In using this ratio, we are assuming that all nonpublic universities are nonprofit. We multiply research in universities by this ratio and add research in other nonprofit institutions to get total nonprofit basic research. This gives us:

$$R = R_{\text{UNIV}} \times \frac{\text{R\&D}_{\text{NPUNIV}}}{\text{R\&D}_{\text{ALL UNIV}}} + R_{\text{OTHER}},$$

where

R	= total nonprofit basic research expenditures.
$R\&D_{\text{NPUNIV}}$	= R&D expenditures by nonpublic institutions of higher education.
$R\&D_{\text{ALL UNIV}}$	= R&D expenditures by all institutions of higher education.
R_{UNIV}	= basic research expenditures by universities and colleges.

R_{OTHER} = basic research expenditures by other nonprofit institutions for the years 1953 to 1981.

R_{UNIV} and R_{OTHER} = for the years 1953 to 1981 are data from the National Science Foundation (1977), taken from NSF 77-310, table B-2. Each of these variables, designated "X", is extrapolated backward for the years 1946 to 1952 in accordance with the formulation,

$$X_t = X_{1953}(1+g)^{t-1953}, \qquad 1 + g = \left(\frac{X_{60}}{X_{53}}\right)^{1/7}$$

$$t = 1946\text{--}52.$$

Data for $R\&D_{NPUNIV}$ and $R\&D_{ALL\ UNIV}$ for the years 1964–81 come from HEW's "Projections of Education Statistics to 1986," table 33, p. 102. For earlier years, HEW's biannual "Statistics of Higher Education: Receipts, Expenditures, Property," is used. Since the data are biannual, off-years are interpolated.

29. Education and training
30. Investment included in BEA personal consumption expenditures
Equal to H + I + J plus the educational part of K, minus nonprofit R&D, as calculated above. Nonprofit R&D is included in item J, and thus is subtracted to avoid double counting.

31. Additional imputed investment
Equal to 21.6 percent of volunteer services plus the percentage of the stocks of nonprofit structures and equipment that is educational multiplied by net imputed interest. Additional imputed investment in education and training may thus be written as

$$AIIET = .216 VOLVAL + \frac{NPSEQ_{ED}}{NPSEQ_{TOT}} \times NETINT.$$

32. Employee training
This is debit, line 3.

33. Health
34. Investment included in BEA personal consumption expenditures
Equal to one-half of item B.

35. Additional imputed investment
Equal to 8.6 percent of volunteer services plus half the percentage of nonprofit structures and equipment which is health multiplied

by net imputed interest. Additional imputed investment in health is thus defined as

$$\text{AIIH} = .086\text{VOLVAL} + .5\frac{\text{NPSEQ}_{\text{HLT}}}{\text{NPSEQ}_{\text{TOT}}} \times \text{NETINT}.$$

36.   Net revaluations
      This is taken from the debit side, line 13.

37. Less: Intermediate product transferred from government
     5-40

38. Less: Intermediate product purchased
     Since nonprofit operating expenses include some intermediate product, this must be subtracted to arrive at gross nonprofit product. It is equal to total nonprofit operating expenses (the sum of A through K) minus labor income, minus interest paid, minus net indirect taxes minus capital consumption allowances.

39. Less: Expenses related to work
     4

40. Gross nonprofit product
     24 + 27 − 37 − 38 − 39

4. Government Enterprise Income and Product

Debits

1. Labor income

2. Compensation of employees
   This is total government enterprise compensation of employees, state and local plus federal: N6.5A-78 + N6.5A-81.

3. Employee training
   See section 13, Investment in Human Capital.

4. Less: Expenses related to work
   This is an estimate of commuting expenses for government enterprise employees. For details of its calculation, see write-up for expenses related to work in appendix B.

5. Capital income
   This item includes only imputed interest on government enterprise inventories. The government sector requires stocks by type of function. Such a breakdown is available only for the combined stocks of government and government enterprises. Hence, government enterprise structures, equipment, residential, and land stocks are included with government stocks. Imputed interest on inventories is calculated as

   $$\text{Interest}_t = .5r_t(\text{Inventories}_t + \text{Inventories}_{t-1}) \qquad t = 1946 \text{ to } 1981.$$

   Data for inventories are year-end figures. They are averaged to estimate mid-year stocks. Inventory data are from the BEA *Reproducible Tangible Capital, Government Enterprises, Current and Constant Cost Valuation* (U.S. Dept. of Commerce, BEA 1980g). The interest rate, r_t, is an economy-wide average after-tax rate of return. (See Section 3, Nonprofit Income and Product, line 8, for details of its calculations.)

6. Surpluses

7. BEA surplus
   This is N3.12-9 + N3.12-17 for 1960 to 1981. Data for 1952 to 1959 are from an unpublished version of N3.12 supplied by D. Tolson of the BEA. Data for 1947 to 1951 are from components of Gross Product Originating, an unpublished table from Dan Eldridge of the BEA. The 1946 BEA surplus is taken to be the same as the 1947 surplus.

8. Sum of absolute values of negative surpluses
   Government enterprise deficits result in a valuation of product less than cost. The absolute value of negative surpluses, in recent years

particularly in the postal service, the commodity credit corporation, and the aggregate of state and local public transit enterprises, is added so that product is valued at cost. Data are taken from N3.12 for 1960 to 1976 and its corresponding unpublished table for 1952 to 1959. For 1946 to 1951, estimates are extrapolated from a regression of negative surplus, NS, on total federal surpluses of government enterprises (N3.12-9), TS, for 1952 to 1959. The resulting equation is:

$$NS_t = 452.001 - .976775 \ TS_t.$$

9. Net revaluations

This includes only net revaluations on the stock of inventories. Stock data are the same as in 5 above. Investment is taken to be the first difference of constant-dollar stocks, converted to current dollars by multiplying by an implicit deflator.

$$I_t = \left(K_t^{72\$} - K_{t-1}^{72\$} \right) \times \frac{K_{t-1}^{cur\$}}{K_t^{72\$}}.$$

10. Net surplus

6 + 9

11. Charges against government enterprise product

1 + 5 + 10

Credits

12. Sales, minus purchases of intermediate goods

2 + 7 + trivial government enterprise indirect taxes.

This is an estimate of the portion of government plus trivial government enterprise indirect taxes that is included in the BEA's personal consumption expenditures.

13. Transfers

14. Capital income plus negative surpluses plus intermediate products from government minus indirect taxes

15. Consumption

Real interest and negative surpluses are allocated between consumption and investment on the basis of consumption and original cost investment in the current dollar totals of TISA table 1. Thus, referring to lines of TISA tables, with 1C designating the credits side of table 1 and 4 designating this table.

Consumption = (4-5 + 4-8)

$$\times \frac{1C\text{-}1 - 1C\text{-}17 - 1C\text{-}18}{1C\text{-}1 - 1C\text{-}17 - 1C\text{-}18 + 1C\text{-}31},$$

where numerator equals consumption, excluding government enterprise consumption and subsidies allocated to consumption, and denominator equals the sum of that consumption and original cost investment.

16.   Investment
       14 − 15

17.   Employee training
       See section 13.

18. Net revaluations
    9

19. Less: Intermediate product from government
    5-43

20. Less: Expenses related to work
    4

21. Gross government enterprise product
    12 + 13 + 18 − 19 − 20

5. Government Income and Product

Debits

1. Labor income includes compensation of federal and state and local government employees, civilian and military, from N6.5, lines 78 and 83, plus the value of employee training, both civilian and military, but less a deduction for expenses related to traveling to and from work. Nonmilitary employee training estimates for the years 1946 and 1966 were derived from unpublished data furnished by John Kendrick. We separated out government and government enterprises from his total government in proportion to compensation of employees. Estimates for the years 1967 to 1981 were then extrapolated on the basis of a regression for the years 1940 to 1966 of the logarithm of Kendrick's government training expenditures per employee on the logarithm of the new hire rate, the logarithm of compensation per employee, and a time trend. The value of military training was estimated as .63075 times military wages (N6.6A-79). The fraction .63075 was obtained from Kendrick worksheets on human capital.

   Utilizing both the 1965 and 1975 time-use studies conducted by the Institute for Social Research at the University of Michigan, time series for 1946–76 were interpolated and extrapolated for time traveling to and from work and for total time traveling. Expenses related to work are taken as total travel expenses multiplied by the ratio of time spent traveling to and from work to total time spent traveling. Total travel expenses are the sum of N2.4, lines 68, 69, 70, 71, 72, 73, and 77 and the imputed interest on the net stock of autos and other motor vehicles. The portion of travel expenditures attributed to government employees is assumed equal to the ratio of government full- and part-time employees to total full- and part-time employees in the domestic economy, that is, N6.7A, (line 75 − line 79 − line 84) ÷ line 2.

2. Compensation of employees

3. Employee training

4. Less: Expenses related to work

5. Capital income
   Capital income is the sum of gross imputed interest on government stock of land, structures and equipment, inventories, and R&D. It is calculated for any year, t, by averaging net stocks of government capital of years t and t-1 and multiplying this average by an economy-wide average after-tax rate of return (for details of its calculation see the nonprofit sector, 3-8). Interest paid is taken from N3.1-13. Net imputed interest is simply gross imputed interest minus interest paid.

Net stock of structues, equipment, and inventories held by government are from printouts of BEA data made available by John Musgrave. The net stocks of government land for 1952 to 1968 are obtained from Milgram (1973). The stocks of R&D are developed from the government R&D investment series, line 38.

6. Interest paid

7. Net imputed interest

8.   Gross imputed interest

9.   Land

10.   Structures and equipment

11.   Inventories

12.   Research and development

13.   Less: Interest paid
For 1945 and 1951 we assume that the ratio of government-held land to private land was the same as it was in 1952, as Milgram's data indicated. Similarly we assume that from 1969 to 1981 the government sector's holding of land was the same percentage of private land as it was in 1968. Then, utilizing private land value estimates provided by the Flow of Funds section of the Federal Reserve Board, we calculate

$$L_{Gt} = \frac{L_{G52}}{L_{Pr52}} \times L_{Pr,t} \qquad t = 1945 \text{ to } 1951,$$

and

$$L_{Gt} = \frac{L_{G68}}{L_{Pr68}} \times L_{Pr,t} \qquad t = 1969 \text{ to } 1981,$$

where

L_{Gt} = value of government land in year t and
$L_{Pr,t}$ = value of private land in the U.S. economy in year t.

14. Net revaluations

15.   Land

16.   Structures and equipment

17.   Inventories
(15, 16, and 17 are obtained from Eisner (1980a) tables 5.55 and 5.56)

18. Income originating in the government sector is the sum of lines 1, 5, and 14, or labor income + capital income + net revaluations.

19. Uncompensated factor services, *UFS,* consist of services of draftees, which are assigned to the national defense function, and jurors' services, which are assigned to general administration.

20.   Draftees
       Our estimates of uncompensated services of draftees are based on Lundberg and Nebhut (1979). They view the supply of volunteers as a function of the draft rate, the relative wage of the military, the civilian employment rate for draft-age males, and the existence of a war for the years 1964 to 1972. A simulated military wage that would have supplied sufficient enlistments to the actual armed forces without the draft is then calculated. The value of uncompensated services is taken as the difference between the actual compensation of first-term members of the armed forces and the implied compensation necessary if all first-termers were to be volunteers.

       For the Vietnam War era Lundburg and Nebhut found no response of volunteers to the relative wage rate. Taken literally this would imply the necessity of an infinite military wage to secure sufficient enlistments in the absence of the draft. We nevertheless apply the pre-Vietnam relative wage function, so that our figures for the Vietnam-War years may be considered very much a lower bound to estimates of the compensation necessary to secure sufficient volunteers. As the last draftees were inducted in 1972 we assume that there were no nonvolunteers in the armed forces after 1975.

21.   Jurors
       We base our estimates of uncompensated juror services largely on procedures employed by Martin (1972). We apply annual data on the number of jury trials and median income by occupation to his estimates of the 1962 occupational composition of jurors to secure estimates of the annual opportunity costs of jury service. We then deduct the amounts of fees actually paid for jury service to arrive at the uncompensated service of jurors.

       The main difference in our analysis is the use of TISA's value of unpaid household work to impute mean income of nonworking jurors,

$$
NWJY_t = DOMWAGE_t
$$
$$
\times \left(\frac{MNON_t \times MHRHW_t + FNON_t \times FHRHW_t}{MNON_t + FNON_t} \right)
$$

where

$NWJY_t$ = mean nonworking jurors' income in year t.
$DOMWAGE_t$ = domestic wage per hour in household sector in year t.
$MNON_t$ = number of nonemployed males in year t.
$FNON_t$ = number of nonemployed females in year t.
$MHRHW_t$ = male's hours expended on household work in year t.
$FHRHW_t$ = female's hours expended on household work in year t.
t = 1946 to 1981

(See appendix A, Valuation of Household Work, for a further explanation of $MHRHW$ and $FHRHW$.)

22. Charges against net government product are the sum of lines 18 and 19, income originating plus uncompensated factor services.

23. Capital consumption allowances on government capital were obtained from the BEA. Since in the case of government capital there is no BEA adjustment necessary to obtain consistent accounting, the revaluations component equals the capital consumption adjustment.

24. Original Cost

25. Revaluations

26. Charges against gross government product are the sum of lines 22 and 23, charges against net government product plus capital consumption allowances.

Credits

27. Consumption to households

The total of gross government product is estimated on the debit side. Line 51, gross government product, is thus set equal to line 26, charges against gross government product. We subtract net revaluations, line 50 (equal to line 14) to arrive at gross government product exclusive of net revaluations, line 49.

We then also subtract change in inventories, line 46, and add intermediate purchases from other sectors, line 47, and expenses related to work, line 48 (equal to line 4), to arrive at gross credits exclusive of change in inventories and net revaluations, line 45.

These gross credits, line 45, must then be allocated among consumption (to households), line 27; capital accumulation, line 28; and intermediate product, line 40. The allocation is based upon the functions or activities into which government output can be categorized. The functional classification also determines the sectors to which government output, which is of course not generally sold, is transferred.

Government research and development is viewed as creating an output which is partly retained in government as a stock of R&D knowledge, line 38, and partly transferred to business, line 29. Education and training, line 31, is considered an output of capital which is transferred to households. Health services are viewed as going half to human capital formation and hence counted under capital going to households, line 36, and going half to households in the form of maintenance or current consumption, included in line 27. Government investment in natural resources is counted as capital accumulated by government, in line 39.

Finally, government output of services of defense, transportation, and general administration is counted as intermediate in other government production or in the output of other sectors. The portion going to other sectors is given on line 40.

Details of the derivation of lines 27, 28, and 40, consumption, capital, and intermediate product, and some of their subdivisions are offered below.

28. Capital accumulation
29.   To business (R&D)
30.   To households
31.   Education and training
32.   Public schools
33.   Employee training
34.   Military
35.   Nonmilitary
36.   Health
37.   To government
38.   Research and development
39.   Natural resources
40. Intermediate product
41.   To business
42.   To nonprofit
43.   To government enterprise

44. To household

45. Gross credits exclusive of change in inventories and net revaluations
    26 − 46 + 47 + 48 − 50

    This is equal to the sum of product transferred and product retained by government: 27 + 28 + 40.

46. Change in inventories
    Unpublished tables from BEA.

47. Less: Intermediate purchases from other sectors
    Government expenditures for goods and services minus government compensation of employees and capital expenditures.

48. Less: Expenses related to work
    This is identical to line 4 above.

49. Gross government product exclusive of net revaluations
    45 + 46 − 47 − 48

50. Net revaluations
    14

51. Gross government product
    49 + 50

    Details of allocations of government product:*

    A. General (a three-step procedure is followed)
       1. We divide all government activities among ten functions.
       2. We estimate for each function the "untransferred product," or its component of gross credits exclusive of changes in inventories and net revaluations.
       3. We classify each function's product as retained by government or transferred to other sectors, and as consumption, investment, or intermediate product.

    B. Government functions
       Government expenditures by type of function, reclassified from N3.16 and N3.17, are as follows:**

---

*All of the rest of this section on government product is essentially taken from Eisner and Nebhut (1981).

**Government enterprise activities are excluded from this classification.

		Federal Gov't.	State and Local Gov't.
1.	National defense and international relations		
	a. National defense	N3.16-11	—
	b. International affairs	N3.16-7	—
	c. Insurance (veterans benefits)	N3.16-49	—
	d. Civilian safety	N3.16-16	N3.17-5
2.	Space	N3.16-10	—
3.	Education and training		
	a. Education	N3.16-20	N3.17-9
	b. Education (veterans benefits)	N3.16-48	—
	c. .064875 × recreational and cultural activities	.064875 × N3.16-56	.064875 × N3.17-28
	d. Labor training and services	N3.16-78	N3.17-40
4.	Health and hospital services		
	a. Health and hospitals	N3.16-24	N3.17-14
	b. Hospital and medical care (veterans benefits)	N3.16-50	—
5.	Housing and community services	N3.16-52	N3.17-23
6.	Transportation and mobility	N3.16-67	N3.17-34
7.	Local parks and recreation		
	.935125 × recreation and cultural activities	.935125 × N3.16-56	.935125 × N3.17-28
8.	Natural resources		
	a. Conservation of agricultural resources	N3.16-64	N3.17-32
	b. Natural resources	N3.16-66	N3.17-33
	c. Conservation and development of energy sources	N3.16-58	—
9.	Welfare	N3.16-25	N3.17-17

10. General administration

a. Central executive and judicial	N3.16-2	N3.17-2
b. Economic development, regulation, and services	N3.16-74	N3.17-39
c. Postal services and others	N3.16-51 + N3.16-60 + N3.16-65 + N3.16-73	N3.17-22

C. The composition of product by functions

In describing the allocation of product to functions we find it useful to develop precise concepts of untransferred product, gross product, and final product, along with the following symbols and definitions.

1) Let VA_i = value added of function i, the sum of factor payments (excluding the value of employee training), uncompensated factor services, and depreciation minus expenses related to work. Thus,

2) $$VA_i = R_i + D_i + CE_i + UFS_i - ERW_i,$$

where

R_i = imputed interest on capital stock in function i,
D_i = capital consumption of capital stock in function i,
CE_i = compensation of employees in function i,
UFS_i = uncompensated factor services in function i, and
ERW_i = expenses related to work incurred by employees in function i.

Interest is distributed by function on the basis of the distribution of land, structures, equipment and inventories, and capital consumption on the basis of the distribution of structures and equipment.

3) Let IP_{io} = purchases of intermediate products (noncapital goods and nonfactor services from outside government) for use in producing output in function i.

4) Let I_i = purchase of capital goods for use in function i.

5) Let PGS_i = total purchases of goods and services for use in producing output in function i.

6) Then $$PGS_i = I_i + IP_{io} + CE_i,$$

and

$$IP_{io} = PGS_i - I_i - CE_i.$$

7) Let ΔH_i = additions to inventories associated with function i.

8) Let UP_i = $VA_i + IP_{io} - \Delta H_i + ERW_i$ = untransferred product in function i, net of additions to inventories, that is, the sum of value added, intermediate product purchased and used in current production, and expenses related to work, but exclusive of intermediate product transferred between functions of government.

9) Let IP_{ij} = transfer of output of function j to function i, $j \neq i$.

10) Let GP_i = gross product of function i = untransferred product plus product transferred to function i from other functions of government.

11) Thus $$GP_i = VA_i + IP_{io} - \Delta H_i + ERW_i + \sum_j I_{ij}.$$

12) Let FP_i = final product of function i = gross product minus transfers of product to other functions.

13) Thus $$FP_i = GP_i - \sum_j IP_{ji}.$$

D. Allocation of capital by function

To calculate value added by function we must assign capital by function. Since precisely appropriate data are rarely available, a variety of more or less complex methods was used to obtain reasonable approximations. We have benefitted particularly from unpublished estimates (later published) by Ott and Austin (1978 and 1980) of stocks of structures by function. They built these up from unpublished BEA tabulations of investment in structures by function.

Data are available for a number of components of capital employed in the defense function. Defense capital is the sum of structures, equipment, inventories, and land used in defense, where defense comprises both military and nonmilitary protection services. Defense structures, S_D, thus includes among its components military structures, S_m, and nonmilitary protection structures, S_p.

Military structures include
S_n = military nonresidential structures,
S_b = industrial buildings, and
S_r = residential structures.
Nonmilitary protection structures involve police protection, fire protection, and correctional institutions.

Thus,

$$S_m = S_n + S_b + S_r,$$

and

$$S_D = S_m + S_p = \text{total defense structures.}$$

Defense equipment, E_D, consists of military equipment plus police, fire, and correctional institutional equipment.

Defense inventories, H_D, consist of police, fire, and correctional institution inventories, and the military share of other government inventories. Aggregate data on structures, equipment, and inventories are from unpublished BEA tabulations. Data on stocks of structures by function are from Ott and Austin.

Land also includes both military and nonmilitary protection components. Military land values are estimated from total federal land values on the basis of acreage proportions. Thus,

$$L_m = (A_m/A_F)L_F,$$

where

L_m = the value of military land,
A_m = military land acreage, from the *Statistical Abstract of the United States* table entitled "Federal Land by Agency and

Predominant Usage,'' (U.S. Dept. of Commerce, Bureau of the Census)

A_F = total federal land acreage from the *Statistical Abstract of the United States* table entitled ''Total Land and Federally Owned Land and Buildings,'' and

L_F = the value of all federal land, from Milgram (1973) for 1952 and 1968, and extrapolated for 1945 to 1951 and 1969 to 1981.

Utilizing the Milgram data on federal land holdings, and the private land value estimates, L_{Pr}, provided by the Flow of Funds section of the Federal Reserve Board, we calculate:

$$L_{Ft} = \frac{L_{F52}}{L_{Pr52}} \times L_{Prt} \qquad t = 1945 \text{ to } 1951,$$

$$L_{Ft} = \frac{L_{F68}}{L_{Pr68}} \times L_{Prt} \qquad t = 1969 \text{ to } 1981.$$

This reduces to

$$L_{Ft} = \frac{L_{F52}}{L_{G52}} \times L_{Gt} \qquad t = 1945 \text{ to } 1951,$$

and

$$L_{Ft} = \frac{L_{F68}}{L_{G68}} \times L_{Gt} \qquad t = 1969 \text{ to } 1981,$$

where L_{Gt} is as described on line 13, p. 320, above.

Somewhat devious methods are applied to allocate the nonmilitary protection portions of defense capital,

$$K_{pD} = S_p + E_p + H_p + L_p.$$

We do so by first estimating the structures component, S_p, and then assuming proportionality for the other components.

We have from Ott and Austin estimates of value of structures for ''Other State and Local Buildings,'' which we may designate S_q.

These are an aggregate of the value of structures in civilian safety, that is, in policy protection, fire protection, and correctional institutions, S_p; structures in local parks and recreational facilities which we designate as S_{LR}; and general purpose and all other state and local buildings which we will designate as S_{LG}, to be included with general administration structures. We do have figures for state and local capital outlays (not values of stocks) for local parks and recreation, I_{LR}, and for general administration, I_{LG}, from the Census of Governments. We also have NIPA figures for total state and local purchases of goods and services for protection, PGS_p, and for general administration, PGS_{LG}. We assume ratios of values of structures to be proportionate both to ratios of capital outlays in parks and recreation and in general administration and to ratios of total purchases of goods and services in protection and in general administration. We can then estimate values of state and local structures in protection, in parks and recreation, and in general administration. Writing,

$$x = PGS_p/PGS_{LG}, \text{ and } y = I_{LR}/I_{LG},$$

we can then have

$$S_p = x\ S_{LG} \text{ and } S_{LR} = y\ S_{LG}.$$

Since

$$S_{LG} + S_p + S_{LR} = S_q,$$

we have

$$S_{LG}(1 + x + y) = S_q.$$

Thus, the value of protection structures may be written:

$$S_p = S_q\ [x/(1 + x + y)].$$

For structures to be counted with parks and recreation we have

$$S_{LR} = S_q\ [y/(1 + x + y)].$$

And for structures to be allocated to general administration we have

$$S_{LG} = S_q \, [1/(1 + x + y)].$$

Then, in our proportionality assumptions, designating S_{nm}, E_{nm}, H_{nm}, and L_{nm}, and K_{nm} as the total nonmilitary government stocks of structures, equipment, inventories, land, and all capital, respectively, and letting $p = S_p/S_{nm}$ we have

$$E_p = pE_{nm},$$
$$H_p = pH_{nm},$$
$$L_p = pL_{nm},$$

and

$$K_p = pK_{nm}.$$

To allocate nondefense government capital to the other functions we utilize the functional breakdown of government's nonmilitary stocks of structures in the tabulation of Ott and Austin. That classification maps into our functions as follows:

Education includes federal education buildings and state and local education buildings.

Health includes federal hospital buildings and state and local hospital buildings.

Sanitation includes state and local sewerage and water structures.

Transportation includes federal and state and local highways and miscellaneous state and local structures.

Natural resources includes federal conservation and development and state and local conservation and development.

Parks and recreation includes the portion of "other state and local buildings," S_{LR}, defined above.

General administration includes other federal buildings, miscellaneous federal structures and the portion of "Other State and Local Buildings," S_{LG}, defined above.

We have been unable to assign capital to the functions designated as space and welfare. These have been included with defense and general administration, respectively.

For all functions but national defense, we allocate nonmilitary net stocks of equipment, E_{nm}, inventories, H_{nm}, and land L_{nm} (= total government land minus military land), on the basis of each function's share of nonmilitary structures, S_i/S_{nm}. Hence equipment, inventories and land in the ith function are

$$E_{it} = E_{nm,t} \times (S_i/S_{nm})_t$$
$$H_{it} = H_{nm,t} \times (S_i/S_{nm})_t$$
$$L_{it} = L_{nm,t} \times (S_i/S_{nm})_t \quad i \neq \text{defense}, t = 1946 \text{ to } 1981.$$

The total capital stock assigned to each function is K_i where

$$K_{it} = S_{it} + E_{it} + H_{it} + L_{it} \quad t = 1946 \text{ to } 1981.$$

E. Gross capital income by function
Gross imputed interest is then allocated to each function in proportion to its share of total capital. Thus

$$R_{it} = R_{Gt}(K_i/K_G)_t \quad t = 1946 \text{ to } 1981,$$

where R_{Gt} is total government gross imputed interest of year t and K_G is again total government capital.

Capital consumption allowances of government are separated into military and nonmilitary components by the BEA. We allocate the nonmilitary capital consumption allowances on the basis of the distribution of nonmilitary structures and equipment. The national defense function's capital consumption allowances are composed of the capital consumption allowances of military capital, D_m, and a portion of the capital consumption allowances of nonmilitary capital, D_{nm}, related to the structures and equipment, S_p and E_D, devoted to protection services. Thus,

$$D_{Dt} = D_{mt} + D_{nmt} \times \left(\frac{S_p + E_p}{S_{nm} + E_{nm}} \right)_t \quad t = 1946 \text{ to } 1981.$$

F. Compensation of employees by function
Compensation of employees (CE) is available separately in NIPA for the federal government as a whole, for the aggregate of state and local governments, for the defense component of federal expenditures and for the educational component of state and local expenditures. The precise sources are
Federal CE: Total, N3.7-7 and N3.7-16, 1946 to 1981
Defense, N3.7-7, 1952 to 1981

State and Local CE: Total, N3.7-23, 1946 to 1981
Education, N3.6-16, 1952 to 1981
Government purchases of goods and services (PGS) are of course also available in NIPA:
Federal PGS: Total, N3.2-13; Defense, N3.2-14, 1946 to 1981
State and Local PGS: Total, N3.3-14, 1946 to 1981

With the exception of federal defense and state and local education, a breakdown of CE is not available for any year. We hence assume that the ratio of federal CE_i to federal PGS_i is identical for all functions, i, other than defense, and similarly that the ratio for state and local CE_i to state and local PGS_i is identical for all functions, i, other than education.

Thus, let $CE_{F,t}$ and $CE_{SL,t}$ designate the federal and state and local compensation of employees, respectively, in the year t, and

$CE_{Fi,t}$ = federal compensation of employees in the ith function in the year t, and

$CE_{SLi,t}$ = state and local compensation of employees in the ith function in the year t.

Then noting that $i = nd$ for national defense and $i = e$ for education, and similarly using PGS to refer to purchases of goods and services, we may use subscripts nnd for nonfederal defense and nse for non-state-and-local education, and write

$$CE_{Fnnd} = CE_F - CE_{nd}, \qquad PGS_{Fnnd} = PGS_F - PGS_{nd}$$
$$CE_{SLne} = CE_{SL} - CE_{SLe}, \qquad PGS_{SLne} = PGS_{SL} - PGS_{SLe}.$$

Then

$$CE_{Fi,t} = CE_{Fnnd,t} \times (PGS_{Fi}/PGS_{Fnnd})_t \qquad i \neq \text{defense},$$
$$t = 1952 \text{ to } 1981,$$

and

$$CE_{SLi,t} = CE_{SLne,t} \times (PGS_{SLi}/PGS_{SLne})_t \qquad i \neq \text{education},$$
$$t = 1952 \text{ to } 1981.$$

For 1946 to 1951 we estimate federal defense compensation of employees as proportional to federal defense purchases of goods and services. Thus,

$$CE_{FD,t} = CE_{F,t} \times \frac{PGS_{FD,t}}{PGS_{F,52}} \qquad i \neq \text{defense}, \ t = 1946 \ \text{to} \ 1951.$$

For other functions we assume compensation of employees was the same proportion of non–national defense compensation that it was in 1952. Thus,

$$CE_{F,it} = CE_{Fnnd,t} \times \frac{CE_{Fi,52}}{CE_{Fnnd,t}} \qquad i \neq \text{defense}, \ t = 1946 \ \text{to} \ 1951.$$

For state and local compensation of employees by function prior to 1952, we multiply each year's total state and local compensation by the share attributed to that function in 1952. Hence,

$$CE_{SL,it} = CE_{SL,t} \times \left(\frac{CE_{SL,i}}{CE_{SL}}\right)_{52} \qquad t = 1946 \ \text{to} \ 1951.$$

For each function, i, other than defense, compensation of employees is the sum of federal and state and local compensation of employees by function:

$$CE_{it} = CE_{F,it} + CE_{SL,it} \qquad t = 1946 \ \text{to} \ 1981.$$

For defense we incorporate three elements of compensation of employees; federal compensation of employees strictly for "national defense," CE_{Fnd}; state and local compensation of employees in "protection," CE_{SLP}; and federal compensation of employees in federal civilian safety programs and international affairs, designated CE_{CS+IA}. This last is estimated as a share of total federal non–national defense compensation of employees proportionate to its share of federal non–national defense purchases of goods and services. Thus,

$$CE_{CS+IA,t} = CE_{Fnnd,t} \times (PGS_{CS+IA} \div PGS_{Fnnd})_t$$

and

$$CE_{Dt} = CE_{Fnnd,t} + CE_{LP,t} + CE_{CS+IA,t} \qquad t = 1946 \ \text{to} \ 1981.$$

The expenses related to work, *ERW*, subtracted from compensation of employees to arrive at labor income, consist of the share of the BEA's personal consumption expenditures for transportation which we consider work-related expenses of government employees. We allocate these expenses to each function in proportion to its share of compensation of employees. Thus, $ERW_i = ERW_G(CE_i/CE_G)$, where ERW_G are the expenses related to work for government as a whole, line 4.

G. Other elements of product and expenditures by function
Purchases of goods and services, PGS, are allocated among our ten functions on the basis of the basic categorization indicated above (section B).

Investment in structures is available from the BEA in the same functional breakdown as the stock of structures discussed above. Investment in equipment is broken down only into military and nonmilitary categories. To retain consistency with NIPA accounts we take total investment in structures and equipment from N3.8-5, N3.8-8, and N3.8-15, and use the BEA proportions to allocate it by function, applying the method for allocation of capital stocks described in section D above.

Change in inventories, $\Delta H_t = H_t - H_{t-1}$, is calculated from constant (1972) dollar tabulations of the BEA. Current dollar change in inventories is then reflated from the constant dollar change by multiplying by an inventory implicit deflator.

Change in inventories, ΔH, is classified in the BEA series as change in nonmilitary inventories, ΔH_{nm}, and change in military inventories ΔH_m. Change in nonmilitary inventories is allocated in proportion to investment in nonmilitary structures, IS. Thus,

$$\Delta H_i = \Delta H_{nm} \times (IS_i/IS_{nm}) \qquad i \neq \text{defense.}$$

The change in defense inventories equals change in military inventories plus change in inventories in state and local protection services.

$$\Delta H_D = \Delta H_m + \Delta H_{nm} \times (IS_p/IS_{nm}).$$

H. The development of untransferred product, gross product, and final product by function
The untransferred product of functions i, UP_i, is the sum of value added, intermediate product purchased from other sectors of the

economy and used in current production, and expenses related to work. Hence,

$$UP_i = VA_i + IP_{io} - \Delta H_i + ERW_i.$$

We define gross product of function i, GP_i, as the sum of untransferred product and intermediate product transferred to function i from other functions of government. This intermediate product transferred within government originates in the functions of defense, D, transportation, T, and general administration, GA. Designating the transfer of the output of function j to function i as IP_{ij} we can write:

$$GP_i = UP_i + IP_{ij} \qquad J = D, T, \text{ and } GA.$$

Final product of function i, FP_i, is defined as gross product of function i minus transfers of product to other functions. Thus for all but the defense, transportation, and general administration functions, the final product and gross product are equal.

For defense, transportation, and general administration functions we subtract from gross product the transfers of intermediate product to other functions in order to arrive at final product. We designate the intermediate product of these functions as IP_j, $j = D, T,$ and GA.

The share of IP_j allocated to any function i, is based on the proportion of untransferred product produced by function i. Thus

$$IP_{ij} = \frac{UP_i}{\sum_i UP_i} \times IP_j \qquad j = D, T, \text{ and } GA.$$

The determination of IP_j, however, proves complex, and differs somewhat for each of the three functions.

We assume that the defense function protects the economy's capital stock. Therefore the amount of defense product retained by government is dependent on the government's share of the total capital stock. We can then write

$$IP_D = b \times GP_D, \qquad \text{where } b = K_G/K,$$

K = the total stock of capital—structures, equipment, land, and inventories—in the economy and K_G = the stock of government capital.

We assume that the gross product of the transportation function is distributed to households and enterprises or retained by government. The nonretained product is distributed on the basis of vehicle miles traveled by the household and enterprise sectors. To determine the proportion retained by government we assume that the production functions for government and enterprises are similar, such that government uses transportation in the same proportion as does the enterprise sector, adjusted for the scale of production, k. Hence, defining Y_G as total or extended product originating in government, and Y_E as total or extended product originating in enterprise sectors (as reported in Eisner, 1978), $k = Y_G/Y_E$.

To estimate the vehicle miles traveled by households and enterprises we assume that all buses and trucks belong to enterprises and that passenger cars may be owned by either households or enterprises. A representative of the Highway Safety Research Institute suggested to us that 15 percent of passenger cars are purchased by enterprises. We then calculated the fraction of government final product of transportation services transferred to enterprises as

$$e = \frac{M_b}{M} + .15 \left(1 - \frac{M_b}{M}\right) = .15 + .85 \left(\frac{M_b}{M}\right),$$

where M_b = bus and truck miles traveled and M = total vehicle miles traveled.

The data are from the *Statistical Abstract of the United States* table entitled "Volume and Characteristics of Travel." The fraction of final product transferred to households is thus $h = 1 - e$.

Recalling that the final product of a function is gross product minus intermediate product transferred to other functions of government, we have

$$(e \times FP_T) + (h \times FP_T) + IP_T = GP_T.$$

Then recalling that k is the ratio of product originating in the government sector to product originating in the enterprise sector, our assumption about the government's use of transportation may be expressed

$$IP_T = k \times e \times FP_T = c \times GP_T,$$

where c is the proportion of GP_T retained by government. Since

$$FP_T = (1 - c) \times GP_T,$$
$$ke\,(1 - c) = c,$$

and

$$c = \frac{ke}{1 + ke}.$$

The gross product of the general administration function is distributed to households and enterprises or retained by government on the basis of product originating in each sector. Hence, recalling that Y_G and Y_E are total product originating in government and enterprises, respectively, and writing Y_H as total product originating in households, we can define

$$d = YG/(Y_G + Y_E + Y_H)$$

and write

$$IP_{GA} = d \times GP_{GA}.$$

Gross product of defense, for example, is the untransferred product of defense plus the defense share of intermediate product of transportation and general administration. Using the definitions of UP_i and GP_i, for gross product of defense, transportation, and general administration we may write

$$GP_i = UP_i + a_i \sum_{k:k \neq i} IP_{ik}, \qquad i = D, T, GA,$$

where

$$a_i = \frac{UP_i}{\sum_i UP_i}.$$

Recalling that the proportions of gross product retained as intermediate within government are respectively b, c, and d, for defense, transportation, and general administration or

$$IP_D = b \times GP_D,$$
$$IP_T = c \times GP_T,$$

and

$$IP_{GA} = d \times GP_{GA},$$

we have

$$GP_D = UP_D + a_D(cGP_T + dGP_{GA}),$$
$$GP_T = UP_T + a_T(bGP_D + dGP_{GA}),$$

and

$$GP_{GA} = UP_{GA} + a_{GA}(bGP_D + cGP_T).$$

These equations are solved simultaneously for GP_D, GP_T, and GP_{GA}. The final product of the three functions may then be expressed as

$$FP_D = (1 - b - a_D b)GP_D,$$
$$FP_T = (1 - c + a_T c)GP_T,$$

and

$$FP_{GA} = (1 - d + a_{GA}d)GP_{GA}.$$

I. The distribution of final product
The final product of each function is classified as consumption, capital, or intermediate product. It is either transferred to households and enterprises or retained by government.

The consumption product transferred to households includes half of that portion of the final product of the space function related to manned space flights, half of the final product of the health and sanitation functions, all of the transportation product transferred to households times the ratio of total travel time not spent traveling to work, and .935125 of the final product of the local parks and recreation function.

NASA classified its expenditures as attributable to manned space flights or associated space science and technology. We assume that the final product of space, FP_S, can be similarly classified. Thus the proportion of FP_S attributable to manned space flight FP_m is calculated as

$$FP_M = m(FP_S)$$

$$\text{where } m = \frac{\text{NASA Expenditures for Manned Space Flight}}{\text{Total NASA Expenditures}}$$

and the data are taken from the *Statistical Abstract of the United States,* table entitled "NASA—Outlays for Research and Development."

Capital transferred to enterprises consists of research and development funded by government and performed by business, universities, and colleges, and other nonprofit institutions. The data are taken from the National Science Foundation, *National Patterns in R&D Resources* (NSF 1982), table B-1.

Capital transferred to households consists of the value of employee training plus final product of education, half of the final product of health, and .064875 of the final product of parks and recreation.

Capital produced by government and retained by government has two components. One is federally funded, federally performed research and development which we assume relates to the defense and space functions. These data are also from the National Science Foundation (1982). The final product of the natural resources function is the other component of retained government capital.

The intermediate product component of government final product which is transferred to households and enterprises includes half of the final product and sanitation, the enterprise share of transportation final product, eFP_T, 33.2 percent of the household share of transportation final product, all of the final product of general administration, all of space final product not allocated to consumption or research and development, and all of national defense final product not allocated to research and development. Putting this in symbols, letting $I_{R\&D,G}$ = federally funded, federally performed research and development, presumed part of defense and space functions in proportions which we do not determine, and noting again that *FP* denotes final product and *IP* intermediate product, and that the subscript *S*, *D* and *M* refer to space, defense, and manned space flights respectively.

$$FP_S + FP_D = .5 \; FP_M + I_{R\&D,G} + FP_S \text{ to } IP + FP_D \text{ to } IP.$$

Thus,

$$FP_{S+D} \text{ to } IP = FP_D + FP_S - .5 \; FP_M - I_{R\&D,G}.$$

6. Household Income and Product

Debits

1. Labor income

2. Compensation of employees
   This is taken from N2.4-42, compensation of employees, private households.

3. Imputations

4. Employee training
   Kendrick's series on training costs is used for 1946 to 1966 and extrapolated for the remaining years. Kendrick's series is for the personal sector, which includes nonprofit institutions. The divisions of these training costs between the household sector and the non-profit sector is made on the basis of compensation of employees in the two sectors. The method for extrapolating Kendrick's series and then dividing it between the two sectors is described in section 13, Investment in Human Capital.

5. Opportunity costs of students
   Students aged 14 and over are assumed to have opportunity costs. For 1946 to 1969 and 1973, Kendrick's series on opportunity costs of students is used. This series was obtained from unpublished worksheets (1978). For 1970 to 1972, interpolations were made on the basis of the growth rate from 1969 to 1973:

$$OPCST_{1969}(1 + g)^4 = OPCST_{1973};$$

$$OPCST_t = OPCST_{1969}(1 + g)^{t-1969},$$

where

$OPCST_t$ = opportunity cost of students at time t and
g = growth rate = 0.125572916.

Kendrick's data are extrapolated on the basis of school enrollment, total civilian labor force and total civilian compensation of employees for the years 1974 to 1981. It is assumed that the percent change in average annual compensation foregone per student is equal to the percent change in average annual compensation per member of the labor force. The total increment in the opportunity costs of students would then reflect both the percent change in average annual compensation foregone per student and the percent increase in student population. Thus for 1974 to 1981:

$$OPCST_t = OPCST_{1973} \, (AVC_t/AVC_{73}) \, (SE_t/SE_{73})$$

where

AVC_t = average compensation of civilian employees at time t.
SE_t = full-time equivalent school enrollment for age $\geq$ 14 at time t.

Average compensation of civilian employees is obtained by dividing total civilian compensation of employees by total civilian labor force. Total civilian compensation of employees is compensation of domestic employees (N6.5B-2) less compensation of military employees (N6.5B-80). Total civilian labor force is full-time equivalent domestic employees (N6.8B-2) less full-time equivalent military employees (N6.8B-80).

School enrollment data are taken from *Current Population Reports,* Series P-20, "School Enrollment—Social and Economic Characteristics of Students" (U.S. Dept. of Commerce, Bureau of the Census, numbers vary each year; example, #303 in 1975).

Students aged 14 to 34 below college level and 14 to 15 in college are taken from table 1. Students aged 16 to 34 in college full-time and part-time are from table 5. Students aged 35 and over below college level, full-time college, and part-time college are from table A3. It is assumed that students below college level or in college but under 16 are full-time. Full-time equivalent of the part-time enrollment is assumed to be 30 percent of those enrolled part-time in college.

6. Unpaid household work
   Unpaid household work is an imputation for the value of time spent by adults on work at home. See appendix A, Valuation of Household Work.

7. Less: Expenses related to work
   Expenses related to work are the costs incurred by domestic employees in commuting to and from work. See appendix B, Expenses Related to Work.

8. Capital Income

9.   Owner-occupied housing
10.   Interest paid
        The interest paid is net interest on owner-occupied nonfarm dwell-
        ings, N8.8-78.
11.   Net imputed interest
12.   Gross imputed interest
13.   Land
14.   Owner-occupied dwellings
15.   Less: Interest paid
16.   Net rental income
17.   Rental income on non-farm owner-occupied dwellings and land
           Rental income of persons with capital consumption adjustment,
           N8.8-79.
18.   Less: Net imputed interest
19.   Consumer goods
20.   Consumer interest
        Interest paid by consumers to business, N2.1-28.
21.   Net imputed interest
22.   Gross imputed interest
           We take the BEA's rental income plus interest paid as an es-
           timate of the return to owner-occupied housing. We divide this
           by the stock of owner-occupied housing, consisting of both
           structures and the associated land value, to obtain an estimate
           of the rate of return to household capital, *RRHHC*. This rate
           is then applied to the stock of household durables, semidura-
           bles, and inventories to provide an imputation of interest return
           to household capital other than housing.

$$RRHHC_t = \frac{IPOOH_t + RIOOH_t}{KOOH_t}$$

where

IPOOH = Net interest paid on owner-occupied non-farm
        housing, N8.8-78.
RIOOH = Rental income of owner-occupied non-farm hous-
        ing, N8.8-79.

KOOH = Current cost valuation of the stock of owner-occupied housing, including land. Data are from the Federal Reserve Board's Flow of Funds section.

23.   Durables

Net stocks of consumer durables, autos, and other motor vehicles are from BEA capital stock tapes.

To the stocks of autos and of other motor vehicles is added 80 percent of the value of the stock of tires, tubes, and other accessories. The BEA capital stocks contain only 20 percent of the value of these items.

24.   Semidurables

Net stocks and depreciation are calculated from gross investment data using the perpetual inventory method with straight-line depreciation and the half-year convention, and an assumed service life of three years. Gross investment which we classify as "semidurables" is taken in current dollars from

NIPA table 2.4, line 12: shoes and other footwear

line 13: clothing and accessories except footwear

line 33: semidurable house furnishings.

Gross investment in constant dollars is from NIPA table 2.5.

Constant dollar stocks are calculated from the constant dollar investment series and then reflated to current dollars using the implicit inflator:

$$\text{DEFLAT}_t = .5(P_t + P_{t+1}),$$

where

$$P_t = I_t^{cur\$}/I_t^{72\$}$$

and I_t = investment in semidurables in year t.

25.   Inventories

Stocks of inventories are assumed to be a two-week supply of NIPA nondurables less semidurables. Thus,

$$H_t = (NONDUR_t - SEMIDUR_t) / 26,$$

where

$NONDUR$ = current dollar investment in nondurables (N1.1-4), and

$SEMIDUR$ = current dollar investment in "semidurables" (N2.4-12 + N2.4-13 + N2.4-33).

26.   Less: Consumer interest
       Equal to line 20.

27. Net revaluations
    The method of calculating net revaluations is described in 2-22.

28. Land
    Net investment in land is assumed to be zero.

29. Owner-occupied dwellings
    Net investment is from BEA capital stock tapes.

30. Consumer goods

31. Durables
    Gross investment and depreciation are from BEA capital stock tapes with an adjustment added for auto accessories (see line 23 above).

32. Semidurables
    Gross investment and depreciation are as described in line 24 above.

33. Inventories
    Since the stock of inventories is assumed to be a two-week supply, depreciation for the year is assumed to be zero, and net investment equals gross investment. Current dollar investment in inventories is the first difference of constant dollar net stocks multiplied by the implicit price deflator.

$$\Delta H_t = (H_t^{72\$} - H_{t-1}^{72\$})(H_t^{cur\$}/H_t^{72\$}),$$

where

$H_t^{72\$}$ = $(NONDUR_t^{72\$} - SEMIDUR_t^{72\$}) / 26,$

$NONDUR_t^{72\$}$ = investment in nondurables in 1972 dollars in year t, from N1.2-4,

$SEMIDUR_t^{72\$}$ = investment in semidurables in 1972 dollars in year t (line 24), and

$H_t^{Cur\$}$ = $(NONDUR_t^{Cur\$} - SEMIDUR_t^{Cur\$})$ / 26.

34. Income originating
    $1 + 8 + 27$

35. Less: Intangible (human) capital consumption
    This is the same as line 41 below, where the procedure is described.

36. Net income originating and charges against net household product
    $34 - 35$

37. Capital consumption allowances

38.   Tangible (nonhuman)
    Tangible capital consumption allowances stem from owner-occupied housing, durables, and semidurables. Straight-line depreciation is applied.

39.   Original cost
    Taken from BEA capital stock tapes. Original cost depreciation of owner-occupied nonfarm dwellings is from N8.8-75; consumer durables depreciation is from BEA; semidurables is calculated from current dollar investment as described in line 24.

40.   Revaluations
    The revaluations component of capital consumption allowances of owner-occupied nonfarm dwellings is from BEA. For durables and semidurables this is calculated as the difference between current cost depreciation and original cost depreciation. Current cost depreciation for durables is obtained from BEA and for semidurables is calculated from constant dollar investment, with 3-year lives, reflating to current costs as explained in line 24 above.

41.   Intangible (human)
    For the method of obtaining investment, current and constant dollars, in human capital and for the average service life for the various types of investment, see section 3, Investment in Human Capital. Straight-line depreciation with the half-year convention is used in calculating stocks and depreciation.

42.   Original cost
    Original cost depreciation of human capital is obtained under the above assumptions using current dollar investment data.

43.   Revaluations
    Revaluations are the difference between current, or replacement cost, and original cost. Current cost depreciation was obtained

by calculating depreciation in 1972 dollars and multiplying the result by the average implicit human capital investment price deflator,

$$.5(PHC_t + PHC_{t+1}),$$

where

$PHC_t = IHC_t^{Cur\$}/IHC_t^{72\$}$ and
IHC_t = investment in human capital.

44. Charges against gross household product
    36 + 37

Credits

45. Consumption

46.　Market (labor services in households)
       This is the same as compensation of employees, debit item from line 2.

47.　Nonmarket

48.　Net space rent on owner-occupied nonfarm dwellings

49.　　BEA net space rent on owner-occupied nonfarm dwellings
         This is N8.8-74, gross housing product (of owner-occupied nonfarm housing).

50.　　Subsidies
         This is N8.8-77, subsidies (of owner-occupied nonfarm housing).

51.　Capital services other than on owner-occupied dwellings
       For each item, capital services is the sum of gross imputed interest and capital consumption allowances. The value of the services of durables also includes personal motor vehicle licenses (N3.4-12) and personal property taxes (N3.4-13).

52.　Durables

53.　　Gross

54.　　Less: Services allocated to investment

55.　　Less: Services to expenses related to work

56.　Semidurables

57. Inventories
    From services of durables we subtract those allocated to investment in education and health and those included in expenses related to work.

58. Labor services

59. Total imputed labor services
    This is the same as line 3 above.

60. Less: Labor services allocated to investment
    This is opportunity costs of students, line 5, and the portion of unpaid household work, line 6, consisting of education and health care to children in the home. These are included in investment in human capital. See appendix A regarding household work allocated to child-rearing.

61. Intermediate product of government to consumption
    Intermediate product of government transferred to household is divided between consumption and investment on the basis of the ratio of consumption to investment exclusive of intermediate product of government. From the consumption portion we then subtract household indirect business taxes, *IBTHH*, which is the sum of the indirect business taxes included in space rent, N8.8-76; personal motor vehicle licenses, N3.4-12; and personal property taxes, N3.4-13. Thus,

$$IPGC = IPGHH \times \frac{MPCHH + NMPCHH}{DENOM} - IBTHH,$$

    where

    $IPGC$ = intermediate product of government to consumption.
    $IPGHH$ = intermediate product of government transferred to households (5-44).
    $MPCHH$ = household market product consumed (line 46).
    $NMPCHH$ = household nonmarket product consumed (line 47).
    $DENOM$ = the sum of household market and nonmarket product consumed, teaching children in the home, the opportunity cost of students, durable services allocated to investment in education and health, and employee training exclusive of intermediate product of government, that is, lines 46 + 47 + 65 + 66 + 67 + 69 + 70.

62. Capital accumulation

63.   Intangible at original cost

64.   Education

65.   Teaching children in home
This is the portion of unpaid household work, line 6 above, spent teaching children in the home. See appendix A regarding unpaid household production.

66.   Opportunity cost of students
This is line 5 above.

67.   Durable services allocated to education
Following Kendrick, .172 of the rental value of the stock of radio and television receivers, records and musical instruments, plus .342 of the rental value of the stock of books and maps, plus .474 of expenditures for magazines, newspapers, and sheet music (N2.4-84) are considered investment in education. Stocks are obtained from the BEA.

68.   Intermediate product of government to education
This is the portion of intermediate product of government transferred to households which is allocated to investment in education.

$$IPGE = IPGHH \times \frac{TC + OPCST + DURINV}{DENOM}$$

where

$IPGE$ = intermediate product of government to households allocated to investment in education.

TC = the imputed value of teaching children in the home (line 65).

$OPCST$ = the opportunity costs of students (line 66).

$DURINV$ = the services of durables allocated to investment in education (line 67).

69.   Health
This is the sum of the value of time spent in the home on the health care of children (see appendix A) half of the rental value of the stock of opthalmic products and orthopedic appliances, and a portion of intermediate product of government to health, *IPGH*, as defined below. Stocks are obtained from the BEA,

$$\text{IPGH} = \text{IPGHH} \times \frac{\text{YHHL}}{\text{DENOM}}$$

where

$IPGH$ = intermediate product of government to health, and
$YHHL$ = household-produced health output.

70.   Employee training
       This is the sum of line 4 above and a portion of intermediate
       product of government to employee training, *IPGET,* where

$$\text{IPGET} = \text{IPGHH} \times \frac{\text{ET}}{\text{DENOM}}$$

where ET = line 4 above.

71.   Net revaluations
       See line 27 above.

72.   Services to expenses related to work
      Equals line 55.

73.   Less: Intermediate product transferred from government
      5-44

74.   Less: Expenses related to work
      Equals line 7.

75.   Gross household product
      45 + 62 + 72 − 73 − 74

7. Gross National Product in 1972 Dollars

Deflators and Additional Procedures

1. Consumption
2. Household expenditures for services and nondurables
3. Gross expenditures included from BEA personal consumption expenditures

   Designating the relevant variables by their labels in our computer program, we have

$$
\begin{aligned}
TOCRK(1) = \; & C\$PCE - C\$DUR - CSEMDUR \\
& - TOCRK(4) - HHDEK(31) - MEDEXP \\
& - PNCRK(1) - CHHINV - PNCRK(5) \\
& - PNCRK(7) - PNCRK(3),
\end{aligned}
$$

where

TOCRK(1)	= gross expenditure included from BEA PCE.
C\$PCE	= personal consumption expenditures in constant dollars, from N1.2-2.
C\$DUR	= personal consumption expenditures for durable goods in constant dollars, from N2.5-2.
CSEMDUR	= constant dollar investment in semidurables equal to N2.5-27 + N2.5-36.
TOCRK(4)	= constant dollar BEA imputations other than owner-occupied nonfarm dwellings: line 6.
HHDEK(31)	= BEA constant dollar net space rent on owner-occupied nonfarm dwellings: 12-5.
MEDEXP	= medical expenses included in BEA PCE. Equals N2.4-44 − N2.4-46 − N2.4-53 − N2.4-54 − .5 × N22.4-50, all deflated by N7.12-71.
PNCRK(1)	= constant dollar nonprofit consumption in BEA personal consumption expenditures: 9-2.
CHHINV	= constant dollar investment in household inventories. Equals (N1.2-4 − N2.5-27 − N2.5-36)/26.
PNCRK(5)	= constant dollar nonprofit investment in health included in BEA PCE: 9-11.
PNCRK(7)	= constant dollar nonprofit investment in R & D: 9-5
PNCRK(3)	= constant dollar nonprofit investment in education included in BEA PCE: 9-7

4.   Less: Personal consumption expenses related to work
This is the sum of the sector expenses related to work, in constant dollars, which we calculate by applying the deflator described in appendix B, Expenses Related to Work.

5.   Expense account items of consumption
This is taken from constant dollar 8-7.

6.   BEA imputations other than housing
This is defined as:

$$TOCRK(4) = RUAL + GHP + SERFIN + FEMP + CLOTH + GFP$$

	= BEA imputations other than owner-occupied nonfarm dwellings.
RUAL	= constant dollar rental value of buildings and equipment owned and operated by nonprofit institutions: N8.8-87/N7.12-48.
GHP	= constant dollar gross housing product: N8.8-82/N7.12-47.
SERFIN	= Constant dollar value of services furnished without pay by financial intermediaries: N8.8-91/N7.12-80.
FEMP	= Constant dollar value of food furnished to employees: N8.8-96/N7.12-23.
CLOTH	= Constant dollar value of standard clothing issued to military personnel: N8.8-97/N7.12-30.
GFP	= Constant dollar value of gross farm product: N8.8-95/N7.12-23.

7.   Subsidies allocated to consumption

8.   Subsidies included in business income
We take the series from constant dollar 8-6.

9.   Less: Amount allocated to investment

10.   Transfers
This is taken from TISA accounts 8 through 12, with the lines below derived in the same manner as the corresponding current dollar lines in account 1 were derived from accounts 2 through 6.

11.   From business

12.   Media support

13.   Total media support

14.   Less: Media support allocated to investment

15.   Health and safety

16.   From nonprofit institutions

17. From government enterprises

18. From government

19. Nonmarket services produced in households
    This is taken from TISA account 12 in the same manner as this line and the line below are derived in account 1 from account 6 for current dollars.

20. Net space rent of owner-occupied nonfarm dwellings

21. Other capital services

22.   Durables

23.   Total durables

24.   Less: Durables allocated to investment

25.   Less: Services of durables to expenditures related to work

26.   Semidurables

27.   Inventories

28. Labor services

29. Less: Labor services allocated to investment

30. Gross domestic capital accumulation

31.   Original cost

32.   Tangible

33.   Structures and equipment and household durables and semidurables

34.   Business

35.   Nonresidential
    From BEA capital stock tapes.

36.   Structures

37.   Equipment

38.   Residential other than owner-occupied nonfarm dwellings
    From BEA capital stock tapes.

39.   Nonprofit institutions
    From BEA capital stock tapes.

40.   Structures

41.   Equipment

42.   Government enterprises
    From BEA capital stock tapes.

43.   Structures

44.   Equipment

45.   Government
       From BEA capital stock tapes for structures and equipment
       and from 11-13, for product accumulated.

46.   Structures

47.   Equipment

48.   Product accumulated

49.   Households

50.   Owner-occupied nonfarm dwellings
       From BEA capital stock tapes.

51.   Durables
       From N2.5-2.

52.   Semidurables
       From an unpublished constant dollar version of N2.5-27
       + N2.5-36.

53.   Fixed GPDI reconciliation

54.   NIPA fixed GPDI
       N1.2-7

55.   Less: Corresponding sector totals
       34 + 39 + 50

56.   Government capital accumulation reconciliation

57.   NIPA government investment
       N3.8B-4 + N3.8B-11 + N3.8B-20 + N3.8B-25

58.   Less: Government and government enterprise totals
       This is equal to the sum of government and government
       enterprises constant dollar investment in structures and
       equipment.
       42 + 46 + 47

59.   Change in inventories

60.   Business
       N1.2-15

61.   Government
       11-20

62.   Households
       Constant dollar stocks of household inventories is equal to
       (N1.2-4 − N2.5-27 − N2.5-36)/26. Investment in inven-
       tories is taken as change in stocks between adjacent years.

63.   Intangible

64. Research and development
    Sources are the same as for current dollars (see 2-20 above) but constant dollar series are used.
65. Business
66. Nonprofit institutions
67. Government
68. Education and training
    See section 13.
69. Health
    See section 13.
70. Subsidies and government enterprises transfers allocated to investment.
    9 + 10-5
71. Net revaluations
    We apply the fixed investment deflator, N7.1-7, to the current dollar series.
72. Land
73. Business
74. Nonprofit
75. Government and government enterprise
76. Households
77. Structures and equipment
78. Business
79. Nonprofit institutions
80. Government
81. Households (owner-occupied dwellings)
82. Household durables and semidurables
83. Durables
84. Semidurables
85. Inventories
86. Business (including nonprofit)
87. Government enterprises
88. Government
89. Households
90. Net exports
91. Net BEA exports

92. Exports
     N1.2-19

93. Imports
     N1.2-20

94. Terms of trade effect

95. Net exports in current dollars, deflated
     1 Credits-90, divided by the BEA GNP implicit price deflator.

96. Less: Net exports in constant dollars without terms of trade effect
     This is BEA net exports, line 91 above.

97. Gross national product
     1 + 30 + 90

Addenda

98. GNP minus net revaluations (NR)

99. Net national product minus net revaluations

100. Net national income minus net revaluations

101. Gross domestic capital accumulation minus net revaluations (GDCA −
     NR)

102. Net domestic capital accumulation minus net revaluations (NDCA −
     NR)

103. NDCA

104. NDCA at original cost (OC)

105. NDCA, tangible, at original cost

106. NDCA, intangible, at original cost

107. GDCA − NR / GNP − NR, percent

108. NDCA − NR / NNP − NR, percent

109. NDCA, tangible, OC / NNP − NR, percent

110. NDCA, intangible OC / NNP − NR, percent

111. Gross business product

112. Gross nonprofit product

113. Gross government enterprise product

114. Gross government product

115. Gross household product

116. Gross domestic product

117. Gross product, rest of world

118. BEA GNP

119. BEA NNP
120. BEA NI
121. BEA GPDI
122. BEA NPDI
123. BEA PCE
124. BEA GPDI / BEA GNP, percent
125. BEA NPDI / BEA NNP, percent
126. TISA GNP / BEA GNP, percent
127. TISA NNP / BEA NNP, percent
128. TISA NNI / BEA NNI, percent
129. (TISA GNP $-$ NR) / BEA GNP, percent
130. (TISA NNP $-$ NR) / BEA NNP, percent
131. (TISA GDCA $-$ NR) / BEA GPDI, percent
132. (TISA NDCA $-$ NR) / BEA NPDI, percent
133. TISA NDCA, TAN, OC / BEA NPDI, percent
134. TISA consumption / BEA PCE, percent
135. GNP
136. Capital consumption allowance (CCA)
137. CCA, tangible
138. CCA, intangible
139. NNP
140. Business transfer payments $+$ uncompensated factor services $+$ net indirect tax $+$ statistical discrepancy
141. Net national income
142. GNP less sum of sectors and rest of world.

8. Gross Business Product in 1972 Dollars

Deflators and Additional Procedures

1. BEA gross domestic product, business
   N1.6-3

2. Less: Net space rent of owner-occupied nonfarm dwellings
   We use the corresponding deflator, N7.12-45.

3. Less: BEA government enterprise product
   We apply a government enterprise implicit deflator calculated as N6.2-24 ÷ N6.1-24.

4. Less: Rental value of buildings owned and used by nonprofit institutions
   We use the housing services, "other" deflator, N7.12-48.

5. BEA-type gross domestic product of TISA business sector
   The deflator applied here is N7.4-3.

6. Subsidies included in business income
   1 − 2 − 3 − 4 − 5

7. Expense account items of consumption
   We apply the implicit deflator for indirect business tax and nontax liability plus business transfer payments less subsidies plus current surplus of government enterprises, N7.5-4, to subsidies less current surplus of government enterprise. To surpluses of federal government enterprises and surpluses of state and local government enterprises we apply the same deflator. We apply the owner-occupied nonfarm dwellings space rent deflator, N7.12-45, to subsidies to owner-occupied dwellings.

8. Less: Expenses related to work
   We apply the implicit deflator for motor vehicles and parts, N7.20-20, to the value of the service of company-owned cars, and the personal consumption expenditures deflator, N7.1-2, to the expense account items of consumption other than the services of company-owned cars.

9. Business investment in research and development
   We use the gross national product deflator, N7.1-1.

10. Training produced in business sector
    We use the constant dollar series described in section 13, Investment in Human Capital.

11. Media support plus health and safety
    We apply the gross business product deflator, calculated as the ratio of current BEA gross business product to constant dollar gross business product (N1.5-3 ÷ N1.6-3), to media support. For health and safety

we take the constant dollar series described in section 13, Investment in Human Capital.

12. Net revaluations
    We use the fixed investment deflator, N7.1-7

13. Less: Intermediate product from government
    We take the constant dollar series from the government account (11-15).

14. Gross business product
    $5 + 6 + 7 - 8 + 9 + 10 + 11 + 12 + 13$

9. Gross Nonprofit Product in 1972 Dollars

Deflators and Additional Procedures

1. Consumption

2.   Consumption included in BEA personal consumption expenditures
    Each component of consumption is deflated separately. Thus

$$\text{line } 2 = (A + F)/\text{N7.12-76} + (.5B)/\text{N7.12-75}$$
$$+ (C + D + E)/\text{N7.12-81} + G/\text{N7.12-84}$$
$$+ (K - .3\text{MUSEUMS} - .25\text{RELIG})/\text{N7.12-89}$$

where $A, B, C, \ldots K$ are as described in section 3, Nonprofit Income
and Product. *MUSEUMS* and *RELIG* refer to portions of part K
(religious and welfare activities) which are used for museums and
religious organizations, respectively.

3. Additional imputed consumption
    This is derived from am implicit deflator constructed from line 2,

$$\text{line } 3^{72\$} = \text{line } 3^{\text{cur\$}} \times \frac{\text{line } 2^{72\$}}{\text{line } 2^{\text{cur\$}}} .$$

4. Capital accumulation

5.   Research and development
    This is deflated by the GNP deflator, N7.1-1.

6.   Education and training

7.   Investment included in BEA personal consumption expenditures
    Each component of investment is deflated individually:

$$\text{line } 7 = (H + I + J)/\text{N7.12-85} + (1.25\text{RELIG} +$$
$$.3\text{MUSEUM})/\text{N7.12-89} - \text{PNCRE(7)}/\text{N7.1-1},$$
    where PNCRE (7) is nonprofit R&D and the
    others are as defined in line 2 above.

8.   Additional imputed investment
    This is deflated using line 7, current and constant.

$$\text{line } 8^{72\$} = \text{line } 8^{\text{cur\$}} \times \frac{\text{line } 7^{72\$}}{\text{line } 7^{\text{cur\$}}}$$

9.   Employee training
      See section 13, Investment in Human Capital, for how series was
      constructed.

10.   Health

11.   Investment in health included in BEA personal consumption
       expenditures
       This equals current dollar series deflated by N7.12-75.

12.   Additional imputed investment
       This equals current dollar series, also deflated by N7.12-75.

13.   Net revaluations
       Deflated by the fixed investment deflator, N7.1-7.

14. Less: Intermediate product transferred from government
    Deflated in the government sector (11-16).

15. Less: Intermediate product purchased
    We apply the implicit deflator calculated from total nonprofit operating
    expenses, current and constant. Thus,

$$\text{line } 15^{72\$} = \text{line } 15^{cur\$} \times \frac{(\text{line } 2 + \text{line } 7 + \text{line } 11)^{72\$}}{(\text{line } 2 + \text{line } 7 + \text{line } 11)^{cur\$}}.$$

16. Less: Expenses related to work
    See appendix B, Expenses Related to Work, above.

17. Gross nonprofit product
    $1 + 4 - 14 - 15 - 16$

10. Gross Government Enterprise Product in 1972 Dollars

Deflators and Additional Procedures

1. Sales minus purchases of intermediate goods
   Current dollar series deflated by N7.22-24 for 1947 to 1981. For 1946
   the deflator is constructed as

$$DEF_{1946} = DEF_{1947} \times \frac{N7.4\text{-}12,1946}{N7.4\text{-}12,1947}.$$

2. Transfers
3. Capital income plus negative surplus plus intermediate product from
   government minus indirect taxes
4. Consumption
   Interest and negative surpluses in current dollars are allocated between consumption and investment on the basis of constant dollar
   consumption and investment at original cost. Once allocated, consumption is deflated with the PCE deflator, N7.1-2. Thus, this
   line is

$$(4\text{-}5 + 4\text{-}8) \times \frac{7\text{-}1}{7\text{-}1 + 7\text{-}31} \div N7.1\text{-}2.$$

5. Investment
   Allocated as above and then deflated with the fixed investment
   deflator, N7.1-7. Thus, this line is

$$(4\text{-}5 + 4\text{-}8) \times \frac{7\text{-}31}{7\text{-}1 + 7\text{-}31} \div N7.1\text{-}7.$$

6. Employee training
   See section 13, Investment in Human Capital.
7. Net revaluations
8. Less: Interest product from government
9. Less: Expenses related to work
   Deflated with the fixed investment deflator, N7.1-7.
10. Gross government enterprise product
    $1 + 2 + 7 - 8 - 9$

11. Gross Government Product in 1972 Dollars

Deflators and Additional Procedures

The undistributed product by function is converted to 1972 dollars using specific deflators in some cases and general deflators for federal, for state and local, or for all government purchases of goods and services in others.

Defense product is deflated by the implicit price deflator for federal purchases of goods and services from N7.1-20, for the years 1946 to 1981. We use the defense product deflator calculated by Ziemer and Galbraith (1979) for the years 1972-76. Space product is deflated for all years with the implicit price deflator for federal purchases of goods and services.

The products of the education, welfare, and local parks and recreation functions are deflated by the implicit deflator for state and local government purchases of goods and services from N7.1-23. The product of the general administration function is deflated by the implicit price deflator for all government purchases of goods and services from N7.1-19.

For the remaining functions we have specific deflators. The product of the health functions is deflated by the implicit price deflator for medical care from N7.12-71. The products of the sanitation function and transportation function are deflated respectively by the implicit price deflator for water and sanitary services, N7.12-52, and the implicit price deflator for transportation services, N7.12-56. The product of the natural resources function is deflated by the implicit price deflator for agricultural services, forestry, and fisheries product from N7.22-6.

For change in inventories we derive an implicit deflator from figures on current and constant dollar end-of-year inventory stocks secured from the BEA. The stock deflator is $P_{Ht} = (H_{t,current\$}) /(H_{t,1972\$})$, for inventories at the end of the year t. We then define our change-in-inventory deflator as

$$P_{\Delta H,t} = (P_{Ht} + P_{H,t-1}) \div (P_{H72} + P_{H71}),$$

thus getting a measure of prices over the year and normalizing to make the index precisely equal to 1.0 in the year 1972.

We construct our own implicit price deflator to convert intermediate purchases from other sectors to constant dollars. This is based on ratios of current to constant dollar government expenditures for nondurables, G_{ND}, and services other than those of employees, G_S. Thus our deflator may be written

$$P_{IP} = \frac{(G_{ND} + G_S)_{cur\$}}{(G_{ND} + G_S)_{1972\$}}$$

We use our transportation services index to deflate expenses related to work.

Constant dollar net revaluations for 1946 to 1976 are from Eisner 1980a. The fixed investment deflator, N7.1-7, is used to convert current dollar estimates to 1972 dollars.

12. Gross Household Product in 1972 Dollars

Deflators and Additional Procedures

1. Consumption

2.   Market (labor services in households)
        Domestic services deflator, N7.12-54, is applied.

3.   Nonmarket

4.   Net space rent on owner-occupied nonfarm dwellings
        The corresponding deflator, N7.12-45, is applied to both BEA net
        space rent and subsidies.

5.   BEA net space rent on owner-occupied nonfarm dwellings

6.   Subsidies

7.   Capital services other than owner-occupied dwellings

8.   Durables
        Services of durables in current dollars are converted to 1972
        dollars with the implicit deflator for durables, N7.11-2. Constant
        dollar series are used directly for services of durables allocated
        to consumption. These are described in section 13, Investment
        in Human Capital.

9.   Gross

10.   Less: Services allocated to investment

11.   Less: Services to expenses related to work

12.   Semidurables
        We apply an implicit deflator calculated from the current and
        constant dollar series for stocks of semidurables described for
        6-24.

13.   Inventories
        We apply an implicit deflator calculated from the current and
        constant dollar series for inventories described for 6-25.

14.   Labor services
        For opportunity costs of students we apply the PCE deflator,
        N7.1-2. A constant dollar series is used directly for employee
        training costs. Unpaid household work is deflated by the domestic
        wage deflator. The latter two series are described in subsection
        2, on education and training of Section 13, below, and in the
        appendix A, Valuation of Household Work.

15.   Total imputed labor services

16.   Less: Labor services allocated to investment

17.   Intermediate product of government to consumption
       A constant dollar series is taken from the government sector. From
       this we subtract current dollar indirect taxes divided by the durable
       goods deflator, N7.11-2.

18. Capital accumulation

19.   Intangible at original cost

20.   Education

21.   Teaching children in the home
       The constant dollar series used is described in appendix A,
       Valuation of Household Work.

22.   Opportunity cost of students
       We apply the PCE deflator, N7.1-2.

23.   Durable services allocated to education
       Current dollar stock series are divided by an implicit deflator
       for services allocated to investment.

24.   Intermediate product of government to education
       Constant dollar series are taken from the government sector
       (11-18).

25.   Health
       The constant dollar series for value of time spent in the home on
       health care is described in appendix A. Constant dollar stocks of
       ophthalmic products and orthopedic appliances are taken from
       the BEA. Intermediate product of government is again from the
       government accounts.

26.   Employee training
       The constant dollar series is described in section 13, in subsection
       2 on education and training.

27.   Net revaluations
       We apply the fixed investment deflator, N7.1-7.

28. Services to expenses related to work
       Constant dollar series are used directly for services of durables related
       to expenses to work, as described in appendix B, Expenses Related
       to Work.

29. Less: Intermediate product transferred from government
       This is from government product in constant dollars.

30. Less: expenses related to work
       See appendix B, Expenses Related to Work.

31. Gross household product
       $1 + 18 + 28 - 29 - 30$

13. Investment in Human Capital

1. Framework: Investment series

1.1 General methodology

Investment in human capital is classified as intangible investment in education and in health. The main components of these, for the years 1929 to 1969, are taken from the series for "education and training" and for "medical and health," listed under the title, "human intangible" in Kendrick (1976). We do not include expenditures for mobility, which Kendrick counts in human investment, and we also exclude rearing costs, which Kendrick considers investment in "tangible" human capital. We add to Kendrick's expenditure series, however, imputations for the value of time spent in the home on education and health care.

Construction of human capital series requires assumptions about service lives of capital. These entail disaggregation of the components of investment in human capital and assignment of lives—on occasion, varying lives—to each component. Investment in education consists of employee training, broken into specific and general, military education, and the major category of "all other education." Investment in health is subdivided into investment in business health and safety and "all other health."

Investment in employee training, military education, and business safety and health are classified as 40 percent specific and 60 percent general. Specific investment in each sector is assumed to have a service life equal to the sector's average length of employment. We assume a service life of 40 years in all sectors for general training and 25 years for general investment in military education and in business safety and health. We assume a service life of 50 years for all other investment in human capital, that is, "all other education" and "all other health."

Our 40/60 percent allocation of investment in business safety and health differs from Kendrick's 50/50 allocation. We gave the greater weight to general investment to reflect expenditures for health and safety equipment, the services of which outlive the employment of current workers. Our assignment of a service life of 50 years to the "all other" categories also differs from Kendrick, who allocates expenditures by age cohorts and then applies population and mortality tables to calculate service lives.

.

1.2 Service lives

1.2.1 Education and training

1. Specific training
Households, nonprofit institutions and business

1925–1929	3 years
1930–1940	4 years
1941–1953	2 years
1954–1966	4 years
1967–1981	3 years

Government and government enterprises

1925–1929	6 years
1930–1940	8 years
1941–1953	3 years
1954–1966	7 years
1967–1981	8 years

2. General training
All sectors   40 years

3. Military Education
Specific   3 years
General   25 years

4. All other education   50 years

1.2.2 Health and medical care

1. Business health and safety
Specific   3 years
General   25 years

2. All other health and medical care   50 years

1.3 Extrapolation for early years

Since human capital is assumed to have lives up to 50 years, to obtain stocks and depreciation beginning in 1946, we need investment data as far back as 1895. We begin by extrapolating total real investment in human capital. This series is carried back to 1929 by assuming the same ratio to Kendrick's series in the years 1929 to 1939 as the average of its ratio to the Kendrick series in the years 1940 to 1949.

$$
(1) \qquad IHC_t = 0.1 \sum_{\tau = 1940}^{1949} (IHC_\tau / IHCKEN_\tau) IHC_t
$$
$$
t = 1929 \text{ to } 1939.
$$

The extrapolation is then extended back to 1895 on the basis of its average annual growth rate for the years 1938 to 1981.

(2) $\text{IHC}_t = \text{IHC}_{29} \times (\text{IHC}_{81}/\text{IHC}_{38})^{(t-1929)/33}$
        $t = 1895 \text{ to } 1928.$

Conversion to current dollars is accomplished by applying an available consumer price index normalized to the implicit deflator for 1929 of the human capital investment series, IHCPI_{29}.

(3) $\text{IHC\$}_t = \text{IHC}_t \times \text{CPI}_t \times \dfrac{\text{IHCPI}_{29}}{\text{CPI}_{29}}$

The consumer price index (CPI) utilized is that for all items, appearing in *Historical Statistics of the United States* (U.S. Dept of Commerce, BEA 1975).

Investment in the 50-year "all other" categories, IAO, is obtained by subtracting the sum of investment in employee training, military education, and business health and safety, designated *ISUM,* from total investment in human capital, *IHC*. The components of *ISUM* are extrapolated as follows.

First, for investment in employee training, *IET,* and investment in business safety and health, *IBSH,* the Kendrick series on investment in human capital, *IHCKEN,* which goes back to 1929, is applied. We simply assume that the ratios *IET/IHCKEN* and *IBSH/IHCKEN* were the same for each of the years 1929 to 1939 as their 10-year average ratios from 1940 to 1949.

(4) $\text{IX}_{jt} = .1 \displaystyle\sum_{\tau = 1940}^{1949} (\text{IX}_{j\tau}/\text{IHCKEN}_\tau)\text{IHCKEN}_t$

$\text{IX}_j = \text{IET, IBSH}$
$t = 1929 \text{ to } 1939.$

Then adding investment in military education, *IME,* taken from Kendrick, we calculate *ISUM = IET + IBSH + IME* for the years 1929 to 1938, that is,

(5) $\text{ISUM}_t = \text{IET}_t + \text{IBSH}_t + \text{IME}_t$

$t = 1929 \text{ to } 1938.$

ISUM is next extrapolated back to 1895 by assuming that the ratio, *ISUM/IHC* is the same for each of those years as the average of its ratios for the years 1929 to 1938.

(6) $\text{ISUM}_t = \text{IHC}_t \times .1 \sum\limits_{\tau=1929}^{1938} (\text{ISUM}_\tau/\text{IHC}_\tau)$

$$t = 1895 \text{ to } 1928.$$

Then,

(7) $\text{IAO}_t = \text{IHC}_t - \text{ISUM}_t \quad t = 1895 \text{ to } 1981.$

The TISA investment series, prior to extrapolation, were converted to current and 1972 dollars. Since Kendrick's constant dollar series were in 1958 dollars, the TISA 1972 dollar series were reconverted to 1958 dollars by dividing them by their implicit deflators for 1958. Extrapolations were accomplished in current dollars and in 1958 dollars. In a final stage, series for all years were reconverted to 1972 dollars.

Investment in military education, employee training, and safety and health are assumed to be 60 percent general. These series are extended back from 1928 to 1895 using the following formula:

(8) $\text{IGEN}_{it} = .1 \sum\limits_{\tau=1940}^{1949} (\text{IGEN}_{i\tau} \div \text{ICH}_\tau) \, \text{IHC}_t$

$$i = 1,2,3$$

$$t = 1895 \text{ to } 1928.$$

$IGEN_{it}$ = TISA general investment in military education, employee training and safety and health.

Historic cost depreciation is calculated from current dollar investment. Constant 1958 dollar stocks and depreciation are calculated from the 1958 dollar investment series. Stocks at the end of each year, t, are then converted to current dollars and to 1972 dollars by applying the averages of investment price deflators for the years t and $t + 1$.

2. Education and training

2.1 Components by sector

The following outline indicates the attribution of investment in education and training by sector. We have allocated Kendrick's "personal" sector investment to our household and nonprofit sectors, and his government investment to our separate government and government enterprise sectors. Our procedures in estimating investment in employee training are described in a separate section immediately below the outline. This is followed by the description of methods, by sector, for obtaining investment in the other categories of education and training.

2.1.1 Nonprofit sector
1. Formal education
2. Informal education
3. Religious education
4. Imputations for volunteer services and interest
5. Employee training

2.1.2 Household sector
1. Formal education
   1. Direct costs
   2. Associated costs
   3. Student opportunity costs
   4. Intermediate product transferred from government
2. Informal education
   1. Radio, TV, records, musical instruments
   2. Books and maps
   3. Magazines, newspapers, and sheet music
   4. Time spent with children
   5. Intermediate product transferred from government
3. Employee training

2.1.3 Business sector
1. Informal education
2. Employee training

2.1.4 Government sector
1. Formal education
2. Informal education
3. Military education
4. Civilian training

2.1.5 Government enterprise sector
Employee training

2.2 Employee training

2.2.1 Derivation, 1946 to 1966
Stock series in 1958 dollars were obtained from Kendrick for 1925–66. These series were broken down into two types of capital stocks, general and specific, for the business sector, the government sector (general government plus government enterprises), and the personal sector (household and nonprofit institutions).

Investment in specific training for the personal and business sectors was derived from the stock series as follows:

$$I_t = K_t - K_{t-1} + K_{t-2}/3 \qquad t = 1925 \text{ to } 1929, n = 3$$
$$I_t = K_t - K_{t-1} + (K_{t-2} + K_{t-3})/8 \quad t = 1930 \text{ to } 1940, n = 4$$
$$I_t = K_t - K_{t-1} + (K_{t-1} + K_{t-2})/4 \quad t = 1941 \text{ to } 1953, n = 2$$
$$I_t = K_t - K_{t-1} + (K_{t-2} + K_{t-3})/8 \quad t = 1954 \text{ to } 1966, n = 4$$

where n = specific investment life (job tenure).

For the government sector, investment series were derived from the following:

$$I_t = K_t - K_{t-1} + (K_{t-3} + K_{t-4})/12 \quad t = 1925 \text{ to } 1929, n = 6$$
$$I_t = K_t - K_{t-1} + (K_{t-4} + K_{t-5})/16 \quad t = 1930 \text{ to } 1940, n = 8$$
$$I_t = K_t - K_{t-1} + K_{t-2}/3 \qquad t = 1941 \text{ to } 1953, n = 3$$
$$I_t = K_t - K_{t-1} + K_{t-4}/7 \qquad t = 1954 \text{ to } 1966, n = 7$$

Investment series for general training are obtained for each of the three sectors with the assumption of a service life of 40 years.* Thus, for each sector, j,

$$I_{jt} = \Delta K_{jt} + (K_{j,t-20} + K_{j,t-21})/80,$$

where j denotes personal, business, and government sectors, respectively.

The investment series are converted from 1958 dollars to current dollars and then back to 1972 dollars by applying the implicit deflator for government purchases of goods and services to the government series and using a weighted average of the PCE deflator and the fixed investment deflator for the personal sector and the business sector:

$$PBP = \frac{2}{3} PPCE + \frac{1}{3} PFI,$$

*Kendrick assumed a 40:60 split between specific and general training investment. An assumption of a 40-year service life for general training, when applied to Kendrick's stock figures, reproduced this distribution. Inspection of data referred to by Kendrick (characteristics of trainees enrolled in institutional training programs) supported the 40-year service life assumption.

where

PBP = deflator for business sector and personal sector (1958
      = 1.0),
PPCE = personal consumption expenditures deflator, and
PFI = fixed investment deflator.

The weights are those used by Kendrick in his estimation of formal training costs but the PCE deflator is substituted for his deflator for compensation of employees (Kendrick 1976, appendix B-4a, on microfiche, pp. 36–37) which was unavailable. And lacking both the breakdown between formal training costs and other training costs and the deflator for other training costs, we used the weighted average, PBP deflator on the series for total training costs.

2.2.2 Extrapolation, 1967 to 1981

The 1972 dollar investment series are then extrapolated to the years 1967 to 1981 on the basis of equations estimated from ordinary least squares regressions of the earlier data. Equation specifications were chosen to relate the main components of Kendrick's employee training series. Employee compensation and the new hire rate are the key explanatory variables, with the latter reflecting costs associated with initial training. The compensation variable captures predominantly the expenditures associated with additional training and retraining. A nonlinear form of the equation is specified to capture the interaction of these variables.

1. Business

The business sector 1972 dollar series is extended to 1981 by regressing the logarithm of total business sector training costs on the logarithm of compensation per business employee, the logarithm of the new hire rate, and the logarithm of total employment in the business sector. The estimated equation is

$$\text{LBTR} = -2.951 + .686 \text{ LBCOEM} + .406 \text{ LNH\%} + 1.400 \text{ LBEMP},$$
$$\qquad\quad (2.024) \quad (.669) \qquad\qquad (.075) \qquad\qquad (.815)$$

$$\hat{R}^2 = .836 \qquad n = 21 \ (1946 \text{ to } 1966)$$

where ·

LBTR   = logarithm of total business sector training costs,
LBCOEM = logarithm of compensation per business employee
        = log [(N6.5A, line 2 − line 4 − line 7)
          ÷ (N6.8A, line 2 − line 4 − line 75)],

LNH%   = logarithm of new hire rate, and
LBEMP   = logarithm of total employment in the business sector
          = log [N6.8A, line 2 − line 4 − line 75].

Current dollar series are obtained by applying the deflators described above.

2. Government

For the government sector the logarithm of government training costs per employee is regressed on the logarithm of compensation per government employee, the logarithm of the new hire rate, and a time trend. All dollar variables are in 1972 dollars. The fitted equation is

$$\text{LGTREM} = .018 + .153 \text{ LGCOEM} + .557 \text{ LNH\%} + .020 \text{ TIME}$$
$$\quad\quad (.592)\quad (.137)\quad\quad\quad (.104)\quad\quad\quad (.006)$$

$$\hat{R}^2 = .637 \quad n = 27 \text{ (1940 to 1966)},$$

where

LGTREM = logarithm of government training costs per employee, 1972 dollars,
LGCOEM = logarithm of compensation per government employee, 1972 dollars (N6.5A, line 75/(N.6.8A, line 75 minus line 79)), deflated as noted above,
LNH%   = logarithm of new hire rate (table D-3, *Employment and Earnings,* U.S. Dept. of Labor, Bureau of Labor Statistics 1975), and
TIME   = time trend.

Consolidated government sector training costs, GTR, are then divided between government and government enterprises on the basis of relative aggregate compensation of employees:

$$\text{GVTR} = \text{GTR} \left(\frac{\text{GVCE}}{\text{GVCE} + \text{GECE}} \right)$$

$$\text{GETR} = \text{GTR} \left(\frac{\text{GECE}}{\text{GVCE} + \text{GECE}} \right),$$

where

GVTR   = government sector training costs,
GETR   = government enterprise sector training costs,

GVCE = government sector compensation of employees (TISA 5-2), and

GECE = government enterprise sector compensation of employees (TISA 4-2).

3. Personal

The personal sector 1972 dollars series is extended to 1981 by regressing the logarithm of total personal training costs on the logarithm of total personal compensation of employees and the logarithm of the new hire rate. Thus,

$$LPTR = -1.621 + .847\ LPCOM + .509\ LNH\%$$
$$ (.172)\quad (.076)\qquad\qquad (.064)$$
$$\hat{R}^2 = .827 \qquad n = 27\ (1940\ \text{to}\ 1966),$$

where

LPTR = logarithm of personal sector training costs in 1972 dollars,

LPCOM = logarithm of personal sector compensation in 1972 dollars, or log (N1.12, line 41 minus N6.5A, line 74), deflated as noted above, and

LNH% = logarithm of new hire rate.

Kendrick's personal sector training costs (PTR) are divided between the household and nonprofit sectors on the basis of compensation of employees, i.e.:

$$HHTR = PTR\left(\frac{HHCE}{HHCE + NPCE}\right)$$

$$NPTR = PTR\left(\frac{NPCE}{HHCE + NPCE}\right),$$

where

HHTR = household training costs,

NPTR = nonprofit sector training costs,

HHCE = compensation of employees in the household sector (TISA 6-2), and

NPCE = compensation of employees in the nonprofit sector (TISA 3-2).

To the imputation for employee training in the household and nonprofit sector is added a portion of intermediate product of government transferred to each of these sectors. For each sector

$$\text{IPGET} = \text{IPG} \left(\frac{\text{ET}}{\text{C} + \text{I} - \text{IPG}} \right),$$

where

$IPGET$ = intermediate product of government allocated to employee training transferred to either nonprofit institutions or households,

IPG = intermediate product of government transferred to either nonprofit institutions or households,

ET = employee training in either nonprofit institutions or households, and

C + I − IPG = consumption plus investment exclusive of intermediate product of government in either sector. This is in TISA table 3 for nonprofit institutions, line 24 + line 27 − line 37, and in table 6 for households, line 45 + line 62 − line 73.

2.3 Other education and training

2.3.1 Business sector

Informal education

This consists of a portion of media support by business for radio, magazines, newspapers, and TV. Kendrick divides these expenditures between nonprofit institutions and business on the basis of income originating. We have retained these expenditures in the business sector, which is consistent with our inclusion of all media transfers in the business sector (TISA 2-32).

Media support by business is described in the write-up for business income and product, 2-32. The portions of media support in each category to be allocated to education are from Fritz Machlup (1962). These are: 50 percent for magazines, 40 percent for newspapers, 22 percent for radio, and 11 percent for TV. For estimates in 1972 dollars, magazine and newspaper expenditures are deflated with unpublished BEA deflators; radio and TV expenditures are deflated by the radio and TV deflator, N7.15-18.

2.3.2 Nonprofit sector

1. Formal education

   Nonprofit expenditures on formal education, or schooling, are from N2.6-98. A finer division of these costs from the BEA includes expenditures by nonprofit institutions and the household sector combined, as well as expenditures on research and development.

   Investment in formal education excludes research and development but includes the rental value of structures and equipment used in education. The BEA data contain an imputation for rent: depreciation plus interest. The difference between the BEA imputation and ours is included under additional imputations.

2. Informal education

   Informal education consists of expenditures on libraries and museums, which are included in N2.6-102, religious and welfare activities. (An unpublished version of this line, listing libraries and museums as a separate item, was obtained from the BEA.) Of this, 30 percent is considered investment; the remaining 70 percent is assumed to be consumption. Kendrick differs by assuming all expenditures on libraries and museums are investment and by taking them to be a constant (1.0415) percent of the unpublished expenditure series for all religious and welfare activities, N2.6-97 (1966).

3. Religious education

   Religious education included in investment is that portion of religious organization expenditures (BEA unpublished data, included as part of line 102 in N2.6) which is devoted to education. We follow Kendrick in taking 25 percent of these expenditures. This percentage was derived by Kendrick from National Council of Churches data.

4. Imputations for volunteer services and interest

   Counted as additional investment in education are the value of volunteer services, interest on nonprofit structures and equipment used in education, and a portion of intermediate product of government transferred to nonprofit institutions, as indicated in the description of procedures in estimating product in section 3, Nonprofit Income and Product. Kendrick does not include volunteer services.

Unpublished data for all the N2.6 items above were obtained from the BEA in 1972 dollars.

2.3.3 Government sector

1. Formal education
   Government expenditures on formal education plus an imputed rental value of plant and equipment are calculated in the government sector. Government informal education is added to this and appears on the credit side of the government accounts as 5-32, public schools.

2. Informal education
   This is the portion of parks and recreation expenditure devoted to practical education. The average ratio of educational recreational expenditures to total recreational expenditures is .12975. It was obtained from data in *City Finances** for cities having a population of over 100,000 for 1932–42 and for the largest 37 cities for 1943–50. Half of total educational recreation expenditures are considered consumption and half investment.

3. Military education and training
   This was calculated as 63.075 percent of military wages (N8.6-78). The percentage is taken from Kendrick worksheets.† For additional detail see general write-up on the government sector, accounts 5 and 11.

2.3.4 Household Sector

1. Formal education

   1. Direct costs
      Direct expenditures on education are taken from N2.6-98: 2.6, line 98: private education and research, minus nonprofit expenditures, minus research and development.

   2. Student opportunity costs
      Current dollar series are described in the write-up for account 6 on household income and product, line 5. Estimates in 1972 dollars were calculated from the current dollar series by applying the PCE deflator (N7.7.1-2).

---

*Post-1950 data are from *City Finances* (U.S. Dept. of Commerce, Bureau of the Census) and are aggregated with no separate listing for educational recreation. Thus, the ratio was calculated from 1932–50 data only, using 1932–42 expenditures of cities of over 100,000 population and 1932–50 expenditures of the 37 largest cities. These were found in a table entitled "Government Cost Payments for Operation and Maintenance of General Departments by Principal Division and Subdivision." (Table number varies from year to year.)

†Kendrick 1976, appendix B-4a, microfiche p. 24, reportedly based on a study by a Colonel Hunt.

3. Associated costs

These costs relate to books, travel and accessories, such as typewriters, used in formal education. They are calculated as 6.32 percent of direct cost and expenditures by federal, state, and local government for education. This percent is taken from the average of the ratio of Schultz's estimates of associated costs for 1950 and 1956 ($.578 and $.911 billion, respectively) to our direct costs for education. Estimates in current and in 1972 dollars were prepared in similar fashion from series in current and in 1972 dollars.

Schultz (1960, 571–83) used 5 percent of the foregone earnings of high school students and 10 percent of the foregone earnings of college students to arrive at his estimate of associated costs. Machlup (1962) took 3 percent and 6 percent of the foregone earnings of high school and college students, respectively, allocating to a publishing category the remainder of the earnings contained in Schultz's 5 percent and 10 percent. However, Machlup's associated costs with the 5 percent and 10 percent estimates still differ from Schultz's since Machlup used different estimates of the foregone earnings of students.

Kendrick follows Machlup's use of 3 percent and 6 percent of the foregone earnings of high school and college students, respectively, to obtain associated costs of education. He also adds 1.5 percent of the foregone earnings of elementary school students but does not include Machlup's publishing category. Kendrick applied these percentages to his own estimate of the foregone earnings of students.

It does not seem appropriate to assume that the associated costs of education vary with the foregone earnings of students. Since there seems to be general agreement with Schultz's original work, we have taken his estimates of the associated costs of education for 1950 and 1956. We have assumed that they vary over the remaining years, however, on the basis of the relationship between these costs and the direct costs of education. Thus, associated costs are calculated as:

$$AC_t = .5 \left(\frac{AC_{s\ 1950}}{DC_{1950}} + \frac{AC_{s\ 1956}}{DC_{1956}} \right) DC_t$$
$$t = 1946 \text{ to } 1981,$$

where

AC_S = Schultz's estimates of associated costs, and
DC = TISA direct costs.

4. Intermediate product transferred from government
   Intermediate product of government transferred to households, IPGHH, is divided between consumption and investment on the basis of the ratio of consumption to investment, exclusive of intermediate product of government. The portion allocated to education is

$$\text{IPGE} = \text{IPGHH} \left(\frac{\text{TC} + \text{OPCST} + \text{DSIE}}{\text{C} + \text{I} - \text{IPG}} \right),$$

where

TC = the imputed value of teaching children in the home (2.4 below),
$OPCST$ = the opportunity cost of students (2.3.4.1.2 above), and
$DSIE$ = durable services allocated to investment in education (2.1 and 2.2 below).

The remaining variables are as defined in 2.2.2.3 above.

2. Informal education
   Costs of informal education are those for radio, TV, records and musical instruments, for books and maps, and for magazines, newspapers, and sheet music.

   For each of these categories, the portion of the total expenditures related to education is taken from Kendrick's unpublished worksheets and the appendix to Kendrick (1976, appendix B-4a, microfiche, pp. 18–19). Kendrick took the proportions from Machlup (1962), who developed weighted averages for each category on the basis of 1954 consumer expenditure data.

   1. Radio, TV, records, musical instruments
      This includes 17.2 percent of the imputed rental value of these items.

$$\text{RENT}_t = \text{DEPR}_t + .5\text{CDI}_t \, (\text{STK}_t + \text{STK}_{t-1}),$$

where

$RENT$ = imputed rental value,
$DEPR$ = current dollar depreciation (BEA, unpublished),
CDI = consumer durable interest rate (Smith 1971; and as described in the write-up for household income and product, 6-22), and
STK = year-end current dollar stocks (BEA, unpublished).

BEA series in 1972 dollars are used for 1972 dollar estimates.

2. Books and maps

This includes 34.2 percent of the imputed rental value of books and maps. Rental value is computed as in 1, immediately above, using stocks of books and maps (BEA, unpublished).

BEA series in 1972 dollars are used for 1972 dollar estimates.

3. Magazines, newspapers, and sheet music

This includes 47.4 percent of total expenditures for magazines, newspapers, and sheet music (N2.6-84). For 1972 dollar estimates, an unpublished version of N2.6-84 is used.

4. Time spent with children

This is the value of time spent teaching children in the home. See appendix A, Valuation of Household Work.

3. Health and Medical Care Investment

Following Kendrick, we have estimated medical investment to be one-half of total medical and health expenditures. We assume the other half to be maintenance, or current consumption, which does not enhance future productivity.

3.1 Business sector

Business sector investment in health and safety care of private, non-farm employees is divided between "specific" investment which yields benefits only as long as workers remain in the employ of the same firm, and "general" investment which is not contingent upon continued employment. We have made the same allocation of 40 percent to specific investment and 60 percent to general investment that we did for employee training, although Kendrick used a 50/50 division between specific and general. We are giving more weight to general investment since not only is some health care taken with employees when they change jobs, but some safety equipment is left in the workplace to be enjoyed by the new employees.

Business sector current dollar investment in safety and health, using Kendrick's method, is the sum of industrial in-plant medical costs and safety costs.

Industrial in-plant medical costs for 1945, and 1950 to 1961 are from *Social Security Bulletin*, Nov. 1962, "Social Security Expenditures." For 1962–66 they are from *HEW Trends*, "Private and Public Expenditures for Health and Medical Care" (U.S. Dept. of Health, Education, and Welfare).

Data for the missing years were interpolated and extrapolated from the regression equation:

$$\text{HEALTH}_t = .072 + .1009\text{INSURANCE}_t$$
$$t = 1945, 1950\text{–}61,$$
$$\hat{R}^2 = .96,$$

where

HEALTH   = estimated in-plant medical costs and
INSURANCE = health insurance expenditures (N2.6-51).

To obtain safety costs, we follow Kendrick in an estimate from Bachman (1952, 262) of $9.14 for expenditures on safety programs per employee in 1949. Each year's average annual earnings (N6.9-1) is then multiplied by .00316, the ratio of $9.14 to average annual earnings in 1949, to obtain expenditures per employee on safety in other years.

Bachman further found that 73.5 percent of companies surveyed had accident prevention programs.* Total safety cost is thus calculated as

$$\text{SAFETY} = .735 + .00316 \times \text{AVEARN} \times \text{EMPLOY},$$

where

AVEARN = average earnings (N3.9-2) and
EMPLOY = full-time equivalent (FTE) employees in domestic industries (N6.8-74) minus PTE employees in agriculture, forestry, and fisheries (N6.8-3).

*Bachman obtained his data from a 1951 National Association of Manufacturers survey. He indicates that it is unclear how much of these expenditures are for personal, nondurables, or capital, but feels they are an understatement. The only additional data available are in McGraw-Hill capital expenditure surveys from 1972 to the present. This series is too short to develop capital stocks and impute a value of service. Calls to HEW, BLS, the National Safety Council, and the National Association of Manufacturers for more data have been futile. Our series clearly do not reflect possibly increased expenditures due to OSHA, passed in 1970, or other factors.

Series in 1972 dollars are obtained by applying the medical care deflator (N7.12-64).

3.2 Nonprofit institutions

Investment in health and medical care by the nonprofit sector is composed of two elements: (1) expenditures included in personal consumption expenditures (a portion of N2.6-50: privately controlled hospitals and sanitariums) and (2) imputed investment, which is primarily volunteer services, imputed interest, and a portion of intermediate product of government transferred to nonprofit institutions. For methodology of calculating the current and constant dollar investment, see the nonprofit sector accounts, 3 and 9.

3.3 Government sector

Here we depart somewhat from the method used by Kendrick. Kendrick used total expenditures minus capital outlays plus the rental value of service of capital in health and medical care and sanitation. We do not incorporate sanitation in our series, viewing this as maintenance or current consumption and not as investment.

Current dollar series are taken and updated from Eisner and Nebhut (1981), table 1, "Final Government Product by Function: Health." Series in 1972 dollars are from Eisner and Nebhut, table 2.

3.4 Household sector

Current dollar investment in health and medical care consists of outlays for health, excluding expenditures for ophthalmic products and orthopedic appliances and also excluding income loss insurance and workers' compensation insurance, but including the imputed rental value of ophthalmic products and orthopedic appliances and imputation for time spent on medical care in the home. Kendrick also includes an imputed net interest on structures which we have omitted since this is included by the BEA in medical care expenses (N2.6-44).

We therefore have

$$HHMED = MEDEXP - APPEXP - NPEXP$$
$$- INSUR + APPRENT + THMCC,$$

where

HHMED = total medical and health output of households.
MEDEXP = medical care expenses (N2.6-44).
APPEXP = ophthalmic products and orthopedic appliances expenditures (N2.6-46).

NPEXP   = nonprofit sector expenditures included in N2.6-50 (TISA 3-34).

INSUR   = income loss insurance and workers' compensation insurance (N2.6-53 and 54).

APPRENT = rental value of ophthalmic product and orthopedic equipment.

THMCC   = value of time spent in the home on the medical care of children. (See appendix A, Value of Household Work.)

Income loss insurance for 1948 to 1981 is from N2.6-53, and for 1946 and 1947 is estimated as .2867 times total health insurance (N2.6-51), where .2867 is the average ratio of income loss insurance to total health insurance for the following 10-year period, 1948–57.

Workers' compensation insurance for 1948 to 1981 is from N2-54 and for 1946 to 1947 is estimated as .3003 times total health insurance (N2.6-51), where .3003 is the average ratio of workers' compensation insurance to total health insurance for the following 10-year period, 1948–57.

To the household expenditures on health is added a portion of the intermediate product of government transferred to households, defined as

$$\text{IPGH} = \text{IPGHH} \times \left(\frac{\text{APPRENT} + \text{THMCC}}{\text{DENOM}} \right),$$

where

IPGH   = intermediate product of government transferred to households allocated to investment in health.

IPGHH   = intermediate product of government transferred to households (TISA, table 5, line 11).

DENOM = the sum of household market and nonmarket product consumed (TISA, table 6, lines 46 and 47), the imputed value of teaching children in the home (TISA, table 6, line 65), the opportunity cost of students (TISA, table 6, line 66), employee training exclusive of *IPGHH* (a portion of TISA, table 6, line 70), *THMCC*, and *APPRENT*.

Series in current dollars in NIPA, table 2.6, are available in 1972 dollars in an unpublished table, or in less detail in N2.7.

14. Total Capital

The estimates in tables 13, 14, and 15 relate to end-of-year net capital stocks. Straight-line depreciation was applied to all capital other than land and inventories.

Tangible capital stock estimates were taken in large part directly from BEA computer tapes. Data up to 1976 were taken originally from BEA (1980a) tabulations, designated by the letters "a" through "k." Hard copy series are now to be found in U.S. Dept. of Commerce, BEA (1987). Estimates for household inventories and semidurables were calculated from NIPA expenditure series and our assumed depreciation rates. The Flow of Funds Section of the Federal Reserve Board was the source of our estimates of land, except for government land.

Intangible capital stock estimates (of R&D and human capital) were generally our own estimates or extensions of Kendrick (1976) estimates. They were sums of components calculated by cumulating successive years of net investment. Construction of the underlying investment series and depreciation for human capital are described in detail in section 13 above. The R&D series and sources are described in section 2, lines 20 and 46, section 3, line 28, and section 5, under "I. The distribution of [government] final product."

Each end-of-year constant dollar stock in principle equaled the previous end-of-year stock plus the current year's investment minus the current year's capital consumption. Discrepancies between end-of-year aggregate stock deflators and component investment flow deflators, in calculations that entailed repeated conversions back and forth among various constant and current dollar magnitudes, contributed to inconsistencies, however, between changes in stock and net investment flows for aggregates of intangible capital as well as many of the sub-aggregates of tangible capital.

The implicit price deflators of table 15 are simply the ratios of corresponding lines in table 13 and table 14. Specific sources for tables 13 and 14 follow.

1. Total capital
    The sum of lines 2, 9, 13, 19 and 23, the capital in each sector.

2. Business

3.   Tangible

4.   Land
            From Flow of Funds accounts. The BEA fixed investment deflator, N7.1-7, is used to convert current land estimates to con-

This section was originally drafted in collaboration with Paul J. Pieper.

stant dollars. Seven percent of nonprofit institution land is added, as explained immediately below.

5.   Structures and equipment

The combined business and nonprofit structures and equipment (e) minus 93 percent of the nonprofit figures (b). The 7 percent of nonprofit structures and equipment attributed by the BEA to wholesale cooperatives is counted as part of the business sector and hence not subtracted. Since Flow of Funds land estimates are tied to structures, 7 percent of them are similarly included in the business sector, as indicated above.

6.   Residential

Total business residential capital (e) minus nonprofit residential capital (k) and minus owner-occupied nonfarm dwellings (i) which TISA includes in the household sector.

7.   Inventories

These correspond precisely, in constant dollars, to the sum of the current change in inventories plus the previous end-of-year stock (e).

8.   Intangible (R&D)

The cumulative sum of previous business net investment in R&D and "transfers" of R&D from government and nonprofit institutions.

9.   Nonprofit institutions

10.   Land

Flow of Funds estimate, again minus 7 percent for wholesale cooperatives.

11.   Structures and equipment

BEA figures (b), again minus 7 percent.

12.   Residential

BEA figures (k).

13.   Government

With the exception of land, government capital here is exclusive of government enterprise capital. TISA income and product accounts, however, include in the government sector reproducible fixed capital used by government enterprises. (This was necessary to impute output by function because capital breakdowns by function are available only for the combined stocks of government and government enterprises.)

14.   Land

Estimates by Milgram (1973) for the years 1952 through 1968. The remaining years are extrapolated from total private land stocks from Flow of Funds accounts.

$$GL_t = PL_t \left(\frac{GL_{1952}}{PL_{1952}} \right) \qquad t = 1945 \text{ to } 1951,$$

$$GL_t = PL_t \left(\frac{GL_{1968}}{PL_{1968}} \right) \qquad t = 1969 \text{ to } 1981,$$

where

GL = government land.
PL = total private land.

15. Structures and equipment
     Government structures and equipment (h) minus government enterprises (g).

16. Residential
     Government residential (h) minus government enterprise residential (g).

17. Inventories
     Government inventories (h) minus government enterprise inventories (g).

18. Intangible (R&D)
     Cumulation of previous net investment not transferred to business.

19. Government enterprise

20. Structures and equipment
     BEA (g)

21. Residential
     BEA (g)

22. Inventories
     BEA (g)

23. Household

24. Tangible

25. Land
     Flow of Funds

26. Residential
     This is owner-occupied nonfarm dwellings, from BEA (f).

27. Durables
     From the BEA consumer durable stock series (a). However, this series capitalizes only 20 percent of N2.6-68, tires, tubes, and auto accessories. We construct a stock series for the remaining 80 percent of N2.6-68, and add it to the BEA's estimate

of the stock of consumer durables. We assume straight-line depreciation, a three-year life and a constant rate of investment within each year. Thus:

$$KD_t = .833ID_t + .5ID_{t-1} + .167ID_{t-2},$$

where

KD = end-of-year constant dollar stock of tires, tubes, and accessories.

ID = N2.7-5, which is N2.6-68 in constant dollars.

For current dollars this series is reflated with an end-of-year implicit deflator, PKD:

$$KD_t^{cur} = KD_t^{72\$}(PKD_t),$$

where

$$PKD_t = .5 \left(\frac{N2.6\text{-}68}{N2.7\text{-}5}\right)_t + .5 \left(\frac{N2.6\text{-}68}{N2.7\text{-}5}\right)_{t+1}$$

28.   Semidurables

In contrast to the BEA, which classifies consumer goods as either durable or nondurable, TISA establishes semidurables as a third category. Semidurables consist of shoes, clothing, and semidurable house furnishings, all of which the BEA classifies as nondurables. We construct our own estimates of semidurable stocks, using N2.6-11, 13, and 33 as the source for investment, and assuming straight-line depreciation and a three-year life:

$$KSD_t = .833ISD_t + .5ISD_{t-1} + .167ISD_{t-2,}$$

where

KSD = end-of-year constant dollar stock of semidurables.

ISD = constant dollar investment in semidurables, equal to N2.7-23 plus line 32.

For current dollars, this series is reflated with the end-of-year implicit deflator, $PKSD$:

$$KSD_t^{cur} = KSD_t^{72\$} (PKSD_t),$$

where

$$PKSD_t = .5 \sum_{\tau = t}^{t+1} \left(\frac{N2.6, \text{lines } 11 + 13 + 33}{N2.7, \text{lines } 23 + 32} \right)_\tau$$

29.   Inventories

Household inventories are stocks of nondurables, which we conservatively estimate as having a two-week life. Our investment data are the BEA's consumer expenditures on nondurables, less our investment in semidurables.

$$KND_t = IND_t/26,$$

where

KND = stock of household inventories and
IND = investment in inventories.
    IND^{cur} = N2.3-6 minus N2.6-11 minus N2.6-13 minus N2.6-33.
    $IND^{72\$}$ = N2.7-16 minus N2.7-23 minus N2.7-32.

30.   Intangible (human capital)

Notes

1. See Carson and Jaszi (1981) for a brief presentation and U.S. Department of Commerce (1954) for some of the basic documents describing Bureau of Economic Analysis (BEA) concepts and methods. A further review and discussion of conceptual issues may be found in Ruggles (1983). Readers may also wish to consult a new series of BEA methodology papers (U.S. Department of Commerce, 1985a, 1985b, 1987a, 1987b, and others to come).

2. See Studenski (1961).

3. For early and classic discussions of some of the basic issues, see Hicks (1940 and 1948), Kuznets (1937, 1946, 1948a, 1948b), and Gilbert et al. (1948).

4. Kuznets 1941, 1948a, 1948b, 1951a, 1951b, and 1952, for example.

5. Other giants in the early construction of accounts included James Meade and Richard Stone, who developed the double entry national accounting system in 1939, in a British Treasury study sponsored by John Maynard Keynes, about the same time as Ragnar Frisch in Norway and Dertisan in Denmark, working independently, and Edward Denison, Milton Gilbert, and George Jaszi in the United States. (See Kendrick 1972, 10–38, for a substantial historical account of the development of the national accounts.) A powerful later voice for extension of the accounts was that of Juster (1970, 1973), and particular support is to be found in the work of Nordhaus and Tobin (1972, 1973), Nancy and Richard Ruggles (1970, 1973), Kendrick (1976, 1979) and Eisner (1971, 1973).

6. In U.S. Department of Commerce (1954, 30; reprinted 1970, 9).

7. As Kuznets stated: "Exclusion of the products of the family economy, characteristic of virtually all national income estimates, seriously limits their validity as measures of all scarce and disposable goods produced by the nation. The line of division between the business and the family economy differs from country to country, and for the same country from time to time. The temporal differences are especially important for estimates, since they occur not only over long periods but also, given violent cyclical fluctuations, over short" (1941, 10; as cited by Campbell and Peskin, 1979, 67).

8. Classic works in the vast literature bearing on investment in human capital include Schultz (1961) and Becker (1965, 1975).

9. Eisner (1988) and, in a somewhat abbreviated version, Appendix E of this volume.

10. The survey did not cover similar initiatives for other nations—a heroic effort in Japan comes particularly to mind (see Economic Council of Japan 1974)—and sets of "satellite" accounts in France (see Archambault and Arkhipoff 1986), most partial reconstructions of particular sectors, usually households, and broader frameworks including a host of social indicators that go clearly beyond what are generally taken to be economic variables. It did not consider the vast literature dealing exclusively with official (BEA) accounts in the United States and other nations and the United Nations System of Standard National Accounts (SNA). It also ignored the much broader social indicator literature.

11. A troublesome issue of consistency may be raised with regard to the treatment of "police services" provided by those who seek security by keeping guns in their homes. None of the extended and revised accounts, including my own, has moved to exclude such firearms, or their services, from our measures of consumption or final product.

12. Referring to government intermediate product, Kuznets stated: "It is particularly true of such activities as are directed at domestic peace and the international position of the country that they provide the pre-condition of economic activity; but that they themselves cannot be conceived as yielding a final economic product, as if economic product could be imagined without the basic social framework of the economy. These activities of government, as well as those specifically designed for the benefit of business firms, are in the nature of costs rather than of returns; and if wisely chosen and pursued, will increase the flow of economic welfare—the latter to be recorded when it materializes in a greater flow of goods to individuals" (1948b, 8; as cited in Campbell and Peskin, 1979, 63).

13. As James Tobin has pointed out in commenting on a draft of this section, "We do have to admit that there are lots of problems in the 'utility' criterion of welfare that we economists love so well. Maybe utility comes from relative position, so universal progress is not possible. Maybe a lot of what we treat as final utility-producing goods is instrumental, but we can't subtract them as intermediate or regrettably necessary. Fuel and utility bills? Soap? Warm clothes? On the other hand, the idea that there is no utility to work is probably wrong. As professors know, some work is fun, and people do get satisfaction out of doing something well and being so perceived."

14. This too was suggested by Kuznets (1941, 39 and 1948a, 157; as cited by Campbell and Peskin, 1979, 71).

15. See NIPA table 8.9, *Survey of Current Business* (U.S. Dept. of Commerce, Bureau of Economic Analysis, July 1987 or July 1988), for a complete list of BEA imputations. An explanation of the rationale used is to be found in *National Income, 1954* (U.S. Dept. of Commerce 1954, 45), included in the *Readings* (1970) cited above.

16. For development and discussion of a conceptual framework and matters of measurement see Reid (1934, 1947), Gronau (1973), Rosen (1974), and Murphy (1978, 1980).

17. See Eisner (1984).

18. See Gates (1982).

19. See Machlup (1962).

20. The calculation of net revaluations generally followed the formulation and procedures described in Eisner (1980a). Thus,

$$NR_t = [K_t - (P_{t,end}/P_{t-1,end}) K_{t-1} - (P_{t,end}/P_t)IN_t] (P_t/P_{t,end}),$$

where NR_t = net revaluations of the year t,

K_t = net value of stock at the end of the year t,

P_t = the GNP implicit price deflator for the year t,

$P_{t,end} = (P_{t,IV} + P_{t+1,I})/2$, with $P_{t,IV}$ and $P_{t+1,I}$ denoting GNP implicit price deflators for the fourth quarter of the year t, and the first quarter of the year $t+1$, respectively, and

IN_t = net investment or net flows in the year t.

21. A particular anomaly may be seen in the application to accounting or book depreciation, and hence to profits, income, and net investment, of a "replacement-cost" capital consumption adjustment for inflation of capital goods prices without, in turn, adjusting measures of profits, income, and the net addition to the value of capital for the increases in the prices of existing, surviving capital. This helps lead many to the, I believe, dubious conclusion that capital-intensive firms and their owners need particular tax relief in times of inflation. Their "losses" due to the higher prices of buying new assets are deplored while their gains from the greater values of their old assets are ignored.

22. This correction is similar to the adjustment in the alternative measure of GNP on a "command" basis introduced by Denison (1981) and available with the BEA NIPAs.

23. What some of these modifications amount to for measures of consumption and investment is shown in tables S.2 and S.3.

24. TISA does not, however, show complete capital accounts and balance sheets, some of which are to be found in Eisner (1980a and 1986).

25. The share of media output allocated to consumption rather than intermediate product was estimated on the basis of the analysis by Cremeans (1980).

26. Estimated by multiplying average hourly earnings of nonsupervisory workers in manufacturing by time in volunteer activities indicated by Szalai (1972) and utilizing further data in Weisbrod and Long (1975).

27. Estimates following the procedures of Martin (1972).

28. This represents the difference between what might have had to be paid for military draftees in a free market and the actual remuneration by government. The estimates were taken and developed from the work of Lundberg and Nebhut (1979).

29. See Martin, Landefield, and Peskin (1982) for other estimates of the value of services of government capital.

30. Taken from Ott and Austin (1978).

31. All this is described in harrowing detail in the massive Sources and Methods section of this volume and, earlier, in Eisner and Nebhut (1981). See Reich (1986) for alternative classifications of government activity, detailed estimates for Canada and the German Federal Republic, and comparisons of broad breakdowns for other countries.

32. Included in household work was time devoted to sets of activities classified as housework, obtaining goods and services, and care of family and others, as reported

in studies conducted by the Survey Research Center at the University of Michigan, discussed in detail in appendix A.

Time estimates were derived from Michigan Survey Research Center time use studies of 1965, 1975, and 1981, using basic data tapes made available by the Inter-University Consortium for Political and Social Research at the University of Michigan. (See Survey Research Center, 1979, 1980, and Inter-University Consortium 1983.)

Mean weekly use of time in a set of household activities related to what is classified as nonmarket output was calculated for respondents and spouses each categorized as male employed, male nonemployed, female employed, and female nonemployed.

Corresponding figures for 1965 were derived by applying to the 1975 data rates of change indicated on a 1965–75 "comparison tape." A panel of common respondents in 1975 and 1981 was used to derive age-adjusted rates of change between those years. These were applied to the 1975 data to secure estimates of mean time use in each of our four categories for 1981 and, by geometric interpolation, the years from 1976 to 1980. The years from 1966 to 1974 were similarly interpolated from the 1965 and 1975 figures. Mean time use from 1946 to 1964, however, was taken to be the same as in 1965. The mean annual time use per person in each category in each year was multiplied by the applicable number of persons in the nation to derive figures for total time in activities related to ordinary housework as well as education of children, medical and health services, volunteer activities, and travel to work.

With the 1975 survey used as a benchmark, estimates of hours per week devoted to household work by individuals generally 18 years of age and over (see tables A.7 and A.8 in appendix A) were

	1965	1975	1981
Employed males	11.70	12.47	13.43
Nonemployed males	16.38	21.27	22.83
Employed females	32.26	27.67	27.67
Nonemployed females	52.41	43.31	42.69
Total population weighted average	29.48	25.77	26.20

The 1975 weighted average corresponded almost exactly (although TISA population weights were for those 16 years and over) to the average weekly time in household work of 26 hours reported for 1975–76, with weighting of more detailed subgroups, by Gates and Murphy (1982, 11). Kendrick apparently derived lesser estimates of time devoted to household work, since he also used the mean wage of household workers for evaluation but came up with considerably lower estimates for the value of household labor product than did TISA.

33. Gross imputed interest on *household* capital is calculated by multiplying net stocks by the rate of return on *housing* capital. That rate of return is calculated as the sum of net interest paid and imputed rental income on owner-occupied housing divided by the value of the net stock of such housing with its associated land values. Informative discussion and alternative measures of services of household capital are to be found in Katz and Peskin (1980) and Katz (1982).

34. Also see U.S. Department of Commerce, Bureau of Economic Analysis, *Fixed Reproducible Tangible Wealth in the United States, 1925–85* (1987c). Net capital

stocks and capital consumption allowances for durable goods are taken directly from the BEA. For semidurables, net stocks and depreciation are calculated from gross investment data using the perpetual inventory method with three-year, straight-line depreciation, and the half-year convention. Inventories of nondurables, on the assumption of an average shelf life of two weeks, are approximately 4 percent of annual purchases. The separate estimates of land in all sectors were generally from series provided by the Flow of Funds Section of the Board of Governors of the Federal Reserve System (1985).

35. See Denison (1981).

36. Compared to 3.50 percent for BEA gross domestic product of business. The difference was due essentially to the subtraction of much larger amounts of intermediate product from government in 1946 than in 1981. If, as with the BEA gross product of business, there had been no such subtraction, TISA gross business product would have shown a growth of only 3.812 percent per annum.

37. The surveys can be identified as (1) the United States sample of the 1965 Multinational Time-Use Study, (2) the first wave of the 1975–76 Study of Americans' Use of Time, and (3) the Time-Use Longitudinal Panel Study: 1975–81. All surveys were conducted by the Economic Behavior Program at the Institute for Political and Social Research, University of Michigan. The data for the 1975–81 study were originally collected by F. Thomas Juster, Martha S. Hill, Frank P. Stafford, and Jacquelynne Eccles Parsons. Neither the collectors of the original data nor the Consortium bear any responsibility for our data processing, aggregation, and analysis.

38. These categories actually describe what was used for 1975–81. Those for the 1965–75 growth rate estimation are not as broad because the 1965 sample contained only a limited number of them. The differences in categories would not appear to have more impact on our results.

39. Since employed women spend less time working in the market than employed men, their greater household work time does not come solely at the expense of leisure time.

40. Murphy (1978, 250) suggests that the maintenance associated with a growing stock of household capital will exert an upward pressure on household work time. Our results support his claim.

41. Our calculation of the value of household work is consistent with estimates by Murphy (1978). Adopting a more detailed market cost approach and a different population breakdown, he estimates the value of unpaid household work in the United States for the years 1960 and 1970. He assumes that time use is the same in both years. Nevertheless, his results are similar to ours. Murphy estimates the values of unpaid household work to be $185.3 billion in 1960 and $335.6 billion in 1970. We estimate the values to be $203.5 billion and $360.6 billion, respectively.

42. See Herfindahl and Kneese (1973), Drechsler (1976), Cremeans (1977), and Marin (1978) for discussions of concepts and problems of measurement and possibilities of bringing the deterioration and maintenance of the environment into national accounts. See also earlier published discussions by Peskin (1975, 1976, and 1981) and, within a broad framework for the measure of nonmarket production, Peskin and Peskin (1978).

43. See Samuelson (1973a and 1973b), for example.

44. Subtraction for disamenities, as such, is not consistent with my concept of a measure of final output contributing to welfare, rather than welfare itself. Nordhaus and Tobin seek explicitly to measure the latter.

45. Amounting to $53.3 billion 1972 dollars or 4.0 percent of GNP in 1977. These are extrapolated from a survey attributed to Liu and Yu (1976), who broke 1970 damage costs of $46.5 billion into $2.7 billion for health, $5.0 billion for soiling, $38.4 billion for material, and $0.3 billion for crops.

46. By far the greatest part of Zolotas's cost of commuting in recent years relates to the welfare cost from the loss of time. He takes this as the excess of commuting time over 20 minutes per day, with total time increasing at two minutes per day each year from 1950 to 1977. It is not clear why Zolotas includes travel time as a welfare cost to be deducted since EAW includes the value of leisure. Increased travel time should automatically reduce Zolotas's measure of welfare by reducing leisure time.

47. Zolotas excludes 40 percent of the services of "technologically advanced products" such as dishwashers and vacuum cleaners as included implicitly in the value of the time saved in household work. Household services are estimated "on the assumption that, for the average household, the required amount of housework— whether supplied within or outside of the market—is equivalent to the employment of one person for five hours a day for 365 days a year" (1981, 91). These hours are then reduced in proportion to the services supplied in the market and the remaining time is imputed to be " 'paid' for at the real average wage rate before taxes in the private urban sector."

48. This is for "EAW Index 2," including depletion cost. For EAW 1, without depletion cost, the rate of growth was 2.17 percent. Zolotas also finds that, on the growth margin, increases in GNP were contributing proportionally less and less to increases in EAW. Specifically, the elasticity of the EAW index with respect to GNP fell from 0.717 during the period 1950–60 to 0.639 from 1960 to 1970 and 0.547 from 1970 to 1977. With deduction of the imputed costs of use of natural resources, the corresponding elasticities were somewhat less, 0.677, 0.583, and 0.511, respectively, in the three periods (Zolotas, p. 102, and table 22, p. 108).

49. The time is calculated as 14 hours per day minus 1,300 hours per year for each person enrolled in school and also minus actual time in market labor. Ten hours per day is presumably reserved for satisfying physiological needs such as eating and sleeping, viewed as maintenance. Thus all of the rest of time not spent in school or on the job is viewed as devoted to consumption.

The time allocated to producing consumption services, whether nonmarket work in the household or leisure, is then evaluated at the average hourly compensation rate after taxes of all employed persons classified by sex, age, and education. The imputed wage for those under 15 and over 74, both presumed to be out of the labor force, is set at zero.

50. The difference is derived from a substantial set of demographic accounts put together from census data. The future incomes are projected on the assumption of 2 percent per annum real growth and present values are calculated on the assumption of a 4 percent real rate of interest.

51. Graham and Webb (1979), noting similarly contrasting estimates, suggest

that it would take a 20 percent rate of discount to equate present values of future incomes to costs.

52. Fraumeni and Jorgenson (1980) did not include human or intangible investment. Their capital inputs or investment comprised producers' durable equipment, consumers' durables, tenant-occupied residential structures and nonresidential structures, owner-occupied residential structures, inventories, and land. In this work, "gross private national saving and capital formation" thus consisted of tangible, nongovernment capital. It amounted in 1975 to $406.4 billion. With replacement and depreciation estimated at $281.4 billion, net private national saving and capital formation was $125.0 billion. Revaluation of $407.8 billion brought the change in wealth to $532.9 billion.

53. Since these foregone earnings are taken to be the students' opportunity costs they should in principle be net of taxes but gross of benefits, such as employer social security contributions (viewed as payments for future receipts from social security) not included in wages. Kendrick does not make these adjustments, but it may be argued that taxes that would have been paid by students if they had been in the labor market would have been low and roughly counterbalanced by the benefits not included in their measured earnings.

54. This is based on work by Machlup (1962).

55. Building on 1967–68 and 1975–76 time-use surveys by Walker and Woods and by Juster, respectively, Kendrick presents average weekly hours of unpaid household work by household members, by type of family and/or household. These figures for females, males, teenagers and preteens, for wives, husbands, and other adults in husband-wife and non-husband-wife households, further categorized by employment status, type of household, and presence and ages of children, are assumed not to change for all the years that Kendrick imputes product. Total hours in the population do change, however, with changes in the total population and its composition.

56. These were benchmarked on a 1964 Labor Department survey and extrapolated backward and forward on the basis of fragmentary data assembled by Wolozin (1966). The estimated hours were then multiplied by an adjusted measure of average hourly compensation in the services sector of the economy.

57. See Ruggles and Ruggles (1970, 1973), for example.

58. The Ruggleses (1970, 1973) had proposed a complete set of moderately extended accounts for national income and product, sector income and outlay, and capital formation. In the enterprise sector they separated out self-employed compensation, imputed interest on plant and equipment, and a net operating surplus. In the government and household sectors they added "imputed income from development and durables." Consumption was increased by nonmarket imputations of capital services in households and government and by enterprise provision of consumption goods and mass media support. And capital formation was extended to include development expenditures for research and development and education and health, as well as government and household expenditures for structures and durables.

References

Government documents and other institutional publications will be found at the end of this reference list.

Archambault, Edith, and Oleg Arkhipoff, ed. 1986. *Etudes de comptabilité nationale.* Paris: Economica.

Bachman, George W. and Associates. 1952. *Health resources in the United States.* Washington, D.C.: Brookings Institution.

Becker, Gary S. 1965. A theory of the allocation of time. *Econ. J.* 75(299): 493–517.

————. 1975. *Human capital.* 2d ed. New York: Columbia Univ. Press.

Bhatia, Kul B. 1970. Accrued capital gains, personal income, and saving in the United States, 1948–64. *Rev. Income Wealth,* 16(4): 363–78.

Boskin, M. J., M. S. Robinson, and Alan Huber. 1989. Government saving, capital formation, and wealth in the United States, 1947–85. In Robert E. Lipsey and Helen Stone Tice, eds., *The measurement of saving, investment and wealth. Studies in Income and Wealth,* vol. 52: 287–353. Chicago: Univ. of Chicago Press for NBER.

Boskin, M. J., M. S. Robinson, T. O'Reilly, and P. Kumar. 1985. New estimates of the value of federal mineral rights and land. *Amer. Econ. Rev.* 75(5): 923–36.

Campbell, Beth, and Janice Peskin. 1979. Expanding economic accounts and measuring economic welfare: A review of proposals. Washington, D.C.: BEA, U.S. Department of Commerce, October.

Carson, Carol S., and George Jaszi. 1981. The National Income and Products Accounts of the United States: An overview. *Surv. Curr. Bus.* 61(2): 22–34.

Chadeau, Ann. 1985. Measuring household activities: Some international comparisons. *Rev. Income Wealth* 31(3): 237–53.

Christensen, Laurits R., and Dale W. Jorgenson. 1969. The measurement of U.S. real capital input, 1929–1967. *Rev. Income Wealth* 15(4): 293–320.

————. 1973. Measuring economic performance in the private sector. In *The measurement of economic and social performance,* 233–338. See Moss 1973.

Cremeans, John E. 1977. Conceptual and statistical issues in developing environmental measures—Recent U.S. experience. *Rev. Income Wealth,* 23(2): 97–115.

————. 1980. Consumer services provided by business through advertising-supported media in the United States. *Rev. Income Wealth* 26(2): 151–74.

Denison, Edward F. 1971. Welfare measures and the GNP. *Surv. Curr. Bus.* 51(1): 1–8.

————. 1973. Comment on Nordhaus and Tobin. In *The measurement of economic and social performance*, 546–548. See Moss 1973.

————. 1981. International transactions in measures of the nation's production. *Surv. Curr. Bus.* 61(5): 17–28.

————. 1982. Comment. *Surv. Curr. Bus.* 62(5): 59–65.

Drechsler, László. 1976. Problems of recording environmental phenomena in national accounting aggregates. *Rev. Income Wealth* 22(3): 239–52.

Eisner, Robert. 1971. New twists to income and product. *Surv. Curr. Bus.*, part 2 (Anniversary Issue—The Economic Accounts of the United States: Retrospect and Prospect) 51(7): 67–68.

————. 1973. Comment on Juster, in *The measurement of economic and social performance*, 99–102. See Moss 1973.

————. 1978. Total incomes in the United States, 1959 and 1969. *Rev. Income Wealth* 24(1): 41–70.

————. 1980a. Capital gains and income: Real changes in the value of capital in the United States, 1946–77. In *The measurement of capital: Studies in income and wealth*, vol. 45, ed. Dan Usher. Chicago: Univ. of Chicago Press.

————. 1980b. Total income, total investment, and growth. *Amer. Econ. Rev.* 70(2): 225–31.

————. 1984. Transfers in a total incomes system of accounts. In *Economic transfers in the United States: Studies in income and wealth*, vol. 49, ed. Marilyn Moon, 9–35. Chicago: Univ. of Chicago Press for NBER.

————. 1985. The total incomes system of accounts. *Surv. Curr. Bus.* 65(1): 24–48.

————. 1986. *How real is the federal deficit?* New York: The Free Press.

————. 1988. Extended accounts for national income and product. *J. Econ. Lit.* 26(2): 1611–84.

Eisner, Robert, and David H. Nebhut. 1981. An extended measure of government product: Preliminary results for the United States, 1946–76. *Rev. Income Wealth* 27(1): 33–64.

Eisner, Robert, and Paul J. Pieper. 1984. A new view of the federal debt and budget deficit. *Amer. Econ. Rev.* 74(1): 11–29.

Eisner, Robert, Emily R. Simons, Paul J. Pieper, and Steven Bender. 1982. Total incomes in the United States, 1946–1976: A summary report. *Rev. Income Wealth* 28(2): 133–74.

Eisner, Robert, and Arthur B. Treadway. 1970. Non-income income: A foreword. In *1970 Proceedings of the Business and Economic Statistics Section*, 131. Washington, D.C.: American Statistical Assoc.

Fraumeni, Barbara M., and Dale W. Jorgenson. 1980. The role of capital in U.S. economic growth, 1948–1976. In *Capital, efficiency and growth*, ed. G. von Furstenberg, 9–250. Cambridge: Ballinger.

Gates, John H. 1982. Education and training costs. A measurement framework and estimates for 1965–79. In *Measuring nonmarket economic activity,* 107–35. *See* U.S. Department of Commerce 1982.

Gates, John H. and Martin Murphy. 1982. The use of time: A classification scheme and estimates for 1975–76. In *Measuring nonmarket economic activity,* 3–22. *See* U.S. Department of Commerce 1982.

Gilbert, Milton, George Jaszi, Edward F. Denison, and Charles F. Schwartz. 1948. Objectives of national income measurement: A reply to Professor Kuznets. *Rev. Econ. Statist.* 30(3): 179–95.

Graham, John W., and Roy H. Webb. 1979. Stocks and depreciation of human capital: New evidence from a present-value perspective. *Rev. Income Wealth,* 25(2): 209–24.

Gronau, Reuben. 1973. The measurement of output of the nonmarket sector: The evaluation of housewives' time. In *The measurement of economic and social performance,* 163–90. *See* Moss 1973.

Hawrylyshyn, Oli. 1976. The value of household services: A survey of empirical estimates. *Rev. Income Wealth* 22(2): 101–131.

———. 1977. Towards a definition of non-market activities. *Rev. Income Wealth* 23(1): 79–96.

Herfindahl, Orris C., and Allen V. Kneese. 1973. Measuring social and economic change; Benefits and costs of environmental pollution. In *The measurement of economic and social performance,* 441–503. *See* Moss 1973.

Hicks, J. R. 1940. The valuation of the social income. *Economica* 7(26): 105–124.

———. 1948. The valuation of the social income—A comment on Professor Kuznets' reflections. *Economica* 15(59): 163–172.

Jaszi, George. 1973. Comment on Juster. In *The measurement of economic and social performance,* 84–99. *See* Moss 1973.

Jorgenson, Dale W., and Barbara M. Fraumeni. 1987. The accumulation of human and non-human capital, 1948–1984. Unpub. ms., Harvard Univ.

Jorgenson, Dale W., and Alvaro Pachon. 1983. The accumulation of human and non-human wealth. In *The determinants of national saving and wealth,* eds. R. Hemming and F. Modigliani, 302–352. London: Macmillan.

Juster. F. Thomas. 1966. *Household capital formation and financing.* New York: NBER.

———. 1970. On the measurement of economic and social performance. NBER 50th Annual Report, 8–24.

———. 1973. A framework for the measurement of economic and social performance. In *The measurement of economic and social performance,* 25–84. *See* Moss 1973.

Juster, F. Thomas, Paul N. Courant, and Greg K. Dow. 1981. A theoretical framework for the measurement of well being. *Rev. Income Wealth* 27(1): 1–31.

Katz, Arnold J. 1982. The value of services provided by the stock of consumer durables, 1947–79: Alternative user cost measures. In U.S. Department of Commerce, *Measuring nonmarket economic activity,* 42–72.

———. 1983. Valuing the services of consumer durables. *Rev. Income Wealth* 29(4): 405–427.

Katz, Arnold J., and Janice Peskin. 1980. The value of services provided by the stock of consumer durables, 1947–77: An opportunity cost measure. *Surv. Curr. Bus.* 60(7): 22–31.

Kendrick, John W. 1972. *Economic accounts and their uses.* New York: McGraw-Hill.

———. 1976. *The formation and stocks of total capital.* New York: Columbia Univ. Press. for NBER.

———. 1979. Expanding imputed values in the national income and product accounts. *Rev. Income Wealth* 25(4): 349–363.

———. 1987a. Happiness is personal productivity growth. *Challenge* 30(2): 37–44.

———. 1987b. The concept and estimation of full personal income in current and constant prices. Prepared for meetings of the International Association for Research in Income and Wealth in August in Rocca di Papa, Italy.

Kuznets, Simon. 1937. *National income and capital formation, 1919–1935.* New York: NBER.

———. 1941. *National income and its composition, 1919–1938.* 2 vols. New York, NBER.

———. 1946. *National income: A summary of findings.* New York: NBER.

———. 1948a. Discussion of the new Department of Commerce income series. *Rev. Econ. Statist.* 30(3): 151–179.

———. 1948b. On the valuation of social income—Reflections on Professor Hicks' article. Part 1. *Economica* 15(57): 1–16.

———. 1951a. National income and structure. *Proceedings of the International Statistical Conferences, 1947.* Vol. 5, 205–239. Calcutta. Reprinted in *Economic change,* 145–191. See Kuznets 1953.

———. 1951b. Government product and national income. *Income and Wealth, Series 1.* Cambridge: Bowes and Bowes.

———. 1952. Long-term changes in the national income of the United States of America since 1870. In *Income and wealth of the United States: Trends and structure, Income and Wealth Series 2,* 163–167. Baltimore, Md.: Johns Hopkins U. Press.

———. 1953. *Economic Change.* New York: Norton.

———. 1973. Concluding remarks. In *The measurement of economic and social performance,* 579–593. See Moss 1973.

Landefield, J. Steven, and James R. Hines. 1982. Valuing non-renewable natural resources: The mining industries. In *Measuring nonmarket activity,* 136–168. See U.S. Department of Commerce 1982. Reprinted in *Rev. Income Wealth,* March 1985, 31(1): 1–20.

Liu, Ben-Chieh, and Eden Yu. 1976. *Physical and economic damage functions for air pollutants by receptor.* Washington, D.C.: U.S. Environmental Protection Agency (EPA).

Lundberg, Shelley, and David Nebhut. 1979. Estimating the uncompensated labor services of draftees in the U.S. Armed Forces: 1953–1973. Unpub. ms., Northwestern Univ.

McElroy, M. B. 1976. Capital gains and social income. *Econ. Inquiry* 14(2): 221–40.

Machlup, Fritz. 1962. *The production and distribution of knowledge in the United*

States. Princeton, N.J.: Princeton Univ. Press.

Marin, A. 1978. National income, welfare, and the environment. *Rev. Income Wealth* 24(4): 415–428.

Martin, Donald. 1972. The economics of jury conscription. *J. Polit. Econ.* 80(4): 680–702.

Martin, Frank, J. Steven Landefield, and Janice Peskin. 1982. The value of services provided by the stock of government-owned fixed capital, 1948–79. In U.S. Department of Commerce, *Measuring nonmarket economic activity,* 73–106.

Menchik, Paul L., and Burton A. Weisbrod. 1987. Volunteer labor supply. *J. Public. Econ.* 32(2): 159–183.

Milgram, Grace. 1973. Estimates of the value of land in the United States held by various sectors of the economy annually, 1952–1968. In *Institutional investors and corporate stock,* ed. Raymond W. Goldsmith, 343–347. New York: NBER.

Moss, Milton, ed. 1973. *The measurement of economic and social performance: Studies in income and wealth.* Vol. 38. New York: Columbia Univ. Press for NBER.

Murphy, Martin. 1978. The value of nonmarket household production: Opportunity cost versus market cost estimates. *Rev. Income Wealth* 24(3): 243–255.

————. 1980. The measurement and valuation of household nonmarket time. Washington, D.C.: BEA, U.S. Department of Commerce, March.

————. 1982a. Comparative estimates of the value of household work in the United States for 1976. *Rev. Income Wealth* 28(1): 29–43.

————. 1982b. The value of household work for the United States. 1976. In *Measuring nonmarket activity,* 23–41. *See* U.S. Department of Commerce 1982.

Nordhaus, William D. and James Tobin. 1972. Is growth obsolete? In *Economic Growth,* Fiftieth Anniversary Colloquium, vol. 5. New York: NBER.

————. 1973. Is growth obsolete? In *The measurement of economic and social performance,* 509–532. *See* Moss 1973.

Okun, Arthur M. 1971a. Social welfare has no price tag. *Surv. Curr. Bus.,* part 2 (Anniversary Issue—The Economic Accounts of the United States: Retrospect and Prospect) 51(7): 129–133.

————. 1971b. Should GNP measure social welfare? *Brookings Bulletin,* Summer.

Ott, Attiat F., and Thomas Austin. 1978. Capital formation by government. Manuscript dated 1978. Published in *The government and capital formation,* ed. G. von Furstenberg, 265–317. Cambridge, Mass.: Ballinger, 1980.

Peskin, Henry M. 1975. Accounting for the environment (A progress report). *Social Indicators Research* 2(2): 191–210.

————. 1976. A national accounting framework for environmental assets. *J. Environ. Econ. Manage.* 2(4): 255–262.

————. 1981. National income accounts and the environment. *Natural Res. J.* 2: 511–537.

————. 1986. Untitled book manuscript on national accounts.

Peskin, Henry M., and Janice Peskin. 1978. The valuation of nonmarket activities in income accounting. *Rev. Income Wealth* 24(1): 71–92.

Reich, Utz P. 1986. Treatment of government activity on the production account. *Rev. Income Wealth* 32(1): 69–85.

Reid, Margaret G. 1934. *The economics of household production.* New York: John Wiley and Sons.

————. 1947. The economic contributions of homemakers. *The Annals of the American Academies of Political and Social Science,* May.

Robinson, J. P., and P. E. Converse. 1967. *66 basic tables of time budget research data for the United States.* Ann Arbor, Mich.: Survey Research Center, Univ. of Michigan.

Rosen, H. S. 1974. The monetary value of a housewife: A replacement cost approach. *Amer. J. Econ. Soc.* 33(1): 65–73.

Ruggles, Nancy, and Richard Ruggles. 1970. *The design of economic accounts.* New York: Columbia Univ. Press.

————. 1973. A proposal for a system of economic and social accounts. In *The measurement of economic and social performance,* 111–146. *See* Moss 1973.

Ruggles, Richard. 1983. The United States National Income and Product Accounts, 1947–1977: Their conceptual basis and evolution. In *The U.S. National Income and Product Accounts,* ed. Murray F. Foss. NBER Studies in Income and Wealth, vol. 47. Chicago: The University of Chicago Press.

Ruggles, Richard, and Nancy D. Ruggles. 1982a. Integrated economic accounts for the United States, 1947–1980. *Surv. Curr. Bus.* 62(5): 1–53.

————. 1982b. Integrated economic accounts: Reply. *Surv. Curr. Bus.* 62(11): 36–53.

Samuelson, Paul A. 1973a. *Economics.* 9th ed. New York: McGraw-Hill.

————. 1973b. *Readings in economics.* 7th ed. New York: McGraw-Hill.

Schultz, Theodore W. 1960. Capital formation by education. *J. Polit. Econ.* 68(6): 571–583.

————. 1961. Investment in human capital. *Amer. Econ. Rev.* 51(1): 1–17.

Shay, Robert. 1965. Rate structure in automobile financing. *45th Annual Report.* New York: NBER.

Smith, James. 1971. The demand for consumer installment credit since 1948: A dynamic stock-adjustment model. Unpub. diss. Southern Methodist University, Dallas, Texas, May.

Soloday, John J. 1980. Measurement of income and product in the oil and gas mining industries. In *The measurement of capital: Studies in income and wealth,* vol. 45, ed. Dan Usher. Chicago: Univ. of Chicago Press.

Solow, Robert M. 1973. Comment on Juster. In *The measurement of economic and social performance,* 102–5. See Moss 1973.

Studenski, Paul. 1961. *The income of nations.* New York: New York Univ. Press.

Szalai, Alexander, ed. 1972. *The use of time.* The Hague: Mouton Press.

Walker, Kathryn E., and William H. Gauger. 1973. Time and its dollar value in household work. *Family Economics Review.* Fall: 8–13.

Walker, Kathryn E., and Margaret E. Woods. 1976. *Time use: A measure of household production of family goods and services.* Washington, D.C.: Center for the Family of the American Home Economics Association.

Weinrobe, Maurice. 1974. Household production and national production: An improvement of the record. *Rev. Income Wealth* 20(1): 89–102.

Weisbord, Burton, and Stephen H. Long. 1975. The size of the voluntary nonprofit sector: Concepts and measures. Discussion paper. Madison: Institute for Research on Poverty, Univ. of Wisconsin.

Wolozin, Harold. 1966. The value of volunteer services in the U.S. economy. Paper prepared for NBER, 1966.

Ziemer, Richard C., and Karl D. Galbraith. 1979. Deflation of defense purchases. Presented to the NBER Conference on Research in Income and Wealth, in May, in Cambridge, Mass.

Zolotas, Xenophon. 1981. *Economic growth and declining social welfare.* Athens: Bank of Greece.

Council of Economic Advisers. 1978. *Economic report of the President.* Washington, D.C.: USGPO.

Economic Council of Japan, NNW Measurement Committee. 1974. *Measuring net national welfare of Japan.* Printing Bureau, Ministry of Finance.

Federal Reserve System. Board of Governors. Flow of Funds Section. 1985 *Balance sheets for the U.S. Economy, 1945–83.* Washington, D.C.

———. 1979 and subsequent dates. *Flow of funds accounts.* Washington, D.C.

———. Issues of 1979 and earlier years. *Federal reserve bulletin.*

———. 1979. Table entitled Finance rate and other terms on new and used car installment credit contracts purchased from dealers by major auto finance companies.

Inter-university Consortium for Political and Social Research. 1983. *Time use longitudinal panel study, 1975, 1981.* Ann Arbor, Mich.

———. 1979. *Time use in economic and social accounts, 1975–1976.* Ann Arbor, Mich.: Survey Research Center, Institute for Social Research.

National Science Foundation. 1977. *National patterns of R&D resources and manpower in the United States, 1953–1977.* (NSF 77-310.) Washington, D.C.

———. 1982a. *National patterns of service and technology resources 1982.* (NSF 82-319.) Washington, D.C.

———. 1982b. *National patterns in R&D resources.* Washington, D.C.

———. 1983. *Research and development in industry, funds, 1981, scientists and engineers, January 1982.* Detailed statistical tables. Washington, D.C.

———. 1980. *Americans' use of time, 1965–1966, and time use in economic and social accounts, 1975–1976, Merged data.* Ann Arbor, Mich.

U.S. Department of Commerce. 1954. *National income, 1954 edition.* Washington, D.C.: USGPO. Reprinted in part in *Readings in concepts and methods of national income statistics,* 5–137. Washington, D.C.: USGPO, 1970.

U.S. Department of Commerce. Bureau of the Census. 1977 and earlier years. *Census of governments.* Washington, D.C.: USGPO.

———. 1978 and earlier years. *Current population reports,* series P-20. School enrollment—Social and economic characteristics of students. Washington, D.C.: USGPO.

———. Various years. *City finances: Financial statistics of cities.* Washington, D.C.

———. Various years. *Population estimates and projections,* series P-25, numbers 98, 310, 311, 519, 721. Washington, D.C. USGPO.

———. 1978 and earlier years. *Statistical abstract of the United States.* Washington, D.C.: USGPO.

———. 1978. Capital consumption allowances, owner-occupied nonfarm dwellings. Washington, D.C.

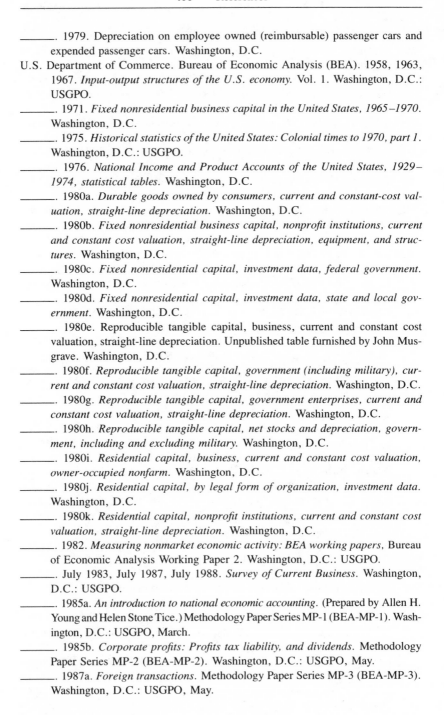

————. 1979. Depreciation on employee owned (reimbursable) passenger cars and expended passenger cars. Washington, D.C.

U.S. Department of Commerce. Bureau of Economic Analysis (BEA). 1958, 1963, 1967. *Input-output structures of the U.S. economy.* Vol. 1. Washington, D.C.: USGPO.

————. 1971. *Fixed nonresidential business capital in the United States, 1965–1970.* Washington, D.C.

————. 1975. *Historical statistics of the United States: Colonial times to 1970, part 1.* Washington, D.C.: USGPO.

————. 1976. *National Income and Product Accounts of the United States, 1929–1974, statistical tables.* Washington, D.C.

————. 1980a. *Durable goods owned by consumers, current and constant-cost valuation, straight-line depreciation.* Washington, D.C.

————. 1980b. *Fixed nonresidential business capital, nonprofit institutions, current and constant cost valuation, straight-line depreciation, equipment, and structures.* Washington, D.C.

————. 1980c. *Fixed nonresidential capital, investment data, federal government.* Washington, D.C.

————. 1980d. *Fixed nonresidential capital, investment data, state and local government.* Washington, D.C.

————. 1980e. Reproducible tangible capital, business, current and constant cost valuation, straight-line depreciation. Unpublished table furnished by John Musgrave. Washington, D.C.

————. 1980f. *Reproducible tangible capital, government (including military), current and constant cost valuation, straight-line depreciation.* Washington, D.C.

————. 1980g. *Reproducible tangible capital, government enterprises, current and constant cost valuation, straight-line depreciation.* Washington, D.C.

————. 1980h. *Reproducible tangible capital, net stocks and depreciation, government, including and excluding military.* Washington, D.C.

————. 1980i. *Residential capital, business, current and constant cost valuation, owner-occupied nonfarm.* Washington, D.C.

————. 1980j. *Residential capital, by legal form of organization, investment data.* Washington, D.C.

————. 1980k. *Residential capital, nonprofit institutions, current and constant cost valuation, straight-line depreciation.* Washington, D.C.

————. 1982. *Measuring nonmarket economic activity: BEA working papers,* Bureau of Economic Analysis Working Paper 2. Washington, D.C.: USGPO.

————. July 1983, July 1987, July 1988. *Survey of Current Business.* Washington, D.C.: USGPO.

————. 1985a. *An introduction to national economic accounting.* (Prepared by Allen H. Young and Helen Stone Tice.) Methodology Paper Series MP-1 (BEA-MP-1). Washington, D.C.: USGPO, March.

————. 1985b. *Corporate profits: Profits tax liability, and dividends.* Methodology Paper Series MP-2 (BEA-MP-2). Washington, D.C.: USGPO, May.

————. 1987a. *Foreign transactions.* Methodology Paper Series MP-3 (BEA-MP-3). Washington, D.C.: USGPO, May.

————. 1987b. *GNP: An overview of source data and estimating methods.* Methodology Paper Series MP-4 (BEA-MP-4). Washington, D.C.: USGPO, September.

————. 1987c. *Fixed reproducible tangible wealth in the United States, 1925–85.* (BEA 1987). Washington, D.C.: USGPO.

U.S. Department of Defense. 1979. *Selected manpower statistics.* Washington, D.C.: USGPO, March.

U.S. Department of Health, Education, and Welfare. 1962 to 1967. *Health, education, and welfare trends.* Washington, D.C.

————. 1962. Social welfare expenditures. *Social Security Bulletin.* November.

U.S. Department of Housing and Urban Development. Financial and Economic Analysis Division. 1979. U.S. average yields on FHA new home mortgages. Unpublished table, July.

U.S. Department of Labor. Bureau of Labor Statistics. 1975. *Handbook of Labor Statistics, 1975.* Washington, D.C.: USGPO.

————. 1979. *Employment and earnings.* Washington, D.C.: USGPO, June.

————. 1980. Employed and unemployed persons by detailed industry group, class of workers, and sex. Unpublished, December.

Index